PARTNERSHIP AND LLP LAW

PARTNERSHIP AND LLP LAW

NINTH EDITION

Geoffrey Morse
Thomas Braithwaite

UNIVERSITY PRESS

Great Clarendon Street, Oxford, OX2 6DP,
United Kingdom

Oxford University Press is a department of the University of Oxford.
It furthers the University's objective of excellence in research, scholarship,
and education by publishing worldwide. Oxford is a registered trade mark of
Oxford University Press in the UK and in certain other countries

© Geoffrey Morse & Thomas Braithwaite 2020

The moral rights of the authors have been asserted

Seventh Edition published in 2010
Eighth Edition published in 2015
Ninth Edition published in 2020

Impression: 1

All rights reserved. No part of this publication may be reproduced, stored in
a retrieval system, or transmitted, in any form or by any means, without the
prior permission in writing of Oxford University Press, or as expressly permitted
by law, by licence or under terms agreed with the appropriate reprographics
rights organization. Enquiries concerning reproduction outside the scope of the
above should be sent to the Rights Department, Oxford University Press, at the
address above

You must not circulate this work in any other form
and you must impose this same condition on any acquirer

Crown copyright material is reproduced under Class Licence
Number C01P0000148 with the permission of OPSI
and the Queen's Printer for Scotland

Published in the United States of America by Oxford University Press
198 Madison Avenue, New York, NY 10016, United States of America

British Library Cataloguing in Publication Data
Data available

Library of Congress Control Number: 2019954555

ISBN 978–0–19–883279–9

Printed and bound by
CPI Group (UK) Ltd, Croydon, CR0 4YY

Links to third party websites are provided by Oxford in good faith and
for information only. Oxford disclaims any responsibility for the materials
contained in any third party website referenced in this work.

PREFACE

When the first edition of this book (intended at that stage purely for undergraduate students) was published in 1986, partnership law was and had been for some time in a virtual steady-state, based on the 1890 Act and several Victorian and Edwardian cases. The intervening years between 1986 and today have however seen many substantial changes to the format, both legislative and judicial. In terms of legislation, there have been significant changes to the Limited Partnerships Act 1907, introducing the new sub-form of Private Fund Limited Partnerships. These changes originated in the recommendations of the Law Commissions of England and Scotland in 2003 and have modernized the LP format as appropriate for investment vehicles. There are probably further changes to come, however, in the light of their uses as vehicles for international fraudulent schemes. Unfortunately, the changes to the basic partnership law suggested by the Commissions proved to be still-born, foundering on substantial opposition to the introduction of legal personality in England and Wales. The baby was indeed thrown out with the bath water.

The judiciary, on the other hand, have instead 'updated' partnership law on a number of substantial issues, in addition to the usual minor adjustments. The interface between common law and the 1890 Act was, for example, explored by the House of Lords in relation first to the application of the doctrine of repudiation to partnership law, the question as to exactly when a contractual relationship of partnership comes into being, and the vicarious liability of partners for equitable breaches by their fellow partners. The courts have also clarified the distinction between capital and income profits and what is capable of constituting partnership property. Sometimes changes come out of left field, such as the recent and sudden application of the equitable doctrine of forfeiture as a remedy for partnership wrongs. Perhaps of even more significance is the suggestion (at least) by members of the Supreme Court that partners could also be employees of each other, a proposition which ignores (and destroys) the very basis of the partnership relationship. There are still a few areas which will also need judicial attention in due course, such as partners' liability for negligence inter se and why there are two totally disparate sections of the Act dealing with terminating a partnership at will.

The English form of partnership still forms the basic model for several Commonwealth countries and cases from Australia and Canada, in particular, can sometimes shed light on areas not covered by our courts, but they are of course non-binding. The format also applies in Scotland but with the important proviso that Scottish partnerships and LPs, unlike their southern counterparts, have legal personality and so the, often insightful, decisions of the Court of Session have to be read in that light. That does not, however, explain the disagreement between the two jurisdictions as to the interpretation of valuation clauses in exit agreements.

These developments of partnership and LP law can best be described as professionalizing the law so as to be suitable for an age far removed from the subject's Victorian roots. Nothing brought this into focus more than the introduction in 2001 of a new business format, lazily called the Limited Liability Partnership or LLP. This vehicle with its legal personality and external corporate regulation is definitely *not* a version of a partnership. Its title is totally misleading; the persons involved (known as members) may or may not be in a similar relationship to each other as partners, but they could equally well be categorized as employees of the LLP (a distinction which may have confused the Supreme Court, above, as the case actually involved an LLP). The 2000 Act expressly excludes partnership law from applying to LLPs unless the contrary is provided by statute. Internally an LLP can in effect decide its own structure and relationships. The LLP form is therefore used substantially by former professional partnerships but also as an investment and business vehicle. It is actually a modified form of company but with partnership connections. The judiciary can be variable as to their approach on the relationship between LLPs and partnerships, sometimes making clear distinctions between them, but on other occasions treating them the same without comment. The connections between the two structures can be quite profound, and for that reason it is convenient for a book such as this to examine both partnerships and LLPs, addressing the similarities and differences as they occur.

This ninth edition of the book, which has taken LLPs on board since 2001, reflects this professionalization of partnership law. It has morphed into a book for practitioners rather than students, although it is hoped that those interested in a more academic study of the subject will still find it useful. In particular the part on LLPs has been expanded to reflect their economic importance. But there is very little case law as yet on LLPs to indicate where the problems are, so that an academic is ill-equipped to deal with LLPs in any comprehensive way. A leading practitioner in the field is of course in a very different position. He or she knows where the potential bodies are buried. So, the book (and I) are very fortunate indeed that Thomas Braithwaite of Serle Court agreed to revamp that part of the book, bringing both insights and clarity of expression which can only enhance the book. I am very grateful to him. I should of course make it clear that he is no way responsible for any errors in the other parts of the book; that falls on me.

The law is as known to the editors on 30 September 2019.

Geoffrey Morse
Worcestershire, October 2019

CONTENTS—SUMMARY

Table of Cases — xxi
Table of Legislation — xxxvii
Table of Statutory Instruments — xliii
Table of European Legislation — xlv
List of Abbreviations — xlvii

PART I PARTNERSHIPS

1. Partnerships and Partnership Law — 3
2. Establishing a Partnership — 45
3. Legal Controls on Partnerships — 85
4. Partners and Outsiders — 107
5. Partners and Each Other — 157
6. Partnership Property — 205
7. Dissolution and Winding Up — 229
8. Partnerships and Insolvency — 281
9. Limited Partnerships — 299

PART II LLPs

10. LLPs: An Introduction — 317
11. The Corporate Structure — 329
12. Membership — 353
13. Rights and Duties of Membership — 365
14. The LLP Agreement — 379
15. Decision-Making — 397
16. Termination of Membership — 409
17. Insolvency and Dissolution — 419

Index — 431

CONTENTS

Table of Cases — xxi
Table of Legislation — xxxvii
Table of Statutory Instruments — xliii
Table of European Legislation — xlv
List of Abbreviations — xlvii

PART I PARTNERSHIPS

1. Partnerships and Partnership Law
   - What is a Partnership? — 1.01
     - Limited liability partnerships — 1.02
     - Further developments in Jersey — 1.03
     - Law Commissions' review of partnership law — 1.04
   - Legal Personality and Continuity — 1.05
     - Continuity — 1.06
     - Contractual and statutory problems — 1.07
     - Legal personality in Scotland — 1.08
   - Partnership Law — 1.09
     - Partnership Act 1890 — 1.09
     - Common law and equity — 1.10
     - Other relevant statutes — 1.11
   - Essentials of a Partnership — 1.12
     - Relationship with joint ventures — 1.13
     - Business — 1.14
       - Contemplated partnerships — 1.15
       - Self-employment and employees — 1.16
       - Single commercial venture — 1.17
       - Excluded relationships—co-ownership — 1.18
       - Forming a company or LLP — 1.19
     - Carried on in common — 1.20
       - Participation in the business — 1.21
       - Control — 1.22
       - Limited partners — 1.23
     - With a view of profit — 1.24
       - Need for agreement to share profits? — 1.25
       - Gross and net profits — 1.26
   - Partnerships Then and Now — 1.27
     - Partnerships up to 1890 — 1.28
     - The growth and development of private companies — 1.29
     - Partnerships today—impact of the LLP — 1.30
   - Partnerships: Variations on a Theme — 1.31
     - Group partnerships — 1.31
       - Extension of fiduciary liabilities — 1.32

x CONTENTS

Identifying a single or multiple firm—multinational firms	1.33
Subpartnerships	1.34
Corporate Partners	1.35
Capacity issues	1.36
Other issues	1.37
The International Dimension—Jurisdiction	1.38
Cases where the Judgments Regulation applies	1.39
Cases where the Judgments Regulation does not apply	1.40
2. Establishing a Partnership	
Questions and Answers	2.01
Importance of establishing a partnership	2.02
Refining the question	2.03
No requirement for written agreement	2.04
Intentional Partnerships	2.05
The partnership agreement or deed	2.05
Commencement	2.06
Duration—partnerships at will	2.07
Relationship between ss 26 and 32(c)	2.08
Partnership at will following a fixed-term partnership	2.09
Current situation	2.10
Form of notice	2.11
Continuing terms into a partnership at will	2.12
Partnerships by Association	2.13
Association by Financial Involvement	2.14
Profit-sharing as evidence of partnership	2.15
Establishing community of benefit or opposition of interest	2.16
Sharing of losses	2.17
Other factors	2.18
Specific cases	2.19
Remuneration of employees	2.20
Provision for dependants	2.21
Partners or creditors	2.22
Examples	2.23
Need for written agreement	2.24
Sale of goodwill	2.25
Effectiveness of s 2(3)	2.26
Deferred debts (s 3)	2.27
Partnership Liability by Representation	2.28
Need for representation	2.29
Knowingly being represented as a partner	2.30
Need for reliance	2.31
Written notice of being a partner	2.32
True nature of liability	2.33
Partners, Employees, and Workers	2.34
Can a partner also be an employee?	2.34
Can a partner also be a worker?	2.35
Importance of the distinction	2.36
Salaried and Fixed Share Partners	2.37
Growth of salaried and fixed share partners	2.37
Early cases—semi-retirement issues	2.38

Decision in *Stekel v Ellice*—the modern approach to salaried partners	2.39
Substance not form	2.40
Subsequent cases on salaried partners	2.41
Fixed share partners	2.42
Persons Having Status as a Partner	2.43

3. Legal Controls on Partnerships

Public and Private Controls	3.01
Areas of public interest	3.02
Restrictions on three freedoms	3.03
Restrictions on the Freedom to Contract	3.04
Capacity and discrimination	3.04
Illegality	3.05
Restraint-of-trade Clauses	3.06
Assessing the validity	3.06
Medical partnerships	3.07
Solicitors' partnerships	3.08
Decision in *Bridge v Deacons*	3.09
Bridge v Deacons distinguished	3.10
Enforcement	3.11
Restrictions on Freedom of Association	3.12
Restrictions on Choice of Business Name	3.13
Application of Part 41 of the Companies Act 2006	3.14
Limitations on choice of name	3.15
Disclosure of names of partners	3.16
Passing-off actions	3.17
Partnerships and the Public Domain	3.18
Partnership litigation	3.19
Right of individual partner to sue for wrong done to the partnership	3.20
Right of partner not to be joined as a claimant in partnership action	3.21

4. Partners and Outsiders

Potential Problem Areas	4.01
Liability of Partners for Contracts	4.02
Agency concepts	4.02
Types of authority	4.03
Limitations in the agreement	4.04
Ratification	4.05
The implied or usual authority of a partner—s 5	4.06
Applying the s 10 vicarious liability test	4.08
'Kind of business'	4.09
Acts or instruments in the firm name	4.10
Pledging credit	4.11
'In the usual way'	4.12
Modern developments	4.13
Another business	4.14
Imputed notice	4.16
Exclusion of implied authority	4.17
Doctrine of the undisclosed principal	4.18
Application to partnership	4.19
Interface with s 5	4.20

Playing word games	4.21
Alternative trust solution	4.22
Liability for Other Wrongs	4.23
Vicarious Liability for Torts, Breaches of Duty, and Crimes	4.24
Ordinary course of business	4.25
Close connection test	4.25
Examples of ordinary course of business	4.26
Personal dealings	4.27
Wrongs within partner's authority	4.28
Limitations on the liability	4.29
Primary liability of wrongdoer	4.30
Wrongs between partners	4.31
Crimes	4.32
Can a firm be convicted of an offence?	4.33
Corporate manslaughter and homicide	4.34
Scottish partnerships	4.35
Liability for Misapplication of Property	4.36
Relationship between ss 10 and 11	4.37
Receipt within apparent authority of partner	4.38
Receipt in course of ordinary business	4.39
Improper employment of trust property in the partnership	4.40
Vicarious liability for dishonest assistance and knowing receipt	4.41
Specific problems with receipts	4.42
Vicarious liability for breaches of express trusts	4.43
Scope of s 13	4.44
Nature of the Liability	4.45
Joint and several liability	4.45
Civil Liability (Contribution) Act 1978	4.46
Liability for costs	4.47
Duration of the Liability	4.48
Effect of a change of partner	4.49
Single continuing contract	4.50
Scottish partnerships	4.51
Novation—English law	4.52
Implied novation	4.53
Guarantees	4.54
Liability for debts incurred after leaving the firm	4.55
Presumption of liability	4.56
Actual notice	4.57
Notice in the Gazette	4.58
Where third party did not know he was a partner	4.59
Summary	4.60

5. Partners and Each Other

Contract and Equity	5.01
Fiduciary relationship	5.01
Effect of agreement	5.02
Interaction between contract and equity	5.03
Duty of Care to Each Other	5.04
Assessing the standard of care and skill	5.04

Fiduciary Duties	5.05
Good faith—the fiduciary principle	5.05
Width of the good faith principle	5.06
Limitations on the good faith principle	5.07
Application to prospective partners	5.08
Application to repudiation and dissolution	5.09
Honesty and Full Disclosure	5.10
Conflict of Interest and Duty—Unauthorized Personal Profit	5.11
The 'no-profit' and 'no-conflict' rules	5.11
Direct profit from partnership transaction	5.12
Use of partnership asset for personal benefit	5.13
Identifying the asset	5.14
Misuse of partnership opportunity	5.15
Analogy with company directors	5.16
Duration of liability	5.17
Errant partner's share of the benefit	5.18
Duty Not to Compete	5.19
Contract: Implied Terms	5.20
Management and Control	5.21
Management rights	5.21
Remuneration—share of the profit	5.22
Majority voting	5.23
Abuse of power	5.24
Access to partnership books	5.25
Financial Affairs	5.26
Principle of equality	5.26
Rebutting the presumption of equality	5.27
Evidential burden	5.28
Losses	5.29
Interest on capital contributions	5.30
Advances	5.31
Indemnities	5.32
Change of Partners	5.33
Implied requirement for unanimous consent	5.33
Contrary intention	5.34
Evidential difficulties	5.35
Conditional clauses	5.36
Expulsion Clauses	5.37
Need for express clause	5.37
Complying with the terms of the clause	5.38
Procedural compliance with the clause	5.39
Application of natural justice	5.40
Abuse of power	5.41
Unreasonableness	5.42
Compulsory retirement	5.43
Assignment of the Partnership Share	5.44
Rights of the assignee whilst the partnership is a going concern	5.45
Rights of the assignee on dissolution	5.46
Entitlement to an account	5.47
Losses	5.48

Charging Orders Against Partners ... 5.49
    Strict interpretation ... 5.50

6. Partnership Property

Problems and Possibilities ... 6.01
    Need to identify partnership property ... 6.01
    Link with insolvency ... 6.02
    Beneficial ownership ... 6.03
    Application of fiduciary duties ... 6.04
    Co-ownership issues ... 6.05
    Doctrine of conversion ... 6.06
What is Partnership Property? ... 6.07
Nature and Consequences of a Partner's Interest ... 6.08
    Enforceable only on partial or total dissolution ... 6.08
    Beneficial interest ... 6.09
    Limits on assets capable of being partnership property ... 6.10
    Land held under a trust ... 6.11
Identifying Partnership Property ... 6.12
    Express or implied agreement—surrounding circumstances ... 6.12
    Use in partnership not always sufficient to create partnership property—business efficacy and necessity ... 6.14
        Farming cases ... 6.15
    Strict construction of agreements ... 6.16
    Property bought with partnership profits ... 6.17
    Purchase of land out of profits made by use of non-partnership land ... 6.18
        Application to improvements ... 6.19
        Contrary intention ... 6.20
    Resulting trusts ... 6.21
Business Premises: Leases and Licences ... 6.22
    Problems of assignment ... 6.22
    Business tenancies ... 6.23
    Ownership by all partners outside the partnership ... 6.24
    Ownership by one or some partners outside the partnership ... 6.25
Goodwill: A Note ... 6.26
    Identifying goodwill ... 6.27
        Professional partnerships ... 6.28
    Consequences of a sale of goodwill ... 6.29
    Goodwill as a partnership asset ... 6.30

7. Dissolution and Winding Up

Dissolution ... 7.01
    General and technical dissolutions ... 7.01
Contractual Grounds for Dissolution ... 7.02
    Implied terms ... 7.02
    Death, bankruptcy, and charging orders ... 7.03
        Contrary intention—s 33(2) ... 7.04
    Express clauses ... 7.05
    Mutual agreement ... 7.06
Illegality ... 7.07
Dissolution by the Court ... 7.08

Grounds for court order	7.08
(a) Mental incapacity	7.09
(b) Permanent incapacity	7.10
(c) Prejudicial conduct	7.11
(d) Persistent breaches of the agreement	7.12
(e) Carrying on the business at a loss	7.13
(f) Just and equitable ground	7.14
Just and equitable ground—'no fault divorce'	7.15
Application to commercial partnerships	7.16
Ouster clauses	7.17
Frustration of the Partnership Agreement	7.18
Rescission of the Partnership Agreement	7.19
Repudiation of the Partnership Agreement	7.20
Contractual effect of repudiation	7.21
Effect of repudiation on partnership relationship—abandonment/mutuality	7.22
General Dissolutions—Winding Up	7.23
Winding Up by the Existing Partners	7.24
Extent of implied authority	7.25
Effect on contracts of employment	7.26
Duty to wind up	7.27
Partnership Receivers	7.28
Appointing a receiver	7.28
Professional partnerships	7.29
Continuation of business	7.30
Single partner or receiver continuing the business	7.31
Remuneration of a receiver	7.32
Liability of a receiver	7.33
Return of Premiums	7.34
Application of Assets on a Winding Up	7.35
Partners' rights in the assets of the firm	7.35
Powers of the court in respect of the assets	7.36
Realization by sale	7.37
Buy out or *Syers v Syers* orders	7.38
Technical Dissolutions	7.39
Problem areas	7.40
Liability of Former Partner	7.41
Valuation of a Partner's Share in the Assets	7.42
Capital, assets, and profits	7.42
Valuation method	7.43
Entitlement to market value—the position in Scotland	7.44
Construction of the agreement—the position in England and Wales	7.45
Income profits	7.46
Construction of terms of the agreements	7.47
Law Commissions' proposals	7.48
Partner's Share in Profits etc after Dissolution	7.49
Choice of profits or interest	7.49
Outgoing partner—technical dissolution only	7.50
No application to capital profits	7.51
Post-dissolution income profits	7.52
Attributable to the use of his share of the partnership assets	7.53

Deductions for management by remaining partner(s)	7.54
Adjustments for management etc in relation to share of capital profits	7.55
Interest option in lieu of share of income profits	7.56
No effect on right to capital profits	7.57
Making an election	7.58
Contracting out	7.59
Transfer of Outgoing Partner's Share	7.60
Distribution of Assets—Solvent Partnerships	7.61
Need for final accounts	7.61
Surplus assets and capital losses	7.62
Surplus assets	7.63
Capital losses	7.64

8. Partnerships and Insolvency

Possibilities and Problems	8.01
Applicable insolvency law	8.02
Partnership and partner insolvencies	8.03
Bankrupt partner but no petition against the firm	8.04
Winding Up of an Insolvent Partnership Only	8.05
Winding Up of an Insolvent Partnership and Concurrent Bankruptcy of the Partners	8.06
Priority of creditors	8.07
Disqualification from management of a company or LLP	8.08
Joint Bankruptcy Petitions	8.09
Winding Up a Partnership after Separate Bankruptcy Petitions	8.10
Partnership Voluntary Arrangements	8.11
Effect of a partnership voluntary arrangement	8.12
Obtaining a temporary moratorium for 'smaller' partnerships	8.13
Partnership Administration Orders	8.14
Purpose of the administration	8.15
Appointment by application to the court	8.16
Exercise of the court's discretion	8.17
Appointment by the partners	8.18
Consequences of an order	8.19
Flexibility of administration	8.20

9. Limited Partnerships

Origins and Development of the Limited Partnership	9.01
The 1907 Act	9.02
The reform process	9.03
Limited Partnerships which are not Private Fund Limited Partnerships (sometimes referred to as private limited partnerships)	9.04
Formation	9.04
Registration—reform proposals adopted	9.04
Effectiveness of the certificate of registration—fraudulent applications	9.05
Other requirements	9.06
Limited Partner's Liability	9.07
Possible reforms on capital	9.08
Trading losses	9.09
Failure to contribute agreed sum	9.10
Interference in management	9.11

Other Modifications of Partnership Law	9.13
Derivative actions	9.14
Dissolution	9.15
Private Fund Limited Partnerships	9.16
Definition, registration, and de-registration of a private fund limited partnership	9.17
Interfering in management—permitted activities	9.18
Capital contributions	9.19
Registered particulars, changes, and Gazette notices	9.20
Other modifications on partnership law	9.21
Winding up	9.22
Proposed Reforms to Counter Abuse of the Limited Partnership Form	9.23
Evidence of abuse	9.23
Proposals for reform to counter abuse	9.24

PART II LLPs

10. LLPs: An Introduction

A Note on Citation	10.01
What is an LLP?	10.02
The Development of LLPs	10.03
The genesis of the Limited Liability Partnerships Act	10.04
The response to the Act	10.05
Criticisms	10.06
The Legislative Scheme	10.07
The Act	10.08
The regulations	10.09
LLPs, Partnerships, and Companies	10.10

11. The Corporate Structure

The Basic Requirements for an LLP	11.01
'Two or more persons'	11.02
'Associated for carrying on'	11.03
'A lawful business with a view to profit'	11.04
The Process of Incorporation	11.05
Name	11.06
Situation and address	11.07
Members' particulars	11.08
Designated members	11.09
Statement of initial significant control	11.10
The Legal Consequences of Incorporation	11.11
Attribution and vicarious liability	11.12
Attribution	11.12
Vicarious liability	11.13
Members' authority	11.14
Apparent authority	11.15
The corporate veil and limited liability	11.16
Exceptions	11.17
Lifting the veil	11.18
Capacity	11.19
Pre-incorporation contracts and deeds	11.20
Post-incorporation contracts and deeds	11.21

Litigation	11.22
Disclosure obligations	11.23
Display of name	11.24
Register of members	11.25
Notification of membership changes to the Registrar	11.26
The PSC register	11.27
Registration of charges	11.28
Annual confirmation statements	11.29
Records and accounts	11.30

12. Membership

Who is a Member?	12.01
Commencement of membership	12.01
The consequences of membership	12.02
Degrees of membership?	12.03
Termination of membership	12.04
'Salaried members'	12.05
Shadow members	12.06
De facto members	12.07
Members and Employees	12.08
Tiffin v Lester Aldridge LLP	12.09
Clyde & Co LLP v Bates van Winkelhof	12.10
Members and Workers	12.11
Disqualification from Membership	12.12
Disqualification of LLP members	12.13
Disqualification of company directors	12.14
Grounds for disqualification	12.15
Undischarged bankrupts	12.16

13. Rights and Duties of Membership

The Member's Share	13.01
The effect of assignment and bankruptcy on a member's share	13.02
The Sources of Members' Rights and Duties	13.03
The LLP Agreement	13.04
Statutory rights and duties	13.05
Common law and equity	13.06
Members' Fiduciary Duties	13.07
Fiduciary duties between members and the LLP	13.08
Informed consent by the LLP	13.09
Remedies	13.10
Fiduciary duties between members themselves	13.11
Members' Duty of Care to the LLP	13.12
Exclusion of liability	13.13
Relief from liability	13.14
Members' Duties to Third Parties	13.15
Liability for one's own wrongs	13.15
Assumption of responsibility	13.16
Said v Butt	13.17
Members' Duties to Creditors	13.18
Minority Protections	13.19
Unfair prejudice	13.20

Excluding the right	13.21
Quasi-partnerships	13.22
Just and equitable winding up	13.23
Standing of members	13.24
Grounds for relief	13.25
Arbitration and other remedies	13.26

14. The LLP Agreement

The Scope of the LLP Agreement	14.01
'Between the members' or 'between the LLP and its members'	14.02
Formalities	14.03
Default Provisions	14.04
(1) Right to an equal share in capital and profits	14.05
(2) Right to an indemnity	14.06
(3) Right to manage	14.07
(4) No right to remuneration	14.08
(5) No right to assign	14.09
(6) Majority rule	14.10
(7) Books and records	14.11
(8) Duty to account	14.12
(9) Duty not to compete	14.13
(10) Improper benefit	14.14
(11) Expulsion	14.15
A Duty of Good Faith	14.16
Amending the Agreement	14.17
Remedies for Breach	14.18
Rescission	14.19
Availability of the remedy	14.20
Application of the remedy	14.21
Repudiation	14.22
Flanagan v Liontrust Investment Partners LLP	14.23
Resignation and a claim for damages	14.24
Frustration	14.25

15. Decision-Making

The Decision-Making Process	15.01
Ordinary matters connected with the business	15.02
Extra-ordinary matters	15.03
Statutory powers	15.04
Corporate decision-making at common law	15.05
The *Duomatic* principle	15.06
The Exercise of Discretion	15.07
Good faith and proper purpose	15.08
Rationality	15.09
Natural Justice and Giving Reasons	15.10
Natural justice	15.11
Natural justice in a corporate setting	15.12
Reasons	15.13
The forensic value of procedural propriety	15.14
Statutory rights	15.15
The Consequences of an Unlawful Decision	15.16

Acting outside the scope of the power	15.17
Improper exercise of the power	15.18

16. Termination of Membership

Methods of Termination	16.01
'By death or dissolution'	16.02
'Agreement with the other members'	16.03
Abandonment?	16.04
Expulsion	16.05
'Reasonable notice'	16.06
Consequences of Termination	16.07
External consequences	16.08
Internal consequences	16.09
Entitlement to profits	16.10
Repayment of capital	16.11
Capital profits and goodwill	16.12
Forfeiture of profits	16.13
Post-Termination Controls	16.14
Covenants in restraint of trade	16.15
Implied restrictions on solicitation?	16.16

17. Insolvency and Dissolution

The Insolvency Act Regime	17.01
Voluntary winding up	17.02
Compulsory winding up	17.03
Voluntary arrangements	17.04
Administration	17.05
Receivership	17.06
The LLP in Liquidation	17.07
Contributions by members	17.08
Voluntary contributions: s 74	17.09
Enforced contributions: s 214A	17.10
Claims by members	17.11
Claims to capital	17.12
Claims to profit	17.13
Arrangements and Reconstructions	17.14
Schemes of arrangement	17.14
Cross-border mergers	17.15
Voluntary reconstructions	17.16
Investigations	17.17
Striking Off the Register	17.18
Striking off consequent to winding up	17.18
Striking off by the Registrar	17.19
Bona vacantia	17.20
Restoration	17.21

Index   431

TABLE OF CASES

975 Duncan v The MFV Marigold Pd 145 2006 SLT 975, CS (OH) 7.25, 7.60
337965 BC Ltd v Tackama Forest Products Ltd (1992) 91 DLR (4th) 129 . . . . .5.02
3464920 Canada Inc v Strother, 2007 SCC 24 . . . . 4.24, 4.26, 4.41

A Akman & Son (Fla) Inc v Chipman (1988) 45 DLR (4th) 481 . . . . .5.09
ACC Bank plc v Johnston [2011] IEHC 108 . . . . 4.56, 7.02
AIB Group (UK) plc v Martin [2002] 2 All ER (Comm) 686 . . . . .5.02
Aas v Benham [1891] 2 Ch 244, CA 5.15, 5.19, 14.14
Abbatt v Treasury Solicitor [1969] 1 WLR 1575, CA 15.16
Abbott v Abbott [1936] 3 All ER 823 . . . . .2.10
Achom v Lalic [2014] EWHC 1888 (Ch) 1.13, 2.04
Acquinas Education Ltd v Miller [2018] EWHC 404, QB 3.11
Adam v Newbigging [1888] 13 AC 308, HL 2.04
Agip (Africa) Ltd v Jackson [1991] Ch 547 . . . . .4.41
Agriculturist Cattle Insurance Co, Baird's Case, Re (1870) LR 5 Ch App 725, CA 4.02
Ali v Torrosian (2018) UKEAT/0029/18/JOJ 3.04
All Link International Ltd v Ha Kai Cheong [2005] 3 HKLRD 65 . . . . 2.32, 2.39
Allen v Aspen Group Resources Corporation 2009 Can LII 67668, Ont SC 4.08, 4.26
Allied Business and Financial Consultants Ltd, Re [2009] 1 BCLC 328 . . . . .5.15
Allied Pharmaceutical Distributors Ltd v Walsh [1991] 2 IR 8 . . . . .4.28
Alton Renaissance I v Talamanca Management Ltd (1993) 99 DLR (4th) 707 . . . . .1.37
Anderson Group v Davies (2001) 53 NSWLR 401 . . . . 1.35, 7.03, 7.30
Antonelli v Allen [2001] Lloyd's Rep PN 487 . . . . 4.38, 4.39
Arbuckle v Taylor (1815) 3 Dow 160 . . . . .4.29
Arden v Roy [1883] 1 NZLR 365 . . . . .4.53
Arif v Yeo [1989] SLR 849 . . . . 5.22, 7.02
Armagas Ltd v Mundogas SA [1986] AC 717, HL 4.03
Armitage v Nurse [1998] Ch 241 . . . . .13.13
Armour Intl Co Ltd v Worldwide Cosmetics Inc 689 F 2d 134 (1982) 1.33
Ashbury Railway Carriage & Iron Co Ltd v Riche (1874-75) LR 7HL 653 . . . . 15.17
Associated Provincial Picture Houses Ltd v Wednesbury Corporation [1948] 1 KB 223 . . . . 5.41, 15.08
Australia & New Zealand Banking Group Ltd v Richardson [1980] QdR 321 . . . . .1.34
Automatic Self-Cleaning Filter Syndicate Co Ltd v Cuningham [1906] 2 Ch 34 . . . . .5.22

Badeley v Consolidated Bank (1888) 38 Ch D 238, CA 2.14, 2.16
Badham v Williams (1902) 86 LT 191 . . . . .7.46
Badyal v Badyal [2018] EWHV 68 (Ch) 6.17
Bagel v Miller [1903] 2 KB 212 . . . . .4.50
Bailey v Manos Breeder Farms Pty Ltd (1990) 8 ACLC 1119 . . . . .1.37
Baker v Lintott [1982] 4 WWR 766 . . . . .3.07
Balmer v HM Advocate [2008] HCJAC 44 . . . . 1.08, 4.36
Bank of Beirut SAL v HRH Prince Adel El-Hashemite [2015] EWHC 1451 (Ch) 9.05
Bank of Scotland v Butcher [2003] 1 BCLC 575, CA 4.07, 4.12, 4.13
Barber v Rasco International Ltd [2012] EWHC 269 (QB) 5.17, 6.10, 7.06, 7.22
Barclays Bank Trust Co Ltd v Bluff [1982] Ch 172 . . . . 7.51, 7.56
Barfield v Loughborough (1872) LR 8 Ch App 369 . . . . .5.31
Barfoot v Goodall (1811) 3 Camp 147 . . . . .4.57
Barnard, Re [1932] Ch 269 . . . . .9.02
Barnes v Youngs [1898] 1 Ch 414 . . . . .5.40
Bartels v Behm (1990) 19 NSWLR 257 . . . . .7.52

TABLE OF CASES

Barton v Morris [1985] 1 WLR 1257 .... 6.05
Bass Breweries Ltd v Appleby [1997] 2 BCLC 700, CA 1.31, 2.33, 4.38, 4.42, 4.44
Bathurst v Scarborow [2004] 1 P & CR 4, CA 6.05
Beale v Trinkler [2009] NSWCA 1093 .... 7.55
Beaver v Cohen [2006] EWHC 199 (Ch) 6.28
Beckman v Canada (2001) 196 DLR (4th) 193 .... 1.25
Beckman v IRC [2000] STC (SCD) 59 .... 7.50
Belfield v Bourne [1894] 1 Ch 521 .... 7.17
Belgravia Nominees Pty Ltd v Lowe Pty Ltd [2015] WASCA 143 .... 7.25
Bell's Indenture, Re [1980] 1 WLR 1271 .... 4.41, 4.42
Bennett v Richardson [1980] RTR 358, Div C 2.36
Bennett v Wallace 1998 SC 457 .... 5.27, 7.42, 7.61
Bentley v Craven (1853) 18 Beav 75 .... 5.12
Bernhard Schulte GmbH & Co KG v Nile Holdings Ltd [2004] EWHC 977 (Comm),
 [2004] 2 Lloyd's Rep 352 .... 15.11
Bevan v Webb [1901] 2 Ch 59, CA 5.25
Bhayani v Taylor Bracewell LLP [2016] EWHC 3360, IPEC 3.17, 6.30, 16.12
Bhullar v Bhullar [2003] 2 BCLC 241 .... 5.16
Bigelow v Powers (1911) 25 OLR 28 .... 4.31
Biliora Pty ltd v Leisure Investments Pty Ltd (2001) 11 NTLR 148, CA 2.12
Bilta (UK) Limited v Nazir (No 2) [2005] UKSC 23, [2006] AC 1 .... 11.12
Bird Precision Bellows Ltd, Re [1984] Ch 419 (Ch) 13.22
Bishop v Goldstein [2014] EWCA Civ 10 .... 5.03, 7.12
Biss, Re [1903] 2 Ch 40 .... 5.17
Bissell v Cole [1997] 12 WLUK 221, CA 1.21, 5.23
Blisset v Daniel (1853) 10 Hare 493 .... 5.41, 15.17
Bloxham, Re [2017] IEHC 664 .... 6.08
Blue Line Hockey Acquisition Co v Orca Bay Hickey Ltd Partnership [2009] BCCA 34 ..... 1.15
Boardman v Phipps [1967] AC 46 .... 5.15, 9.18
Boehm v Goodall [1911] 1 Ch 155 .... 7.32
Boghani v Nathoo [2011] EWHC 2101 (Ch) 7.25
Bohachewski v Bohachewski 2018 SKQB 229 .... 7.04
Bonnin v Neame [1910] 1 Ch 732 .... 5.45
Bonzalie v Cullu [2013] NSWSC 1576 .... 7.22
Boston Deep Sea Fishing & Ice Co v Ansell (1888) 39 Ch D 339 .... 5.12
Bottrill v Harling [2015] EWCA Civ 564 .... 5.02
Bourne, Re [1906] 2 Ch 427 .... 7.25
Boutsakis v Kakavelakis 2010 BCSC 1077 .... 5.32
Braganza v BP Shipping Ltd [2015] 1 WLR 1661 .... 5.41, 15.08, 15.14
Braymist v Wise Finance Co [2002] EWCA Civ 127, [2002] Ch 273 .... 11.20
Brenner v Rose [1973] 1 WLR 443 .... 5.17
Brettel v Williams (1849) 4 Ex 623 .... 4.13
Brew v Rozano Holdings Ltd 2006 BCCA 346 .... 7.22
Brewer v Yorke (1882) 46 LT 289 .... 7.34
Brice v Garden of Eden Ltd [1965–70] 2 LRB 204 .... 2.29
Bridge v Deacons [1984] AC 705, PC 3.06, 3.08–3.10, 6.30, 16.15
Briggs & Co, Re [1906] 2 KB 209 .... 4.10
Briggs v Oates [1990] ICR 473 .... 2.36, 2.41, 3.06
Bristol and West Building Society v Mothew [1998] Ch 1, CA 13.07
British Airways plc v Airways Pension Scheme Trustee Ltd [2018] EWCA Civ 1533,
 [2018] Pens LR 19 .... 14.17
British Homes Assurance Corporation Ltd v Paterson [1902] 2 Ch 404 .... 4.38
British Shoe Corporation Ltd v Customs and Excise Commissioners [1998] V & DR 348 ..... 1.07
Britton v Commisisoners of Customs & Excise [1986] VATTR 204 .... 1.24
Bromhead v Graham [2007] NSWCA 257 .... 7.26
Brooks v AH Brooks & Co [2010] EWHC 2720 (Ch) 3.19

Brooks v Brooks (1901) 85 LT 453	2.12
Browell v Goodyear, The Times, 24 October 2000	7.42
Brown Economic Assessments Inc v Stevenson (2003) 11 WWR 101	2.28
Brown, Janson & Co v Hutchinson (No 2) [1895] 2 QB 126, CA	5.48
Brown v Oakshot (1857) 24 Beav 254	6.05
Brydges v Branfill (1842) 12 Sim 369	4.41
Buchanan v Nolan [2013] CSIH 38	7.61, 7.62
Buckingham v Dole 1961 3 SA 384 (T)	1.18
Burchell v Wilde [1900] 1 Ch 551	6.30
Byford v Oliver [2003] FSR 39	6.30
Byrne v Reid [1902] 2 Ch 735, CA	5.34, 5.36
C & M Ashberg, Re *The Times*, 17 July 1990	2.28
CMS Dolphin Ltd v Simonet [2001] 2 BCLC 704	5.06, 5.16
Campbell v Campbell [2017] EWHC 182 (Ch)	5.10, 6.10, 7.36
Campbell v McCreath 1975 SLT 5	4.16
Canadian Pacific Ltd v Telesat Canada (1982) 133 DLR (3d) 321	1.22
Canny Gabriel Castle Jackson Advertising Pty Ltd v Volume Sales (Finance) Pty Ltd (1974) 131 CLR 321	6.09
Cappe v Tsung [2018] NSWCA 86	5.23
Carmichael v Evans [1904] 1 Ch 486	5.37, 7.05
Carter Bros v Renouf (1962) 36 ALJR 67	6.21
Carver v Duncan [1985] 1 AC 1082	7.55
Casson Beckman & Partners v Papi1 [1991] BCLC 299CA	2.41
Castledine v RSM Bentley Jennison [2011] EWHC 2363 (Ch)	6.27
Catch a Ride Ltd v Gardner [2014] EWHC 1220 (Ch)	7.28, 7.31
Certain Limited Partners in Henderson PFI Secondary Fund II LLP v Henderson PFI Secondary Fund II LP [2012] EWHC 3259 (Comm)	3.20, 9.14
Chahal v Mahal [2005] 2 BCLC 655, [2005] EWCA Civ 898, CA	7.06, 7.22
Chan, Leung & Cheung v Tse Mei Lin [2004] 2 HKC 283	3.21
Chan Sau-kut v Gray & Iron Construction and Engineering Co [1986] HKLR 84	2.04, 2.22, 5.03
Chan v Zacharia (1984) 154 CLR 178	5.09, 5.11, 5.17, 7.24
Chandroutie v Gajadhar [1987] AC 147, PC	7.51, 7.57
Cheema v Jones [2017] EWCA Civ 1706	1.10, 2.04, 7.06, 7.22
Cheeseman v Price (1865) 35 Beav 142	7.12
Chiam Heng Hsien v Chiam Heng Chow [2014] SGHC 119	7.60
Chickabo Pty Ltd v Zphere Pty Ltd [2019] VSC 73	5.10
Chittick v Maxwell (1993) 118 ALR 728	4.27
Choudary v Minhas [2006] EWHC 2289 (Ch)	3.04
Choudhri v Palta [1994] 1 BCLC 184, CA	7.32
Christie Owen & Davies plc v RAOBGLE Trust Corporation [2011] EWCA Civ 1151	1.15
Chua Ka Seng v Bounchai Sumpolpong [1993] 1 SLR 482, CA	2.41
Churton v Douglas (1859) John 174	6.29
Clark v Fahrenheit 451 (Communications) Ltd [2000] 6 WLUK 65, EAT	16.06
Clark v Leach (1863) 1 de GJ & S 409	2.12, 5.37
Clark v Watson 1982 SLT 450	7.44, 7.45
Clarke v Newland [1991] 1 All ER 397	3.07
Clifford v Timms [1908] AC 112	7.05
Clode v Barnes [1974] 1 All ER 1176	4.32
Cloutte v Storey [1911] 1 Ch 18, CA	15.17
Clyde & Co LLP v Bates van Winklehof [2012] EWCA Civ 1207	2.34, 2.35, 12.10
Clyde & Co LLP v Bates van Winklehof [2014] UKSC 32, [2014] 1 WLR 2047	1.07, 1.08, 2.34, 2.35, 12.10, 12.11
Cobbetts LLP v Hodge [2009] EWHC 786 (Ch)	2.41
Cole v Lee [2017] NSWCA 1011	2.07, 2.08, 2.10

TABLE OF CASES

Commissioner of Taxation v Everett (1980) 143 CLR 440 . . . . .5.44
Company (No 005685 of 1988), Re a [1989] BCLC 427 (Ch) 13.22
Conlon v Simms [200] EWHC 401 (Ch) 5.08, 5.10
Connell v Bond Corporation Pty Ltd (1992) 8 WAR 352 . . . . .6.09
Const v Harris (1824) Turn & R 496 . . . . .5.01
Construction Engineering (Aust) Pty Ltd v Hexyl Pty Ltd (1985) 155 CLR 541 . . . . 4.20, 4.22
Continental Bank Leasing Corporation v The Queen (1998) 163 DLR (4th) 385 . . . . 3.05, 7.07
Cook v Rowe [1954] VLR 309 . . . . .6.22
Coope v Eyre (1788) 1 HBL 37 . . . . .1.18
Courage Group's Pension Schemes, Re [1987] 1 WLR 495 (Ch) 15.08
Court v Berlin [1897] 2 QB 396 . . . . .4.50
Coward v Phaestos Ltd [2013] EWHC 1232 (Ch) 1.10, 6.13, 6.14
Cowell v Quilter Goodison Co Ltd [1989] IRLR 392 . . . . 2.34, 12.08
Cox v Coulson [1916] 2 KB 177, CA 1.26
Cox v Hickman (1860) 8 HL Cas 268, HL 1.24, 2.14–2.16, 2.22, 2.26, 9.12
Craven v Knight (1682) 2 Rep in Ch 226 . . . . .8.07
Crouch and Lyndon v IPG Finance Australia Pty Ltd [2013] QCA 220 . . . . .4.24
Crowder, ex p (1715) 2 Vern 706 . . . . .8.07
Crown Dilmun v Sutton [2004] 1 BCLC 468 . . . . .5.16
Cruikshank v Sutherland (1922) 92 LJ Ch 136, HL 7.43–7.45
Cruttwell v Lye (1810) 7 Ves Jr 335 . . . . .6.27
Curl Bros Ltd v Webster [1904] 1 Ch 685 . . . . .6.29
Customs & Excise Commissioners v Evans [1982] STC 342 . . . . .1.07
Cutts v Holland [1965] Tas SR 69 . . . . .7.22
Cyril Henschke Pty Ltd v Commissioner of State Taxation [2010] HCA 43 . . . . .6.09

D & H Bunny Pty Ltd v Atkins [1961] VLR 31 . . . . .2.29
DB Rare Books Ltd v Antiqbooks [1995] 2 BCLC 306 . . . . .5.07
DKLL Solicitors, Re [2008] 1 BCLC 112 . . . . .8.17
DTR Nominees Pty Ltd v Mona Homes Pty Ltd (1978) 138 CLR 423 . . . . .7.22
Dallas McMillan & Sinclair v Simpson 1989 SLT 454 . . . . .3.10
Dao Heng Bank Ltd v Hui Kwai-wing [1977] HKLR 122 . . . . 2.30, 2.32
Darby v Meehan, The Times, 25 November 1998 . . . . .6.29
Dave v Robinska [2003] ICR 1248 . . . . .1.07
Davidson v Waymen [1984] 2 NZLR 115, CA 7.01
Davies v H and C Ecroyd Ltd (1996) 2 EGLR 5 . . . . 6.03, 6.15, 6.16
Davis v Davis [1894] 1 Ch 393 . . . . 2.15, 2.18, 6.19, 6.20
Davy v Scarth [1906] 1 Ch 55 . . . . .7.32
Daw v Herring [1892] 1 Ch 284 . . . . .2.12
De Renzy v De Renzy [1924] NZLR 1065 . . . . .7.53
Dhaliwal v Toor 2010 BCSC 1065 . . . . .1.13
Dickensen v Gross (1927) 11 TC 614 . . . . .2.06
Doak v GJ & BP Chard [2015] NSWSC 431 . . . . .4.31
Dockrill v Coopers & Lybrand Chartered Accountants (1994) 111 DLR (4th) 62 . . . . .5.06
Dodson v Downey [1901] 2 Ch 620 . . . . .5.46
Dollar Land (Cumbernauld) Ltd v CIN Properties Ltd 1996 SLT 186, CS (OH) 1.12
Dollars & Sense Finance Ltd v Rerekohu [2008] NZSC 20 . . . . .4.25
Don King Productions Inc v Warren [1999] 2 All ER 218, CA 5.03, 5.09, 5.11, 5.17,
6.04, 6.10, 6.13, 7.24, 7.25, 7.31, 7.35
Drake v Harvey [2011] EWCA Civ 838 . . . . .7.45
Dubai Aluminium Company Ltd v Salaam [2003] AC 366, HL 4.08, 4.09, 4.14,
4.15, 4.25, 4.37, 4.41, 4.43
Duke of Portland v Lady Topham (1864) 11 HLC 32, HL 15.08
Duncan v Lowndes and Bateman (1813) 3 Camp 478 . . . . .4.13
Duncan v The MFV Marigold Pd 145, 2006 SLT 975 . . . . .7.53
Dungate v Lee [1967] 1 All ER 241 . . . . 2.05, 3.05
Duomatic Ltd, Re [1969] 2 Ch 365 (Ch) 15.06

Dutia v Geldof [2016] EWHC 547 (Ch) 1.10, 1.19, 2.04
Dyce v Fairgreave [2013] CSOH 155 . . . . 7.56
Dyke v Brewer (1849)2 Car & kir 828. . . . . 4.50
Dymoke v Association for Dance Movement Psychotherapy UK Ltd [2019] EWHC 94 (QB). . . . 15.12

Eardley v Broad (1970) 120 NLJ 432 . . . . 6.16
Eaton v Caulfield [2011] EWHC 173 (Ch), [2011] BCC 386. . . . . 10.10, 12.02, 13.25, 16.05
Ebrahimi v Westbourne Galleries Ltd [1973] AC 360, HL 1.29, 5.21, 7.14, 9.11, 13.22
Eclairs Group Ltd v JKX Oil & Gas plc [2015] UKSC 71, [2016] BCC 79 . . . . 15.08, 15.12
Edwards v Bairstow [1956] AC 14, HL. 2.03
Edwards v Worboys (1983) 127 SJ 287, CA 3.08
Egon Zehender Ltd v Tilman [2019] UKSC 32 . . . . 3.06
Elite Business Systems UK Ltd v Price [2005] EWCA Civ 920 . . . . 2.30
Ellerforth Investments Ltd v The Typhon Group Ltd, 429/07, 9 September 2009, Ont SC 7.14
Ellis v Joseph Elis & Co [1905] 1 KB 234 . . . . 2.34
Emerson v Emerson [2004] 1 BCLC 575, CA 5.26, 5.27, 7.51, 7.55
Energy Corrector Ltd, Re [2019] EWHC 144 (Ch). 11.22
Ernst & Young v Stuart (1997) 144 DLR (4th) 328 . . . . 3.11
Espley v Williams [1997] 08 EG 137, CA 3.06
Esso Petroleum Co Ltd v Harper's Garage (Stourport) Ltd [1968] AC 269HL 16.15
Estate of Edith Rogers Deceased [2006] EWHC 753 (Ch). 1.30
Eva v Yin [2018] HKDC 4 . . . . 2.11, 7.02
Ewing v Buttercup Margarine Co Ltd [1917] 2 Ch 1 . . . . 3.17

F & C Alternative Investments (Holdings) Ltd v Barthelmy
 [2011] EWHC 1731 (Ch). 11.06, 13.08, 13.11, 14.16
Faber Image Media Pte Ltd v Patrician Holding Pte Ltd [2009] SGHC 16. . . . . 4.57
Facchini v Facchini [2002] WADC 127 . . . . 4.31
Fairman v Scully 1997 GWD 29-1942 . . . . 5.40
Faria v Bush [2018] ONSC 7288 . . . . 1.18
Fassihi v Item Software (UK) Ltd [2004] BCC 994. . . . . 5.16
Faulks v Faulks [1992] 1 EGLR 9. . . . . 6.03, 6.15
Fazio v Fazio [2012] WASC 72 . . . . 6.09, 7.06, 7.22
Featherstone v Staples [1986] 1 WLR 861 . . . . 6.23
Federal Commissioner of Taxation v Everett (1980) 54 AJLR 196 . . . . 6.09
Feetum v Levy [2005] EWCA Civ 1601, [2006] Ch 585. . . . . 10.09
Fengate Developments v CEC [2005] STC 191, aff'g [2004] STC 772 . . . . 6.08
Filkow v D'Arcy & Deacon LLP 2019 MBCA 61 . . . . 5.10
Finlayson v Turnbull (No 1) 1997 SLT 613 . . . . 5.06, 6.28, 6.30
First Energy (UK) Ltd v Hungarian International Bank Ltd [1993] 2 Lloyd's Rep 194. . . . . 4.03
Firth v Amslake (1965) 108 SJ 198 . . . . 7.06
Flanagan v Liontrust Investment Partners LLP [2015] EWHC 2171 (Ch) 14.16, 14.18, 14.23, 14.25
Floydd v Cheney [1970] Ch 602 . . . . 5.06, 7.29
Flynn v Robin Thompson & Partners *The Times*, 14 March 2000. . . . . 4.29
Forster v Ferguson, Forster, Macfie and Alexander [2010] CSIH 38 . . . . 7.22
Fort, ex p Schofield, Re [1897] 2 QB 495 . . . . 2.24, 2.27
Foss v Harbottle (1843) 2 Hare 461. . . . . 3.20
Foster Bryant v Bryant [2007] 2 BCLC 239, CA 5.06
Fox Hayes v Financial Services Authority 2010 WL 1944393 . . . . 2.36, 2.42
Franich v Harrison [2006] NZHC 1059 . . . . 1.25
Frank Mills Mining Company, In re (1883) 23 Ch D 52. . . . . 5.03
Franklin and Swaythling's Arbitration, Re [1929] 1 Ch 238 . . . . 5.36
Fraser Edmiston Pty Ltd v AGT (Qld) Pty Ltd [1988] 2 QdR 1 . . . . 5.08
Frauenstein v Farinha [2007] FCA 1953 . . . . 1.37
Fred Drughorn Ltd v Rederiaktiebolaget Transatlantic [1919] AC 203, HL 4.18
Fry v Oddy [1999] 1 VR 542, CA 7.54
Fulham Football Club (1987) Ltd v Richards [2011] EWCA Civ 855, [2012] Ch 333 . . . . 13.26

TABLE OF CASES

Fulton v AIB Group (UK) plc [2014] NICh 8 .... 8.19
Fung v Heung [2006] HKEC 631 .... 1.18
Fung v Kit [2018] HKDC 1252 .... 4.26

Gadd v Gadd (2002) 08 EG 160 .... 7.45
Gaiman v National Association for Mental Health [1971] Ch 317, CA 15.11, 15.12
Gallagher v Shultz [1988] 2 NZBLC 103 .... 5.04
Garner v Murray [1904] 1 Ch 57 .... 7.64
Garty v Garty [1997] 3 NZLR 66 .... 6.28
Garwood's Trusts, Re [1903] 1 Ch 236 .... 5.43, 5.48
Geisel v Geisel (1990) 72 DLR (4th) 245 .... 1.09, 4.31
Gian Singh v Devraj Nahar [1965] 2 MLJ 12 .... 6.14
Gieve, ex p Shaw, Re [1899] WN 41, CA 2.27
Giltej Applications Pty Ltd v Moschello [2005] NSWSC 599 .... 2.11
Glenn v Watson [2018] EWHC 2016 (Ch) 1.13
Goldberg v Miltiadous [2010] EWHC 450 (QB) 4.25
Golstein v Bishop [2014] EWCA Civ 10, [2014] Ch 455 .... 7.22, 14.24
Goldup v Cobb [2017] EWHC 182 (Ch) 6.10, 6.13
Golstein v Barnes [2016] EWHC 2187 (Ch) 8.12
Goode v Harrison (1821) 5 B & Ald 147 .... 3.04
Gorne v Scales, 14 November 2002 .... 5.06, 6.04
Goudberg v Herniman Associates Pty Ltd [2007] VSCA 12 .... 1.15
Grace v Smith (1775) 2 W Bl 998 .... 2.14
Grant v Langley, 5 April 2001, QBD 1.12
Grays v Haig (1855) 20 Beav 219 .... 7.61
Greck v Henderson Asia Pacific Equity Partners (FP) LP [2008] CSOH 2 ...... 15.13
Greek Taverna, Re [1999] BCC 153 .... 8.17
Green v Hernum, 2006 NLCA 46 .... 7.02
Green v Herzog [1954] 1 WLR 1309 .... 5.03
Green v Howell [1910] 1 Ch 495 .... 5.40
Greenbank v Pickles The Times, 7 November 2000, CA 7.42
Greville v Venables [2007] EWCA Civ 878 .... 1.10
Griffiths v Martinez [2019] NSWSC 664 .... 5.03
Gross Klein & Co v Braisby (2005) SPC 00463, 16 February 2005 .... 5.22, 5.30
Grupo Torras SA v Sheikh Fahad Mohammed Al-Sabah [1996] 1 Lloyd's Rep 7, CA 1.39
Gwembe Valley Development Co Ltd v Koshy [2004] 1 BCLC 131 .... 5.01

HF Pension Trustees Ltd v Ellison [1999] PNLR 894 .... 4.53
HMRC v Pal [2008] STC 2442 .... 1.07, 2.28
Hadlee v Commissioner of Inland Revenue [1993] AC 524, PC 5.43, 5.44, 6.09, 7.01, 7.04
Hailes v Hood [2007] EWHC 1616 (Ch) 13.20, 16.12
Halliwells LLP, Re [2010] EWHC 2036 (Ch), [2011] 1 BCLC 345 .... 17.05
Ham v Bell [2016] EWHC 1791 (Ch) 6.15
Ham v Ham [2013] EWCA Civ 1301 .... 7.45
Hamerhaven Pty Ltd v Ogge [1996] 2 VR488 .... 4.56, 4.57
Hamlyn v Houston & Co [1903] 1 KB 81, CA 4.26, 4.28
Hammond v Brearley, 10 December 1992, CA 7.38
Hammonds v Danilunas [2009] EWHC 216 (Ch) 2.05, 3.04, 3.19, 4.31
Hammonds v Jones [2009] EWCA Civ 1400 .... 2.05, 3.19, 7.47
Handyside v Campbell (1901) 17 TLR 623 .... 7.13
Hanlon v Brookes, 9 October 1997, CA (Aus) 5.39, 5.40
Harris v Burgess & Thorne (1937) 4 DLR 219 .... 7.02
Harris v Microfusion 2003-2 LLP [2016] EWCA Civ 1212 .... 11.22
Harrison-Broadley v Smith [1964] 1 WLR 456 .... 6.25
Hashwani v Jivraj [2011] UKSC 40 .... 2.35
Hasleham v Young (1844) 5 QB 833 .... 4.13

Hawkes Hill Publishing Co Ltd, Re [2007] BCC 937 . . . . .17.10
Hawthorn v Smallcorn [1998] STC 591. . . . . 3.18, 7.47
Heather Capital Ltd v Levy & McRae [2015] CSOH 115 . . . . .4.51
Hebei Enterprises Ltd v Livasiri & Co [2008] HKEC 1164 . . . . .4.37
Hedley Byrne & Co v Heller & Partners Ltd [1964] AC 465, HL. 13.16
Henry Butcher International Ltd v KG Engineering [2004] EWCA Civ 1597 . . . . .8.02
Hensman v Traill, *The Times*, 22 October 1980. . . . . .3.07
Heybridge Ltd v Chan Sze Sze [2007] HKCA 418. . . . . .2.10
Higgins v Beauchamp [1914] 3 KB 1192, DC 4.12, 4.13
Highly v Walker (1910) 26 TLR 685 . . . . .5.23
Hill, Re [1934] Ch 623 . . . . .2.38
Hill v CA Parsons & Co Ltd [1972] Ch 305, CA 16.06
Hills v Niksun Inc [2016] EWCA Civ 115, [2016] IRLR 715. . . . . .15.08
Hilton v D IV LLP [2015] EWHC 2 (Ch). 5.25, 10.10, 14.04, 14.11
Hirst v Etherington *The Times*, 21 July 1999, CA 4.09
Hitchman v Crouch Butler Savage Associates (1983) 127 SJ 441 . . . . 5.39, 7.22
Ho Lai Ming v Chu Chik Leung [2007] HKEC 1721 . . . . .7.61
Hodson v Hodson [2010] EWCA 1042 . . . . .7.06
Holdgate v The Official Assignee [2002] NZCA 66 . . . . 7.06, 7.61
Hole v Garnsey [1930] AC 472, HL 14.17, 15.08
Hopper v Hopper [2008] EWCA Civ 1417 . . . . 5.26, 7.50
Hopper v Hopper [2008] EWHC 228 (Ch) 7.36
Horizon Electric Ltd v Larry Hassen Holdings Ltd (1990) 71 DLR 273. . . . . .4.59
Horner v Hasted [1995] STC 766 . . . . .2.43
Hosking v Marathon Asset Management LLP [2016] EWHC 2418 (Ch) 5.03, 5.22, 13.10, 16.13
Howard Smith Ltd v Ampol Petroleum Ltd [1974] AC 821, PC 15.18
Hraiki v Hraiki [2011] NSWSC 656 . . . . .4.25
Hudgell Yeates & Co v Watson [1978] 2 All ER 363 . . . . 2.31, 2.33, 7.07
Humble v Hunter (1848) 12 QBD 310 . . . . .4.18
Hungerford v Richardson [2018] NSWSC 1543. . . . . .7.61
Hunter v Wylie 1993 SLT 1091 . . . . .7.05
Hurst v Bennett [2001] 2 BCLC 290, CA 7.21, 7.61
Hurst v Bryk [1997] 2 All ER 283, CA 7.41
Hurst v Bryk [2002] 1 AC 185, HL 1.10, 2.10, 5.03, 5.09, 7.06, 7.18, 7.21, 7.22, 14.22, 14.25, 16.04
Hussar Estate v P & M Construction Ltd, 7 March 2005, Ont SC. 5.13
Hussar Estate v P & M Construction Ltd (No 2), 13 May 2005, Ont SC. 7.49, 7.50
Huston v Burns [1955] Tas SR 3 . . . . .4.31
Hutchinson v Tamosius (1999) LTL, 20 September 1999 . . . . .5.28
Hydrodan (Corby) Ltd (in liquidation), Re [1994] BCC 161 (Ch). 12.06

IAC (Singapore) Pte Ltd v Koh Meng Wan (1978-1979) SLR 470. . . . . 1.07, 4.13
IRC v Gray [1994] STC 360. . . . . .6.08
Ilott v Williams [2013] EWCA Civ 645 . . . . 1.15, 1.19, 7.06
In Plus Group Ltd v Pyke [2002] 2 BCLC 201 . . . . .5.16
Inco Europe v First Choice Distribution [2000] 1 WLR 586, HL 10.09
Industrial Development Consultants Ltd v Cooley [1972] 1 WLR 443 . . . . .5.16
Ingenious Games Ltd v HMRC [2019] UKUT 226 (TCC) 1.25, 11.01, 11.04
Inland Revenue Commissioners v Graham's Trustees 1971 SC (HL) 1 . . . . 1.08, 7.04, 7.25
Inland Revenue Commissioners v Williamson (1928) 14 TC 335 . . . . 2.03, 2.06
Institute of Chartered Accountants (British Columbia) v Stone, 2009 BCSC 1153 . . . . .4.49
Inversiones Friera SL v Colyzeo Investors LP [2011] EWHC 1762 (Ch),
    [2012] EWHC 1450 (Ch). 5.25, 9.12, 14.11
Investment and Pensions Advisory Service Ltd v Gray [1990] BCLC 8. . . . . .8.05
Investors Compensation Scheme v West Bromwich BS [1998] 1 WLR 896 . . . . .2.05
Irvine v Talksport Ltd [2002] EWHC 367 (Ch). 3.17
Island Export Finance Ltd v Umunna [1986] BCLC 460. . . . . .5.16

TABLE OF CASES

JE Cade and Son Ltd [1992] BCLC 213 .... 6.25
JJ Coughlan Ltd v Ruparelia [2004] PHLR 4, CA 4.08, 4.09, 4.13, 4.25, 4.29, 4.30
JJ Harrison (Properties) Ltd v Harrison [2002] 1 BCLC 162, CA 5.01
Jack v Jack [2016] CSIH 75 .... 6.15
Jackson v White [1967] 2 Lloyd's Rep 68 .... 2.05
Jacobs v Chaudhuri [1968] 2 QB 470 .... 6.23
James & Wells Patent and Trade Mark Attorneys & Snoep [2009] NZ Emp C 97 .... 2.39
James Hay Pension Trustees Ltd v Hird [2005] EWHC 1093 (Ch) 5.02
Jardine-Paterson v Fraser 1974 SLT 93 .... 7.01
Jassal's Executrix v Jassal's Trustees 1988 SLT 757 .... 7.06
Javelin Wholesale Ltd v Waypharm Limited Partnership 22 May 2014,
  Case No 6563 of 2013 (Ch) 8.04
John Taylors v Masons [2001] EWCA Civ 2106 .... 5.11, 5.13
John v Rees [1970] Ch 345 (Ch) 15.11
Johnson v Stephens & Carter [1923] 2 KB 857, CA 3.21
Jones v Jones (1870) 4 SALR 12 .... 6.17
Joyce v Morrisey [1998] TLR 707, CA 5.28

Kaliszer v Ashley, 14 June 2001, Ch 3.06, 3.07
Kao, Lee & Yip v Edwards [1994] HKLR 232, CA 2.36, 2.41, 3.06, 3.10, 3.21
Karstein v Moribe 1982 2 SA 282 (T) 3.05, 4.18
Keech v Sandford (1726) Sel Cas King 61 .... 5.17
Keegan v Fitzgerald, Claim No HC11C01028, 3 November 2011 .... 5.03
Keen v Commerzbank AG [2006] EWCA Civ 1536, [2007] IRLR 132 .... 15.13
Keith Spicer Ltd v Mansell [1970] 1 All ER 462, CA 1.19
Kelly v Denman (1996) LTL, 17 September 1996 .... 5.41
Kelly v Fraser [2012] UKPC 25 .... 4.03, 4.09
Kelly v Northern Ireland Housing Executive [1999] 1 AC 428, HL 1.07
Kendal v Wood (1871) LR 6 Ex 243, CA 4.11
Kendall v Hamilton (1879) 4 App Cas 504, HL 4.45, 4.46
Kennedy v Malcolm Bros (1909) 28 NZLR 457 .... 4.11
Kerr v Morris [1987] Ch 90, CA 3.07, 5.40, 5.41
Khan v Khan [2006] EWHC 1477 (Ch) 2.10, 5.26, 6.14
Khurll v Poulter, 8 April 2003 .... 7.15
Kidsons v Lloyds Underwriters Subscribing Policy No 621/PK10000101
  [2008] EWHC 2415 .... 7.01, 7.24
Kilpatrick v Cairns (1994) LTL, 28 December 1994 .... 2.41
Kingsley v Kingsley [2019] EWHC 1073 .... 7.36, 7.61
Kirkintilloch Equitable Co-operative Society Ltd v Livingstone 1972 SLT 154 .... 4.28
Kiwak v Reiner [2017] EWHC 3018 (Ch) 1.13
Klaue v Bennett (1989) 62 DLR (4th) 367 .... 5.31, 7.52
Kommalage v Sayanthakumar LTL 19 November 2014 CA (Civ) 3.19
Konsult One CC v Strategy Partners (Pty) Ltd [2013] ZAWCH 55 .... 1.25
Kotak v Kotak [2014] EWHC 3121 (Ch) 7.37
Kotak v Kotak [2017] EWHC 1821 (Ch) 4.12, 4.13
Kovats v TFO Management LLP 2009 WL 1062968, 21 April 2009 .... 12.09
Kriziac v Ravinder Rohini Pty Ltd (1990) 102 FLR 8 .... 1.21, 1.22, 6.03
Kyrris v Oldham [2003] 2 BCLC 35 .... 8.19

Lane v Bushby [2000] NSWSC 1029 .... 5.04, 5.32, 13.12
Langley Holdings Ltd v Seakens (2000) LTL, 5 March 2000 .... 4.26, 4.36
Latcham v Martin (1984) 134 NLJ 745, PC 7.37
Latchman v Pickard, 12 May 2005, Ch 7.28
Law v Law [1905] 1 Ch 140 .... 5.10
Lawson v Wenley, Davies, Willis and Cross [2012] NZHC 204 .... 7.04, 7.49, 7.61
Leather Goods case, Re 11 ER 1435 .... 3.17
Lee v The Showmen's Guild of Great Britain [1952] 2 QB 329, CA 15.11

Lewis v Narayanasamy [2017] EWCA Civ 229	2.21, 2.41
Lewis v Ramachandren [2017] EWCA Civ 229	1.26
Lictor Anstalt v Mir Steel UK Ltd [2011] EWHC 3310 (Ch), [2012] 1 All ER (Comm)	13.17
Liddle v Liddle [2019] EWCA Civ 346	7.40
Lie v Mohile [2014] EWCA Civ 728	6.23
Lie v Mohile [2014] EWHC 3709 (Ch)	6.25
Lie v Mohile [2015] EWHC 200 (Ch)	5.38, 7.12, 7.15, 7.22, 7.61
Liggins v Lumsden Ltd [1999–01] MLR 601	4.41
Lim Kok Koon v Tan Cheng Yew [2004] 3 SLR 111	4.41, 4.43
Lo-Line Electric Motors Ltd, Re [1988] Ch 477	12.07
Lon Eagle Industrial Ltd v Realy Trading Co [1999] 4 HKC 675	2.30, 4.56
Lonergan, ex p Sheil, Re (1877) 4 Ch D 789, CA	2.27
Longhorn Group (Pty) Ltd v Fedics Group (Pty) Ltd 1995 SA 836 (W)	1.20
Longmuir v Moffat [2009] CSIH 19	6.17
Lovell and Christmas v Beauchamp [1894] AC 607, HL	3.04
Lovett v Carson Country Homes Ltd [2009] EWHC 1143 (Ch), [2009] 2 BCLC 196	11.21
Lowson v Lowson (1894) 17R 571	1.08
Ludwig Professional Corporation v BDO Canada LLP 2017 ONCA 292	5.39, 5.40
Lujo Properties Ltd v Green 1997 SLT 225	7.25
Lukin v Lovrinov [1998] SASC 6614	7.22
Lynch v Stiff (1944) 68 CLR 428	2.31, 2.33
Lyne-Pirkis v Jones [1969] 1 WLR 1293, CA	3.07
M Young Legal Associates Ltd v Zahid [2006] EWCA Civ 613, [2006] 1 WLR 2562	1.25, 2.42
McClean v Chadwick [2016] EWHC 2650 (Ch)	8.07
McGowan v Chadwick [2002] EWCA Civ 1758	7.33
McHugh v Kerr [2003] EWHC 2985 (Ch)	4.08, 4.26
McInnes v Onslow-Fane [1978] 1 WLR 1520 (Ch)	15.11
Mackenzie v Richard Kidd Marketing Ltd [2007] WSSC 41	1.13
McKeown v Small [2015] NZHC 1043	6.17, 7.04
MacKinlay v Arthur Young McClelland Moores & Co [1990] 2 AC 239, HL	3.18
Maclag (No 11) Pty Ltd v Chantay Too Pty Ltd [2010] QSC 299	5.41
McLeod v Dowling (1927) 43 TLR 655	2.11
McPhail v Bourne [2008] EWHC 1235 (Ch)	1.10
Macquarie International Health Clinic Pty Ltd v Sydney South West Area Health Service [2010] NSWCA 268	14.16
McTear v Eade [2019] EWHC 1673 (Ch)	13.08, 13.18, 17.10, 17.12, 17.13
Magi Capital Partners LLP, Re [2003] EWHC 2790	7.15, 7.17, 13.26
Maidstone Palace Varieties Ltd, Re [1909] 2 Ch 283	7.33
Maillie v Swanney 2000 SLT 464 (OH)	2.07, 2.09, 2.10, 2.12
Mair v Wood 1948 SL 83	4.31
Major v Brodie [1998] STC 491	1.08
Manley v Sartori [1927] 1 Ch 157	7.53, 7.54
Mann v D'Arcy [1968] 1 WLR 893	1.22, 4.14, 4.15
Manufacturing Integration Ltd v Manufacturing Resource Planning Ltd (2000) LTL, 19 May 2000	2.17
Manville Canada Inc v Ladner Downs (1993) 100 DLR (4th) 321	1.32
Mara v Browne [1896] 1 Ch 199	4.41
Marks & Spencer plc v BNP Paribas Securities Services Trust Co (Jersey) Ltd [2015] UKSC 72, [2016] Ac 742	14.16
Marr, Re [1990] Ch 773, CA	8.02
Marsden v Guide Dogs for the Blind Association [2004] 3 All ER 222	4.09, 4.53
Marsh v Stacey (1963) 107 SJ 512, CA	2.38
Marshall v Bullock [1998] EWCA Civ 561	5.03, 6.08, 7.61
Marshall v Marshall [1999] 1 QdR 173, CA	1.20
Martin v Norton Rose Fulbright Australia (No 2) [2019] FCA 96	5.06
Martin v Thompson 1962 SC (HL) 28	5.35

TABLE OF CASES

Martinez v Prick Me Baby One More Time Ltd [2018] EWHC 776, IPEC 3.17, 6.27
Matthews v Ruggles-Brise [1911] 1 Ch 194. . . . . .5.32
Meagher v Meagher [1961] IR 96 . . . . .7.57
Meekins v Henson [1964] 1 QB 472 . . . . .4.30
Megevand, ex p Delhasse, Re (1878) Ch D 511 . . . . .2.23
Mehra v Shah, 1 August 2003, Ch. 1.14
Mehra v Shah [2004] EWCA Civ 632. . . . . .6.03
Menon v Abdullah Kutty [1974] 2 MLJ 159, FC. 6.14, 6.22
Mephistopheles Debt Collection Service v Lotay [1995] 1 BCLC 41 .3.19
Mercantile Credit Co Ltd v Garrod [1962] 3 All ER 1103 . . . . .4.13
Merchants of the Staple of England v The Governor and Company of the Bank
  of England (1887) 21 QBD 160, QB 15.05
Meridian Global Funds Management Asia Ltd v Securities Commission [1995] 2 AC 500, PC 11.12
Metropolis Motorcycles Ltd, Re [2007] 1 BCLC 520 . . . . .5.08
Miah v Khan [2000] 1 WLR 1232, HL, revs'g [1998] 1 WLR 477, CA
  (sub nom Khan v Miha). 1.15, 1.19, 5.02, 9.05
Miles v Clarke [1953] 1 All ER 779 . . . . 6.14, 6.16, 6.26
Milne v Rashid [2018] CSOH 23, [2018] 2 BCLC 673 . . . . .17.10
Ministry of Health v Simpson [1951] AC 251, HL 4.40
M'Lure v Ripley (1850) 2 Mac & G 274 . . . . .5.09
Momentum Productions Pty Ltd v Scotts [2009] FCAFC 30 . . . . .7.61
Moore v Moore, 27 February 1998, HC (NI) 2.18, 5.13, 5.22, 6.15
Moore v Moore [2016] EWHC 2202 (Ch) 7.11, 7.12, 7.14, 7.15
Moray Estates Development Co v Butler [1999] SLT 1338 . . . . .1.08
Morris Wentworth-Stanley [1999] 2 QB 1004 . . . . .4.46
Morrison v Aberdein Considine & Company UKEAT/0018/17/JW 2.36, 2.41
Mortgage Trust Ltd v Wilmett Solicitors [2018] EWHC 488 . . . . .8.01
Moss v Elphick [1910] 1 KB 846, CA 2.08–2.10, 2.12
Mullins v Laughton [2002] EWHC 2761, [2003] 4 All ER 94 (Ch) . . .5.09, 7.18, 7.22, 7.38, 14.22, 14.25
Murray v Feros [2019] NSWSC 260 . . . . 7.14, 7.28
Murray v Lesicar [2016] SASC 71. . . . . .5.25
Murray v Maclay Murray & Spens LLP [2018] IRLR 710, EAT. 3.04, 16.03

Nadeem v Rafiq [2007] EWHC 2959 (Ch) 6.17
Naish v Bhardwaj, 29 March 2001, unreported. 2.07
Natal Land & Colonization Co Ltd v Pauline Colliery & Development Syndicate Ltd
  [1904] AC 120, PC 11.20
National Commercial Banking Corporation of Australia Ltd v Batty
  (1986) 160 CLR 251 . . . . 4.08, 4.09, 4.29
National Westminster Bank plc v Jones [2001] 1 BCLC 98 . . . . .7.06
National Westminster Bank plc v Msaada Group [2011] EWHC 3423 (Ch); [2012] BCC 226. . . . .8.16
Nationwide Building Society v Lewis [1997] 3 All ER 498; [1998] Ch 482 . . . . 2.28, 2.32, 2.33, 2.41
Neath Rugby Ltd, Re [2009] 2 BCLC 487, CA 7.14, 7.15
Neilson v Mossenf Iron Co (1886) 11 App Cas 298, HL. 2.12
Nelson v Moorcraft [2014] WASCA 212 . . . . .2.10
Neutral Capital CP LLC v 1156062BC Ltd 2019 BCCA 258 . . . . .7.19
Newstead v Frost [1980] 1 All ER 363, HL. 1.25, 1.36
Newtherapeutics ltd v Katz [1991] Ch 226 . . . . .1.39
Newtons Coaches Ltd, Re [2016] EWHC 3068 . . . . .8.03
Ng Chu Chong v Ng Swee Choon [2002] 2 SLR 368. . . . . 6.08, 6.13
Nigel Lowe & Associates v John Mowlem Construction plc 1999 SLT 1298, CS (HL). 3.16
Noble v Noble 1965 SLT 415 . . . . .7.44
Noonan, Re [1949] St R Qd 62 . . . . .5.22
North Cheshire & Manchester Brewery Co Ltd v Manchester Brewery Co Ltd [1899] AC 83, HL. 3.17
Northampton Regional Livestock Centre Company v Cowling [2015] EWCA Civ 651 . . . . .4.26
Northern Bank Ltd v Taylor [2014] NICh 9. . . . . .8.16
Northern Sales (1963) Ltd v Ministry of National Revenue (1973) 37 DLR (3d) 612. . . . . .2.17

O'Donnell v Shanahan [2009] EWCA Civ 751 .... 5.15, 14.14
Official Receiver v Hollens [2007] EWHC 753 (Ch) 8.02, 8.10
Old v Hodgkinson [2009] NSWSC 1160 .... 7.34
Oldham v Kyrris, 21 July 1997 .... 8.20
Olson v Gullo (1994) 113 DLR (4th) 42 .... 5.18
Olver v Hillier [1959] 1 WLR 551 .... 7.17
O'Neill v Phillips [1999] 1 WLR 1092, HL 1.29, 5.21, 7.15, 7.38, 13.22
Ong Kay Eng v Ng Chiaw Tong [2001] 2 SLR 213, CA 7.28
Ontario Realty Corporation v Gabriele & Sons Ltd 2009 00-CL-3726 (Ont SC) 4.47
O'Sullivan v Management Agency & Music Ltd [1985] 3 All ER 351, CA 3.04
Oswald Hickson Collier & Co v Carter-Ruck [1984] AC 720, HL 3.08
Oxnard Financing SA v Rahn [1998] 1 WLR 1465 .... 3.19

PWA Corporation v Gemini Group Automated Distribution Systems Inc
 (1993) 103 DLR (4th) 609 .... 7.13, 7.16
Page v Cox (1852) 10 Hare 163 .... 5.34, 5.36
Pallant v Morgan [1953] Ch 43 .... 1.13
Palter v Zeller (1997) 30 OR (3d) 796 .... 1.14
Palumbo v Stylianou (1966) 1 TR 407 .... 2.36
Patel v Mirza [2016] UKSC 42 .... 3.05
Patel v Patel [2007] EWCA Civ 1520 .... 7.60
Patel v Patel [2019] EWHC 298 (Ch) 5.28
Pathirana v Pathirana [1967] 1 AC 233, PC 5.13, 7.50
Patley Wood Farm LLP v Brake [2016] EWHC 1688 (Ch) 8.15–8.18
Paton v Reck [2000] 2 QdR 619, CA 5.09, 5.14
Peake v Carter [1916] 1 KB 652, CA 5.48
Pearn v Berry, 17 May 1998, CA 7.37
Peskin v Anderson [2001] BCC 874, CA 13.11
Peso Silvermines v Cropper [1966] 58 DLR (2d) 1 .... 5.15
Petrodel Resources v Prest [2013] UKSC 34, [2013] BCC 571 .... 11.18
Peveril Gold Mines Ltd, Re [1898] 1 Ch 122, CA 13.26
Peyton v Mindham [1972] 1 WLR 8 .... 3.07, 5.40, 7.05, 7.10
Pham v Doan [2005] NSWSC 201 (16 March 2005) 3.05
Phillips v Melville [1921] NZLR 571 .... 7.02
Phillips v Symes [2002] 1 WLR 853 .... 1.39
Phillips v Symes [2006] EWHC 1721, Ch 7.23
Pick v Pick [20017] All ER (D) 318 .... 7.36
Pine Energy Consultants Ltd v Talisman Energy (UK) Ltd [2008] CSOH 10 .... 1.15
Pitt v Holt [2013] UKSC 26, [2013] AC 108 .... 15.17, 15.18
Pocock v Carter [1912] 1 Ch 663 .... 6.25
Polkinghorne v Holland (1934) 51 CLR 143 .... 4.09
Pooley v Driver (1877) 5 Ch D 458, CA 1.25, 2.23, 2.27
Popat v Schonchhatra [1997] 3 All ER 800, CA 5.17, 5.20, 5.26, 5.27,
                                                               6.08, 7.42, 7.51, 7.53, 14.05, 16.11
Proceedings Commissioner v Ali Hatem [1999] 1 NZLR 305, CA 4.26
Promontoria (Chestnut) Ltd v Craig [2017] EWHC 2405 (Ch) 8.19
Prothroe v Adams [1997] 10 WWR 101 .... 5.07
Prudential Assurance v Newman (no 2) [1982] Ch 204, CA 11.22
Public Trustee v Mortimer (1985) 16 DLR (4th) 404 .... 4.28, 4.38
Purewall v Purewall [2008] CSOH 147 .... 7.60

Quarter Master UK Ltd v Pyke [2005] 1 BCLC 245 .... 5.06
Queensland Mines Ltd v Hudson (1978) 18 ALR 1, PC 5.15
Quinlan v Essex Hinge Co Ltd [1996] 2 BCLC 417 .... 7.14

R (Sword Services Ltd) v HMRC [2016] EWHC 1473 (Admin), [2016] 4 WLR 113 .... 10.10
R v Kupfer [1915] 2 KB 321 .... 7.07

R v Local Government Board ex p Arlidge [1914] 1 KB 160, CA 15.11
R v Register of Stock Companies ex p A-G [1991] BCLC 476........................11.04, 11.11
R v Register of Stock Companies ex p More [1931] 2 KB 197 ....11.04
RBS v Etridge [2002] 2 AC 773 ....3.04
Rabiah Bee Bte Mohamed Ibrahmim v Salem Ibrahim [2007] SGHC 27 ....1.13
Ralls Builders Ltd, Re [2016] EWHC 243 (Ch), [2016] BCC 293............................17.10
Ravindran v Rasanagayam (2000) LTL, 24 January 2001.................................1.14
Rayner & Co v Rhodes (1926) 24 Ll L Rep 25 ....9.10
Rayner (Mincing Lane) Ltd v Department of Trade [1989] Ch 72 ....11.16
Reckitt & Colman Products Ltd v Borden Inc (No 3) [1990] 1 WLR 491 ....3.17
Recovery Partners GP Ltd v Rukhazde [2018] EWHC 2918 (Comm), [2019] Bus LR 1166......13.08
Reed v Young [1986] 1 WLR 649, HL..9.09
Regal (Hastings) Ltd v Gulliver [1942] 1 All ER 378....................................5.16
Reinhard v Ondra LLP [2015] EWHC 26 (Ch)............................. 12.01, 12.05, 13.01
Reinhard v Ondra LLP [2015] EWHC 1869 (Ch)................................. 12.05, 12.10
Revenue & Customs Commissioners v Holland [2010] UKSC 51,
    [2010] 1 WLR 2793 ....12.06, 12.07
Rhodes v Moules [1895] 1 Ch 236 ....4.38
Richardson v Bank of England (1838) 4 My & Cr 165 ....5.31
Richmond Pharmacology Ltd v Chesters Oversear Ltd [2014] EWHC 2692 (Ch) 5.16
Riley v Reddish LLP [2019] WLUK 96 (Ch) 13.08
Roberts v Wilsons Solicitors LLP [2016] ICR 659 (EAT), affd [2018] EWCA Civ 52,
    [2018] ICR 1092 ....12.11
Rochwerg v Truster (2002) 212 DLR (4th) 498.......................... 5.05, 5.10, 5.15, 5.18, 5.19
Rock Advertising Ltd v MWB Business Exchange Centres Ltd [2018] UKSC 24,
    [2019] AC 119 ....14.03
Rodway v Landy [2001] EWCA Civ 471 ....6.26
Rojoda Pty Ltd v Commissioner of State Revenue [2018] WASCA 224..............6.09, 7.61
Rolfe v Flower Salting & Co (1866) LR 1 PC 27..4.53
Root v Head [1996] 20 ASCR 160..7.15
Rosanove v O'Rourke [1988] 1 QdR 171, SC...7.32
Rose v Dodd [2005] ICR 1776..7.26
Rose v Rose [2009] NZSC 46...6.09
Ross Harper and Murphy v Banks 2000 SLT 699 CS (OH) 5.04
Ross River Ltd v Wavely Commercial Ltd [2013] EWCA Civ 910 ....1.13
Rosserlane Consultant Ltd v Appointment of a judicial factor [2008] CSOH 120 ....7.28
Rowella Pty Ltd v Abfam Nominees Pty Ltd (1989) 168 CLR 301, HC 7.63
Rowella Pty Ltd v Hoult [1988] 2 QdR 80, SC................................ 1.22, 4.15, 5.23
Rowlands v Hodson [2009] EWCA Civ 1025 ....1.20, 1.25, 2.42, 7.06
Roxburgh Dinardo & Partners' Judicial Factor v Dinardo 1993 SLT 16.....................5.09
Ruben v Great Fingall Consolidated [1906] AC 439, HL.................................11.21
Russell v Clarke [1995] 2 QdR 310 ....5.38
Ryder v Frolich [2004] NSWCA 472 ....7.22
Rye v Rye [1962] AC 496, HL 1.07, 2.34, 6.24

Sagacity Professional Corporation v Buchanan Barry LLP 2010 ABQB 151................5.10
Sagkeen/Wing Development Partnership v Sagkeen (2003) 5 WWR 245..................4.31
Sahota v Sohi [2006] EWHC 344 (Ch)... 1.03, 7.23
Said v Butt [1920] 3 KB 497 ....13.17
Salford Estates (No 2) Ltd v Altomart [2015] Ch 589, CA...............................13.26
Salomon v A Salomon & Co Ltd [1897] AC 22, HL 1.01, 1.28, 11.16
Sandhu v Gill [2006] Ch 466; rev'g [2005] 1 All ER 990.................................7.53
Sandilands v Marsh (1819) 2 B & Ald 673 ....4.13
Sangster v Biddulphs, 22 March 2005, unreported.....................................2.29
Saul D Harrison & Sons plc, Re [1995] 1 BCLC 14, CA 13.22
Say-Dee Pty Ltd v Farah Constructions Pty Ltd [2005] NSWCA 469 ....7.02
Saywell v Pope (1979) 53 TC 40 ....1.21, 1.22, 2.03, 2.06

TABLE OF CASES xxxiii

Scally v Southern Health and Social Services Board [1992] 1 AC 294 ....14.03
Scarborough Building Society v Howes Percival, 5 March 1998, CA 4.26
Scher v Policyholders Protection Board [1994] 2 AC 57, HL 1.37
Schooler v Customs & Excise Commissioners [1995] 2 BCLC 610, CA 8.04, 8.11
Scottish Pension Fund Trustees Ltd v Marshall Ross & Munro [2018] CSIH 39................4.51
Seaconsar (Far East) Ltd v Bank Markazi Jomhouri Islami Iran [1994] 1 AC 438 ....1.50
Seal & Edgelow v Kingston [1908] 2 KB 579 ....3.21
Secretary of State for Health v R (Malik) [2007] EWCA Civ 265 ....6.26
Seiwa Australia Pty Ltd v Beard [2009] NSWCA 240.......................................4.38
Seldon v Clarkson Wright & Jakes [2012] UKSC 16................................. 3.04, 16.03
Senanayake v Cheng [1966] AC 63, PC 7.19
Shanmugathaas v Paramanipurupen [2018] NSWSC 1232................................7.02
Sharma v Sharma [2013] EWCA Civ 1287 ....5.16
Sharp v Blank [2015] EWHC 3220 (Ch), [2017] BCC 187 ....13.11
Sharp v Taylor (1849) 2 Ph 801 ....5.12
Shaw v Shaw 1968 SLT (Notes) 94..7.44
Sheppard & Cooper Ltd v TSB Bank plc [1997] 2 BCLC 222 ....1.07
Sheveleu v Brown [2018] CSIH 68 .... 7.25, 7.50
Short v Gray HC Auckland Civ-2008-404-2232, 9 June 2010...............................6.26
Shorter v CEC, 1 June 2001, VADT 6.26
Sim v Howat [2011] CSOH 115...4.51, 5.03, 5.10
Simpson v Chapman (1853) 4 De GM & G 154 ....7.53
Sims v Brutton (1850) 5 Ex 802..4.39
Singh v Nahar [1965] 1 WLR 412...6.16
Skipp v Harwood (1747) 2 Swans 586 ....7.35
Skyepharma v Hyal Pharmaceutical Corporation [2001] BPIR 163, Ont CA 7.33
Smith, Re 1999 SLT (Sh Ct) 5...8.03
Smith v Baker [1977] 1 NZLR 511 ....2.11
Smith v Gale [1974] 1 WLR 9 ....7.47
Smithton Ltd v Naggar [2014] EWCA Civ 939, [2015] 1 WLR 189 ....12.07
Snook v London and West Riding Investments Ltd [1967] 2 QB 786, CA....................12.03
Sobell v Boston [1975] 1 WLR 1587..7.01, 7.30, 7.50, 7.56
Socimer International Bank v Standard Bank London [2008] EWCA Civ 116,
    [2008] 1 Lloyd's Rep 558 ....15.08
Solicitor's Arbitration, Re A [1962] 1 WLR 353 ....5.38
Speed Investments Ltd v Formula One Holdings (No 2) [2004] EWCA Civ 1512,
    [2005] 1 WLR 1936 ....11.25
Spiliada Maritime Corp v Consulex Ltd [1987] AC 460 ....1.40
Spire Freezers Ltd v Canada (2001) 196 DLR (4th) 210...................................1.25
Spiro v Com [2015] ONSC 609..1.18, 1.26
Springer v Aird & Berlis LLP 2009 WL 953083 (Ont SC) 5.01, 5.06
Sri Alam Sdn Bhd v Newacres Sdn Bhd [1995] 4 MLJ 73..................................1.20
Standard Chartered Bank v Pakistan National Shipping Co (Nos 2 & 4) [2002] UKHL 43,
    [2003] 1 AC 959 ....13.15
Steinberg v Scala (Leeds) Ltd [1923] 2 Ch 452 ....3.04
Steingarten v Burke [2003] MBQB 43 ....6.09
Stekel v Ellice [1973] 1 WLR 191 .... 1.25, 2.37–2.39
Stocking v Montila [2005] EWHC 2210 (Ch)..6.03
Strathearn Gordon Associates Ltd v Commissioners of Customs & Excise
    [1985] VATTR 79 .... 1.20, 1.24
Strover v Strover [2005] EWHC 860 (Ch) 6.13
Strydom v Protea Eiendomsagente 1979 (2) SA 206 (T) 1.07
Summers v Smith [2002] EWHC 694 (Ch) 6.30, 7.01, 7.04
Sutherland v Barnes, 8 October 1997, CA 7.15
Sutherland v Gustar [1994] 4 All ER 1; [1994] Ch 304 ....1.05, 3.20, 3.21
Syers v Syers (1876) 1 App Cas 174, HL 7.38
Sze Tu v Lowe [2014] NSWCA 462..6.09, 7.02

TABLE OF CASES

Tan Boon Cheo v Ho Hong Bank Ltd [1934] (Vol 111) MLJ 180 .... 4.57
Tan Liang Chong v Chou Lai Tiang [2003] 4 SLR 775 .... 6.08, 7.61
Tann v Hetherington [2009] EWHC 445 (Ch) 5.04
Taylor v Good [1974] 1 WLR 556, CA 1.17
Taylor v Grier (No 3), Case No 1995/8125, 12 May 2003, Ch 1.09, 7.53
Taylor v Mazorriaga (1999) LTL, 12 May 1999, CA 1.14, 2.16
Tecle v Hassan 2012 ONSC 2233 .... 7.15
Tendring Hundred Waterworks Co v Jones [1903] 2 Ch 615 .... 4.39
Thames Cruises Ltd v George Wheeler Launches Ltd [2003] EWHC 3093 (Ch) 1.20, 2.04
Thomas v Atherton (1878) 10 Ch D 185 .... 5.04
Thompson's Trustee v Heaton [1974] 1 WLR 605 .... 5.17
Thom's Executrix v Russel & Aitken 1983 SLT 335 .... 7.44
Tiffin v Lester Aldridge LLP [2012] EWCA Civ 35 .... 2.34, 2.36, 2.37, 2.42, 12.09
Toker v Akgul, 2 November 1995, CA 7.31
Tomlinson v Broadsmith [1868] 1 QB 386 .... 3.21
Toogood v Farrell [1988] 2 EGLR 233, CA 2.11, 6.25
Touche Ross and Company v Bank Intercontinental Ltd 1986 CILR 156 .... 1.33, 1.38
Tower Cabinet Co Ltd v Ingram [1949] 2 KB 397 .... 2.30, 4.59
Tower Taxi Technology LLP v Marsden [2005] EWHC 1084 (Ch) 10.10, 13.25
Trego v Hunt [1896] AC 7, HL 6.27, 6.29, 16.16
Trimble v Goldberg [1906] AC 494 .... 5.19
Trinkler v Beale [2009] NSWCA 30 .... 5.09, 5.10
Truong v Lam [2009] WASCA 217 .... 7.01, 7.50
Tucker v Kelly (1907) 5 CLR 1 .... 5.27
Tugboba v Adelagun (1974) 1 ALR 99 .... 5.12
Turkington v Telegraph Group Ltd [1998] NIQB 1 .... 3.19
Turner v Haworth Associates, 8 March 1996, CA 2.32

UCB Home Loans Corporation Ltd v Soni [2013] EWCA Civ 62 .... 2.29, 2.30
Unical Properties v 784688 Ontario Ltd (1991) 73 DLR (4th) 751 .... 3.19
Unioil International Pty Ltd v Deloitte Touche Tohmatsu (1997) 17 WAR 98 .... 1.30, 1.32
United Bank of Kuwait Ltd v Hammoud [1988] 1 WLR 1051, CA 2.37, 4.03, 4.09, 4.12
United Builders Pty Ltd v Mutual Acceptance Ltd (1980) 144 CLR 673 .... 1.37
United Dominions Corporation Ltd v Brian Pty Ltd (1985) 60 ALR 741 .... 5.08
United Tankers Pty ltd v Moray Pre-Cast Pty Ltd [1992] 1 QdR 467 .... 1.19, 2.18
Unsworth v Jordon [1896] WN 2 .... 7.02

Valrut Investments Ltd v Norstar Commercial Developments 2008 WL 949777, Ont SCJ 7.38
Vankerk v Canada 2005 TCC 292 .... 1.14
Vanquish Properties (UK) LP v Brook St (UK) Ltd [2016] EWHC 1508 .... 9.02
Varley v Coppard (1872) LR 7 CP 505 .... 6.22
Vatcher v Paull [1915] AC 372 .... 15.08
Vekaria v Dabasia (1998) LTL, 1 February 1998, CA 1.18
Voaden v Voaden, 21 February 1997 .... 3.11

W Stevenson & Sons v R [2008] EWCA Crim 273 .... 4.33
Waddington v O'Callaghan (1931) 16 TC 187 .... 2.06
Walker v European Electronics Pty Ltd (1990) 23 NSWLR 1 .... 4.28
Walker v Hirsch (1884) 27 Ch D 460 .... 2.17
Walker v Stones [2000] 4 All ER 412, CA 4.41–4.43
Walker West Development Ltd v FJ Emmett Ltd [1979] 252 EG 1171, CA 2.18
Wallace v Altan [2018] NZHC 1337 .... 6.26
Walters v Bingham [1988] FTLR 260 .... 2.10–2.12, 5.37, 5.41
Waltham Forest NHS Primary Care Trust, Secretary of State for Health v R (Malik) [2007] EWCA Civ 265 .... 6.26
Wang v Rong [2015] NSWS 1419 .... 5.22
Ward v Newalls Insulation Co Ltd [1998] 1 WLR 1722 .... 5.21

Waterer v Waterer (1873) LR 15 Eq 6.20
Watson v Haggitt [1928] AC 127, PC 7.46
Watson v Imperial Financial Services Ltd (1994) 111 DLR (4th) 643 .....3.20
Watteau v Fenwick [1893] 1 QB 346 .....4.19, 4.20
Watts v Driscoll [1901] 1 Ch 294, CA 5.45
Waugh v Carver (1793) 2 H Bl 235 .....1.24, 2.14
Wedge v Wedge (1996) 12 WAR 489, SC 7.31
Weiner v Harris [1910] 1 KB 285 .....2.04
Welsh Development Export Agency v Export Finance Co [1992] BCLC 148, CA 13.17
Welsh v Knarston 1972 SLT 96 .....7.27
West Park Golf & Country Club, Re [1997] 1 BCLC 20 .....8.16
Whealy v Canada 2004 TCC 377 .....1.25
Wheatley v Smithers [1906] 2 KB 321, CA 4.12
White, Re [2001] Ch 393, CA 7.45
White v Jones [1995] 2 AC 207, HL 13.07
Whitehead v Hughes (1834) 2 C&M 318 .....3.21
Whitehill v Bradford [1952] 1 All ER 115 .....3.07
Whiteman Smith Motor Co v Chaplin [1934] 2 KB 35, CA 6.27
Whitwell v Arthur (1863) 35 Beav 140 .....7.10
Whywait Pty Ltd v Davison [1997] 1 QdR 225 .....1.12, 1.17
Wild v Wild [2018] EWHC 2197 (Ch) 6.15
Wilkinson v West Coast Capital [2007] BCC 717 .....5.15
Willett v Blanford (1842) 1 Hare 253 .....7.53
William S Gordon & Co Ltd v Mrs Mary Thompson Partnership 1985 SLT 112 .....7.04
Williams v Natural Life Health Foods Ltd [1998] 1 WLR 830, HL 13.16
Williams v Williams [1999] 9 CL 457 .....7.56
Williamson v Barbour (1877) 9 Ch D 529 .....4.16
Wilson v Dunbar 1988 SLT 93 .....7.44
Wilsons Solicitors LLP v Roberts [2018] EWCA Civ 52, [2018] 1 BCLC 306 .....14.23, 14.24
Wilton-Davies v Kirk [1997] BCC 770 .....7.31
Windle v Farada ULEAT/0339/13/RN 2.35
Winsor v Schroeder (1979) 129 NLJ 1266 .....1.17, 5.04
Winter v Winter, 10 November 2000 .....7.39
Wise v Perpetual Trustee Co [1903] AC 139, HL 1.18
Wood v Fresher Foods Ltd [2007] NZHC 1466 .....4.56, 4.57
Wood v Scholes (1866) LR 1 Ch App 369 .....5.31
Woodfull v Lindsley [2004] 2 BCLC 131 .....5.17
Worbey v Campbell [2017] CSIH 49 .....1.10, 1.20
Wright v Van Gaalen 2011 BCSC 707 .....5.15

Yard v Yarhoo Pty Ltd [2007] VSCA 35 .....7.14
Yates v Finn (1880) 13 Ch D 839 .....7.53
Yazhou Travel Investment Co Ltd v Bateson Starr [2005] PNLR 31 (HK CFI) 13.16
Yenidje Tobacco Co Ltd, Re [1916] 2 Ch 426 .....7.14, 7.15
Younes v Chrysanthou [2016] EWHC 3269 (QB) 1.10

Zafiris v Liu (2005) 149 SJLR 147 .....6.23

TABLE OF LEGISLATION

Age of Majority (Scotland) Act 1969 . . . . . . .3.04
Agricultural Holdings Act 1986 . . . . .6.23
Agricultural Holdings (Scotland) Act 2003 . . . 9.01
Agricultural Tenancies Act 1995. . . . . .6.23
Arbitration Act 1996 . . . . .3.03
Betting and Gaming Act 1960. . . . . .3.05
Bribery Act 2010. .4.33
Business Names Act 1985 . . . . 1.11, 3.13
Civil Jurisdiction and Judgments Act 1982
   s 43 . . . . .1.39
   sch 4 . . . . .1.38
Civil Liability (Contribution) Act 1978 . . . . .5.32
   s 3 . . . . 4.46, 4.60
Companies Act 1907 . . . . .1.29
Companies Act 1980 . . . . .1.29
Companies Act 1981 . . . . 1.29, 3.13
Companies Act 1985 . . . . 10.09
   s 44A. 17.17
   s 431 . . . . 17.17
   s 431(2). 12.01
   s 432(1). 17.17
   s 432(2). 17.17
   s 433 . . . . 17.17
   s 434(1). 17.17
   s 434(2). 17.17
   s 436 . . . . 17.17
   s 437 . . . . 17.17
   s 441 . . . . 17.17
   ss 442–446 . . . . 17.17
   ss 447–447A 17.17
   s 448 . . . . 17.17
   ss 449–450 . . . . 17.17
Companies Act 2006 . . . . . 1.09, 1.29, 1.36, 1.37,
                   2.30, 3.01, 3.20, 5.05, 10.01,
               10.09, 10.10, 13.05, 13.08, 15.04
   Pt 15 . . . . 10.09
   Pt 16 . . . . 10.09
   Pt 21A. 11.27
   Pt 41 . . . . 1.11, 3.03, 3.13, 3.16, 4.57
   s 7(2). 11.04
   s 12A. 11.10
   s 15 . . . . 11.11
   s 39(1). 1.36
   s 40 . . . . .1.36
   s 41 . . . . .1.36
   s 43 . . . . 11.21
   s 44 . . . . 11.21, 12.07
   s 44(4). 11.21
   s 44(5). 11.21
   s 51 . . . . 11.20
   s 51(2). 11.20
   ss 53–57 . . . . 11.06
   s 65 . . . . 11.06
   ss 66–68 . . . . 11.06
   ss 69–74 . . . . 11.06
   s 76 . . . . .3.15
   s 82 . . . . 11.24
   s 83 . . . . 11.24
   s 86 . . . . 11.07
   s 87 . . . . .10.01, 11.07
   s 88 . . . . 11.07
   s 112(2). 11.25
   s 156 . . . . 11.02
   s 156A. 11.02
   s 161 . . . . 12.07
   s 162 . . . . .11.08, 11.25
   s 162(1). 11.25
   s 163 . . . . .11.08, 11.25
   s 164 . . . . .11.08, 11.25
   s 164(d) 11.02
   s 165 . . . . 11.25
   s 165(1). 11.25
   ss 167A–167E 11.25
   ss 170–180 . . . . .5.11
   s 170(4). 13.08
   s 171(b) 15.08
   s 174 . . . . 13.12
   s 175 . . . . 13.09
   s 177 . . . . 13.09
   s 232 . . . . 13.13
   ss 241–246 . . . . 11.26
   ss 260–264 . . . . .3.20
   s 386 . . . . 11.30
   s 387 . . . . 11.30
   s 388 . . . . .11.30, 14.11
   s 389 . . . . 11.30
   s 394 . . . . 11.30
   s 441 . . . . 11.30
   s 442 . . . . 11.30
   ss 451–453 . . . . 11.30
   s 539 . . . . 14.01
   ss 743–748 . . . . 11.28
   ss 790D–790J. 11.27
   s 790K. 11.27
   s 790M 11.27
   s 790M(1). 11.25
   ss 790N–790O. 11.27
   s 790T. 11.27

ss 790W–790ZD 11.25, 11.27
ss 853A–853B 11.29
s 853L 11.29
ss 859A–859E 11.28
ss 859A–859Q 11.28
s 859F 11.28
s 859H 11.28
s 859I 11.28
s 859K 11.28
s 859L 11.28
ss 859P–859Q 11.28
ss 895–900 . . . . 17.14
s 899(1) 17.14
ss 942–965 . . . . .3.01
s 993 . . . . 12.15
s 994 . . . . 5.21, 5.24, 10.10, 14.07
s 994(3) 13.21, 14.03
s 996 . . . . 7.38, 14.01
s 1000 . . . . 17.19
s 1000(4)–(5) 17.19
s 1000(6)–(7) 17.19
s 1001 . . . . 17.19
s 1003 . . . . 11.17
ss 1003–1011 . . . . 17.19
s 1003(5)–(6) 17.19
ss 1012–1023 . . . . 17.20
ss 1024–1034 . . . . 17.21
s 1028 . . . . .1.37
s 1030 . . . . 17.21
s 1032 . . . . .1.37
s 1064 . . . . 11.11
s 1080 . . . . 11.25
ss 1085–1086 . . . . 11.23
s 1086 . . . . 11.05
s 1087A 11.26
s 1096 . . . . 11.25
ss 1103–1107 . . . . 11.07
s 1116 . . . . 11.11
ss 1139–1140 . . . . 11.22
s 1157 . . . . 13.14
s 1173 . . . . 14.01
s 1192 . . . . .3.14
ss 1193–1197 . . . . .3.15
s 1194(3) 3.15
s 1196 . . . . .3.15
s 1198 . . . . .3.15
s 1200 . . . . .3.14
s 1201 . . . . .3.16
ss 1201–1204 . . . . .3.16
s 1206 . . . . .3.16
sch 1A 11.27
Company Directors Disqualification
    Act 1986 . . . . 8.02, 8.05, 8.08, 10.09,
                12.06, 12.07, 12.12, 12.13
s 1A 12.15
s 2 . . . . 12.15
s 3 . . . . 12.15
s 4 . . . . 12.15
s 5 . . . . 12.15
s 5A 12.15
s 6 . . . . 12.15
s 7 . . . . 12.15
s 8 . . . . 12.15
s 8ZA 12.15
s 8ZD 12.15
s 9A 12.15
ss 9A–9E 12.15
s 11(1) 13.02
s 13 . . . . 12.15
s 15 . . . . 11.17, 12.15
s 15(4) 12.15
s 15A 17.08
s 22(4) 12.07
sch 1 . . . . 12.15
Consumer Rights Act 2015 . . . . 13.16
Contracts (Rights of Third Parties)
    Act 1999 . . . . 2.05, 14.02
s 6(2A) 14.02
Corporate Manslaughter and Corporate
    Homicide Act 2007 . . . . 1.07, 4.34
s 1(1) 4.34
s 1(2) 4.34
s 1(3) 4.34
s 1(4)(c) 4.34
s 2 . . . . 4.34
s 14 . . . . .1.07
s 14(1) 4.34
s 14(2) 4.34
s 14(3) 4.34
Corporation Tax Act 2009
s 1273 . . . . 11.04
County Courts Act 1984 . . . . 12.16
Courts and Legal Services Act 1990 . . . . . . .3.12
Employment Relations Act 1999
s 10 . . . . 15.15
Employment Rights Act 1996 . . . . 2.35, 12.10
s 230 . . . . 12.10
s 230(3)(b) 2.35, 12.11
Enterprise Act 2002 . . . . 8.02, 8.14
para 22 . . . . .8.18
para 23 . . . . .8.18
paras 29–34 . . . . .8.18
para 42 . . . . .8.19
para 43 . . . . .8.19
para 105 . . . . 8.18, 8.19
sch B1 . . . . .8.14
    para 3 . . . . .8.15
    paras 14–21 . . . . .8.15
Equality Act 2010 . . . . 3.04, 5.37, 16.03
s 19 . . . . .3.04
s 44 . . . . .3.04
s 45 . . . . 16.03
Fair Employment (Northern Ireland) Act 1976
s 17 . . . . .1.07

TABLE OF LEGISLATION xxxix

Family Law Reform Act 1969 ....3.04
Finance Act 1972
   s 22 ....1.07
Finance Act 1985 ....3.18
   s 48 ....9.09
Finance Act 2001
   s 76 .... 10.10
Finance Act 2014 .... 12.05
Financial Services and Markets
   Act 2000 .... 10.09
   s 235 ....9.17
   s 235(5)....................................9.03
   s 367 ....8.19
Health Act 1986 ....4.33
Income Tax (Trading and Other Income)
   Act 2005
   s 863 ....10.10, 11.04
   s 863A......................................2.42
   ss 863A–863G 10.10, 12.05
   s 863B......................................2.42
Insolvency Act 1985.....................8.02
Insolvency Act 1986 ...... 1.11, 2.14, 7.14, 8.02,
        8.05, 8.09, 8.11, 10.09, 12.06, 13.02,
        14.01, 15.04, 17.01, 17.06, 17.11
   Pt I 8.11, 8.13
   Pt II..8.14
   Pt V..8.03
   s 74 .... 11.16, 17.08, 17.09, 17.11, 17.12
   s 74(2)(f) 17.11
   s 79 .... 13.24
   s 79(1).................................. 13.24
   s 84(1)................................... 17.02
   s 86(1)................................... 17.02
   s 110 .... 17.16
   s 110(6)................................ 17.16
   s 111 .... 17.16
   s 112(1)(c) 11.02
   s 122(1)................................. 17.03
   s 122(1)(b) 11.11
   s 122(1)(c) 11.17, 17.03
   s 122(1)(d) 17.03
   s 122(1)(e) 11.04, 13.23, 17.03
   s 122(1)(f) 17.03
   s 122(1)(g) 5.21, 13.23, 17.03
   s 123 .... 17.03
   s 124 .... 11.04
   s 124(1)................................ 13.24
   s 124A.................................. 17.17
   s 125 .... 13.26
   s 145 .... 13.02
   ss 165–168.............................. 17.07
   ss 201–205.............................. 17.18
   s 212 ....8.19, 12.07
   s 213 .... 17.08
   ss 213–214.............................. 12.15
   s 214 .... 12.06, 12.07, 13.12, 17.08, 17.10
   s 214A........ 12.06, 12.07, 13.24, 17.08, 17.10
   s 214A(2)(a) 17.10
   s 214A(2)(b) 17.10
   s 214A(3)............................. 17.10
   s 214A(4)............................. 17.10
   s 214A(5)............................. 17.10
   s 214A(6)............................. 17.10
   s 216 ....8.03, 11.06
   s 217 .... 11.06
   s 221 ....8.04
   s 238 .... 17.08
   s 239 ....17.08, 17.10
   s 251 ....12.06, 12.07
   s 267(1)...................................8.04
   s 303 ....8.10, 10.01
   s 306 .... 13.02
   s 390 ....8.15
   sch 4 .... 17.07
   sch A1..........................8.11, 8.13
   sch B1.................................. 17.05
      para 3 .... 17.05
Insolvency Act 2000 .... 8.02, 8.11, 8.13
Interpretation Act 1978
   s 11 .... 12.07
   sch 1 .... 11.02
Joint Stock Companies Act 1856............1.28
Landlord and Tenant Act 1954 ....6.25
   Pt II..6.23
   s 41A.......................................6.23
Law of Property Act 1925............6.11, 14.03
   s 61 ....5.38
   s 72 .... 2.34, 6.24, 6.25
   s 82 ....2.34, 6.24
Law of Property Act 1969
   s 9 ....6.23
Law of Property (Miscellaneous
   Provisions) Act 1989 .... 14.03
   s 2 ....2.04
Legal Services Regulation Act 2015
   (Ireland)........................... 10.05
Limitation Act 1980
   s 21(1)(a) 5.01
   s 21(1)(b) 5.01
Limited Liability Partnership Act 2017
   (Pakistan) 10.05
Limited Liability Partnership Law 2017
   (Cayman Islands) 10.05
Limited Liability Partnerships Act 2000 .....1.01,
        1.02, 10.01, 10.04–10.08, 11.02, 13.03
   s 1 ....1.01, 10.08
   s 1(2)–(3) 10.04
   s 1(3)................................... 11.19
   s 1(4).........................11.16, 17.08
   s 1(5) 10.10, 13.11, 14.22
   s 2 ....10.08, 11.01, 11.05, 11.11
   s 2(1)(a) 11.01, 11.05
   s 2(1)(b) 11.05
   s 2(1)(c) 11.05

TABLE OF LEGISLATION

s 2(2)(f) 11.09
s 2(2ZA) 11.08
s 3 .... 10.08
s 4 .... 10.08, 12.07
ss 4-9 .... 10.08
s 4(1) 11.11, 12.07, 14.20, 16.03
s 4(2) 12.01, 12.03, 12.07, 13.02, 14.20
s 4(3) 14.20, 14.23, 16.01–16.04, 16.06
s 4(4) 2.34, 12.08–12.10
s 4A 11.17
s 5 .... 10.08, 13.07, 14.03
s 5(1) 13.04, 14.01–14.04, 14.23
s 5(1)(a) 14.01, 14.02
s 5(1)(b) 14.23
s 5(2) 11.20
s 6 .... 4.21, 11.15, 13.08, 16.08
s 6(1) 11.12, 11.14, 11.16, 13.11
s 6(2) 11.15, 12.07, 15.16
s 6(3) 16.08
s 6(4) 11.13
s 7 .... 10.08, 13.02
s 7(1) 13.01, 13.02
s 7(1)(a) 16.02
s 7(1)(d) 14.09
s 7(2) 13.02, 16.09
s 7(2)(b)-(d) 13.02
s 7(3) 13.02
s 8 .... 10.08, 11.09
s 9 .... 10.08, 11.09, 11.26
s 9(1) 16.08
s 10 .... 10.10
ss 10–13 .... 10.08
ss 14–17 .... 10.08
s 15(c) 12.14, 14.01
s 18 .... 12.07
s 19(4) 10.05
sch. 10.08
  para 2 .... 11.06
  para 2(2) 11.07
  para 4 .... 11.06
  para 5(4) 11.06
  para 6 .... 11.06
  para 7 .... 11.06
Limited Liability Partnerships Act 2005
  (Singapore) 10.05
Limited Liability Partnerships Act
  2008 (India) 10.05
Limited Liability Partnerships Act 2012
  (Malaysia) 10.05
Limited Liability Partnerships Act 2016
  (Mauritius) 10.05
Limited Liability Partnerships (Guernsey)
  Law 2013 .... 10.05
Limited Liability Partnerships (Jersey)
  Law 1997 .... 10.04
  Art 2 .... 10.04
  Art 6 .... 10.04
Limited Liability Partnerships (Jersey)
  Law 2013 .... 10.04
Limited Partnerships Act 1907 .... 1.01, 1.02,
              1.20, 1.29, 9.01–9.03, 9.10
s 4 .... 9.01
s 4(2) 3.12
s 4(2A) 9.07
s 4(2B) 9.19
s 4(3) 9.07, 9.19
s 4(3A) 9.19
s 4(3B) 9.19
s 6 .... 1.23, 9.10, 9.13, 14.11
s 6(1) 9.11–9.14, 14.11
s 6(3A) 9.22
s 6(3B) 9.18, 9.22
s 6(3D) 9.22
s 6(5) 9.21
s 6(5)(f) 9.21
s 6(6) 9.21
s 6A 1.23, 9.18
s 6A(2) 9.18
s 6A(3) 9.18
s 6A(4)(a) 9.18
s 6A(4)(b) 9.18
s 7 .... 9.02
s 8 .... 9.03
s 8(3) 9.17
s 8A 9.04, 9.05, 9.17
s 8A(3) 9.20
s 8B 9.04, 9.06
s 8C 9.04, 9.05
s 8C(4) 9.04
s 8C(5) 9.17
s 8C(7) 9.17
s 8C(8) 9.17
s 8C(9) 9.17
s 8D 9.17
s 8D(1) 9.17
s 8D(2) 9.17
s 9 .... 9.06, 9.20
s 9(1) 9.05
s 10 .... 9.07, 9.13
s 10(1A) 9.20
s 10(1B) 9.20
s 10(1C) 9.20
s 11 .... 9.13
s 13 .... 9.06, 9.13
s 14 .... 9.06
s 14(1) 9.13
s 28 .... 9.21
s 36(2) 9.21
Mental Capacity Act 2005 .... 7.09
Mental Health Act 1959 .... 7.09
Misrepresentation Act 1967 .... 7.19
s 2(1) 7.19, 14.19
s 2(2) 7.19, 14.19

National Health Service Act 1977
 s 54 ....3.07
Partnership Act 1890 ..... 1.02, 1.04, 1.09, 1.10,
     1.27, 1.31, 3.01, 4.12, 4.45, 9.03, 12.05
 s 1 ......1.08, 1.10, 1.18, 1.25, 1.26, 1.35, 2.01,
        2.22, 2.26, 7.22, 9.05, 11.01, 11.04
 s 1(1)................................1.01
 s 1(2)................................1.01
 s 2 .... 2.01, 2.14, 2.26
 s 2(1)...................... 1.18, 2.01, 6.18
 s 2(2)...................... 1.26, 2.01, 2.15
 s 2(3)....... 1.09, 1.24, 1.26, 2.01, 2.15, 2.16,
        2.18, 2.19, 2.22, 2.25–2.27, 2.40, 9.15
 s 2(3)(a) 2.22, 9.12
 s 2(3)(b) 2.20
 s 2(3)(c) 2.21, 2.27
 s 2(3)(d) 2.22–2.24, 2.27, 8.07, 9.12
 s 2(3)(e) 2.25, 2.27, 8.07
 s 3 .... 2.14, 2.27, 8.07
 s 4(1).......................... 1.05, 1.08
 s 4(2)................................1.08
 s 5 .... 1.09, 4.02, 4.04, 4.06, 4.08–4.11,
        4.13, 4.14, 4.17, 4.19–4.22, 6.23, 7.24
 ss 5–8 ....4.02
 ss 5–18 ....4.01
 s 6 .... 4.10, 4.11
 s 7 ....4.11
 s 8 .... 2.05, 4.04, 4.11
 s 9 .... 4.45, 4.47
 s 10 .... 1.09, 4.07, 4.08, 4.23–4.26, 4.29,
        4.30, 4.32, 4.33, 4.36–4.43, 4.45, 11.13
 s 11 .... 4.23, 4.36–4.38, 4.40–4.45
 s 11(a)........................... 4.37, 4.38
 s 11(b) 4.37–4.39
 s 12 .... 4.45, 4.47
 s 13 .... 4.23, 4.37, 4.40, 4.42–4.44
 s 14 .... 2.32, 4.01, 4.03, 4.48, 4.55,
              4.56, 4.59, 5.46, 7.07, 7.41
 s 14(1)................ 2.28, 2.30–2.33, 2.36,
              4.59, 4.60, 9.13, 16.08
 s 14(2).................................2.30
 s 15 ....4.09
 s 16 ....4.16
 s 17 ....4.48
 s 17(1)......................... 4.49, 4.52
 s 17(2)......................... 4.49, 4.52
 s 17(3)......................... 4.52, 4.53
 s 18 ....4.54
 s 19 .... 1.09, 2.05, 5.02, 5.20
 s 20 .... 6.09, 6.10
 s 20(1)...............6.07, 6.08, 6.12–6.14
 s 20(2)...............................6.11
 s 20(3)..........................6.18–6.20
 s 21 .... 6.09, 6.17, 6.20
 s 22 ....6.06
 s 23 .... 1.09, 5.47, 7.03
 s 23(1)......................... 5.47, 5.48
 s 23(2)......................... 5.47, 5.48
 s 23(3)...............................5.48
 s 23(5)...............................5.47
 s 24 .... 5.20, 5.30, 5.33, 7.53, 14.04
 ss 24-30 .... 14.04
 s 24(1)............ 5.26–5.29, 5.32, 7.51, 14.05
 s 24(2)......................... 5.32, 14.06
 s 24(2)(a) 5.32
 s 24(3)......................... 5.31, 7.52
 s 24(4)...............................5.30
 s 24(5).................. 5.21, 5.22, 14.07
 s 24(6)......................... 5.22, 14.08
 s 24(7).................. 4.14, 5.33, 14.09
 s 24(8).....3.20, 5.23, 5.24, 5.33, 14.10, 15.02
 s 24(9)......................... 5.25, 14.11
 s 25 .... 5.20, 5.37, 5.38, 14.15, 16.05
 s 26 .... 2.07–2.10, 2.12, 7.02, 7.03
 s 26(1).................. 2.07, 2.08, 2.10, 2.11
 s 26(2)................................2.11
 s 27 .... 2.09, 2.12
 s 28 ....5.10, 5.11, 5.48, 9.12, 13.11, 14.12
 ss 28–30 .... 1.10, 5.09
 s 29 .... 5.10, 5.11, 5.13, 5.18, 5.19
 s 29(1)............................. 14.14
 s 30 .... 5.10, 5.19, 14.13
 s 31 .... 5.43, 5.48
 s 31(1)................... 5.43, 5.44, 5.46
 s 31(2)......................... 5.44, 5.45
 s 32 .... 2.08, 2.10, 7.02
 s 32(a)........................... 2.08, 7.02
 s 32(b) 2.08, 7.02
 s 32(c) 2.08–2.11, 7.02
 s 33(1)......................... 7.03, 7.04, 7.18
 s 33(2)................... 5.48, 7.03, 7.04
 s 34 .... 2.31, 7.07, 7.18
 s 35 .... 7.08, 8.13, 8.19
 s 35(a)........................... 7.09, 7.10
 s 35(b) 7.10, 7.18
 s 35(c) 7.11, 7.14
 s 35(d) 7.12, 7.14, 7.22, 14.22
 s 35(e)................................7.13
 s 35(f) 7.12, 7.14, 7.15, 7.17
 s 36 ....2.30, 4.01, 4.48, 4.55, 4.60, 7.41
 s 36(1)................... 4.56, 4.59, 16.08
 s 36(2)......................... 4.57, 4.58
 s 36(3)..........................4.57–4.59
 s 37 ....7.41
 s 38 ....7.24–7.27
 s 39 .... 6.08, 7.35, 7.37, 7.53
 s 40 ....7.34
 ss 40–43 ....6.08
 s 41 .... 7.19, 14.18
 s 41(a)...............................7.53
 s 42 ....7.30, 7.50–7.53, 7.55, 7.56, 7.60, 16.10
 s 42(1)................. 7.49, 7.54, 7.57–7.59
 s 42(2)...............................7.59
 s 43 .... 7.56, 7.60

TABLE OF LEGISLATION

s 44 .... 6.08, 7.53, 7.62
s 44(a) 7.64
s 44(b) 7.64
s 45 ....1.14
s 46 ....1.09
Partnership Law Amendment Act 1865
   (Bovill's Act) 1.09, 1.28, 2.14, 2.23
Partnerships (Prosecution) (Scotland)
   Act 2013 .... 1.08, 4.35
Policyholders Protection Act 1975 ....1.37
   s 6(7)(b) 1.37
Race Relations Act 1976 ....1.07, 3.04
Registration of Business Names Act 1916 .... 3.13
Revised Uniform Partnership Act 1994 .....1.10
Sex Discrimination Act 1975 ....3.04
   s 11 ....1.07
Small Business, Enterprise and
   Employment Act 2015 .... 3.01, 11.10

Small Business, Enterprise and
   Employment Act 2015 .... 1.29, 8.11,
                                  11.25, 11.27
   Pt 9 ....8.02
   Pt 10 ....8.02
Solicitors Act 1974 ....7.07
Taxation of Chargeable Gains Act 1992
   s 59A 10.10
Trade Descriptions Act 1968
   s 15 ....4.32
Trade Marks Act 1994 ....6.30
Trusts of Land and Appointment of
   Trustees Act 1996 ....6.06
   s 14 ....7.36
Unfair Contract Terms Act 1977 .... 13.16
VAT Act 1994
   s 45 ....1.07

TABLE OF STATUTORY INSTRUMENTS

Civil Jurisdiction and Judgments Order
    2001 (SI 2001/3929) 1.38, 1.39
Civil Procedure Rules 1998 (SI 1998/3132)
    PD 7A
        para 5A. 3.19
        para 5B. 3.19
        para 5B.1 . . . . .3.19
    PD 70, para 6A 3.19
    Pt 6 . . . . 1.40, 11.22
    r 6.20(3) 11.21
    rr 6.3–6.6 . . . . .3.19
    r 6.3(3) 11.22
    r 6.9. . . . . 3.19, 11.22
    r 6.9(2) 3.19
    r 7.2. . . . . .3.19
    r 19.9C 11.22
Collective Investment in Transferable
    Securities (Contractual Scheme)
    Regulations 2013 (SI 2013/1884) 9.03
Companies Act 2006 (Substitution of
    Section 1201) Regulations 2009
    (SI 2009/3182). 3.16
Companies (Cross-Border Mergers)
    Regulations 2007 (SI 2007/2974) 17.15
Companies and Partnerships (Accounts
    and Audit) Regulations 2013
    (SI 2013/2005). 1.29, 1.37
Companies, Partnerships and Groups
    (Accounts and Reports) Regulations
    2015 (SI 2015/980) 1.37
Deregulation and Small Business
    Enterprise and Employment Act
    (Consequential Amendments)
    (Savings) Regulations 2017
    (SI 2017/540). 8.02
Insolvency (Miscellaneaous Amendments)
    Regulations 2017 (SI 2017/1119) 8.02
Insolvency Partnerships (Amendment)
    (No 2) Order 2002 (SI 2002/2708) 1.11
Insolvency Partnerships (Amendment)
    (No 2) Order 2007 (SI 2007/2708) 1.11
Insolvency Partnerships (Amendment)
    Order 1996 (SI 1996/1308) 1.11
Insolvency Partnerships (Amendment)
    Order 2001 (SI 2001/767) 1.11
Insolvency Partnerships (Amendment)
    Order 2002 (SI 2002/1308) 1.11
Insolvency Partnerships (Amendment)
    Order 2006 (SI 2006/622) 1.11

Insolvent Partnerships (Amendment)
    (No 2) Order 2002
    (SI 2002/2708). 8.02, 8.05, 8.11, 8.13
Insolvent Partnerships (Amendment)
    Order 1996 (SI 1996/1308) 8.02, 8.05
Insolvent Partnerships (Amendment)
    Order 2001 (SI 2001/767) 8.02
Insolvent Partnerships (Amendment)
    Order 2002 (SI 2002/1308) 8.02, 8.05
Insolvent Partnerships (Amendment)
    Order 2005 (SI 2005/1516). . . . 1.11, 8.02, 8.14
Insolvent Partnerships (Amendment)
    Order 2006 (SI 2006/622) 8.02
Insolvent Partnerships Order 1986
    (SI 1986/2142). 8.02, 8.04
Insolvent Partnerships Order 1994
    (SI 1994/2421). 1.11, 8.02–8.04, 8.07
    art 4. . . . . .8.11
    art 5. . . . . .8.11
    art 6. . . . . .8.14
    art 7. . . . . .8.05
    art 8. . . . . .8.06
    art 9. . . . . .8.05
    art 10 . . . . .8.06
    art 11 . . . . 8.09, 8.10, 8.12, 8.13
    art 14(2) 8.10
    art 16 . . . . .8.08
    sch 1 . . . . .8.11
    sch 3 . . . . .8.05
    sch 4 . . . . .8.06
    sch 5 . . . . .8.05
    sch 6 . . . . .8.06
    sch 7 . . . . .8.09
    sch 8 . . . . .8.08
Large and Medium-Sized Limited Liability
    Partnerships (Accounts) Regulations
    2008 (SI 2008/1913) 10.09, 11.30
Legislative Reform (Limited Partnerships)
    Order 2009 (SI 2009/1940) 9.03
Legislative Reform (Private Fund
    Limited Partnerships) Order 2017
    (SI 2017/514). 9.03, 9.16
Limited Liability Partnerships (Accounts
    and Audit) (Application of Companies
    Act 2006) Regulations 2008
    (SI 2008/1911). 10.01, 10.09
    reg 6 . . . . 11.30, 14.11
    reg 9 . . . . 11.30
    reg 17 . . . . 11.30

reg 22 .... 11.30
reg 47 .... 14.01
reg 48 .... 14.01
Limited Liability Partnerships (Application
   of Companies Act 2006) Regulations
   2009 (SI 2009/1804) 10.01, 10.09,
                         10.10, 12.07, 17.14
pt 8A................................ 11.27
reg 4 .... 11.21, 12.07
reg 7 .... 11.20
regs 8–10 .... 11.06
reg 11 .... 11.06
reg 12 .... 11.06
reg 14 .... 11.24
reg 16 .... 10.01, 11.07
reg 17 .... 11.07
reg 18 .... 11.02, 11.08, 11.25
reg 18A............................. 11.25
reg 19 .... 11.25, 11.26
reg 21 .... 11.28
reg 30 .... 11.29
regs 31A–31N 10.09
reg 31B............................. 11.27
reg 31C............................. 11.27
regs 31D–31E 11.27
reg 31E....................... 11.25, 11.27
reg 31F............................. 11.27
reg 31H............................. 11.27
reg 31K....................... 11.25, 11.27
reg 31M............................ 11.27
reg 31ZA 11.29
reg 32 .... 11.28
reg 45 .... 17.14
reg 46 .... 17.15
reg 48 .... 13.20, 13.21, 14.03
reg 50 .... 17.19
reg 51 .... 11.17, 17.19
regs 52–55 .... 17.20
regs 56–58 .... 17.21
reg 57 .... 17.21
reg 60 .... 11.05, 11.11
reg 61 .... 11.11
reg 66 .... 11.23, 11.26
reg 67 .... 11.25
reg 68 .... 11.07
reg 75 .... 11.29
reg 77 .... 13.14
reg 79 .... 14.01
Limited Liability Partnerships (Application
   of Companies Act 2006 Regulations)
   (Amendment) Regulations 2013
   (SI 2013/618)
   reg 8 .... 11.27
Limited Liability Partnerships and
   Business Names (Sensitive Words
   and Expressions) Regulations 2014
   (SI 2014/3140)...................... 3.15

Limited Liability Partnerships and Business
   (Names and Trading Disclosures)
   Regulations 2015 (SI 2015/17)
   Pt 6 .... 11.24
   reg 17 .... 3.14, 3.15
   reg 24 .... 11.24
   reg 25 .... 11.24
   sch 2 .... 3.14, 3.15
Limited Liability Partnerships (Register
   of People with Significant Control)
   Regulations 2016 (SI 2016/340) 11.27
Limited Liability Partnerships
   Regulations 2001 (SI 2001/1090) 8.08,
              10.01, 10.09, 12.07, 17.08, 17.16
   reg 2 .... 12.06, 14.01
   reg 4 .... 13.02
   reg 4(2)................ 12.06, 12.12–12.14
   reg 5 .... 17.01
   reg 7 ..... 14.01, 14.04, 14.09, 14.15, 14.23
   reg 7(5)..................... 12.01, 13.01
   reg 7(6)........................... 13.09
   reg 7(7)........................... 14.04
   reg 7(8)........................... 13.11
   reg 8 .... 14.01, 14.03, 14.04,
                  14.15, 14.23, 16.05
   sch 2 .... 12.01, 12.12, 17.17
   sch 3 ...... 11.01, 11.04, 11.06, 11.11, 11.16,
            11.17, 12.06, 13.02, 13.12, 13.23,
            13.24, 14.01, 17.01, 17.02, 17.09,
                  17.10, 17.16–17.18
Partnerships (Accounts) Regulations 2008
   (SI 2008/569).................. 1.29, 1.37
Persons with Significant Control
   Regulations 2016
   (SI 2016/339)................. 1.29, 11.27
Primary Medical Services (Sale of Goodwill
   and Restrictions on Sub-contracting)
   Regulations 2004 (SI 2004/906)..... 3.07, 6.26
reg 3A of LLP Regs 2009 (SI 2009/1804) 11.10
Regulatory Reform (Business Tenancies)
   (England and Wales) Order 2003
   (SI 2003/3096)....................... 6.23
Regulatory Reform (Removal of 20 Member
   Limit in Partnerships) Order 2002
   (SI 2002/3203)....................... 3.12
Scottish Partnerships (Register of People
   with Significant Control) Regulations
   2017 (SI 2017/694) 1.29, 9.03, 9.24
Small Business, Enterprise and Employment
   Act 2015 (Consequential Amendments,
   Savings and Transitional Provisions)
   Regulations 2019 (SI 2019/1058) 8.02
Small Limited Liability Partnerships
   (Accounts) Regulations 2008
   (SI 2008/1912)............... 10.09, 11.30
Working Time Regulations 1998
   (SI 1998/1883)....................... 2.35

TABLE OF EUROPEAN LEGISLATION

DIRECTIVES

Dir 78/660/EEC [1978] OJ L222/78
    Company Directive 1.37, 11.08
Dir 83/349/EEC [1983] OJ L193/83
    Company Directive 1.37
Dir 90/605/EEC [1990] OJ L317/90
    Company Directive 1.37
Dir 2006/43/EC [2006] OJ L157/06
    Company Directive 1.37
Dir 2013/334/EU 1.37
Dir 2017/1132 [2017] OJ L169/46 . . . . .1.37

REGULATIONS

Regulation 1215/2012/EU
    Art 4 (ex Art 2) 1.39
    Art 24(2) 1.39
Regulation 1346/2000 [2000] OJ L160/1 . . . .8.02

TREATIES AND CONVENTIONS

Brussels Convention 1968
    art 16 . . . . .1.39

LIST OF ABBREVIATIONS

BEIS	Department for Business, Energy and Industrial Strategy
CPR	Civil Procedure Rules
DBERR	Department for Business, Enterprise and Regulatory Reform
DBIS	Department for Business, Innovation and Skills
DTI	Department of Trade and Industry
EEIG	European Economic Interest Grouping
FCA	Financial Conduct Authority
FSA	Financial Services Authority
HMRC	HM Revenue & Customs
ICC	Insolvency and Companies Court
LLP	limited liability partnership
LP	limited partnership
LPA	Limited Partnership Act 1907
LRO	legislative reform order
PAYE	pay as you earn
PFLP	private fund limited partnership
PSC	people with significant control
PVA	partnership voluntary arrangement
RLE	Relevant Legal Entities
SI	statutory instrument
SLP	Scottish limited partnership

PART I
PARTNERSHIPS

1
PARTNERSHIPS AND PARTNERSHIP LAW

What is a Partnership?

A partnership is defined, with misleading simplicity, in s 1(1) of the Partnership Act 1890 as 'the relation which subsists between persons carrying on a business in common with a view of profit'. All legal definitions have exceptions, however, and s 1(2) is quick to exclude all forms of company (from ICI plc to Jones the Butchers Ltd) which would otherwise fall within the definition. Also excluded are limited liability partnerships (or LLPs) formed under the Limited Liability Partnerships Act 2000, despite their name. Section 1 of the 2000 Act makes that clear, although some aspects of partnership law do apply to LLPs (see below). The definition in the 1890 Act, however, does provide the three essential ingredients for a partnership, namely, a business, carried on in common, and with a view of profit, and we will return to those later on in this chapter. For the moment, however, the key word in the definition is the word 'relation'. Partnership is a relationship: it is not, except in Scotland, an organization in its own right with a separate legal personality. Unlike a company, therefore, a partnership cannot of itself make contracts, employ people, commit wrongs, or even be sued, any more than a marriage can. Where we talk of a partnership (or frequently of a firm) we simply mean the partners who comprise the partnership. Rather like a marriage or a civil partnership, a commercial partnership is a relationship arising from a contract, which if established governs the rights and duties between the parties and their relationships vis-à-vis the rest of society. **1.01**

The other key difference between a partnership and a company or LLP is that a partnership does not confer any limited liability on the partners. Thus it is possible for each partner to be liable without limit for debts incurred by the other partners in the course of the partnership business. This is seen by the business community as an obvious drawback but an early attempt in 1907 by the Limited Partnerships Act to create partnerships in which some of the partners would have limited liability was doomed to failure as a general business medium. This was partly because of the weaknesses of the form itself (if the limited partner for example interferes in the management of the firm he loses his immunity) but also because private companies arrived at the same time, providing both limited liability and a separate legal personality to hide behind. The presumed advantages of Mr Salomon in the famous case of *Salomon v A Salomon & Co Ltd*[1] would not have been available to him under either of the true partnership forms currently available in the United Kingdom.

---

[1] [1897] AC 22, HL.

Limited partnerships (LPs) have, however, become a very important vehicle of choice for several specialized purposes, eg for venture capital, and, until recently, for Scottish agricultural leases. As such, that form of partnership fulfils a totally different role from the general partnership.[2] LPs have been the subject of a number of recent changes to the 1907 Act, enacted in response to their increasing popularity with the financial sector. Since 2017, there is therefore now a modified form of LP available to that sector, known as the private fund LP. The apparent attractiveness of Scottish LPs (they have legal personality) to those involved in somewhat suspicious financial transactions has led the Government to apply further regulation to them and to consider further changes to the 1907 Act. All these matters are considered in Chapter 9. For the moment it is enough to recognize that an LP is a very different animal in practice to an ordinary partnership.

Until the advent of the limited liability partnership, partnership remained the preferred medium for the professions, initially due to the flexibility of both its financial and constitutional provisions when compared with a company, but also because of the tax and privacy advantages for the partners. Although the number of partnerships is falling slightly, they are still used by many small and family businesses, including agriculture, the music industry, and the retail trade. There are over 450,000 of them in the United Kingdom.[3] Partnership disputes continue to occupy the courts. Even the growing LLP litigation often involves disputes over partnership concepts.

Limited liability partnerships

1.02 During the 1990s, however, the accountancy profession in particular became concerned about the potential liability of partners, often quite remote from the activity in question, for the substantial damages being awarded against the larger firms for negligence. In 1997, in response to this pressure and the creation of a potentially available limited liability partnership form in Jersey, the Department of Trade and Industry (DTI) published a consultation paper entitled *Limited Liability Partnership—A New Form of Business Association for Professions*. Following lengthy consultations a draft Bill was published in 1998 and the result was the Limited Liability Partnerships Act 2000, which came into force on 6 April 2001. As a result of the consultations, this new form of business association, the LLP, became open to all businesses and not just specified professions as originally envisaged. In effect it is a hybrid between a company and a partnership, although much more like the former than the latter, despite its name. It has legal personality and provides limited liability for its members, in return for which it must publish its accounts and comply with several other regulatory requirements adapted from company law. It is *not*, however, based on the partnership form with

---

[2] In March 2018 there were 49,287 LPs on the register (Companies House, *Statistical Tables on Companies Registration Activities 2017–18*).
[3] BEIS, *Business Population Estimates for the UK and Regions: 2018*.

limited liability added on; and thus should not be confused with an LP formed under the 1907 Act, which is still a true partnership.

The connection between an LLP and a partnership formed under the 1890 Act derives mainly from the fact that the relationship between its members (as opposed to its dealings with outsiders) may be modelled on partnership law and that it, or rather its members, will be taxed as if it were a partnership and not, as it really is, a body corporate. The major features of this new business form are set out in Chapters 10 to 12. Whilst there is clear evidence that it has been adopted by most of the professional firms,[4] the important thing to grasp is that, despite appearances, in reality it has very little in common with partnerships as set out in the rest of this book.

Further developments in Jersey

1.03 The previous influence of Jersey which led to the introduction of the UK LLP raises an issue as to whether recent developments in that jurisdiction will have any effect on UK law. In August 2019, a revised LLP form was introduced, and in September 2019 legislation providing for a new business entity, an LLC (limited liability company) was passed. The latter is based on a US form and is clearly aimed at the US market.[5] It is unlikely that either of these developments will affect the United Kingdom's business forms, not least because our LLP is not too dissimilar from an LLC.

Law Commissions' review of partnership law

1.04 In general, partnership law has been allowed to develop organically through a steady stream of court decisions since the 1890 Act. But in 1998 the DTI, as part of its 'think small first' policy, also applied to company law reform, asked the Law Commissions of England and Wales and of Scotland to undertake a review of partnership law generally,[6] including LPs. After a lengthy consultation process,[7] the two Commissions published a joint Report in November 2003, which made a considerable number of recommendations for changing the law and included a draft Bill to replace the existing legislation.[8] Some members of the legal profession were quite hostile in their immediate opposition to the Report, homing in on the issue of legal personality, and the response from Government was somewhat underwhelming. In April 2004, the DTI issued a

---

[4] In October 2017 there were 53,848 registered LLPs (Companies House, *Statistical Tables on Companies Registration Activities 2017–18*).
[5] Jersey Finance, *New LLC Legislation Set to Provide Attractive Proposition for US Institutions and Fund Managers*, 12 September 2018.
[6] Excluding insolvency.
[7] See the Law Com Consultation Papers Nos 159 (2000) and 161 (2001). All of these documents are available on the Law Commission's website: <http://www.lawcom.gov.uk>. See also Morse, 'Partnerships for the 21st Century—Limited Liability Partnerships and Partnership Law Reform in the UK' [2002] SJLS 455.
[8] Cm 6015 (Law Com No 283; Scot Law Com No 192)—referred to as 'Law Com' hereafter.

consultation document seeking views not as to the merits of the recommendations as such but as to the economic and business costs and benefits of those changes.[9] In 2006, the Government baldly announced that it was not proposing to take forward any of the Law Commissions' proposals on general partnership law. In response, however, to favourable comments from the venture capital industry, it said that it would consult with a view to enacting the, quite separate, proposals on the reform of LP law.[10] That process, which after a small beginning initially seemed to have stalled, was revived by the Government for collective investment schemes using the LP form, leading to the private fund LP being introduced in 2017. The current state of play is set out in Chapter 9.

But in the main the reform proposals are dead in the water. Many of these related to the process of resolving partnership disputes and dissolution where the current law often produces litigation costs out of all proportion to the amounts involved.[11] The Report foundered, above all, on its pervasive recommendation that partnerships should have legal personality, an issue which the Commissions were specifically invited to address. Although the other proposals were largely independent of that, they were predicated on the basis of legal personality and would have to be rewritten if it were abandoned. As such, however unfortunate the result, they fell with it. It is appropriate therefore to consider legal personality and its linked issue of continuity at this point.

Legal Personality and Continuity

1.05 English partnerships do not have legal personality.[12] They are only relationships, but the confusion which arises from this lack of legal personality is not helped by the fact that in common usage a partnership often looks like and is regarded as a separate entity. The words 'and Co' are sometimes found at the end of the name used by a firm. This signifies nothing in legal terms and does not make the firm into a company. Most private limited companies use the word 'limited' or the abbreviation, 'Ltd', at the end of their names. Further, partners can sue and be sued in the firm's name and tax assessments are raised on the firm, although the fact that the latter is a smokescreen is shown by the decision in *Sutherland v Gustar*[13] that an assessment may be challenged by any partner irrespective of the wishes of the other partners. Partnerships, as distinct from partners, can even be prosecuted. Further s 4(1) of the Partnership Act itself provides that:

---

[9] *Reform of Partnership Law: The Economic Impact*, April 2004.
[10] Written Ministerial Statement 20 July 2006.
[11] See, eg *Sahota v Sohi* [2006] EWHC 344 where a dispute over £50,000 incurred costs of over half a million pounds.
[12] The reasons for this are historical, reflecting the common law's separate development from the law merchant applicable in continental Europe and in Scotland: see Holdsworth, *A History of English Law*, Vol V, p 84, Vol VIII, pp 194–8.
[13] [1994] 4 All ER 1.

Persons who have entered into partnership with one another are for the purposes of this Act called collectively a firm, and the name under which their business is carried on is called the firm-name.

But in England this provides nothing more than a useful shorthand to describe the partnership. The word 'firm' is in effect no more than a collective noun. At all times remember that an English partnership is in law a contractual relationship which affects the rights and duties of those concerned and no more.

Continuity

1.06 There are many problems associated with this lack of legal personality. Not least are the practical difficulties in relation to the ownership of property and the continuation of contractual rights and obligations of the partners when there is a change in the membership. If X contracts with A, B, and C as partners, how does that continue if, say, either A leaves the firm or D joins it? That is the related issue of continuity. The Law Commissions recommended that, in addition to legal personality, there should be a default rule[14] that in such a case the partnership should continue so long as two partners remained.[15] Continuity of contractual liability could therefore have been achieved without legal personality. The problems associated with an outgoing or incoming partner are dealt with in Chapter 4 so far as third parties are concerned, and in Chapter 7 as to dealings between the partners.

Contractual and statutory problems

1.07 There are many other problems associated with this lack of legal personality, however, and the following may serve as examples. In the South African case of *Strydom v Protea Eiendomsagente*[16] a firm of estate agents sold a property for another firm on terms that the vendor firm would pay the commission unless the purchasers defaulted, in which case the purchasers would be liable. The purchasers duly defaulted and the estate agents now sued them for the commission. It transpired, however, that the same people were the partners of both the vendor and estate agent firms and the court held that since a person could not contract with himself, neither could the two firms in this case, so that the contract was a nullity. The court did, however, point out that there was no evidence that the two firms were conducting separate businesses and hinted that if they had been then the position might have been different. It is difficult to see why that should be. The position is unclear in English law; one firm can bring an action against another even

---

[14] This is one that applies unless the partnership agreement provides otherwise: Law Com, para 4.58.
[15] Law Com, para 8.30. The draft Bill would not have made a change of partner a ground for breaking up the firm.
[16] 1979 (2) SA 206 (T).

if they have partners in common (see Chapter 3) but in *Rye v Rye*[17] it was held by the House of Lords that partners who owned some premises could not lease the property to themselves under English land law. But since one partner can clearly lease premises (although paradoxically he cannot grant a licence) to the firm, is he not in that case contracting at least partly with himself? That paradox was raised by two members of the Supreme Court in relation to a discussion as to whether a partner could also be an employee.[18] The traditional view is that one cannot employ oneself. This issue is discussed in Chapter 2.

A second example occurred in the case of *Sheppard & Cooper Ltd v TSB Bank plc*.[19] A company appointed a firm of accountants to conduct a financial investigation into its affairs. Under the terms of the contract, signed by one of the partners, the firm agreed that it would never become involved in the management of that company. The bank now proposed to appoint two partners of that firm as receivers of the company (which would amount to managing it). The question was whether one of those partners was excluded by the earlier agreement since he had not been a partner at the time when it had been made. The Court of Appeal actually decided the issue on the basis that it was a joint appointment and the other partner, who had been a member of the firm at the date of the contract, was clearly bound by the agreement; but it also said that to construe the agreement as only applying to persons who were partners at the time it was entered into would not be realistic in accordance with modern commercial practice in the case of large professional firms. This might be thought of as amounting to de facto legal personality.

A compromise approach was taken by the House of Lords in an appeal from Northern Ireland in *Kelly v Northern Ireland Housing Executive*.[20] The issue was whether a partner in a firm of solicitors, who applied unsuccessfully for her firm to be included on a panel to act for the Executive and who had named herself as the designated solicitor to be responsible for the work, could complain to the relevant body on the grounds of discrimination under s 17 of the Fair Employment (Northern Ireland) Act 1976. Such a complaint required Mrs Kelly to be seeking 'a contract personally to execute any work'. The Court of Appeal in Northern Ireland refused her application on the ground that it was the firm which was seeking the work and a firm cannot contract personally to do anything, but the House of Lords (only by a majority of three to two) reversed that decision. Two members of the majority thought that the relevant legislation was wide enough to include a firm acting personally through a designated partner and only Lord Griffiths thought that in fact there was in law no contract with the firm as such but one with each of the

---

[17] [1962] AC 496, HL. Nor can they guarantee their own debts: *IAC (Singapore) Pte Ltd v Koh Meng Wan* (1978–1979) SLR 470.
[18] *Clyde & Co LLP v Bates van Winklelhof* [2014] UKSC 32. The actual dispute concerned an LLP but was argued by reference to partnership law.
[19] [1997] 2 BCLC 222.
[20] [1999] 1 AC 428, HL.

partners so that each partner could be said to be seeking the contract personally. One anomaly of that construction is that if Mrs Kelly had been an assistant solicitor and not a partner there could have been no complaint since there would have been no contract with her.

The interface of partnerships with modern regulatory and invasive statutory law also throws up problems associated with the lack of legal personality. In *Dave v Robinska*,[21] the Employment Appeal Tribunal allowed one partner to bring an action against her only other partner under the Sex Discrimination Act 1975 on the basis that that other partner could be 'the firm' as required by s 11 of that Act for that purpose. If it had been a ten-partner firm she could have sued the other nine and there should be no difference for a two-partner firm.[22] This is another example of the solution being a de facto legal personality. A similar solution was adopted, amongst others, in the Corporate Manslaughter and Corporate Homicide Act 2007. That Act applies to some partnerships, but only the firm and not its members can be prosecuted.[23]

The final example concerns the all too familiar imposition of value added tax. Under s 22 of the Finance Act 1972 (now s 45 of the VAT Act 1994), registration for VAT could be in the firm name and no account was to be taken of any change in the partnership. But Glidewell J in *Customs & Excise Commissioners v Evans*[24] was forced to conclude that, since a partnership was not a person but only a group of taxable persons trading jointly, an assessment could only be made against the individual partners and further that such assessments must be notified to each partner. Since the particular firm involved, which ran a wine bar known as the 'Grape Escape', had had a change of personnel during the year and not all the partners had been so notified, the assessment was, therefore invalid. The authorities were forced to change the law in the Finance Act 1982 to cover the specific case. But it has since been held by the VAT Tribunal in *British Shoe Corporation Ltd v Customs and Excise Commissioners*[25] that a summons served on a partnership to produce documents for VAT purposes had no effect—the relevant rules required service either on a body corporate or an individual and neither could include a partnership. Problems involving VAT and partnerships continue to occur.[26] In *HMRC v Pal*[27] it was held that the registration of a partnership could have no effect on individuals who, although they had been represented as such, were not in fact partners at all.

---

[21] [2003] ICR 1248.
[22] That situation could not have arisen under the Race Relations Act 1976 since that did not apply to firms with less than six members. Discrimination generally is considered in Ch 3, below.
[23] The 'firm' may thus also be convicted. See s 14 of the 2007 Act and Ch 4, below.
[24] [1982] STC 342.
[25] [1998] V & DR 348.
[26] See [2000] BTR 406.
[27] [2008] STC 2442.

Legal personality in Scotland

1.08 The position in relation to Scottish partnerships is on the face of it very different. In accordance with Scots common law, s 4(2) of the Partnership Act provides: 'In Scotland a firm is a legal person distinct from the partners of whom it is composed.' It might be thought therefore that none of the problems associated with the lack of legal personality of a partnership in England would apply. Following the case of *Major v Brodie*,[28] however, this seems to be far from the case. The case was actually heard in England but concerned a question of the income tax liability of partners in a Scottish partnership. The taxpayers carried on a farming business in Scotland in partnership under the name 'Skeldon Estates'. They each borrowed money which was used partly to acquire another farm owned by the Murdoch family. The Skeldon Estates partnership then entered into an agreement with Mr Murdoch to carry on a farming business on both farms under the name 'W Murdoch & Son'. The balance of the loans was then used as working capital by W Murdoch & Son.

The taxpayers claimed tax relief on the interest paid on the loans. That could only be done, under the tax legislation, if the loan were used 'wholly for the purposes of the business carried on by the partnership'. The Revenue refused to allow the claim for tax relief on the basis that the money had not been used wholly for the purposes of the business of the Skeldon Estates partnership but for the business of W Murdoch & Son. In other words they argued that each partnership was a separate legal entity which owned the business carried on by it so that the two could not be merged.

The Special Commissioner who heard the taxpayers' appeal was therefore faced with the question as to what exactly were the consequences of the separate legal personality of a Scottish partnership. He was presented with two contradictory opinions by eminent Scots lawyers. In one opinion it was said that the Revenue were correct and that the partners in Scotland only acted as agents for the firm. The business is always carried on by the firm and not by the partners as such. The other opinion was that, whilst the firm owned the business, it was carried on by the partners as principals. This was because s 4(2) is subject to s 1 of the Partnership Act, ie that the firm, which is only defined as being a collective noun for the persons who have entered into partnership by s 4(1) and to which legal personality has been attributed in Scotland under s 4(2), is only created by the fact of persons carrying on a business with a view of profit.

It was this latter opinion which found favour with the Commissioner. The persons who are carrying on the business as required by s 1 of the Act are the partners in Scotland and they are not mere agents of the legal persona, even if 'given a quasi- corporate veneer, since if they are not, there can be no partnership'. Thus either the Skeldon Estates partnership or the taxpayers as partners of it were carrying on the business of farming

---

[28] [1998] STC 491.

in partnership with Mr Murdoch under the firm name of W Murdoch & Son. The taxpayers' claim would be allowed.

On appeal to the High Court the Revenue did not dispute that finding by the Commissioner but reserved the right to argue it before the House of Lords if the case proceeded that far. The real problem is that if s 4(2) of the Act does indeed create full legal personality for Scottish partnerships, which would seem to be the clear intention on its wording, this sits very uneasily with s 1 and other sections of the Act which are designed for the English situation. For example, as we shall see in Chapter 4, every partner is an agent 'of the firm and his other partners'. If the firm has full legal personality how can a partner be an agent for his fellow partners? The firm would be the sole principal and all the partners mere agents of it. The alternative construction, adopted in this case, would allow the Act to apply fully in Scotland but at the expense of regarding 'legal personality' as a type of 'bolt-on' extra to the other concepts of partnership law.

There are also problems with continuity in respect of Scottish partnerships. The cases have been concerned with the effect of the death of one partner on a pre-existing contract with the firm.[29] Does the firm continue to exist; does it have perpetual succession so that the contract is still valid as against the firm? One possible solution, canvassed in the cases, is to regard such a contract as being 'with the house', although that has never actually been applied. The position appears to be far from settled.[30] A different effect of the Scottish partnership's legal personality appeared when Lady Hale used it as part of her discussion as to whether a partner in a UK partnership could also be an employee of the partnership in *Clyde & Co LLP v Bates van Winklehof*.[31] That issue is considered in Chapter 2.

Another difficulty with reconciling the legal personality of a Scottish partnership with other parts of the Act arose in the criminal appeal case of *Balmer v HM Advocate*.[32] The question was whether the firm, as a separate entity, could be prosecuted after it had been dissolved. The court held that it could not as the legal personality ended on dissolution and the relevant sections of the Act only applied to secure the necessary contractual and other obligations associated with a winding up.[33]

Following that decision and the apparent uncertainty, as we have seen, as to whether the legal personality of a Scottish partnership survives changes in the membership of the partnership[34] it was also arguable that a partnership could not be prosecuted after a change in personnel for any offence committed prior to that change. Further, it would not be possible to enforce a fine against the partnership which has ceased to exist as

---

[29] *Lowson v Lowson* (1894) 17R 571; *IRC v Graham's Execs* [1971] SC 1, HL; *Moray Estates Development Co v Butler* [1999] SLT 1338.
[30] For a recent analysis of this problem and others see Stephen Chan, *A Practical Guide to Scottish Partnership Law*, Sweet and Maxwell, 2018.
[31] [2014] UKSC 32.
[32] 2008 HCJAC 44.
[33] See ss 38 and 43 in Ch 7, below.
[34] See also Law Com, para 8.7.

it can no longer be said to own the assets. As a result the Partnerships (Prosecution) (Scotland) Act 2013 was enacted. It is now possible to prosecute a dissolved Scottish partnership notwithstanding its dissolution providing proceedings are commenced within five years of the dissolution. A fine imposed on the partnership may be enforced as if the partnership had not been dissolved and a partnership can be prosecuted for a prior offence despite a change in personnel.

Partnership Law

Partnership Act 1890

1.09 Where then do we find the law relating to partnerships? Partnership law in fact developed in a very traditional way through the courts, both of common law and equity, particularly during the latter half of the nineteenth century. The Partnership Law Amendment Act 1865 (known as Bovill's Act) was a brief statutory incursion aimed at clarifying the distinction between partners and their creditors (of which much more in Chapter 2) but in 1890 the Partnership Act was passed, based on a Bill drafted by Sir Frederick Pollock in 1879. This short Act forms the basis of partnership law today and has remained virtually unscathed through over a century of change.

But it is far from being a straightforward Act in modern terms. It was, and is, largely declaratory of the law—there were virtually no 'new' rules (s 23 is an exception to this). But it is neither a codifying nor a consolidating Act. Large areas of the subject remain open to the vagaries, or delights, according to taste, of case law. Section 46 preserves all equitable and common law rules applicable to partnerships 'except so far as they are inconsistent with the express provisions of this Act'. Thus cases decided prior to 1890 will be authoritative unless they are inconsistent with the clear meaning of the Act.[35] Further, the ordinary rules of law and equity apply unless there is an express inconsistency with the Act. In the Canadian case of *Geisel v Geisel*,[36] the personal representatives of a deceased partner brought an action against the other partner under the Fatal Accidents Acts following an accident in the course of the firm's business. The defendant argued that in the Manitoba Act, which contained an equivalent of s 46, liability of a partner was limited in respect of injuries caused in the course of the firm's business to 'any person *not* being a partner in the firm'. (We have a similar provision in s 10.) Thus, it was argued, an action by one partner against another partner for such an injury was inconsistent with the Act and so not preserved by the equivalent to s 46. This argument was rejected on the basis that the Act was not intended to prevent such actions being brought.

---

[35] See, eg *Taylor v Grier (No 3)*, Case No 1995/8125, 12 May 2003, Ch, para 49 per Behrens J.
[36] (1990) 72 DLR (4th) 245.

The Partnership Act is again, also by modern standards, a short Act with short sections (fifty sections or seventy-nine subsections in total) with a total lack of modern legislative jargon and cross-referencing.[37] The draftsman rejected the temptation to define every conceivable concept and whilst this does occasionally cause difficulties (we shall for example agonize over ss 2(3) and 5 later on) it makes it readable. Turning from the Partnership Act 1890 to the Companies Act 2006 is to experience the culture shock of the time traveller. Like man and the apes they are cousins but the relationship is sometimes difficult to imagine.

Comparing the Partnership Act to the Companies Act also demonstrates another facet of the 1890 Act. It is on the whole a voluntary code.[38] Section 19 allows all its provisions as to the rights and duties of partners vis-à-vis each other to be varied by consent, express or implied (from a course of dealings). Other sections are also subject to contrary intention. This feature can be traced to the contractual nature of the relationship called a partnership. As with other contracts the parties can, within certain defined limits, agree to whatever terms they wish as between themselves (and thus the parts of the Act covering those areas are also subject to contrary agreement) but they cannot rely on any such agreement vis-à-vis third parties on the well-known principles of privity of contract (and thus those sections of the Act relating to third parties are not voluntary). The third type of section in the Act, by which the courts are allowed to interfere in the relationship, either to establish liability or to end the partnership, are, of course, also non-negotiable.

Common law and equity

Since the 1890 Act is both declaratory in nature and partial in scope, it follows that the many cases decided before that date are relevant either to explain or amplify the Act itself or to cover areas outside its scope. It must be true that, for a declaratory Act above all others, earlier cases can be relied on to clarify the draftsman's (and also Parliament's) intentions. It goes almost without saying that cases decided since 1890 are of great importance in deciphering the law. In this context, however, it is important to realize that the Partnership Act 1890 applies equally to Scotland and that cases decided in Edinburgh are of strong persuasive authority, although they must sometimes be read in the context of the fact that Scottish partnerships have legal personality. The English concept of partnership was also exported, among other countries, to India, Hong Kong, Canada, Singapore, Malaysia, Australia, and New Zealand and their statutes bear a strong resemblance to our own. Several of the United Kingdom's partnership concepts were also adopted in South Africa although that country has no statute. Cases decided

1.10

---

[37] The draft Bill proposed by the Law Commissions had fifty-three sections and five Schedules dealing with general partnerships.
[38] The Law Commissions' objectives included the preservation of partnership 'as a flexible, informal and private business vehicle'.

in those and other common law jurisdictions are therefore also important (and in many instances of a more recent vintage). Only in the USA has partnership developed along different lines.[39]

Although s 1 does not expressly say so, it is clear that unless there is a binding contractual relationship between the parties there can be no partnership.[40] It follows that an executory contract is ineffective to form a partnership so long as it remains executory. But where an agreement is made after the partners have already embarked on the activities of the partnership, the agreement is not thereby an executory one.[41] Such a partnership agreement may be express or implied. In one case, the court held that if the evidence from the express conversations is that the parties discussed but failed to agree on forming a partnership, it is difficult, although not impossible,[42] to imply a partnership from conduct.[43] Similarly, if the written documents and other evidence do not indicate an intention to enter into a partnership, there will be no implied contract.[44] Occasionally the courts will imply a partnership contract in order to give 'business reality' to the activities of those involved. In *Cheema v Jones*,[45] five doctors, having failed to agree on the terms of a written partnership agreement, were held nevertheless to have made an implied oral agreement since they had acted and treated each other as partners, and intended to create a contractual relationship. Such a contract was necessary to give business reality to their provision of medical services under the NHS contract. The evidence in that case was very strong—two of them had been in partnership and the intention was to bring in the other three. The issue is obviously very fact specific and the evidence in support must be sufficient.[46]

The common law rules relating to formation, variation, and vitiation of a contract all apply to partnerships (although it appears that acceptance of a repudiatory breach of the agreement is an exception to this).[47] Tort also plays a part—in particular, the concepts of passing off and vicarious liability. But these are mainly areas where partnership is in one sense incidental—the problem arises from tort or contract not from the relationship between partners. In one area of the common law, however, the partnership concept is central. The liability of partners for partnership debts (the central issue of any firm) is based upon an understanding and specific application of the law of agency. Each partner is an agent of his fellow partners (and a principal in relation to the acts of his fellow partners); agency is a consequence of partnership. The application, not

---

[39] See the Revised Uniform Partnership Act 1994.
[40] If there is such a binding arrangement the next question of course, dealt with below, is whether it is a contract of partnership embracing the criteria of s 1 or of something else such as a joint venture. See, eg *McPhail v Bourne* [2008] EWHC 1235 (Ch) explaining a dictum of Lord Millett in *Hurst v Bryk* [2002] 1 AC 185 at 194F.
[41] *Coward v Phaetos Ltd* [2013] EWHC 1292 (Ch) at [187] per Asplin J.
[42] This is because a partnership may exist even if parties expressly agree that there is none.
[43] *Greville v Venables* [2007] EWCA 878.
[44] *Dutia v Geldof* [2016] EWHC 547 (Ch).
[45] [2017] EWCA Civ 1706.
[46] See, eg *Younes v Chrysanthou* [2016] EWHC 3269 (QB).
[47] See Ch 7, below.

always consistent, of the agency concept to partnership is a problem that will be considered in Chapter 4.

Yet partners are more than contracting parties—they had been established by the courts of equity as owing a duty of good faith and subsequently fiduciary duties to each other by the time of the Act, and developments in the law of equity in recent times have strengthened rather than diminished such duties. It is therefore also an equitable relationship and partners are expected to behave towards each other as if they were trustees for each other, making full disclosure and being scrupulously fair in their dealings. Equity does not require fault or dishonesty to establish a breach of such a duty (unlike the common law) and such duties can be enforced by the equitable remedies of account (which does not require proof of loss), equitable compensation and full restitution. The Act merely cites three examples of these 'higher' duties (in ss 28 to 30) and one of the largely untested areas in modern times is how some of the more venerable decisions on those and other duties should be read in the light of the recent expansion of the law of constructive trusts and fiduciary duties in other areas, especially of company directors (see Chapters 5 and 6). As a result of this equitable or fiduciary element, partnership is more than a contract; it creates an equitable relationship which is also subject to the Partnership Act. In Scotland this has been neatly described as creating a status.[48] One consequence has been the decision that acceptance of a repudiatory breach of the contract does not dissolve the partnership. That is discussed in Chapter 7.

Partners are, therefore, contractors, agents, principals, fiduciaries, and beneficiaries all at the same time. The potential chaos suggested by such an analysis is, however, for the most part lacking.

Other relevant statutes

Although partnerships are for the most part exempt from those aspects of public control which have caused company law to expand in a geometrical progression since 1967 there are nevertheless areas where such control exists. Chapter 3 is concerned with such intrusions. The two most important for the purposes of this book, since they affect the creation and dissolution of partnerships *qua* partnerships, are, first, Part 41 of the Companies Act 2006, which replaced the Business Names Act 1985. This regulates the use and disclosure of firm names. The other is the Insolvency Act 1986, as applied by the Insolvent Partnerships Order 1994,[49] concerning the insolvency of the firm and/or the partners. There are many other cases, of course, where partnerships cannot avoid

1.11

---

[48] *Worbey v Campbell* [2017] CSIH 49 at [35].
[49] SI 1994/2421, as amended by the Insolvent Partnerships (Amendment) Order 1996, SI 1996/ 1308, the Insolvent Partnerships (Amendment) Order 2001, SI 2001/767, the Insolvent Partnerships (Amendment) Order 2002, SI 2002/1308, the Insolvent Partnerships (Amendment) (No 2) Order 2002, SI 2002/2708, the Insolvent Partnerships (Amendment) Order 2005, SI 2005/1516, and the Insolvent Partnerships (Amendment) Order 2006, SI 2006/622.

the complexities of modern life—employment law and taxation, for example—but in general the problems that arise in such cases are caused by adapting the complex provisions of those areas of the law to partnerships—problems not helped, as we have already seen, by the schizophrenic nature of the concept of partnership as a relationship which is dressed up to look like a separate being. Insolvency law tries to solve this conundrum by treating a partnership as if it were an unregistered company.[50]

Having established that a partnership is an equitable relationship founded on contract and that we must find the law relating to it from many sources, we must now turn to those three legal criteria we ran into at the beginning which make the contract one of partnership—a business, carried on in common, and with a profit motive.

Essentials of a Partnership

1.12 Chapter 2 will deal in rather more detail with the rules governing precisely how and when a partnership is or is not established and the circumstances in which the question might be raised. For the moment it is sufficient to note, as we have seen, that a partnership can arise by implying an agreement from an association of events as well as from an express contractual agreement and that the question of whether or not a partnership has been established can crop up in such varied areas as property law, employment law, taxation, insolvency, national insurance, and the statutory powers of corporations, as well as the more obvious example of making one person liable for the debts incurred by another. In all such cases, however, the courts must always bear in mind the three essential criteria contained in s 1 of the Act without which there cannot be a partnership.[51] In deciding such matters the courts will look at all the aspects of the relationship, applying the legal criteria to the facts. But as has been said by the courts for many years, most recently in the Scottish case of *Dollar Land (Cumbernauld) Ltd v CIN Properties Ltd*,[52] there is no one feature which is absolutely necessary to the existence of a partnership once the essential criteria have been established, although if those criteria are missing there cannot be a partnership.

Relationship with joint ventures

1.13 The term 'joint venture' was originally used in the USA to get round the then prohibition on companies there forming partnerships. In modern commerce it has no specific legal definition. Thus what the parties describe as a joint venture may or may not be a partnership, depending upon whether the criteria for a partnership are fulfilled.[53] It

---

[50] See Ch 8, below.
[51] In some cases only s 1 is used: see, eg *Grant v Langley*, 5 April 2001, QBD.
[52] 1996 SLT 186, CS (OH).
[53] Simply calling it a joint venture does not affect the issue. See, eg *Whywait Pty Ltd v Davison* [1997] 1 QdR 225.

has been suggested that joint ventures are more commonly used for one-off adventures than for a continuing business;[54] or that they are more often used for the exploitation of a product than for a business at a profit.[55] Whilst many of the criteria for joint ventures and partnerships overlap, one difference is that it is possible to have a joint venture without actually carrying on a business.[56]

Whether a particular joint venture was also a partnership was discussed in detail by the Inner House of the Court of Session in the case of *The University Court of the University of St Andrews v Headon Holdings Ltd*.[57] The court considered the carefully negotiated agreement, the fact that it had been registered as a partnership for VAT purposes, the specific restrictions on the ambit of the joint venture, the restriction of the activities and powers of each party being set out, and the fact that there was both a dispute resolution procedure and a profit-sharing agreement. It did, however, remit the case to the court below to decide the issue—in particular whether the exploitation of land was a business.

If the activity is not a partnership, the court then has to decide on the legal consequences of the joint venture. Given that that the term joint venture has no specific legal meaning, it does not automatically give rise to fiduciary duties, so that each has to be examined on its own facts.[58] If there is a failure even to establish any concluded agreement as to a joint venture, there is the possibility that one party who has conferred an advantage on the other or has suffered a detriment as a consequence of the arrangement or understanding, may recover their position by means of a constructive trust.[59]

Business

Partnerships are business media—they cannot, unlike companies, be formed for benevolent or artistic purposes. Section 45 of the Act defines 'business' for this purpose as including every trade, occupation, or profession, subject, of course, to those professions, such as the Bar, where a partnership is forbidden by professional rules. It was therefore established prior to the Act that the occupation of a landowner cannot form the basis of a partnership whereas that of a market gardener clearly can. In other words there must be some commercial venture— a selling of goods or services for a reward— before there can be a partnership. The relationship must arise in connection with that business. Difficulties arise when the parties are also in a personal relationship. Thus in the Canadian case of *Palter v Zeller*[60] Mr and Mrs Palter had been friends for a number

1.14

---

[54] See, eg *Rabiah Bee Bte Mohamed Ibrahim v Salem Ibrahim* [2007] SGHC 27 at paras 64–6.
[55] See, eg *Mackenzie v Richard Kidd Marketing Ltd* [2007] WSSC 41 and the cases referred to therein.
[56] See the clear analysis of this issue in the Canadian case of *Dhaliwal v Toor* 2010 BCSC 1065.
[57] [2017] CSIH 61.
[58] See, eg *Ross River Ltd v Wavely Commercial Ltd* [2013] EWCA Civ 910; *Glenn v Watson* [2018] EWHC 2016 (Ch).
[59] *Kiwak v Reiner* [2017] EWHC 3018 (Ch), applying *Pallant v Morgan* [1953] Ch 43. Failure to prove a detriment or an advantage is fatal—see, eg *Achom v Lalic* [2014] EWHC 1888 (Ch).
[60] (1997) 30 OR (3d) 796.

of years with Ms Lieberman and through her had come to know Mr Zeller, a lawyer. Ms Lieberman also studied to be a lawyer and, having married Zeller, joined his practice. The Palters as a result engaged Zeller and, following a dispute, now sought to recover damages from Lieberman on the sole basis that she was in partnership with her husband. The judge found that there was no evidence that the spouses had been in partnership. The mere fact that they behaved in an equal social and marital relationship did not mean that their business relationship was the same. The fact that the Palters had wrongly made the assumption was of no consequence. For an alternative conclusion on the facts see *Taylor v Mazorriaga*[61] and *Ravindran v Rasanagayam*.[62] The latter case involved a brother and sister rather than spouses. In that case it was said that, in deciding whether a partnership existed, the closer the non-business relationship the less formality was to be expected in their business relationship. In some cases disentangling family and business relationships can be very complex.[63]

Contemplated partnerships

1.15 Similarly there will be no partnership if there is merely an agreement to set up a business activity which has not begun to be implemented. Such an agreement is known as a contemplated partnership.[64] All that is required for an actual partnership, however, is the carrying on of some business activity by the persons involved. That includes anything which could be regarded as a business activity if done by a sole trader. There is no requirement that the business itself must actually be trading before a partnership can be said to have come into existence. That was the decision of the House of Lords in *Miah v Khan*.[65] Mr Khan and three others agreed that he would fund the opening of an Indian restaurant, to be run by two of the defendants. A joint bank account was opened, a bank loan obtained, premises acquired, furniture and equipment bought, a contract made for laundry, and the opening of the restaurant was advertised in the local press. Before the restaurant opened for business, however, the parties had fallen out. Mr Khan now sought a declaration that there had been a partnership in existence before the restaurant opened.

The majority of the Court of Appeal held that, although there was no need to show the actual receipt of profits, it was not enough to show that necessary preparations for the business had been made—the business itself, ie the restaurant, had to be up and running for there to be a partnership. The House of Lords disagreed (as did Buxton LJ in the Court of Appeal). They said that there was no rule of law that the parties to a joint venture do not become partners until actual trading commences. The rule is that persons who agree to carry on a business activity as a venture do not become partners until they actually embark on the activity in question. Setting up a business often

---

[61] (1999) LTL, 12 May 1999.
[62] (2000) LTL, 24 January 2001.
[63] eg *Mehra v Shah*, 1 August 2003, Ch. Similarly in tax cases: see *Vankerk v Canada* 2005 TCC 292.
[64] See, eg *Pine Energy Consultants Ltd v Talisman Energy (UK) Ltd* [2008] CSOH 10 at para 28 per Lord Glennie.
[65] [2000] 1 WLR 1232, HL, reversing [1998] 1 WLR 477, CA (sub nom *Khan v Miah*).

involves considerable expense and such work is undertaken with a view of profit. It may be undertaken as well by partners as by a sole trader. It can be a business activity and if done by those involved in common there will be a partnership.

Applying that test to the facts of the case, Lord Millett said:

> The question in the present case is not whether the parties 'had so far advanced towards the establishment of a restaurant as properly to be described as having entered upon the trade of running a restaurant', for it does not matter how the enterprise should properly be described. The question is whether they had actually embarked upon the venture on which they had agreed. The mutual rights and obligations of the parties do not depend on whether their relationship broke up the day before or the day after they opened the restaurant, but on whether it broke up before or after they actually transacted any business of the joint venture. The question is not whether the restaurant had commenced trading, but whether the parties had done enough to be found to have commenced the joint enterprise in which they had agreed to engage. Once the judge found that the assets had been acquired, the liabilities incurred and the expenditure laid out in the course of the joint venture and with the authority of all parties, the conclusion inevitably followed.

Although the decision in *Miah v Khan* has been accepted in other jurisdictions as well it is far from easy in practice to distinguish between acts which are preparatory to carrying on a business and those which are business activities in their own right so far as to amount to embarking on the venture. In the Australian case of *Goudberg v Herniman Associates Pty Ltd*,[66] the Court of Appeal in Victoria held that doing market research, making demographic studies, and travelling twice to the USA to study franchise models with a view to running a restaurant franchise business, could not reasonably amount to carrying on a business. Similarly in the Canadian case of *Blue Line Hockey Acquisition Co v Orca Bay Hockey Ltd Partnership*,[67] the British Columbian Court of Appeal held that an agreement between the parties to hold exploratory talks to acquire an (ice) hockey team and the making of expressions of interest to the vendor were not enough to establish the carrying on of a business. They only agreed to share their lawyer's fees; they neither established an office nor borrowed funds.

The problem has also since been discussed twice by the Court of Appeal in England. In *Christie Owen & Davies plc v RAOBGLE Trust Corporation*,[68] the purchase of a building with a view in the short term of running it as a form of hotel, and in the long term to redevelop the site, was held to be sufficient even though those plans lay in the future. The purchase of the building was the first step in the venture and the Court thought that simply buying the restaurant would have been sufficient in *Khan v Miah* although in that case there were other activities involved.

---

[66] [2007] VSCA 12.
[67] [2009] BCCA 34.
[68] [2011] EWCA Civ 1151.

In *Ilott v Williams*,[69] however, the Court of Appeal refused to overturn the judge's decision that there was no business when those involved had merely made presentations on the basis that they were willing to go into an investment business. Whilst preparatory work can form part of a business there was still a distinction between preparatory arrangements and partnership. It was not enough simply to identify the proposed business. The judge had made an evaluation from the facts (eg no property had been acquired) and the Court of Appeal would not interfere unless he was clearly wrong.

Self-employment and employees

1.16 The concepts of trade and profession are well known to income tax lawyers and two difficulties which have arisen in that context have also arisen in partnership law, ie the distinction between the self-employed trader or professional and an employee, and the status of a single commercial venture.

Partners are by definition self-employed. An employee is not a trader and thus it is thought cannot be a partner and the distinction is primarily the common one between a contract of service and a contract for services. This is an increasingly complex issue, however, which we will reserve for consideration in Chapter 2.

Single commercial venture

1.17 For tax purposes a trade can include an adventure in the nature of trade and it now seems to be accepted that for a partnership a business can exist even if it is only for a single commercial venture. Thus, for example, when a lady found herself contracted to purchase two houses without having sufficient funds and so agreed with a local property dealer to purchase the houses jointly and share the profits equally: *Winsor v Schroeder*.[70] Woolf J admitted that where there was only one transaction involved it was less likely to be regarded as a partnership but that this situation had all the elements of partnership. In the Queensland case of *Whywait Pty Ltd v Davison*[71] it was conceded that a single venture could constitute a partnership. The emphasis must be, as in the tax cases, not on whether it is a single venture but whether it is a commercial venture and not, for example, simply realizing an investment, eg buying a house, finding that one's spouse won't live there, and having the property improved and sold at a profit: *Taylor v Good*.[72] Factors used in tax cases have included a profit motive, a commercial organization, the subject matter of the transaction (some things are more likely to be held as investments than others), repetition, and the circumstances of the realization (eg insolvency).

---

[69] [2013] EWCA Civ 645.
[70] (1979) 129 NLJ 1266.
[71] [1997] 1 QdR 225.
[72] [1974] 1 WLR 556, CA.

Excluded relationships—co-ownership

This need for a business has excluded several relationships which might otherwise have been construed as partnerships. For example, most members' clubs and other non-profit-making associations cannot be said to be carrying on a business and are thus not partnerships: see *Wise v Perpetual Trustee Co.*[73] Nor does the simple co-ownership of property constitute partnership. One of the rules for determining the existence of a partnership in s 2(1) of the Act provides that no form of co-ownership (both the English and Scottish forms are set out) shall 'of itself' create a partnership as to anything so held or owned *whether or not they share any profits made by the use of the property.*[74] Co-ownership without a business attached does not create a partnership, it is simply co-ownership,[75] which is, incidentally, not the position in most of our European neighbours.

1.18

An example of the operation of s 2(1) is the Court of Appeal decision in *Vekaria v Dabasia.*[76] Two individuals purchased a long lease and declared that they would hold any profits in the proportions they had contributed to the purchase price. The Court of Appeal upheld the judge's statement that co-owners who share profits are almost indistinguishable from partners and that in essence the issue comes back to the basic questions of s 1. The question was whether they were carrying on a business or simply making an investment with a view to profit. Co-ownership with a view to profit was not enough. In finding that this was a joint investment and not a partnership the Court of Appeal noted that: the two individuals only dealt with each other through an intermediary; one of them only put up part of the purchase price because the other had insufficient funds; and there was no agreement as to the carrying on of the business, merely as to the distribution of profits. On the other hand the fact of co-ownership can be used as an indication of the existence of a partnership: see the South African case of *Buckingham v Dole.*[77] This distinction between co-ownership and partnership also creates many problems in the field of partnership property and we will return to it in Chapter 6.

A similar situation arises with an agreement for a joint purchase only of property (eg to achieve a discount). This equally cannot amount to a partnership. For example, if Mr Smith and Mr Jones agree to purchase a case of wine for their own consumption because it proves to be cheaper than buying six bottles each and Mr Smith sends in the order, intending to recover a share of the cost from Mr Jones, it is not suggested that they are thereby partners. It might, of course, be different if they intended to resell the wine at a profit. This basic distinction was made as early as 1788 in a case called *Coope*

---

[73] [1903] AC 139, HL.
[74] In the Hong Kong case of *Fung v Heung* [2006] HKEC 631 it was said that, in particular, purchasing property as joint tenants mitigated against a partnership, which usually requires a tenancy in common to negate the right of survivorship.
[75] See, eg *Faria v Bush* [2018] ONSC 7288.
[76] (1998) LTL, 1 February 1998, CA.
[77] 1961 3 SA 384 (T).

v Eyre.[78] Mr Eyre purchased some oil on behalf of what we would now refer to as a syndicate, dividing it up after purchase. Eyre failed to pay and the seller sought to recover from the other members. Gould J said no, there was no community of profit:

> But in the present case there was no communication between the buyers as to profit or loss. Each party was to have a distinct share of the whole, the one having no interference with the share of the other, but each to manage his share as he judged best.

This approach has also been applied to negate a partnership between joint purchasers of a lottery ticket.[79]

Forming a company or LLP

1.19 Nearly 200 years later yet another relationship was excluded from a partnership by the Court of Appeal. It is not unusual for persons intending to set up a company to prepare the ground whilst waiting for the incorporation procedure to take place—in technical terms they are known as promoters. In *Keith Spicer Ltd v Mansell*[80] the question was whether, in carrying out these preliminary activities, the promoters could be regarded as partners. In that case one of the promoters ordered goods from the plaintiff company intending them to be used by the proposed company and the goods were delivered to the other promoter's address. The promoters opened a bank account in the name of the proposed company, omitting the all-important 'Ltd' at the end. The bank account was never used and the promoter who had ordered the goods became insolvent. The county court judge found that there was insufficient evidence of partnership and this was upheld by the Court of Appeal. Harman LJ said that the promoters were merely working together to form a company, they had no intention of trading prior to incorporation—they could not be partners because they had never carried on business as such. The issue is whether the parties embarked on the business in the period before the company or LLP was formed or whether it was envisaged that only the company or LLP would carry on the business.[81] The position is different from that in *Khan v Miah*,[82] discussed above, where the parties have decided to form a partnership and the question is when did it start.[83] The question is not whether the work amounted to embarking on the intended business activity but whether it referred to an agreement to carry on a business together or only to the setting-up of a business to be carried on by the company or LLP.[84]

In the Australian case of *United Tankers Pty Ltd v Moray Pre-Cast Pty Ltd*[85] the intention was to convert an existing partnership into a company. Mr Savage, who was not a

---

[78] (1788) 1 HBL 37.
[79] *Spiro v Com* [2015] ONSC 609.
[80] [1970] 1 All ER 462, CA.
[81] See *Dutia v Geldof* [2016] EWHC 547 (Ch) at [100].
[82] [2000] 1 WLR 1232, HL.
[83] But see the decision in *Ilott v Williams* [2013] EWCA Civ 645, where a partnership was never contemplated as being the business vehicle.
[84] [2016] EWHC 547 (Ch) at [99].
[85] [1992] 1 QdR 467.

member of the existing partnership, agreed to invest some money into the business in return for a one-third interest in the company when it was formed. The court held that he did not thereby become a partner in the business prior to incorporation. He had taken an interest in the company when formed rather than an immediate interest as a partner. Thus, whereas in the cases above the absence of a business was the key factor, in this case it was the non-participation of Mr Savage in the business prior to incorporation which decided the matter. This leads us into the next requirement for a partnership, involvement in the business.

Carried on in common

1.20 A partnership of necessity requires the involvement of two or more persons, however limited,[86] in the business. The importance of the need for carrying on the business in common is one of the major distinctions between a partnership and other business relationships. For example, without it a company and its employees would be in a partnership or those working together in anticipation of concluding a contract. This requirement leads to the fiduciary obligations which partners owe to each other.[87] With the singular exception of a limited partner under the Limited Partnerships Act 1907, it follows that one distinction in this context is between participation *in* the business and a connection *with* the business, such as that of a supplier of goods or services. In *Strathearn Gordon Associates Ltd v Commissioners of Customs & Excise*,[88] the company acted as a management consultant and was paid fees plus a share of the profits of seven separate developments. It argued that these were receipts of a partnership carrying out the various developments and that the company was not supplying services for the purposes of VAT. The VAT Tribunal rejected this argument. The parties had not made any agreement to carry on a business together. What the company had actually agreed to do was to supervise the carrying out of the work and in essence that was an agreement for the provision of services. The mere fact that the consideration was measured by reference to a share in the profits was not enough to convert it into a partnership. In other words they were not involved in the business, they simply provided services for the business. On a similar basis it has been held in South Africa that a franchise agreement does not as such amount to a partnership: *Longhorn Group (Pty) Ltd v Fedics Group (Pty) Ltd*.[89]

Sometimes the question is whether two or more persons are carrying on separate businesses or a joint business. In the Queensland case of *Marshall v Marshall*,[90] the court found that there were two separate businesses being carried on, one by each of two

---

[86] Thus a solicitor whose sole role is the supervision of a newly qualified solicitor, as required by law, and who has to be a partner, is carrying on the business in common: *Rowlands v Hodson* [2009] EWCA 1025.
[87] See eg *Worbey v Campbell* [2017] CSIH 49 at [64].
[88] [1985] VATTR 79.
[89] 1995 SA 836 (W).
[90] [1999] 1 QdR 173, CA. See also *Sri Alam Sdn Bhd v Newacres Sdn Bhd* [1995] 4 MLJ 73.

builders who alleged that they were in partnership—they traded on their own accounts with their own stock. The so-called partnership was in fact a device intended to allow one of them to act as a builder although not licensed to do so since a licence was not necessary for someone in partnership with a licensed builder. In *Thames Cruises Ltd v George Wheeler Launches Ltd*,[91] a number of Thames boat companies set up an association to provide a single ticketing operation, available on any of the boats. They worked to an agreed timetable and the net profits were distributed according to the number of boats involved. The judge held that the companies each maintained their individual businesses—they were each responsible for their own costs. The association was simply one method of jointly contracting with the public. There was no single business carried on in common.

Participation in the business

1.21 If there is no joint participation in the common business then it seems that, even if there is an intention to draw up a partnership agreement and some discussion between the parties as to the consequences of it, the courts will not declare a partnership. In *Saywell v Pope*,[92] Mr Saywell and Mr Prentice were partners in a firm dealing in and repairing agricultural machinery. In January 1973 the firm obtained a marketing franchise from Fiat which expanded the work of the firm. Until that time Mrs Saywell and Mrs Prentice had been employed by the firm to do a small amount of work but they then began to take a more active part in the business. At the suggestion of the firm's accountant the four drew up a written partnership agreement but this was not signed until June 1975. The bank mandate in force before 1973 enabling Mr Saywell and Mr Prentice to sign cheques was, however, unchanged, and no notice of any change in the firm was given to the bank or the creditors or customers of the firm. Neither of the wives introduced any capital into the business and had no drawing facilities from the partnership bank account. A share of the profits was credited to them for 1973 and 1974 but they never drew on them. In April 1973 the wives had been informed that if they became partners they would become liable for the debts of the firm and they had not objected. The Inland Revenue refused to accept that the wives had become partners before 1975.

Slade J agreed with the Revenue. The written agreement could only apply from the date it was signed and even though it contained a statement that the partnership had actually begun earlier that could not make them partners during that period unless that was the true position. There was no evidence that in 1973 the parties had contemplated such an agreement and neither the partnership agreement nor the discussion of liability could be taken as creating an immediate partnership. There was no evidence that during the relevant time they did *anything in the capacity of partners*. The crediting of the net profits was of more significance and we shall return to this below at para 1.25. What is important is that despite the fact that there was a business and a 'sharing' of

---

[91] [2003] EWHC 3093 (Ch).
[92] (1979) 53 TC 40.

profits no partnership existed since in effect the wives had never been integrated into the firm.

That decision was approved by the Court of Appeal in *Bissell v Cole*.[93] The question asked in that case was whether an individual had an involvement in the business and it was said that undue reliance should not be placed on statements in brochures or letterheads.

On the other hand where there is participation in a business those involved will be partners even before they have drawn up the formal agreement to that effect. Thus in *Kriziac v Ravinder Rohini Pty Ltd*[94] an agreement to redevelop a hotel site with a formal agreement to be executed in due course was held by the Australian court to establish a partnership prior to that agreement (which never happened) because of the evidence of participation in a business such as the creation of a joint bank account, the joint engagement of an architect, and the joint application for planning permission.

Control

Another way of making the distinction between a partner and a business 'contact', for want of a better word, is whether the alleged partner has any control over the property or ultimate management control. In one sense neither of the wives in *Saywell v Pope* had either of these whereas the two developers in *Kriziac* clearly did. It is possible to enter into a business venture with another party without establishing a partnership, particularly if that other party is itself a separate business entity, whether incorporated or not.

1.22

In the Canadian case of *Canadian Pacific Ltd v Telesat Canada*,[95] the Telesat Canada Corporation had only those powers allowed to it by its founding statute and these did not permit it to enter into a partnership. A shareholder of the company sought to establish that an agreement between the corporation and the nine principal Canadian telephone companies setting up the Trans-Canada Telephone System had established just such a forbidden partnership. The Ontario Court of Appeal decided that, since the arrangement did not involve the corporation's abandoning control over its property or delegating ultimate management control, it did not amount to a partnership. Similarly, in *Mann v D'Arcy*,[96] Megarry J held that an agreement between a firm of produce merchants and another merchant to go on a joint account on the sale of some potatoes did not amount to a new and separate partnership. It was a single venture controlled by the existing firm in the ordinary course of its existing business. 'The arrangement was merely one made of buying and selling what [the negotiating partner] was authorised to buy and sell'. The position may, however, be different if the new venture effectively determines the partnership business and transfers control of it to others. This was

---

[93] [1997] 12 WLUK 221, CA.
[94] (1990) 102 FLR 8.
[95] (1982) 133 DLR (3d) 321.
[96] [1968] 1 WLR 893.

suggested but not decided by the Full Court of the Supreme Court of Queensland in *Rowella Pty Ltd v Hoult*.[97]

Limited partners

1.23 The exception to this requirement of participation is a limited partner in an LP. Such a person is forbidden to take part in the management of the firm.[98] What exactly that means is discussed in Chapter 9, below.

With a view of profit

1.24 Many of the earlier problems concerning the existence of a partnership revolve around the concept of profit motive and profit-sharing. It is impossible to establish a partnership if there is no intended financial return from the business—it would hardly be a business if no financial return was contemplated. Far more problems arise in practice in the reverse situation—ie when a financial return from a business is argued *not* to constitute the recipient a partner because, for example, it is really a wage paid to an employee, or interest paid to a creditor, or a contractual return for the supply of goods or services rendered. At one time a mere receipt of a share of the profits established a partnership: *Waugh v Carver*;[99] but this was repudiated by the House of Lords in *Cox v Hickman*[100] and that repudiation was codified into s 2(3) of the 1890 Act. It is now well established that mere receipt of a share of the profits of a business does not automatically make the recipient a partner. Thus the VAT Tribunal in *Strathearn Gordon Associates Ltd v Commissioners of Customs & Excise*[101] were able to declare in a sentence that: 'The mere fact that this consideration was measured by reference to a share of the net profit does not in our judgment convert the agreement into a partnership'. An agreement for the supply of services was exactly that and no more. Further, another VAT Tribunal in *Britton v Commissioners of Customs & Excise*[102] found that, although a wife took a share of the profits of her husband's business, this was a domestic as distinct from a commercial arrangement. The profits had been paid into their joint bank account which continued as both a domestic and business account. 'The profit was Mr Britton's and Mrs Britton as his wife had access to it.' Sharing profits did not amount to partnership. The precise circumstances under which the receipt of a share of the profits will turn an employee, creditor, or supplier into a partner are discussed in Chapter 2.

---

[97] [1988] 2 QdR 80, SC.
[98] See ss 6 and 6A of the Limited Partnerships Act 1907.
[99] (1793) 2 H Bl 235.
[100] (1860) 8 HL Cas 268.
[101] [1985] VATTR 79.
[102] [1986] VATTR 204.

Need for agreement to share profits?

1.25 There must, however, be a profit motive[103]—but then all businesses are designed to make money and a simple requirement of a profit motive might not, at first sight, seem to add anything to the business criterion already discussed. It has been argued, however, that that is the only requirement as to profit imposed by s 1 of the 1890 Act. Returning to the words of that section, there must be a 'business carried on in common with a view of profit'. These words, so the argument goes, require only a profit motive and not necessarily a *share* in the profits for each partner, ie only the business need be carried on 'in common', not necessarily the profits. Another, equally appropriate interpretation, however, is that it is a business with a view to profit which must be carried on in common. A share of the profits must on that basis be contemplated for a partnership to be established. That was certainly the view taken by the pre-1890 cases such as *Pooley v Driver*.[104]

Academic commentaries have differed as to whether the wording of s 1 altered the pre-Act law, if indeed that was the position then. The matter in England was clarified to some extent by the Court of Appeal in *M Young Legal Associates Ltd v Zahid*.[105] The court held that a person receiving a fixed sum from a firm unrelated to the firm's profits could nevertheless be a partner.[106] But only Hughes LJ expressly addressed the issue as to whether a person receiving no form of return from a firm could still be a partner. In his opinion, if the other essentials of partnership were present,

> the partners are free under the Act to arrange for remuneration of themselves in any manner they choose, including by agreement that one or more shall receive specific sums or that one or more receive nothing, in either case irrespective of profits.[107]

The Court of Appeal in *Rowlands v Hodson*,[108] however, took the view that the decision in *M Young Legal* etc was that the receipt of a share of profits was not a pre-requisite of a claim to partnership. In that case the person was entitled to receive a nominal share of the profits but had waived her claim in two successive accounting periods. It was held that she could still be a partner since all the criteria in s 1 had been complied with. The court was also unimpressed by the argument that if she had permanently waived her right to the money that would have ended the partnership.

This point is also relevant in tax cases where the partnership is formed to achieve a tax benefit, as in the case of *Newstead v Frost*.[109] David Frost, the late television personality,

---

[103] See, eg *Franich v Harrison* [2006] NZHC 1059. In the South African case of *Konsult One CC v Strategy Partners (Pty) Ltd* [2013] ZAWCH 55, the lack of any immediate intention to make a profit was held to negative partnership.

[104] (1877) 5 Ch D 458, CA.

[105] [2006] EWCA Civ 613, [2006] 1 WLR 2562.

[106] Following the decision of Megarry J in *Stekel v Ellice* [1973] 1 WLR 191. That was a case as to whether a 'salaried partner', ie a person described as a partner but paid a fixed salary, was in fact a true partner or an employee. See Ch 2, below.

[107] [2006] EWCA Civ 613 at [41].

[108] [2009] EWCA Civ 1025.

[109] [1980] 1 All ER 363, HL.

formed a partnership with a Bahamian company to exploit his highly profitable activities in the USA. The major purpose behind this was the common one of tax avoidance, the general idea being to isolate the income produced from the individual and thus from the United Kingdom and the Inland Revenue. The latter attacked this partnership on two fronts—one, as to the capacity of the company to enter into such a partnership (of which more anon) and two, as to the existence of the partnership itself. The Revenue argued that this agreement was designed largely as a tax avoidance scheme and so did not constitute carrying on a business with a view of profit. The House of Lords, however, disagreed. The partnership was in fact formed to create a profit from the exploitation of the entertainer's activities and the fact that it was hoped such profits would avoid tax did not affect that basic idea. There was a view of profit.

The question of the influence of a tax motive on the existence of a partnership has been discussed in a number of cases in Canada. The Canadian Supreme Court has ruled in three cases that an ancillary profit-making purpose will suffice and that neither a tax motivation nor a short duration will invalidate a partnership if that purpose exists.[110] It is of course a question of fact in each case as to whether that purpose does exist. In the tax case of *Ingenious Games Ltd v HMRC*,[111] the Upper Tribunal, applying the Canadian cases, said that the issue was to be resolved by looking at the subjective intentions of the parties. The question is whether there was a real and serious intention to make a profit.

Gross and net profits

1.26 So far we have been discussing the question of the intention to create and share in *profits*. In one sense that is not entirely accurate since it has long been clear that the profits in question must be *net* profits—ie those calculated after accounting for the expenses incurred in making them. Another of the rules for establishing the existence of partnership, in s 2(2) of the 1890 Act, makes this clear: 'The sharing of gross returns does not of itself create a partnership, whether the persons sharing such returns have or have not a joint or common right or interest in any property from which . . . the returns are derived'. Thus an author who is paid a 10 per cent royalty (at the least, one hopes) on the published price of his book is not a partner with his publisher—duties of good faith might well be stretched otherwise![112]

Another example can be found in the case of *Cox v Coulson*.[113] Mr Coulson was a theatre manager who agreed with Mr Mill to provide his theatre for one of Mill's productions. Mr Coulson was to pay for the lighting and the posters etc, Mr Mill to provide the company and the scenery. Under the agreement Mr Coulson was to receive 60 per cent

---

[110] *Beckman v Canada* (2001) 196 DLR (4th) 193; *Spire Freezers Ltd v Canada* (2001) 196 DLR (4th) 210; *Whealy v Canada*, 2004 TCC 377.
[111] [2019] UKUT 0226 (TCC).
[112] Nor are persons sharing lottery winnings on a joint ticket—those are gross returns: *Spiro v Cam* [2015] ONSC 609.
[113] [1916] 2 KB 177, CA.

of the gross takings and Mr Mill the other 40 per cent. The play must have been heady stuff since the plaintiff in the case was shot by one of the actors during a performance. She sought to make Mr Coulson liable on the basis that he and Mr Mill were partners and so responsible for the outrage. The Court of Appeal had little difficulty in rejecting any claim based on partnership since s 2(2) made it quite clear that the sharing of gross returns did not of itself create such a partnership.

Implicit in the idea of sharing net profits is the sharing of expenses and thus if necessary in net losses (except for the limited partner of course). Sharing of gross returns or turnover points towards not taking risks and not sharing losses and so is not enough to indicate a partnership.[114]

Before we leave this topic two points should now be borne in mind. First that there are, in addition to the concepts just discussed, the other provisions of s 2(3) of the 1890 Act which were intended to draw the often fine distinctions between a partner and a creditor where a share of the profits is undoubtedly being received. These provisions form the basis of part of Chapter 2 but they must always be read subject to s 1 of the Act and the essentials of a partnership. Second, it may perhaps occur to the reader that in this general area, as with others in the law, the result often seems to depend upon the question being asked and the consequences of the answer. It may well be that the emphasis may vary between, say, one case where the parties are trying to convince a doubting HM Revenue & Customs (HMRC) of the existence of a partnership, and another where an unpaid supplier is seeking to make someone liable as a partner of the person who ordered the goods.

Partnerships Then and Now

Before embarking on a more detailed study of the creation, operation, and extinction of partnerships it is useful to have some idea of the changing role of partnerships in the commercial life of the country. The nineteenth century, which saw the establishment of the partnership as a popular business medium, culminated in the Act of 1890 and the basic partnership rules which still apply today. By the turn of the century, however, the demise of the partnership as the universal form for small businesses was well under way, although, as we have seen, a substantial number of partnerships still exist; whilst until recently the development of professional partnerships, especially those of solicitors and accountants, and the influence of taxation presented new challenges and brought new uses for the partnership form. The introduction of the LLP has, however, significantly lowered the number of professional partnerships.

1.27

---

[114] *Lewis v Ramachandren* [2017] EWCA Civ 229 at [46].

Partnerships up to 1890

1.28 Partnerships, as we have seen, developed naturally (in the sense of slowly through the case law system) out of the laws of contract, agency, and equity. They were hedged in with few compulsory rules and since they conferred neither legal personality nor limited liability they rarely raised issues of a sufficient concern to merit the interference of Parliament. They provided freedom to operate on any terms which could be agreed and did not allow those responsible to avoid the consequences of their actions. The courts responded to any problem with an ease and calm assurance which typifies the so-called 'golden era' of English law. Only rarely did they cause confusion—Bovill's Act of 1865 being the exception, since it was deemed necessary to clarify the distinction between partners and creditors following the volte-face, already mentioned, about whether simply taking a share of the profits meant an automatic partnership or not. But in general the fact that in 1890 only one real change was made by the Act to the existing case law rules is a testimony to the nineteenth-century judges who created much of the present law.

Partnerships thrived and multiplied. This was due in part to their compatibility with utilitarian philosophy, much in evidence in the early nineteenth century, as anyone with even a passing acquaintance with the novels of Charles Dickens must be aware. But it was also due to the fact that in the early part of the century there were really no alternatives for the small or medium-sized business. Companies could be formed with both legal personality and limited liability but only by a royal charter or a private Act of Parliament. This may have been ideal for the East India Company or the canal and railway companies and other vast enterprises but it was slow and very expensive and not at all in tune with the growing needs of the age. The earlier problems of the South Sea Bubble and other fiascos, however, prevented any easier form of incorporation. At common law, companies, known as deed of settlement companies, were in effect merely large partnerships.

The expansion of industrial and commercial life during that period, however, soon provided the pressure for legislation to provide a cheaper and quicker access to the twin benefits of incorporation and limited liability. Partnerships were inappropriate for entrepreneurs turning their attention to world markets. By 1855 the modern concept of the registered limited company was possible and the Joint Stock Companies Act 1856 allowed promoters to register and thus create a company simply by filing the requisite documents—a process still in force today. Decisions such as *Salomon v A Salomon & Co Ltd*[115] pressed home the benefits of limited liability; the concept entered into popular mythology, as can be discovered from listening to the Company Promoter's song from the Gilbert and Sullivan comic opera, *Utopia Ltd*. To explain the distinction between a company and its members, Gilbert invented the story of a monarch whose rule

[115] [1897] AC 22, HL.

was absolute except that he could at any time be exploded by the 'Public Exploder' on the word of two 'Wise Men'. To avoid this the king turned himself into a limited company and confronted his tormentors with the thought that although they could wind up a company they could not blow it up.

The registered company was to be the major business medium from then on. Administratively and economically it was more attractive than a partnership and by the time of the Partnership Act itself partnerships were on the decline. There were, however, still some disadvantages for the small business in selecting the corporate form, such as increased formality and disclosure and less flexibility, especially if a dispute arose, but company law itself was to develop so as to reduce most, if not all, of them.

The growth and development of private companies

One of the consequences of this growth in companies was the LP, introduced by the Limited Partnerships Act 1907. We have already come across this 'commercial mongrel' and much more will be said in Chapter 9. As an attempt to revive the partnership form as a general business medium, however, it was a dismal failure. By the Companies Act 1907 the private company was introduced and, initially, sank its rival almost without trace until its revival as a financial sector medium. A private company allowed management participation by the director-shareholders without loss of limited liability and it could raise money by means of a floating charge (ie a charge over all its assets, which can nevertheless be utilized by the company until disaster strikes)—a popular method of finance which for technical reasons has always been denied to partnerships. **1.29**

As company law became more complex and above all more interventionist so that greater public disclosure was demanded of such things as accounts and exactly who owned what, it might have been expected that small businesses would return to the partnership fold. But this never happened on a large scale—partly at least because company law itself sought to protect the small private company from the more inconvenient aspects of this policy. In recent years the attractiveness of the small private company has been enhanced by two important developments. The first was a consequence of our membership of the EU. Most European countries differentiate between the public and private company form to a far greater extent than we do—for example, they have separate codes for each form. The vast majority of EU-inspired changes to company law therefore were applicable only to public companies, and to accommodate this approach the Companies Act 1980 created a much clearer distinction between public and private companies in the United Kingdom—one visible effect of which is the use of a different abbreviation at the end of a company's name. When dealing with Marks & Spencer for example, the ending is not 'Ltd' but 'plc'. Many of the more Draconian rules are only applicable to public companies and the Companies Act 1981 exempted 'small' and 'medium- sized' companies from many of the accounting disclosure rules. The Companies Act 1989 introduced the concept that private companies may elect to dispense with certain internal requirements such as the holding of an annual general meeting, the laying of accounts at a meeting, and the annual appointment of auditors. Further, private companies may pass resolutions without holding a formal meeting of the members. One of the major themes of the latest review of company law was to 'think small first'[116] and this policy was adopted by the Government.[117] The resulting Companies Act 2006 relieved private companies of many of the existing controls, not least from the onerous rules on the giving of financial assistance for the acquisition of its shares and the obligation to hold any formal meetings.[118] The application of the Persons with Significant Control Regulations of 2016 to all companies[119] under the Small Business, Enterprise and Employment Act 2015, rather bucks this trend. They require publication of the details of anyone with significant control over the company. It is also the case that some corporate accounting requirements are applicable to partnerships whose partners are all companies.[120]

The courts also evolved the concept of the 'quasi-partnership' company, that is, a company which, although legally a company, is in economic and management terms a partnership, particularly where there is an underlying right for the shareholder-directors to take part in the management of the company. In *Ebrahimi v Westbourne Galleries Ltd*,[121] the House of Lords decided that a breach of that underlying obligation, typically a dismissal of one of the directors, although perfectly in accord with the formal procedures of the Companies Act, could lead to a winding up of the company on the just and equitable ground. (Incidentally Lord Wilberforce in that case rejected the term 'quasi-partnership' as being misleading but the term has stuck and provided it is used only as a general description little harm will be done.) Since then that concept has been skilfully blended with the unfairly prejudicial conduct remedy for minority shareholders by Lord Hoffmann in *O'Neill v Phillips*.[122] Small companies are therefore protected one way or another from most of those areas of company law which would otherwise prove to be a drawback.

Partnerships today—impact of the LLP

1.30 Whilst the importance of the private company as a business medium should not be underestimated the fact remains that there are still many small businesses, roughly 450,000, which operate under the partnership form. There are undoubtedly some tax and national insurance advantages attached in some cases to the partnership form, not

---

[116] The Company Law Review presented its Final Report to the DTI in July 2001.
[117] *Modernising Company Law* (Cm 5553, DTI, July 2002).
[118] See also *Company Law Reform* (Cm 6456, DTI, March 2005).
[119] SI 2016/339. These have, however, also been extended to LLPs and even some Scottish partnerships and all Scottish LPs (SI 2017/694).
[120] SI 2008/569 as amended by SI 2013/2005.
[121] [1973] AC 360, HL.
[122] [1999] 1 WLR 1092, HL.

least in the areas of capital gains tax and the payment of retirement annuities. In other cases the tax advantages will go the other way. It is always a question of balancing tax with other factors in choosing a business medium. Partnerships remain more flexible and private as a vehicle for small owner-managed businesses and it is true that in practice the concept of limited liability for the owner-managers of a small company is more illusory than real since the bank will almost certainly require them to use their own houses as security for a loan to the company.

The impact of the LLP form on partnerships has been substantial in respect of professional firms. The advantages are legal personality and increased borrowing powers. But if it is seen merely as an attempt to avoid joint and several liability for partnership debts the benefits may be debatable.[123] The merits and otherwise of the LLP form have been debated in print.[124] The evidence so far is that there was initially a substantial increase in the number of LLPs since it was introduced and that most professional firms have adopted it. The numbers have steadied in recent years.[125] So far as partnerships are concerned, the change to an LLP will be largely tax-neutral.

There is a further point in that, by adopting the LLP form, with legal personality, large professional firms may possibly expose themselves to greater liability with regard to their fiduciary duties to their clients. Thus where a member in one office has knowledge relevant to another member in another office acting for a client, that knowledge could be imputed to the second member, giving rise to an obligation to disclose that information and to liability for failure to disclose. Under partnership law it is much less likely that such an obligation will be implied since it would be settled under the laws of agency: see, eg *Unioil International Pty Ltd v Deloitte Touche Tohmatsu*.[126]

One example of a solicitors' firm switching from the partnership to the LLP form was where the partnership had been appointed as executors under a client's will, but the client died after the change to an LLP. The question arose whether the successor LLP could still act as those executors. In *The Estate of Edith Lilian Rogers Deceased*,[127] a test case was brought after the local Probate Registry (following a national agreement) refused to allow the LLP to obtain probate of the will. Lightman J, taking a practical and common-sense view and noting that the Law Society had assimilated partnerships and LLPs of solicitors so far as clients were concerned, decided that the deceased's intentions would be best served by allowing the LLP to obtain probate as executors of the will.

The LLP form, which is based substantially on the corporate and not the partnership form, is the subject of Chapters 10 to 12, below.

---

[123] See Freedman and Finch [1997] JBL 387.
[124] Finch and Freedman, 'The Limited Liability Partnership. Pick and Mix or Mix-up?' [2002] JBL 475; cf Morse, 'Partnerships for the 21st Century—Limited Liability Partnerships and Partnership Law Reform in the UK' [2002] SJLS 455.
[125] In 2001–2 there were 1,936 LLPs on the register. In October 2013 there were 56,297 and in March 2008 there were 53,848.
[126] (1997) 17 WAR 98.
[127] [2006] EWHC 753 (Ch).

Partnerships: Variations on a Theme

Group partnerships

1.31 Partnerships served a wider variety of economic functions than those at the time of the 1890 Act. So flexible and successful are the provisions of that Act, however, that legal draftsmen were able to adopt the form to meet the new demands of both the professions and taxation. It was mainly the perceived threat of substantial personal liability that led to the LLP alternative. For many years partnerships were limited in size—initially the limit was twenty, but this limit had been waived since 1967 for most professional partnerships, including solicitors and accountants, and was removed completely for all firms in 2002. Clearly a single partnership of three or four-figure numbers was possible but not very workable and, prior to the arrival of the LLP, such firms often organized themselves into a group partnership which was in essence nothing more than a partnership between partnerships. In this way each branch office was in effect a semi-autonomous partnership but each one was linked by a partnership deed to the 'head' office, usually in London. Smaller firms and individuals carrying on independent businesses may also combine into a group association, often under a group management agreement. Such an association may or may not amount to a partnership, since members may not share the profits of the individual businesses.

Much care must be taken, of course, in the drafting of such agreements: voting and financial matters are obvious areas of concern. But it is essentially a matter for agreement. There are potential problems: for example, as to the liability of a partner in one branch for the debts incurred by the head office or by another branch, but many of them will be capable of solutions based on the ordinary principles of agency. Thus, in *Bass Brewers Ltd v Appleby*,[128] liability was fixed by the application of the 'holding-out' principle, ie that the defendant had been held out as a partner by another firm in the same 'group'. It was therefore unnecessary to decide whether the group association agreement itself constituted a partnership.

Extension of fiduciary liabilities

1.32 Similar problems could arise in connection with the potential fiduciary liabilities of partners in a professional group partnership prior to the arrival of the LLP. Such professional partners, eg solicitors or accountants, owe fiduciary duties to their clients, so that they must not put themselves in a position where their duty to the client and their personal interest conflict. Similarly they are under a duty to disclose all relevant information to their client. The potential problems with a group partnership are shown by the Australian case of *Unioil International Pty Ltd v Deloitte Touche Tohmatsu*.[129]

---

[128] [1997] 2 BCLC 700, CA.
[129] (1997) 17 WAR 98.

Unioil had engaged a firm of accountants and a firm of lawyers to report on another company with a view to investing in that company. The lawyers were based in Perth but there were other offices under the same name in each of the main centres in Australia, including Sydney. It transpired that one of the partners in the Sydney office was acting in another capacity for the company under investigation and that there was contact between the two individual partners. Each office of the firm was a separate 'profit centre' and a separate partnership. Nevertheless the judge found that the group were able to practise de facto as a national firm and that the partners of one firm regarded themselves as de facto partners in the others. He was not required to decide whether all the partners of each firm were also legally partners of the others, although he doubted whether they were, following the Canadian case of *Manville Canada Inc v Ladner Downs*,[130] where every effort was made to keep the various firms apart in terms of clients etc.

But the judge did decide that the partner advising Unioil, being aware of the Sydney office's work for the company being investigated, would have been tempted, consciously or unconsciously, to deal with the matter in a way which was least embarrassing to the Sydney office. Thus there was a conflict of interest and duty on his part and consequent liability (despite a favourable report being made to Unioil, the investment proved to be disastrous). On the other hand the judge rejected an alternative claim that all the information known to the Sydney office should be imputed to the partner in Perth so that he should have told Unioil about it. But the judge did that, even on the assumption that the group partnership was one partnership, by reference to the law of agency. It would be impracticable and even absurd to suggest that in large firms (whether as groups or a single entity) partners were under a duty to reveal to each client and use for that client's benefit any knowledge possessed by any one of their partners or staff.

The internal issues still arising from group partnerships will also fall to be resolved by reference to the law of agency and the fiduciary duties which partners owe to each other.

Identifying a single or multiple firm—multinational firms

If litigation is brought against a firm it may be important to establish that the firm is subject to the jurisdiction of the court and whether any other court may also/instead be seised of the case. That issue is considered generally at the end of this chapter, but one side effect may be to determine whether a firm is a single multinational firm based in a particular country or a series of separate firms working in their own jurisdictions. This was the situation before the Grand Court of the Cayman Islands in *Touche Ross and Company v Bank Intercontinental Ltd*.[131] The defendant bank had sued the plaintiffs in Florida in relation to an alleged negligent audit in Cayman and the plaintiffs now asked the Cayman court to issue an injunction against the bank preventing it bringing proceedings anywhere but Cayman. The actual decision of the court was that there

1.33

---

[130] (1993) 100 DLR (4th) 321.
[131] 1986 CILR 156.

were separate substantive issues triable in both jurisdictions and so it refused to make the order.

One of those issues, however, which was before the Florida court, was the exact nature of the firm or firms known as Touche Ross International. That organization's brochure included the phrase: 'The parties in each country are joined together through membership in Touche Ross International, a legal entity formed under Swiss law'. The judge commented that:

> I think it has to be said (whatever the 'Touche Ross' label may eventually be held to mean in law in any given situation) that these materials undoubtedly convey and must be taken to convey, at first sight, the impression not only that there is a multinational entity called 'Touche Ross' but also that it is one which at least has a professional relationship with its constituent elements, and more than that... one which controls in terms of *quality* and *financial responsibility* the work done in the Touche Ross name.[132]

Consequently the judge held that the allegation of there being a worldwide firm was not unsustainable.[133] This case shows not only the case-by-case approach which has to be taken in such situations but also the potential exposure to liability within a group partnership where such responsibility has been assumed. On the facts of that case much may have depended on the precise nature of the Swiss *Verein* at the centre of affairs.

Subpartnerships

1.34 A similar variation on the partnership theme is the subpartnership, that is, a partnership where one of the partners agrees to divide his share of the main partnership profits and losses with others. There are in effect two partnerships, one of which is a partner of a 'head partnership' together with individual partners. Thus a partnership of A, B, and C can have a subpartnership if C agrees to subcontract his profit and losses from the head partnership with D and E. The questions which arise are whether this is possible; if it is, what are the liabilities of D and E with respect to the debts of the head partnership, and what are the fiduciary duties of A, B, and C towards D and E? Rather surprisingly the answer to the first question is yes. Whilst it might at one time have been possible to argue that C, D, and E are not actually carrying on a *business* (whereas in a group partnership it is envisaged that each 'branch office' will be doing so), such arrangements have been accepted by the courts of England, Scotland, and Australia. Presumably the business is the management of the interest in the principal partnership.

The answer to the second question was given by Connolly J in the Queensland case of *Australia & New Zealand Banking Group Ltd v Richardson*.[134] The bank had lent

---

[132] At 170.
[133] See also the US case of *Armour Intl Co Ltd v Worldwide Cosmetics Inc* 689 F 2d 134 (1982).
[134] [1980] QdR 321.

$30,000 to a newsagents' firm of which Mr Gary and Mr Richardson were partners. They later discovered that a Mrs Vernon had an association with the business in that she had advanced $25,000 to Richardson, her son-in-law, to fund his half-share of the partnership. In 1976 Mrs Vernon and Richardson agreed in writing that they would be equal partners in the half-share and were each entitled to withdraw $200 per week from the business so long as the cash flow of the business allowed. She played very little part in the affairs of the business itself. The bank now sought to recover the debt directly from Mrs Vernon. The judge, having ruled that in no way could she be regarded as a full partner in the business, had to decide whether her subpartnership with Richardson nevertheless made her fully liable for the debts of the head partnership.

In short the judge's answer was no. The liability of a subpartner is limited to the extent of his subcontract with the subpartner who is also a full partner in the head partnership:

> [A] subpartner's only interest in and relationship with the partnership lies in his right to a share of such of its profits as reach his partner. He has no rights against the partnership and can only enforce his right to profits which have actually been received by his subpartner.... He has no say in the running of the business for that would involve rights which cannot be conferred on him by one partner alone. It follows that he cannot be liable for the partnership debts on the footing that they were authorised by him.

In effect, therefore, a subpartner will simply suffer loss in revenue arising from main partnership losses but if the principal partner is liable to contribute further to the debts he may be able to call on a contribution from the subpartner.

Since the only conceivable business of the subpartnership is the management of the interest in the main partnership, few fiduciary problems will arise as between the subpartners since their interests are solely financial, consequential on the success or failure of the main partnerships. On the other hand it is possible that if the main partner were to involve the subpartners in the management of the main firm he would be in breach of his duties to the other main partners. At least on a formal level, therefore, the subpartnership will simply be a vehicle for the economic consequences of the share in the main partnership.

By way of postscript it should, however, be remembered that if the subpartner is regarded as a full partner by a third party, such as the bank in this case, he will be liable as such whatever the agreements involved. It is significant that in this case the bank had no knowledge of Mrs Vernon's existence until they commenced the proceedings. At no time did they rely on her being a partner when the credit was being extended.

Corporate Partners

It is perfectly possible for a company to be a partner. (Section 1 of the Partnership Act relates to persons and the Interpretation Acts have always defined a person as including

1.35

a company unless the contrary is provided.) This is so, even though some sections of the Act refer to the bankruptcy of a partner[135] rather than to the insolvency of a partner. Since companies cannot become bankrupt it has been said that such a provision cannot apply to them.[136] There is in fact nothing to prevent a partnership being composed entirely of companies. Companies as partners can fulfil many roles. For example, they were used to enable the former size limits of a partnership to be overcome[137]—partnerships which were limited to twenty by having, say, twenty companies as partners, each company having as many members as it wished. Companies also provide some means of limited liability for partnerships since although the company partner would be liable for all the partnership debts without limit, the partnership creditors in pursuing their debts could only recover from the company's own resources and not those of its members.

Capacity issues

1.36 There are problems, however, as always. Companies are artificial legal persons and there are historically two limits on their ability to do things. As an eminent judge once remarked, 'A company cannot eat nor sleep'; or, in other words, there are those physical things which a company simply cannot do.

In *Newstead v Frost*[138] the Revenue attacked the partnership between David Frost and the Bahamian company on that ground. Mr Frost and the company formed the partnership to exploit 'the activities of television and film consultants and advisers... and of producers, actors, directors, writers and artistes'. In fact the only entertainer so exploited was Mr Frost himself. The argument put forward by the Revenue, who needed to negative the partnership, was that physically a company cannot be a television entertainer or an author and so could not form a partnership for such purposes since the only other partner could not exploit his own skills. The House of Lords rejected this. There was nothing in the agreement which required the company to entertain or write books and there was nothing to prevent the company and the individual jointly agreeing to exploit the individual's skills. The Court of Appeal had earlier commented that even if a company cannot 'do' the act in question, if the partnership as a whole could do it then it would be part of the partnership business and would have to be brought into account between the partners accordingly.

Traditionally, companies were also limited by their constitution. They had no capacity to act outside their objects. The 2006 Companies Act, however, abolished the need for any objects. In any event, this second restriction had been removed so far as the

---

[135] See, eg s 33.
[136] *Anderson Group v Davies* (2001) 53 NSWLR 401 at 404, SC.
[137] These have been abolished: see Ch 3, below.
[138] [1980] 1 All ER 363, HL.

capacity of a company to enter into a partnership is concerned, by what is now s 39(1) of the Companies Act 2006, which provides that:

> The validity of an act done by a company shall not be called into question on the ground of lack of capacity by reason of anything in the company's memorandum.

Further, if the directors by agreeing to bind the company into a partnership, act contrary to the company's constitution, that act will still be valid unless the other partners have acted with actual understanding that it was contrary to the company's constitution. Even then the agreement may be ratified by the company. Section 40 of the 2006 Act which so provides is subject only to s 41. That section would apply where the company entered into a partnership with one or more of its directors, and even in that case the agreement would only be voidable at the instance of the company. Restrictions in the company's constitution are therefore largely an internal matter between the directors and the members. The right of a member to prevent a company acting outside its constitution by seeking an injunction is in practice theoretical only.

Other issues

Other problems have arisen as a result of the increasing growth of corporate partners and no doubt will continue to do so. We have already referred to the fact that if all the partners are limited companies then there is in effect indirect limited liability for the firm's debts. This prompted the EU to extend the accounting requirements (both as to content and publication) imposed on companies by the Fourth and Seventh EC Company Directives to such partnerships by an amending Directive of 1990.[139] A further Directive of 2006 also applied the requirements as to the appointment and dismissal of auditors, the signature of auditors' reports, and disclosure of auditors' remuneration to corporate partners.[140] These requirements are set out in the Partnership (Accounts) Regulations 2008.[141] In effect the requirements of the Companies Act 2006 as to the format and content of accounts and as to auditors[142] are applied to partnerships each of whose partners is either a limited company wherever formed or an unlimited company or Scottish firm, each of whose members is a limited company wherever formed.

1.37

Other examples may serve to indicate the type of problem which can arise from having a corporate partner. In *Scher v Policyholders Protection Board*,[143] the House of Lords

---

[139] Dir 90/605/EEC, OJ L317/90, amending Dir 78/660/EEC [1978] OJ L222/78 and Dir 83/349/EEC [1983] OJ L193/83. See now Dir 2017/1132 which consolidated the previous directives.
[140] Dir 2006/43/EC [2006] OJ L157/06 as amended by Dir 2013/334/EU. See now Dir 2017/1132.
[141] SI 2008/569 as amended by the Companies and Partnerships (Accounts and Audit) Regulations 2013, SI 2013/2005 and the Companies, Partnerships and Groups (Accounts and Reports) Regulations 2015, SI 2015/980.
[142] Including those relating to statutory auditors.
[143] [1994] 2 AC 57, HL.

had to interpret the application of the Policyholders Protection Act 1975 to a partnership with some corporate partners. That Act is designed to provide a safety net for those who take out policies with insurance companies which subsequently fail to pay out on a claim because they have become insolvent. This protection applies, however, only to private individuals and not to companies. Section 6(7)(b) of the Act accordingly provided that a partnership is to be treated as a private individual if, but only if, it consists of private individuals. The problem with that approach is that in legal terms an insurance policy taken out by a partnership is a bundle of contracts between the insurer and each of the partners. The House of Lords decided that the section must nevertheless be interpreted as treating a partnership as a single entity so that if any partner is a company then the Act cannot apply to the firm's policies. Lord Mustill spelt out the consequences of this decision as follows:

> This undoubtedly leads to harsh results in some cases and also creates a distinctly unsystematic regime, since the same partner may during the life of the policy gain the protection of the Act, or lose it, according to whether a single corporate partner leaves or joins the firm.

That case demonstrates the problems of corporate partners under the general law (apart from being yet another example of the problems caused by the lack of legal personality). Two further examples show the problems that can occur from the nature of companies themselves. As we shall see a partnership is automatically dissolved by the death of an individual partner. The equivalent for a corporate partner would be its liquidation and dissolution. But, unlike an individual, the court may declare the dissolution of a company to be void so that it is in effect restored to life. The question arises therefore as to the effect of such a restoration on the partnership. Under the law of Ontario it was held in *Alton Renaissance I v Talamanca Management Ltd*[144] that the effect was to revive an LP. It is arguable that this is also the position in England since on the restoration of a dissolved company by the court under the Companies Act 2006, ss 1028 and 1032, the court may make such provision as if the company had not been dissolved. The nature of a company is also relevant to the question as to whether it is a partner at all. A company has no existence until it is formed so that it cannot be regarded as a partner on the basis of evidence as to the acts etc of individuals prior to formation. Further there must be evidence of actual partnership activities by the company itself after formation, eg making contracts etc in its own name.[145]

A final example arises from the fact that a company, unlike individuals, can raise money on the security of a floating charge, ie a charge over all its assets, present and future, including its stock in trade, and not just a fixed charge on its fixed assets. For various reasons it may be important to decide whether a charge is a fixed

---

[144] (1993) 99 DLR (4th) 707.
[145] *Frauenstein v Farinha* [2007] FCA 1953.

or floating charge. What is the position therefore when a corporate partner creates a charge over its partnership interests? This is a very complex issue, requiring an analysis of the nature of a partner's interest, which we will return to in Chapter 6, and it has not yet come before the English courts. In Australia the distinction has been made between a charge over the corporate partner's interest in the partnership which creates a fixed charge (*United Builders Pty Ltd v Mutual Acceptance Ltd*[146]) and a series of charges by all the corporate partners, where there are no individual partners, over all the assets of the firm which creates a floating charge (*Bailey v Manos Breeder Farms Pty Ltd*[147]).

The International Dimension—Jurisdiction

We have already seen in relation to group partnerships the problems which can arise where there is an allegation as to the existence of a multinational firm, especially as to the issues of whether a particular national court has jurisdiction to hear the case and whether any other court may also be properly seized of the issue.[148] But such issues can arise in far less glamorous surroundings. This is a very complex and specialist area, part of the conflict of laws, and reference should be made to the specialist works on the subject. But put simply the question is when will the English courts have jurisdiction to hear a partnership dispute,[149] given that a partnership is not an entity and in reality it is the partners who are involved. The answer depends entirely upon whether it is a case which falls within the scope of the EU Judgments Regulation 2015 or not, that Regulation being of course automatically part of United Kingdom law. In very general terms the answer in turn depends upon whether the defendant is domiciled in a Member State of the EU.[150]

1.38

Cases where the Judgments Regulation applies

The basic rule under the Regulation is that the court has jurisdiction only if the claim is made against a partner domiciled in England.[151] However, under Art 25 of the Regulation, if the defendant is domiciled in an EU Member State, the court has exclusive jurisdiction if the defendant has submitted to the jurisdiction or there is a valid

1.39

---

[146] (1980) 144 CLR 673.
[147] (1990) 8 ACLC 1119.
[148] See, eg *Touche Ross and Company v Bank Intercontinental Ltd* 1986 CIR 156.
[149] Similar rules apply to the Scottish courts. There are also special rules for establishing the jurisdiction of the English and Scottish courts in relation to partnerships located entirely within Britain: see Sch 4 to the Civil Jurisdiction and Judgments Act 1982, as amended by SI 2001/3929. In essence the court where the defendant is domiciled will have jurisdiction with exceptions for proprietary issues. For more details see Dicey, Morris, and Collins, *Conflict of Laws* 15th edn, with supplements, London: Sweet & Maxwell, 2012, 11.109–11.114.
[150] Excluding Denmark, but that has a parallel agreement with the United Kingdom in similar terms. Again for detailed analysis, see Dicey and Morris, ch 11.
[151] Reg 1215/2012, Art 4, ex Art 2.

choice of jurisdiction clause in its favour in any contract. More specifically, under Art 24(2) of the Regulation, the English court will have exclusive jurisdiction in proceedings which have as their object the validity of the constitution, the nullity or the dissolution of companies, or other legal persons or *associations of natural or legal persons*, or the validity of the decisions of their organs, if the company, legal person, or association has its seat in England.

It has been held in the case of *Phillips v Symes*[152] that this applied to English partnerships. In that case a claim by the executors of a Greek domiciliary to recover movable assets in England was brought in England. The defendant, an English domiciliary, now resident in Switzerland, had brought proceedings in Greece seeking to establish his ownership of those assets and he now sought to have the English proceedings stayed. One of the issues was as to whether the disputed assets were in fact assets of a partnership between the deceased and Mr Symes. It was assumed that the 'seat' of any such partnership was in England. Having decided that Art 24(2) could apply to a partnership,[153] the further issue was whether the ownership dispute fell within 'the validity of the constitution... or dissolution' of a partnership. The judge decided that it did, on the basis that dissolution included also the winding up of a partnership's affairs consequent on a dissolution.[154] Consequently he granted an injunction preventing the defendant from pursuing the partnership issues before the Greek court.

In establishing where a partnership has its seat for this purpose the Regulation allows the court to apply its own rules. These are contained in s 43 of the Civil Jurisdiction and Judgments Act 1982,[155] whereby a partnership has its seat in the United Kingdom if, and only if: (a) it was formed here; (b) its head office is here; or (c) its central management and control is exercised here.

Cases where the Judgments Regulation does not apply

1.40 If the defendant is domiciled in a State not subject to the Regulation, process can be served on any person, wherever domiciled, who is in England at the time of service, partnership being no exception to this basic rule. In addition since any two or more persons, wherever domiciled, carrying on or alleged to be carrying on business as

---

[152] [2002] 1 WLR 853.
[153] The case was actually fought on Art 16 of the Brussels Convention but the wording was the same.
[154] It is reasonable to assume that this could also include a partial dissolution of a partnership, where the dispute would be as to the outgoing partner's share. That could also fall under the heading of the constitution of the partnership. It seems sensible to apply Art 24(2) to any issue where partnership law, as opposed to the general law, is in issue. On this point see the company cases of *Newtherapeutics Ltd v Katz* [1991] Ch 226 and *Grupo Torras SA v Sheikh Fahad Mohammed Al-Sabah* [1996] 1 Lloyd's Rep 7, CA, where an issue as to excess of authority by the board was held to fall within this article, but there was some doubt as to whether the scope of the fiduciary duty of the board did so.
[155] As amended by SI 2001/3929.

partners in England can sue and be sued in the firm name, and service can be at the firm's business, it seems that a partner outside England at the time will be caught, although only the assets within the jurisdiction will be involved.[156] There are also provisions for service on partners abroad, but only with the permission of the court, and on restricted grounds.[157]

---

[156] The defendant can apply for a stay of proceedings by showing that there is a better forum, unless the claimant can in turn show that it would be unjust to deprive him of the right to sue here: *Spiliada Maritime Corp v Consulex Ltd* [1987] AC 460.
[157] See CPR Part 6 and *Seaconsar (Far East) Ltd v Bank Markazi Jomhouri Islami Iran* [1994] 1 AC 438.

2
ESTABLISHING A PARTNERSHIP

Questions and Answers

A partnership is therefore a relationship arising from a contract between persons carrying on a business in common with a view of profit. Having digested that, the next question for a lawyer is how such a relationship can be established. In this respect, although s 1 of the Partnership Act 1890 provides the criteria which must be satisfied, s 2 provides more detailed guidance on specific issues. That section, according to the marginal note, contains rules for determining the existence of a partnership and they are intended to be of practical assistance in dealing with specific situations. In effect s 2 is intended to assist in the quest for the criteria required by s 1. We have already mentioned the rules as to co-ownership (s 2(1)) and the sharing of gross returns (s 2(2)) in the hope of shedding some light on the concepts of business and profit as required by s 1. The main force of s 2 is, however, in s 2(3), which deals with the connection between receiving a financial return from a business and the creation of a partnership—whether the recipient is involved in a partnership or whether the recipient is involved simply in a debtor–creditor or employer–employee relationship, or is involved in risk-taking.

2.01

Importance of establishing a partnership

The question of establishing a partnership or partnership liability arises in three basic situations. First, when a person who has dealt with a business seeks to make another person liable as a partner in that business—sometimes this is called the 'outsider question'. It is usually about recovery of a debt or other liability from a person on the basis that he is a partner—if he or she is not a partner they will not be liable and so the issue is crucial. There are in fact two aspects of this particular question, since such a person may be liable as a partner either because of a financial and managerial interest in the business, which makes him or her a true partner, or because, without actually being a partner, he or she has been represented as a partner to the third party. Partnership liability can be incurred either way.

2.02

The second situation arises when one person seeks to enforce a duty or obligation on another on the basis that they are partners with each other and such duties or obligations will not otherwise apply if there is no partnership—this can be called the 'insider question'. Since partners owe both a duty of good faith and fiduciary duties to each other (over and above the common law duties of reasonable care etc) this is often very important. There are also property issues involved. In some cases, the reverse situation arises, that is where a person contends that he or she is not a partner so that they may instead take advantage of statutory rights given to employees or workers. That in turn raises questions as to whether a person can be both a partner and an employee of the firm at the same time, or a partner and a 'worker' (which has a specific statutory definition). This is compounded by the use of the imprecise terms 'salaried partner' and 'fixed share partner' in many of the cases. These issues, of considerable topical interest, are discussed towards the end of this chapter. The third case is in the field of taxation and other public regulation areas,[1] since it may be in the parties' interest to establish a partnership for such purposes (or, alternatively, for the authorities to establish one). There are no special rules in the tax legislation to determine the existence of a partnership and the general law applies.

Refining the question

2.03 Sometimes the difficulties become clearer if the question asked is: if they are not partners, what are they? The answer will usually be either debtor and creditor or employer and employee. In essence, therefore, many of the disputes as to the existence of a partnership resolve themselves into a distinction between either a partner and a creditor or a partner and an employee. There are no absolutes in this area, simply rules and guidelines which can bend with the facts. One essential factor is the burden of proof and in general this is, of course, on the person alleging that a partnership exists. This is particularly relevant in tax cases where the taxpayers are seeking to establish a partnership. In *Saywell v Pope*,[2] for example, Slade J placed the burden of proof fairly and squarely on the taxpayer, an obligation which can be traced to the Scottish case of *Inland Revenue Commissioners v Williamson*.[3]

One note of caution when reading tax cases as to the existence of a partnership for those uninitiated in the mysteries of taxation: tax cases are first heard by a first instance specialist tribunal, and only proceed to the upper tribunal and then the Court of Appeal and Supreme Court on an appeal on a point of law. It is for the tribunal to establish the facts and the court will only reverse their decision if either the law as applied to those facts is wrong or if the tribunal could not reasonably have come to the conclusion which they reached: see *Edwards v Bairstow*.[4] This can be a nuisance for those seeking to build elaborate arguments on tax cases since in many instances the courts will simply be saying that the tribunal was not so obviously wrong that its conclusions should be overruled.

---

[1] Such as employment and disability legislation.
[2] (1979) 53 TC 40.
[3] (1928) 14 TC 335.
[4] [1956] AC 14, HL.

No requirement for written agreement

Inherent in all these questions is the assumption, quite rightly, that partnerships, being largely unregulated by the law in modern terms, can arise informally, sometimes without the partners even realizing it—in effect by association and a consequent implied agreement. As we have seen in Chapter 1, the courts require clear evidence of a concluded contract of partnership to imply such an agreement.[5] If one is implied, perhaps on the business efficacy test, it will probably be a partnership at will (see below).[6] In fact it seems that, even if the partnership involves interests in land, no written agreement is needed despite the apparent requirements of s 2 of the Law of Property (Miscellaneous Provisions) Act 1989 for a written agreement. But many are formed intentionally and it would present a false picture to assume that 'accidental' partnerships by association form the majority. For obvious reasons, however, such partnerships do give rise to far more difficulties in the particular area of formation. One important point to note is that, even if there is some form of written agreement, a statement in it to the effect that it is, or more likely is not, to constitute a partnership, is not regarded by the courts as being conclusive either way. The court will be concerned with the substance and not the form of the relationship.[7] As Cozens-Hardy MR put it in *Weiner v Harris*:[8] 'Two parties enter into a transaction and say "It is hereby declared there is no partnership between us." The court pays no regard to that. The court looks at the transaction and says "Is this, in point of law, really a partnership?"' Before examining the problems associated with establishing an informal partnership relationship, however, it is appropriate to consider those formed intentionally.

2.04

Intentional Partnerships

The partnership agreement or deed

In general a partnership agreement or deed is no different from any other contract. There are no formalities arising from the fact that it is a partnership agreement and the general rules as to the formation of contract apply. Thus a partnership agreement can arise from a course of dealings provided that the courts can discover a *consensus ad idem*. In *Jackson v White*[9] the court refused to hold that there had been a partnership agreement since no particular contractual intention could be attributed to the parties,

2.05

---

[5] See, eg *Achom v Lalic* [2014] EWHC 1888; *Dutia v Geldof* [2016] EWHC 547 (where neither side was found to be a credible witness).
[6] *Cheema v Jones* [2017] EWCA Civ 1706.
[7] *Adam v Newbigging* [1888] 13 AC 308, HL at 315 per Lord Halsbury LC; *Chan Sau-kut v Gray & Iron Construction and Engineering Co* [1986] HKLR 84.
[8] [1910] 1 KB 285 at 290, CA. That was not itself a partnership case, however, and in *Thames Cruises Ltd v George Wheeler Launches Ltd* [2003] EWHC 3093 (Ch), it was said that the parties' statement was not to be ignored entirely but was simply one factor to be considered by the court in considering the substance of the agreement.
[9] [1967] 2 Lloyd's Rep 68.

whereas in *Dungate v Lee*[10] such an agreement was inferred. Being a contract, the partnership agreement is also subject to various contractual rules as to the formation of that contract such as those relating to capacity, illegality, misrepresentation, and mistake which apply to all contracts. It seems, however, that a partnership agreement may not be subject to the contractual doctrines of acceptance of repudiatory breach and frustration.[11]

Usually the partnership agreement takes the form of a deed setting out the conditions of the partnership and the terms upon which it is to be conducted. Standard forms of partnership deeds are included in many of the larger works on partnership and in books of precedents. Within very few limits, usually those associated with public policy such as restraint of trade clauses,[12] partners may include whatever terms they wish. In fact the Partnership Act itself encourages this. Section 19 provides that:

> The mutual rights and duties of partners, whether ascertained by agreement or defined by this Act, may be varied by the consent of all the partners, and such consent may be either express or inferred from a course of dealing.

Thus the implied terms as to management, accounts, indemnity etc found in the Act[13] can be varied by the partnership deed. Further, the section envisages that the express terms of the deed itself can be varied by consent and that such consent can be 'inferred from a course of dealing'. At the end of the day each case will thus depend upon the particular contractual agreement.

Sometimes such questions of construction are quite complex. In *Hammonds v Danilunas*,[14] the judge had to decide whether a clause dealing with the partnership accounts was binding on partners who had left the firm during the accounting year in question. The partnership agreement provided that any challenge to the accounts was to be decided by a majority of the partners and that their decision would be binding on all the partners. The judge applied the established principles of construction—the search being for the meaning of the document. That is what the parties would reasonably have been understood to mean, using the words which they have against the relevant background.[15] The Court of Appeal in the case, now called *Hammonds v Jones*,[16] agreed with the judge that it did apply to departed partners, even though that meant that the term 'partners' meant different things in the same sentence of the agreement. To decide otherwise would be contrary to the purpose of the clause.

---

[10] [1967] 1 All ER 241.
[11] See Ch 7, below.
[12] See Ch 3, below.
[13] See Ch 5, below. The Law Com referred to these as default terms. In general they recommended retention of the existing regime.
[14] [2009] EWHC 216 (Ch).
[15] See *Investors Compensation Scheme v West Bromwich BS* [1998] 1 WLR 896 at 913, per Lord Hoffmann.
[16] [2009] EWCA Civ 1400. All the other parties had settled their differences before the appeal hearing.

This freedom to contract is, however, just that. It is subject to the restrictions placed by English law on the scope of contract and in particular by the doctrine of privity of contract. Thus, even after the Contracts (Rights of Third Parties) Act 1999, although A and B may agree as to restrictions as to who may do what etc as between themselves, this clearly cannot affect a third party who has no notice of their terms. Section 8 of the Partnership Act 1890 provides indirect statutory confirmation of this:

> If it has been agreed between the partners that any restriction shall be placed on the power of any one or more of them to bind the firm, no act done in contravention of the agreement is binding on the firm with *respect to persons having notice* of the agreement.

Since there is no central registry of partnership deeds there is no general concept of constructive notice in this context and although it is possible to think of situations where a third party could have constructive notice they are unlikely and the usual requirement will be one of actual notice.

It is not within the scope of a book of this size to analyse a specimen partnership deed. There are, however, two areas where the agreement will usually touch on matters relating to the establishment of the partnership itself. First it will purport to give a starting date to the partnership and second it may well make some provision for the duration of the agreement and thus of the partnership and it seems appropriate to consider these topics at this point.

Commencement

'You do not constitute or create or form a partnership by saying that there is one', said Lord President Clyde in *Inland Revenue Commissioners v Williamson*.[17] Thus any statement in the partnership agreement as to the date when the partnership commenced is always subject to contrary proof if the circumstances show that the date is incorrect. Sometimes, therefore, the courts have declared that the execution of a partnership deed will not even operate to create a partnership from the date of the deed if the external evidence clearly shows that there is no partnership in fact: *Dickenson v Gross*.[18] Usually, however, the problem arises when the deed declares that a partnership has existed from a date preceding the execution of the deed itself. Such a statement cannot in law operate retrospectively. At best it may accurately reflect the past position but if in fact there was no partnership during that period such a statement in the deed cannot retrospectively alter the situation: *Waddington v O'Callaghan*.[19] Thus in *Saywell v Pope*[20] a partnership agreement signed in June 1975 which stated that the partnership had commenced in April 1973 was held to be of 'little assistance' in establishing the existence

2.06

---

[17] (1928) 14 TC 335, CS.
[18] (1927) 11 TC 614.
[19] (1931) 16 TC 187.
[20] (1979) 53 TC 40.

of a partnership at the earlier date. It is, of course, equally possible for a partnership to exist prior to the date specified in the deed if the circumstances so dictate.

Duration—partnerships at will

2.07 Whilst it may seem unduly pessimistic, most partnership agreements provide for some method of ending the partnership or at least some time span by which the partnership is to be measured. These clauses vary tremendously in nature, some providing an ending on certain dates or events whilst others use more uncertain or variable criteria. Some partnerships have no such provision at all. In general, for the purposes of duration the Act divides partnerships into those entered into for a fixed term and others. The latter are known as partnerships at will. The distinction is of some importance since a partnership for a fixed term can only be ended in accordance with the terms of the agreement or the express provisions of the Partnership Act (eg death or bankruptcy of a partner) or by a court order if there is a serious dispute. A partnership at will, on the other hand, can be ended under English law at any time by one partner giving notice to his other partners to that effect. The presumption is that a partnership is a partnership at will unless there is an express or implied agreement to the contrary. This was confirmed by Blackburne J in *Naish v Bhardwaj*,[21] where the judge refused to imply any such term into a medical partnership, on either of the accepted grounds of business efficacy or obviousness.

The right to dissolve a partnership at will by notice is contained in s 26(1) of the Act. This provides that:

> Where no fixed term has been agreed upon for the duration of the partnership, any partner may determine the partnership at any time on giving notice of his intention so to do to all the other partners.

In the Scottish case of *Maillie v Swanney*[22] there was a strong suggestion, but no concluded decision, that in Scotland s 26 does not deal either with the full dissolution of a partnership or its consequences and may be limited to allowing one partner in such a case to terminate his or her concern in the partnership, leaving the remaining partners to carry on the business without any dissolution as between themselves. That is not thought to be the law in England, where of course the firm has no legal personality. A similar view was canvassed by Parker J in the Australian case of *Cole v Lee*,[23] mainly by tracing the antecedents of s 26, which he suggested applied to a retirement from a partnership rather than a full dissolution. But he expressed no concluded view and that is not the position in English law.

---

[21] 29 March 2001.
[22] 2000 SLT 464, CS (OH).
[23] [2017] NSWCA 1011.

Relationship between ss 26 and 32(c)

Section 26(1) cannot, however, be read in isolation since s 32 of the Act provides, *subject to contrary intention*, that a partnership is dissolved (a) if entered into for a *fixed term*, by the expiration of that term; (b) if entered into for a single adventure or undertaking, by the termination of that adventure or undertaking; (c) if entered into for an *undefined time*, by any partner giving notice to the other or others of his intention to dissolve the partnership; and in that case the partnership is dissolved from the date mentioned in this notice as the date of dissolution or, if no date is mentioned, as from the date of the communication of the notice.

2.08

Section 32(c), therefore, whatever the position vis-à-vis s 26, clearly provides for dissolution at any time by one partner giving notice to that effect, but unlike s 26(1) it applies to partnerships for an *undefined time* rather than to partnerships with *no fixed term*. There is another difference in that s 32 is subject to contrary agreement whereas s 26(1) appears to be mandatory (unless it could be regarded as a right or duty of a partner and so subject to contrary agreement by virtue of s 19, mentioned above). However, it has been possible to reconcile these two sections by a particular construction of the phrases 'no fixed term' and 'undefined term'. This is made somewhat easier by the fact that s 32(a) speaks of a partnership for 'a fixed term' and it would be strange therefore if an 'undefined time' in s 32(c) meant anything other than the opposite, ie a partnership with no 'fixed term', although in *Maillie v Swanney*[24] it was suggested that the different terminologies were deliberately selected.

This balancing act was achieved by the Court of Appeal in *Moss v Elphick*.[25] The facts were very simple in that the partnership agreement between the two partners contained no mention of any time limit or other limiting factor except to provide that it could be terminated 'by mutual arrangement only'. Moss gave Elphick a notice of his intention to dissolve the partnership and the question was whether he had the right to do so under either s 26(1) or s 32(c). The Court of Appeal had little difficulty in rejecting his right under s 32(c) since, although this was a partnership for an undefined time, the provision as to mutual consent was a clear contrary intention which the Act provided for. What then of s 26(1) where such contrary intention was (it was apparently accepted in that case) not provided for? The argument that 'no fixed term' simply meant a partnership with no definite term in the deed was rejected. Instead the section was construed as applying only 'to cases in which the partnership deed is silent as to terms with regard to the duration of the partnership', or in other words to those for 'an undefined time'. The deed was far from silent in this case and s 26(1) could not therefore apply.

The practical consequence of this decision is that any provision in the agreement as to termination, however vague or tenuous, will prevent s 26(1) applying since it will not be for 'no fixed term' (apologies for the double negative but it makes the

---

[24] 2000 SLT 464 (OH).
[25] [1910] 1 KB 846, CA.

position clearer) and will also amount to a contrary intention for the purposes of s 32(c), so that neither section will be available for a dissolution by notice. It presumably follows that a provision such as the one in *Moss v Elphick* will make the partnership one for a fixed term under s 32(a), although that would seem to be a generous interpretation of the phrase and perhaps renders s 32(b) redundant. The Court of Appeal in coming to their decision were much concerned that s 26 should not conflict with freedom of contract in partnership matters. It should be realized that if s 26(1) had applied in that case the provision as to mutual consent would have been meaningless.

A different approach to s 32 was taken by Parker J in the Australian case of *Cole v Lee*.[26] He said that a 'fixed term' in s 32(a) must be contrasted with s 32(b) so that where a partnership was expressed to continue so long as the business continued, that fell within (b) (termination of the undertaking) and not (a). Since (a), (b), and (c) were mutually exclusive, if (b) applied, (c) could not and so there was no ability to dissolve by notice. It also followed that a fixed term in s 32(a) was not exactly the same as 'no fixed term' in s 26 since it had to be construed in the light of s 32(b) and (c). Section 26 therefore only applied to partnerships at will. On the other hand, he was also quite prepared to follow the *Moss v Elphick* construction as an alternative.

Partnership at will following a fixed-term partnership

2.09 In *Maillie v Swanney*[27] the Scottish court, having ruled out s 26 as being inapplicable to a full dissolution as sought by the petitioner, also appears to have decided that s 32(c) could not apply to a partnership at will arising after the expiry of a fixed term. This was because the section could only apply where the partnership was entered into without the partners making provision, expressly or by implication, for the duration of the firm in the circumstances which have come about and, in that case, they had done so. It is not clear, however, in such a case, how there could have been a partnership at will at all since effective implied or express terms as to duration would negate such a conclusion. Further, if it had been a partnership at will, how could those provisions as to duration have had any effect since, as we shall see, s 27 excludes any terms of the original agreement which are incompatible with a partnership at will (see below)? The better explanation is, surely, that there was contrary intention which negatived the application of s 32(c) in that case. The position must clearly be different if there were no such provisions as to duration, since a partnership at will, or for an undefined time, would then have arisen. Such an explanation would better accord with *Moss v Elphick*[28] and the judge in *Maillie v Swanney* regarded the two decisions as being compatible.

---

[26] [2017] NSWSC 1011.
[27] 2000 SLT 464 (OH).
[28] [1910] 1 KB 846, CA.

Current situation

There are therefore some problems still associated with the operation of s 26 and s 32. But most are solved by the practical, if slightly contrived, decision in *Moss v Elphick* and that case was (lukewarmly) supported in *Maillie v Swanney*. It was also used as an alternative solution in *Cole v Lee*, and it is clear that the *Moss v Elphick* solution does reconcile two disparate but overlapping sections of the Act. The complexity and difficulties of the reasoning in the other cases suggests that the practical approach will still be followed in England. So, if ss 26 and 32(c), as so construed, apply then the right to dissolve the partnership by notice will apply. There is no need to give reasonable notice of such intention.[29] The only question is whether unequivocal notice of dissolution has actually been given.[30]

2.10

The initial question therefore is whether the sections apply or whether in any particular agreement there is any form of provision limiting the right to dissolve by notice. (If anyone is still confused, the result of *Moss v Elphick* is that if there is such a provision it will take the partnership out of s 26(1) since it will not be one 'not for a fixed term' and it will also be contrary intention for the purpose of s 32(c).) Examples of whether such a limitation exists or not can be found in *Abbott v Abbott*[31] and *Walters v Bingham*.[32] In the latter case a well-known firm of solicitors were in the habit of renewing their partnership deed every three years, usually late. The partners decided that a new permanent deed was needed and that until it was ready, the existing deed having expired, the partnership should continue on the terms of a 'final draft'. The judge somewhat reluctantly regarded that as being a partnership based on the final draft, to last until a formal deed was prepared, although he was clear that the partners never addressed their minds to the question. Having decided that, he was able to apply the reasoning of *Moss v Elphick* and deny the right of dissolution by notice.

The reasoning in Moss v Elphick has also been applied by the Court of Appeal in Western Australia in the case of *Nelson v Moorcraft*.[33] In that case the parties had agreed that the partnership should last until either one party voluntarily retired from it on giving one month's notice, or was determined by one party being in default (as specified), by mutual agreement,[34] or under the Act. That was held to be both a 'fixed term' and a 'defined time'.

Form of notice

If the right to dissolve or terminate a partnership by notice does exist, the next question is as to what form of notice will be sufficient. Section 32(c), as we have seen, states

2.11

---

[29] See, eg *Heybridge Ltd v Chan Sze Sze* [2007] HKCA 418.
[30] See, eg *Khan v Khan* [2006] EWHC 1477 (Ch).
[31] [1936] 3 All ER 823.
[32] [1988] FTLR 260.
[33] [2014] WASCA 212.
[34] See *Hurst v Bryk* [2002] 1 AC 185, 195. The mutual agreement constitutes a variation of the prior agreement as to duration.

that the notice takes effect either from the date specified in the notice or from the date of communication. Section 26(2) provides that in a partnership constituted by a deed any form of written notice will suffice, which allows for other forms of notice for less formally constituted firms. Both sections therefore allow for written or other forms of notices, but is it permissible to dissolve a partnership set up by deed otherwise than by written notice if it is served under s 32(c) and not s 26(1)? Alternatively do the rules as to the effect of the notice under s 32(c) have any effect on a notice served under s 26(2)? Unfortunately there are no answers to these questions but the wording used in s 26(2) being permissive in nature would hardly seem to negative s 32(c).

There are, however, examples of what can amount to a notice and when a written notice is communicated. With regard to the former it appears that simply denying the existence of a partnership at will in the course of legal proceedings can amount to a notice of dissolution if the court actually finds that one exists. This was recognized in the New Zealand case of *Smith v Baker*,[35] which was based on UK authorities. Mere denial of a partnership's existence may, however, prove less effective as a notice. The problems of establishing whether effective notice has been given where written notice has not been specified can be seen from the case of *Toogood v Farrell*.[36] One of three partners in a firm of estate agents walked into the office and said, 'I am resigning'. After a trial lasting twenty days and an appeal lasting nine days, that was held to constitute sufficient notice. It is also clear from that case and others,[37] that once given, the notice binds the partner giving it unless the parties subsequently agree otherwise. It cannot be unilaterally revoked.

As to the form of communication it appears that a written notice which does not itself specify a date of dissolution will only be effective at the time it is received rather than at the time it is posted, thus reversing the usual contractual postal rules. This was the decision in *McLeod v Dowling*[38] where the partner sending the notice died between the posting and receipt of the notice. The judge decided that the partnership had in fact been dissolved by the death before it had been dissolved by the notice. On the other hand in *Walters v Bingham*[39] delivery of written notices to the firm's office in envelopes addressed to each partner individually was considered to be sufficient communication even to partners who were away on business or on holiday. The judge in that case, however, also decided that notices of dissolution served with intention to conceal the partner's own fraud would have no effect. In Hong Kong it has been held that provided the notice was clear and unambiguous it could be given electronically via a 'WhatsApp' link.[40] That is not something which has yet troubled the English courts.

---

[35] [1977] 1 NZLR 511.
[36] [1988] 2 EGLR 233, CA. See also Ch 6, below.
[37] See *Giltej Applications Pty Ltd v Moschello* [2005] NSWSC 599 (14 June 2005) and cases discussed therein.
[38] (1927) 43 TLR 655.
[39] [1988] FTLR 260.
[40] *Eva v Yin* [2018] HKDC 4.

Continuing terms into a partnership at will

2.12 One final point on duration. If there is a partnership for a fixed term (as construed in *Moss v Elphick*) and after that has expired the partners continue the partnership then, as we have seen, the partnership will be automatically converted into a partnership at will. This was the position prior to the Act: see *Neilson v Mossend Iron Co*;[41] and it is now expressed in s 27 as follows:

> Where a partnership entered into for a fixed term is continued after the term has expired, and without any express new agreement, the rights and duties of the partners remain the same as they were at the expiration of the term, so far as is consistent with the incidents of a partnership at will.

The question which arises, therefore, is as to which of the terms of the original agreement will continue to apply.

For an original provision to continue in force under the section, it must (a) have been in existence at the *expiration* of the fixed term, and (b) be consistent with a partnership at will. The former is a question of fact and it must be borne in mind that the original written terms may have been varied by a course of dealing or other agreement. The latter depends upon its consistency with the concept of dissolution by notice since that is the hallmark of a partnership at will. Thus it is impossible for any term which restricts that right (and as we have seen that means any term as to the ending of a partnership at all) to continue into a partnership at will. It was held in *Clark v Leach*[42] that a power to expel a partner would not survive, but this was rejected as binding authority in *Walters v Bingham*.[43] In that case such a power was allowed to continue in the case of a large modern partnership, since there is then a real difference between an expulsion, which leaves the remaining partners intact, and dissolution, eg by notice, where the whole firm is wound up. In addition, terms as to the consequences of a dissolution may also be consistent with a partnership at will. In particular it seems that a provision allowing one partner to purchase the share of another at a valuation within a certain time limit is perfectly acceptable—see, for example, *Daw v Herring*,[44] *Brooks v Brooks*,[45] and the Australian decision in *Biliora Pty Ltd v Leisure Investments Pty Ltd*.[46] An arbitration clause has been allowed to continue and it is also clear that the fiduciary and agency rules continue to apply.

In *Maillie v Swanney*, as we have seen, the Scottish court did not consider how the terms as to duration could be said to have continued after the expiration of the fixed term if the partnership had indeed then become a partnership at will. It is axiomatic that any terms as to duration are by definition incompatible with such a partnership and in fact

---

[41] (1886) 11 App Cas 298, HL.
[42] (1863) 1 De GJ & S 409.
[43] [1988] FTLR 260.
[44] [1892] 1 Ch 284.
[45] (1901) 85 LT 453.
[46] (2001) 11 NTLR, 148, CA.

prevent it arising. The reason for this failure to consider s 27 is that the court regarded s 27 as being, like s 26, irrelevant to a full dissolution by notice, being concerned solely with a withdrawal by the partner serving the notice under s 26 without a dissolution of the whole firm.

Partnerships by Association

2.13 Children, and others, are frequently told that if they play with fire they might expect to be burned. The same is true of partnerships. Someone who takes part in the running of a business and receives a share of the net profits cannot expect to avoid the consequences of his acts; there is an implied agreement as to the existence of a partnership. Equally a person who allows himself to be represented or represents himself to another as a partner cannot then escape liability on the basis that he is only an employee or a consultant etc. There are in fact two distinct strands. In the first case the person involved will be a partner in the full sense of the word, whereas in the second the person will only be liable *as if he were* a partner: he will have no rights *as a* partner. In the first case the law has to distinguish between the genuine creditor or outsider on the one hand and a partner who simply wishes to take the benefits of partnership without accepting the burdens on the other. The second case is basically an example of estoppel and is designed to protect persons extending credit or making supplies on the strength of the representation. For the sake of convenience we can divide this topic into association by financial involvement, which creates a partnership, and association by representation, which only creates liability to outsiders *as if* the person concerned was a partner, provided these labels are not regarded as tablets of stone.

Association by Financial Involvement

2.14 In the early days the courts took the view that participation in the profits of a business created a partnership so that a creditor who was to be repaid out of the profits of a business automatically became a partner and was liable as such: see, eg *Waugh v Carver*.[47] In 1860 this idea was rejected by the House of Lords in *Cox v Hickman*.[48] In that case a partnership business which was in financial difficulties was transferred by the original partners to trustees who were to run the business and to divide the profits between the various creditors. If the creditors were repaid in full the business was to be transferred back to the original partners. Two of the creditors acted as trustees and Hickman now

---

[47] (1793) 2 H Bl 235. One of the reasons for this approach was that, had the transaction been characterized as a loan with interest payments, it would have been void under the then Draconian laws on usury. To characterize it as a partnership allowed the courts to hold the parties to their agreement. See also *Grace v Smith* (1775) 2 W Bl 998.
[48] (1860) 8 HL Cas 268, HL.

sought to make them liable as partners. The House of Lords decided that since they had not been represented as partners the mere fact that they were sharing in the profits of the business did not of itself make them partners. Thus there was association neither by representation nor by financial involvement.

Cox v Hickman established that the sharing of profits, although in certain cases strong evidence of the existence of a partnership, does not raise an irrebuttable presumption of its existence. This major change in the law caused some confusion and led to Bovill's Act of 1865 which to all intents and purposes is now ss 2 and 3 of the 1890 Act. As Lindley LJ remarked in *Badeley v Consolidated Bank*[49] the former rule was artificial in that it took only one term of the contract and raised a whole presumption on it. From 1860 onwards, therefore, the courts have refused to be bound by a rigid application of the profit-sharing concept. It is a question of looking at all the facts and terms of the agreement. *Cox v Hickman* concerned a deed of arrangement with creditors—in effect a very early form of the administration procedure introduced by the Insolvency Act 1986, ie an attempt to save the concern by continuing the business and if successful handing it back to the original controllers (see Chapter 8). The creditors remained creditors.

Profit-sharing as evidence of partnership

The current position is set out in s 2(3) of the 1890 Act which provides: **2.15**

> The receipt by a person of a share of the profits of a business is prima facie evidence that he is a partner in the business, but the receipt of such a share, or of a payment contingent on or varying with the profits of a business, does not of itself make him a partner in the business.

The section then goes on to provide five specific cases to which the first half of that sentence does not apply. In those cases, therefore, receipt of a share of the profits does not of itself make the recipient a partner. Before examining the effects of this somewhat contradictory section we should perhaps remind ourselves that we are dealing with net profits in this context (remember s 2(2) makes it clear that a share of gross receipts is no evidence of partnership).

By way of introduction to s 2(3) it must be said at once that the wording could have been better. In particular the use of the words 'prima facie' is unfortunate since one interpretation of the phrase is that, since a receipt of a share of profits is prima facie evidence of a partnership, if there is no other evidence at all then a partnership exists. On the other hand the second part of the section makes it quite clear that such a receipt does not *of itself* make the recipient a partner, ie exactly the opposite of such an interpretation of the first part. Either 'prima facie' must mean something else (eg evidence

---

[49] (1888) 38 Ch D 238, CA.

upon which the court *may* act) or the section cancels itself out by providing conflicting burdens of proof: the first part suggesting that if evidence of profit-sharing is produced it must be rebutted and the second part suggesting that additional supporting evidence of a partnership is required. One simple (perhaps too simple) way out of that impasse is to apply the basic rule that he who alleges must prove.

However that may be, the courts have treated s 2(3) as simply re-enacting the original test in *Cox v Hickman*.[50] The classic statement of the effect of s 2(3), which is still used by judges, was given by North J in *Davis v Davis*:[51]

> Adopting then the rule of law which was laid down before the Act, and which seems to me to be precisely what is intended by s 2(3) of the Act, the receipt by a person of a share of the profits of a business is prima facie evidence that he is a partner in it, and, if the matter stops there, it is evidence upon which the court must act. But, if there are other circumstances to be considered, they ought to be considered fairly together; not holding that a partnership is proved by the receipt of a share of profits, unless it is rebutted by something else; but taking all the circumstances together, not attaching undue weight to any of them, but drawing an inference from the whole.

Establishing community of benefit or opposition of interest

2.16 Whilst this statement seems to suggest that evidence of receipt of a share of the profits, if it is the only evidence, requires the courts to find that a partnership exists, it should be pointed out that the courts have always found other evidence to consider, if only from the circumstances by which the profits came to be shared, so that it is the last sentence of that quotation which is relevant and applied today. North J also quoted with approval the somewhat shorter test of Lindley LJ in *Badeley v Consolidated Bank*:[52] 'I take it that it is quite plain now, ever since *Cox v Hickman*, that what we have to get at is the real agreement between the parties'. In discovering this the courts have refused to be dogmatic or to lay down universal rules so that ultimately each case must depend upon its facts—is it a partnership agreement or some other form of contract such as one of loan, employment, or a joint venture between two separate businesses? The statement by Stuart-Smith LJ in *Taylor v Mazorriaga*,[53] to the effect that receipt of a share of profits falling within the first part of s 2(3) was a 'powerful support' for the existence of a partnership, has to be read in the context of the case overall. Neither of the other judges in that case referred to s 2(3) at all.

---

[50] (1860) 8 HL Cas 268, HL.
[51] [1894] 1 Ch 393.
[52] (1888) 38 Ch D 238, CA.
[53] (1999) LTL, 12 May 1999, CA.

Sharing of losses

One of the most persuasive factors in establishing a partnership by financial association is an agreement to share losses as well as profits, for that is an indication of the true participation in a business—the so-called risk factor. The strength of this factor is illustrated by the Canadian case of *Northern Sales (1963) Ltd v Ministry of National Revenue*.[54] Three companies made an agreement for the marketing of rape-seed for the 'crop year' 1960–1, each being entitled to a share of the profits. Collier J, after stating that a share in the profits was not conclusive evidence, turned to examining the surrounding circumstances. He found that the agreement provided for the sharing of losses as well as profits, which he regarded as characteristic of a partnership contract. He also relied on the fact that the agreement provided for consultation between the parties and there had been some consultation. The judge therefore found the companies to be carrying on a partnership even though there was 'no contribution of capital, no common management, no common assets, no common facilities, no common bank account and no common firm-name'. Such features were not essential for the existence of a partnership. In *Manufacturing Integration Ltd v Manufacturing Resource Planning Ltd*,[55] on the other hand, Sullivan J found that the notable absence of a shared risk between the parties, coupled with minimal financial transparency, rebutted the presumption of a partnership based on profit-sharing.

2.17

But the sharing of losses is not conclusive—remember there are no absolutes in this area. For example, in *Walker v Hirsch*,[56] Walker was employed as a clerk by two partners and he agreed with them that in return for his advancing £1,500 to the firm he was to be paid a fixed salary for his work in the business and to be entitled to one-eighth of the net profits and be liable for one-eighth of any losses. The agreement could be determined by four months' notice on either side. Walker continued to work exactly as he had done before the agreement and was never represented to the customers as a partner. The partners determined the agreement and excluded him from the premises. He now asked for a dissolution of the firm on the basis that he was a partner. The Court of Appeal decided by reference to the agreement and those famous surrounding circumstances that this was not a partnership agreement but simply a contract of loan repayable where he left the firm's employment.

Other factors

In *Davis v Davis*,[57] North J was persuaded to discover a partnership by the fact that the parties drew exactly similar sums from the business and had represented themselves as partners to outsiders. In *Walker West Development Ltd v FJ Emmett Ltd*,[58] the Court of Appeal, faced with a complex agreement between property developers and builders

2.18

---

[54] (1973) 37 DLR (3d) 612.
[55] (2000) LTL, 19 May 2000.
[56] (1884) 27 Ch D 460.
[57] [1894] 1 Ch 393.
[58] [1979] 252 EG 1171, CA.

in relation to a housing development did not consider the absence of joint liability for losses as crucial. Rather they approached the issue by asking whether there was in reality one business carried on in common or two separate businesses, the one employing the other. Since the agreement referred to 'the project', to be advertised as a joint project of the two companies and the net profits were to be divided in equal shares, the Court of Appeal felt able to conclude that a partnership existed although both Goff LJ and Buckley LJ admitted to some amount of indecision.

More recently in the Australian case of *United Tankers Pty Ltd v Moray Pre-Cast Pty Ltd*[59] there was held to be no partnership where one party agreed to invest a sum as working capital in a partnership business on the basis that he would receive a one-third interest in the company which was to be formed to acquire that business. He took none of the benefits of being a partner such as remuneration and had no involvement in the business prior to incorporation. The surrounding circumstances indicated that he had taken an interest in the company rather than in the partnership. In *Moore v Moore*,[60] the Northern Irish High Court found that the parties were partners with respect to the dairy part of a family farm but not the pig-breeding or arable parts. Thus it seems that s 2(3) can apply to those who share in the profits of part of a business so as to make them partners in respect of that part only.

Specific cases

2.19 Having established this basic rule as to the sharing of profits, s 2(3) goes on to specify five particular instances in which such a receipt 'does not of itself' make the recipient a partner. In these cases such a receipt is not even prima facie evidence of partnership. The practical difference between a specific receipt within one of these heads and a receipt subject to the general wording of the section is in reality small except that it is quite clear that in the specific cases the burden of proof will always be firmly on those alleging that a partnership does exist to adduce additional evidence: conflicting burdens of proof clearly cannot exist in these cases. With due respect to the draftsman of the Act it will be easier if we leave para (a) of the section until we come to para (d) since they are related.

Remuneration of employees

2.20 The first specific receipt covered is therefore in s 2(3)(b):

> A contract for the remuneration of a servant or agent of a person engaged in a business by a share of the profits of the business does not of itself make the servant or agent a partner in the business or liable as such.

---

[59] [1992] 1 QdR 467.
[60] 27 February 1998, HC (NI).

This provision is quite self-evident, for, as we have seen, it is generally thought that the relationship of employer and employee is inconsistent with partnership, and that of an independent agent (eg an estate agent engaged to sell the partnership offices) is clearly distinguishable on the basis that there is no involvement in the business. What this paragraph does, therefore, is to make it quite clear that if such a relationship has been established by other factors suggesting either a contract of service or an independent contractor, the mere fact that he is to be paid out of the net profits of the business will not make him a partner.[61] The basic question of course remains—is he an employee or a partner? We shall return to that question at the end of this chapter.

Provision for dependants

Nor need we dwell long on s 2(3)(c). It provides that: **2.21**

> A person being the widow or child of a deceased partner, and receiving by way of annuity a portion of the profits made in the business in which the deceased person was a partner, is not by reason only of such receipt a partner in the business or liable as such.

It is not unusual for partners to make provision for their dependants in the event of their death and one way is to provide in the partnership agreement that a partner's widow or children are to receive a specified proportion of the profits of the business after his death. Such a receipt is clearly no evidence of partnership. In practice the agreement might also provide that a proportion is payable to the partner after his retirement, but this may well be regarded as the purchase price of his share of the business or as his 'remuneration' as a consultant partner and is not within this paragraph.

On a contemporary note we should remember that, when the Act became law, widows for the purpose of this paragraph would rarely have included widowers and children would have been legitimate ones only. There is little doubt that a modern court would apply the paragraph widely to include anyone who was dependent on the deceased partner, including civil partners, former spouses and civil partners, and children, however acquired. The important point is that the provision of an annuity for a dependant after a partner's death does not make him or her a partner.

Partners or creditors

The central issue in s 2(3) is, however, the distinction between a partner and a creditor. **2.22** As we have seen, it was this issue in *Cox v Hickman*[62] which led to the section being passed at all. Two paragraphs, (a) and (d), provide more specific guidance on this issue. Section 2(3)(a) states that:

> The receipt by a person of a debt or other liquidated amount by instalments, or otherwise out of the accruing profits of a business does not of itself make him a partner in the business or liable as such.

---

[61] *Lewis v Narayanasamy* [2017] EWCA Civ 229 at [46].
[62] (1860) 8 HL Cas 268, HL.

Section 2(3)(d) continues:

> The advance of money by way of loan to a person engaged or about to engage in any business on a contract with that person that the lender shall receive a rate of interest varying with the profits, or shall receive a share of the profits arising from carrying on the business, does not of itself make the lender a partner with the person or persons carrying on the business or liable as such. Provided that the contract is in writing, and signed by or on behalf of all the parties thereto.

Paragraph (a) therefore relates to the repayment of the loan itself out of profits whereas para (d) applies to the payment of interest on a loan out of profits. In practice the former presents few problems and is in effect no more than a statutory version of the actual decision in *Cox v Hickman*. If the trick is to distinguish between a creditor and a partner, it is unlikely that the latter would require capital repayments out of profits; it is much more likely that this will be a compromise method of paying off a creditor and so avoiding an insolvency, as in fact happened in this case. On the other hand, if there are other factors not present in that decision then a partnership can exist, eg if the creditors take over the business completely and are not obliged to return it to the original partners when their debts have been satisfied.

An income return by reference to the profits of a business is a different matter entirely. A person wishing to invest in a business would take a share of the profits as his return and the fact that this can be called 'interest' does not turn an investment into a loan. The tax courts have spent many complex hours distinguishing between genuine and false 'interest' payments. If we remember s 1 of the Act, it is the hallmark of a partnership that those involved are running a business together for an income return based on net profits. The courts approach this problem by ascertaining the intention of those involved. Did they intend to form a partnership and to avoid the consequences of being partners or did they always envisage only a debtor–creditor relationship? In answering this question, s 2(3)(d) seems to have been of little practical assistance—it will always be a question of ascertaining the intention of the partners although, of course, this must be gleaned objectively from all the facts and not necessarily the expressed intention of the parties. One way of putting it is whether there is community of benefit (partnership) or an opposition of interests (debtor/creditor).[63]

Examples

2.23 In *Re Megevand, ex p Delhasse*,[64] Delhasse lent £10,000 to a business run by two partners. The agreement provided that this was to be a loan and was not to make Delhasse a partner. On the other hand he was to receive a fixed proportion of the profits and was given rights to inspect the accounts and, if necessary, to dissolve the firm. This 'loan' was not repayable until after a dissolution and in fact the £10,000 formed the

---

[63] *Chan Sau-kut v Gray & Iron Construction and Engineering Co* [1986] HKLR 84.
[64] (1878) Ch D 511.

basis of the partnership's capital. The court had little difficulty in holding that Delhasse was indeed a partner despite the express wording to the contrary. In effect he was the classic sleeping partner or 'banker' who puts up the money for others to exploit their skills. Section 2(3)(d) (already in existence in Bovill's Act) could not save him since the surrounding circumstances, objectively construed, indicated the intention to set up a partnership.

The leading case in this area is still, however, *Pooley v Driver*.[65] In that case the loan agreement with the 'lender' contained a covenant by the admitted partners that they would observe all the covenants in their own partnership agreement. In effect this gave the 'lender' an equal right with the partners to enforce the partnership agreement. The partnership agreement itself provided strong evidence against this being a loan. For example twenty parts of the sixty equal parts of capital were to be allocated to persons advancing money by way of loan and the profits were to be divided amongst the holders of capital in proportion to their capital holding. This combined evidence of profit-sharing and control convinced the court that this was a clear case of a partnership and that the parties intended to be partners. 'What they did not intend to do was to incur the liabilities of partners', said Jessel MR.

No doubt both these cases are examples of partnership draftsmen being carried away with the forerunner of s 2(3)(d) and giving that paragraph far more strength than it in fact has. In *Pooley v Driver* Jessel MR put para (d) firmly in its place:

> I take it to mean this, that the person advancing must be a real lender; that the advance must not only profess to be by way of loan, but must be a real loan; and consequently you come back to the question whether the persons who entered into the contract of association are really in the position of creditor and debtor, or in the position of partners.... But the Act does not decide that for you. You must decide that without the Act; and when you have decided that the relation is that of creditor and debtor, then all the Act does is this: it says that a creditor may take a share of the profits, but... if you have once decided that the parties are in the position of creditor and debtor you do not want the Act at all, because the inference of partnership derived from the mere taking a share of profits, not being irrebuttable, is rebutted by your having come to the conclusion that they are in the position of debtor and creditor.

Need for written agreement

2.24 It should perhaps be noted that whatever benefit is conferred by s 2(3)(d) it cannot apply if the loan is made under an oral rather than a written agreement since the proviso to the paragraph is quite clear: 'Provided that the contract is in writing, and signed by or on behalf of all the parties thereto'. Confirmation that this means what it says was

---

[65] (1877) 5 Ch D 458, CA.

given by Smith LJ in *Re Fort, ex p Schofield*.[66] The Law Commissions sensibly suggested that this proviso to s 2(3)(d) should be repealed as being a relic of the days when there was a greater emphasis on written contracts.[67]

Sale of goodwill

2.25 Section 2(3) concludes with para (e):

> A person receiving by way of annuity or otherwise a portion of the profits of a business in consideration of the sale by him of the goodwill of the business is not by reason only of such receipt a partner in the business or liable as such.

The intention is clear: to protect the vendor of a business who agrees to sell the goodwill of that business by reference to the future profits of the business. Since goodwill is notoriously difficult to value except by reference to profits this is a sensible provision. Like the other paragraphs in s 2(3), however, it really adds little to the realities of any decision. The courts will be concerned to see whether or not this is the relationship of vendor and purchaser. If it is then there will be no partnership. On the other hand, if the reality is that one partner is taking on another active partner who is buying his way into the business nothing in s 2(3)(e) will save him.

Effectiveness of s 2(3)

2.26 Section 2(3) taken as a whole, therefore, merely states rather than solves the problems associated with the financial returns from a partnership and adds little to *Cox v Hickman*.[68] Indeed the Law Commissions asked for views as to whether s 2 as a whole should be repealed, leaving the question as to the existence of a partnership to be determined by whether there is an agreement within the terms of s 1. Having considered the case law, the reader may well agree that s 2 has in fact served its purpose of clarifying ancient doubts and is now past its sell-by date. Others did not think so, however, and it would have been preserved in the proposed Bill.

Deferred debts (s 3)

2.27 Ironically the only time when the actual wording of at least part of s 2(3) has been crucial has arisen not in relation to the existence of a partnership but in connection with s 3 of the Act. This section provides that a person who has lent money to a business 'upon such a contract as is mentioned' in s 2(3)(d) or who has sold the goodwill 'in consideration of a share of the profits of the business' (ie within s 2(3)(e)) is postponed to (will only be paid after) all the other creditors of the business. In other words such a lender or seller will only be able to recover his debt if the partnership is dissolved after all the

---

[66] [1897] 2 QB 495.
[67] Report, para 4.53.
[68] (1860) 8 HL Cas 268.

other partnership creditors have been paid in full. It can therefore be important to decide whether a particular loan or sale is within s 2(3)(d) or (e) simply for repayment purposes.

Two cases illustrate the importance of such matters. In *Re Fort, ex p Schofield*,[69] Schofield lent £3,000 to Fort on an oral agreement that they should share in net profits until the loan was repaid. On Fort's insolvency Schofield asked for repayment. The issue was simple. Was this loan within s 2(3)(d) and so caught by s 3 so that Schofield would come last in the queue of creditors (and so receive nothing in practice)? Schofield argued that since this was an oral and not a written agreement it was within the proviso to s 2(3)(d) (ie that the contract must be in writing and signed by the parties) and so outside the terms of that paragraph and naturally therefore outside s 3. The Court of Appeal rejected this argument. Section 3 applies to 'such a contract' as is specified by s 2(3)(d) and this was taken to refer to any contract of loan providing for a return out of net profits. The proviso related only to those wishing to take advantage of s 2(3)(d) to avoid being partners.

In *Re Gieve, ex p Shaw*,[70] the widow of a businessman sold the business to Gieve and Wills under an agreement by which she was to be paid an annuity of £2,650. They carried on the business. Gieve died and Wills became insolvent. Could the widow sue for the annuity (which would be capitalized for the purposes of a claim in bankruptcy) or was she subject to s 3? In this case the Court of Appeal found that she could sue. Section 2(3)(c) requires a person to be receiving, by way of annuity, 'a portion of the profits of a business' in return for the sale of the goodwill. On the facts she had simply required that an annuity be paid to her: there was nothing in the agreement that it should be paid out of the profits of the business. The fact that without the business the purchasers could not have paid the annuity was irrelevant. In reality this agreement was neither one of partnership nor the sale of the goodwill in return for a share of the profits but a sale coupled with an annuity.

Although s 3 is a penal section in that it deprives a creditor of his rights, it has limits. In *Re Lonergan, ex p Sheil*[71] the Court of Appeal made it clear that although the section postponed the debt it had no effect on any security the creditor might have, such as a mortgage over the partnership property. As a mortgagee such a creditor retained his full rights. The opposite conclusion was said to be equivalent to confiscating the property of the mortgagee and there was nothing in this section to suggest that.

By way of postscript it could have been argued that the mere presence of s 3 might have lent more weight to s 2(3)(d) in cases such as *Pooley v Driver*[72] in that such a creditor although having the benefits of s 2(3)(d) would suffer the burden of s 3. The current state of play is that s 2(3)(d) confers precious few benefits, whereas s 3

---

[69] [1897] 2 QB 495.
[70] [1899] WN 41, CA.
[71] (1877) 4 Ch D 789, CA.
[72] (1877) 5 Ch D 458, CA.

remains a real burden. The Law Commissions recommended its repeal as being a relic of the days when such a person might have been a partner and as being at variance with modern insolvency rescue procedures such as a voluntary arrangement where such a loan may be the best solution.[73] Above all, why should such a lender be disadvantaged over others, eg one who charges a fixed rate of interest which in practice absorbs all the profits?

Partnership Liability by Representation

2.28 Partnerships which arise as the result of financial involvement are true partnerships in that the relationship is established both within and outside the firm. But it is equally possible for a person to be liable *as if he or she were* a partner even though he or she is in no way carrying on a business in common with a view of profit. This liability is known variously as a partnership by holding out, partnership by estoppel, or a quasi-partnership. In reality there is no partnership, at least not one involving the person concerned, but simply liability to a third party. That liability arises where a person by words or conduct represents to another that he or she is a partner, on the strength of which that other person incurs a liability, believing the representation to be true. Whether this is phrased as an action for misrepresentation, breach of warranty of authority, or fraud, the significance is that such a person cannot turn round and claim that he or she is in fact not a partner and so should not be liable as such. He or she is estopped by his actions from denying that he or she is a partner and so is liable as such. Such a person is not a partner, however, so that if A is held out as being a partner of B, A and B are not carrying on a partnership business, A is only liable *as if he were* a partner. Thus there is no partnership capable of being wound up by the court in that situation. This was decided in *Re C & M Ashberg*,[74] where the contrary argument that A would be estopped from denying the existence of the firm for all purposes was rejected by the judge. Similarly it was held in *HMRC v Pal*[75] that simply putting one's name on a VAT partnership registration form as being a partner in the firm being registered did not make such non-partners liable for the VAT subsequently due from the firm, which is the taxable person. That liability required an actual partnership and not simply individuals holding themselves out as partners, even if they were guilty of deception on a third party. The liability simply fell on the true partners.[76]

All this stems from s 14(1) of the Act:

> Every one who by words spoken or written or by conduct represents himself, or who knowingly suffers himself to be represented, as a partner in a particular firm, is

---

[73] Report, para 4.53.
[74] The Times, 17 July 1990. See also *Brown Economic Assessments Inc v Stevenson* (2003) 11 WWR 101.
[75] [2008] STC 2442.
[76] Quaere what would happen if there were no true partners at all? The solution suggested was to cancel the firm's VAT registration and substitute one of those actually carrying on the business.

liable as a partner to any one who has on the faith of any such representation given credit to the firm, whether the representation has or has not been made or communicated to the person so giving credit by or with the knowledge of the apparent partner making the representation or suffering it to be made.

The section only applies if the third party has 'given credit' as a result of the representation. In *Nationwide Building Society v Lewis*,[77] it was accepted that this was narrower than the common law requirement for estoppel of acting to one's detriment, but made no attempt to go any further. In *HMRC v Pal*,[78] the judge held that on any definition of that phrase it did not include public law issues such as liability to the tax authorities. It required a private law transaction with the firm concerned which arose either directly or indirectly out of reliance on the representations made. Thus the main issues are as to the representation and the reliance upon it.[79]

Need for representation

Central to this concept, therefore, is the representation that a person is a partner in a particular firm. **2.29**

The use of the words 'particular firm' can limit the scope of the section. In *UCB Home Loans Corporation Ltd v Soni*,[80] there was a representation by S that A was a partner in a firm under the generic name of S & Co. In fact S operated a number of solicitors' businesses under that name from a number of different addresses, some in partnership and some as a sole practitioner. The representation made generally by S, which A had allowed, was that she was a partner in S & Co operating from four business addresses. But the specific (fraudulent) representation made by S to X was that A was a partner in S & Co operating at a different address and nowhere else. In fact that business had ceased (it had been S's sole practice) and the letterhead normally used by S & Co did not refer to it. The Court held therefore that A had not knowingly allowed herself to be represented as a partner in that particular firm operating from that specific address. The representation made to X was not within the scope of the representation she had suffered to be made.

On the other hand there is apparently no requirement that the particular firm specified actually exists provided the other requirements of s 14 are satisfied. That was the decision in the Australian case of *D & H Bunny Pty Ltd v Atkins*[81] where two men, Atkins and Naughton, approached the credit manager of the company and asked for extended credit facilities, stating that they had agreed to become partners with each other. Goods

---

[77] [1998] Ch 482.
[78] [2008] STC 2442.
[79] In the *Pal* case there was no evidence that HM Revenue & Customs (HMRC) had actually relied on the registrations so as to either give credit or suffer a detriment.
[80] [2013] EWCA Civ 62.
[81] [1961] VLR 31. See also *Sangster v Biddulphs*, 22 March 2005.

were supplied to Naughton on credit debited to an account opened in their joint names. Atkins was held liable for the purchase price on the basis of his representation of partnership even where no such firm existed. The fact that the section refers to the representation being as to a partner 'in a particular firm' was held not to require the evidence of an actual firm.

It is submitted that this is correct on general principles despite some dicta to the contrary.[82] The need for there to be a partnership only goes to the effectiveness of the representation that he or she is a partner, which must mean in a firm whether illusory or not.

Knowingly being represented as a partner

2.30 Problems are much more likely to arise, however, over the liability of someone who does not actually make the representation himself but is represented by another as being a partner. In such cases the section requires that he has *knowingly* suffered himself to be so represented.[83] Three separate factual situations can arise here: one where the person concerned knows of the representation before it is made and knows that it is going to be made; another where he has no actual knowledge of the representation but a reasonable person would have known of it; and yet another where he or she has failed to take steps to correct a representation which he has since discovered. The first case produces no problems except of fact, but what is the position with regard to negligence in either of the other two? Does negligently failing to realize that a representation is being made, or negligently failing to correct a representation once known, amount to 'knowingly' suffering the representation for the purposes of s 14(1)?

Some assistance can be gained from the decision of Lynskey J in *Tower Cabinet Co Ltd v Ingram*.[84] Christmas and Ingram carried on a partnership business selling household furniture under the name 'Merry's' (unlikely as that may seem). The partnership was dissolved by mutual agreement in 1947. Christmas continued to run the business and ordered several suites of furniture from the plaintiffs. By mistake he confirmed the order on old notepaper which had Ingram's name on it. The plaintiff not having been paid by the business sought to make Ingram liable under s 14(1). The plaintiff had never dealt with the firm before and apart from the notepaper had no knowledge of Ingram's existence. The judge held that it was impossible to conclude that Ingram had knowingly suffered himself to be represented as a partner since he neither knew of nor authorized the use of the old notepaper. The fact that he might have been negligent or careless in not seeing that all the old notepaper had been destroyed when he left was not sufficient. (Since this case involved the liability of a former partner for debts incurred after he ceased to be a partner s 36 of the Act was also relevant and we shall return to the case in Chapter 4.)

---

[82] See, eg *Brice v Garden of Eden Ltd* [1965–70] 2 LRB 204 at 207.
[83] In that particular firm: *UCB Home Loans Corporation Ltd v Soni* [2013] EWCA Civ 62.
[84] [1949] 2 KB 397.

Negligently allowing a misrepresentation is not therefore the same as knowingly allowing it. It has been said that it is a far step from saying that X ought to have realized that the impression that he was a partner might have been given, to saying that therefore he 'knowingly' created that impression.[85] This decision is also relevant in the case of former partners in relation to the provisions in the Companies Act 2006 that the names of all the partners should be included on all business correspondence or available, on demand, for inspection (see Chapter 3). It is unlikely that simply because X's name is so disclosed, without his or her knowledge, there would be any holding out.[86] But, if a partner on retirement fails to destroy all the notepaper bearing his name, is he or she now within s 14(1) of the 1890 Act? There may well be a distinction between negligence and recklessness in such a case, ie the difference between not realizing the consequences and realizing but not caring about the consequences. It is possible to argue that the latter does amount to an implied authorization to use his name. There is no authority as to the failure to correct an unauthorized misrepresentation once known but again the distinction may be between negligence and recklessness in such failures. It is a question of achieving a balance between the person so represented and the person being misled. In cases such as *Ingram* the position will often be solved by reference to s 36 of the Act (see Chapter 4).

Section 14(2) further provides:

> where after a partner's death the partnership business is continued in the old firm-name, the continued use of that name or of the deceased partner's name as part thereof shall not of itself make his executors or administrators estate or effects liable for any partnership debts contracted after his death.

Need for reliance

Section 14(1) also requires the person misled to have acted on the strength of the representation and implicit in that, of course, is that he or she must believe it to be true. But that is all the person misled need show—he or she does not have to prove that he or she would not have given credit if he or she had known it to be untrue. Once again this is best illustrated by an Australian case, *Lynch v Stiff*.[87] Mr Lynch was employed as a solicitor in a practice. Although his name appeared as a partner in the heading of the firm's notepaper, he remained at all times an employee of the firm. He had previously been employed by the employer's father and had always been Mr Stiff's solicitor, handling his business on behalf of the firm. When the son took over the business he assured Mr Stiff that his affairs would continue to be handled by Mr Lynch and it was clear that Mr Stiff

2.31

---

[85] *Elite Business Systems UK Ltd v Price* [2005] EWCA Civ 920, per Lord Phillips MR at [15].
[86] By analogy with *Dao Heng Bank Ltd v Hui Kwai-wing* [1977] HKLR 122; *Lon Eagle Industrial Ltd v Realy Trading Co* [1999] 4 HKC 675.
[87] (1944) 68 CLR 428.

kept his business there at least partly because of that statement and the apparent statement on the new notepaper that Mr Lynch was now a partner. Mr Stiff gave the firm money for investment which the son misappropriated and Mr Stiff now sued Mr Lynch under a provision identical to s 14(1). One point that arose was whether it made any difference that Mr Stiff had entrusted his affairs to the firm because of his confidence in Mr Lynch prior to the representation being made in the notepaper and thus may well have done so even if no such representation had been made. The court held that so long as Mr Stiff could prove reliance and belief he need show no more.

But reliance is necessary and without it there can be no liability under the doctrine of holding out. An unusual example of this arose in the case of *Hudgell Yeates & Co v Watson*.[88] In January 1973, Mr Watson instructed one of the partners in the plaintiff firm of solicitors, a Mr James, to act for him in a case. This work was passed to another partner, Miss Griffiths, who together with a managing clerk (who appears to have done most of the actual work) acted for Mr Watson in 1973. There was a third partner, a Mr Smith, who worked in a different office and took no part at all in Mr Watson's case. Mr Smith forgot to renew his solicitor's practising certificate for 1973 until 2 May and so was disqualified from acting as a solicitor from 1 January to 2 May 1973. When Mr Watson was sued for failure to pay his bill for legal costs he argued that since for part of that time Mr Smith had been disqualified from acting as a solicitor the whole firm was precluded from acting as such, since work done by one partner was done as an agent for the others. Accordingly the charges for work done during that period could not be enforced.

The Court of Appeal by a majority dismissed this argument, finding that on Mr Smith's disqualification the partnership between himself and the other two partners was automatically dissolved[89] and reconstituted as between the two qualified partners who could thus sue for the money used. For present purposes, however, the important point is that this was not affected by the doctrine of holding out since at no time did Mr Watson give any credit on the basis that Mr Smith was at any time a partner in the firm. Put another way there was a holding out of Mr Smith as a partner, but no estoppel arose since Mr Watson had at all times thought that he was only dealing with Mr James.

Written notice of being a partner

2.32 But in the absence of such a clear finding of fact, will the use of headed notepaper representing a defendant, who is not a partner but merely an employee or associate, as being a partner, as distinct from a former partner who has left the firm, suffice to establish both a holding out and reliance so as to give rise to an estoppel? In *Nationwide Building Society v Lewis*,[90] the Nationwide instructed a firm of solicitors to act for it in a mortgage transaction. The matter was handled solely by Mr Lewis and instructions were given to Bryan Lewis & Co, 'ref Mr B Lewis'. Two days later the firm accepted the

---

[88] [1978] 2 All ER 363, CA.
[89] Under s 34: see Ch 7, below.
[90] [1997] 3 All ER 498, [1998] Ch 482, CA.

instructions by letter enclosing the firm's report on title. The firm's notepaper showed there to be two partners, Mr Lewis and Mr Williams. In fact Mr Williams was not a partner but an employee. Mr Williams sought to avoid liability on the transaction on the basis that although he had been held out as a partner the Nationwide had never placed any reliance on that fact, having in fact instructed only Mr Lewis. This argument was rejected by the judge because the acceptance letter and enclosures sent to the Nationwide came apparently from a two-partner firm. The enclosed report (the subject of the action) carried the implied *imprimatur* of both apparent partners and it was upon that report that the Nationwide had relied. But his argument was accepted by the Court of Appeal. The only person ever instructed or relied upon by the Nationwide to carry out the transaction was Mr Lewis.[91]

Further, in *Turner v Haworth Associates*[92] the plaintiff had dealt with a firm where there was in fact a sole trader and a person held out as a partner by having his name on the notepaper. The plaintiff had been sued unsuccessfully by the sole trader. In an action to recover his costs from the person so held out, the Court of Appeal refused his claim based on estoppel by representation when he said that it had made no difference to him whether he had been dealing with a partnership or a sole trader. An alternative claim based on estoppel by convention also failed on the basis that this can only work if both parties believed the representee to have been a partner and the defendant clearly had no such belief. Similarly in *Dao Heng Bank Ltd v Hui Kwai-wing*,[93] where the bank, having dealt with X as the sole proprietor of a ginseng business in Hong Kong, subsequently discovered that there were three others listed as partners in the Business Registration records. Since the bank continued to deal only with X and extended no additional credit whatsoever as a result of the additional three 'partners', it could not make them liable for the loan to the business.[94]

True nature of liability

These cases also show the clear distinction between liability on the holding-out ground and the creation of a true partnership. In *Lynch v Stiff*[95] and *Nationwide Building Society v Lewis*[96] the defendants remained at all times employees, and in *Hudgell Yeates & Co v Watson*,[97] it was precisely because Mr Smith was not at the relevant time a partner that there was no viability in Mr Watson's defence. It should be remembered that, if there is a holding out under s 14(1), not only will the person so represented be liable as if he

2.33

---

[91] But if the client has only ever dealt with, and so has relied on, the apparent partner as being a member of the firm, s 14 will apply: *All Link International Ltd v Ha Kai Cheong* [2005] 3 HKLRD 65.
[92] 8 March 1996, CA.
[93] [1977] HKLR 122.
[94] An alternative ground was that the bank had elected to deal only with X.
[95] (1944) 68 CLR 428.
[96] [1998] Ch 482, CA.
[97] [1978] 2 All ER 363, CA.

were a partner, those actually making the representation will also be liable for the consequences of making that representation. Thus in *Bass Breweries Ltd v Appleby*,[98] where a sole trader and a partnership operated under a group association agreement using a common trade name and including all the members of the group in their brochures, the Court of Appeal had little difficulty in finding that the partnership had held the sole trader out as a partner. It is less clear, however, if A holds B out as being a partner of A and C, what the precise circumstances are in which C will be liable. Section 14(1) has no direct application and thus presumably the basic rules of estoppel will apply.

For the present, however, the situation remains as expressed by Waller LJ in the *Hudgell Yeates* case:[99]

> The doctrine of holding out only applies in favour of persons who have dealt with a firm on the faith that the person whom they seek to make liable is a member of it.' [*Lindley on the Law of Partnership* (13th edn., 1971) p 108.] The fact, if it be the fact, that Mr Smith was held out as being a partner might well make the other partners liable for his actions in contract because they were holding him out as a partner. Similarly, in so far as he was holding himself out as a partner he would be making himself liable for the debts of the firm. But in each case this would not be because he was a partner but because on the facts he was being held out. When the different question is asked, was there a partnership so that the acts of the others must have been the acts of Mr Smith, my answer is no.

(It was because Bridge LJ in that case failed to make this distinction that he disagreed with the other two judges.)

Partners, Employees, and Workers

Can a partner also be an employee?

2.34 It has always been stated both judicially and academically that the concepts of partnership and employment are mutually exclusive so that one cannot be both a partner and an employee.[100] One cannot employ oneself. As recently as 2012 Rimer LJ was able to say: 'That is because in law an individual cannot be an employee of himself. Nor can a partner in a partnership be an employee of the partnership, because it is equally not possible for an individual to be employee of himself and his co-partners.'[101] The Law Commissions, recognizing that there was some doubt as to whether a Scottish partnership with its legal personality could employ a partner, consulted on the possibility of

---

[98] [1997] 2 BCLC 700, CA.
[99] [1978] 2 All ER 363, CA.
[100] See eg *Ellis v Joseph Elis &Co* [1905] 1 KB 234 and *Cowell v Quilter Goodison Co Ltd* [1989] IRLR 392.
[101] *Tiffin v Lester Aldridge LLP* [2012] EWCA Civ 35 at [31]. See also per Elias J in the CA in *Clyde & Co LLP v Bates van Winklehof* [2012] EWCA Civ 1207. At [64]–[65].

allowing all partnerships (which they suggested would have legal personality) to employ partners. Following that consultation their recommendation for all partnerships even with legal personality was negative.[102]

It came as something of a bolt out of the blue therefore when that proposition was questioned by four out of five members of the Supreme Court in *Clyde & Co LLP v Bates Van Winkelhof*.[103] That case actually involved the employment status of a member of an LLP, which, as we have seen, does have legal personality. But because of the opaque test imposed by s 4(4) of the LLP Act 2000 the issue also involved consideration of whether a partner could be an employee. Lady Hale,[104] having decided that the partnership/employment issue did not have to be decided since s 4(4) did not apply in that case,[105] nevertheless questioned why a partner could not also be an employee. She referred first to the effect of s 82 of the Law of Property Act 1925 which makes it clear that if a person contracts with himself and others it can be enforced as if it were made solely with the others. Second she pointed out that a partner could lease property to his partnership thus being both landlord and tenant, and lend money to the partnership, thus being both debtor and creditor. As a result she asked 'so why should it be legally impossible to be employed... by the partnership'.[106] That question she left hanging in the air.

Only Lord Carnwath considered that the status quo was settled law. In his view the effect of s 82 was limited to leases, and took account of the fact that partners are co-adventurers not employees. Above all there is no contract between the partner as employee and the firm but with the partners, his or her co-adventurers.[107]

Of the specific examples given by Lady Hale to suggest that partners can operate in a dual capacity, the situation on leases is far from clear. The authority quoted, *Rye v Rye*,[108] is a technical decision on s 72 of the Law of Property Act, the results of which are far from clear. The other example, loans made to a partnership by a partner, are not recoverable in the way that a normal creditor could.[109] It is all part of the distribution of assets in a solvent partnership (see Chapter 7). Although the earlier cases denying the double capacity relied on the impossibility of one person contracting with him or herself, which has clearly been altered by s 82 of the 1925 Act, they also stressed the incompatibility of being both a partner and employee. That is the real issue. Employment requires a hierarchical relationship (which is why the employee is given statutory rights) which is incompatible with an equitable relationship such as partnership, with the attendant rights and duties. The mistake is to treat the partnership as

---

[102] 'The status, right and obligations of a partner were wholly different from those of an employee' (para 13.52).
[103] [2014] UKSC 32.
[104] With whom Lord Neuberger and Lord Wilson agreed. Lord Clarke also considered that the matter should be looked at again: [2014] UKSC 32 at [54].
[105] We will return to the complex issue of LLP members and employment in Ch 12.
[106] [2014] EWSC 32 at [29].
[107] Ibid at [59].
[108] [1962] AC 496.
[109] *Green v Hertzog* [1954] 1 WLR 1309, CA.

an entity.[110] Further, the relationship is a mutual one—they are carrying on the business in common. Partnership is a unique relationship which is the antithesis of an employer–employee relationship.[111] The conflicts between the one person acting in two capacities with disparate duties owed to the same persons in each capacity would be legion.

The general question, however, has now been raised and will no doubt fall one day to be resolved, given the rights available to employees, such as unfair dismissal, which a disaffected partner might wish to use. If the answer is ever given in the positive then subsidiary questions will also arise such as to whether employment can be ascertained from the partnership agreement or whether there must be a separate contract.

For the time being, however, we must assume that one can either be a partner or an employee but not both. An employee, but not a partner, will have employment but no partnership rights (or liabilities). That of course then begs the question as to how one decides into which category a particular individual falls. But before we can consider that question, there is a second one to consider. The position is complicated by the fact that some more limited rights are given to 'workers' which has a wider definition than employees as generally understood. So could a partner also be a worker for those purposes?

Can a partner also be a worker?

2.35 The Employment Rights Act 1996 gives certain rights not just to those who work under a contract of employment (so called limb (a) workers) but also under s 230(3)(b) of that Act to any individual who has entered into or works under

> any other contract... whereby the individual undertakes to do or perform personally any work or services for another party to the contract whose status is not by virtue of the contract that of a client or customer of any profession or business undertaking carried on by the individual.

These are so called limb (b) workers. These rights include protection given to 'whistle blowers', protection against unauthorized deduction from wages, and protection under the Working Time Regulations 1998. But they do not have rights such as unfair dismissal. This category of worker therefore falls somewhere between employees under a contract of employment and those who are entirely self-employed and act entirely independently. They are in effect self-employed persons whose activities are restricted by contract. These are people who are essentially working for themselves but who in the course of carrying on their own business or profession personally perform work or services for other parties other than their clients or customers. In *Clyde & Co LLP*

---

[110] That is not so in Scotland, another point raised by Lady Hale.
[111] I have developed these points further at (2018) 6 NIBLeJ 4.

v Bates Van Winkelhof,[112] the Supreme Court held that it could include a member of a solicitors' LLP as she could not market her services as a solicitor to anyone other than the LLP.

The Supreme Court made that decision on the basis that partnership law was irrelevant to the issue but the Court of Appeal had decided that the issue had to be answered by analogy with partnership law and that being a limb (b) worker was inconsistent with partnership. They decided this on the basis that even a limb (b) worker required a degree of subordination which was incompatible with the joint venture ethos of a partnership. As Elias LJ said: 'The partnership concept is the antithesis of subordination. It is true that the contractual arrangements between the parties may, and typically do, confer different powers on different groups of partners. But the essential nature of the relationship with each partner acting as an agent for, and being responsible for the acts of other partners places them outside the sphere of employment relations entirely.'[113] Although the statutory language on its face could apply to the solicitor in question, that was negatived by the fact that partnership took the partners out of employment law altogether.

In the Supreme Court, Lady Hale was unimpressed by the subordination argument. In her view there was no single test to describe a limb (b) worker: 'There will be cases where that is not easy to do. But in my view they are not solved by adding some mystery agreement of "subordination" to the concept of employee or worker.'[114] The issue therefore is whether partnership law excludes all employment rights, however defined, or whether if, as in the cases, the words of the statute apply to the partner in question, limb (b) rights are available to such partners irrespective of that relationship. They are self-employed but they in effect perform their services for others. In the *Clyde & Co* case itself, the member of the LLP was held to be a worker even though she was involved in management, shared profits, and was subject to a duty of good faith, because her activities fell within the wording of the section. The question of incompatibility was not considered by Lady Hale. If that approach is taken with regard to partnerships it is hard to see why it would not encompass many if not all of most partners.[115]

The difference of course between a partnership and an LLP is that the 'others' in this case are the partners and not the separate legal person, the LLP. Given that the cases which established the dichotomy between partnership and employment predate the concept of a limb (b) worker it is by no means certain that partnership is incompatible with the wording of the section. A self-employed person acting only for 'the firm' might well have the rights of a limb (b) worker. If the wording of the section is applied it may not be incompatible with partnership simply on the basis of lack of legal personality.

---

[112] [2014] EWSC 32.
[113] [2012] EWCA Civ 1207 at [64]–[65].
[114] [2014] UKSC 32 at [39]. There is considerable authority, however, that the question of subordination is relevant. See eg *Windle v Farada* ULEAT/0339/13/RN citing especially *Hashwani v Jivraj* [2011] UKSC 40.
[115] See (2018) NIBLeJ 4.

That question may well be particularly apposite in respect of a fixed share partner (see below).

Importance of the distinction

2.36 The importance of the current distinction between partners and employees is, as we have seen, mainly evident in relation to their rights as against each other. An employee is entitled to the protection of the law in relation to such things as redundancy and unfair or wrongful dismissal, whereas a partner enjoys no such protection (see eg, *Tiffin v Lester Aldridge LLP*).[116] Not surprisingly therefore the question does come up before the Employment Appeal Tribunal and other industrial tribunals. The approach of the Employment Appeal Tribunal is to identify the nature of the agreement and its true meaning. To do so it is permissible to take the written agreement as the starting point and then assess all the evidence, although there is no rule to that effect.[117]

In *Palumbo v Stylianou*,[118] for instance, a hairdresser who opened a new shop left his assistant in charge of the old one, allowing him to keep the net profits (after deducting his 'wage' of £3 per week). When the assistant was dismissed the tribunal held that he was a partner and so unable to claim any redundancy payment. The result of such a finding is, of course, that the partnership had been dissolved by the dismissal and the assistant could have asked for a winding up. It is generally a question of swings and roundabouts in such situations. Thus in *Briggs v Oates*,[119] an employee who had a contract with the two partners was able to avoid a restraint of trade clause when the partnership was dissolved. The dissolution was a breach of the contract of employment and had brought it to an end. Sometimes the question arises as to whether the individual is liable for a penalty imposed upon the partnership, eg for a breach of some regulatory regime. A partner but not an employee will be subject to that penalty.[120] The setting may be different: it may be a national insurance or tax problem, but the question remains the same—is the recipient a partner under the general law of partnership—is he carrying on a business in common with a view of profit?

On the other hand, the distinction so far as persons dealing with the partnership is concerned may be far less relevant, since a person who is in law an employee may nevertheless be represented to an outsider as a partner and liable as such under s 14(1) of the Act. So that although an employee does not enjoy the implied authority of a partner to bind the firm he can easily acquire apparent authority as the result of a representation and make the whole firm liable for his acts. There are occasions, however, when the

---

[116] [2012] EWCA Civ 35.
[117] *Morrison v Aberdein Considine & Company* UKEAT/0018/17/JW.
[118] (1966) 1 TR 407.
[119] [1990] ICR 473. See also *Kao, Lee & Yip v Edwards* [1994] HKLR 232, CA.
[120] *Fox Hayes v Financial Services Authority* 2010 WL 1944393.

distinction is vital. In *Bennett v Richardson*,[121] for instance, Mr Richardson, who was blind, was sitting in the rear of a van hired by a partnership which consisted of himself and the person driving the van. The van 'had certain defects' and was uninsured. Mr Richardson was charged with using the van in contravention of various road traffic regulations all of which referred to his using, causing, or permitting the use on a road of a vehicle defective in various ways. He was acquitted by the magistrates and on appeal to the Divisional Court that acquittal was upheld. That court decided that where a person was charged with using, or causing or permitting the use of a defective vehicle which he was not actually driving, he could not be convicted unless he was the driver's employer. The fact that he was in partnership with the driver was irrelevant.

Salaried and Fixed Share Partners

Growth of salaried and fixed share partners

The distinction between partners and employees has been blurred by the development of what were initially called salaried partners and more recently fixed share partners. These positions are created to give middle ranking members of a professional firm status and rights by way of career development within the firm above an associate but which fall short of a full 'equity' partnership. They will have restricted rights as to voting and finance. They also seek to enable the holders to be taxed as self-employed rather than as employees.[122] Such a person may well be represented to the world as a partner and they may bind the firm in the same way as a full partner. Thus in *United Bank of Kuwait Ltd v Hammoud*,[123] a salaried partner in a firm of solicitors was treated by the Court of Appeal as having actual authority to represent himself as being a partner in the firm.

2.37

A judicial description of a salaried partner and the legal issues raised by such a person was given by Megarry J in *Stekel v Ellice*:[124]

> Certain aspects of a salaried partnership were not disputed. The term 'salaried partner' is not a term of art, and to some extent it may be said to be a contradiction in terms. However, it is a convenient expression which is widely used to denote a person who is held out to the world as being a partner, with his name appearing as partner on the notepaper of the firm and so on. At the same time, he receives a salary as remuneration, rather than a share of the profits, though he may, in addition to his salary, receive some bonus or other sum of money dependent upon the profits. *Quoad* the outside world it often will matter little whether a man is a full partner or a salaried partner; for a

---

[121] [1980] RTR 358, Div C.
[122] This has caused a change in tax law to identify which members of an LLP are taxable as employees. These may well be relevant to partnerships as well and are set out below.
[123] [1988] 1 WLR 1051, CA.
[124] [1973] 1 WLR 191.

salaried partner is held out as being a partner, and the partners will be liable for his acts accordingly. But within the partnership it may be important to know whether a salaried partner is truly to be classified as a mere employee, or as a partner.[125]

When it was found that salaried partners were not always being treated as self-employed by HMRC for tax purposes, a different category, the fixed share partner, was created so as to satisfy the tax authority's requirements. A typical fixed share partner is as described by the Court of Appeal in *Tiffin v Lester Aldridge LLP*.[126] A fixed share partner is usually one with some voting rights, a limited requirement to contribute some capital into the firm, and a potential right to a share of any surplus if the firm was wound up. But their remuneration is a limited and fixed share of the profits, but that is often guaranteed.

The question which now arises is whether such persons are partners or employees (or possibly also limb (b) workers as described above).

Early cases—semi-retirement issues

2.38 Prior to *Stekel v Ellice*, there was little authority as to the criteria by which to decide whether a salaried partner was merely an employee or a partner, albeit with some restricted rights. In *Re Hill*,[127] the issue arose only peripherally in connection with the equitable rule that a trustee who is a solicitor cannot make a profit from acting as a solicitor for the trust. Such a person may employ his partner as the solicitor provided it has been expressly agreed between the partners that the trustee shall himself derive no benefit from the charges made. In this case, however, there was no such agreement, but the trustee argued that since he was, by virtue of a general agreement with his partners, limited to a 'salary' of £600 a year out of the profits, and the profits without the trust work would easily cover that amount, he was not benefiting from the trust work undertaken by his partners. In deciding that the exception would not be extended so far, the Court of Appeal clearly regarded the trustee as a partner and not as an employee even though he was to do only a limited amount of work in connection with the business and take a small salary out of the profits (small compared with the firm's profits that is).

Re Hill[128] was of course concerned with the case of a salaried partner at the opposite end of the spectrum from most modern examples since the partner was semi-retired rather than aspiring to greatness. The issues are the same (ie is the individual a partner or an employee?) but it is more likely perhaps that he will be regarded as a partner since he will usually have negotiated his agreement from a position of strength as an established partner. Such partners are frequently described as 'consultants' to outsiders.

---

[125] Similar problems arise in the context of LLPs. See Ch 12, below.
[126] [2012] EWCA Civ 35 at [59].
[127] [1934] Ch 623.
[128] Ibid.

In *Marsh v Stacey*,[129] however, it is far from clear what the semi-retired partner became. One of two partners, by agreement between them, reduced his activities and instead of taking a percentage of the profits (indicative perhaps of a full partner) he agreed to accept 'a fixed salary' of £1,200 a year 'as a first charge on the profits'. In the course of his judgment in the Court of Appeal, Upjohn LJ said that he 'really became a salaried partner, as it is called, that is to say an employee of the partnership'. On the other hand the Court of Appeal held that this 'employee' could wind up the firm provided the profits amounted to more than £1,200. Employees clearly have no such rights so he must have been more than an employee. One possible explanation for this decision is that the court treated him as a creditor who was entitled to recover his debt.

Decision in *Stekel v Ellice* —the modern approach to salaried partners

Not surprisingly therefore when Megarry J in *Stekel v Ellice*[130] was faced with deciding whether a salaried partner in the modern sense was really a partner or an employee he reverted to basic principles rather than legal precedents: 'I have found it impossible to deduce any real rules from the authorities before me, and I think that, while paying due regard to those authorities, I must look at the matter on principle'. The facts of the case are illustrative of the modern salaried partner. Ellice was an accountant and in partnership when his partner died. He then agreed to employ Stekel, another accountant, at a salary of £2,000 'with a view to partnership'. In August 1968 Stekel asked about a partnership, but Ellice preferred to wait until the final account with his deceased partner's executors had been agreed and so he suggested that Stekel become a salaried partner. An agreement was signed to this effect on 1 October 1968 which was to last until 5 April 1969 when Stekel was to be entitled to a deed making him a full partner. Amongst the terms of this agreement, which continued the salary provision, was one that either 'partner' should be able to give a notice determining the partnership for specified breaches of the partnership agreement and another that all the capital, except for a few items, was to belong to Ellice. Stekel's name appeared on the firm's notepaper and he acted as a partner within the firm. His salary, however, was paid without deduction of tax (an employee's tax is deducted before payment under a system known as Pay As You Earn or PAYE whereas self-employed persons pay later directly to HMRC, which has the merit of delay but the pain of actually signing a cheque). In the event no new agreement was made in April 1969 and by August 1970 the two had separated.

2.39

Stekel now sought a dissolution and winding up of the firm. His argument was that the 1968 agreement had simply amounted to a contract of employment which had been replaced as from April 1969 by a partnership at will and, as we have seen, under such a partnership any partner may dissolve the partnership at any time by simply serving a notice

---

[129] (1963) 107 SJ 512, CA.
[130] [1973] 1 WLR 191. Followed in *All Link International Ltd & Ha Kai Cheong* [2005] HKLRD 65; *James & Wells Patent and Trade Mark Attorneys & Snoep* [2009] NZ Emp C 97.

on the other partners, which he had duly done. Ellice, on the other hand, argued that the 1968 agreement had set up a full partnership agreement between them and that this had been implicitly renewed in April 1969 by the conduct of the parties. Under that agreement there could only be a dissolution on certain specified grounds and no possibility of a general right to dissolve by notice existed. The issue was clear—did the 1968 agreement make Stekel a partner or an employee?

Having decided to revert to matters of principle, Megarry J admitted that:

> It seems to me impossible to say that as a matter of law a salaried partner is or is not necessarily a partner in the true sense. He may or may not be a partner, depending on the facts.

Substance not form

2.40 It is a question of looking at the substance of the relationship between the parties and not necessarily the labels used. Whilst Megarry J thought that many salaried partners would in fact be employees held out as being partners it was quite possible for a salaried partner to be a true partner, in particular if he was entitled to share in the profits in a winding up. On the facts of this case the terms of the agreement as to capital, dissolution, management, and accounting, indicated the existence of a partnership and the conduct of the parties and the tax position all pointed in that direction. The judge, therefore concluded that the 1968 agreement had constituted a full partnership which continued to apply.

To decide this, Megarry J had to consider s 2(3) of the Act since Mr Stekel had no 'share of the profits' within that section. But he decided that this simply meant that there was no 'prima facie' evidence of a partnership under the particular head; it did not negative the other evidence of partnership. The provisions relating to salary and capital were unusual but the remainder of the evidence pointed towards a contract of partnership and not a contract of employment. 'If it is merely a contract for employment, then it is one of the most remarkable contracts for employment that I have seen', he confirmed.

Subsequent cases on salaried partners

2.41 Subsequent cases have largely found salaried partners to be employees even though they were held out as being partners. In *Briggs v Oates*[131] Scott J analysed the position as follows:

> No doubt it was intended that the defendant would, following his appointment, be held out to the public as a partner. Nonetheless, the terms of the agreement make it clear, in my opinion, that as between [the true partners] on the one hand and the defendant on the other hand, the defendant was not a partner but remained an employee. The agreement gave him no share of the profits and imposed on him no liability for

---

[131] [1990] 1 CR 473. See also *Kao, Lee & Yip v Edwards* [1994] 1 HKLR 232, CA, where it was held that there was no mutuality as between the parties.

losses. He was to be remunerated by a combination of salary and commission on bills delivered.

Similarly in *Casson Beckman & Partners v Papi*[132] the partners of a firm of accountants were seeking to recover fees paid to Mr Papi for acting as liquidator or receiver whilst successively an employee, salaried partner, and consultant to the firm. The Court of Appeal regarded him as having been promoted to a salaried partner but it was agreed by all sides that for the purposes of this liability he should still be regarded as an employee. Since the court found that as such he had to account for the fees under a fiduciary duty it made no difference whether he was a true partner or not.

In *Nationwide Building Society v Lewis*[133] Rimer J also found that a salaried partner who had joined a sole principal in a law practice remained an employee. He was paid a fixed salary, paid tax under PAYE, had no right to any further share in the profits, and had only been willing to become a signatory on the firm's bank accounts on the bank giving him a written assurance that he would not be liable for the firm's overdraft. The fact that his name appeared on the firm's notepaper was insufficient to make him a partner. In *Summers v Smith*,[134] it was accepted that, before becoming a full partner, the individual had previously been employed by the firm, first as an assistant solicitor and then as a salaried partner.

In *Cobbetts LLP v Hodge*,[135] the defendant solicitor was held to be an employee as the deed made a clear distinction between partners and employees and placed him clearly in the latter category. The fact that he enjoyed a great deal of autonomy was consistent with his being a senior employee and the fact that he was taxed as a self-employed person was something arranged for his benefit and which did not alter his basic position.

In *Kilpatrick v Cairns*[136] it was also agreed that the salaried partner was not an employee, although he would have been better protected if he had been. His position was regulated by the partnership deed, which gave him no rights as to a share of the net assets on a dissolution. Since the partnership subsequently became a partnership at will, the salaried partner's rights ended once due notice of dissolution had been given. He had no statutory rights as an employee. The influence of the burden of proof should not be underestimated. In an internal dispute, eg as to financial entitlements, it will be on the person alleging he is a full, or equity, partner.[137]

In each case it is therefore a matter of analysing the relationship from all the evidence, written and oral. Sometimes the person wishes to be regarded as an employee (eg to

---

[132] [1991] BCLC 299, CA.
[133] [1997] 3 All ER 498.
[134] [2002] EWHC 694 (Ch).
[135] [2009] EWHC 786 (Ch).
[136] (1994) LTL, 28 December 1994.
[137] *Chua Ka Seng v Bounchai Sumpolpong* [1993] 1 SLR 482, CA.

claim for unfair dismissal), in others to be a partner (eg to wind up the firm). As we have seen one day the courts may say that one can be both, but that is not currently the law. There are no decisions yet as to a person being a worker and/or a partner (see the discussion above). Two recent examples as to the status of a salaried partner, using similar analyses, have found the person in one case to be a partner,[138] and in the other to be an employee.[139] The analyses in both cases focussed on the amount or lack of financial risk involved, the control in fact which existed between the parties eg as to supervision or independence (a matter of degree), and the nature of the remuneration, including bonuses.

Fixed share partners

2.42 In *M Young Legal Associates Ltd v Zahid*,[140] a young solicitor took on a senior solicitor as a fixed salaried partner in order to comply with the solicitors' practice rules which forbid a newly qualified solicitor from practising as a sole practitioner. The Court of Appeal held that the fixed share partner was a partner and not an employee—it was not necessary for a person to receive an actual share of the profits to be a partner so long as the business was being carried on with a view of profit. The arrangement was genuine and not a sham.

In *Fox Hayes v Financial Services Authority*,[141] the Upper Tribunal had to decide the potential liability of a number of 'partners' working for a firm to a penalty imposed by the Financial Services Authority on the firm. Two of them were described as 'salaried partners'—they did not share in the profits or goodwill, made no contribution of the firm's capital and were indemnified by the partners in respect of liabilities of the partnership. Accordingly they were not partners but employees (it being assumed that the two were mutually exclusive). Two of them were 'fixed share equity partners' who were entitled to a share of fees billed by them together with a fixed sum out of the first £505,000 of profits. They were to be regarded as partners.

In *Tiffin v Lester Aldridge LLP*,[142] Mr Tiffin was described in the members' agreement of an LLP as fixed share partner. The Court of Appeal decided that had the LLP been a partnership, Mr Tiffin would have been a partner and not an employee (which was the test required by LLP law). As in the previous case this was contrasted with the salaried partners under that agreement. Rimer LJ set out the reasoning for this:

> a reading of the members' agreement shows…[what] could fairly be regarded as a partnership relationship between the full equity partners and the fixed share partners.

---

[138] *Morrison v Aberdein Considine & Company* UKEAT/0018/17/JW.
[139] *Lewis v Narayanasamy* [2017] EWCA Civ 229.
[140] [2006] EWCA Civ 613. See also *Rowlands v Hodson* [2009] EWCA Civ 1025.
[141] 2010 WL 1944393.
[142] [2012] EWCA Civ 35.

Of course their respective commercial interests in the firm were materially different, with the full equity partners putting a good deal more into it in the way of capital and also expecting to get a good deal more out of it in the way of profits, as well as having a materially greater voice in its management. But the character of the interests in the firm of these two classes of the LLP's members was nevertheless essentially the same. All had to contribute capital. All had a prospect of a share of the profits depending upon the performance of the LLP in any particular accounting period (and it makes no difference that...the basic fixed share return of the fixed share partners was guaranteed: those partners points allocation also gave them a true interest in and share of the firm's profits). All had a prospect of a share in the surplus assets on a winding up. All had a voice in the management of the affairs of the LLP.'[143]

In the Australian case of *Griffiths v Martinez*,[144] Mr Griffiths was described as a 'fixed draw partner'. The court did not have to decide whether that made him a partner or an employee, however, as the partnership deed provided that such 'partners' could be dismissed for any ground justifying the dismissal of an employee, which was the subject of the dispute.

Tax law now has specific provisions which would designate a member of an LLP as a 'salaried member' and so taxable as an employee. Whilst this does not as such apply to partnerships, it may well form a template as to how to avoid a fixed share partner being taxed as an employee. The three criteria are: (i) receipt of payment by way of a disguised salary (ie one not in practice affected by the firm's overall profits or losses; (ii) no significant influence over the affairs of the firm; and (iii) a contribution of less than 25 per cent of the disguised salary.[145]

At the very least these are the classic indicators of the rights of fixed share partners which will be scrutinized to ascertain the true nature of the position.

Persons Having Status as a Partner

By way of contrast with the typical modern salaried or fixed share partner who is seeking a full or equity partnership in due course and whose name is included on the firm's notepaper as a first step, developments in some professional firms have seen the appointment of senior figures who are given partnership status within the firm but who cannot lawfully be partners because they are not members of the profession concerned and the rules of the profession forbid it.

2.43

The question arises whether, despite the professional rules, such a person could be in law a partner. Since the firm concerned will have taken steps not to represent an

---

[143] Ibid at [59].
[144] [2019] NSWSC 664.
[145] Income Tax (Trading and Other Income) Act 2005, ss 863A, 863B.

unqualified person as being a partner so as not to infringe professional rules, the question here is not whether he or she would be liable to third parties but whether for internal or tax purposes he is a partner or an employee. In that respect the issues are the same as for salaried partners.

Such an issue arose in the tax case of *Horner v Hasted*.[146] Mr Horner, having worked for the Inland Revenue, joined the accounting firm of Kidsons. Not being a chartered accountant he could not be made a partner, although it was clear that if it had been possible he would have been. Thus his name was never included on any document as being a partner. But he was of such importance to the firm that he was given the status equivalent to that of a partner and he was remunerated by reference to a share of the profits. He attended and voted at partnership meetings, participated in the management of the firm, and signed important internal documents. He lent money to the firm of an amount equivalent to a partner's capital contribution and received interest on it in the same way as a partner.

Despite all those factors, Lightman J held that Mr Horner remained at all times an employee—none of those factors was inconsistent with a contract of employment. It was an unusual contract of employment in unusual circumstances. The fact that he was not under the control of anyone else was no longer of prime importance in defining an employee. In addition there were factors which pointed to his being an employee. He contributed to the firm's pension scheme and paid income tax and national insurance as an employee; he could not sign cheques.

If this decision is correct, it is difficult to envisage circumstances in which such 'partner status' individuals would be treated as partners. It is perhaps interesting to observe, however, that Lightman J, being concerned only as to whether the decision of the Special Commissioner that the taxpayer was an employee was justified, concentrated on the criteria for being an employee and never asked himself the question whether Mr Horner was carrying on a business in common with the other partners with a view of profit. Once again the answer to a question may be seen to depend upon the question being asked. The position may not therefore be quite as clear as at first sight.

---

[146] [1995] STC 766.

3
LEGAL CONTROLS ON PARTNERSHIPS

Public and Private Controls

I have already stressed the essentially voluntary nature of the 1890 Act in relation to partnerships. This is not surprising in that the major formative developments took place in a laissez-faire age, but what is rather more surprising is that to a large extent the extensive review conducted by the Law Commissions showed that this attitude still applies today. This is in sharp contrast with modern companies legislation.[1] Company law is not simply more technical than it was 100 years ago, it has also become more pervasive and inquisitive. Companies are regarded as part of the public domain, so that not only is there compulsory registration of information on formation (which is then open to all who take the trouble to look), but a continuing and ever-expanding disclosure requirement whilst the company is a going concern. Even after the 2006 reforms there is still a considerable amount of regulation applicable to small, closely held businesses operating as companies.[2] If public investment is required there are also all the rules for admission to listing on the Stock Exchange to be complied with. There are provisions for instigating both company and Department of Business, Innovations and Skills investigations into the ownership or conduct of companies. Even such historically unregulated areas as take overs are now governed by a complex code of rules devised by the City itself.[3]

3.01

A considerable amount of the law relating to the public control of companies has also been applied to LLPs, including the intrusive Persons with Significant Control (PSC) Regulations. It is the price of limited liability (see Chapter 10). Limited partnerships too, because of suspected misuse, are coming under increasing scrutiny in that regard. The PSC Regulations already apply to Scottish limited partnerships (LPs) (see Chapter 9).

Partnerships, on the other hand, have in the main avoided such restrictions—there is no public disclosure[4] (a weak form of registration where a business name was used disappeared after 1981) and no machinery for public inquiries into their activities. The historical reasons for this are many. Partnerships on the whole were small concerns in

---

[1] The Companies Act 2006 originally had 1,300 sections and 16 schedules. It has also spawned a plethora of secondary legislation.
[2] The 2006 Act removed some of these, eg as to meetings and financial assistance for the acquisition of shares. The Small Business, Enterprise and Employment Act 2015 has, however, added more back on.
[3] Now under a statutory framework: see the Companies Act 2006, ss 942–965.
[4] Except for limited partnerships.

economic terms, whilst the larger ones were professional firms controlled by codes of conduct and disciplinary bodies. Above all, perhaps, they do not have limited liability. In short, partnerships rarely enter the public domain and their regulation is largely left to the settlement of private disputes either between partners inter se or between partners and those who deal with them. In such cases, of course, the law is called upon to resolve those disputes, but those usually involve the application of accepted private law concepts such as agency and constructive trusts.

Areas of public interest

3.02 There are nevertheless three general areas where the public interest, either directly by legislation or through the doctrine of public policy worked out by the courts, does limit partnership activities and it is with those areas that this chapter is principally concerned. In addition there are areas where the State or its institutions, having devised a system for a particular purpose, for example, to collect taxes or national insurance or to regulate the investment industry, has to assimilate partnerships into such a system. One example is the legal system itself which requires a set form of procedure for litigation and has to include partnerships. It has also long been established that the fact of an insolvency requires intervention in an attempt to provide an orderly and civilized compromise between the defrauding of creditors and the debtors' prison—again partnerships have to be incorporated into the system. In fact it is in this general area, the assimilation of partnerships into systems designed for individuals, that their lack of legal personality has caused most problems (companies and LLPs, being separate legal persons, present far fewer problems—they are either regarded as equivalent to individuals for this purpose, eg the legal system, or an entirely different system is evolved for them, eg corporation tax). Even if the Law Commissions' proposals as to legal personality had been implemented, the intention was to leave the tax position of partnerships as transparent as it mainly is for LLPs. As it is, the other problems of assimilation are still with us and are dealt with at the end of this chapter.

Restrictions on three freedoms

3.03 As mentioned above there are public controls on three general areas of partnership life. The first of these is the area of freedom of contract. Partnerships are in essence a specialized form of contract and thus require all the elements needed for a contract (above all an offer and acceptance or *consensus ad idem*). In addition, however, they are subject to those restrictions on the power to contract which apply generally—questions such as capacity, undue influence, and illegality. They are also subject to the control of the courts if the terms of the agreement are contrary to public policy—this is particularly true of restraint-of-trade clauses in professional partnership agreements. These are clauses which attempt to limit a partner's business activities both in area and scope if he leaves the firm. They seem in recent times to have caused particular problems for doctors and solicitors. Another common clause, an arbitration clause, is also regulated in the sense that if arbitration is desired it becomes subject to the specialized laws on arbitration and its procedures, especially the attempt by the Arbitration Act 1996 to limit any subsequent appeal to the courts.

The second area of control relates to the freedom of association. Partnerships were until comparatively recently limited in size (usually by provisions in the Companies Acts—a historical anomaly that was perpetuated by the 1948 and 1985 consolidations) although it is true that such limitations had been relaxed considerably by the time of their repeal. Whilst that restriction no longer applies, there are still other restrictions relating to the composition of particular professional partnerships. The third area of control is a mixed area of legislation and case law. It applies to the freedom to trade under a chosen business name. This freedom is now restricted by Part 41 of the Companies Act 2006 in that certain names are prohibited, others need permission, and most require disclosure of the partners' names on relevant documents and buildings. Choice of business name is also restricted by the common law tort of passing off whereby one trader is prevented from diverting trade from another by the use of a similar name.

Restrictions on the Freedom to Contract

Capacity and discrimination

Capacity used to be a more dominant issue than it is today. One of the reasons for this is that two of the potential categories of parties who had limited capacity to contract, namely married women and companies, now have full capacity. In fact the pendulum swung the other way with the Sex Discrimination Act 1975 and the Race Relations Act 1976, both of which applied to partnerships. Discrimination is now governed by the Equality Act 2010 which prohibits both direct and indirect discrimination[5] in a number of activities on grounds of age,[6] disability, gender reassignment, marriage and civil partnership, race, religion or belief, sex, and sexual orientation. Section 44 of the Act specifically provides that partnerships (or proposed partnerships) must not so discriminate, harass, or victimize a person on the appointment or non-appointment of a partner, on the terms and internal conduct of the partnership relationship, on the expulsion of a partner or by subjecting that person to any other detriment. Some guidance on what this means can be found from the case of *Ali v Torrosian*,[7] where one doctor employed by a family medical practice was dismissed on grounds of capability, after having a heart attack and then damaging his shoulder. The Employment Appeal Tribunal held that since there was a possibility of his being able to work part time, the

3.04

---

[5] That is where A applies a discriminatory provision, criterion, or practice against B. Equality Act 2010, s 19. See, eg *Murray v Maclay Murray Spens LLP* [2018] IRLR 710.
[6] This is not an absolute ground as social policy is also taken into account. See eg *Seldon v Clarkson Wright and Jakes* [2010] EWCA Civ 899 in the partnership context on compulsory retirement at 65.
[7] (2018) UKEAT/0029/18/JOJ.

failure to discuss it with him made the dismissal potentially unfair on discriminatory disability grounds. The position would surely have been the same if he had been a partner. There is also a duty to make reasonable adjustments for disabled persons.

The liability of partners for discrimination against a partner (including a corporate partner whose principal shareholder is discriminated against)[8] was discussed by Warren J in *Hammonds v Danilunas*.[9] Whilst it was clear that if all the other partners were guilty of discrimination they could all be sued as being 'the firm', the judge was less clear whether if, say, there had been a 7/3 split between the other partners, the three dissentient partners could be sued. That was on the basis that the majority who committed the unlawful act, of discrimination, would be in breach of their duty of good faith both to the partner discriminated against and the dissenting partners. The position would be even more complicated if there were two partners so discriminated against. Could each of them sue the other as being part of the firm? With respect to the judge it does seem that such issues are really best solved by the law of agency and the authority of the discriminators to bind the firm.[10]

The remaining categories of limited capacity are minors, enemy aliens, and persons of unsound mind. The latter have capacity, it seems, so long as they are capable of appreciating the nature of the agreement. Great care is needed in such cases, however, since intervening insanity no longer automatically dissolves a partnership. The modern law, quite rightly, is concerned to protect the mental patient and not his partners.

Since the Family Law Reform Act 1969 and the Age of Majority (Scotland) Act 1969, the age of majority in the United Kingdom has been 18, so that on attaining that age an individual attains full legal capacity. Until that age he or she is no longer referred to as an infant but as a minor. A minor does have the capacity to become a partner—the law is still very much as laid down by the House of Lords in *Lovell and Christmas v Beauchamp*.[11] That case established that although a minor can become a partner and be entitled to a share in the profits of a firm he or she cannot personally be sued for the firm's debts, whereas the adult partners are fully liable for debts incurred by the minor on behalf of the firm. The adult partners are, however, entitled to have any capital contributed by the minor applied in satisfaction of the firm's debts and to deduct any losses from his undrawn or future share of the profits. It is not possible, however, for the adult partners to hide behind the minor in order to evade responsibility for partnership debts.

Prior to reaching 18, a minor may repudiate the partnership agreement but once he or she has reached that age he must decide within a reasonable time whether to do so. By simply carrying on he or she will automatically become a full partner although

---

[8] *EAD Solicitors LLP v Abrams* UKEAT/0054/15/DM.
[9] [2009] EWHC 216 (Ch).
[10] For the position with LLPs see *Murray v Maclay Murray Spens LLP* [2018] IRLR 710.
[11] [1894] AC 607, HL.

he or she will still not be liable for debts incurred during his or her infancy: *Goode v Harrison*.[12] If he or she repudiates a contract to enter into a partnership he or she can recover any premiums paid on the basis that there has been a total failure of consideration: *Steinberg v Scala (Leeds) Ltd*.[13]

Closely linked to questions of capacity are the equitable concepts of undue influence and unconscionable bargain. If it can be established that a person entered into a partnership contract on unfavourable terms due to the undue influence of the other party,[14] the court may declare the agreement to be void and order the return of any property and award damages. It seems, however, that in some cases the other partners may be able to retain part of the firm's profits—see *O'Sullivan v Management Agency & Music Ltd*.[15] To establish that the person was a vulnerable person who was persuaded into an unconscionable bargain, it is not enough to show that the agreement was commercially disadvantageous. The agreement will only be set aside if there is an element of moral culpability on the part of the defendants, eg having behaved in a morally reprehensible way.[16]

Illegality

In general terms a partnership is illegal if it is formed for a purpose prohibited either by statute or at common law. The latter relates to the upholding of current ideas of morality, religion, or public policy. Clearly such grounds are continually shifting and the older cases should be read with some care. In times of war it is illegal for a person resident in this country to form a partnership with a person resident in an enemy country. A partnership formed to commit, or assist in, or benefit from a criminal offence is equally obviously illegal. (If you dig back through the old cases you can find a partnership dispute involving two highwaymen—much good it did them for it appears that they were both hanged.)

3.05

A partnership agreement is illegal not only if the purpose for which the partnership is formed is illegal but also, although the purpose is one which could be attained by legal means, it is carried out in an illegal way. For an unpleasant example of this see the South African case of *Karstein v Moribe*[17] involving the apartheid laws.

The modern cases as to whether there is any illegality involve the application of regulatory statutes to partnerships. In some cases the public policy is the protection of personal welfare (eg the legal and medical professions). In others it is a matter of economic or social regulation. In each case the purpose of the statute is central. Thus in

---

[12] (1821) 5 B & Ald 147.
[13] [1923] 2 Ch 452.
[14] For a detailed analysis of undue influence see *RBS v Etridge* [2002] 2 AC 773 and the speech of Lord Nicholls.
[15] [1985] 3 All ER 351, CA.
[16] *Choudary v Minhas* [2006] EWHC 2289 (Ch).
[17] 1982 2 SA 282 (T).

Dungate v Lee[18] Dungate and Lee agreed to set up a bookmaking business at Newhaven, contributing £500 each to the business. Lee obtained a betting licence. Dungate had no bookmaker's permit. Although there was no written agreement it was orally agreed that only Lee was to deal directly with customers over the counter and that in fact became the practice. Dungate handled credit betting on the telephone. Following a dispute, Dungate brought an action for dissolution of the partnership and Lee argued that the partnership was in any event illegal under the Betting and Gaming Act 1960 which required every bookmaker to have a permit. Buckley J refused to allow the argument since the 1960 Act did not require every *partner* to have a permit and since the agreement did not require Dungate to carry on the practice of bookmaking himself it could not be said that the partnership was formed for an illegal purpose.

Similarly, in the Canadian case of *Continental Bank Leasing Corporation v The Queen*,[19] a question arose as to the validity of a partnership between the subsidiary of a bank and other companies. Under the Bank Act of Ontario a bank may not directly or indirectly participate in a partnership in Canada. The Supreme Court of Canada held that the business of the partnership was not rendered illegal merely because the investor bank held shares in a corporate partner in the partnership when the law said it should not. The partnership had to be distinguished from those who may invest or support the partners that make it up.

But if the partnership business is contravening the purpose of the statute then it will be illegal. Thus in *Pham v Doan*,[20] where a registered pharmacist and a non-pharmacist were partners in a pharmacy business, this was held to be illegal as being contrary to the New South Wales statute which prohibited any non-pharmacists from being involved in the financial benefits of such a business.

The consequences of illegality as a defence to a civil claim (in our case relating to an illegal partnership) were radically reset in 2016 by the Supreme Court in *Patel v Mirza*.[21] The court consisted of no fewer than nine justices, and the majority (six) held that it was no longer the law that a party to an illegal agreement could not enforce a claim against the other party simply because he had to rely on his own illegal conduct to establish the claim. Instead it was for the court to assess whether the public interest would be harmed by enforcing the illegal agreement. This requires consideration of (a) the underlying purpose of the relevant prohibition and whether that purpose will be enhanced by denial of the claim; (b) any other relevant public policy which might be impacted; and (c) whether denial of the claim was a proportionate response to the illegality, given that punishment is a matter for the criminal courts. Within that framework various factors may be relevant but a principled and transparent approach is needed, not a dogmatic

---

[18] [1967] 1 All ER 241.
[19] [1998] 2 SCR 298.
[20] [2005] NSWSC 201 (16 March 2005).
[21] [2016] UKSC 42.

Restraint-of-trade Clauses

Assessing the validity

Many partnerships contain a clause prohibiting a partner who leaves the firm from subsequently competing with it, usually within a stated area and for a specified time. If such a clause is regarded as unreasonable by the courts it will be void as being in restraint of trade. The basic presumption is that such clauses are unreasonable as being in breach of the public's interest in everyone being able to carry on his trade or profession freely, so that if the remaining partners wish to enforce it they must show that the clause is reasonable both as between the parties and also in the interests of the public. The courts have, in deciding what is reasonable, paid great attention to the type of contract involved and the relative bargaining strength of the parties. Thus they are suspicious of any such clause in a contract of employment but much more lenient with regard to a clause inserted by the purchaser of a business and its goodwill on the vendor. The issue is perhaps best expressed as to whether there was mutuality as between the parties as to benefits and burdens and did they make the agreement on an equal footing? Restraint-of-trade clauses in partnership agreements are usually akin to the latter type since the partners will have negotiated on an equal basis. But that might not be true if, say, a junior doctor is seeking to join an established practice,[22] or one of the parties is in fact an employee, although referred to as a salaried partner.[23] Where the salaried partner is found to be an employee, a restraint of trade clause may cease to be enforceable if there is a dissolution of the firm, since the dissolution may be a breach of the contract of employment. This was held in *Briggs v Oates*[24] but on the basis that the contract was with both of the true partners and not with the proprietor(s) of the business for the time being.

3.06

In *Bridge v Deacons*[25] Lord Fraser of Tullybelton suggested that it was pointless to equate partnership clauses with either the vendor–purchaser or employer–employee categories, and that the courts should simply ascertain what the legitimate interests of the remaining partners are which they are entitled to protect, and then see whether the proposed restraints are more than adequate for that purpose. As to the ascertainment of these 'legitimate interests', that, he said, will depend largely on the nature of the firm and the position of the former partner within that firm. Questions of mutuality are

---

[22] See, eg *Kaliszer v Ashley*, 14 June 2001, Ch, per Judge Reid QC.
[23] *Kao, Lee & Yip v Edwards* [1994] 1 HKLR 232, CA. There is also no mutuality—a salaried partner does not receive the full benefits of an equity partner.
[24] [1990] 1 CR 473.
[25] [1984] 1 AC 705, HL.

inherent in this. If to this test is added the criterion of a possible public interest in the prevention of restraint of trade in a particular area then the test would appear to be complete. It should be stressed that if the clause is wider than is reasonable in such circumstances it may be cut down entirely, although the offending part may be severed (see below).

In *Espley v Williams*[26] the Court of Appeal said that there were three questions to be answered before such a clause could be enforced: (a) does the complainant have a legitimate interest capable of being protected, ie is the firm still trading? (b) is the covenant no more than adequate to protect that interest in terms of area, duration, and prohibited activities? and (c) without the enforcement of the covenant, could the interest be damaged? In that case the Court of Appeal upheld a covenant in an estate agents' partnership which prohibited a former partner from acting as an estate agent within a radius of two miles. The remaining partner had a legitimate interest to protect as he was continuing the business and the two-mile radius was essential since that covered the area of which the former partner would have specialist knowledge and within which the firm was operating.

A significant development in the effectiveness of restraint of trade clauses was the unanimous Supreme Court decision in *Egon Zehender Ltd v Tilman*.[27] Although it was not a partnership case, it concerned a professional employee in a very similar position to a partner. Ms Tilman, although an employee of the company, was promoted to 'partner' within the company and became the co-global head of the financial services practice group. She then gave notice to the company, which put her on garden leave and then terminated her appointment. She now wished to work for a US firm, but Egon sought to apply a detailed restrictive covenant which, inter alia, prevented her from being 'interested in any business carried on in competition with any of their businesses' for six months after termination. The Supreme Court agreed with the Court of Appeal that this wording would prevent her from owning any shares, even a minority holding, in a competitor and so was unreasonable and unenforceable. It was irrelevant that she was not proposing to buy any such shares. But the Supreme Court, disagreeing with the Court of Appeal and reversing previous cases, held that the words 'interested in' could be severed from the clause, thus leaving the remainder of the clause specifically preventing employment with a rival, enforceable. The test for severance was whether removal of the provision would not generate any major change in the overall effect of all the post-employment restraints in the contract.

Medical partnerships

3.07 A medical partnership may have two different types of goodwill to protect—that attaching to its National Health Service practice and that attaching to its private practice.

---

[26] [1997] 08 EG 137, CA.
[27] [2019] UKSC 32.

In *Hensman v Traill*,[28] Bristow J decided that no restriction at all could be taken by the remaining partners in relation to the National Health Service since any restriction on a doctor from complying with his obligations to care for patients under the then National Health Service Act 1977 was contrary both to the Act (s 54 of which prohibited the 'sale' of such goodwill) and public policy. However, the Court of Appeal in *Kerr v Morris*[29] overruled that decision. Although the NHS goodwill still cannot generally be sold,[30] it is a valuable asset of the firm which the partners were entitled to protect by a reasonable restraint-of-trade clause; nor is such a restraint contrary to public policy per se, since a doctor's patients had no right to require him to stay in a particular area. For an example of the public interest in a country without the NHS see the Canadian case of *Baker v Lintott*.[31]

The test of reasonableness with respect to medical partnerships has not been applied uniformly over the years. In *Whitehill v Bradford*[32] a covenant not to 'carry on or be interested or concerned in carrying on the business or profession of medicine, surgery, midwifery or pharmacy or any branch thereof' within ten miles and for twenty-one years was upheld, whereas in *Lyne-Pirkis v Jones*[33] the Court of Appeal rejected a clause which required the former parties 'not to engage in practice as a medical practitioner' as being too wide. This approach was approved by Plowman J in *Peyton v Mindham*[34] when he rejected a clause that the outgoing doctor should not 'advise, attend, prescribe for or treat any person who is or has during the subsistence of the partnership been a patient of the partnership'. The reason given in both cases was that the clauses could preclude consultancy work and such a prohibition was unnecessary to protect the remaining partner, who therefore lost his entire protection for the goodwill of the practice.

On the other hand in *Clarke v Newland*,[35] the Court of Appeal upheld a clause which prohibited a partner in a general medical practice from practising within a defined area for three years after leaving the firm. The defendant who had set up a general practice within 100 yards of the firm's surgery claimed that the prohibition was too wide since it could include all forms of medical practice such as consultancy. The Court of Appeal decided that such agreements should be construed in context in the light of the factual matrix and by reference to the object sought. The restriction on 'practising' clearly needed some clarification and there was no good reason why it should not be construed as 'practising as a *general* medical practitioner'. As such it was clearly reasonable to protect the plaintiff's business. Further in *Kaliszer v Ashley*[36]

---

[28] The Times, 22 October 1980.
[29] [1987] Ch 90, CA.
[30] See the complex rules under the Primary Medical Services (Sale of Goodwill and Restrictions on Subcontracting) Regs 2004 (SI 2004/906) which make a basic distinction between essential and other services.
[31] [1982] 4 WWR 766.
[32] [1952] 1 All ER 115.
[33] [1969] 1 WLR 1293, CA.
[34] [1972] 1 WLR 8.
[35] [1991] 1 All ER 397.
[36] 14 June 2001, Ch.

94 LEGAL CONTROLS ON PARTNERSHIPS

the court upheld a covenant which restricted an outgoing general practitioner from treating existing patients of the practice for one year within a radius of three miles. It was manifestly reasonable— they could set up practice in any area, even next door to the existing surgery.

Solicitors' partnerships

3.08 In the case of solicitors, the Court of Appeal, in *Oswald Hickson Collier & Co v Carter-Ruck*,[37] stated that it is contrary to public policy for a solicitor to be prevented from acting for a client when that client wants him to act, particularly in litigation. It followed, therefore, that a restraint-of-trade clause in a partnership deed which prevents one of the partners acting for a client in the future would be contrary to public policy since there is a fiduciary relationship between a solicitor and his client and the client ought reasonably to be entitled to the services of whichever solicitor he wishes. However, the same court in *Edwards v Worboys*[38] refused to regard this as a matter of general principle and the Privy Council in *Bridge v Deacons*[39] 'respectfully and emphatically' declined to agree with it. It was said to be unjustified either on the authorities or in principle.

Decision in *Bridge v Deacons*

3.09 *Bridge v Deacons* is in fact also an interesting example of the application of the reasonableness test in relation to solicitors. The firm, established in Hong Kong, had twenty-seven partners and forty-nine assistant solicitors. It worked through self-contained specialist departments. Mr Bridge became a full partner in 1974 in charge of the intellectual property division (about 10 per cent of the total work of the firm). He was charged a nominal amount for goodwill. In 1982 he resigned from the firm and received a substantial amount for his share in the firm although only a nominal amount for his goodwill. He then set up practice on his own account in Hong Kong. The firm now sought to enforce a clause in the partnership agreement that no former partner should act as a solicitor in Hong Kong for five years for any client of the firm or any person who had been a client in the three years before he left. Applying the test of legitimate protection of the remaining partners, the Privy Council regarded this clause as being reasonable both in scope and time. In particular they rejected Mr Bridge's argument that since he had only been concerned with 10 per cent of the firm's clients he was being unreasonably restricted in respect of the other 90 per cent. The firm was a single practice for the mutual benefit of all the partners—whilst a partner he had enjoyed the protection of this clause. The low nominal value paid for the goodwill was irrelevant since he had paid a nominal amount for it. The court not only rejected the

---

[37] [1984] AC 720, HL, (1982) 126 SJ 120, CA.
[38] (1983) 127 SJ 287, CA.
[39] [1984] AC 705, PC.

argument that such clauses were always void for public policy reasons but in fact regarded this clause as being in the public interest since it encouraged younger people to join the firm and also tended to secure continuity of the firm which was beneficial to clients.

Bridge v Deacons distinguished

However, in *Dallas McMillan & Sinclair v Simpson*,[40] the Court of Session held as unreasonable a clause preventing a partner in a firm of solicitors in Glasgow from directly or indirectly carrying on business as a solicitor, except with the firm, within twenty miles of Glasgow Cross. Such a clause was too wide, both geographically since it covered about half the law firms in Scotland, and in scope, since it prevented the former partner from practising as an employee or even as a duty legal aid solicitor, a field of law in which the firm was not concerned. *Bridge v Deacons* had only applied to former clients; this was a very different clause. The court reaffirmed the basic principle that a restraint-of-trade clause will be invalid unless it is reasonable to protect the legitimate interests of the firm.

3.10

Bridge v Deacons was also distinguished by the Hong Kong Court of Appeal in *Kao, Lee & Yip v Edwards*.[41] In that case the defendant had been an employed salaried partner and so the court found that the concept of mutuality of benefit and burdens as between the parties, present in *Deacons*, was missing. Nor had there been equality of bargaining power. The court then found that a five-year worldwide ban on doing 'any work or act normally done by solicitors' was far wider than necessary to protect the plaintiffs' interests. In *Deacons* it had been limited to Hong Kong. The firm was not an international firm and had no interest, therefore, in whether the defendant practised in England during that period. It was a covenant aimed at stifling competition and not a protection of legitimate interests.

Enforcement

If the court decides that a restraint-of-trade clause can be upheld, it may grant an injunction to enforce its terms. The granting of an injunction is entirely discretionary and can be subject to undertakings from the plaintiffs. One example is *Voaden v Voaden*.[42] In that case a partner was obliged to give one year's notice of his intention to leave the partnership and could not within one year of leaving act as a chartered surveyor (the business of the firm). The defendant in fact left the firm by negotiation three months after giving his notice. He then proceeded to break various undertakings he had given as to his activities after leaving the firm. The judge granted an injunction against him

3.11

---

[40] 1989 SLT 454.
[41] [1994] 1 HKLR 232, CA.
[42] 21 February 1997. For a recent example as to the protection of confidential information in a professional employee case, see *Acquinas Education Ltd v Miller* [2018] EWHC 404, QB.

acting in any way as a chartered surveyor (subject to minor exceptions) up to the end of the year's notice but subject to an undertaking by the plaintiffs that they would remunerate him for that period as if he had been a partner.

Even if the restraint-of-trade clause is held to be unreasonable, a partner who leaves without agreement in breach of a notice provision may be liable in damages—but the non-enforceability of the clause may reduce those damages. This happened in the Canadian case of *Ernst & Young v Stuart*[43] where, because the restraint-of-trade clause was held to be unenforceable, the damages payable by the errant partner were reduced on the basis that even if due notice had been given he might not have stayed the full year as required and that the business he obtained for his new firm might not have gone to his former firm.

Restrictions on Freedom of Association

3.12 People used to be restricted from forming partnerships in two ways. First for most partnerships there was a maximum number of twenty partners allowed by law. There was no limit, however, for specified partnerships such as solicitors, accountants, stockbrokers, general medical practitioners, patent agents, surveyors, valuers, actuaries, consulting engineers, building designers, loss adjusters, town planners, lawyers in a multinational firm, members of the Stock Exchange, those carrying on an authorized investment business, and trade mark agents.

The Law Commissions initially suggested that the restrictions on size were outdated. They arose out of the need to prevent difficulties in enforcing claims which had long since disappeared. In any event there were a number of exceptions, many ways to avoid the restriction (eg by having corporate partners), and they were a barrier to multi-disciplinary partnerships. This view was also shared by the DTI, which, having consulted[44] on the abolition of the twenty-partner limit, abolished it.[45] There are thus now no numerical limits on partnerships of any kind.[46]

The remaining restriction on association stems from the regulation of individual professions. Thus, despite the Courts and Legal Services Act 1990, there are still some restrictions on solicitors forming partnerships with non-lawyers. There are also restrictions in many other areas and barristers are prohibited from forming partnerships at all.

---

[43] (1997) 144 DLR (4th) 328.
[44] URN 01/752. Over 75% of the responses were in favour of abolition.
[45] Regulatory Reform (Removal of 20 Member Limit in Partnerships) Order 2002 (SI 2002/ 3203).
[46] The 2002 Order also amended s 4(2) of the Limited Partnership Act 1907 to remove a similar restriction on limited partnerships.

Restrictions on Choice of Business Name

Until 1982 all business names used by firms had to be registered under the Registration of Business Names Act 1916 at a central registry. Registration was of little legal significance since it did not lead to constructive notice of the facts so registered. The 1916 Act and the register were abolished by the Companies Act 1981. The 1981 Act replaced the old system with a new one which is designed to control the use of certain words or expressions in business names and to require disclosure of the partners' names to potential customers and suppliers. These provisions were then consolidated in the Business Names Act 1985. They are now in Part 41 of the Companies Act 2006.

3.13

Application of Part 41 of the Companies Act 2006

The restrictions apply by virtue of ss 1192 and 1200 to all partnerships in the United Kingdom which carry on a business here under a name which does not consist only of the surnames of all individual partners and corporate names of all the corporate partners and certain 'permitted additions'. These additions are the forenames or initials of the partners, the letter 's' at the end of a surname which belongs to two or more of the partners, and anything which merely indicates that the business is being carried on in succession to a former owner of the business. Thus any partnership which is of any size must be caught by the sections together with any firm using a trade name rather than the surnames of the partners. It is an interesting question as to whether a group partnership is a separate partnership for this purpose. Even the addition of '& Co' at the end will render the firm liable to the provisions of the Act. (It is a criminal offence for a partnership to use the abbreviation 'Ltd' by virtue of the Company, Limited Liability Partnerships and Business (Names and Trading Disclosures) Regulations, 2015.[47])

3.14

Limitations on choice of name

If the sections apply, then ss 1193 to 1197 provide limitations on the choice of business name. The written approval of the Secretary of State for Business, Energy and Industrial Strategy is needed before a business can use any name which is likely to give the impression that the business is connected with any of the UK the governments, or any local authority, or specified public authority. In addition, for certain other words and expressions, such approval is required and, if appropriate, a written request must first be made to 'the relevant body' for their comments which must then be forwarded to the Department of Business, Energy and Industrial Strategy. These words and expressions, which include their plural and possessive forms, and the relevant body, if any, can be found in the Company, Limited Liability Partnerships and Business Names (Sensitive

3.15

---

[47] SI 2015/17, reg 17 and Sch 2.

Words and Expressions) Regulations 2014.[48] These words or expressions run from 'accredit' to 'Windsor' through such words as 'Chamber of Commerce', 'midwife', and 'university'. To take one practical example of how the system works, any firm wanting to use the phrase 'district nurse' in its name must ask the Panel of Assessors in District Nurse Training for its opinion which must then be sent on to the Department of Business, Energy and Industrial Strategy (which must have been informed that such an opinion has been sought) for its decision. If approval is given it may be subsequently withdrawn on public policy grounds, under s 1196. Unapproved use of any such names is a criminal offence under s 1194(3).

There is also a general prohibition on a partnership using a name 'that gives so misleading an indication of the nature of the activities of the business as to be likely to cause harm to the public'.[49] This restriction, new in the 2006 Act, simply provides that a breach will be a criminal offence and unlike its, older, equivalent for company names (s 76) does not allow the Secretary of State to order a change of name.

Disclosure of names of partners

3.16 The Act also provides, in ss 1201[50] to 1204, that a partnership subject to Part 41 must disclose the name of each partner, and an address for each of them at which service of a writ or similar document will be effective, on all its business documents (letters, orders, receipts, invoices etc) and at the business premises by a notice displayed in a prominent place. If the firm has a place of business in the UK, that address must be in the UK. If the partnership does not have a place of business in the United Kingdom, then there must be an effective address in the UK for service of documents. Business premises for this purpose include premises to which suppliers as well as customers have access. The same information must be given to any one who asks for it during the course of the business. The obligation to list each partner on a business document would clearly be inconvenient for a very large firm and so if there are more than twenty partners that requirement will be satisfied by the keeping of a list of the partners at the firm's principal place of business and a statement in the document of the existence and location of such a list and of its availability for public inspection. No partner's names must then be on the document except in the text or as signatory. The list must be so available during office hours—refusal of inspection is a criminal offence. Such firms must, however, comply with the display requirement at their premises and in addition any partner must produce a written list of the partners 'immediately' on a request from 'any person with whom anything is done or discussed in the course of the business'.

Failure to comply with these disclosure requirements may have limited civil consequences for the firm. Section 1206 provides that the firm cannot enforce an action based on any contract made whilst it was in breach of the sections if the defendant has

---

[48] SI 2014/3140.
[49] Section 1198.
[50] Section 1201 was substituted by SI 2009/3182.

shown either that he could not pursue a claim against the partnership because of the breach or that he has suffered financial loss as a result of it. This protection is only available to the other party as a defendant, however, and lapses if he brings a counterclaim. But in circumstances where s 1206 does not apply, the Scottish case of *Nigel Lowe & Associates v John Mowlem Construction plc*[51] decided that a firm which it was alleged had made a contract in breach of that section's predecessor could confess its breach of that section and show by other means that the contract was in fact made by the partnership and not just the person whose name was on the letterhead.

Passing-off actions

The Companies Act does not prevent more than one firm from using the same or a similar name nor does it prevent a firm from using a business name similar to that of a registered company, LLP, or partnership or vice versa. To protect the goodwill and reputation of the firm, therefore, the partners may be forced to rely on the tort of passing off. This is designed to provide a remedy by way of damages or, more usefully, by way of injunction for an injury to the legitimate trading reputation of a company, partnership, or other business. This rationale was expressed by Astbury J in *Ewing v Buttercup Margarine Co Ltd*:[52]

3.17

> The ground of interference by the court in these name cases is that the use of the defendant['s] name, or intended name, is calculated to deceive, and 'so to divert business from the plaintiff to the defendant', or 'to occasion a confusion between the two businesses': *Kerly on Trade Marks*, 4th ed., p. 568.

To establish a passing-off action the claimant must show: (i) that their goods or services had acquired goodwill in the market and were known by some distinguishing name or other indication; (ii) there was a misrepresentation by the defendants which could lead the public to believe that goods or services offered by them were those of or connected with the claimants; and (iii) the claimants had suffered damage from the misrepresentation.[53] Mere confusion on the part of customers (as ordinary members of the public) is not enough. There has to be deception or risk of deception.[54] In the case of a partnership, the goodwill so acquired for that purpose usually belongs to the firm and not an individual partner,[55] but it is possible if the acts are outside the partner's duties to the firm.[56] The goodwill generated by a solicitor's work as a solicitor therefore vests in the firm.[57]

---

[51] 1999 SLT 1298, CS (OH).
[52] [1917] 2 Ch 1.
[53] *Reckitt & Colman Products Ltd v Borden Inc* (No 3) [1990] 1 WLR 491.
[54] This is more difficult if the businesses are not alike: *Martinez v Prick Me Baby One More Time Ltd* [2018] EWHC 776, IPEC.
[55] *Leather Goods Case, Re* 11 ER 1435.
[56] *Irvine v Talksport Ltd* [2002] EWHC 367 (Ch).
[57] *Bhayani v Taylor Bracewell LLP* [2016] EWHC 3360, IPEC.

Partnerships and the Public Domain

3.18 Partnerships do not operate in a vacuum. Partners pay taxes, business rates, and national insurance and they use the legal system. Because partnerships do not have a separate personality their assimilation into these state systems is not always easy. We have already seen the continuing problems encountered with VAT. Another issue which arose in connection with that tax was whether a repayment of VAT which fell due as a result of overpayment by a firm and which was to be repaid under the legislation to the 'person' paying the overdue amount, was payable to the partnership generally or to each partner proportionately. In *Hawthorn v Smallcorn*[58] the judge preferred the latter construction but added that in any event the amount repaid would be an asset available to all the partners. The complexities of fitting partnerships into the income tax system have also filled many weighty publications. The basic solution for income tax is to regard the partnership as one person for the purposes of an assessment but to calculate the assessment according to the tax position of each partner. Since a change in the membership of the firm is technically a cessation of the old firm's business and the commencement of the new firm's trade or profession this can have far-reaching consequences for tax assessment. In fact partners may elect to regard the old and new firm as continuing the same business and the Finance Act 1985 stopped most tax advantages from such a change of partners.

Although a partnership is regarded as a separate entity for the purposes of assessment to income tax that assessment is then transparent so that this does not affect the calculation of the amount subject to that assessment. In *MacKinlay v Arthur Young McClelland Moores & Co*[59] the House of Lords refused to allow payments made to a partner to cover the costs of moving house when moving from one part of the country to another to work in another partnership office, as expenses against the profits of the firm. Lord Oliver of Aylmerton rejected the idea that there could be a distinction between the partnership's purpose and that of the partner concerned. Since the partner's purpose was partly to achieve domestic satisfaction the expenditure could not be regarded as wholly and exclusively for the purposes of the business. Partners are not employees, as we have seen, and so no analogy with payments made by employers to employees moving in the course of their employment could be made.

Insolvency is also an area where partnerships present special problems. Either one partner may be insolvent or all the partners, with the consequence that the firm is insolvent, and rules have had to be worked out whereby the firm's creditors and the individual partners' creditors are dealt with as fairly as possible. A further description of insolvency can be found in Chapter 8, below.

---

[58] [1998] STC 591.
[59] [1990] 2 AC 239, HL.

Partnership litigation

The legal systems has also assimilated the partnership into its procedure. The Civil Procedure Rule (CPR) 7.2 requires the use of the firm's name either as complainant or defendant in legal proceedings for all actions by or against the partnership. But this will not apply if it is inappropriate to do so.[60] The other party to the litigation may request a 'partnership membership statement' which is a list of the names and addresses of all the partners at the time when the cause of action accrued.[61] Because the action is nevertheless one against a number of individuals and not the 'firm', the procedural rules must ensure that each partner is identified and notified of the action. This is particularly important where there has been a change of partners between the time when the cause of action accrued and the time when the claim is served. Thus under CPR 6.9(2) the claimant has the option to serve notice on all or any of the partners at either their usual or last known address, or at the usual or last known business address of the firm. Service on the firm at that address will constitute service on all or any of the partners. But what is the position if the claimant knows that there are those who were partners at the date the cause of action accrued but are not so at the date of service? This was the issue in *Brooks v AH Brooks & Co*,[62] where the judge decided that in such a case the claimant will not be able to rely on service at the business address but must seek an alternative address or method of service.[63] Acknowledgment of service by some partners may however bind others who have not been served if they are authorized to do so.[64]

3.19

A judgment against the firm may be enforced against any partnership property in the jurisdiction and anyone who was a partner at the material time.[65] In *Kommalage v Sayanthakumar*,[66] it was held, however, that a costs order only bound those who had been partners at the date when the cause of action accrued and not those who had become partners by the date of the order. Only the former were those liable to be sued.

In general this system works well for disputes between a firm and a third party. There are occasional problems. In *Turkington v Telegraph Group Ltd*,[67] the Northern Irish court held that in an action for defamation brought in the firm's name, the damages were limited to the loss of reputation suffered by the firm as a whole and not specific damage to one partner personally. In *Oxnard Financing SA v Rahn*,[68] the Court of Appeal had to decide whether an action brought in England against a Swiss partnership, which had legal personality under Swiss law, could be brought as an action against the partners

---

[60] See para 5A of the Practice Direction 7A to Part 7 of the CPR.
[61] The list must be provided within fourteen days of the request, which must specify the date of accrual: para 5B.1 of the Practice Direction 7A.
[62] [2010] EWHC 2720 (Ch).
[63] Construing CPR 6.9 and applying CPR 6.3 to 6.6.
[64] *Brooks v AH Brooks & Co* [2010] EWHC 2720 (Ch).
[65] Practice Direction—Enforcement of Judgments and Orders PD 70, para 6A. There are additional provisions for non-resident partners.
[66] LTL 19 November 2014 CA (Civ).
[67] [1998] NIQB 1.
[68] [1998] 1 WLR 1465.

individually as defendants. It held that since under English law a partnership could be sued in the names of the partners and the partners in this case were being sued purely in that capacity, suing them would amount to suing the firm. Finally in *Mephistopheles Debt Collection Service v Lotay*,[69] it was held that where one partner was subject to a restriction order which prevented him from bringing an action without permission, the firm could not bring the action.

But there are more difficulties when the dispute is between the partners themselves. If the partnership has ended, disputes between the former partners are personal matters not involving the firm.[70] But where the dispute is between continuing and former partners the position is more complex. This was the situation in *Hammonds (a firm) v Danilunas*.[71] A number of partners had left the law firm of Hammonds and were now being sued by the firm for the return of sums which had allegedly been overpaid to them whilst they were partners. Warren J was much exercised as to the use of Hammond's (a firm) to describe the complainants when the defendants had also been partners in that firm operating under that name. Counsel for the complainants indicated that it was intended to be a reference to the partners at the date when the claim form was issued. Warren J summed up the position as follows:

> Whether the use of 'Hammonds (A Firm)' is a correct way of describing those claimants seems to me to be doubtful and appears to be an unconventional use of a partnership name in the context of litigation. But if I proceed on the basis that the firm name is being used to describe the partners at the time of the issue of the claim form and also ignore any changes in the partnership membership since the date of issue, then it would appear that the action is properly constituted and the right claimants are making their claim against the Defendants... It must however be recognised that the claimants... are together suing each of the... Defendants as the persons collectively entitled to whatever amounts are owing.[72]

Right of individual partner to sue for wrong done to the partnership

3.20 In company law there was for many years a rule known as the rule in *Foss v Harbottle*[73] that where a wrong was done to a company only the company could sue to redress that wrong so that if a majority of the members of the company did not wish to proceed that was the end of the matter. Another rationale of the rule was that it prevents a multiplicity of actions being brought on the same facts, eg by each shareholder. There were exceptions to that rule, however, where the wrong could not lawfully be ratified by the members, eg fraud by those in control or illegal acts. These were known as derivative claims in that the minority may pursue the action, deriving their rights from the

---

[69] [1995] 1 BCLC 41.
[70] See, eg *Unical Properties v 784688 Ontario Ltd* (1991) 73 DLR (4th) 751.
[71] [2009] EWHC 216, Ch. This issue was not discussed by the Court of Appeal in that case, heard under the name of *Hammonds v Jones* [2009] EWCA Civ 1400.
[72] Ibid at para 115.
[73] (1843) 2 Hare 461.

company. The Companies Act 2006 repealed that common law rule insofar as it applied to companies and replaced it with a statutory procedure for a minority shareholder to bring a derivative action on behalf of the company against a director for breach of duty.[74] That procedure is subject to a considerable amount of control by the courts, but the right to sue on behalf of the company when the majority do not wish to do so still exists, albeit in a more limited form.

The application of derivative actions to companies can be explained by the separate legal personality of a company from its members. Could something similar be applied to partnerships, however, where there is only a relationship and each partner has his or her right of action against the wrongdoer, so that if a majority of the partners do not wish an action to be brought (eg to avoid publicity) there will be no action unless a derivative claim is possible? In British Columbia a derivative action was allowed in *Watson v Imperial Financial Services Ltd*.[75] This was an action by the limited partners against a bank for breach of trust. The general partners did not wish to sue, as they were allegedly implicated in the breach. The judge applied the rule and made no play of the fact that it was a limited partnership. Having applied the rule he also decided that an action would lie as a derivative claim by virtue of the fraud-by-those-in-control exception. The judge explained his reasoning as follows:

> Even if it could be said that each of the 845 partners was owed a transmitted or transferred fiduciary duty by the respondent bank, I do not think it would be open to those partners to individually commence actions against the bank. That would expose the bank to any number of lawsuits within the limitation period. I do not think that can be right.... In my opinion, this emphasises the point made by the respondent bank that this claim, in substance, is one of the partnership and not the individual partners. This, in my opinion, is no less so just because the partnership itself is not a legal entity.

The matter is further clouded by the fact that the judge hinted that he would have allowed a representative action, ie where some individuals sue on behalf of an affected class for wrongs done to them. Given the reasoning on avoiding multiple actions, this is really what he did.

The question has also arisen in England in the context of a limited partnership where the limited partners (who generally have no rights of management) were seeking permission to bring a derivative action against a third party since the general partner (who has such powers) declined to do so. This was the case of *Certain Limited Partners in Henderson PFI Secondary Fund II LLP v Henderson PFI Secondary Fund II LP*.[76] The judge accepted that such an action was possible as a matter of principle[77] where there

---

[74] Sections 260–264. The common law may still apply to 'double derivative' actions, ie where a member of a holding company wishes to sue a director of a subsidiary.
[75] (1994) 111 DLR (4th) 643.
[76] [2012] EWHC 3259 (Comm).
[77] Which he said had not been discussed in *Watson v Imperial Financial Services Ltd*, above.

was a need for such an action in order to avoid injustice. Thus there had to be special circumstances. That is a category which has never been defined and is not closed.

In the case itself the special circumstances were the conflict of interest involving the general partner and the proposed defendant. The judge considered that as the question was raised as a preliminary issue the merits or otherwise of the claim would play little part unless it was clearly a hopeless case. If it was strong case that might go to establishing special circumstances. A possible alternative remedy might also be a factor to consider. The basic issue is whether there would be injustice if the claim were not allowed to proceed.

The question is whether this reasoning and decision can be transplanted to an ordinary partnership. There is an obvious difference, highlighted in *Sutherland v Gustar*,[78] where one partner was permitted to appeal against a tax assessment despite the opposition of his fellow partners on the basis of implied authority under s 24(8); but the majority who were opposed were absolved from any liability for costs.[79] That related to a personal liability of the complainant but it could well apply to more general commercial contracts. In practical terms the issue may well be one where the partner seeking to bring the action seeks an indemnity for costs from the reluctant partners. It would seem that the issues at stake there would be similar to those where permission is sought to bring the action. Further, what would be the position if the partnership agreement expressly forbids any action to be brought on behalf of the firm other than with the approval of a majority (or management group) of the partners? That might well then replicate the limited partnership situation.

Right of partner not to be joined as a claimant in partnership action

3.21 The second situation is the reverse. If a majority of partners wish to sue X and one or more of the minority do not wish to do so, or do not wish to continue, can they avoid being parties to the litigation? This question has been discussed in two cases in Hong Kong. In *Kao, Lee & Yip v Koo Hoi Yan Donald*,[80] Ma J postulated three possibilities: (a) that the unwilling partner be joined as a co-plaintiff; (b) that he may be joined as a defendant; and (c) that he be excluded from the action. The second possibility would bind the dissenting partner as to the result in the same way as the company is joined as a defendant in a derivative action. It also happens to a reluctant joint contractor. The third possibility would seem not to be a practical proposition since a partnership action/liability by its very nature affects all the partners.

But more interesting is the first possibility. Normally no one can be made a complainant against their will, but there is a line of English cases which suggest that partnership is an exception. These cases seem to be based on the fact that, unusually, partnership is

---

[78] [1994] Ch 304.
[79] Quaere what would happen if that opposition was improper?
[80] [2002] 3 HKC 323.

a relationship of mutual agency and so they have joint responsibility to third parties and each other.[81] These cases were referred to as the *Whitehead* line of cases, and Ma J quoted Bayley B in *Whitehead v Hughes*:[82]

> One of several partners has a clear right to use the names of the other partners. If they object to their names being used, they may apply for an indemnity against the costs to which they might be subjected by the use of their names.

The correctness of that rule has, however, subsequently been left open by the English Court of Appeal.[83] Ma J, in *Kao, Lee & Yap*, decided that the unwilling partner, originally a co-claimant, should continue to be one, but granted her an indemnity from her co-partners not only as to her future costs but also any future liability on her part for the defendant's costs. Further he granted her a security to back up the indemnity for those future costs because, having left the firm, she had nothing to gain and much to lose from the litigation.

The issue was also discussed by Ng J in *Chan, Leung & Cheung v Tse Mei Lin*,[84] where she refused to strike out the dissenting partner's name as co-complainant, allowing the other partners to use the firm name, subject again to an indemnity for costs. There was, she said, no legal obligation on the other partners to make the unwilling partner a defendant rather than a complainant (except possibly where there was an action against that partner). The indemnity rule would otherwise be redundant. The position in England is still unresolved but the Hong Kong cases seem to have much to recommend them.

---

[81] This liability in England is now joint and several: see Ch 4, below.
[82] (1834) 2 C&M 318 at 319. The other cases which approved this statement were *Tomlinson v Broadsmith* [1868] 1 QB 386 at 392 and *Seal & Edgelow v Kingston* [1908] 2 KB 579 at 582.
[83] *Johnson v Stephens & Carter* [1923] 2 KB 857, CA; *Sutherland v Gustar* [1994] Ch 304, CA.
[84] [2004] 2 HKC 283.

4

PARTNERS AND OUTSIDERS

Potential Problem Areas

Sections 5 to 18 of the Partnership Act 1890 are included in that Act under the heading: 'Relations of Partners to Persons Dealing with Them'. The title of this chapter, 'Partners and Outsiders', is simply a more modern way of saying much but not quite the same thing. To be strictly accurate we are concerned here with the effect of the partnership relationship on the partners vis-à-vis their individual and collective liability to those who are outside that relationship. Such people are usually referred to as 'outsiders' or 'third parties' and in fact they may not actually be 'dealing' with the partnership at all. For example, someone who is injured by one partner driving his car on partnership business may well seek to make the other partners liable, but he can hardly be said to have been dealing with the firm as the Act impliedly requires. In fact, however, the Act does provide for liability in two areas, contracts and other (non-contractual) wrongs, and we can examine the scope of the liability of one partner for the acts of his fellow partners under those two general heads, although the concepts to some extent overlap. 4.01

But it is not enough to know the basic scope of this liability. Assuming that a partner is liable for a particular breach, the next question is how and to what extent will he be liable? Finally because partnership is a potentially fluid form of business medium it is important to know for how long a partner may be liable, eg if he retires is he liable for debts incurred before and after he retires? In seeking the answers to these questions we need to consider ss 5 to 18 of the Act (with the exception of s 14 which we have already discussed in Chapter 2 in relation to a partnership by representation) and s 36 which applies in practice in this context and so may be allowed to trespass from the part of the Act dealing with dissolution.

Liability of Partners for Contracts

Agency concepts

Of one thing there is absolutely no doubt whatever—each partner is an agent of his fellow partners simply by virtue of the relationship. Unlike other agency relationships, however, that same partner is also a principal with regard to his other partners who are also his agents. Thus each partner is an agent and a principal at the same time. This rather confusing position may explain why the application of the law of agency to 4.02

partnerships is not always straightforward. The basic position can, however, be simply stated in the form of a question and answer. If A, B, and C are partners and A orders goods from X, which X delivers but has not been paid for, in what circumstances can X recover the purchase price from B and C? Since A is an agent of B and C, who are his principals, he can bind them to any contract provided that he is acting *within his authority*. This is no more than an application of the basic concept of agency—if an agent makes a contract on behalf of his principal then, provided the agent is acting within his authority, the contract is binding on the principal, who can then sue and be sued on it by the third party without reference to the agent—it is a clear and well-established exception to the doctrine of privity of contract.

That such a relationship exists between partners has been stated many times in the courts. The common law position was explained by James LJ in *Re Agriculturist Cattle Insurance Co, Baird's Case*[1] and this has been substantially codified by ss 5 to 8 of the 1890 Act. Section 5 itself confirms the position quite clearly: 'Every partner is an agent of the firm and his other partners for the purpose of the business of the partnership'. We shall return again to the phrase 'business of the partnership' but it is in one sense misleading, for it is possible for a partner to bind his co-partners for acts entirely unconnected with the firm's business if he has the authority to do so. A partner is an agent and if he has the requisite authority his principals (the other partners) will be bound by his acts. It is time, therefore, that we looked at exactly what can amount to authority for this purpose and thus have such drastic and far-reaching effects on the liability of others.

Types of authority

4.03 There are three ways in which an agent (or partner) can have this authority. Confusion arises not from any doubts as to the nature of these three types of authority but simply as to what each type should be called. Judges and writers disagree with each other and there is little point in worrying about the correct titles. For our purposes we can divide authority into actual, implied, and apparent authority. Implied authority is sometimes referred to as usual or presumed authority and apparent authority as ostensible authority, although the terms apparent or ostensible can be used to mean implied or usual authority—see what I mean?

Actual authority is the easiest to grasp—an agent may bind his principal to any act which he is expressly authorized by his principal to do. Thus if a principal authorizes his agent to buy 100 tons of wheat and the agent does so the principal will be bound by the contract. Implied or usual authority is the authority which arises from the status of the particular type of agent involved. If an agent does an act which the third party would regard as a normal thing for that type of agent to do then the principal will be bound by it. Apparent or ostensible authority arises where the principal has held out the agent as having authority to do a particular thing so that the third party relies on the

---

[1] (1870) LR 5 Ch App 725, CA.

representation to his detriment. It is another example of the doctrine of estoppel—the principal cannot in such circumstances deny the agent's authority.

Both implied and apparent authority, therefore, are based on the idea that the agent looks as though he has authority to do the particular thing and the third party should be able to rely on appearances. It is also implicit in both these ideas that, even though the agent has no actual authority from his principal, the principal will still be bound. The difference is that implied authority arises from the nature of the agency (eg what it is usual for an estate agent to do) whereas apparent authority arises from a representation by the principal (eg if the agent has in fact made such contracts with the third party before and the principal has always honoured them). Apparent authority can even extend in some circumstances so that those who have no actual or implied authority to approve a transaction can nevertheless have apparent authority to assert that it has been approved by those who are authorized to approve it, or that some particular agent has been duly authorized to approve it.[2] This is very close to self-certification. In both cases, of course, the third party cannot rely on the authority if he knows that the agent has no actual authority. These rules are based on commercial realities and the necessities of trade. The third party cannot be expected to check every item with the principal to see if the agent has authority. An example of the confusion caused by the terminology can be found in the judgments of the Court of Appeal in *United Bank of Kuwait Ltd v Hammoud*,[3] where what was clearly a case of implied or usual authority, on our analysis, was dealt with in terms of apparent or ostensible authority because it involved the perception of the third party.

Applying these concepts to partnership it is clear that actual authority is a question of fact in each case. One partner may be given actual authority either by the terms of the partnership agreement (eg to contract debts up to a limited amount) or by the oral or written agreement of the other partners. As such it has no other limits. Apparent authority is also largely a question of fact—did the other partners by words or conduct represent that one partner had the authority to enter into the particular transaction or certify that he or she has such authority? The law is similar to that applicable to persons being held out as partners under s 14 of the Act, which we came across in Chapter 2. The main difference is that it is not a question of whether the representation was that X was a partner, but whether X has the authority to act on behalf of the partnership.[4] (Of course, if the representation is that X is a partner, X will also then have the implied authority of such a partner.) Implied authority, on the other hand, is a question of law to be ascertained in respect of each type of agent—what exactly is it usual for a particular partner to be able to do? The answer depends upon an examination of various sections of the Act and the relevant cases.

---

[2] *First Energy (UK) Ltd v Hungarian International Bank Ltd* [1993] 2 Lloyd's Rep 194, CA; *Kelly v Fraser* [2012] UKPC 25 cf *Armagas Ltd v Mundogas SA* [1986] AC 717, HL.
[3] [1988] 1 WLR 1051, CA.
[4] It is not clear whether the extension to apparent authority in *Kelly v Fraser* (above) would apply to s 14.

Limitations in the agreement

4.04 Because a partner's implied and apparent authority will usually be much wider than a partner's actual authority there will often be provisions in the partnership agreement seeking to limit any given partner's activities. But since such authority is, as we have seen, based on the idea that the third party can rely on appearances, no internal agreement between the partners can affect him unless he knows of the restriction, and he has no duty to inspect or check the partnership agreement. For partnerships the position is the same as for any other agency relationship and is codified in s 8 of the 1890 Act:

> If it has been agreed between the partners that any restriction shall be placed on the power of any one or more of them to bind the firm, no act done in contravention of the agreement is binding on the firm with respect to persons having notice of the agreement.

It is not entirely clear from that wording whether the third party has to have notice both of the restriction and the fact that the firm will not be bound, or simply of the restriction. The Law Commissions suggested that there is little doubt that only the latter is needed, particularly since, as we shall see, s 5 negatives any liability if the third party knows that the partner has no authority.[5]

Ratification

4.05 There is one other agency concept which applies in a straightforward way to partnerships. If the partner making the contract has no authority under any of the three heads then the other partners may nevertheless ratify the contract and thus adopt it as binding on all concerned. Ratification may be express or implied by words or conduct. The only problem would be whether the ratification was effective under the general law. Otherwise there are no partnership-specific problems. This is because there are no limits as to the capacity of a firm: the partners may do anything they like, whether or not it has anything to do with the usual business of the firm. Provided the partners agree, they can do anything within the law.

The implied or usual authority of a partner—s 5

4.06 As we have seen, the implied authority of any agent depends upon the status of the agent giving rise to the presumption that he has the authority to carry out the transaction. For partnerships this authority stems from s 5 of the Act:

> Every partner is an agent of the firm and his other partners for the purpose of the business of the partnership; and the acts of every partner who does any act for carrying on in the usual way business of the kind carried on by the firm of which he is a member

---

[5] In their final report the Commissions recommended the repeal of s 8 since the law of apparent authority covered the situation.

bind the firm and his partners, unless the partner so acting has in fact no authority to act for the firm in the particular matter, and the person with whom he is dealing either knows that he has no authority, or does not know or believe him to be a partner.

In *Bank of Scotland v Butcher*,[6] Chadwick LJ analysed this section as having two limbs. The first was where the act was actually done for the purpose of the business of the firm. That in itself would be sufficient. In effect that is equivalent to actual authority. Failing that, then the remainder of the section imposes implied authority if: (a) the act relates to the kind of business carried on by the firm; (b) if so, it was in the usual way of carrying on that business; and (c) if so, the third party either did not know that the partner had no authority or did not believe that he was not a partner. Part (c) is clearly separate but (a) and (b) are equally clearly closely linked. They are discussed below on the basis that (a) is concerned with the scope or ambit of the business activities and (b) is concerned with the method of carrying out such activities. But it is to some extent an artificial division and the concepts should be read together. In fact, however, they may well have been superseded by a de facto replacement of those words by the application by the courts of the concept of ordinary course of business taken from s 10 of the Act. 4.07

Applying the s 10 vicarious liability test

This apparent substitution arises from the fact that s 10 of the Act, which imposes vicarious liability on partners for wrongs (such as torts) committed by a partner, uses the words 'ordinary course of business'. Those words were subject to considerable scrutiny by the House of Lords in *Dubai Aluminium Company Ltd v Salaam*,[7] and in the subsequent Court of Appeal case of *JJ Coughlan Ltd v Ruparelia*,[8] the tests for liability under both ss 5 and 10 were taken to be the same, based on the House of Lords' analysis of s 10. Their Lordships in *Dubai* never alluded to s 5, but the Court of Appeal in *Coughlan* accepted that there was no material difference between 'ordinary course of business' and 'usual way of business of the kind carried on' and so cheerfully concentrated only on the former, even for s 5.[9] We shall deal in some detail with s 10 later, but since it may well be that in the future the *Dubai* s 10 analysis will also be so applied to s 5, it is appropriate to summarize it here. This summary is adapted from that made by Lawrence Collins J in *McHugh v Kerr*,[10] a subsequent case on s 10. 4.08

The principles are the same as those applicable to the vicarious liability of an employer for the acts of its employees. What amounts to the ordinary course of business is a question of fact but whether an act is to be regarded as being done in the ordinary course of

---

6 [2003] 1 BCLC 575, CA.
7 [2003] AC 366, at 113, HL.
8 [2004] PNLR 4, CA. The *Bank of Scotland* case, n 6 above, was decided only a few days after the *Dubai* case and made no mention of it. The equivalent in s 10 of Chadwick LJ's first limb of s 5 in that case is 'with the authority of his co-partners'.
9 In Australia it has been suggested that the wording of s 5 may be narrower than that of s 10. See, eg *National Commercial Banking Corporation of Australia Ltd v Batty* (1986) 160 CLR 251 at 298. But in Canada the two seem to be regarded as one: see *Allen v Aspen Group Resources Corporation*, 2009 Can LII 67668.
10 [2003] EWHC 2985 (Ch).

that business is a question of law. It does not require that the partner was specifically authorized to do the act, it is enough that the partner was authorized to do acts of the kind in question. The test is then whether *the act was so closely connected with the acts that the partner was authorized to do that, for the purposes of the liability of the firm to third parties, the act may fairly and properly be regarded as done by the partner in the ordinary course of the firm's business*. Whether there is such a close connection requires an evaluative judgement in each case. It can include performing an act in an improper manner, or for an improper purpose, or by an improper means. But even if the act is within the general category of acts which are in the ordinary course of business, it may be so far removed from normality as to be excluded.

With that warning in mind, it is still helpful, at the least, to consider the cases in terms of the actual wording of s 5.

'Kind of business'

4.09 Whether a particular activity is or is not related to the business of the firm is a question of fact and clearly depends upon the type of business involved. In many cases the answer will be obvious. For example, a contract by A, without any actual or apparent authority, to buy 100 tons of wheat from X will not bind A, B, and C as partners in a firm of patent agents—there can be no sense in which X has been misled. In other cases it may be less obvious. What exactly is the scope of the business of a firm of stockbrokers, surveyors, or solicitors? The latter has given rise to some recent litigation. A good starting point is the Australian case of *Polkinghorne v Holland*.[11] Mrs Polkinghorne dealt with Mr Holland who was one of three partners in a firm of solicitors. After consulting him she altered her investments as a result of which she lost a great deal of money, and acted as a guarantor of a bank overdraft of a company in which she was a shareholder and Mr Holland was a director. She sought to make the other partners liable for the loss on the investment and, when forced to pay the bank on the guarantee, for that amount as well. The question was whether the investment advice and the guarantee were part of the firm's business. The court took the view that, although investment analysis was not part of the firm's business, when a solicitor is approached on such questions he is required by the nature of his office to make enquiries and suggest where competent advice may be obtained. Thus his failure to do this was related to the business of the firm. On the other hand, the guarantee, although arising from her confidence in him as a solicitor, had nothing to do with the firm's business. He gave her no advice as a solicitor nor did he act on her behalf—it was a business engagement between them as contracting parties, not as solicitor and client.

In *JJ Coughlan v Ruparelia*,[12] the Court of Appeal, applying the vicarious liability criteria of *Dubai Aluminium*, held that a solicitor who had been involved in promoting a purported investment scheme which was variously described by the judge below as

[11] (1934) 51 CLR 143.
[12] [2004] PNLR 4, CA.

preposterous, abnormal, and incredible,[13] was far beyond the ordinary course of business of a solicitor. The Court did not need to discuss whether investment advice was part of the business of a solicitor since, even if it was, this was so far off-beam as to take it outside. Even if the third party had thought it was part of the ordinary course of business it would not, without specific representations by the other partners, have been—this part of the criteria for implied authority is objective. Equally of course it would not have been 'business of the kind' as required by the wording of s 5 so that nothing in fact fell on the use of s 10 wording.

In *United Bank of Kuwait Ltd v Hammoud*,[14] the Court of Appeal was concerned with the authority of a solicitor to give undertakings to a bank as to money allegedly held by the firm on behalf of a client, namely, that money would be transferred to the bank at a future date, so that the bank advanced money to the client. The court held that the solicitor had 'ostensible' authority to make such (false) representations but was in effect applying the usual authority criteria. Staughton LJ held that two requirements were necessary for such an undertaking to be within the 'ordinary' authority of a solicitor. First that there is a reasonable expectation that the funds will come into the firm's hands and second that the funds do come into their hands in the course of their business. Neither factor was actually present in that case but the bank did not know that. However, since the court held that the bank had acted reasonably in not checking further, the partner had been 'held out' by the firm as having that authority. A simpler analysis would have been that a solicitor has usual authority to give such undertakings if it was reasonable for the bank to assume that it was within the partner's implied authority. Implied or usual authority is based on the reasonable expectations of the third party arising out of the type of business involved, and that is exactly the position in that case. Such an analysis would have avoided the further complication put by Lord Donaldson of Lymington MR that to achieve this holding out, the solicitor had actual authority to hold himself out as a solicitor in the firm and thus his representation bound his partners since the bank could rely on the fact that solicitors are to be taken as persons of good character

> whose word is their bond and whose statements do not require that degree of confirmation and cross-checking which might well be appropriate in the case of statements by others who are not members of so respected a profession.

The *United Bank* case was considered by a different Court of Appeal in *Hirst v Etherington*.[15] In that case a solicitor/partner, Mr Etherington, gave an undertaking to Mr Hirst that he would guarantee repayment of a loan to be made by Mr Hirst to one of the firm's clients. This was to be paid out of funds becoming available to the client on completion of a property deal. Mr Etherington assured Mr Hirst that this undertaking was being given in the normal way of business and would bind his sole partner, Miss

---

[13] It would, if true, have produced a risk-free investment with a return of 6,000% per annum!
[14] [1988] 1 WLR 1051, CA.
[15] The Times, 21 July 1999, CA.

Bassett. Mr Hirst made no further inquiries. The loan was never repaid, Mr Etherington was made bankrupt and now Mr Hirst was suing Miss Bassett for the money on the basis of s 5.

The Court of Appeal applied the approach of Glidewell and Staughton LJJ in the *United Bank* case on the basis that the question whether an act is in the ordinary course of business of a firm is to be judged by whether it would appear to be so to a reasonably prudent third party, in this case the lender, and not necessarily by whether it is actually in the ordinary course of business. Thus, although it is not part of the usual or normal business of a solicitor either to receive money or a promise from a client that without more they can give such an undertaking, the position is to be viewed from the perspective of such a third party. On the facts, apart from the assertion by Mr Etherington himself that this was part of the ordinary business of the firm, there was nothing else to elevate the undertaking into the ordinary course of business. As to that assertion, the Court of Appeal rejected the idea that simply because it is given by a solicitor it somehow commands special respect. The law is quite clear—a partner cannot simply by his own assertion as to his own authority bind the other partners—it would require such an assertion to be within his authority[16] to make.[17]

As such the *Hirst* case clearly preserves the distinction between implied and apparent authority. Implied authority arises from the reasonable assumptions of the third party as to what is the ordinary course of business. Apparent authority is concerned with specific representations by others (ie the other partners) which are relied on by the third party.

Acts or instruments in the firm name

4.10 Two other sections of the Act are relevant here. Section 6 provides that:

> An act or instrument relating to the business of the firm and done or executed in the firm-name, or in any other manner showing an intention to bind the firm, by any person thereto authorised, whether a partner or not, is binding on the firm and all the partners.
>
> Provided that this section shall not affect any general rule of law relating to the execution of deeds or negotiable instruments.

Clearly this applies mainly to the specific problem of negotiable instruments and deeds and the problem usually resolves itself into a question of whether the partner signing the deed etc intended to act on his own account or on account of the firm. Where a deed is necessary for the transaction to be valid it appears that a partner cannot have

---

[16] This may be possible under apparent authority. See *Kelly v Fraser* [2012] UKPC 25, discussed above.
[17] A representation made by a partner concerning the partnership affairs and in the ordinary course of its business is, under s 15 of the Act, evidence against the firm. That section, introduced to circumvent a now obsolete aspect of the hearsay rule, was to be repealed under the Law Commissions' proposals. It does not apply to statements by non-partners: *Marsden v Guide Dogs for the Blind Association* [2004] 3 All ER 222.

any implied authority to bind his partner. In other cases, however, the basic position is the same as for the general law: has the third party the right to rely on the appearance of the deed as being that of the firm? Thus in *Re Briggs & Co*,[18] where a two-partner firm of father and son were being pressed by a creditor, the son agreed to assign the book debts (money owed to the firm) to the creditor in order to play for time. The father knew nothing of this. The deed of assignment stated that it was to be made between 'RB Briggs and HR Briggs, trading under the style or firm of Briggs & Co', but the father's name was forged by the son. The question arose as to whether the father was liable on this deed. The court applied s 6 since it related to the business of the firm and was done in a manner showing an intention to bind the firm and executed by a partner. It is implicit in this decision that the son had implied or apparent authority to do this qua partner (he clearly had no actual authority) and that the phrase 'thereto authorised' in s 6 must be read accordingly. Read as such, s 6 adds little to s 5 of the Act and would have been repealed under the Law Commissions' proposals.

Pledging credit

Section 7 of the 1890 Act deals with another specific activity: 4.11

> Where one partner pledges the credit of the firm for a purpose apparently not connected with the firm's ordinary course of business, the firm is not bound, unless he is in fact specially authorised by the other partners; but this section does not affect any personal liability incurred by an individual partner.

In reality this is again simply declaratory of what we have already said in that a person who deals with a firm can only make the firm liable for that debt if the partner with whom he dealt had authority to contract it.[19] Two phrases, however, could give rise to concern. First, it appears that for implied authority to exist the purpose need only be 'connected with the firm's ordinary course of business' rather than actually being in the course of the business (as is required by ss 5, 6, and 8). Is there a difference so that implied authority in this case is wider than in the general areas under s 5? If these sections are construed literally it might on one level be so—to take a New Zealand example, it has been held in *Kennedy v Malcolm Bros*[20] that, whilst the purchase of a new farm is not within the ordinary course of business of a farming partnership, if it is an adjoining farm to be used with the existing farm then it is connected with that business. In reality, however, that is simply an example of apparent authority since the partners showed by their conduct that it was to be acquired as part of the business and so in effect held each other out as having authority to bind the firm to the transaction.

The second problem arises from the curious use of the word 'specially' in relation to the authority given by the other partners which will make them liable. Clearly this

---

[18] [1906] 2 KB 209.
[19] It was destined for repeal under the Law Commissions' proposals.
[20] (1909) 28 NZLR 457.

will include actual authority but if that was all that was meant why was the word 'specially' used? Does it therefore include something other than actual authority? The answer must surely be yes, since all the basic concepts of agency and commercial reality point to the fact that the other partners can be liable if they have represented the partner as having that authority. Prior to the Act there was a judicial disagreement in the case of *Kendal v Wood*[21] but a majority of two to one took the view that in such cases apparent authority would suffice and this was followed in Australia. In *Kennedy v Malcolm Bros* itself, decided after the Act, it is clear that this was also regarded as the position and in the absence of any UK cases to the contrary it can be assumed to be the position here.

In short, therefore, ss 6 and 7 add little to what has already been said. For implied authority to exist the act must relate to the business of the firm—how else can an impression of authority be given simply by the partner's status as a partner? But there is no such requirement if the third party is relying on either actual or apparent authority where authority stems from actual permission or words or conduct by the other partners. It is not enough, however, for implied authority, simply for the act to relate to the business—it must also be a 'usual' act within that context.

'In the usual way'

4.12 This area raises such questions as does one partner have the implied authority to borrow money, insure the premises, convey land, give guarantees, sack employees etc in the course of the firm's business? What amounts to carrying on the business 'in the usual way'? Remember it must look all right to the third party if he is to take advantage of a partner's implied authority and this must stem from the Act itself in the context of the particular business. What is it usual for one or more partners to do on their own? The answer can be gleaned from several cases, decided both before and after the 1890 Act, although the courts tend to be wary of the early cases.[22] The distinction traditionally was between general commercial or trading partnerships on the one hand and non-trading partnerships on the other. The former enjoyed a much wider implied authority than the latter, particularly with respect to the borrowing of money.

A trading partnership was defined by Ridley J in *Wheatley v Smithers*[23] as one that required the buying and selling of goods. Applying that test he was able to decide that an auctioneer's partnership was not a trading partnership—an auctioneer does not buy anything. This test was followed by Lush J in *Higgins v Beauchamp*[24] in relation to a partnership carrying on a cinema house business 'and all other forms of entertainment'.

---

[21] (1871) LR 6 Ex 243, CA.
[22] See, eg *United Bank of Kuwait Ltd v Hammoud* [1988] 1 WLR 1051, CA; *Bank of Scotland v Butcher* [2003] 1 BCLC 575, CA; *Kotak v Kotak* [2017] EWHC 1821 (Ch).
[23] [1906] 2 KB 321, CA.
[24] [1914] 3 KB 1192, DC.

Giving the judgment of the Divisional Court, Lush J, noting that Ridley J's test was approved by the Court of Appeal in that case, continued:

> In my opinion it would be wrong to say that every business which involves the spending of money is a trading business. To my mind a trading business is one which involves the purchase of goods and the selling of goods.

The cinema business could not come under that head so that it seems that the purchase of goods and the selling of services will not suffice—thus excluding most, if not all, modern professional partnerships.

Modern developments

The actual decision in *Higgins v Beauchamp* was that since the firm was not a trading partnership one partner could not bind his fellow partner to a debt incurred by him without any other authority. The other partner was in fact a dormant partner (ie one who takes no active interest in the firm's business) and as we shall see it is these partners who feature heavily in the case law on this topic and create special problems with regard to the final part of s 5. In practice many of the problems relating to implied authority for professional firms relate to the other form of liability (for misapplication of clients' funds etc) and we shall return to those later. Their implied authority otherwise was quite limited, although, since many of the cases are quite old, it seems that the modern judges will extend this authority in the light of commercial developments.

4.13

This was the approach of the Court of Appeal in *Bank of Scotland v Butcher*.[25] The issue was whether a guarantee signed on behalf of the firm and themselves by four out of the thirteen partners in favour of the bank bound the other partners who were unaware of it. The guarantee was given in connection with negotiations between the debtor and the firm as to a joint venture, the latter receiving a share of the profits in return for giving the guarantee. There were a number of venerable cases which stated that in a professional partnership there was no general implied authority to give guarantees.[26] The Court of Appeal counselled caution on relying on such authorities in relation to s 5 generally but in fact followed one of them, *Sandilands v Marsh*,[27] on the narrower point that there was implied authority if the guarantee was an integral part of a partnership contract. That was the situation in the case: where a contract entered into by a partnership for the purpose of its business requires an act to be done, that act when done is itself to be regarded as done for the purpose of the partnership business, notwithstanding that (absent the contract) the act would have been outside the usual business of the partnership.[28] It should be remembered here that since a partnership does not

---

[25] [2003] 1 BCLC 575, CA.
[26] *Duncan v Lowndes and Bateman* (1813) 3 Camp 478; *Sandilands v Marsh* (1819) 2 B & Ald 673; *Hasleham v Young* (1844) 5 QB 833; and *Brettel v Williams* (1849) 4 Ex 623.
[27] (1819) 2 B & Ald 673.
[28] On that basis Chadwick LJ held that it fell within the first limb (actual authority) of s 5. The equivalent in s 10 is 'with the authority of his co-partners'.

have legal personality the partners cannot guarantee a partnership debt—one cannot guarantee one's own debt.[29]

This modern approach was encapsulated in *Kotak v Kotak*,[30] involving a property development partnership. The case concerned the implied authority of a partner in such a partnership to borrow money. Noting that such businesses were today financed in whole or in part on borrowed money and that a rational, competent, and prudent lender would know this, it was decided that it would be archaic and outdated to suggest that borrowing was not something which arose in the usual way of carrying out that business. To apply the old cases limiting that to trading partnerships would be 'utterly unrealistic'.

Partners in trading partnerships have always had implied authority to borrow money and to buy and sell trading stock in connection with the firm's business. They can also incur debts on account of the firm, instigate civil proceedings on its behalf, and even lend money to outsiders. To take one example of these—selling goods—this can apparently apply to selling goods which do not belong to the firm. In *Mercantile Credit Co Ltd v Garrod*,[31] Parkin was the active and Garrod the dormant partner in a business mainly concerned with the letting of lock-up garages and repairing cars. The partnership agreement prohibited the buying and selling of cars but Parkin, without any express authority, sold a car to the credit company so that it could be let on a hire-purchase contract to a customer. It then appeared that Parkin did not own the car and the company claimed the £700 paid for it from Garrod. Applying s 5 of the Act, Mocatta J held that Parkin did have implied authority to sell the car. In coming to this decision the judge stressed the central concept of implied authority:

> I must have regard in deciding this matter to what was apparent to the outside world in general and Mr Bone [the company's representative] in particular, and to the facts relevant to business of a like kind to that of the business of this partnership so far as it appeared to the outside world.

Judged on those criteria it was a usual way of carrying on the business of the firm. It should be noted that the provision of the partnership agreement to the contrary was of no avail—the company had no notice of it and, as we have seen, s 8 makes it clear that in such circumstances such limitations do not apply.

It is less clear what the implied authority of a trading partner is with respect to insurance, deeds, and conveyances. Modern practice may again outweigh established and venerable cases.[32]

---

[29] *IAC (Singapore) Pte Ltd v Koh Meng Wan* [1978–1979] SLR 470.
[30] [2017] EWHC 1821 (Ch).
[31] [1962] 3 All ER 1103.
[32] Bearing in mind the caveat given by the Court of Appeal in *JJ Coughlan v Ruparelia* [2004] PNLR 4, above.

Another business

4.14 It is clear, however, that one partner has no implied authority to bind his fellow partners into a partnership with other persons in another business. This is an obvious consequence of the nature of partnership as a relationship involving mutual trust. Since any partner may bankrupt another by his actions it would be ridiculous if one partner could simply on his own initiative bind his fellow partners to another partnership, so that they could be liable for debts incurred by those other partners. Thus if A, B, and C are partners, A has no implied authority to make D a partner, nor has he the implied authority to involve A, B, and C with a firm of D, E, and F in a new business venture. Section 24(7) of the Act confirms this by providing that subject to contrary agreement no new partner may be introduced without the consent of all the existing partners.

But this restriction does not apply if the agreement between A and D, E, and F does not amount to another business but simply amounts to a single joint trading venture between the two firms which is simply one method of carrying out the business of A, B, and C, even though that venture may amount to a partnership for its duration. This is the result of the decision of Megarry J in *Mann v D'Arcy*.[33] D'Arcy & Co was a partnership, consisting of three partners of which only D'Arcy was an active partner, carrying on a business as produce merchants. D'Arcy made an agreement with Mann to go on a joint account as to the purchase and resale of some 350 tons of potatoes on board a particular ship. It was clear that buying and selling potatoes was part of the ordinary business of the firm and that control of the venture remained with D'Arcy. In the event the venture produced a profit of approximately £2,410 but Mann had never received anything. He now sued one of the sleeping partners for his share (D'Arcy and the other partner no longer being 'men of substance') whose defence was that he had no knowledge of anything to do with this affair and that D'Arcy had no implied authority to make him a partner with Mann in this joint-venture partnership.

4.15 After examining the authorities, Megarry J upheld the basic rule that in general there is no implied authority so as to make one firm liable as partners in another business concern but that this did not apply on the facts of the case. He emphasized that the existing prohibition only applied to 'another business' and this could not be said to be another business since it remained under D'Arcy's control, and was in any event part of the existing business of the firm. The fact that the venture was a partnership in its own right did not automatically prevent authority from being implied—there are partnerships and partnerships, and a single-venture agreement was different from a general partnership for a longer period. Turning to s 5 the judge decided that the venture was related to the ordinary business of the firm and could be related to that business being carried out 'in the usual way', even though there was no evidence relating to produce merchants generally or this firm's previous conduct in particular.

---

[33] [1968] 1 WLR 893.

In effect the judge regarded the whole transaction as a method of buying and selling potatoes so as to minimize potential losses (the market was, as ever, uncertain), ie as a form of insurance underpinning a commercial venture which was within the ordinary business of the firm:

> In my judgment the reality of the matter is that what in substance D'Arcy & Co. were doing through [D'Arcy] was to buy and sell potatoes; and this was plainly carrying on business 'in the usual way'. The terms on which [D'Arcy] bought and sold the potatoes were also plainly matters within his authority. Clearly he could agree the prices and other terms both for purchases and sales. Equally, I think, it was within his implied authority to insure the goods, whether during transit or otherwise. In my judgment the arrangement for sharing the profit and the loss which he made with [Mann] falls within this sphere of authority. The arrangement was merely one mode of buying and selling what he was authorised to buy and sell on behalf of the partnership; and he was mitigating the risk at the expense of reducing the profit. Accordingly, it was within his authority.

I have analysed this case not just because it provides an example of the general concept of implied authority but because it indicates the modern judicial approach to the whole issue. The judge was faced with a general rule enunciated in cases decided before the Act and enshrined in legal folklore ever since. What he did was to apply the wording of s 5 to the problem rather than to rely on general principles as to the nature of implied authority. The result was to provide a pragmatic solution on the particular facts rather than to provide such general rules—perhaps the only real general principle now is the wording of the section itself. That is certainly the modern approach although, as we have seen, this may in fact be on the basis of the House of Lords' comments in *Dubai Aluminium Co Ltd v Salaam*.[34]

The decision in *Mann v D'Arcy* was approved by the Full Court of the Queensland Supreme Court in *Rowella Pty Ltd v Hoult*.[35] In that case the managing partner (the remaining partners were all limited partners) entered into a joint venture agreement with Hoult whereby all the partnership's interest in mining leases would be transferred to the joint venture, giving 65 per cent to Hoult and conceding to him the sole right to conduct all operations dealing with the exploitation of the leases. Applying the test laid down by Megarry J that a partner has implied authority to bind the firm to a joint venture if that did not amount to 'another business', the court decided that this case fell on the other side of the line. Ryan J put it this way:

> The limited partnership ceased to carry on its business; instead it transferred assets to Hoult and entrusted him with the carrying on of the business. It may be that this was a sensible arrangement to make in the interests of the members of the limited partnership... That is not however relevant to the question whether the arrangement was one

---

[34] [2003] AC 366, HL.
[35] [1988] 2 QdR 80.

for the carrying on in the usual way of the business of the kind carried on by the firm. The business to be carried on by the joint venture was in my view 'another business' within the principle referred to by Megarry J.

Imputed notice

Section 16 provides that '[n]otice to any partner who habitually acts in the partnership business of any matter relating to partnership affairs operates as notice to the firm, except in the case of a fraud on the firm committed by or with the consent of the partner'. This is an example of the common law concept of 'imputed' notice and is declaratory of the pre-existing common law. The notice must be given to a partner at a time when he is a partner so that notice to a person who subsequently becomes a partner is not within the section—that was also the position prior to the Act (*Williamson v Barbour*[36]). This may be important, for example, where an employee becomes a partner. The notice must also relate to the affairs of the firm so that notice to one firm cannot be transferred to another even when there is common membership, distinguishing between knowledge relating to partnership affairs and knowledge relating to a client's affairs: see *Campbell v McCreath*.[37] The Law Commissions received representations that this section was potentially dangerous in respect of confidential information received by a partner. Accordingly the Commissions recommended its repeal on the basis that a literal interpretation would 'lead to unacceptable results and the separation of partnership law from the general law of agency in relation to the imputation of knowledge'.[38]

4.16

Exclusion of implied authority

Section 5 of the Act, having established that an act done in the usual way and in the course of the business of the firm will be within a partner's implied authority, then proceeds to exclude such authority in two situations. The first is unexceptional: where the partner has no actual authority and the third party knows that he has no such authority. Knowledge of lack of authority destroys the essence of implied authority since the third party cannot then be said to be relying on appearances. The second situation, however, presents some problems: where the partner has no actual authority and the third party 'does not know or believe him to be a partner'. Taken at face value this could suggest that if A, without any actual authority, orders 100 tons of wheat from X on behalf of a partnership of A and B, X will only be able to rely on s 5 to make B liable for the contract if he knew or believed that A was a partner with B. Various permutations could also arise. For instance, what if X knew that A was a partner with someone but had no idea with whom? Again, suppose A has two partners, B and C, and X knows that A is a partner with C but has no idea of B's existence—can X sue B under s 5?

4.17

---

[36] (1877) 9 Ch D 529.
[37] 1975 SLT 5.
[38] Report, para 6.21.

Construing this last part of s 5 is in fact far from easy. Does the third party simply have to know that A is a partner with some person or persons unknown, as they say, or does he have to know the identity of some or all of the other partners? Is there any validity in drawing a distinction between the case where X thinks that A is a sole trader but in fact he has a partner, B, and where X thinks that A is a partner with C, but has no knowledge of partner B? Why should B be liable in the second case and not in the first? Before we can even attempt to solve these problems thrown up by the wording of s 5 we must first take on board a doctrine of the law of agency which further complicates matters in this area—the doctrine of the undisclosed principal.

Doctrine of the undisclosed principal

4.18 This doctrine states that where an agent has authority to act for a principal but does not tell the third party that he is acting as an agent, the third party may sue either the agent or the principal, if and when it is discovered who he is, and either the agent or the principal may sue the third party on the contract. This rather surprising doctrine has never been very popular in the business world—it means, of course, that the third party can sue or be sued by someone of whose existence it was totally unaware. The justification for it is said to be the injustice that would otherwise be caused, ie if the third party has sold goods to an agent acting for an undisclosed principal and delivers the goods to the agent and, before the price is paid, the agent becomes insolvent, the goods could be taken by the agent's creditors to pay for his debts unless the principal can demand their return. This has always seemed a rather thin basis for such a strong departure from the rules that only a party to a contract can enforce it. It is not inconceivable that the third party might not have entered into the contract at all if he had known the true identity of the principal involved. It is generally agreed that the doctrine is anomalous and at complete variance with the accepted principles of contract—it is justifiable only on grounds of commercial convenience.

There are, however, some limitations on this doctrine. First, the agent must have had authority at the time of the contract, otherwise anyone could later adopt the agent's contract and claim that the agent was acting on his behalf. Second, if the contract shows either expressly or by implication that it is to be confined in its operation to the parties (ie the agent and the third party) themselves, the possibility of agency is negatived and no one else can intervene as a principal. This is a question of construction of the contract in each case. For example, where the alleged agent was described as the 'owner' of a ship it was held that evidence was not admissible to show that he was in fact acting as agent for the real owner; the agent appeared to be the sole owner of the subject matter of the contract: *Humble v Hunter*.[39] However, in a similar case where the alleged agent was described as the 'charterer' (hirer) of a ship, evidence was allowed to show who the principal was. To describe oneself as owner precludes the existence of another owner, but 'charterer' simply means no more than a contracting party and does not therefore

---

[39] (1848) 12 QBD 310.

preclude the existence of another owner: *Fred Drughorn Ltd v Rederiaktiebolaget Transatlantic*.[40]

Third, there is a possible restriction on the application of the doctrine if it would result in prejudice to the third party which was unforeseen at the time when he entered into the contract. The obvious example of this would be where the identity of the undisclosed principal was material and the third party would not have contracted if he had known of his existence. An example of this is the poignant South African case of *Karstein v Moribe*.[41] The owner of a farm in an area designated as a 'black' area under the apartheid laws leased the farm to Moribe, who was classed as a black person for that purpose. In fact Mr Moribe was being financed by another person who was a 'white' under the system. The law provided that no white person could lawfully lease land in a black area. Accordingly it was argued that Mr Moribe had taken the lease on behalf of a partnership of himself and his partner, the latter being an undisclosed principal, and on that basis the lease was illegal and void. The judge, applying the prejudice exception to the undisclosed principal rule, held that the lease was simply between the owner and Mr Moribe and so not illegal.

Application to partnership

Ignoring s 5 of the Act for the moment, the doctrine of the undisclosed principal, if applied to partnerships, would mean that, subject to the above limitations, any partner could sue or be sued on a contract made by another partner within the scope of his implied authority, even though his existence was unknown to the third party. Since each partner is a principal of his fellow partners he could equally well be an undisclosed principal. The wording of s 5, however, suggests that this cannot be so, for if the third party does not know or believe that the contracting partner is a partner he cannot rely on that partner's implied authority so as to bind the other partners. This whole problem therefore resolves itself into two questions. Does s 5 negate the doctrine of the undisclosed principal so far as the implied authority of a partner is concerned? If it does, then in what circumstances will an unknown partner be liable under the section itself? Somewhat surprisingly neither of these issues troubled the Law Commissions.

4.19

In answering the first question it is clear that s 5 operates equally in relation to the unknown partner suing the third party, thus avoiding the problems of prejudice, as it does in the more usual reverse situation of the third party suing the unknown partner. Judicial authority, such as it is, suggests that, at least in the second case, in fact s 5 does *not* prevent the general rule from applying. In *Watteau v Fenwick*,[42] a hotel manager appointed by the brewers ordered certain goods from the plaintiff in breach of his agreement with the brewers. The plaintiff believed the manager to be the owner of the hotel (the hotel licence was in his name and his name appeared over the hotel door) but was

---

[40] [1919] AC 203, HL.
[41] 1982 2 SA 282 (T).
[42] [1893] 1 QB 346.

nevertheless allowed to sue the brewers under the doctrine of the undisclosed principal. For our purposes the significance of this case is what the position would have been if the manager and the brewers had been partners. The plaintiff clearly did not know or believe the manager to be an agent (or partner in our scenario). The judge, Wills J, suggested that the result would have been the same:

> But in the case of a dormant partner it is clear law that no limitation of authority as between the dormant and active partner will avail the dormant partner as to things within the ordinary authority of a partner. The law of partnership is, on such a question, nothing but a branch of the general law of principal and agent.

Interface with s 5

4.20 But how can this possibly be reconciled with the actual wording of s 5? Professor JL Montrose, in a well-known article, 'Liability of Principal for Acts Exceeding Actual and Apparent Authority',[43] points out that the application of any of the possible meanings of the words 'does not know or believe him to be a partner' would have produced an entirely different result on the facts of *Watteau v Fenwick* as applied to a partnership. He also makes the point that, unless there was an intention to protect unknown (or dormant) partners in such circumstances, why was this part of s 5 added in 1890? To follow Wills J is to ignore this part of the section entirely. The judge's views can of course be technically dismissed as an obiter dictum since the case was not in fact about partnerships but an ordinary case of agency. Further he does not actually refer to s 5 and declare it to have no such effect.

The doctrine of the undisclosed principal is in many ways illogical. (If implied authority is based on appearances to the third party then the appearance in such cases is that the agent or partner is acting on his own behalf and the third party, having given credit etc accordingly, has little room to complain—why should he have an alternative source of redress?) If the doctrine is applied to partnerships it puts dormant partners in a vulnerable position. Further s 5 does exist and it would be strange indeed if the last line, unlike the rest of the section, is to have no effect. We must therefore assume that the views of Professor Montrose as to its effect on *Watteau v Fenwick* are correct, particularly since full effect was given to the last line of s 5 by the High Court of Australia in *Construction Engineering (Aust) Pty Ltd v Hexyl Pty Ltd*.[44] That does not, however, solve the problem. If the end of s 5 does mean something, what exactly does it mean? Remember the words: 'does not know or believe him to be a partner'. It seems clear that in the *Watteau v Fenwick* situation this should negative the application of the doctrine of the undisclosed principal. Thus if A, without any actual authority, contracts with X, apparently on his own account, X cannot sue any of A's undisclosed partners since X did not know or believe A to be a partner. That was the position in the *Hexyl* case. The position is also clear if A, again without actual

---

[43] (1939) 17 *Canadian Bar Review* 693.
[44] (1985) 155 CLR 541.

authority, contracts with X who knows that A has a partner or partners although he has no idea of their actual identity. Since A is contracting as an agent, the fact that X does not know the actual identity of the other partners is of no consequence: X does know or believe that A is a partner.

Playing word games

Suppose, however, that in such a case X knew that A and B were partners but had no idea of the existence of C, another partner. In such a case Professor Montrose suggests that if X is contracting with A and B jointly, C will not be liable, whereas if X contracts only with A, C will be liable. This rather startling conclusion is based on the idea that the words 'does not know or believe him to be a partner' must include the plural 'does not know or believe them to be partners' and that this plural form must be read with the addition 'of another'. Thus if X contracts with A and B jointly, he does not know or believe them to be partners of another, C, and so C cannot be made liable under the section. If X only contracts with A, however, he does know or believe that A is a partner and so both B and C are liable. A contrary argument has been put by JC Thomas in an article entitled 'Playing Word Games with Professor Montrose'.[45]

4.21

I suspect that for those who appreciate word games this is a potentially endless area of fun. But what should the position be? Surely it should depend solely upon whether X believes or knows that he is dealing with a firm or whether he thinks he is dealing solely with an individual. Such a solution would be simple to apply and it would be consistent with the concept of partnership liability. Once again the real culprit in all this is the fact that a partnership is not a separate legal entity. Thus to say that it depends upon whether X believes or knows that he is dealing with a firm is in some ways misleading. More accurately it should depend upon whether X knows or believes he is dealing with a person who has partners in that business. Put that way it should then be irrelevant whether he knows how many or who they are, since a partnership is by its very nature a fluid form and X could quite easily imagine that there are dormant partners involved. (In practice, of course, since X will not be a lawyer he will in any event assume that a firm in this context is some form of 'being' and that he is dealing with all its members.) The only suggestion put forward by the Law Commissions was to change the wording of the end of s 5 to 'does not know or believe him to be a partner *in the partnership*'. But that was predicated on there being a legal person, the partnership.[46] It would, however, solve some of the Montrose/Thomas issues.

Alternative trust solution

An interesting alternative solution to the problems of this part of s 5 was adopted by the High Court of Australia in *Construction Engineering (Aust) Pty Ltd v Hexyl Pty*

4.22

---

[45] (1977) 6 VUWLR 1.
[46] See s 6 of the Limited Liability Patnerships Act 2000, Ch 12, below.

Ltd.[47] Hexyl and another company, Tambel, were partners in a land development and management scheme. Tambel entered into a building contract with Construction which described Tambel as being the proprietor of the land (although it had in fact been purchased by the partners in equal shares). A question arose as to whether Hexyl was bound by a provision in the contract. The judge held that it was on the basis of the doctrine of the undisclosed principal, despite the identical wording of s 5 of the New South Wales Act. That decision was, however, reversed by the New South Wales Court of Appeal, whose decision was upheld by the High Court of Australia. The High Court held that Tambel had no actual authority to act as an agent for Hexyl in making the building contract and could have no implied authority because it was agreed that Construction neither knew nor believed Tambel to be a partner. In other words, s 5 negatived any application of the doctrine of the undisclosed principal.

Instead the High Court decided that Tambel had contracted with Construction as a trustee for the partnership rather than as an agent acting for an undisclosed principal. That had been the effect of the partnership agreement between Tambel and Hexyl. Thus, although Tambel would hold the benefit of the contract as a trustee for itself and Hexyl, Tambel had contracted solely as a principal and not as an agent so far as Construction was concerned. Trustees do not contract as agents for the beneficiaries of the trust. This solution has much to recommend it since it reconciles the wording of s 5 on liability to third parties with the fiduciary nature of partnership as between the partners.

Liability for Other Wrongs

4.23 Partners may be vicariously or directly liable for wrongs committed by their fellow partners quite independently of any contract. Thus they may be liable, in certain circumstances, for torts, crimes, misapplication of property entrusted to one partner or the firm, and for some breaches of trust, either by a partner/trustee or under the doctrines of 'knowing receipt' and 'dishonest assistance', and other equitable wrongs. The Act provides for liability under three sections: 10, 11, and 13. In general, s 10 applies vicarious liability for all 'wrongs', s 11 provides a primary liability for misapplications, and s 13 applies only to one aspect of breach of trust. These sections were, however, drafted before the growth of the equitable liability for 'dishonest assistance' and 'knowing receipt' and the courts have struggled with the interface between the three sections in relation to such liability and for equitable wrongs in general. The best way to set out the current position is to consider first liability for torts, breaches of duty, and crimes under s 10, next liability for misapplications under s 11, in each case ignoring any liability for any breach of trust or other equitable liability, and then to consider liability for all forms of equitable wrong as a separate head in relation to all three sections.

---

[47] (1985) 155 CLR 541.

Vicarious Liability for Torts, Breaches of Duty, and Crimes

Section 10 of the Act explains the general rule for liability for torts and crimes: **4.24**

> Where, by any wrongful act or omission of any partner acting in the ordinary course of the business of the firm, or with the authority of his copartners, loss or injury is caused to any person not being a partner in the firm, or any penalty is incurred, the firm is liable therefor to the same extent as the partner so acting or omitting to act.

Thus each partner is vicariously liable for the wrongful acts or omissions of his fellow partners. This applies in respect of any consequential loss, injury, or penalty, which would seem to include not only damages but also the equitable remedy of account and any statutory or common law criminal or regulatory penalty,[48] provided either that they are acting in the ordinary course of the firm's business or with the authority of their co-partners. The courts must therefore make a finding that the wrongful act was committed either in the ordinary course of the firm's business or with the authority of the partners. These are not necessarily the same since the partners may by their conduct represent that the wrongdoer was acting within his authority (ie his apparent authority) even though that is not necessarily within the ordinary business of the firm.[49] For liability to exist it must also be shown that what was done by the errant partner in the ordinary course of the firm's business or with the other partners' authority was a wrongful act.

Ordinary course of business

Close connection test

The concept of ordinary course of business in s 10 as establishing vicarious liability for torts and other wrongs was discussed in some detail by Lords Nicholls and Millett in *Dubai Aluminium Ltd v Salaam*.[50] Both of their Lordships regarded the matter as being essentially the same as the vicarious liability of an employer for the acts of an employee. Both phrased the test as to whether the wrongful conduct is so closely connected with the acts that the partner was authorized to do that, for the purpose of the liability of the firm to third parties, the wrongful conduct may *fairly and properly be regarded* as done by the partner in the ordinary course of the firm's business. Whether that close connection test is fulfilled is a matter for the court to evaluate in the light of its primary findings of fact.[51] **4.25**

Once the question is seen as being one as to the closeness of the connection between the wrongdoing and the class of acts which the partner was authorized to perform there

---

[48] See, eg 3464920 *Canada Inc v Strother*, 2007 SCC 24.
[49] For an example see *Crouch and Lyndon v IPG Finance Australia Pty Ltd* [2013] QCA 220.
[50] [2003] AC 366, HL.
[51] For Lord Nicholls that was a question of law. For Lord Millett it was a question of fact.

is no relevant distinction between performing an act in an un-authorized manner and performing it for an improper purpose or by improper means, eg fraudulently. This is because, as Lord Millett said, vicarious liability is a loss distribution device based on grounds of social and economic policy. That is, that liability is so imposed for wrongs which can fairly be regarded as reasonably incidental risks to the type of business being carried on. Only if the partner goes beyond that will there be no vicarious liability.[52] The Supreme Court in New Zealand has formulated the question as being whether the conduct of the partner fell within the scope of the task which the partner was engaged to perform.[53] The court, it said, must concentrate on the nature of the tasks to be performed on behalf of the firm and on how the use of the partner for that purpose has created risk for the third party. The wrong must be seen as a materialization of the risk inherent in the task.

The specific question of the impact on s 10 of one partner acting fraudulently was discussed by White J in the New South Wales case of *Hraiki v Hraiki*.[54] If a partner is acting purely for his own interests and is not pursuing the business of the firm, s 10 will not apply, even if the acts in question are those usually done by the firm in the course of its business. But if the firm has undertaken to do work for the defrauded complainant and the fraud is committed in the wrongful performance of that work then s 10 will apply. On the other hand, a partner doing work of the kind customarily done in the ordinary course of the business of the firm might so act for his own improper purpose such that it should be concluded that he is not acting as a partner of the firm but is engaged on a 'frolic of his own'. As Lord Millett pointed out in *Dubai*, if a partner is engaged only in furthering his own interests, the mere fact that he was doing an act of a kind which he was authorized to do will not, in the absence of apparent authority, make the other partners liable. But if he is engaged in furthering the firm's business, however misguidedly, then the firm will be liable.

Which of those situations applies is a matter of detailed analysis of the facts. Thus in *Goldberg v Miltiadous*,[55] after 220 paragraphs of close factual analysis, the judge decided that fraudulent investment advice given by one of three partners in an accountancy firm was within its ordinary course of business. Although the other two partners had no idea as to what the fraudulent partner was doing: 'there was nothing to dispel the impression given on the firm's writing paper and elsewhere that the partners were authorized to give financial advice.'[56]

---

[52] See, eg *JJ Coughlan v Ruparelia* [2004] PNLR 4, CA, where a solicitor was involved in an investment scheme which was described as being 'preposterous, abnormal and incredible'.
[53] *Dollars & Sense Finance Ltd v Rerekohu* [2008] NZSC 20.
[54] [2011] NSWSC 656 at [83] and [84].
[55] [2010] EWHC 450 (QB).
[56] Ibid at [137].

Examples of ordinary course of business

Thus, whilst it is possible to argue that it is never in the ordinary course of the business of a firm to commit a wrong, the partners will be liable if the erring partner in committing the wrong is simply carrying out the ordinary business of the partnership in such a way as to commit a tort. The original example of this is the case of *Hamlyn v Houston & Co*.[57] A partner was engaged by the firm to obtain information by legitimate means about the business contracts etc of its competitors. He bribed the clerk of a rival firm to divulge confidential information about that firm to him and thus committed the tort of inducing a breach of contract. The bribe came out of the firm's money and the resulting profits went into its assets. The rival firm who had lost money as a result sued the other partners in tort. The Court of Appeal allowed the action to succeed. It was within the ordinary scope of the partner's business to obtain the information, so that his object was lawful, and the fact that it was obtained by unlawful means did not take it outside the ordinary course of the firm's business.[58]

4.26

A classic example of this concept is the decision of the New Zealand Court of Appeal in *Proceedings Commissioner v Ali Hatem*.[59] In that case one of two partners was primarily responsible for staffing matters and he was found to have committed the statutory tort of sexual harassment against two female employees. The other partner was found to be vicariously liable on the basis that, although sexual harassment was not part of the ordinary business of the firm, the perpetrator, when acting as he did, was acting within the ordinary course of the firm's business, ie dealing with staff members in the work environment, and in doing that he committed the tort. The court therefore concluded that '[h]e thereby did tortiously something which he was generally authorised to do' and the other partner was liable accordingly. That is the classic doctrine of vicarious liability enshrined in s 10.

In *Langley Holdings Ltd v Seakens*,[60] the issue was as to what constituted the ordinary business of a firm of English solicitors. One of the partners had received money from Langley into the firm's client account. Langley was not a client of the firm, but the intended payee of the money was. The whole thing was a fraud and the money disappeared. The partner involved was facing fraud charges and Langley sought to recover the money from the other partner in the firm, who had no knowledge at all of what was going on. The judge held (after examining the Solicitors' Accounts Rules) that it would be in the ordinary course of the business of a firm of solicitors to receive money from A, a non-client, pending payment to B, a client, provided it is in the course of a transaction between A and B in which the solicitor is acting for B. The fact that the recipient partner was acting dishonestly would not, of itself, alter that position, but if there was in fact no transaction between the parties which they intended to carry out, so that any

---

[57] [1903] 1 KB 81, CA.
[58] In Hong Kong it has been held that s 10 can apply to the tort of defamation: *Fung v Kit* [2018] HKDC 1252.
[59] [1999] 1 NZLR 305, CA.
[60] (2000) LTL, 5 March 2000.

supposed legal work by the solicitor was in fact spurious, such a receipt of non-client money would not be in the ordinary course of business. On the facts, one of the parties (the payee) knew that there was no such transaction and the other (the non-client) was reckless as to whether there was one (they were 'blinded' by the apparent proposed profits). On that basis it could not be said that the receipt was in the course of the firm's business.

In *McHugh v Kerr*,[61] Lawrence Collins J held that it was common knowledge that firms of accountants, including the appellant firm, bought and sold shares for their clients. The partner in question was not of course authorized to make fraudulent statements in respect of such dealings but that did not matter. He was authorized to carry out such dealings. The firm received the fees from the share transaction and it was therefore clearly within the ordinary business of the firm, albeit a small part.

A different point came before the Court of Appeal in *Scarborough Building Society v Howes Percival*.[62] One partner in a firm of solicitors was involved in a mortgage fraud, partly in his capacity as the secretary of the company used for the fraud and partly as the solicitor carrying out the legal work involved. The firm was the company's solicitors. It was conceded that the legal work, basic conveyancing, was within the ordinary course of the firm's business but it was argued that nothing he did *qua* solicitor was a wrongful act. The fraud had been carried out in his capacity as company secretary. This argument was rejected by the Court of Appeal. The conspiracy involved doing the necessary conveyancing work and as such those were wrongful acts. They were part of the conspiracy. The innocent partners were, accordingly, liable for his actions under s 10.

Section 10 also applies to breaches of fiduciary duty. The Supreme Court of Canada has held that a breach of fiduciary duty by a solicitor to his client (not divulging relevant information which he knew in relation to a transaction he was retained to provide advice on) was within the ordinary course of the firm's business.[63] The wrongful act could not be disentangled from the ordinary business of the firm. The errant partner was not indulging in a 'frolic of his own'. In *Allen v Aspen Group Resources Corporation*,[64] the judge in the Ontario Superior Court discussed whether the firm would be liable for the acts of a lawyer who also sat as a director on the board of a company. The judge thought that if the lawyer was acting for the company and also sat on the board it was arguable that in doing so the lawyer would be acting in the ordinary course of business.

A similar approach has been applied here by the Court of Appeal in *The Northampton Regional Livestock Centre Company v Cowling*.[65] Mr Cowling was a partner with a Mr Lawrence in a firm of property consultants. They were entrusted by the Centre to sell its property. Mr Lawrence, in breach of his fiduciary duty to the Centre, made a substantial

---

[61] [2003] EWHC 2985 (Ch).
[62] 5 March 1998, CA.
[63] *3464920 Canada Inc v Strother*, 2007 SCC 24.
[64] 2009 Can LII 67668 (Ont SC).
[65] [2015] EWCA Civ 651.

personal profit out of the transaction, which he had to account for to the Centre. Mr Cowling knew nothing of this, but was he vicariously liable for his partner's breach? The Court of Appeal held that on the facts Mr Lawrence was not acting on 'a frolic of his own' but that he was acting both in his own interests and those of the firm. His actions had to be viewed in context and not just on the wrongful act itself. By introducing a purchaser, he was performing the very task which the firm had agreed to perform.

Personal dealings

On the other hand if it can be shown that a person intended to deal with the partner exclusively and not with him as a member of the firm, such personal dealings will not be regarded as taking place in the ordinary course of the firm's business even if they otherwise would be. This can be illustrated by the Australian case of *Chittick v Maxwell*.[66] The Chitticks agreed to build a house on land belonging to their daughter and son-in-law, the Maxwells. There was an agreement that the parents should have the right to occupy the house until their deaths when it would pass to the Maxwells or their children. Mr Maxwell was a solicitor and drew up the agreement. This was defective in that it did not protect the Chitticks' right to possession against third parties and the Maxwells repeatedly mortgaged the land without disclosing the Chitticks' occupation of it. The mortgagees successfully enforced an order for possession and the Chitticks were forced to leave. The Chitticks sued Mr Maxwell's partners for his negligence in drafting the agreement. This claim was rejected by the court. Even though the firm were the Chitticks' regular solicitors and the work was of a type normally done by solicitors the facts and circumstances showed that Mr Maxwell was doing something on his own account. In particular, Mr Chittick had not requested the services, he had simply accepted the document and signed it and it had been signed in the Maxwells' house.

4.27

Wrongs within partner's authority

Alternatively the partners will be liable for wrongs committed by a partner if they are committed in obtaining some object which is within the partner's actual, implied, or apparent authority. In *Hamlyn*'s case,[67] for example, an alternative ground was that the partner had actual authority to obtain the information, and the fact that he obtained it by unlawful means, did not take it outside that authority. The position would be the same if the partner is acting within his implied authority (by virtue of his position and status), but in such cases it will also usually be the case that he is acting within the ordinary course of the firm's business. But the partners will also be liable if the wrong is committed by a partner doing something within his apparent authority (ie by virtue of

4.28

---

[66] (1993) 118 ALR 728.
[67] [1903] 1 KB 81, CA.

a representation by words or conduct to that effect) and that is by no means necessarily the same as acting within the ordinary course of business of the firm.

This distinction was also made in the Irish case of *Allied Pharmaceutical Distributors Ltd v Walsh*[68] where a partner in a firm of accountants was a member and director of Allied. Its books and accounts were audited by the firm and the partner's fees as a director were paid to the firm. He caused the company to invest in an unlimited company which he controlled even though it was insolvent. When Allied brought an action against the partners to recover its loss they argued that it was not in the ordinary course of the firm's business to give investment advice and so they were not liable for the partner's negligence. The court held that, although this was true and that the partner had no actual authority from the firm to give investment directions, by auditing the books and failing to challenge the loan transactions the firm had represented that he had such authority. In particular the judge commented that where one partner is put into a position of trust with a client that is itself enough to represent that the partnership trusts that partner and will stand over whatever he does.

The court in *Allied Pharmaceutical Distributors Ltd v Walsh* also approved the earlier Scottish case of *Kirkintilloch Equitable Co-operative Society Ltd v Livingstone*[69] where a partner in a firm of accountants negligently carried out an audit ostensibly in his private capacity. In fact, however, he used the firm's staff and premises and the fee was paid to the firm. He was judged to have been acting in the ordinary course of the firm's business for the purposes of s 10—in effect, he either had implied authority from his position as a partner in an accountancy firm or apparent authority from his permitted use of the partnership facilities. A similar result was obtained in Canada in the case of *Public Trustee v Mortimer*[70] where a solicitor was held to be acting within his apparent authority as a solicitor in the practice when he acted as an executor for a client and as such used all the partnership facilities, and in the Australian case of *Walker v European Electronics Pty Ltd*,[71] where one partner in a firm of accountants handled all the receivership work and misappropriated property whilst doing so.

Limitations on the liability

4.29 However, if the partner has no authority at all to achieve the end sought or there is insufficient connection between the wrongful act and the firm's ordinary business, then his partners will not be liable for any tort he may commit in seeking to achieve that end. To go back 180 years from the last case, an illustration of this point is the case of

---

[68] [1991] 2 IR 8.
[69] 1972 SLT 154.
[70] (1985) 16 DLR (4th) 404.
[71] (1990) 23 NSWLR 1.

Arbuckle v Taylor.[72] One partner of a firm instituted a criminal prosecution on his own account against the plaintiff for an alleged theft of partnership property. The prosecution failed and the plaintiff now sued the firm for the torts of false imprisonment and malicious prosecution. The claim against the other partners failed. It was not within the general scope of the firm's activities to institute criminal proceedings and the other partners were not liable simply because the property allegedly stolen had belonged to the firm. In the absence of any actual or apparent authority, therefore, the partners could not be liable.

A more modern example of a case where the firm were held not liable is the Australian case of *National Commercial Banking Corporation of Australia Ltd v Batty*.[73] One of the two partners misappropriated cheques payable to a company of which he was a director, deposited them in the firm's account, withdrew the proceeds and used them for his own purposes. The firm's bank was sued for conversion of the cheques and now sought to recover its loss from the innocent partner under s 10, as liability for the fraudulent conversion by his fellow partner. By a majority of four to one the High Court of Australia decided that in depositing the cheques in the firm's account the fraudulent partner was not acting in the ordinary course of business of the firm. Although the fraudulent partner had authority to deposit cheques into the account these were cheques payable to the firm and only in exceptional cases cheques payable to third parties. These cheques were substantially larger than other third-party cheques previously paid in. Thus the fraudulent partner had no apparent authority to pay in the cheques since the bank should have been put on notice that he had no authority.

Similarly in *Flynn v Robin Thompson & Partners*,[74] an assault by a solicitor in the court precincts was held to be outside the law firm's ordinary business, as was the assistance by a solicitor in a potently fraudulent investment scam.[75]

Primary liability of wrongdoer

Of course nothing in s 10 relates to a partner's primary liability as a wrongdoer in his own right. Thus if two partners commit a tort which is not within their authority, each can still be liable for the tort, not vicariously but primarily as joint tortfeasors. So in *Meekins v Henson*[76] where one partner wrote a letter defamatory of the plaintiff but could rely on the defence of qualified privilege since he had not acted maliciously, the other partner was held liable since he had acted maliciously. That was on the basis that he was a joint publisher of the letter and so a joint tortfeasor. The plaintiff did not have to rely on s 10—the liability was *primary*, ie being responsible for one's own wrongful act,

4.30

---

[72] (1815) 3 Dow 160.
[73] (1986) 160 CLR 251.
[74] The Times, 14 March 2000.
[75] *JJ Coughlan v Ruparelia* [2004] PNLR 4.
[76] [1964] 1 QB 472.

rather than vicarious, ie being responsible for the wrong of another. Since the partner writing the letter had committed no tort there would of course have been no liability on the other under s 10 since there had been no wrongful act by him.

Wrongs between partners

4.31 The position becomes more complex where one partner commits a tort against another partner in the ordinary course of the partnership business. The Scottish case of *Mair v Wood*[77] decided that the partners not directly involved will not be liable in such a case since if it becomes a partnership liability the plaintiff partner will in effect be suing himself. On the other hand, the Canadian case of *Bigelow v Powers*[78] suggests that such an action against all the other partners is sustainable, with the plaintiff partner's share of the damages being deducted from the final award. This was followed in another Canadian case, *Geisel v Geisel*,[79] where the widow of a deceased partner was allowed to sue the other partner under the Fatal Accidents Acts following a farming accident. Although the judge in that case suggested that the whole firm could be liable, it was in fact simply an action by one partner against the only other partner so that the defendant partner was in effect being sued as a tortfeasor in his own right.

In *Hammonds v Danilunas*,[80] Warren J refused to provide a definitive answer on a striking-out application on a question which raised similar issues. If a misrepresentation is made by one partner to the other partners in the course of the partnership business, does another partner who has acted to his detriment in reliance on the misrepresentation and suffered loss as a result, have a claim against the firm and not just the misrepresentor? Whilst he described this as a developing area of the law, the judge also clearly tended to favour the answer yes, despite the problems of the complainant having to bear a share of his own damages award. The matter must, however, await a later case as this issue was settled between the parties even before the application reached the Court of Appeal.

The position in Australia is equally uncertain. In *Huston v Burns*,[81] an action by one partner against the other two partners, alleging negligence by one of them, was allowed to proceed against the negligent tortfeasor—the action was against him personally and the fact that he was a partner was 'incidental and not the gist of the action'. In *Doak v GJ & BP Chard*,[82] on a preliminary issue, the judge held that the matter depended upon whether the liability of the tortfeasor was a personal one and not a partnership liability. That question could only be determined at trial. The question was whether the

---

[77] 1948 SL 83.
[78] (1911) 25 OLR 28.
[79] (1990) 72 DLR (4th) 245. *See also Sagkeen/Wing Development Partnership v Sagkeen* (2003) 5 WWR 245.
[80] [2009] EWHC 216 (Ch).
[81] [1955] Tas SR 3
[82] [2015] NSWSC 431. See also *Facchini v Facchini* [2002] WADC 127.

Crimes

4.32 Section 10 also applies to crimes ('any penalty'). Again, therefore, a partner can be liable vicariously for the crimes of his partners if they fall within the authority etc of the criminal partner in the sense explained above, unless the instrument creating the offence provides otherwise. Similarly a partner can be liable primarily for the crimes committed by his partners if the offence applies to more than the immediate offenders. For example in *Clode v Barnes*[83] a dormant partner was convicted of an offence under the Trade Descriptions Act 1968 since he was deemed to be a joint supplier of the car with the active partner who had actually sold the car.

Can a firm be convicted of an offence?
4.33 At first sight it seems strange that a distinctly non-corporeal firm can be convicted of a crime in addition to, or even instead of, the constituent partners. Unlike companies and LLPs, partnerships, except in Scotland, only exist as a shorthand description of the relationship between the partners. But many modern regulatory and criminal statutes do provide for the firm to be so liable to a separate conviction, including the modern crime of corporate manslaughter (dealt with below) and various offences under the Bribery Act 2010.[84] The general situation was discussed at some length by the Criminal Division of the Court of Appeal in *W Stevenson & Sons v R*.[85]

In that case, the firm was convicted at Truro Crown Court of eight breaches of the regulations regarding fishing quotas. None of the partners were so charged. When confiscation proceedings were brought against them, however, they appealed to the Court of Appeal on the basis that the conviction of the firm was wrong—it was not possible to treat a partnership as an independent legal entity in this way. The relevant regulation stated that where an offence under it was committed by a partnership, any partner who consented or connived in the offence should be guilty of the offence 'as well as the partnership'. Thus the offence for the firm was one of strict liability, whereas for a partner it required *mens rea*.

The Court of Appeal first noted that under the Interpretation Acts it was apparently permissible to treat a 'person' in a statute as including a partnership unless the context otherwise required. This was a strict liability crime, and the court thought it might be difficult as a general proposition, to convict a firm for a crime requiring *mens rea* if the consequence would be to make a partner liable who had no involvement in the offence.

---

[83] [1974] 1 All ER 1176.
[84] See s 15 of that Act.
[85] [2008] EWCA Crim 273.

Thus they thought that whether a 'person' could include a partnership in any given offence may well depend upon whether there was any restriction on the assets available to pay any penalty.[86] But if, as in this case, the statute expressly provides for the conviction of the firm, then that was the end of the matter.[87]

More difficult was the question as to what were the consequences of such a conviction. Most statutes provide that fines can only be imposed against partnership assets. The one under discussion did not. But the Court was clear. Since a partner could not be personally convicted unless complicit in the crime, it would negative that scheme if their personal assets could be used to pay the fine. If that had been the case then they should have had the right to challenge the validity of the firm's conviction. The fine could only be levied against the assets of the partnership. Further, confiscation orders only lie against offenders, which the partners were not in this case. It is not clear, however, how such an analysis sits in relation to partnership law. First, the argument as to lack of personal liability seems to lie uneasily with s 10 of the Partnership Act;[88] and second, it is a major exception to the rule that the partners are personally liable to fulfil all partnership debts. The partnership assets after all must be replenished by the partners if there is a shortfall in available funds, so restricting liability to those assets may be fruitless. It may also lead to many happy hours establishing what is and what is not partnership property. Firms who may be wary of breaking the law would do well to reduce that to a minimum, which would not be difficult to achieve as they could expressly own the property as co-owners as individuals and not as partners (see Chapter 6, below).

Corporate manslaughter and homicide

4.34 Despite its title, the Corporate Manslaughter and Corporate Homicide Act 2007 applies to the definitely non-corporate English partnership.[89] The offence is set out in s 1(1) of the 2007 Act. It requires an organization to have managed or organized its activities in such a way as to have caused a person's death as the result of a gross breach of the relevant duty of care owed by the organization to the deceased. This is not a book on criminal law so the difficulties of the concepts of causation, gross breach, and relevant duty of care must be found elsewhere. Our question is, given that, how does this offence apply to partnerships?

Under s 1(2) of the 2007 Act a partnership is an organization subject to s 1(1) only if it is an employer.[90] As with all organizations, under s 1(3) the offence will only lie if the defaults of its senior management are a substantial element in the breach. The Act makes

---

[86] But that seems to ignore the effect of s 10 of the Partnership Act.
[87] The Court cited the Health Act 1986 by way of example.
[88] But it might be argued that s 10 only applies if the crime is committed by another partner and not by the firm, which possibility, I suspect, was not envisaged in 1890.
[89] It applies anyway to both LLPs and Scottish partnerships as they have legal personality.
[90] Although, oddly, if it is an employer, it is not only a breach of the duty of care owed to employees which may render the firm liable to prosecution. All the relevant duties in s 2 apply; including eg that owed as an occupier. Thus if eg a client is killed by a falling ceiling, only if the partnership is an employer will the offence lie.

no attempt to apply the concept of senior management to partnerships.[91] Under s 14(1) of the 2007 Act a partnership is to be treated as owing all the duties of care as if it were a body corporate. More significantly for our purposes, s 14(2) states that an offence under the Act may only be committed by the firm and not by the individual partners. Thus they would only be liable under the ordinary offence of gross negligence manslaughter which requires direct personal negligence etc. Then s 14(3) limits the payment of any fine to the funds of the partnership. That would seem again to misunderstand partnership law. If the partnership funds are inadequate to pay the partnership liability then they must surely be replenished by the partners out of their own assets.

Scottish partnerships

In Scotland a partnership has legal personality and so there are no difficulties in convicting one of a crime. But a problem arose because that legal personality disappears immediately on the dissolution of the partnership[92] so that it could no longer be prosecuted. It was even possible that the same thing would happen if there was a change of membership of a partnership. Further, no fine could be levied against it as it had ceased to exist and so could no longer hold assets. The situation was remedied by the Partnerships (Prosecution) (Scotland) Act 2013 which allows a prosecution against a dissolved partnership for up to five years after its dissolution and at any time after a change in membership. Finally, for the avoidance of doubt it provides that criminal proceedings may be brought against any partner irrespective of any dissolution or change of membership.

4.35

Liability for Misapplication of Property

As we have seen it is quite possible for the general liability under s 10 of the Act to cover the liability of partners where another partner misappropriates money or other property in the course of acting in his actual, implied, or apparent authority or in the ordinary course of business of the firm. The words of s 10, 'any wrongful act or omission', are wide enough to include such misapplications. But liability for misappropriations is also specifically covered by s 11. There is no doubt some overlap and in *Langley Holdings Ltd v Seakens*,[93] the court therefore considered that, in the context of that case, s 11 raised the same issue as s 10.

4.36

Section 11 provides:

> In the following cases; namely—
> (a) where one partner acting within the scope of his apparent authority receives the money or property of a third person and misapplies it;

---

[91] The general definition is in s 1(4)(c). They are those who play significant roles in decisions about the whole or a substantial part of the organization or management of the firm's activities, or actually manage or organize the whole or a substantial part of those activities.
[92] *Balmer v HM Advocate* [2008] HCJAC 44.
[93] (2000) LTL, 5 March 2000.

and

(b) where a firm in the course of its business receives money or property of a third person, and the money or property so received is misapplied by one or more of the partners while it is in the custody of the firm;

the firm is liable to make good the loss.

Paragraph (a) therefore applies where the receipt, but not necessarily the misapplication, is by a partner acting 'within the scope of his apparent authority'. Paragraph (b) requires the receipt to be by the firm in the course of its business and to be still in the firm's custody at the time it is misapplied.

Relationship between ss 10 and 11

4.37 In *Dubai Aluminium Ltd v Salaam*,[94] Lord Millett discussed the relationship between ss 10 and 11, having been pressed by counsel for the defence that if s 10 was now to be applied to all liability for misapplications and not just torts, s 11 would be rendered redundant. Section 10 should therefore deal with common law wrongs and s 11 with equitable wrongs. For Lord Millett that analysis was faulty. Section 10, as we shall see, was held in that case to be concerned with vicarious liability for all wrongs, both at common law and in equity, committed by a partner, either with authority or in the ordinary course of the firm's business. Section 11, on the other hand, is not concerned with vicarious liability at all but with the direct liability of the firm to account for misappropriated receipts in certain circumstances and provides that it cannot plead a partner's wrongdoing as an excuse. As such the two sections distinguish between the vicarious and primary liability of the other partners for a misapplication by one partner.[95]

If that is so, the further question is whether both sections are actually needed now. On careful analysis it is clear that they are not identical. Section 11(a) requires the receipt to be within the scope of the partner's authority and s 11(b) requires that the receipt be in the course of the firm's business. Both those correspond to the requirements in s 10 of authority and ordinary course of business. But if the subsequent misapplication is so fraudulent or unusual that it falls into 'the frolic of his own' category that would negative vicarious liability under s 10, whereas the liability under s 11, being primary, would still apply, whatever the circumstances of the misappropriation. All that is needed is a misapplication. That would only be the case in practice for common law liability.[96] Equitable liability for misapplications depends upon the character of the receipt not the misapplication and liability under s 10 for the latter would not be affected by the circumstances of the misapplication. The Law Commissions in fact suggested the repeal

---

[94] [2003] AC 366, HL.
[95] There is also s 13 which further muddies the waters here, but that is dealt with in the next part on trust liability.
[96] See, eg *Hebei Enterprises Ltd v Livasiri & Co* [2008] HKEC 1164.

of s 11.[97] We will return to this issue in the section below on liability for knowing assistance and knowing receipt.

Receipt within apparent authority of partner

4.38 The first important point to grasp is that 'apparent authority' in s 11(a) does not just mean authority created by a representation by words or conduct (ie in the sense in which I have used that term in this book) although it does include that. It also means authority derived from the nature of the business and the status of the partner (ie what I have termed implied authority). As we saw at the beginning of this chapter there is no one meaning of any of the terms applied to authority. Thus s 11(a) applies where the partner receives the property in the course of his implied or apparent authority—the misapplication need not, of course, be part of that authority. In *Antonelli v Allen*,[98] a solicitor who accepted a banker's draft for payment into his firm's client account unconnected with any current or proposed transaction and without any 'solicitor-type' instructions as to what he was to do with it, was not acting within the scope of his apparent authority.

In such cases where the dishonest partner has no such authority there is, therefore, no liability. The best example of this is where the third party is consciously dealing with that partner as an individual and not in his capacity as a partner. Thus in *British Homes Assurance Corporation Ltd v Paterson*,[99] the plaintiffs engaged Atkinson to act as their solicitor vis-à-vis a mortgage and Atkinson later informed them that he had taken Paterson into partnership. The plaintiffs nevertheless sent a cheque ignoring the new firm name, which was then misappropriated by Atkinson, and sought to recover the amount from Paterson under s 11(a). The judge, Farwell J, held that Paterson could not be liable because at all times the plaintiffs had dealt with Atkinson as an individual and had elected to continue the contract as one with an individual even after notification of the existence of the firm. A different question is whether receipt by a company controlled by a partner is a receipt for s 11(a). The point was left open by the Australian court in *Seiwa Australia Pty Ltd v Beard*.[100]

Whether a receipt by a partner is in the course of his apparent or implied authority for the purpose of s 11(a) depends upon establishing one or other of the concepts. If he receives it in the course of his implied authority it will almost certainly be a receipt in the ordinary course of business by the firm and so also fall within s 11(b), as happened in *Bass Brewers Ltd v Appleby*.[101] In *Rhodes v Moules*,[102] the plaintiff sought to raise money

---

[97] Report, para 6.40.
[98] [2001] Lloyd's Rep PN 487.
[99] [1902] 2 Ch 404.
[100] [2009] NSWCA 240.
[101] [1997] 2 BCLC 700, CA.
[102] [1895] 1 Ch 236.

by way of a mortgage on his property. He used a solicitor in a firm who told him that the lenders wanted additional security and so he handed the solicitor some share warrants to bearer (ie transferable by simple delivery and a fraud's delight). This solicitor misappropriated them and the plaintiff now sued the firm under s 11. The Court of Appeal held that the firm was liable under both heads. On the evidence the certificates were received in the ordinary course of the firm's business and also within the apparent authority of the partner.

On the other hand there will be occasions where, because liability under para (a) is based on authority arising from a representation by the other partners rather than from the business of the company, para (b) will not be available. Thus in the Canadian case of *Public Trustee v Mortimer*[103] where a solicitor acting as an executor and trustee of a will misapplied the funds under his control his partners were held liable under para (a) of this section (numbered 12 in the Ontario statute). The judge was unsure whether the solicitor qua trustee and executor was acting in the ordinary course of business of the firm but:

> There can be no doubt, in my view, that the firm, by permitting Mortimer to use the stationery, accounts, staff and other facilities of the firm in connection with his activities as executor and trustee, had vested Mortimer with apparent authority to receive the money or property of the estate which he subsequently misapplied.

The judge also found the other partners liable under the Ontario equivalent of s 10 since it was a wrongful act of a partner acting with the authority of his fellow partners. They could not, however, in view of the judge's doubts, have been liable under the Ontario equivalent of s 11(b) since the receipt (as distinct from the misapplication for the purposes of s 10) was not clearly within the ordinary course of business of the firm.

Receipt in course of ordinary business

4.39 If s 11(b) is relied upon, the receipt must be by the firm in the course of its ordinary business and the misapplication must have been whilst the money or property was still in the firm's custody. Thus the receipt must in effect be by a partner acting within his implied authority[104] and if the misapplication takes place after the property ceases to be in the custody of the firm, eg where the money is loaned out again by the firm to a company and a partner fraudulently persuades the company to repay the money to him, there can be no liability under s 11(b): *Sims v Brutton*.[105] Whether the property is in the custody of the firm at the relevant time is a question of fact—the answer would appear to be no if it is in the custody of an individual partner in his own private capacity. In *Tendring Hundred Waterworks Co v Jones*,[106] the company employed a firm of

---

[103] (1985) 16 DLR (4th) 404.
[104] If not, then there is no liability. *Antonelli v Allen* [2001] Lloyd's Rep PN 487.
[105] (1850) 5 Ex 802. It is unlikely that s 10 would apply either in this situation.
[106] [1903] 2 Ch 615.

solicitors, Garrard and Jones, to negotiate a purchase of land. Garrard was the company secretary and his fees as such were regarded as partnership income. The company stupidly arranged for the land to be conveyed into Garrard's name and the vendors gave him the title deeds. Garrard used the deeds to raise money by way of a mortgage. The company now sought to make Jones liable for Garrard's misapplication.

Farwell J held that this did not fall within s 11(b) since the deeds were given to Garrard not in his capacity as company secretary or partner but as a private individual who was named in the conveyance as the legal owner. Thus the deeds were not in the custody of the firm—they were in Garrard's custody as a private individual. It is, of course, equally true that the receipt by Garrard was not in the ordinary course of the firm's business—it is not part of the ordinary duty of a solicitor to accept conveyances of land belonging to his clients into his own name. It would be different if a client leaves his deeds with his solicitors in the ordinary course of business and a member of the firm fraudulently deposits them with another in order to raise money on them. In such a case the misapplication would take place whilst they were in the custody of the firm.

Improper employment of trust property in the partnership

Section 13 of the Act provides: **4.40**

> If a partner, being a trustee, improperly employs trust-property in the business or on account of the partnership, no other partner is liable for the trust-property to the persons beneficially interested therein.
>
> Provided as follows:—
> (1) This section shall not affect any liability incurred by any partner by reason of his having notice of a breach of trust; and
> (2) Nothing in this section shall prevent trust money from being followed and recovered from the firm if still in its possession or under its control.

This section is, misleadingly, apparently quite straightforward. It only applies to one specific fact situation, ie where a partner/trustee improperly brings trust money *into* the firm (without any subsequent misapplication, which might trigger s 11, or any other subsequent breach, which might trigger s 10), eg as his capital contribution. In such a case it is quite proper to excuse the innocent partners under the basic principles of knowing receipt, since how would they know where it came from? Partners with notice of the breach are liable and the beneficiaries are not prevented from tracing the trust property (ie recovering the property itself (if identifiable) or the proceeds of that property) under the principles laid down in *Ministry of Health v Simpson*.[107] There are some immediate difficulties with the section, however: eg does it apply only to a

---

[107] [1951] AC 251, HL.

partner who is an express trustee or does it also apply to a partner/constructive trustee? Further, will a partner who has constructive but no actual notice of the breach be liable even though that is no longer enough to establish liability for either dishonest assistance or knowing receipt? But the greatest difficulty raised by s 13 is how it affects any possible partnership liability for constructive trusts under ss 10 and 11 since it protects innocent partners, whereas neither of those do so, being formulated instead on concepts of apparent authority and the ordinary course of business. Before coming back to s 13 itself, it is now time to consider partnership liability for breaches of a constructive trust under ss 10 and 11.

Vicarious liability for dishonest assistance and knowing receipt

4.41 Section 10 makes partners vicariously liable for all *wrongs* committed by a partner either in the scope of his apparent authority or in the ordinary course of business of the firm. The question first therefore is whether a breach of a constructive trust, eg dishonest assistance or participation in breach of fiduciary duty, by a partner can be a *wrong* for this purpose. Of course, even if it can, the other aspects of s 10 would have to be fulfilled before any vicarious liability on the other partners could arise. If it cannot, then there can be no vicarious liability under s 10 and the other partners would only be liable if they themselves had become constructive trustees in their own right, ie by their own dishonest assistance or receipt. (For the moment let us leave s 11 out of our calculations—that section could only apply in any event to the specific case of knowing receipt.)

The answer to whether s 10 could apply to liability for dishonest assistance was quite clearly given as a yes by the House of Lords in *Dubai Aluminium Co Ltd v Salaam*.[108] The policy[109] and history[110] of s 10 both required that construction—it applied to all fault-based liability not just to common law liability. For Lord Millett there was no rational ground for restricting s 10 to torts.[111] The only issue which then remained was whether the actual dishonest assistance was done whilst the partner was acting in the ordinary course of the firm's business or with the authority of his co-partners.

In the *Dubai Aluminium* case itself the dishonest assistance had been given by a partner in a firm of solicitors. It was argued by the defendants that as a matter of law it is not within the implied authority of a solicitor to constitute himself a constructive trustee and so the dishonest assistance could not have been given within the firm's ordinary

---

[108] [2003] AC 366, HL. The same conclusion was arrived at in 2001 by the Manx Court (Staff of Government Division) in *Liggins v Lumsden Ltd* [1999 – 01] MLR 601.
[109] The reference to penalties in the section shows that it applies to statutory liability.
[110] Lord Millett referred to *Brydges v Branfill* (1842) 12 Sim 369 as establishing the principle of vicarious liability for equitable wrongdoing. See also *Agip (Africa) Ltd v Jackson* [1991] Ch 547, CA. It thus applies to breaches of fiduciary duty by a partner to a client etc: *3464920 Canada Inc v Strother*, 2007 SCC 24.
[111] His Lordship also, as we have seen, rejected the argument that s 11 applied to equitable wrongs and s 10 therefore only to common law wrongs; the distinction instead being between vicarious and primary liability.

business. They relied on apparently clear statements to that effect by the Court of Appeal in *Mara v Browne*,[112] which were followed and applied by Vinelott J in *Re Bell's Indenture*.[113] The House of Lords in *Dubai Aluminium* explained *Mara v Browne* as applying only to the facts of that case which were that the solicitor had intermeddled in a trust so as to become a de facto trustee. Thus the use of the words constructive trustee meant only that particular type. It had no application to dishonest assistance and *Re Bell's Indenture* was wrong on that point and should be overruled.[114] On the facts the House of Lords in *Dubai Aluminium*, reversing the Court of Appeal, then held that by undertaking drafting work in furtherance of the fraud the partner liable for dishonest assistance had acted in the ordinary course of business of the firm. Accordingly the other partners were vicariously liable for his acts. This finding in itself has considerably widened the potential for vicarious liability since the errant partner had with another actively also conceived and executed the scheme, which, for the Court of Appeal, took it so far outside the scope of the ordinary business of the firm as to negative liability.[115]

Lord Millett was, however, adamant that it would never be part of any solicitor's ordinary course of business to receive money as an express trustee or, as in *Mara v Browne*, as a trustee *de son tort*. This was followed in Singapore in *Lim Kok Koon v Tan Cheng Yew*,[116] but the express trust in that case was very unusual involving the partner concerned in an area of practice which was outside his expertise and it is respectfully suggested that the blanket approach of Lord Millet is too sweeping—after all there are still 'family solicitors', even if they rarely impinge upon the Supreme Court.

Specific problems with receipts

If s 10 applies in principle to all wrongs, it must clearly also apply to liability for knowing receipt, but of course it can again do so only if the actual receipt by the partner (with the requisite knowledge) is within his apparent authority or the ordinary course of business of his firm. This is because the receipt by the partner itself is the breach for which vicarious liability is sought. Section 11, to establish primary liability on the other partners, actually requires the receipt to be either by a partner in the course of his apparent authority or by the firm in the ordinary course of its business. Since, under that section, that will establish liability whether or not the subsequent misapplication of the property is within that authority or ordinary business, the application of ss 10 and 11 to liability for knowing receipt would appear to be the same. In *Re Bell's Indenture Trusts*,[117] Vinelott J categorized the receipt by the firm as being as agents, which negatived primary liability on the partners as constructive trustees. The question which remains to

4.42

---

[112] [1896] 1 Ch 199.
[113] [1980] 1 WLR 1271.
[114] See also *Liggins v Lumsden Ltd* [1999–2001] MLR 601; *Lim Kok Koon v Tan Cheng Yew* [2004] 3 SLR 111.
[115] In *Liggins v Lumsden Ltd*, the Manx court took the view that the acts were within the ordinary course of a solicitor's business because they related to legal work carried for the fraudsters and he was not centrally involved in the administration of the scheme, which they thought would take it outside.
[116] [2004] 3 SLR 111. See also *Walker v Stones* [2000] 4 All ER 412, CA.
[117] [1980] 1 WLR 1271. This part of the judgment is not affected by *Dubai Aluminium*.

be answered, therefore, is whether receipt in such a capacity could fall within the concepts of apparent authority or ordinary business of the firm. Contemporary practice would suggest that in certain circumstances a receipt of trust moneys is now common practice among solicitors and so falls within those criteria. But, as we have seen, the courts have recently[118] stated that a solicitor acting as an express trustee is not within the ordinary business of a firm of solicitors and so the position is far from clear.

Finally, some confusion has arisen as to the interface between s 11 and s 13 in relation to trust property received by the firm. The difference between the two sections was, however, explained by Millett LJ in *Bass Brewers Ltd v Appleby*:[119]

> Section 11 deals with the money which is properly received by the firm (or by one of the partners acting within the scope of his apparent authority) for and on behalf of the third party but which is subsequently misapplied. The firm is liable to make good the loss. Section 13 is concerned with money held by a partner in some other capacity, such as a trustee, which is misapplied by him and then improperly and in breach of trust employed by him in the partnership business. His partners can be made liable only in accordance with the ordinary principles of knowing receipt.

The question therefore ought to be whether the partner's knowing receipt was also a 'proper receipt' by the firm within s 11 (or presumably s 10) so as to establish vicarious liability, or whether it was an 'improper' receipt (ie outside the firm's business etc) which is then put into the firm by the constructive trustee in breach of his trust. In the latter case only a partner with 'notice' will be liable.

Vicarious liability for breaches of express trusts

4.43 In *Walker v Stones*[120] the question arose as to whether a partner in a firm of solicitors could be vicariously liable for a breach of an express trust by a partner/trustee under s 10. The Court of Appeal decided that the ordinary course of business requirement in s 10 could not apply to such a breach because if it did it would be impossible to reconcile that section with s 13. Their argument was that if s 10 could apply it would presuppose that individual trusteeships which a partner may undertake are in the ordinary course of business of a firm and would therefore cover the exact situation as described in s 13, which protects innocent partners. In enacting s 13, therefore, the legislature must have treated such breaches of trust committed by a trustee/partner as being outside s 10 (and s 11). They also relied on the statement by Rix J, as approved by Aldous LJ in the *Dubai Aluminium* case, to the effect that s 13 'appears to assume that the individual trusteeships which a partner may undertake are not something undertaken in the ordinary

---

[118] The Court of Appeal in *Walker v Stones* [2000] 4 All ER 412, approved by Lord Millett in *Dubai Aluminium Co Ltd v Salaam* [2003] AC 366, HL, who was followed in *Lim Kok Koon v Tan Cheng Yew* [2004] 3 SLR 111.
[119] [1997] 2 BCLC 700 at 711.
[120] [2000] 4 All ER 412, CA.

course of business, otherwise it would be inconsistent with s 11'. The case was settled shortly before a scheduled hearing in the House of Lords.

Lord Millett in *Dubai Aluminium Co Ltd v Salaam*[121] was equally adamant:

> If, as I think, it is still not within the ordinary scope of a solicitor's practice to act as a trustee of an express trust, it is obviously not within the scope of such a practice voluntarily to assume the obligations of trusteeship and so incur liability as a de facto trustee.

With respect that simply seems a very strange statement to anyone who has ever dealt with a family firm. Further the argument based on s 13 is surely misplaced. That section only applies to one specific fact situation, ie a breach of trust by a partner by bringing the money into the firm. It cannot apply, eg, to the situation where a firm receives money from a client, one of the partners then becomes a trustee of it, and it is subsequently misapplied by him. The better course is surely to apply ss 10 and 11 on their wording except where to do so would be inconsistent with s 13. As we have seen there is a difference between s 11 and s 13 in scope and the differences between s 10 and s 13 are obvious.

Scope of s 13

4.44 That does of course lead on to the question as to what is the scope of s 13. It clearly applies to a partner who is a trustee under an express trust who uses trust money in the business or in the account of the firm. But could it also apply to a partner who is a constructive trustee or fiduciary and does the same? Further, what is the position of a partner who has intermeddled in a trust and then does the same? Finally, if s 13 applies, what notice do the other partners have so as to be outside the protection of that section? In the *Bass Brewers*[122] case Millett LJ equated that with sufficient notice to make them liable for knowing receipt, which as we have seen, is a long way from constructive notice.

Nature of the Liability

Joint and several liability

4.45 The Partnership Act itself makes a clear distinction between the nature of the liability of partners for debts and obligations on the one hand and for torts, crimes, and other wrongs on the other. Section 9 provides that every partner in a firm is liable *jointly*

---

[121] [2003] AC 366, HL. Followed in *Lim Kok Koon v Tan Cheng Yew* [2004] 3 SLR 111.
[122] [1997] 2 BCLC 700, CA.

with the other partners for all debts and obligations of the firm incurred while he is a partner—this in effect creates the unlimited liability of a partner which gave rise to the demands for the limited liability partnership. Section 12, on the other hand, provides that for liability under ss 10 and 11 of the Act every partner is liable *jointly* with his co-partners and also *severally* for everything for which the firm becomes liable whilst he is a partner. Strangely, however, s 9 does provide several liability for debts once the partner is deceased. The distinction in the Act, therefore, is between joint liability for contracts and joint and several liability for torts etc. This distinction has never applied to Scotland where it has always been joint and several liability for all debts and fines etc, nor does it apply against the estate of a deceased partner—again joint and several liability is imposed, although in that case any liability is postponed until the deceased's non-partnership debts have been paid.

What then is the distinction between joint liability and joint and several liability? The difference is that if liability is only joint the claimant has only one cause of action against all the partners in respect of each debt or contract. In *Kendall v Hamilton*[123] the practical consequence of this was spelt out. A creditor sued all the obvious members of a firm and was awarded judgment against them. He failed to recover the debt in full, however, and when he subsequently discovered a wealthy dormant partner he sought to sue him for the balance of the debt. The House of Lords decided that since the debt was a joint one only, by suing the apparent partners the creditor had elected to sue only them and could not now commence fresh proceedings against the other partner. He had exhausted the cause of action. No such restriction applies to liability under s 12 for there the liability is several as well as joint so that each partner can be sued in turn or all together until the full amount is recovered—the complainant is never put to his election.

Civil Liability (Contribution) Act 1978

4.46 The injustice caused by the decision in *Kendall v Hamilton* was relieved partly by the disclosure of partners' names on notepaper and partly by the rules of practice which allowed creditors to obtain lists of who were the partners at the relevant time. But it was finally laid to rest so far as civil liability is concerned by s 3 of the Civil Liability (Contribution) Act 1978. This provides that:

> Judgment recovered against any person liable in respect of any debt or damage shall not be a bar to an action, or to the continuance of an action, against any other person who is (apart from any such bar) jointly liable with him in respect of the same debt or damage.

Although that section clearly disposes of the anomalies of *Kendall v Hamilton*[124] it has its limitations. Thus in *Morris v Wentworth-Stanley*,[125] where the plaintiff was found to

---

[123] (1879) 4 App Cas 504, HL.
[124] Ibid.
[125] [1999] 2 QB 1004.

have settled his claim against the firm with one of the partners in circumstances where he had not reserved, either expressly or impliedly, the right to go against the other partners, the defence of accord and satisfaction was available to another partner whom he then sued for the same debt (having appropriated most of the original payment made to him to costs). Nothing in the section affected such a defence if properly made out.

Liability for costs

In *Ontario Realty Corporation v Gabriele & Sons Ltd*,[126] the question arose as to the liability of partners for the costs of litigation under ss 9 and 12. The judge in the Ontario Superior Court thought that if costs on a substantial basis were awarded because of the misconduct by a partner or partners during the proceedings, that would not make another partner liable for the higher award caused by that partner or partners. That was because they would not be acting in the ordinary course of business of the partnership in conducting the litigation. But that would not be the case if the higher award was caused by the misconduct in the circumstances giving rise to the litigation.

4.47

Duration of the Liability

We have seen, therefore, that partners are liable without limit for all debts, obligations, torts, crimes, misapplications, etc committed by the firm *whilst they are partners*. But partnerships are not static—partners come and go and therefore it is necessary to find out when a retiring partner ceases to be liable for the debts etc of the firm and when a new partner assumes such liability. The answers are to be found in ss 17 and 36 of the Act, but it should always be remembered that, irrespective of these rules, a person can always be liable as if he were a partner under s 14 of the Act if he either allows himself to be represented as such by the other partners or indeed represents himself as such. This may be particularly relevant where a former partner is involved. Bearing that in mind we should turn our attention to s 17 which provides the basic rules on a change of partners.

4.48

Effect of a change of partner

Section 17(1) states that '[a] person who is admitted as a partner into an existing firm does not thereby become liable to the creditors of the firm for anything done before he became a partner', and s 17(2) accordingly rules that '[a] partner who retires from a firm does not thereby cease to be liable for partnership debts or obligations incurred before his retirement'.[127] Applying these rules therefore presents a neat picture. Suppose A, B,

4.49

---

[126] 2009 00-CL-3726 (Ont SC).
[127] It has been held in Canada that the word 'obligations' applies to private law debts and not public protection matters such as professional regulatory inspections: *Institute of Chartered Accountants (British Columbia) v Stone*, 2009 BCSC 1153.

and C are partners. C retires and D joins the firm. C is liable for the debts etc incurred up to the change by virtue of s 17(2) and D becomes liable only for those debts incurred after the change under s 17(1). In theory this is perfectly correct—D had no control over debts incurred before he became a partner and C should not be allowed to escape liability for existing debts simply by retiring from the firm. But practice is as usual far less tidy than theory. Contracts made with the firm before the date of change may produce liabilities after the date of change—is the new partner liable for such debts or the old partner absolved?

Single continuing contract

4.50 The answer seems to depend in England upon whether the contract is a single continuing contract, in which case the former partner remains liable and the new partner is exempt, or whether it is a series of individual contracts in which case the new partner replaces the old for liabilities incurred after the change. An example of a single continuing contract giving rise to a single liability already incurred at the date of change is *Court v Berlin*.[128] Court was a solicitor retained by a partnership to recover a debt due to it. The firm consisted of Berlin, the sole active partner, and two dormant partners. During the solicitor's work for the firm the two dormant partners retired. After the proceedings for recovery of the debt were completed the solicitor sued Berlin and the former partners for his costs. The dormant partners claimed that they were only liable for costs incurred up to the date of their retirement. The Court of Appeal held that they were fully liable. The contract entered into whilst they were partners was 'one entire contract to conduct the action to the end'; the solicitor did not need to come for fresh instructions at each step of the action. The dormant partners' liability for costs was for all the costs in the action—it did not arise on a day-to-day basis. Presumably it would have been different if Berlin had then decided to take the matter to an appeal court—that would not have been a single continuing liability since fresh instructions would have been needed.

It was suggested in *Court v Berlin* that the retiring partners could avoid liability under a single continuing contract by giving the solicitor in that case express notice of their retirement—in which case presumably the solicitor would have to choose to continue on a new basis or end the contract. If, however, the liabilities accrue on a day-by-day basis, albeit under a single general contract, the retiring partner will cease to be liable on retirement and the new partner will take over from the date of joining. An example of this type of contract is in *Bagel v Miller*[129] where a firm contracted to purchase various shipments of goods. One of the partners died and it was held that his estate was only liable for the goods delivered before his death and not for deliveries afterwards. Those were liabilities accruing after his death. In such standing supply contracts it is the new partner who assumes responsibility: see *Dyke v Brewer*.[130]

---

[128] [1897] 2 QB 396.
[129] [1903] 2 KB 212.
[130] (1849) 2 Car & Kir 828.

Scottish partnerships

The position in Scotland is very different because on a change of partner a new firm (with legal personality of its own) replaces the old firm. The issue therefore is whether the new firm is liable for the debts of the old firm. The position is that there is a presumption to that effect if the business taken over is substantially the same as the old firm and that business continues without interruption. But it is a presumption only and the real question in effect is whether in each case the new firm has so agreed—which may be inferred from circumstances or a course of dealing. The most recent authoritative decision on this issue is *Scottish Pension Fund Trustees Ltd v Marshall Ross & Munro*.[131]

4.51

Novation—English law

All this can be inconvenient and so the Act and the common law allow an alternative to s 17(1) and (2). Section 17(3) accordingly provides that:

4.52

> A retiring partner may be discharged from any existing liabilities, by an agreement to that effect between himself and the members of the firm as newly constituted and the creditors, and this agreement may be either express or inferred as a fact from the course of dealing between the creditors and the firm as newly constituted.

There is no doubt that, since this is simply declaratory of the position at common law in England, similar principles would apply equally to an incoming partner accepting a liability. What is required is a contract of novation between the creditor, the new or retiring partner, and the other partners. This is a tripartite agreement by which the creditor accepts the new firm as taking over liability for the debt from the old firm—it must be a three-way agreement, an internal agreement between the partners cannot limit the rights of the creditor on basic principles of privity of contract. The basic contractual principles of novation require consent of all the parties and consideration.

Implied novation

If such an agreement is express then few problems occur but it is far more likely to be implied from the acts of all concerned. What amounts to a novation in such circumstances is, of course, a question of fact in each case. It is less likely where there is no incoming partner to take over responsibility for the debt but more likely if the debts are difficult to quantify as between before and after the change. The creditor must, however, be aware of the change and that he is looking to the new firm for payment. There are several examples of novation in such circumstances. In *Rolfe v Flower Salting & Co*[132]

4.53

---

[131] [2018] CSIH 39. See also *Sim v Howat* [2011] CSOH 115 and *Heather Capital Ltd v Levy & McRae* [2015] CSOH 115.
[132] (1866) LR 1 PC 27.

three partners took two of their clerks into partnership. The newly constituted firm continued to trade under the old name and no change was made to the business; even the accounts were continued in the same way. The company was owed £80,000 by the old firm (without the clerks). That debt and the interest payable on it had been kept in the accounts and was regularly entered up. The new partners had access to the books. The company continued to trade with the new firm. The Privy Council, agreeing with the Supreme Court of Victoria, found the new partners liable for the old debt on the basis of implied novation. The company, by dealing with the new firm with full knowledge of the change of membership, had impliedly agreed to accept the new firm as debtors in place of the old firm, and the partners, by not objecting to the accounts, had impliedly agreed to accept liability for the debt.

The issue of implied novation in relation to the liabilities of incoming partners was discussed by Lloyd J in *Marsden v Guide Dogs for the Blind Association*.[133] He said that it would not be difficult to find the basis of novation in relation to a continuing contract where the client knows that there has been a change of partner from A and B to B and C. But if the client is unaware of the change then there can be novation.[134] In the case itself, however, the situation was different. There had been a change from a sole proprietorship of A to a partnership of A, B, and C. Again it was considered reasonably easy in that situation to infer novation for future liabilities on a single continuing contract with a client but much more difficult with respect to A's existing liabilities under such a contract, ie those incurred prior to the change. There was no evidence that the client had been made aware of any change in respect of the previous liabilities.

Merely setting up the new firm would not be enough to infer novation of such liabilities[135] nor would any internal agreement between the partners.[136]

If reliance had been sought on a representation by A that B and C would become liable for the existing debts that would have been insufficient without everyone else's consent. If they did consent then consideration might also be inferred for that agreement. Alternatively if reliance is placed on a statement by B or C that they accepted responsibility for A's existing debts then the problem would again be that such statements unsupported by consideration would not be enforceable and it would depend on the facts whether such consideration could be inferred.

---

[133] [2004] 3 All ER 222. The situation in respect of an outgoing partner's release, which is the only one mentioned specifically in s 17(3), is discussed below.
[134] The judge used the example of a long administration of an estate by a firm of solicitors where the partners but not the firm name change and the client is unaware of the changes.
[135] *Arden v Roy* [1883] 1 NZLR 365.
[136] *HF Pension Trustees Ltd v Ellison* [1999] PNLR 894 at 898–9 per Jonathan Parker J.

Guarantees

4.54 From the point of view of an outsider a change in the firm will often terminate his contract, eg to supply goods, and a new contract (usually implied) will be needed. In the case of a guarantee of a debt owed by the firm or a debt owed to the firm, s 18 of the Act makes it quite clear that such a guarantee comes to an end on a change in the firm—it will only cover debts incurred before the change. This is fine where the guarantee is by a third party covering a debt owed by the firm, because if X guarantees a debt owed by A, B, and C to Y and is called upon to pay, he takes over Y's rights against A, B, and C. If C retires, X will lose his rights for the future against C and so the guarantee lapses. But it is much harder to justify where the guarantee is given to the firm in respect of the debt owed to it, ie where the firm is in effect the primary creditor. On the other hand guarantors could always insert what terms they wish to protect themselves—s 18 is subject to contrary intention.

Liability for debts incurred after leaving the firm

4.55 So far we have been discussing the liability of a partner for the debts etc incurred before he retires. He may, however, also be liable for debts incurred *after* he retires, not only under the doctrine of holding out under s 14, but more specifically under the provisions of s 36. In effect this provides a retirement procedure whereby the former partner can escape liability for future debts. It provides for three specific situations although all three subsections have to be read together in order to make this clear. The section is as follows:

(1) Where a person deals with a firm after a change in its constitution he is entitled to treat all apparent members of the old firm as still being members of the firm until he has notice of the change.
(2) An advertisement in the [*London* or *Edinburgh Gazette*]...shall be notice as to persons who had not dealings with the firm before the date of dissolution or change so advertised.
(3) The estate of a partner who dies, or who becomes bankrupt, or of a partner who, not having been known to the person dealing with the firm to be a partner, retires from the firm, is not liable for partnership debts contracted after the date of the death, bankruptcy, or retirement respectively.

Presumption of liability

4.56 Section 36(1) thus extends the liability of a former member of the firm to debts contracted after his departure if he is an 'apparent member' of the firm and the creditor has no notice of his retirement. This is based on estoppel. There is some debate as to the meaning of s 36(1). On one view the requirement to give notice of the retirement applies only if the former partner was an apparent partner both before and after his retirement, but this was rejected by the Court of Appeal in Victoria in *Hamerhaven Pty Ltd v Ogge*.[137] Callaway JA put the other view, and its consequences, as follows:

> In my opinion it means that a person who was an apparent member of the old firm... may for that reason alone continue to be treated as a member of the firm after the change in its constitution until the plaintiff has notice of the change. 'Apparent' is used only in relation to membership of the old firm and 'still' relates to continuing membership not the appearance thereof.

This view was also expressed in the Hong Kong case of *Lon Eagle Industrial Ltd v Realy Trading Co*.[138] The liability is independent of holding-out liability under s 14. The claimant does not have to prove any form of reliance other than the fact that he dealt with the firm.

An argument was put in the Irish case of *ACC Bank plc v Johnston*[139] that s 36(1) could not apply where one partner in a two-partner firm left the firm, since what would be left to be dealt with by the third party would be a sole trader and not a firm. That was rejected on the basis that the common law position prior to the Act was that notice was required in such a situation and there was no reason to find that the Act had altered the common law.

Actual notice

4.57 How then does such a partner escape liability for debts incurred after he has retired? The answer is by giving the complainant actual notice of his retirement or by invoking the provisions of s 36(2) or (3). In *Hamerhaven Pty Ltd v Ogge* the question arose as to what could amount to actual notice for this purpose. The evidence relied on by the retired partner in that case as constituting actual notice was the fact that subsequent to his retirement his name had initially been changed on the firm's letterhead from being a partner to being a consultant and had then been removed altogether. The Court of Appeal in Victoria held first that it was for the retiring partner to show that actual notice had been given to the plaintiff and not for the latter to show that he had no notice.

Second, the court held that the plaintiff was under no obligation to scrutinize the letterhead on the firm's letters and was not to be regarded as having a lawyer's appreciation of what a consultant was or indeed what the consequences were of taking the former partner's name off the letterhead altogether. It might have been different if the firm had spelt out the fact that there had been a change in the firm's constitution either on the letterhead or in the body of the letter. Implicit in this decision is the idea that for a plaintiff to have notice of a partner's retirement he must have some form of knowledge or understanding of that fact.

---

[137] [1996] 2 VR 488. Followed in the New Zealand case of *Wood v Fresher Foods Ltd* [2007] NZHC 1466.
[138] [1999] 4 HKC 675.
[139] [2011] IEHC 108.

The court distinguished the ancient English case of *Barfoot v Goodall*,[140] where a person dealing with a banking partnership was held to have notice of a partner's retirement from that firm because that person's name had been omitted from the firm's cheques. Lord Ellenborough commented that it was well known that banking houses communicated a change of partner in this way and having received such a cheque the plaintiff should have made inquiries. This enabled Callaway JA in the *Hamerhaven* case to say that in *Barfoot* Lord Ellenborough was saying that having noticed the change the plaintiff should have made inquiries whereas in that case the plaintiff was under no obligation even to notice the change.

With respect that is not what Lord Ellenborough was saying. The important point in *Barfoot* was that it was a well-known method of indicating change in the banking field, whereas in *Hamerhaven* that is not so with letterheads. The most sensible solution is surely that the complainant will have notice if he actually appreciates that there has been a change, or a reasonable man would in all the circumstances have so appreciated, and a change in the letterhead, in compliance with the requirements of Part 41 of the Companies Act 2006, may achieve that. If notice can be established, the manner is irrelevant, eg a notice in a newspaper which the customer can be shown to have seen and understood.[141]

But it is clear that the burden of proof rests squarely with the outgoing partner. Thus in *Wood v Fresher Foods Ltd*,[142] where the outgoing partner told a customer that he was retiring, that was construed as referring only to his ceasing work and not as to leaving the firm.

Notice in the Gazette

4.58 There is no need for a retiring partner to give notice if either of s 36(2) or (3) apply. Section 36(2) applies if the creditor has never dealt with the firm before the change. In that case it will be sufficient if the retiring partner has placed an appropriate announcement in the *London Gazette* (for England and Wales), or the *Edinburgh Gazette* (for Scotland). Actual notice, therefore, need only be given to existing customers: prospective customers must read the small print.[143]

Where third party did not know he was a partner

4.59 Under s 36(3) no notice at all need be given if the former partner has died or become bankrupt, or if the customer dealing with the firm did not know him to be a partner. The relationship between s 36(1) and (3) was explained in *Tower Cabinet Co Ltd v Ingram*,[144] a case we have already discussed in Chapter 2 in relation to s 14. To recap

---

[140] (1811) 3 Camp 147.
[141] See, eg *Tan Boon Cheo v Ho Hong Bank Ltd* [1934] (Vol 111) MLJ 180. Notice can be given orally. See *Faber Image Media Pte Ltd v Patrician Holding Pte Ltd* [2009] SGHC 16.
[142] [2007] NZHC 1466.
[143] If the customer has actually read the item that will amount to actual notice. See n 126 above.
[144] [1949] 2 KB 397.

the facts, Christmas and Ingram were partners in a firm which was dissolved in 1947, Christmas carrying on the business under the same name as a sole trader. In 1948, the company agreed to supply some furniture to the business. The order was later confirmed by Christmas on old notepaper which included Ingram's name on its heading. Ingram had no idea that this was being done. The price was never paid and the company now sought to recover the money from Ingram as an apparent partner under s 36(1). (If you remember they also tried s 14 but it was held that Ingram had not 'knowingly' allowed himself to be represented as a partner.) The judge rejected the claim under s 36, holding that s 36(3) applied and provided a complete defence to the claim.

In coming to this conclusion the judge interpreted the words 'apparent partner' in s 36(1) as meaning apparent to the particular creditor and not to the public at large. This could arise either because he had dealt with the firm before or he had some other indication of the former partner's existence, including the notepaper as in this case. Section 36(1), however, has to be interpreted in the light of s 36(3). The company had no knowledge that Ingram was a partner at the date of his retirement, ie he was not an apparent partner as far as the company was concerned at that time, and in such cases there can be no liability under s 36(1) because s 36(3) gave him complete protection. Lynskey J was quite clear:

> If the person dealing with the firm did not know that the particular partner was a partner, and the partner retired, then as from the date of his retirement, he ceases to be liable for further debts contracted by the firm to such person. The fact that later the person dealing with the firm may discover that the former partner was a partner seems to me to be irrelevant, because the date from which the subsection operates is from the date of the dissolution. If at the date of the dissolution the person who subsequently deals with the firm had no knowledge at or before that time that the retiring partner was a partner, then subsection (3) comes into operation, and relieves the person retiring from liability.

A former partner cannot therefore be an apparent partner within s 36(1) if the creditor never knew him to be a partner before his retirement. This case has been followed in a number of Commonwealth cases. The most recent example is the Canadian case of *Horizon Electric Ltd v Larry Hassen Holdings Ltd*,[145] where a partnership between the defendant company and Desrosiers Farms Ltd was dissolved in 1985. Larry Hassen Holdings Ltd continued the business of house building under the firm name of Hassen Homes. The plaintiffs installed electrical wiring and fixtures into new houses built by Hassen Homes in 1986 and had not been paid. They failed to make Desrosiers Farms Ltd liable since they did not know of Desrosiers' connection with Hassen Homes at the time when they were doing business with the 'firm'. Desrosiers was not an apparent partner and so was not liable. Liability for being an apparent partner should stand or

---

[145] (1990) 71 DLR 273.

fall with s 14(1) and not s 36(1) which is specifically related to retirement formalities. The essence of the company's case was that they had been misled by the notepaper but it was equally clear that at no time had that actually been the case.

Summary

Section 36 is confusing enough to require a summary to make things clear. A partner who retires will be liable for debts incurred after he retires unless: (a) he gives actual notice of his retirement to existing creditors at the time of his retirement; (b) he puts a notice in the relevant *Gazette* for prospective creditors; or (c) the creditor did not know that he was a partner at the time when he retired. Of course, if he knowingly allows himself to be subsequently represented as a partner none of these will apply; instead liability will fall quite clearly under s 14(1). If a partner is liable under s 36 it is an interesting question whether the creditor must choose to sue the new firm, without the retired partner, or the old, and having chosen one it cannot then sue the other. This was the position at common law and it is far from clear whether s 3 of the Civil Liability (Contribution) Act 1978, which allows a creditor to sue joint debtors in sequence, will apply as between two groups who do not, vis-à-vis each other, have joint liability.

4.60

5
PARTNERS AND EACH OTHER

Contract and Equity

Fiduciary relationship

Partnership is a relationship based on mutual trust which can have far-reaching consequences as respects the partners' liabilities to outsiders. For precisely that reason it has long been established that partners owe each other a duty of good faith, ie to act honestly and for the benefit of the partnership as a whole. Thus in 1824 in *Const v Harris*[1] Lord Eldon could say: 'In all partnerships, whether it is expressed in the deed or not, the partners are bound to be true and faithful to each other'. The foundation of partnership is mutual faith and trust in each other and ever since the development of equity in the nineteenth century partners have always been regarded as being subject to the equitable duties, sometimes expressed in terms as the 'good faith' principle. **5.01**

As a result, partners owe specific fiduciary duties to each other, such as full disclosure and of not making any unauthorized profit from the firm's business (the so-called 'no profit rule'). The good faith principle continues to exist, however, and the Law Commissions recommended its retention as a separate principle. Although it is sometimes used as another way of stating the fiduciary relationship, in its true sense it is not a specific fiduciary duty and can be used where to apply a fiduciary duty would be inappropriate. Thus in the Canadian case of *Springer v Aird & Berlis LLP*,[2] the allegation was that the Executive Committee of a large professional firm had treated a partner unfairly in terms of allocating income units. The court held that such a decision could not be subject to the fiduciary duty applicable to a trustee, ie that the Committee must act only in the interests of the partner concerned. It would have to apply that to each partner in turn, which simply could not work. Instead the Committee's actions must be judged on whether it had acted in good faith in making the allocation and was not motivated by irrelevant considerations. In any event, partners are not as such trustees for each other even as fiduciaries. That has consequences for limitation periods.[3]

---

[1] (1824) Turn & R 496.
[2] 2009 WL 953083 (Ont SC).
[3] See the cases on company directors: *Gwembe Valley Development Co Ltd v Koshy* [2004] 1 BCLC 131; *JJ Harrison (Properties) Ltd v Harrison* [2002] 1 BCLC 162, CA; and the Limitation Act 1980, s 21(1)(a) and (b).

Effect of agreement

5.02 But partnership is more than a fiduciary relationship: it is above all a contractual agreement and therefore subject to the terms of that agreement, which as in contracts generally may be express or implied.

In the absence of any written agreement, disputes as to the precise terms of oral discussions can be difficult to ascertain and lead to expensive litigation. Thus, in *Bottrill v Harling*,[4] there was a dispute as to the financial terms on a change of partner, in particular the money owed to the retiring partner. Both the original partnership agreement and the negotiations for the change were mainly carried on in the local public house and never written down. The case ended up in the Court of Appeal with QCs and junior counsel on both sides with only a relatively modest amount (in terms of the costs involved) at issue.

In relation to its express terms, the partners will be bound by them, subject of course to the general law of contract, eg as to the consequences of misrepresentation or mistake.[5] In addition to the application of general contract law as to implied terms, the Partnership Act itself contains several implied or default terms, but these can always be excluded or amended either by the express terms of the agreement or by the conduct of the partners. As Lord Millett said in *Khan v Miah*,[6] they are not statutory presumptions but default provisions and only very slight evidence is needed to exclude them. Once again we can say that the Act imposes a largely voluntary framework as between the partners themselves. They may even agree to accept liability not only for partnership debts but also for any separate debt a partner may have with a creditor, whether known or not: see, eg *AIB Group (UK) plc v Martin*.[7] On similar principles even the express terms of the agreement may be varied by a course of conduct. Section 19 of the Act makes all this quite clear:

> The mutual rights and duties of partners, whether ascertained by agreement or defined by this Act, may be varied by the consent of all the partners, and such consent may be either express or inferred from a course of dealing.

As we shall see this means that the partnership agreement or the equitable duties may be varied by agreement, express or implied.

Any such variation under s 19 must therefore be unanimous. If that is express then the position is straightforward. But in order to ascertain whether there has been unanimous implied consent the court may have to infer this from a course of dealing. It will only do so if the evidence shows objectively that all the partners were aware of the

---

[4] [2015] EWCA Civ 564.
[5] Rectification of the agreement is possible but may be difficult to obtain: see, eg *James Hay Pension Trustees Ltd v Hird* [2005] EWHC 1093 (Ch). Not all contractual remedies may be available, however: see Ch 7, below.
[6] [2000] 1 WLR 1232, HL.
[7] [2002] 2 All ER (Comm) 686.

consequences of the dealings and that either by positive action or passive assent they have accepted that the effect was to vary their mutual rights and duties.[8]

Further, it is always a defence to a breach of fiduciary duty or, indeed, the common law duty of care that the other party consented to the breach and such consent may be derived from the terms of the partnership agreement. For a modern example of this see the Canadian case of *337965 BC Ltd v Tackama Forest Products Ltd*.[9]

Interaction between contract and equity

5.03 These two aspects of internal partnership relations, fiduciary duties arising out of the fiduciary relationship and contractual duties and obligations arising from the agreement, are the subject of this chapter. In *Don King Productions Inc v Warren*[10] these two aspects interacted so that, where the partners had agreed to assign contracts, to which either partner was a party, to the firm, the agreement was construed as a declaration by each partner that he held the entire benefit of the contracts on trust for the partnership which was enforceable in equity. This was so even though the contracts could not be assigned under the law of contract since they were for personal services and contained provisions expressly forbidding an assignment.

The exact relationship between these two elements is not always so clear. One of the problems relates to remedies. In one sense some of the duties of good faith etc. may be said to be contractual duties, ie they arise out of a contractual arrangement between the partners as applied by the Act,[11] whereas others arise out of the relationship. The question then arises as to whether the remedies available would be those for breach of contract (ie damages) or those for breach of the equitable duty such as equitable compensation or account. They are not the same as damages. This issue was discussed but not resolved by the Court of Appeal in *Bishop v Goldstein*.[12]

The interaction of contractual and equitable remedies came sharply into focus with the decision of Newey J in *Hosking v Marathon Asset Management LLP*.[13] Mr Hosking had been entitled until his retirement under the LLP agreement (which the judge did not distinguish from a partnership agreement) to an annual share of the profits as an executive member. It now appeared that for a few years prior to his retirement he had been guilty of serious breaches of duty to the firm. The firm now sought to recover half of his profit share during that period (he was entitled to keep 50 per cent under the LLP agreement as a retired non-executive member) under the equitable principle of forfeiture.

---

[8] *Griffiths v Martinez* [2019] NSWSC 664, applying dicta *In re Frank Mills Mining Company* (1883) 23 Ch D 52, CA at 56 and 59.
[9] (1992) 91 DLR (4th) 129.
[10] [1999] 2 All ER 218, CA.
[11] See eg *Sim v Howat* [2012] CSOH 171 at [43].
[12] [2014] EWCA Civ 10.
[13] [2016] EWHC 2418.

That principle can apply where a fiduciary who acts in breach of his duties can lose his right to remuneration. In vain, he argued that forfeiture had never been applied to a partnership and that the matter was one of contractual rights. Although the text books and cases did not refer to forfeiture as a remedy in partnership law, they did not exclude it. The judge rejected any idea of a distinction between remuneration and a profit share in partnership law (see below). Yet Mr Hosking's right to keep 50 per cent was based on his contractual rights on retirement not during the period beforehand—forfeiture was not applied to the whole amount. So was the equitable remedy in fact restricted by the contract? Muddy waters indeed. In the case, the arbitrator had also awarded equitable compensation (rather than damages) for loss caused to the firm by the breaches of duty.

Another problem is that it is far from settled in English law whether one partner may sue another partner for damages for breach of the partnership agreement without a full account being taken. It is a fundamental principle of partnership law that a debt owed by a partner to the other partners (or vice versa) is only recoverable, save in exceptional circumstances, by such an account being taken.[14] This was recently affirmed by the Court of Appeal in *Marshall v Bullock*.[15] One partner discharged the firm's debts after it had been dissolved. No final account was taken. He now brought an action against the other partner to recover his share of those liabilities. Although that action had been brought within six years of the discharge of the liabilities (six years being the limitation period) it was more than six years after the dissolution. Since the final account was the only remedy, the action was time-barred. In the Hong Kong case of *Chan Sau-kut v Gray & Iron Construction & Engineering Co*,[16] it was expressly stated that the action for account was the only remedy available in a partnership dispute over the return of money.[17]

Although those cases were concerned with recovery of loans made to the partnership by a partner, the matter was expressed as a matter of general principle by Lord Millett in *Hurst v Bryk*:[18]

> Neither during the continuance of the relationship nor after its determination has any partner any cause of action at law to recover monies due to him from his fellow partners. The amount owing to a partner by his fellow partners is recoverable only by the taking of an account in equity after the partnership has been dissolved.[19]

In *Keegan v Fitzgerald*,[20] this principle was applied to a claim of unjust enrichment by a partner against the other partners, but the position with regards to say, an account of a secret profit remains open.

---

[14] *Green v Herzog* [1954] 1WLR 1309.
[15] 30 March 1998, CA.
[16] [1986] HKLR 84.
[17] The Law Commissions regarded this as a theoretical rather than a practical issue.
[18] [2002] 1 AC 185. The liability there was to pay a share of rent.
[19] Ibid at 194.
[20] Claim No HC11C01028, 3 November 2011.

Duty of Care to Each Other

Assessing the standard of care and skill

Although there is no express statement in the Act it is clear that as agents partners owe each other a duty of care in relation to the conduct of the partnership affairs. Thus, in certain circumstances, where a partner is negligent and in breach of his duty of care to a third party so that the firm sustains a loss, he may be liable in damages to his fellow partners. The problem is, however, first to define the standard of skill to be expected of such a partner. Is it objective, in the sense of what might reasonably be expected of anyone performing those functions, or is it limited to (or extended by) the individual partner's particular skills and experience? It seems that a partner will be judged by the skill which he possesses or claims to posess. Thus in, *Winsor v Schroeder*,[21] the court defined the test as being 'culpable negligence' and that a partner/businessman must show at least the standards of a reasonable businessman in the situation. In the New Zealand case of *Gallagher v Shultz*[22] the special skills of the partner as an experienced property valuer were taken into account over and above any objective standard. It is more difficult, however, to ascertain the standard of care involved.

5.04

In Scotland the question arose in *Ross Harper and Murphy v Banks*.[23] Lord Hamilton rejected the test of the standard of care as being that which a partner would show in his own affairs. Instead he said that the standard should be that:

> which requires the exercise of reasonable care in all the relevant circumstances. Those circumstances will include recognition that the relationship is one of partnership (which may import some tolerance of error), the nature of the particular business conducted by that partnership (including any risks or hazards attendant on it) and any practices adopted by that partnership in the conduct of that business.

Whilst this would import a more objective standard it would also depend upon the way the firm carried on its business. Thus, as the Law Commissions pointed out in their initial consultation document, on the facts of that case the failure by a solicitor to spot an onerous condition in a title deed may well be regarded as a failure to take reasonable care, but it might not be so, from the point of view of his liability to the other partners, if (say) he had been inadequately trained. Such an approach would also mean that a breach of a duty of care to a client is not necessarily also a breach of duty to the firm, as Lord Hamilton himself recognized. Further, of course, the partnership agreement might excuse any such breach, although in the case itself it was held not to do so.

At about the same time, however, the New South Wales Supreme Court applied a different approach in the context of a negligent partner's implied liability to indemnify his

---

[21] (1979) 129 NLJ 1266.
[22] [1988] 2 NZBLC 103.
[23] 2000 SLT 699 CS (OH).

co-partners for his negligence.[24] That court, in *Lane v Bushby*,[25] took the view that a greater degree of culpability than the normal standard of reasonable care was needed to found inter-partner liability. It had to be gross or culpable negligence.[26]

The most recent case in England is *Tann v Herrington*.[27] Unusually, this involved the alleged negligence of a partner in running the administrative affairs of the firm (failure to renew an insurance policy) rather than in incurring liability to a third party. There the judge rejected the idea of a higher test such as in *Lane v Bushby*. The partner should be judged by whether he had exercised reasonable care and skill to an objective standard. That must be regarded as the current state of the law in England.

Fiduciary Duties

Good faith—the fiduciary principle

5.05 The major consequence of partnership as a fiduciary relationship is that partners owe a wide variety of fiduciary duties to each other—in fact since the boundaries of equity in this respect are never closed it is impossible to provide a definitive list.[28] Whilst there have been some recent cases involving partners, many of the current developments have involved their nearest equivalent, the company director. The law of fiduciaries is under constant development and many questions remain unresolved.[29] The Act itself provides for three specific fiduciary duties which reflect the three main aspects of such liability but it is clear that these duties are applicable in a wider context to modern situations. In addition, as we have seen, there is the pervasive good faith principle which underpins the fiduciary duties.[30]

Width of the good faith principle

5.06 There are several modern examples of the good faith principle operating beyond the three specific instances of fiduciary duties in the Act. In some cases it is used instead of a fiduciary duty,[31] in others it allows a different fiduciary duty to be applied.

---

[24] Under s 24(2)—see below.
[25] [2000] NSWSC 1029.
[26] See, eg *Thomas v Atherton* (1878) 10 Ch D 185.
[27] [2009] EWHC 445 (Ch).
[28] This is in contrast to the list of such duties for directors in the Companies Act 2006.
[29] See also the clear views expressed by the Ontario Court of Appeal in *Rochwerg v Truster* (2002) 212 DLR (4th) 498 at 518.
[30] It has been argued that in Scotland, the good faith principle should only apply between a partner and the firm, given its legal personality. But this does not seem to be the practice. There are echoes of this in relation to LLPs (see below).
[31] *Springer v Aird & Berlis LLP* 2009 WL 953083 (Ont SC) and *Floydd v Cheney*, below.

In *Floydd v Cheney*[32] Floydd, an architect, engaged an assistant, Cheney, with a view to partnership. There was some dispute as to whether a partnership was ever formed, and when Floydd returned from a trip abroad, Cheney told him he was leaving. Floydd then discovered that certain papers were missing and that others had been photographed. He now sued for the return of all the documents and negatives and for an order restraining Cheney from making use of confidential information. Megarry J decided that even if there was a partnership rather than an employer–employee relationship, the duty of good faith would prevent Cheney from acting as he had:

> Such acts seem to me to be a plain breach of the duty of good faith owed by one partner to another. I cannot think it right that even if a partnership is marching to its doom each of the partners should be entitled to a surreptitious free-for-all with the partnership working papers, with the right to make and remove secretly copies of all documents that each partner thinks himself especially concerned with, so that he may continue to work upon them elsewhere.

A similar example is the Scottish case of *Finlayson v Turnbull (No 1)*[33] where three partners in a firm of solicitors resigned from the partnership, left the two branch offices where they worked, taking a large number (at least 1,000) of clients' files with them and opened up a new partnership in two offices close to the ones they had left. The judge had little difficulty in finding that this was a clear breach of their fiduciary duty not to damage the interests of the partnership they were leaving. The judge rejected the arguments of the defendants that these were files relating to legal aid cases and since they were the nominated solicitors in relation to each of them (as is required) there was no damage to the firm. The defendants had no right of ownership in the files and their removal would not only give the defendants a substantial commercial advantage it would also damage the commercial interests of the remaining partners. The proper course would have been to have consulted each client on what he or she wished and to have agreed between the partners on what was to be done about the business already transacted. In the absence of express instructions the clients remained clients of the firm.[34]

The good faith principle also applies the equitable duties of confidentiality as to confidential information relating to the business of the partnership, eg customer indices, in card or electronic form.[35]

A somewhat surprising use of the principle was provided by the Canadian case of *Dockrill v Coopers & Lybrand Chartered Accountants*[36] in which a large firm of accountants decided to reduce their size and to remove one partner, Mr Dockrill. The other

---

[32] [1970] Ch 602.
[33] 1997 SLT 613.
[34] See also the company law cases on similar actions by directors, eg *CMS Dolphin Ltd v Simonet* [2001] 2 BCLC 704; *Quarter Master UK Ltd v Pyke* [2005] 1 BCLC 245, and *Foster Bryant v Bryant* [2007] 2 BCLC 239, CA, which suggest limits to this concept where the fiduciary has severed his connection prior to the business being set up.
[35] *Gorne v Scales*, 14 November 2002.
[36] (1994) 111 DLR (4th) 62.

partners consulted a lawyer who gave advice on how to do this. Mr Dockrill brought an action for wrongful termination and sought to obtain a copy of the advice prepared by the lawyer for the partners. They replied that it was a privileged document since it was prepared by the lawyer for them as clients. This argument was rejected by the court. At the time when the advice document was produced Mr Dockrill was a partner and it was thus available to him in the same way as the other partners.

That proposition was, however, roundly rejected by the Federal Court of Australia in *Martin v Norton Rose Fulbright Australia (No 2)*.[37] The judge described it as being as surprising as it was unsound and one which must be firmly rejected.[38] Partners in an intra-partnership dispute were entitled to obtain legal advice as to their respective rights and obligations, to which legal privilege could attach.

Limitations on the good faith principle

5.07 A somewhat more restrictive view of the mutual trust nature of a partnership was taken by the majority of the Court of Appeal in *DB Rare Books Ltd v Antiqbooks*.[39] The partnership was set up in 1990 to deal and invest in antiquarian books and prints. The partnership agreement contained a clause that each partner should be just and faithful to each other and should at all times act in the best interests of the partnership. Another clause provided that if any partner committed a serious breach of the partnership agreement the other(s) should be able to buy that partner's share. By 1992 the partners were seriously at odds with each other. One of the partners, Mr Brass, without consulting the others or seeking any explanation, asked his accountants to write to the Customs and Excise notifying them of an apparent under-declaration of VAT by the firm. These are known as 'voluntary disclosure letters' and are designed to avoid unpleasant investigations and penalties. That request did not allege any fraud on the part of the others but the letter actually written to the Customs and Excise by the accountants did. In fact it subsequently transpired that there had been no irregularities in the firm's VAT returns.

The other partners now argued that this action was a material breach of the partnership agreement, ie of the duty of good faith. Two members of the Court of Appeal held that it was not. They did so on the basis that Mr Brass had made no allegations of fraud against the other partners, that it was not unreasonable of him to have taken this action to preserve the firm's good name with the VAT authorities, given that there may well have been irregularities, that Mr Brass had not done this in order to further his dispute with the other partners, and that his actions could hardly have damaged the mutual trust of the partners since that had gone already. Since it was not unreasonable it could not amount to a material breach. Dillon LJ dissented and agreed with the trial judge that Mr

---

[37] [2019] FCA 96.
[38] At [160] and [161].
[39] [1995] 2 BCLC 306.

Brass's failure to consult the other partners and seek an explanation was grossly unreasonable and unjust.

The majority decision would seem to be far from in line with the established view of partnership as a relationship of mutual trust. The failure to consult or to seek an explanation before writing to the Customs and Excise, in the absence of very special circumstances such as obvious fraud and an imminent investigation, would seem to be a clear breach of that concept, even if relations were by that time strained. It may be that the majority of the Court of Appeal were too preoccupied with whether there had been a breach of the agreement rather than with the concept of good faith itself. In the event it mattered little because all the judges involved agreed that in the circumstances the firm should be wound up.

The good faith principle may also be negatived by the actions of the complainant. In the Canadian case of *Prothroe v Adams*,[40] the issue was the extent of the duties owed by a committee of the partners set up to negotiate the terms of a merger with another firm. The complainant, one of the other partners, argued that the committee had ignored his interest in the goodwill of the firm in selling it to the new firm for $1. The judge held that, whilst the committee clearly owed duties to the other partners in carrying out the negotiations, they had assumed their duties on the basis that they would report back to the others at reasonable intervals. The others, including the complainant, had a corresponding duty of their own to participate in that process. The complainant had received all material information and had chosen not to participate in the process. Why should the committee then anticipate and protect his interests if he did not do so himself? The committee had acted properly in the light of their mandate.

Application to prospective partners

The good faith principle and the fiduciary duties can apply before a formal partnership agreement has been concluded. The High Court of Australia in *United Dominions Corporation Ltd v Brian Pty Ltd*[41] agreed that such duties can apply even if the parties have never reached full agreement on the terms of the partnership. In particular this will be the case where the prospective partners have embarked upon the conduct of the partnership business before the precise terms of any partnership agreement have been settled. Thus in the Australian case of *Fraser Edmiston Pty Ltd v AGT (Qld) Pty Ltd*,[42] where two companies were negotiating for a partnership, one prospective partner applied for a renewal of its business lease and left the relevant documents which gave it a favourable chance of such renewal with the other company as part of the negotiations. The other promptly applied for and was granted the lease using the documents. It was

5.08

---

[40] [1997] 10 WWR 101.
[41] (1985) 60 ALR 741.
[42] [1988] 2 QdR 1.

held that the second negotiator was in breach of its fiduciary duty and held the lease on trust for the partnership.

In *Conlon v Simms*,[43] Lawrence Collins J accepted that the duty of full disclosure applied to prospective partners. Similarly it was held in *Re Metropolis Motorcycles Ltd*[44] that it also applied to partners negotiating the incorporation of the business; so the position seems clear in England as well.

Application to repudiation and dissolution

5.09 On the other hand it has been held that the fiduciary duties cease when one partner repudiates the partnership agreement, eg by refusing to honour its financial obligations. This principle dates back to *M'Lure v Ripley*[45] which was applied in the Canadian case of *A Akman & Son (Fla) Inc v Chipman*.[46] In that case two partners were attempting to sell some land, the only partnership asset. One of them indicated its intention to withdraw from the firm since prospects for a sale were bleak. Arrangements were made for its share to be purchased but before the deal was concluded the remaining partner found a purchaser and the sale went through. The court held that once one partner had repudiated its partnership obligations the duty of good faith etc ceased to operate and no account would be ordered. Husband JA explained the decision thus:

> The plaintiff, having refused to participate further, is not entitled to information which comes to light after repudiation, on which it might reconsider its position. The plaintiff is not entitled to stay out if the news continues to be bad, but opt back in should the outlook improve.

There is, however, recent judicial authority to the effect that acceptance of repudiation does not dissolve either the partnership or end the partnership agreement, and so the specific principle in *M'Lure v Ripley* may now be open to some doubt.[47]

Fiduciary duties have, however, been held to apply in the case of a lawful dissolution for the purposes of winding up the affairs of the partnership, so that each partner remains under a fiduciary obligation to cooperate in and act under the agreed procedure for the realization, application, and distribution of the partnership assets. Thus a partner who takes the assets of the firm is liable to compound interest on his use of them, at least in Scotland, according to *Roxburgh Dinardo & Partners' Judicial Factor v Dinardo*.[48] For examples of the position on a dissolution see the Australian cases of *Chan v Zacharia*[49]

---

[43] [2006] EWHC 401 (Ch).
[44] [2007] 1 BCLC 520.
[45] (1850) 2 Mac & G 274.
[46] (1988) 45 DLR (4th) 481.
[47] *Hurst v Bryk* [2002] 1 AC 185, per Lord Millett at 189. Only Lord Nicholls in that case left the point open. This was then applied by Neuberger J in *Mullins v Laughton* [2003] 4 All ER 94. See Ch 7, below.
[48] 1993 SLT 16.
[49] (1984) 154 CLR 178.

and *Trinkler v Beale*,[50] and the Court of Appeal decision in *Don King Productions Inc v Warren*[51] which are dealt with later in this chapter. They also apply where the partnership business has ceased, without a dissolution, at least where the possibility of reviving the business exists: see *Paton v Reck*,[52] also dealt with later in this chapter.

The three main aspects of fiduciary duties incorporated into the Act in ss 28 to 30 relate to honesty and full disclosure, unauthorized personal profits, and conflict of duty and interest.

Honesty and Full Disclosure

A partnership agreement is one of *uberrimae fidei* (utmost trust) and it is quite clear that each partner must deal with his fellow partners honestly and disclose any relevant fact when dealing with them. A failure to disclose will suffice for a breach of the duty—there need be no proof of common law fraud or negligence. Section 28 is a statutory version of this duty: **5.10**

> Partners are bound to render true accounts and full information of all things affecting the partnership to any partner or his legal representatives.

This strict duty applies to 'all things affecting the partnership'. In *Law v Law*,[53] the two Laws, William and James, were partners in a woollen manufacturer's business in Halifax, Yorkshire. William lived in London and took little part in the running of the business. James bought William's share for £21,000. Later William discovered that the business was worth considerably more and that various assets unknown to him had not been disclosed. The Court of Appeal held that in principle this would allow William to set the contract aside. Cozens-Hardy LJ explained this decision:

> Now it is clear law that, in a transaction between copartners for the sale by one to the other of a share in the partnership business, there is a duty resting upon the purchaser who knows, and is aware that he knows, more about the partnership accounts than the vendor, to put the vendor in possession of all material facts with reference to the partnership assets, and not to conceal what he alone knows.

Thus the ordinary principle of a contract of sale, *caveat emptor* (let the buyer beware), was varied by the fiduciary duty owed by one partner to another. There was no misrepresentation in the common law sense of the word, no actual lies were told, but nevertheless the contract was voidable.

---

[50] [2009] NSWCA 30.
[51] [1999] 2 All ER 218, CA.
[52] [2000] 2 QdR 619, CA.
[53] [1905] 1 Ch 140.

This duty of disclosure applies whilst the partnership is operating. In *Campbell v Campbell*,[54] there was a dispute between two brothers involving a partnership jewellery business in London and disputed parts of that business carried on by various companies in Bangkok and New York. The overseas businesses were controlled by one brother, Robert, although both brothers had traded in Bangkok. In the course of a lengthy judgment, having to unravel the facts, the judge found that Robert had committed 'striking breaches of duty' to his brother, Richard. These were failure to provide even basic information about the acquisition of a Bangkok factory, refusal to provide information relating to one of the overseas companies (and removing him as a director), and failure to respond to clarify Richard's interests (and those of his Thai family) in several other of the companies. In Canada it has also been applied to negotiations between the executors of a deceased partner and the remaining partners as to a settlement agreement.[55]

Of course the duty under s 28 is not owed at all times. As Lord Hodge said in *Sim v Howat*,[56] partners are not obliged to inform their colleagues of everything which occurs in the course of partnership business as otherwise one could not delegate management powers to a managing partner while allowing others to concentrate on earning income for the firm. It applies in specific circumstances such as partnership negotiations or assets as noted in the cases just discussed.[57] These limits may be explained by the fact that, as we have seen, fiduciary duties may be varied by agreement, express or implied.

The duties of disclosure and not to mislead in partnership dealings are in any event limited to precisely that. If those obligations are complied with then the other partners cannot complain if they do not receive 'full value'.[58] There is probably no common law remedy in damages for simple non-disclosure, rescission being the only remedy, but if there is evidence of fraud or dishonesty then damages will be available.[59] It may also be that in an appropriate case, the equitable remedies of account and compensation will be available.

But this absolute duty of disclosure is potentially wider and on one level may be seen to subsume the other duties under ss 29 and 30. This premise is based on the idea that where a partner is making an unauthorized profit (s 29 below) or is acting in competition with the firm (s 30 below), his failure to disclose that fact will also be a breach of the duty of disclosure. Thus in the Canadian case of *Rochwerg v Truster*,[60] the Ontario Court of Appeal held that where a partner had taken advantage of his position as such to obtain benefits from certain directorships, he was under a duty under s 28 to disclose

---

[54] [2017] EWHC 182 (Ch).
[55] *Filkow v D'Arcy & Deacon LLP* 2019 MBCA 61.
[56] [2012] CSOH 171.
[57] But see the Canadian case of *Sagacity Professional Corporation v Buchanan Barry LLP* 2010 ABQB 151, where the judge refused to apply s 28 to negotiations for a new partnership agreement where the partners were operating on an equal footing.
[58] See *Trinkler v Beale* [2009] NSWCA 30, in the context of a partnership dissolution agreement.
[59] *Conlon v Simms* [2006] EWHC 401. That case also contains a discussion of when relevant professional disciplinary hearings may be used as evidence of fraud etc.
[60] (2002) 212 DLR 498.

all information about the directorships and the associated benefits, irrespective of any breach of s 29. A similar decision as to double breach was made in the Australian case of *Chickabo Pty Ltd v Zphere Pty Ltd*,[61] although the remedy under s 29 was considered sufficient. But liability under s 28 was also extended in that case to a corporate partner which, although it had not breached s 29 itself, had full knowledge of all relevant matters to the breach of s 29 by the other partner. Only full disclosure and consent could have remedied that breach. The remedy against the partner liable solely under s 28 was not fixed by the court at that time.

Conflict of Interest and Duty—Unauthorized Personal Profit

The 'no-profit' and 'no-conflict' rules

5.11 It has long been established that since a trustee must never put himself in a position where his duty to the beneficiaries and his personal interest might conflict, he must not profit from his trust and this concept has been broadly applied to fiduciaries such as partners. This duty is commonly divided into two: the 'no-conflict rule' and the 'no-profit rule'. The no-conflict rule is also often divided into what are known as transactional conflicts (an interest in a partnership transaction) and situational conflict (a situation where a partner would have a potential conflict of interest between his or her personal interests and those of the partnership). If the fiduciary concerned makes no profit from such conflicts then the remedies might lie in damages, rescission, or an injunction. But any un-authorized benefit or gain made by the fiduciary out of his or her position must be accounted for. For company directors these different duties and their consequences are now codified in the Companies Act 2006, although in such a way as to permit case law development.[62]

For partners, however, the Partnership Act in s 29 deals only with the no-profit rule. But it seems clear that the general developments since the Act in the law of fiduciaries, especially company directors, will be applied unless there is a compelling reason otherwise. Simple non-disclosure in a transaction (transactional conflict) is covered by s 28. Situational conflict will surely be addressed even if there is no profit. The ban on unauthorized personal profit in the partnership context can be found in s 29 of the Act:

> Every partner must account to the firm for any benefit derived by him without the consent of the other partners from any transaction concerning the partnership, or from any use by him of the partnership property name or business connection.

The section has two parts, one relating to partnership transactions and the other to the use of property etc. But it is very wide—'any use of the business connection', for

---

[61] [2019] VSC 73.
[62] Companies Act 2006, ss 170–80.

example, can extend beyond use of the partnership assets or exploitation of a partnership transaction. A modern version of this duty to account was set out by Deane J in the Australian case of *Chan v Zacharia*,[63] as approved by the Court of Appeal in both *Don King Productions Inc v Warren*[64] and *John Taylors v Masons*.[65] The duty of account owed by one partner to another applies to any benefit or gain 'which was obtained or received by use or by reason of his fiduciary position or of opportunity or knowledge resulting from it'.

Direct profit from partnership transaction

5.12 The clearest example of liability under this section is a secret profit, ie where one partner makes a personal profit out of acting on behalf of the partnership, eg in negotiating a contract. Thus in *Bentley v Craven*,[66] Bentley, Craven, and two others were partners in a sugar refinery at Southampton. Craven was the firm's buyer and as such he was able to buy sugar at a discount on the market price. Having bought the sugar at the discounted price he then sold it to the firm at market price. The other partners only discovered later that he had been buying and selling the sugar to them on his own behalf. The firm now successfully claimed Craven's profits from these dealings. It would have made no difference if the other partners could not have obtained a discount so that they in fact suffered no loss since they would have had to pay the market price anyway—the point is that Craven made a profit out of a partnership transaction and he had to account for it. This can be deduced from a similar situation involving a company director in *Boston Deep Sea Fishing & Ice Co v Ansell*,[67] where even though the company could not have obtained the discount the director had to account for it as a secret profit.

The liability also clearly extends to simply misappropriating partnership receipts, eg for services invoiced on partnership invoices. In such a situation the fact that the services were illegal since they were provided without a licence, is no defence.[68]

Use of partnership asset for personal benefit

5.13 It is equally clear that if a partner uses a partnership asset for his own benefit he must account to the other partners for that benefit. Thus in *Pathirana v Pathirana*,[69] RW Pathirana and A Pathirana were partners in a service station in Sri Lanka. The station belonged to Caltex (Ceylon) Ltd which had appointed them as agents. RW gave three

---

[63] (1984) 154 CLR 178.
[64] [1999] 2 All ER 218, CA.
[65] [2001] EWCA Civ 2106.
[66] (1853) 18 Beav 75.
[67] (1888) 39 Ch D 339.
[68] *Tugboba v Adelagun* (1974) 1 ALR 99, citing *Sharp v Taylor* (1849) 2 Ph 801.
[69] [1967] 1 AC 233, PC.

months' notice determining the partnership and during that period he obtained a new agreement with Caltex transferring the agency into his name alone. RW then continued to trade in the same way at the same premises under his name. A successfully applied through the Supreme Court of Ceylon to the Privy Council for a share of the profits from that business under s 29. The agency agreement was a partnership asset and RW's unauthorized use of it was a clear breach of fiduciary duty. Similar use of any asset of the firm will lead to the same result, whether it is a physical or an intangible asset as here. A similar situation, involving the renewal of an auctioneers' licence by some partners in the firm which had held the previous licence arose in *John Taylors v Masons*.[70] The Court of Appeal come to the same conclusion—the partners had used the partnership goodwill as a springboard for the renewal. Thus where one partner uses the firm's money for his own purposes, the other partners will be able to recover that money with interest. An example of this is the Northern Irish case of *Moore v Moore*,[71] where one partner in a farming business used funds, inter alia, to modernize his house.

Identifying the asset

Sometimes the difficulty may be to define the partnership asset and to show that it has been used to gain a personal benefit and so give rise to the duty to account. In the Queensland case of *Paton v Reck*[72] there was a partnership between A, B, C, and D, carrying on the business of prawn farming. At all times the land was owned by A and B and it was never argued that it had become partnership property. To carry on the business, however, several permits and licences had to be obtained and this had involved considerable time and expense. They were in fact obtained in the name of A and C. The business failed but there was never any dissolution. A and B sold the land to X, who intended also to use it for prawn farming (although for a different type of prawn). The question was whether A and B had to account for any part of that sale price to C and D. The Queensland Court of Appeal held that they had such a duty. Two of the judges held that X had paid a premium for the land partly because he knew that since the firm had obtained the necessary permits etc he would be likely to be similarly able to do so, even though those permits etc could not be assigned to him. (This seems to equate almost with the goodwill of a business.) A and B had therefore received part of that sum on account of a benefit (the permits etc) which had been obtained by and for the partnership business and that amount could be quantified. The other judge held, less convincingly on the facts, that this was a case of some partners using partnership property (again the permits etc) to obtain a personal benefit. Such cases very much depend upon the findings of fact that there was a partnership benefit and that it did lead to an unauthorized gain.

5.14

---

[70] [2001] EWCA Civ 2106. See also *Hussar Estate v P & M Construction Ltd*, 7 March 2005 (Ont SC), where this liability survived an apparent agreement to the contrary.
[71] 27 February 1998.
[72] [2000] 2 QdR 619, CA.

Misuse of partnership opportunity

5.15 The question of liability is less certain when we look at the misuse of the business 'connection' of the firm. A partner may acquire information, contacts etc from the firm's business. Is he then forbidden to use such information etc in any other enterprise not directly connected with the firm's business and, if so, for how long? Is there liability, in modern terminology, for misuse of a partnership opportunity? In *Aas v Benham*,[73] the defendant was a member of a firm of shipbrokers dealing with the chartering of vessels. He gave considerable assistance in the formation of a company whose objects were the building of ships. He used information and experience gained as a shipbroker in the promotion of the company, even using the firm's notepaper from time to time. He was paid a fee for this work and became a director of the company at a salary. The other partners sought to claim an account of the fee and salary. The Court of Appeal rejected this claim. Information gained in the course of a partnership business could not be used for a partner's own benefit in that type of business, but using it for purposes outside the scope of that business was allowed. In their view it was the use of the information which counted and not the source.

The position is slightly different in Canada where the need is for the transaction to concern the partnership. That requires a link between the transaction and the partnership, which has been said to include, but is not limited to, activities or services within the scope of the partnership business.[74]

The decision in *Aas v Benham* limiting the scope of the no-profit rule to the firm's business or potential business has been the subject of three recent cases involving company directors. In two of them the decision was approved, applied, and refined in the corporate context. In *Wilkinson v West Coast Capital*,[75] it was held that use of information given to a director for a purpose outside the scope of the company's business was exempt from the rule provided that it was not given to him as a director, ie for the company's use. Second, in *Re Allied Business and Financial Consultants Ltd*,[76] it was held that the *Aas v Benham* limitation applied to both the no-profit and no-conflict rules. The difficulty arose if the information was gained in a confidential situation but then used for a purpose outside the company's business. The answer was that if it was confidential to the giver only, there would be no liability; but if it was confidential to the company the situation would be different.[77]

But the Court of Appeal in *O'Donnell v Shanahan*[78] firmly rejected the idea that *Aas v Benham* had any role to play outside partnership law. Whilst that is not a matter for

---

[73] [1891] 2 Ch 244, CA.
[74] *Rochweg v Truster* (2002) 212 DLR (4th) 498 at [58]. See also *Wright v Van Gaalen* 2011 BCSC 707.
[75] [2007] BCC 717.
[76] [2009] 1 BCLC 328.
[77] The answer then may well depend on whether the company has subsequently released its interest in the information. See *Peso Silvermines v Cropper* [1966] 58 DLR (2d) 1; cf *Queensland Mines Ltd v Hudson* (1978) 18 ALR 1, PC. For a stricter view see *Rochwerg v Truster* (2002) 212 DLR (4th) 498.
[78] [2009] EWCA Civ 751.

this book, their interpretation of the case is. The decision was, said Rimer LJ, explicable only on the basis that the width of the partner's fiduciary duties was circumscribed by the partnership agreement. Using partnership information for a purpose outside the business of the firm was thus not subject to the no-profit rule. (Companies, he said, were not so circumscribed.)[79] But, what would happen if there was no express partnership agreement on this issue? Would *Aas* not then apply? The question which the Court of Appeal ought perhaps to have asked was, given that in the *O'Donnell* case the information was clearly given to the directors as directors (they had first sought to use it as part of the company's business), was there anything to take their use of it outside the no-profit rule? The answer on the facts was in fact no and there was no need unduly to restrict the effect of *Aas v Benham*. *O'Donnell* would, I suggest, have been decided the same way even it had been a partnership case.

Analogy with company directors
There are many examples of breaches of the 'no-profit' rule by company directors, which can easily be applied to partnerships by analogy.[80] Thus in *Regal (Hastings) Ltd v Gulliver*,[81] the directors of a company who invested their own money in the purchase of another company as a subsidiary (their original company could only afford to buy 40 per cent of the shares in the second company) and who made a profit when the two companies were later sold, had to account for their profits to the shareholders. Again there was no loss to anyone and no deprivation of an opportunity—further, the only real winners in this case were the new shareholders, ie the purchasers, who in effect received a rebate on their purchase price. The House of Lords in deciding this, however, may have doubted the propriety of those who decided that the company could not afford a greater investment since they were the very people who later made the profit.

5.16

A similar approach was taken in *Industrial Development Consultants Ltd v Cooley*.[82] Cooley was appointed as managing director of the company expressly to attract work from the public sector. He failed to interest the West Midlands Gas Board since the Board did not employ development companies but because of Cooley's record as a public works architect they offered the contract to him personally. Cooley then resigned from the company on the spurious grounds of ill health and took the contract personally. The company now sued for an account of his profits from the contract and won, although it was clear that the company would under no circumstances have been awarded the contract. It has to be said that Cooley's behaviour could not really be described as totally honest and he was specifically employed to obtain for the company that which he so successfully obtained for himself. He had used information given to him in his capacity as a director for his own advantage. However, in *Island Export*

---

[79] Gleaned from the speeches of the majority of the House of Lords in *Boardman v Phipps* [1967] AC 46.
[80] The test is said to be objective and requires no intent on the part of the director: *Richmond Pharmacology Ltd v Chesters Oversear Ltd* [2014] EWHC 2692 (Ch).
[81] [1942] 1 All ER 378.
[82] [1972] 1 WLR 443.

Finance Ltd v Umunna,[83] liability was limited to the appropriation by the managing director of a 'maturing business opportunity' belonging to the company rather than a mere hope of further business. It was also held that use of information about a particular market obtained whilst a director did not preclude his acting in that market after he ceased to be a director. Only very specialized knowledge would found liability.

But if the director knew that the company would have been interested in the opportunity, eg to buy some property, then the director will be liable, since he has a duty both to exploit any opportunity for the benefit of the company and to inform it of the situation.[84] As in *Cooley*, this duty applies even after he has left the company if he has resigned to acquire the opportunity for himself,[85] but not where the director was effectively excluded from the company and the alleged misuse took place some six months later.[86] The most recent general statement of this liability was given by the Court of Appeal in *Bhullar v Bhullar*,[87] where two directors, having seen that a property was up for sale, bought it for themselves. In fact the property was adjacent to the company's existing property and it would have been worthwhile and commercially attractive for the company to have bought it. The company was in fact unaware of the opportunity. The Court of Appeal held that the two directors were liable. There was a clear conflict of interest and duty. The test was whether a reasonable person looking at the facts of the case would think that there was a real possibility of a conflict of interest. More recently, the Court of Appeal in *Sharma v Sharma*,[88] explained that directors would be liable if they exploit for personal gain: (a) opportunities which come to their attention in their role as director; or (b) any other opportunity which they could and should exploit for the benefit of the company. The Court of Appeal have also extended this duty in some cases to require directors to disclose their own misconduct to the company—such a failure being itself a breach of the duty.[89] There seems little reason why these cases should not be applied to partners.

Duration of liability

5.17 There is little doubt that the full scope of the duty to account applies in full to partners. This includes the rule in *Keech v Sandford*[90] whereby a trustee of a trust which includes a lease as trust property and who acquires a renewal of the lease for his own benefit must hold that lease as a constructive trustee for the beneficiaries. The application of the rule in *Keech v Sandford* to partners is that it will apply if the renewal was obtained

---

[83] [1986] BCLC 460.
[84] *Crown Dilmun v Sutton* [2004] 1 BCLC 468.
[85] *CMS Dolphin Ltd v Simonet* [2001] 2 BCLC 704.
[86] *In Plus Group Ltd v Pyke* [2002] 2 BCLC 201.
[87] [2003] 2 BCLC 241.
[88] [2013] EWCA 1287 Civ.
[89] *Fassihi v Item Software (UK) Ltd* [2004] BCC 994; see above. This would be the more true of partnerships.
[90] (1726) Sel Cas King 61.

by a partner by use of his position as a partner. This is rebuttable as a question of fact (ie that it was not so obtained) as happened in *Re Biss*,[91] but the principle was applied by the High Court of Australia in *Chan v Zacharia*,[92] where a partnership between two doctors was dissolved and, before the affairs of the partnership were wound up, one of them refused to exercise a joint option to renew the lease of the partnership premises and instead negotiated an agreement for a lease of the premises for himself. The court held that the lease had been obtained by the partner by use of his partnership position in breach of his fiduciary duty and so a constructive trust arose. The court also held that this duty to account for anything so obtained or received by a partner by use or by reason of his fiduciary position or opportunity or knowledge resulting from it applied equally to the period between dissolution and winding up.

In coming to that conclusion the court upheld the earlier English decision in *Thompson's Trustee v Heaton*.[93] Thompson and Heaton were partners and as such acquired a leasehold interest in a farm in 1948. In 1952 the firm was dissolved by mutual consent when it was occupied by Heaton and later by William T Heaton Ltd, a company controlled by Heaton and his wife. Thompson consented to this occupation. Following the dissolution, the ex-partners made no effective new arrangements with respect to the lease, which thus remained an undistributed asset of the partnership. In 1967 Heaton died and Thompson claimed a half-share in the lease. In 1967 Heaton's executors purchased the freehold reversion and in 1971 sold the farm with vacant possession for £93,000. Thompson's trustee in bankruptcy sought a declaration that the executors held the reversion as trustees for themselves and Thompson. Pennycuick V-C granted the declaration on the basis that where someone holding a leasehold interest in a fiduciary capacity acquires the freehold reversion he must hold that reversion as part of the trust as being a 'well-known' principle. In doing so he considered both that the duty to account applied equally to a partner acquiring the reversion on a partnership lease as it did to the renewal of a lease, and that this applied to the post-dissolution period until there was a final dissolution. Despite some earlier authority to the contrary,[94] both those propositions are now fully accepted. They were accepted, for example, without argument by the Court of Appeal in *Popat v Schonchhatra*,[95] where the dispute was as to the shares of the partners in the subsequent freehold.

The decisions in both *Chan* and *Thompson's Trustee* were expressly approved and applied, by analogy, by the Court of Appeal in *Don King Productions Inc v Warren*.[96] Two boxing promoters set up a partnership relating to the promotion and management of boxing in Europe. Warren assigned the benefit of all his existing management and promotion agreements with boxers to the firm. Warren subsequently entered into an

---

[91] [1903] 2 Ch 40.
[92] (1984) 154 CLR 178.
[93] [1974] 1 WLR 605.
[94] See, eg *Brenner v Rose* [1973] 1 WLR 443.
[95] [1997] 3 All ER 800, CA.
[96] [1999] 2 All ER 218, CA. See also *Barber v Rasco International Ltd* [2012] EWHC 269 (QB).

agreement for his own benefit which was held to justify King's determination of the partnership. The question was whether King was entitled to a share in the benefit of the agreements entered into by Warren. Once it was established that all such agreements entered into by Warren, before or during the partnership, were assets of the partnership and held on trust for it, even though, being personal contracts with boxers, they were not themselves assignable (see Chapter 6), there was no difficulty in holding that King was entitled to a share in the profits from them. Further, by analogy with the principle in *Keech v Sandford*, the duty to account also applied to the renewal by Warren of such contracts during the period between the dissolution and the winding up. They were contracts obtained by a partner from property held by him as a partner. The duty to account did not, of course, apply to contracts entered into after the dissolution with boxers who had not been contracted to Warren during the partnership.

The apparent unlimited duration of Warren's liability by including renewals etc, was based on the fact that the goodwill belonging to the firm gave rise to the probability of renewal. Thus both the goodwill and the advantages it gave rise to were partnership assets. This liability may, however, be restricted by express agreement between the partners, so that the errant partner may, after a certain date, no longer be under a duty to account.[97]

Errant partner's share of the benefit

5.18 One thing which s 29 does not make clear is whether, assuming that a partner has to account to his co-partners under that section, he is entitled to keep his share of the benefit or whether it belongs to the other partners alone. This question does not arise in the straightforward trustee–beneficiary relationship since all benefits belong to the beneficiary. Similarly a company director must account for the whole amount to the company as the beneficiary. But in the absence of legal personality a partner is both fiduciary and beneficiary. The question arose before the Ontario Court of Appeal in *Olson v Gullo*[98] where one of two equal partners sold part of the partnership land at a profit to himself of some $2.5 million. (There was also some evidence that he had sought to have his co-partner killed, although by the time of the action he himself was dead.) Mr Olson now sued Mr Gullo's estate for recovery of that money and the trial judge had awarded him the whole amount. This was reversed on appeal, however, so that Mr Olson was awarded only half of that amount under s 29. The profit was a partnership profit and so belonged to the partners equally. This decision was based on principles of restitution, ie to restore the innocent partner to the position he would have been in had the breach not occurred, rather than on principles of constructive trust. Morden ACJO, giving the judgment of the court, expressed the issues as follows:

---

[97] *Woodfull v Lindsley* [2004] 2 BCLC 131.
[98] (1994) 113 DLR (4th) 42. Followed in *Rochwerg v Truster* (2002) 212 DLR (4th) 498.

I have no doubt that stripping the wrongdoing partner of the whole of the profit, including his or her own share in it, is a strong disincentive to conduct which breaches the fiduciary obligation. Further, as a host of equity decisions have shown for at least two centuries, the fact that this would result in a windfall gain to the plaintiff cannot, in itself, be a valid objection to it.

I do not, however, think that it can accurately be said that the defaulting partner does profit from his wrong when he receives his pre-ordained share of the profit. With respect to this share, the partner's conduct in the impugned transaction does not involve any breach of duty.

The court did, however, express its disapproval of the defendant's conduct (whether for the alleged crime or not is not clear) by making a penal order in costs against him.

Duty Not to Compete

5.19 A clear example of a breach of fiduciary duty is where a partner operates a business in competition with the firm. Section 30 of the Act codifies this:

> If a partner, without the consent of the other partners, carries on any business of the same nature as and competing with that of the firm, he must account for and pay over to the firm all profits made by him in that business.

The sole question in this area is whether the business is in competition with that of the firm. If it is, then the liability to account is established and there is no need to show any use of partnership assets etc in that business as with the previous section.

Whether there is a competitive business is a question of fact. By analogy with the law of trusts it may depend upon how specialized the business is—a yacht chandlery, for example, may require greater protection in terms of area than a firm of newsagents. Thus whilst two yacht chandleries in separate roads may well be in competition it is hard to say the same about newsagents. In the case of *Aas v Benham*[99] which we have just encountered with respect to misuse of the partnership business connection, the Court of Appeal also held that there was no liability under this head. A shipbuilding business was neither the same as nor in competition with the firm's business of shipbroking. The relationship between ss 29 and 30 was clarified by the Ontario Court of Appeal in *Rochwerg v Truster*.[100] Section 29 requires misuse of a partnership asset etc giving rise to a personal profit but it does not require competition with the firm, simply a link between the partnership and the transaction; whereas s 30 requires actual competition within the partnership's scope but no actual use of partnership assets.

---

[99] [1891] 2 Ch 244, CA.
[100] (2002) 212 DLR (4th) 498.

Of course some cases will involve both concepts—misuse of a 'partnership opportunity' and competition with the partnership business. One example is the case of *Trimble v Goldberg*,[101] a decision of the Privy Council on appeal from the Court of Appeal of the Transvaal. In 1902 Trimble, Goldberg, and Bennett formed a partnership to try to acquire some properties belonging to a Mr Holland. These properties consisted of 5,500 shares in a company, Sigma Syndicate, and various plots of land, known as 'stands', mainly in Johannesburg. Trimble was given a power of attorney by the others to negotiate the sale and this went very smoothly, the purchase price being satisfied by a down-payment and mortgage over the properties. Subsequently Trimble made an offer, through Holland, for other 'stands' belonging to the syndicate, and was granted an option to buy them for £110,000. He then asked Bennett to join him in this speculation which was accepted. Goldberg knew nothing of these other purchases until nearly a year later. He now applied for a share of the profits of the separate speculation on the basis of a breach of their fiduciary duties by Trimble and Bennett.

The Privy Council rejected this claim, reversing the court below. Lord Macnaghten giving the judgment rejected claims based on both s 29 and s 30 of the Act:

> The purchase was not within the scope of the partnership. The subject of the purchase was not part of the business of the partnership, or an undertaking in rivalry with the partnership, or indeed connected with it in any proper sense. Nor was the information on which it seems Trimble acted acquired by reason of his position as partner, or even by reason of his connection with the Sigma Syndicate.

Contract: Implied Terms

5.20 The contractual framework within which a partnership operates and the fiduciary and other duties of partners apply, depends upon the terms of the agreement between the partners. As we have seen, both the written terms and those imposed by the Act may be varied by express or implied agreement under s 19, and the opening part of s 24 confirms this.

> The interests of partners in the partnership property and their rights and duties in relation to the partnership shall be determined, subject to any agreement express or implied between the partners, by the following rules.

Remember these 'rules' are default provisions and not statutory presumptions. In effect this section, in addition to s 25 which relates to expulsion clauses, provides nine rules which apply to a partnership unless there is evidence of contrary intention, express or implied.

---

[101] [1906] AC 494, PC.

Leaving aside expulsion clauses for the moment, we can divide these implied terms into three general categories: management and control; finance; and change of partners. Since these are all areas where the actual agreement is of supreme importance we can only ascertain guidelines as to the effect and practicality of the rules in s 24. Following the decision of the Court of Appeal in *Popat v Schonchhatra*[102] it seems that none of these implied terms actually relate to the interests of the partners in partnership property as such. The Law Commissions were in general happy to endorse the existing terms.[103]

Management and Control

Management rights

We have seen enough about partnerships by now to know that they depend upon a joint venture based on mutual trust. It will not surprise anyone therefore that s 24(5) provides that '[e]very partner may take part in the management of the partnership business'. A right to management participation is a necessary consequence of unlimited liability for the debts of the firm (remember that limited partners have no rights of management and if they interfere in the business they will lose their limited liability). So basic is this right that even in company law the courts have applied it by analogy to the so-called partnership company cases (ie a company which is in economic and relationship terms a partnership but in legal terms remains a company) so that withdrawal of the right to participate in the management of such a company can lead to a winding up,[104] or more likely now to an automatic exit right,[105] even though no canon of company law has been infringed. In fact such companies are defined by reference to mutual trust and an implied right of management participation. It is obvious, therefore, that breach of such a fundamental right can also lead to a dissolution of a partnership and it has also in the past been enforced by injunction. On the other hand it should be noted that there is no implied term that a partner is obliged to take part in the management process. Sleeping partners are well known and accepted by HM Revenue & Customs as being entitled to a share of the profits.[106]

5.21

Of course the partners may agree differently. It is not uncommon to have a managing partner and/or a management group. In such cases the courts have held that the other partners would have no rights to restrict his/their activities or to interfere with the

---

[102] [1997] 3 All ER 800, CA.
[103] Report, para 10.29.
[104] Under s 122(g) of the Insolvency Act 1986. See *Ebrahimi v Westbourne Galleries Ltd* [1973] AC 360, HL.
[105] Under s 994 of the Companies Act 2006. See *O'Neill v Phillips* [1999] 1 WLR 1092, HL.
[106] eg *Ward v Newalls Insulation Co Ltd* [1998] 1 WLR 1722.

management of the firm. The only exceptions would be if there was misconduct or a total dissolution of the firm.[107]

Remuneration—share of the profit

5.22 The nature of partnership as a joint venture is also reflected in s 24(6), which follows naturally from s 24(5): 'No partner shall be entitled to remuneration for acting in the partnership business'. The idea is that each partner will receive his reward by a straightforward share of the profits and, possibly, interest on his original capital investment. The basic rule therefore is no additional 'salaries'. (There is an exception, as we shall see in Chapter 7, where one partner continues the business for the purpose of a winding up following a dissolution.) On the other hand, it is not unknown for some partners to be more active in the business than others and for those partners to take in addition to a share of the profits a 'salary' to be deducted before the net profits are shared out. Many permutations are possible invoving 'senior' partners, 'middle' partners, and 'junior' partners who only receive a 'salary'—we have already encountered the problem of 'salaried partners' in Chapter 2. The important point to grasp in all this is, of course, that such 'salaries' are not salaries in the ordinary sense of the word but merely a way of apportioning the profits by agreement. For tax purposes, for example, all the profits of a partnership received by a partner are taxable as the receipts of a trade or profession and not as a salary under a contract of employment. The partnership does not 'exist', remember, and a partner cannot employ himself.[108]

If the partnership agreement does make a provision for the payment of a 'salary' or 'enhanced remuneration' in return for undertaking some responsibilities or activities, the question arises as to what happens if a partner fails to undertake those duties. One solution is that this will be dealt with as a breach of contract so that either he or she loses the right to receive the salary or, more likely because of the time line involved, having already received it, becomes liable to pay damages of at least that amount.[109] But in *Hosking v Marathon Asset Management LLP*,[110] the equitable remedy of forfeiture was applied to recover the additional amount, treating such remuneration as simply a share of the profits. This was on the basis of the fiduciary position of a partner rather than the contract. That right was, however, limited by a contractual right to a lower share.

Section 24(6) is therefore frequently altered by the partnership agreement, although there must be evidence of such alteration—the fact that one partner is required to do all the work will not in itself, apparently, be sufficient to provide contrary intention. There

---

[107] *Automatic Self-Cleaning Filter Syndicate Co Ltd v Cuningham* [1906] 2 Ch 34 at 44 per Cozens-Hardy LJ; *Arif v Yeo* [1989] SLR 849.
[108] For a very clear example of all this see *Gross Klein & Co v Braisby* (2005) SPC 00463, 16 February 2005, a decision of John Avery Jones, a Special Commissioner of Taxes.
[109] See, eg *Wang v Rong* [2015] NSWSC 1419.
[110] [2016] EWHC 2418 (Ch). This case has been discussed above.

is Australian authority in *Re Noonan*,[111] for the proposition that if all the partners are required to devote all their time etc to the partnership business and one fails to do so then the others will automatically be entitled to additional remuneration for covering for him, but this has been widely criticized in its own country and it seems preferable to sue for breach of contract in such circumstances. In *Moore v Moore*,[112] the Northern Irish High Court refused to find that s 24(6) was excluded simply because one partner claimed a contribution for extra work carried out by her during a period of tension between the other two partners. The combined effect of s 24(5) and (6) is therefore that in the absence of contrary agreement the law implies that each partner has a right to participate equally in the work and rewards of the joint venture, guided and controlled by their fiduciary duties to each other.

Majority voting

5.23 Equal rights of management presuppose give and take between the partners in the actual decision-making process. Section 24(8) accordingly provides:

> Any difference arising as to ordinary matters connected with the partnership business may be decided by a majority of the partners, but no change may be made in the nature of the partnership business without the consent of all existing partners.

The distinction is therefore between day-to-day business decisions and the fundamental nature of the business itself (unlike a company, therefore, a partnership cannot alter its 'objects' except by unanimous consent, subject, as ever, to contrary intention). If the matter goes to the fundamental nature of the firm it is equally clear that the implied rule is unanimity—eg the admission of a new partner (see below), changes in the deed, sale of a substantial part of the undertaking. It will be a question of fact in each case whether (a) the implied term applies, and (b), if it does, whether the dispute relates to the running or the structure of the firm. On the second issue, in *Bissell v Cole*[113] the Court of Appeal held that a decision to expand the business of the firm from travel agency to tour operator was a change in the nature of the business which required the consent of all the partners. The absence of any such consent meant that the firm's business remained that of a travel agency only for the purposes of the partnership accounts. The tour operator business was not a business of the firm.

On this point see also the Australian case of *Rowella Pty Ltd v Hoult*,[114] which has been dealt with in Chapter 4 in relation to the implied authority of a partner to bind the firm to a new venture. That issue is clearly linked to s 24(8), and in many cases will involve the same points. There is a similar linkage between s 24(8) and the possible application

---

[111] [1949] St R Qd 62.
[112] 27 February 1998.
[113] [1997] 12 WLUK 221, CA.
[114] [1988] 2 QdR 80.

of the derivative action to partnerships as to the question of whether a majority of the partners can prevent an action being brought in the firm's name.[115]

In *Highly v Walker*[116] three partners ran a large and profitable business. Two of the partners agreed to allow the son of one of them to be taken on as an apprentice to learn the business. The other partner objected and applied for an injunction. Warrington J decided that since the majority had acted properly, discussing the matter with the other partner, listening to his arguments, and generally acting bona fide, their decision should stand. It was an ordinary matter connected with the partnership business within s 24(8) and thus a question for majority decision.

If there is a specific clause in the partnership agreement devolving certain matters to a special majority of the partners, matters which are not covered by that clause were held in an Australian case to revert to being governed by the provisions of s 24(8). Thus, they may then require the consent of all the partners.[117]

Abuse of power

5.24 The powers given to the majority by s 24(8) must be exercised bona fide under the good faith principle and not so as to deprive the minority of their rights, or to gain an unfair advantage over them. What happens if a minority partner suspects that he is being unfairly treated by the majority? He can sue for breach of contract and/or an account if there has been a specific breach of a particular agreement; he can apply for the appointment of a receiver or,[118] in the last analysis, he can apply for a dissolution on the just and equitable ground. There is, however, no equivalent to s 994 of the Companies Act 2006 which allows the court to make any order it wishes to protect a minority shareholder in a company who has been the victim of unfairly prejudicial conduct. All the possible remedies are, however, very public and it is very common to include in the partnership agreement a clause whereby disputes between the partners are to be referred to arbitration. Whether a particular clause is wide enough to cover the dispute is a question of fact but assuming it is, in the majority of cases the courts will enforce the arbitration agreement and under recent legislation appeals to the court from a decision of an arbitrator are difficult to sustain—it is no longer enough, for example, to allege that the arbitrator might have made a mistake as to the law involved.

Access to partnership books

5.25 One problem for a minority partner is to prove unfair treatment. To assist him or her in this, s 24(9) provides:

---

[115] See Ch 3, above. The Law Commissions recommended that it should be made clear that bringing or defending actions was an ordinary matter for the purpose of s 24(8): Report, para 10.30.
[116] (1910) 26 TLR 685.
[117] *Cappe v Tsung* [2018] NSWCA 86.
[118] See Ch 7, below.

The partnership books are to be kept at the place of business of the partnership (or the principal place, if there is more than one), and every partner may, when he thinks fit, have access to and inspect and copy any of them.

This right to inspect the books is a valuable one and again flows from the nature of a partnership. The 'books' which a partner may inspect have been considered recently in the contexts of a limited partnership and an LLP, where the same wording applies.[119] Any such limitations in the partnership context may depend upon the management rights of the partner. A very sensible modern approach to s 24(9) was taken in the South Australian case of *Murray v Lesicar*.[120] The term 'partnership books', said the court, was wide enough to include electronic records so that, in that case, a partner was granted full access to the email database held on the server operated by the main office. That was created and maintained for the use of the business of the partnership. The fact that a staff member may have used that email address for private purposes could not maintain an objection on the grounds of confidentiality.

The courts have in fact strengthened this right by allowing a partner to appoint an agent to inspect the books on his behalf. In *Bevan v Webb*[121] the dormant partners in a business were about to sell out to the active partners. They employed a valuer to inspect the books but the active partners refused him access, arguing that s 24(9) only referred to partners and not to their agents. The Court of Appeal ordered that he be allowed to inspect the books. The purpose of s 24(9) is to allow partners to inform themselves as to the position of the firm so that if a partner needs an agent to assist him in understanding the position the agent may inspect the books.

The main objection to the use of agents is that they will then have access to confidential information about the other partners. The Court of Appeal in *Bevan v Webb* had an answer for this. Henn Collins LJ said:

> There is, of course, a natural common-sense limitation of such a right of inspection. The inspection is to be of books and documents in which all the partners are interested, and the inspection cannot be made in such a way as to curtail the rights or prejudice the position of the other partners. They are all interested in the matter, and one partner cannot assert his right in derogation of the rights of the others. But the interests of the others can be amply safeguarded by placing a limitation upon the particular agency which the inspecting partner desires to employ. The agent employed must be a person to whom no reasonable objection can be taken, and the purpose for which he seeks to use the right of inspection must be one consistent with the main purposes and the well-being of the whole partnership.

---

[119] *Inversiones Friero SL v Colyzeo Investors LP* [2011] EWHC 1762 (Ch), [2012] EWHC 1450 (Ch); *Hilton v DIV LLP* [2015] EWHC 2. See Chs 9 and 11.
[120] [2016] SASC 71.
[121] [1901] 2 Ch 59, CA.

An agent who is employed by a rival firm can thus be excluded. Partners and their agents cannot, of course, misuse any information gained in breach of their fiduciary duties.

Financial Affairs

Principle of equality

5.26 The essential criterion for a partnership is mutual sharing of profits and losses. It is of little surprise therefore that s 24(1) provides that, subject to contrary agreement:

> All the partners are entitled to share equally in the capital and profits of the business, and must contribute equally towards the losses whether of capital or otherwise sustained by the firm.

Before going any further it is very important to understand what is meant by capital in the partnership context. As was made clear by the Court of Appeal in *Popat v Schonchhatra*[122] there is a clear distinction between partnership capital on the one hand and partnership assets (or property) on the other. Partnership capital is the amount which each partner has agreed to contribute to the business (ie it is the sum total of their investment in the business). This may be in cash or in kind (eg a partner's skill and reputation) which must be given a monetary value. Thus the partnership capital is a fixed sum. There is no minimum required by law and, subject to contrary agreement,[123] the capital cannot be increased or reduced without the consent of the partners—it cannot, therefore, be withdrawn. Partnership assets, including capital gains, on the other hand include everything which belongs to the firm and clearly can vary from day to day in value. What amounts to partnership assets or property is the subject of Chapter 6. The important thing to realize at this stage is that there may be a clear distinction between a partner's aliquot share in the capital of the firm and his aliquot share in its assets over and above the amount of that capital figure, ie in the capital profits or gains. In this respect the position is entirely different from that of a shareholder in a company, where surplus assets are distributed according to the interests of the shareholders in the share capital of the company.

Section 24(1) provides that both capital and profits are presumed to be shared equally between the partners. Since, as we have seen, capital in this context does not mean surplus assets, ie the value of the partnership assets over and above the capital invested by the partners, a partner's share in those assets must be ascertained either by treating the surplus assets as capital profits, and so as 'profits' within the equality presumption of s

---

[122] [1997] 3 All ER 800, CA. Approved in *Emerson v Emerson* [2004] 1 BCLC 575, CA.
[123] For an example of a contrary agreement see *Hopper v Hopper* [2008] EWCA Civ 1417, where there was found to have been an implied agreement that undrawn profits would be added to the capital. Cf *Khan v Khan* [2006] EWHC 1477 (Ch) where no such contrary agreement was found.

24(1), or by the old-established presumption that in the absence of any contrary agreement all partners share equally in partnership property. In *Popat v Schonchhatra*[124] both alternatives appear to have been used—the result of course being the same.

The end result of this financial analysis is that it is quite possible for the partners to have agreed, expressly or impliedly, to negative the presumption of equality in the case of their right to a return of capital but not as to their right to share in capital profits, ie surplus assets over and above that capital figure. It is a question of looking at the facts in each case to establish whether there has been any such contrary express or implied agreement.

Rebutting the presumption of equality

The courts will almost always find that if the partners have made unequal contributions to the capital of a partnership, that will be sufficient to negative the equality presumption as to 'capital' in s 24(1). See, for example, the Australian case of *Tucker v Kelly*.[125] But if that is the only evidence before the court, the presumption of equality as to 'profits' in s 24(1) will not be ousted. To affect that presumption there would have to be some agreement about profit-sharing ratios. Remember that in this context profits include capital profits or surplus assets, whatever you wish to call them.

5.27

That was the actual decision in *Popat v Schonchhatra* itself. The two partners contributed unequally to the capital of the business. The partnership was determined by the plaintiff and the defendant continued the business. Two-and-a-half years later the defendant sold the business and realized a capital profit (ie he sold it for far more than the capital originally invested). In the absence of any agreement of any sort to the contrary the Court of Appeal held that, after the partners had received their capital back (in proportion to their contributions, s 24(1) having been ousted in respect of capital), the surplus assets must be divided equally between them as being a profit under s 24(1).

In coming to that conclusion the Court of Appeal also held that s 24(1) applied to post-dissolution profits just as it did when the business was a going concern.[126] We shall return to that aspect of the case in Chapter 7. For the moment remember that there are three elements involved in this puzzle: (a) a partner's share in the capital originally invested in the business; (b) a partner's share in the income profits of the business; and (c) a partner's share in the capital profits of the business. The presumption of equality applies to all three and it is a question of fact which if any of them have been negatived by contrary agreement. The point about *Popat v Schonchhatra* is that an implied contrary agreement about the first had no effect on the third. The second was not in

---

[124] [1997] 3 All ER 800, CA.
[125] (1907) 5 CLR 1.
[126] See also *Emerson v Emerson* [2004] 1 BCLC 575, CA.

issue—it involved post-dissolution profits which are subject to special rules as we shall see in Chapter 7.

The Law Commissions recommended that the section might be amended so as to displace the presumption as to equality in respect of the return of capital contributions.[127] Since the courts usually find a contrary intention from unequal contributions to capital (as in the *Popat* case itself) that would seem to be the least of the problems posed by the case. A more important related problem may be the fact that where there is a change of partners, the decision, by distinguishing between capital and capital profits, underlines the fact that an incoming partner might well be entitled to a share in the capital profits which accrued prior to his entry, ie in effect to a hidden capital profit. This has been doubted, however, in the Scottish case of *Bennett v Wallace*,[128] where it was held that, subject to contrary agreement, an incoming partner would only be credited with capital profits accruing after his entry.

Evidential burden

5.28 Inherent in s 24(1), however, is the issue as to how a partner may rebut the presumption of equality as to a share of the profits (however ascertained) in the absence of any express agreement. In *Joyce v Morrissey*,[129] there was a dispute as to the profit-sharing ratio of a successful band, 'The Smiths'. This was run by the four members of the band in partnership and the question was whether Mr Joyce, the drummer, was an equal partner and entitled to 25 per cent of the profits. Originally it was clear that the presumption of equality under s 24(1) did apply, although there was never any express agreement of any kind. Mr Morrissey now argued that the presumption had been subsequently displaced by an implied agreed profit-sharing ratio of 40:40:10:10, with Mr Joyce being entitled only to 10 per cent. He relied on several grounds as establishing this implied contrary agreement but three in particular concerned the Court of Appeal.

First it was said that the defendant and one other member of the band had in fact done most of the work so that the unequal division was appropriate. That was rejected—unequal contribution to a business in no way displaces the presumption of equality of profits. Second it was alleged that the defendant had refused to continue unless the profit-sharing ratio was changed and the acceptance by the others in the form of continuing with the band amounted to an implied variation. That was rejected on the basis that, whilst it was possible to have a variation in such circumstances in an informal agreement, it must be possible to spell out a specific agreement as to the new ratios before a variation can be established and the evidence did not support this. Finally it was argued that the partners had never challenged accounts subsequently drawn up on the basis of the new ratios and so had impliedly accepted the variation by their silence. That

---

[127] Report, para 10.30(1).
[128] 1998 SC 457.
[129] [1998] TLR 707, CA.

too was rejected by the Court of Appeal. There was no evidence that Mr Joyce had understood the significance of the accounts and, in the absence of some communication clearly alerting him to the change and its consequences, it was impossible to construe his silence as amounting to acceptance.

Joyce v Morrisey was followed in *Patel v Patel*.[130] In that case the two partners, A and B, had agreed to share the profits equally, but in the first two years A had foregone his right to his share. The partners fell out and A now claimed an equal share of the profits. B claimed that the division of profits had been varied by A's conduct. The judge held that only clear and unambiguous conduct could amount to a variation of the partnership agreement. A's conduct could equally well be construed as a waiver for the year and not as a variation of contract. Further there was no consideration for any such variation (usually that is agreeing to extending the partnership).

In *Hutchinson v Tamosius*,[131] the position was reversed. In that case the express agreement provided for an unequal division of the profits and the argument was whether that had been displaced by a subsequent agreement as to equality. The judge considered that nothing in s 24(1) required him to assume that such a change had taken place—all that the parties had in fact agreed was that they would move to a position of equality and there was no evidence that they had actually done so.

Losses

Of course the partnership may have no surplus assets and may in fact have made a loss so that the amount remaining in the firm is less than the capital originally invested. In this case the implied term in s 24(1) is quite clear—losses, even of the capital originally invested by the partners, are to be borne in the same proportion as the profits are shared, even though the original contributions to capital were unequal.

5.29

An example may help to explain the position. Suppose A, B, and C are partners sharing profits equally. A invested £9,000, B £6,000, and C £3,000 into the business. After paying off all the creditors only £12,000 remains. Does each partner bear one-third of the £6,000 loss or do they share the losses in a ratio of 3:2:1 in accordance with their capital contributions? The answer is that, subject to contrary intention, each partner bears an equal share of the losses so that each will receive £2,000 less than originally invested. If C had invested nothing, he would still be equally liable and would have to reimburse A and B for his share of the losses.

---

[130] [2019] EWHC 298 (Ch).
[131] (1999) LTL, 20 September 1999.

Interest on capital contributions

5.30 The concept of partnership capital as being simply the amount which the partners have agreed to invest in the business as distinct from profits, capital, or otherwise, is important in relation to other parts of s 24. Section 24(4) provides that '[a] partner is not entitled, before the ascertainment of the profits, to interest on the capital subscribed by him'. Again this is subject to contrary intention and it is not unusual to find a clause authorizing the payment of interest on capital to be paid before the net profits are ascertained. In a sense this is the counterbalance to the payment of a 'salary' to an active partner and it is no more 'interest' in the true sense of that word than the latter is a salary. It is another way of slicing up the profits prior to applying the profit-sharing ratio and, just as a partner cannot employ himself, he cannot truly pay himself interest, and tax is charged accordingly with the interest simply being regarded as an allocation of business profits.[132] (The tax position is more complex when the partner receiving the interest has retired from the firm but has left his capital in the business in return for interest.)

Advances

5.31 The Act does, however, distinguish between a contribution of capital by a partner and a further advance so as to create a form of partner/creditor in such cases. This is yet another example of the problems caused by lack of legal personality. Section 24(3) provides:

> A partner making, for the purpose of the partnership, any actual payment or advance beyond the amount of capital which he has agreed to subscribe, is entitled to interest at the rate of five per cent per annum from the date of the payment or advance.

This section is not without its difficulties, however. The fixed rate of interest payable may well be at variance with the prevailing interest rates so that it is unlikely to be used without contrary agreement with respect to a straightforward cash advance. It is more likely to occur where the partner settles a partnership debt out of his own pocket. One other possible application of the section, to non-cash advances by a partner, was firmly rejected by the British Columbia Court of Appeal in *Klaue v Bennett*.[133] In that case the court refused to apply the equivalent section of the British Columbia Partnership Act to award interest on a loan of some equipment by a partner to the firm. An advance under the section means an advance of money unless the parties specifically agree to the contrary. It should be noted that the British Columbia section allows for the partner to receive a fair rate of interest on such an advance.

---

[132] See, eg the decision of John Avery Jones as Special Commissioner in *Gross Klein & Co v Braisby* (2005) SPC 00463, 16 February 2005.
[133] (1989) 62 DLR (4th) 367.

Another difficulty is to decide on the exact status of an advance under s 24(3). In *Klaue v Bennett* the Canadian court, applying the English case of *Richardson v Bank of England*,[134] stated that the advance cannot amount to a debt whilst the partnership is a going concern, and further held that the section has no application once the firm is in the process of dissolution, where of course the distinction between a debt payable to a creditor and an internal matter of account between the partners would be important, since creditors are paid before partners. On the other hand it does seem possible for the partnership agreement to provide for a debtor–creditor relationship which could continue into a dissolution so that interest continues to run. This appears to be the result of *Wood v Scholes*[135] and *Barfield v Loughborough*.[136]

Indemnities

If one partner does settle a partnership debt, either willingly or unwillingly because he or she is the one who has been sued (remember all are liable for such debts but any one can be sued for the whole amount), he or she has a right to claim an indemnity from his or her fellow partners. Thus, s 24(2) provides that: **5.32**

> The firm must indemnify every partner in respect of payments made and personal liabilities incurred by him—
> (a) In the ordinary and proper conduct of the business of the firm; or,
> (b) In or about anything necessarily done for the preservation of the business or property of the firm.

Part (a) is reasonably straightforward and is declaratory of any agent's right to reimbursement of expenses etc incurred whilst acting within his authority as well as providing a machinery for equal sharing of losses under s 24(1). It probably does not extend to physical as opposed to financial loss, and it must be the 'ordinary' and 'proper' way of conducting the business, which may imply some financial limit.

Provided the expenditure is so authorized it must be made good by the firm even if it proves to be useless. On the other hand expenditure inconsistent with the partnership agreement cannot be so charged even it would otherwise be proper and even necessary for the conduct of the partnership business.[137]

Section 24(2)(a) was applied in the case of *Matthews v Ruggles-Brise*.[138] Coupe and Matthews took a lease for forty-two years from 1879 as trustees for themselves and eight other partners. In 1886 the firm was incorporated and the company took over all the assets and liabilities of the firm. Coupe died in 1886 and in 1887 Matthews assigned

---

[134] (1838) 4 My & Cr 165.
[135] (1866) LR 1 Ch App 369.
[136] (1872) LR 8 Ch App 369.
[137] See eg *Boutsakis v Kakavelakis* 2010 BCSC 1077.
[138] [1911] 1 Ch 194.

the lease to the company. He died in 1891. In 1909 the landlord sued Matthews's executors for arrears of rent and breach of covenant in the lease. The company was insolvent and the action was settled by a surrender of the lease and a payment by Matthews's executors to the landlord of £5,750. They now claimed a contribution from Coupe's executors and the judge agreed. The lease remained the liability of Coupe and Matthews—the company's liability was in addition to it. Thus the payment was a partnership debt and Coupe had to indemnify Matthews for the loss in proportion to their shares in the firm. The assignment to the company did not affect the original nature of the liability.

In *Lane v Bushby*,[139] the New South Wales Supreme Court held that liability incurred as the result of fraud, illegality, wilful default, or culpable or gross negligence would not be within 'ordinary' and 'proper' conduct for the purposes of requiring an implied indemnity. Ordinary negligence in the course of business was said to be covered, however.

Part (b) of s 24(2) is in effect an extension of the agency of necessity whereby an agent can be indemnified even if he acts outside his authority, provided he was unable to communicate with his principal and acted in good faith in doing what was necessary in the principal's interest. This statutory right of indemnity is also backed up by the common law and the Civil Liability (Contribution) Act 1978 where a partner has, for example, committed a tort in the authorized conduct of the business. He may not be so entitled, however, if he has acted carelessly in incurring the liability.

Change of Partners

Implied requirement for unanimous consent

5.33 Partnership being based on mutual trust, the introduction of a new partner is usually a sensitive issue since the new partner will have the power to impose severe financial burdens on the other partners. It is not surprising, therefore, that the Act does not regard such a matter as one for the majority to decide under s 24(8); instead it provides in s 24(7) that '[n]o person may be introduced as a partner without the consent of all existing partners'. This has always been the case, even in Roman law, and goes to the root of partnership. However, it is, like all the other provisions of s 24, subject to contrary intention and a contrary clause in the partnership agreement will be given effect to. Sometimes such clauses are very wide and allow the introduction of a new partner with virtually no restrictions at all, in other cases they are limited to the introduction of a specific person or class of person (eg children of existing partners) or limited by some form of veto in the other partners.

---

[139] [2000] NSWSC 1029.

Contrary intention

5.34 In *Byrne v Reid*[140] a clause in the partnership agreement gave each partner the right to nominate and introduce any other person into the firm. Byrne nominated his son who was employed in the firm, but the other partners refused to admit him. They then consented to his admission but failed to execute any of the documents necessary for this. The Court of Appeal decided that since the clause was so wide and contained no restrictions the other partners had consented in advance to the son's nomination. There was no reason why they should not so agree or give their consent in advance. Thus even without the consent order he would still have had the right to become a partner. The court applied the doctrine in *Page v Cox*,[141] that if there is a person validly nominated as a partner under a clause in a partnership agreement, the result is that a trust is created with reference to the partnership assets for the purpose of enabling the nominated person to take that to which he is entitled under the deed—he is a partner in equity.

Since the son could be regarded as a beneficiary under a trust in such a case he was entitled to the equitable remedy of specific performance to ensure that the trust was carried out. He was thus entitled to the execution of two deeds by the other partners—one whereby he was bound to observe the terms of the existing agreement (that appears to have been the real source of the dispute) and one vesting his share of the partnership assets in him—in fact he was to take over his father's share of the business. Provided, therefore, a person has been validly nominated as a partner and there are no conditions to be fulfilled he will be able to obtain specific performance of the trust created by such nomination under the agreement. But this depends, of course, on the nomination's being valid and unconditional— unless both can be established there can be no trust and in the absence of a contract to which he is a party there can be no specific performance—equity will not assist a volunteer.

Evidential difficulties

5.35 The Scottish case of *Martin v Thompson*[142] illustrates the difficulties of proving a valid nomination. The agreement between two partners provided that on the death of one of them control of the business was to pass to the survivor but that either partner could by will 'nominate' his widow to his share of the partnership. On the death of one of the partners his whole estate passed under his will to his widow. The House of Lords held that this did not make her a partner, it simply operated as an assignment of her husband's share in the assets. A general bequest of all the estate to his widow could hardly be regarded as a nomination for the purpose of the clause. It might have been different if he had specifically bequeathed her the partnership share—there was no

---

[140] [1902] 2 Ch 735, CA.
[141] (1852) 10 Hare 163.
[142] 1962 SC (HL) 28.

evidence that the widow was being given the right to become a partner. The problems associated with an assignment of a partner's share of the assets (voluntary and involuntary) are dealt with at the end of this chapter. For the moment it is sufficient to note the distinction between a person introducing a replacement for himself into a partnership as a partner[143] and an assignment of his share of the assets as in this case—an assignee as such does not become a partner.

Conditional clauses

5.36 Sometimes there are conditions attached to the right to nominate a new partner. Thus in *Re Franklin and Swaythling's Arbitration*,[144] the clause allowed a partner to introduce any qualified person as a new partner provided that the other partners should consent to his admission—such consent not to be unreasonably withheld. Franklin nominated his son as a new partner but the other partners refused to admit him. The judge decided that the fact that consent was necessary and had not been given (whether reasonably or unreasonably had not been established) prevented the trust doctrine of *Page v Cox* from applying.[145] Maugham J put the point this way:

> The applicant admittedly is not at present a partner. The applicant admittedly has no contractual rights. The applicant may be able to establish hereafter that he is a cestui que trust under the doctrine of *Page v Cox*, but at the present he cannot do anything of the sort; because, for aught I know, the general partners have properly exercised their rights, and in that case he has no more interest in the partnership assets than a stranger.

In fact the son in *Franklin's* case was in even deeper trouble, for the nomination clause went on to say that any dispute as to whether the consent had been unreasonably withheld should be referred to arbitration and his actual application in that case was for the matter to be referred to arbitration. Since he could not take the benefit of a trust without proving that the consent had been unreasonably withheld and that was the issue for arbitration, and since he was not a party to the original arbitration agreement, he had no rights under it to force the matter to arbitration. The position would have been different, however, if the clause had been similar to that in *Byrne v Reid*[146] so that by simply being nominated he became a partner in equity. In enforcing that trust the court might well allow the nominee to invoke an arbitration clause to perfect his entry into the firm.

---

[143] See *Byrne v Reid* [1902] 2 Ch 735.
[144] [1929] 1 Ch 238.
[145] (1852) 10 Hare 163.
[146] [1902] 2 Ch 735.

Expulsion Clauses

Need for express clause

The law has always been keen to protect a partner from being victimized by his fellow partners and s 25 of the Act is quite clear: **5.37**

> No majority of the partners can expel any partner unless a power to do so has been conferred by express agreement between the partners.

Thus there can be no expulsion without an express clause to that effect. Without such a clause, however, the partners are potentially at the mercy of a rogue partner unless the whole firm is dissolved since the court has no power to remove a partner without a dissolution. An expulsion may or may not involve a dissolution; thus if A and B expel C the partnership in effect continues, but if A 'expels' his sole partner B there is in effect a full dissolution—this overlap may explain some of the problems associated with such clauses. Thus in *Walters v Bingham*,[147] it was held that an express expulsion clause is not necessarily inconsistent with a partnership at will which operates when the firm continues after the partnership agreement has expired. The earlier decision to the contrary, *Clark v Leach*,[148] only involved two partners so that an expulsion amounted to a dissolution which, in a partnership at will, can be effected by notice. In *Walters v Bingham* the firm was a large firm of solicitors where the judge regarded an expulsion as being fundamentally different from a dissolution.

There are three questions, in addition to any discrimination issues under the Equality Act 2010,[149] involved in considering expulsion clauses: (a) is the expulsion within the terms of the clause itself; (b) do the rules of natural justice apply to the expulsion procedure and if so have they been complied with; and (c) did the expelling partners act in good faith?[150]

If the answer to all these questions is yes then the courts will support an expulsion. Thus in *Carmichael v Evans*[151] where a junior partner in a draper's firm was convicted of travelling on a train without paying his fare and so defrauding the railway company (on more than one occasion) he was held to have been validly expelled under a clause which allowed expulsion for any 'flagrant breach of the duties of a partner'. This was so, even though the offence was not committed whilst on partnership business, because it was inconsistent with his practice as a partner and would adversely affect the firm's business (an account had appeared in the press). Honesty, generally, was regarded as a duty of a partner, inside or outside the firm. It would clearly depend upon the offence

---

[147] [1988] FTLR 260.
[148] (1863) 1 De GJ&S 409.
[149] See Ch 3, above.
[150] The possibility of a fourth issue, unreasonableness, is discussed below.
[151] [1904] 1 Ch 486.

as to whether a criminal conviction would amount to a flagrant breach of the duties of a partner—crimes of strict liability might not always be so regarded.

Complying with the terms of the clause

5.38 The first question is therefore whether the expulsion falls within the terms of the clause. Adultery, for example, may be many things but it does not amount to financial misconduct likely to damage a banking business. In *Re a Solicitor's Arbitration*,[152] a clause stated that '[i]f any partner shall commit or be guilty of any act of professional misconduct the other partners may by notice in writing expel him from the partnership'. One partner, Egerton, served a notice of expulsion on *both* his fellow partners on the grounds of alleged misconduct, claiming that the word 'partner' in the clause could include the plural. This argument was based on s 61 of the Law of Property Act 1925 which implies the plural for the singular in all deeds unless the context otherwise provides. The judge found that the context did provide otherwise—this clause was designed to allow two partners to expel the third: it did not cover the situation here for that would allow the minority to expel the majority which would be strange when read against the background of s 25.

Similarly in the Queensland case of *Russell v Clarke*[153] the court held that a clause authorizing the 'other partners' to expel a partner in certain circumstances could not apply where eight partners (out of a ten-partner firm) signed expulsion notices against each of the other two. All the other partners (ie nine) had to sign each notice for it to be valid. Further, in *Lie v Mohile*,[154] the clause allowed for an expulsion for 'grave or persistent breaches' of the partnership agreement. The judge held that the act of the other partner in serving an invalid dissolution notice had been negated by the expelling partner continuing the business for three years thereafter. The expulsion notice therefore was invalid.

Procedural compliance with the clause

5.39 Sometimes the question is whether the partners have complied with the procedural requirements set out in the partnership agreement for the exercise of an expulsion power. An example is the decision of the Court of Appeal of Victoria in *Hanlon v Brookes*.[155] The partnership deed provided for two days' notice to be given to each partner of partnership meetings and for seven days' notice to be given if a special resolution (ie one requiring a 75 per cent majority in favour) was on the agenda. A special resolution was needed to affirm the expulsion power in the deed. But the deed also provided that no meeting was necessary prior to making any decision to expel a partner, nor was the

---

[152] [1962] 1 WLR 353.
[153] [1995] 2 QdR 310.
[154] [2015] EWHC 200 (Ch).
[155] 9 October 1997, CA (Aus).

partner proposed to be expelled entitled to be included in any deliberations or to be present at any meeting where that decision was to be taken. A partner was expelled at a meeting which he neither received any notice of nor attended. The court held that, contrary to that partner's arguments, there was no requirement for there to be two meetings, a preliminary one at which the matter was to be decided (of which, it was agreed, the expelled partner was not entitled to notice) and a second one at which it was to be affirmed (where he would have been entitled to receive a notice). Only the first was necessary so that the notice provisions in the deed did not apply.

In the Canadian case of *Ludwig Professional Corporation v BDO Canada LLP*,[156] the power of expulsion in a large firm was in the hands of a committee. The court found that that committee had failed to exercise any independent judgment and had merely ratified the concluded decision of the chief officer. Each member of the committee was required to reach an independent decision. As a result of that failure to comply with the terms of the power, the court awarded the plaintiff aggravated damages for harm to his reputation. That has not been applied yet in English law, where the traditional view is that the expulsion is simply set aside.

On the other hand the courts will not strictly apply the letter of an expulsion clause if that would produce a nonsensical situation. Thus in *Hitchman v Crouch Butler Savage Associates*,[157] an expulsion clause required the signature of the senior partner in order for it to be valid. This was held not to apply where the partner to be expelled was the senior partner himself. Although such clauses are strictly construed they must give effect to the intention of the parties in view of the document as a whole. It was not possible for a partner to expel himself since expulsion was dismissal against the will of the person being expelled and so the clause had to be construed so as to dispense with the requirement of the signature.

Application of natural justice

The second question is whether the rules of natural justice apply to such expulsion procedures and if so whether they have been complied with. Specifically this would require that the partner concerned should be given the precise cause of the complaint against him and be afforded an opportunity to defend himself. In cases where the deed itself sets out a procedure and the expulsion power is not predicated on fault (such as breach of duty) then compliance with the procedure is sufficient.[158] But if those two criteria are not present, the position is less clear-cut.

5.40

---

[156] 2017 ONCA 292.
[157] (1983) 127 SJ 441.
[158] *Hanlon v Brookes*, 9 October 1997, CA (Aus).

In *Barnes v Youngs*,[159] the clause allowed the majority to expel a partner for breach of certain duties and also provided that in the case of a dispute the matter should go to arbitration. The majority purported to expel Barnes but gave no detail of the particular act complained of (he was in fact living with his common law wife). Romer J declared the expulsion to be unlawful—the majority had failed to inform him as to the cause of complaint and to allow him to answer the allegation. Good faith required this. However, this approach was totally rejected by the Court of Appeal in *Green v Howell*.[160] In that case one partner expelled his fellow partner for what were admittedly flagrant breaches of the agreement—the clause allowed this and provided for reference to an arbitrator in the case of a dispute. The partner protested that he had been given no opportunity of providing an explanation. The Court of Appeal decided that in such circumstances there was no need to observe the rules of natural justice since the expelling partner had otherwise acted in good faith. The expelling partner was acting in an administrative character—he was not acting in a judicial capacity since he was simply serving a notice which could lead to an arbitration where the matter would be considered judicially.

There is some doubt, therefore, as to whether these procedural requirements apply to expulsion clauses. In an article, 'The Good Faith Principle and the Expulsion Clause in Partnership Law',[161] Bernard Davies argued that *Green v Howell* was really a case of dissolution masquerading as an expulsion (only one partner was left) and that it only applied to a notice setting such a dispute on its way to arbitration. *Barnes v Youngs* should continue to apply to a genuine expulsion to be decided on by a majority of the partners who must discuss the matter and act in a quasi-judicial manner. Since that article, Plowman J was faced with a similar problem in the case of *Peyton v Mindham*.[162] The two doctors had been partners for eight years. The deed provided that if either partner was incapacitated from performing his fair share of the work of the practice for more than nine consecutive months the other partners could determine the partnership by notice. Peyton suffered a cerebral haemorrhage on 2 January 1970 and although he returned on 1 October 1970 he was in fact incapable of performing his share of the practice. On 9 October Mindham served the notice and Peyton argued that this notice was invalid because it was issued before either Mindham could ascertain or Peyton could demonstrate that he could perform his fair share. The judge rejected this defence and allowed the notice to stand since Mindham had otherwise acted bona fide. The reasoning was on a par with *Green v Howell*; Mindham had not been acting judicially when serving the notice.

It is therefore an open question under English law whether *Barnes v Youngs* is good law since both *Green v Howell* and *Peyton v Mindham* can be distinguished on the grounds of being dissolution cases in reality and that in both cases the actual complaint had

---

[159] [1898] 1 Ch 414.
[160] [1910] 1 Ch 495.
[161] (1969) 33 Conv NS 32.
[162] [1972] 1 WLR 8.

been substantiated by the time of the decision on natural justice. Dillon LJ in *Kerr v Morris*,[163] however, seems to have regarded natural justice as a requirement in a true expulsion case.[164] In Scotland, however, there seems no doubt that the rules of natural justice do apply to an expulsion: see, eg *Fairman v Scully*.[165]

In the Canadian case of *Ludwig Professional Corporation v BDO Canada LLP*,[166] the judge amplified the position re natural justice in more detail than the UK cases. He distinguished between a power framed in subjective terms (eg unfit to practice) and one framed in objective terms (eg being convicted of an offence of dishonesty). In the latter case, if the evidence supports the grounds for expulsion that is really all that is required. So, if all the expelling partners have independently formed the view that objective grounds for the expulsion exist there is no need to give the defendant any opportunity to explain. But if one or more of them seek to persuade the others that such grounds exist, it is advisable to allow the defendant an opportunity to explain. If the power is subjective in nature, however, then the defendant should always be given the opportunity to explain their conduct. That analysis has much to recommend it.

Abuse of power

One certain requirement is that the partners must act in good faith, so that in exercising a power of expulsion the partners must have been acting bona fide for the benefit of the firm as a whole and not for their own ends. The classic example is *Blisset v Daniel*.[167] The expulsion clause was being exercised by the majority in order to obtain the other partner's share at a discount. The court had little difficulty in holding that the power had been improperly exercised. The judge, Page Wood V-C, said that it was quite clear that the power was being used solely for the majority partners' exclusive benefit and that such use of the power was an abuse and would not be allowed. The power must be used for the purpose for which it was intended. In *Walters v Bingham*,[168] it was also said that a power of expulsion would be invalid if it was expropriatory, ie if the expelled partner would be disadvantaged by a dissolution. On the other hand, the presence of other motives does not necessarily mean that a power exercised for a legitimate reason will be in bad faith. Thus in *Kelly v Denman*[169] one partner was expelled on the basis that he had been engaged in a tax fraud. Since that was a legitimate reason and within the terms of the power, the fact that the other partners had wanted to exclude him for some time did not invalidate its exercise.

5.41

---

[163] [1987] Ch 90, CA.
[164] See the next paragraph.
[165] 1997 GWD 29–1942.
[166] 2016 ONSC 2225, affirmed 2017 ONCA 292.
[167] (1853) 10 Hare 493.
[168] [1988] FTLR 260.
[169] (1996) LTL, 17 September 1996.

The decision in *Blisset v Daniel*, was qualified by McMurdo J in the Queensland case *of Maclag (No 11) Pty Ltd v Chantay Too Pty Ltd*,[170] on the basis that the expulsion power in the first case had been given to the partners without any requirement of misconduct by the partner to be expelled. The situation would be different where the power required misconduct on the part of the expelled partner and that had been established. On that basis the expelling partners were not bound to consider what was in the economic interests of the defaulting partner. Nor were they bound to consider his interests in deciding whether to act upon his misconduct at all. That can be explained on the basis that in such a case, by acting as they did the expelling partners were in fact preserving the partnership and so acting in good faith in that sense.

In relation to good faith and natural justice, when Dillon LJ in *Kerr v Morris*[171] spoke of the need to exercise a power of expulsion in good faith, he seems to have suggested the possibility of including in that the need to give reasons and to afford the expelled partner a hearing. That was a case of a true expulsion, ie by three against one, and did not therefore amount to a dissolution. Whilst making it clear that he was not expressing any conclusive view on the matter, the Lord Justice said (emphasis added):

> Prima facie it may be said, therefore, with some force that, if the other partners are giving the defendant a 12 months' notice of expulsion, *they must specify a reason for giving it . . . which must prima facie be a reasonable reason . . . So it may well be that, apart from the question whether they were bound to afford him a hearing, and a hearing that went further than the meeting in January 1985 . . . the question . . .* will come down to whether they were justified in their honest belief that the trust necessary between partners had been breached by the defendant.

Unreasonableness?

5.42 There is a possibility that a fourth requirement might be applied to the exercise of an expulsion clause. In *Braganza v BP Shipping Ltd*,[172] the Supreme Court had to decide whether a decision by an employer as to the facts surrounding the death of an employee which affected his widow's rights against the company had been properly made. The majority decided that since the decision maker had a potential conflict of interest, the well-known *Wednesbury* test of reasonableness/irrationality[173] should apply both as to the process and the outcome of the decision (was it reasonable on the evidence?). This could potentially be applied to expulsion decisions in partnership, but it is too early to say. If the decision is one which no reasonable person could make, that would in any event negative good faith.

---

[170] [2010] QSC 299.
[171] [1987] Ch 90, CA.
[172] [2015] 1 WLR 1661.
[173] *Associated Provincial Picture Houses Ltd v Wednesbury Corporation* [1948] 1 KB 223.

Compulsory retirement

Similar rules to expulsion clauses will also apply to the exercise of a compulsory retirement provision in a partnership agreement, ie one whereby a partner must retire after a period of notice. **5.43**

Assignment of the Partnership Share

There is a clear distinction between the introduction of A as a replacement partner for B and the assignment of B's share in the partnership to A. As we have seen, the introduction of a new partner requires the consent of all the other partners unless the agreement provides to the contrary and the intended partner is able to enforce that agreement. In such cases A replaces B totally in the firm and acquires all his rights and liabilities vis-à-vis the other partners. An assignment, on the other hand, does not, unless the contrary is agreed, make A a partner in B's place, it simply assigns B's rights in the partnership assets and/or profits to A: A does not become a partner. Such assignments may be commercial, eg a mortgage, or personal, eg a divorce agreement. An assignment may also occur involuntarily, ie, by a judgment creditor who, having been awarded judgment against a partner for a private debt, then wishes to levy execution of that debt over the partner's share of the firm's assets. Let us look at the position of these two types of assignee, voluntary and involuntary, in turn. **5.44**

Rights of the assignee whilst the partnership is a going concern

The rights of an assignee of a share in a partnership are set out in s 31 of the Act. It is not entirely clear whether the section applies to both voluntary and involuntary assignments or only the former. These rights are set out first whilst the partnership is a going concern: **5.45**

(1) An assignment by any partner of his share in the partnership, either absolute or by way of mortgage or redeemable charge, does not, as against the other partners, entitle the assignee, during the continuance of the partnership, to interfere in the management or administration of the partnership business or affairs, or to require any accounts of the partnership transactions, or to inspect the partnership books, but entitles the assignee only to receive the share of profits to which the assigning partner would otherwise be entitled, and the assignee must accept the account of profits agreed to by the partners.

Assignees are therefore considerably restricted in their control of the assigned assets. They cannot interfere in any way in the running of the firm; they cannot in any circumstances inspect the books or demand an account—all they have is the right to the assignor's share of the profits so that the assignment under s 31(1) transfers no capital assets to the assignee. Thus in *Hadlee v Commissioner of Inland Revenue*,[174] the Privy Council found that for New Zealand tax purposes the income which accrued to the assignee arose not from a capital asset but from the performance by the assignor of his obligations under the partnership agreement. Further, an assignee must accept the other partner's accounts as to the amount of those profits.

This obligation to accept the other partners' accounts was taken to extreme lengths in *Re Garwood's Trusts*.[175] Garwood was one of three partners in a colliery business who received an equal share of the profits but took no 'salary' since all the work was done by employees. In 1889 Garwood charged his share of the partnership with payment of £10,000 to two trustees of a settlement for the benefit of his wife on his separation from her. He later agreed to pay all his share of the profits into the settlement. In 1893 the partners, including Garwood, decided to take part personally in the running of the business and that accordingly they should each be paid a salary before net profits were ascertained. Garwood received nothing by way of salary after 1895. Mrs Garwood, whose income under the settlement was thus reduced by the salaries payable to the other two partners, sought to have these payments stopped. Buckley J, applying s 31(1), held that the decision to pay the salaries was a matter within the administration or management of the firm and so a matter entirely for the decision of the partners and one which could not be challenged by Mrs Garwood as an assignee. She had to accept the account of profits as agreed between the partners.

On the other hand it is clear that in coming to this decision the judge was impressed by the fact that the actions of the partners were bona fide, in the sense that they were not done with the intention of defeating Mrs Garwood's rights, nor were they improper or fraudulent. The reason for the partners' increased activity was to superintend sales at the pithead so as to stop thefts which were occurring. Stopping such thefts would, of course, actually increase the net profits. It follows that if the partners' actions had not been bona fide the result might well have been different. The rule as to s 31(1) is therefore as laid down by Buckley J in that case:

> The intention of the Acts was to substitute the assignee for the assignor as the person entitled to such profits as the assignor would have received if there had not been an assignment, but to give the assignee no right to interfere at all with anything bona fide done in management or administration.

It is an open point whether a decision to alter the actual profit-sharing ratios would fall within this exception. Presumably if it was done bona fide for management reasons there could be no objection—in any event the practical effect of a 'salary' payment such as in *Re Garwood's Trust* is the same as an adjustment of the profit-sharing ratio. As we have seen they are all simply different methods of allocating the profits.

---

[174] [1993] AC 524, PC.
[175] [1903] 1 Ch 236.

Rights of the assignee on dissolution

5.46 The position of an assignee changes when the partnership goes into dissolution. In such cases s 31(2) applies:

> In case of a dissolution of the partnership, whether as respects all the partners or as respects the assigning partner, the assignee is entitled to receive the share of the partnership assets to which the assigning partner is entitled as between himself and the other partners, and, for the purpose of ascertaining that share, to an account as from the date of dissolution.

Thus where the assigning partner is leaving the firm and taking out his share or when the whole firm is being dissolved the assignee has two rights: (a) to the assigning partner's share and (b) to an account as from the date of dissolution to ascertain that share. He is no longer interested in profits as they arise, he needs to quantify the actual share of the assets and so, unlike s 31(1), he is entitled to an account. If there is no such account the assignee is not bound by the actions of the other partners. In *Hadlee v Commissioner of Inland Revenue*[176] the Privy Council, after considering the nature of the assigning partner's share, decided that since he had no proprietary interest in the assets, s 31(2) effected an assignment of income and not capital for New Zealand tax purposes. However, in *Commissioner of Taxation v Everett*[177] a distinction was made between the total assignment by a partner of his share (proprietary interest in the assets) and a partial assignment (income only) for Australian tax purposes. The reason for the difference in approach flows from the difficulty of defining the nature of a partner's interest in the partnership.[178]

Entitlement to an account

5.47 In *Watts v Driscoll*,[179] a father lent £1,900 to his son to set him up in partnership, and he secured that sum by taking an assignment of his son's share in the firm. The son fell out with the other partner and sold his share to him for £500. The father claimed an account to enable him to ascertain the value of the son's share irrespective of the agreement. The Court of Appeal agreed. Section 31(2) was intended to give the assignee a right to an account whenever a dissolution takes place irrespective of whether there is a private agreement between the other partners. On the facts no accounts had been taken. The son made up his mind to leave the partnership and made a bargain without the father's knowledge or consent to sell his share for £500. There was no evidence that this was the correct valuation since the agreement took no account of the goodwill—it could not therefore be construed as an unofficial account. The father was entitled to an account properly drawn up to ascertain the true value of the son's share.

---

[176] [1993] AC 524, PC.
[177] (1980) 143 CLR 440.
[178] See Ch 6, below.
[179] [1901] 1 Ch 294, CA.

Two points need to be made here. First, that the Court of Appeal came to this decision even though there was no evidence of fraud in the conduct of the partners in fixing the share at £500. The decision was that an account had to be taken by virtue of the Act and the existing partners simply could not agree otherwise as between themselves. Second, that the right to have an account is simply the right to an account 'bona fide taken in the course of the partnership on the footing of its being a going concern' according to the Court of Appeal in *Watts*'s case. Thus if a bona fide account had shown the share to be worth only £500 that would have been the end of the matter. This was in fact the position prior to the Act and the court was anxious to make it clear that this section had not altered the law by giving a right to a different type of account.

But an assignee is entitled to an account on that basis. Thus in *Bonnin v Neame*,[180] assignees were held not to be bound by an arbitration agreement in the deed under which the partners wished to resolve their dispute as to the valuation of their shares on a dissolution. Since the assignees were not parties to the agreement they could not be bound by the arbitration clause—they were entitled to rely on their statutory right to ask the court to order an account. The court refused to stay the action pending the arbitration. Swinfen Eady J summed up the position:

> Then how can an account taken behind their backs, and to which they are not parties, bind them? If I were to determine that they were bound by an account taken as between the partners, it would be not to allow them the right which the statute confers upon them. They are entitled to an account, and to hold that they are to be bound by an account taken in their absence and that unless they can show some fraud or some manifest error they are not to be entitled to come to the court for an account would be to ignore the language of the statute altogether.

Losses

5.48 There is some doubt as to whether an assignee as such acquires any liability for partnership losses. Of course he will be liable to third parties, by virtue of s 14, if he represents that he is a partner, but it would seem that otherwise the effect of s 31(1) is to exempt him—he is by definition not a partner. This is the view taken in Australia but there is some doubt cast on that sensible proposition by the English case of *Dodson v Downey*,[181] where Farwell J found that an assignee was liable to indemnify his assignor against partnership losses. This decision has been much criticized and seems to have been based on a misunderstanding of the law of vendor and purchaser which was used by way of analogy. Clearly since an assignee is not a partner he should not be liable as such either—he has no right of management and the law would be inconsistent if the Australian cases were held not to apply here.

---

[180] [1910] 1 Ch 732.
[181] [1901] 2 Ch 620.

Charging Orders Against Partners

Prior to the Partnership Act, if a creditor was awarded judgment against an individual partner in respect of a private (non-partnership) debt he was able to enforce this judgment against the partnership assets. This could have dramatic effects on the firm—it could, for example, paralyse its business and injure the other partners who were not concerned in the dispute. For once, the Act changed the law and s 23(1) now provides that 'a writ of execution shall not issue against any partnership property except on a judgment against the firm'. Only firm debts can be enforced against the firm's assets. Instead a private creditor has to rely on s 23(2):

5.49

> The High Court, or a judge thereof, or a county court, may, on the application by summons of any judgment creditor of a partner, make an order charging that partner's interest in the partnership property and profits with payment of the amount of the judgment debt and interest thereon, and may by the same or a subsequent order appoint a receiver of that partner's share of profits (whether already declared or accruing), and of any other money which may be coming to him in respect of the partnership, and direct all accounts and inquiries, and give all other orders and directions which might have been directed or given if the charge had been made in favour of the judgment creditor by the partner, or which the circumstances of the case may require.

Thus a judgment creditor can ask the court to make him in effect an assignee of the debtor's share in the partnership. He is entitled to ask for any order to effect this, including the appointment of a receiver—but such a receiver will only be able to collect the sums due to the debtor, he cannot interfere in the running of the firm. Section 23 does not apply to Scotland (s 23(5)).

Strict interpretation

The courts have interpreted this section strictly against the judgment creditor. In *Peake v Carter*,[182] the Court of Appeal held that if there was a dispute as to whether particular assets were partnership assets or belonged solely to the debtor there could be no execution against the assets without the other partners' being given a chance to interplead in the proceedings making the order. Further if the dispute, as in that case, related to whether the assets were partnership assets or the sole property of an innocent partner, no execution at all could be levied against the property because of s 23(1). The matter would have to be resolved by an inquiry under s 23(2) to ascertain the particulars of the partnership assets and of the debtor's share and interest in them. Further in *Brown, Janson & Co v Hutchinson (No 2)*,[183] where an order had been made under s

5.50

---

[182] [1916] 1 KB 652, CA.
[183] [1895] 2 QB 126, CA.

23(2) charging a partner's interest in the firm for payment of a private debt, the Court of Appeal refused to make an additional order for an account. Such an order, although provided for in s 23(2), will only be made in exceptional circumstances.

The reasoning behind this is that the court regards an involuntary assignment under s 23(2) as being similar to an assignment under s 31 where there is, as we have just seen, no right to demand an account. This analogy should be adhered to in ordinary cases. As the Court of Appeal said: 'As a general rule, a judgment creditor of a partner must be treated in the same way as the assignee of the share of a partner'. If this is so, it is conceivable that the judgment creditor's rights may be frustrated by a device such as used in *Re Garwood* to reduce the debtor's share of the profits,[184] provided of course it is a bona fide management decision. One snag to that is, of course, that the creditor would simply hang around for longer than he would otherwise do with the additional possibility that he would go back to the court for an order for account, which he could not do as an assignee under s 31.

If the other partners object to the imposition of a charge under s 23(2) they have two alternative courses of action. First, under s 23(3) they are 'at liberty at any time to redeem the interest charged, or in case of a sale being directed, to purchase the same'. Alternatively, under s 33(2), they may dissolve the partnership and in that case all will be worked out in the winding-up process which will follow. If they redeem the charge by paying the amount owed into court then, of course, the debt will be transferred to them and they can recover it from the debtor at their own convenience. Dissolution is a rather drastic step and would have the same practical effect as if s 23 had never been passed, ie bringing a possibly prosperous business to an end because of the private folly or ill luck of one of the partners.

If the other partners decide to purchase the debtor's share, and s 23(3) seems to give them a pre-emptive right to do so (although the language of the section is not that strong, such an interpretation would be in accord with the other parts of the section), they must be careful not to fall foul of s 28 and their fiduciary duty of avoiding a conflict of interest. A trustee may not purchase trust property and although this may not apply strictly to fiduciaries it would be very wise to employ an independent valuer to advise the debtor. The fact that it was sold to a partner at an auction will not in itself suffice to negative the obligation of full disclosure etc. It seems that, at least prior to the Act, where such a sale was set aside on the grounds of breach of a fiduciary duty, the other partners lost their right to dissolve the firm. Nor can partnership money be used to purchase the share since it will then simply become partnership property itself.

---

[184] [1903] 1 Ch 236.

6
PARTNERSHIP PROPERTY

Problems and Possibilities

Need to identify partnership property

In the previous chapters we have seen something of the importance of distinguishing between property which belongs to all the partners as partners (ie to the firm) and property which remains that of an individual partner, or partners, as individuals. Sometimes the distinction is quite clear but it can become blurred in relation to assets used by the firm. It is then possible for such an asset to be owned by one partner and used by the firm under some form of agreement or even for it to be owned by all the partners as individuals and used by them as partners under a similar arrangement. On the other hand such assets can be owned and used by the firm as partnership property. Circulating assets, eg stock in trade, work in progress etc, are highly likely to be partnership property, but much more difficulty arises with fixed assets in the name of one partner, eg the freehold or leasehold business premises, plant and machinery etc.

6.01

Link with insolvency

Before we attempt to solve some of these problems, however, we should clarify why this distinction between partnership and other property needs to be made. There are five potential problem areas, although one is now of historical interest only. First, as we shall see in Chapter 8, when there is an insolvency both of the firm and its partners there will be two sets of creditors—the creditors of the firm and the creditors of each individual partner. Under the current regime for insolvency, introduced in 1994, the firm's creditors have first go at the partnership assets (or estate as it is called then) in priority to the individual creditors whereas both sets of creditors rank equally with respect to the individual (ie non-partnership) estates of the partners. It is therefore of great importance to sort out which assets belong to which estate in circumstances where, by definition, not all the creditors are going to be paid in full.

6.02

Beneficial ownership

Second, if an asset is identified as partnership property, as opposed, say, to it being family property, it belongs only to the partners, and not the family as a whole. This was

6.03

the subject of the dispute in *Mehra v Shah*,[1] which involved an extended family, originally of twelve siblings. The action concerned the ownership of several properties. The Court of Appeal agreed with the judge that they were partnership assets, owned by six of the siblings who had been the only members of the firm. The other six siblings therefore had no interest in the properties.

Also, if an asset increases in value, that increase will be attributed to the firm if it is partnership property although, if the increase is due to the expenditure of one partner, he or she is entitled to have that amount treated as a capital contribution on the taking of final accounts on a dissolution.[2] Of course if the asset remains the property of an individual partner, any increase in its value will belong to that partner. There is an exception to this, however, if that increase is caused by the partnership business itself when the other partners will become entitled to a share in such increase. Thus in the Australian case of *Kriziac v Ravinder Rohini Pty Ltd*[3] one partner brought a hotel into the firm as its property but the business of the firm was to demolish the hotel and develop the site. The firm was dissolved before this was accomplished but not before planning permission had been obtained by the partners' efforts thus raising the value of the site by some $444,000. On those facts it was held that all the partners were entitled to the increase, which was not merely an accidental or incidental increase, but had arisen from the special efforts of the partners.

On the other hand, *Davies v H and C Ecroyd Ltd*[4] involved a dairy-farming partnership in which the farm was expressly reserved as the property of one of the partners. A milk quota (ie the right to produce and sell milk under EC law) was subsequently allocated to the farm. Blackburne J held that there was no partnership entitlement to any increased value of the farm as a result of obtaining the milk quota:

> There is no suggestion that, owing to the exceptional efforts of the partnership, a greater amount of quota was allocated to the farm than might otherwise have been expected. There is nothing to indicate that, as a result of the introduction of quota and in order to maintain the amount of quota allocated to the farm, the partnership incurred any significant expenditure which it might not otherwise have undertaken.

Blackburne J set out the basis for giving the partners rights in relation to the asset of a partner as follows:

> It arises where a partnership expends money for the benefit of a partner in circumstances where justice requires that, in taking partnership accounts, some allowance should be made to the partnership against that partner for some or all of the amount of the expenditure or of the enhanced value brought about by the expenditure.

---

[1] [2004] EWCA Civ 632.
[2] *Stocking v Montila* [2005] EWHC 2210 (Ch).
[3] (1990) 102 FLR 8.
[4] (1996) 2 EGLR 5.

From that statement it will be seen that the principle could apply even where there is no increase in the asset's value but where, for example, the firm has spent partnership money in effecting repairs to a partner's asset so reducing a fall in its value. In all these cases, however, the asset would not, it seems, on that basis alone, become owned by the partnership, it would simply be a matter of adjusting entitlements between the partners (see per Chadwick J in *Faulks v Faulks*[5]). On the other hand the cases so far have all involved disputes between partners and not their creditors, where ownership would be central.

Application of fiduciary duties

6.04 The third reason is that, as we have seen in Chapter 5, where an asset is a partnership asset the rules of equity will apply to any profit or benefit derived by a partner from that asset. Thus in *Don King Productions Inc v Warren*[6] where contracts originally entered into by one partner had become partnership property, renewal of some those contracts by one partner for his own benefit prior to the final winding up of the firm meant that the benefit of the renewed contracts was also partnership property and not that of the individual partner. Similarly in *Gorne v Scales*,[7] where, having decided that confidential files etc were partnership property, the equitable duty of confidentiality was applied.

Co-ownership issues

6.05 The fourth reason is the technical, but important, one that partnership property is presumed to be held by the partners as trustees for themselves beneficially as tenants in common whereas it is possible for other property to be held by the individual owners as joint tenants.[8] The difference is that tenants in common own an 'undivided share' in the property (ie an unseparated but otherwise quantifiable share in the whole) which they can sell, mortgage, bequeath, etc. Joint tenants, on the other hand, have no such share: each one owns everything and so they have no 'share' to sell etc. In particular joint tenants cannot leave their shares in a will so that with a joint tenancy the right of survivorship applies. Thus if A and B own an office block and A dies leaving all his property to X, X can only inherit A's 'half' if A and B were tenants in common. Otherwise B becomes the sole owner.

Equity has always presumed partners to be tenants in common even if the formal transfer of property to them suggests that they are joint tenants. Normally this distinction depends upon whether 'words of severance' such as 'equally' or 'in equal shares' are

---

[5] [1992] 1 EGLR 9.
[6] [1999] 2 All ER 218, CA.
[7] 14 November 2002.
[8] *Brown v Oakshot* (1857) 24 Beav 254.

used—at common law only if there are such words of severance will there be a tenancy in common. Equity, however, regards a joint tenancy, with its right of survivorship, as being incompatible with a commercial enterprise such as a partnership and so implies a tenancy in common behind a trust. Particularly in the older cases, therefore, this has been the cause of the dispute as to the nature of an asset's ownership—ie are the partners co-owners as individuals, and so possibly as joint tenants, or as partners and so as tenants in common?

Although the presumption against partnership property accruing only to the surviving partner is very strong, it can be rebutted by clear evidence that the partners did intend that to be the consequence of the property being held by them both legally and beneficially as joint tenants. As in other matters partnership law is substantially subject to the express or implied agreement of the partners. This was established in *Barton v Morris*,[9] on the basis that both partners understood the consequences of declaring themselves to be joint tenants. But in that case the property, a guest house, was also the partners' home in which they co-habited. A more difficult case was that before the Court of Appeal in *Bathurst v Scarborow*.[10] The partners in that case were two friends, one with a girlfriend, the other married with two children. The former died in an accident. They had bought a house from an old lady on terms that she could live there during the rest of her life. The partners thought of this partly as an investment and partly to store partnership goods. They bought the house as joint tenants and the evidence of the lawyer was that they understood the survivorship consequences of this. The Court of Appeal held that the presumption of tenancy in common was negatived by this evidence,[11] even though, as the judge below had said, it seemed inconceivable that the surviving partner with a family would have agreed to losing his share had he died first.

Doctrine of conversion

6.06 Finally, it was formerly the rule that the equitable doctrine of conversion applied to partnership property. This meant that even partnership land was regarded as being personal property, since it was held upon a trust for sale, and equity, looking upon that as done which ought to be done, treated the partners' interests as being in the proceeds of sale. This consequence was codified by s 22 of the Act. Land which remained the property of an individual partner was of course regarded as real property. Prior to 1925 this also applied to land which remained the property of one or more of the partners without it becoming partnership property. This distinction between realty and personalty was important in connection with intestacy (one went to the 'heir' and the other to the 'next of kin') so that on the death of a partner intestate it was important to decide whether land was partnership property or not.

---

[9] [1985] 1 WLR 1257.
[10] [2004] 1 P & CR 4, CA.
[11] Evidence is a problem in these cases since, by definition, only the survivor is around to give his or her story.

The 1925 property law reforms effectively ended this distinction and also put all land held in co-ownership, whether partnership property or not, into a statutory trust for sale so that the doctrine of conversion applied in every case except where the land was owned by a single partner. By the Trusts of Land and Appointment of Trustees Act 1996, however, all land held on trust is now held under a trust of land rather than a trust for sale and the doctrine of conversion no longer applies. That Act also repealed s 22 of the Partnership Act 1890. It follows that the doctrine of conversion no longer plays any role in the distinction between partnership and other property but it does explain some of the disputes in the earlier cases.

What is Partnership Property?

The Act provides only a basic definition of what amounts to partnership property, although as we shall see later, it does provide additional guidelines for subsequent acquisitions out of profits. Section 20(1) provides: **6.07**

> All property and rights and interests in property originally brought into the partnership stock or acquired, whether by purchase or otherwise, on account of the firm or for the purposes and in the course of the partnership business, are called in this Act partnership property, and must be held and applied by the partners exclusively for the purposes of the partnership and in accordance with the partnership agreement.

This section covers two distinct features: one the existence of partnership property and the other the nature of a partner's interest in the property. Identifying the property is one thing, describing the partner's interest in it another. Let us cover these two aspects in reverse order (it is actually easier that way round).

Nature and Consequences of a Partner's Interest

Enforceable only on partial or total dissolution

Section 20(1) requires partnership property to be held for partnership purposes and in accordance with the partnership agreement. It seems clear that this gives each partner an interest in the assets of the firm. In *Popat v Schonchhatra*[12] Nourse LJ set out the nature of that interest in English law as follows: **6.08**

> Although it is both customary and convenient to speak of a partner's 'share' of the partnership assets, that is not a truly accurate description of his interest in them, at all events so long as the partnership is a going concern. While each partner has a

---

[12] [1997] 3 All ER 800, CA.

proprietary interest in each and every asset he has no entitlement to any specific asset, and, in consequence no right, without the consent of the other partners or partner to require the whole or even a share of any particular asset to be vested in him. On dissolution the position is in substance not much different, the partnership property falling to be applied, subject to ss. 40 to 43 (if and so far as applicable), in accordance with ss. 39 and 44 of the 1890 Act. As part of that process, each partner in a solvent partnership is presumptively entitled to payment of what is due from the firm to him in respect of capital before division of the ultimate residue in the shares in which profits are divisible.... It is only at that stage that a partner can accurately be said to be entitled to a share of anything, which, in the absence of agreement to the contrary, will be a share of cash.[13]

We shall deal with those sections in Chapter 7. What is clear, however, is that a partner's interest in the assets of the firm is ultimately only enforceable by an action for a partnership account—it is a chose in action. It follows that a partnership share confers no interest as such in any specific partnership asset. One consequence was that where partners had sold their shares to companies controlled by them, a receiver appointed by a bank under a loan agreement with the companies could not recover funds directly from the partnership assets themselves.[14]

As the Law Commissions put it, there is a clear distinction between the external perspective, the undivided share of each partner, and the internal perspective, the restrictions on realizing such a share.[15] In Scotland, where there is legal personality, the position is different.[16] In *Fengate Developments v CEC*,[17] the issue was as to whether a transfer of partnership land was a transfer by the firm of the entire interest in it or was simply a transfer of one partner's interest in the land.[18] The judge said that under partnership law one partner could sell her interest in the land by an assignment, but the purchaser could not have realized that interest without a dissolution of the firm. There are limited exceptions to this principle, eg where the partnership accounts have been settled on a dissolution and an asset is subsequently recorded, but they do not go to the nature of the interest (see *Marshall v Bullock*[19]). But the interest is also a beneficial interest (the proprietary interest referred to by Nourse LJ), which arises from the fact that all partnership property is held in trust for the partners.

---

[13] See also *IRC v Gray* [1994] STC 360 at 377 per Hoffmann LJ; *Ng Chu Chong v Ng Swee Choon* [2002] 2 SLR 368; *Tan Liang Chong v Chou Lai Tiang* [2003] 4 SLR 775.
[14] *Bloxham, Re* [2017] IEHC 664.
[15] Report, para 9.67.
[16] Ibid, para 9.68. Had English law adopted legal personality, the situation would also have been different.
[17] [2005] STC 191, CA, affirming [2004] STC 772.
[18] There were complex VAT and conveyancing points involved.
[19] 30 March 1998, CA.

Beneficial interest

The fact that the partners have such an interest has posed two problems. The first is exactly what type of interest it is. The Australian courts have examined this question in various contexts. In *Canny Gabriel Castle Jackson Advertising Pty Ltd v Volume Sales (Finance) Pty Ltd*,[20] partners were held to have an equitable interest capable of taking priority over a later equitable interest such as an equitable charge ('where the equities are equal the first in time prevails'). In *Federal Commissioner of Taxation v Everett*,[21] the court preferred to class the interest as an equitable interest in the nature of a chose in action. In *Connell v Bond Corporation Pty Ltd*,[22] Malcolm CJ had to decide whether a partner's interest was registrable for land law purposes. After an extensive review of the cases he decided that the interest was more than a 'mere equity'. It was an equitable chose in action which gave a partner a present beneficial interest in every asset of the firm although it could take effect in possession only on the dissolution of the partnership. As such it was registrable. In *Cyril Henschke Pty Ltd v Commissioner of State Taxation*,[23] it was decided that this equitable chose in action could be ended, on being bought out, by accord and satisfaction. It is regarded there as a proprietary interest.[24] The decision in Australia that a partner's interest with respect to each individual item of partnership property is more than a mere equity, it is an equitable interest which can give the partner priority as against outsiders, was reaffirmed in 2018 by the Western Australia Court of Appeal in *Rojoda Pty Ltd v Commissioner of State Revenue*.[25]

On the other hand, as we have seen in Chapter 5, the Privy Council in *Hadlee v Commissioner of Inland Revenue*[26] decided that for New Zealand tax purposes partners do not have a proprietary interest in the assets of the firm. Against this, the New Zealand Supreme Court has since held that a partner has a beneficial interest for the purposes of defining 'relationship property' under New Zealand law.[27] And in Canada such an interest has been held to be capable of being insured. In *Steingarten v Burke*,[28] it was described as a property interest, the partners having 'units' in the firm's client accounts. In *Sze Tu v Lowe*,[29] the New South Wales Court of Appeal held, in the context of a claim for tracing partnership funds mixed with other funds to acquire properties, that neither ss 20 nor 21 as such created a trust 'in the strict sense' nor trust property for the purposes of their Limitation Act. Something more would be required.

6.09

---

[20] (1974) 131 CLR 321.
[21] (1980) 54 ALJR 196.
[22] (1992) 8 WAR 352.
[23] [2010] HCA 43.
[24] *Fazio v Fazio* [2012] WASC 72.
[25] [2018] WASCA 224.
[26] [1993] AC 524, PC.
[27] *Rose v Rose* [2009] NZSC 46.
[28] [2003] 6 WWR 729.
[29] [2014] NSWCA 462.

Since the basic rights of a partner with regard to partnership property, as set out by Nourse LJ above, are not in dispute, perhaps the best course is to regard a partner's interest as unique and not to attach labels to it but to decide its nature with respect to the context in which the issue arises (such as the question of floating charges referred to in Chapter 1).

Limits on assets capable of being partnership property

6.10 The second problem is whether the existence of such a beneficial interest in partnership property limits the type of asset which may be regarded as partnership property. This was the principal issue before the Court of Appeal in *Don King Productions Inc v Warren*.[30] Warren, a boxing promoter, had purported to transfer the benefit of certain contracts, which he had previously made with various boxers as to managing and promoting their careers, to the partnership with King. It was now argued that, being personal contracts of service, Warren could not legally assign the benefit of them and therefore they could not have become partnership property. The benefit of such contracts could not be sold and so would not be available to pay partnership debts on a dissolution, as required by s 39, and if, as partnership property, they became subject to a trust in favour of the partners this would give the other partner a right to interfere in what were personal contracts to the potential prejudice of the boxers.

These arguments were rejected by the Court of Appeal. They regarded the fact that the contracts were non-assignable as being entirely consistent with the benefit of them being held on trust for the partnership. Partnership property within s 20 included that to which a partner was entitled and which all the partners expressly or by implication agreed should, as between themselves, be treated as partnership property. Ability to actually assign that property to the other partner was immaterial as between the partners. The fact that this effected a trust of the property for the partnership did not mean that the other partner could interfere with the personal obligations of the boxers. Rules to give effect to such a trust would not be allowed to jeopardize the trust property itself—not all the principles of trust law would be applied to every type of trust. Once again, therefore, there is the idea that this equitable interest of a partner in partnership property is to some extent *sui generis*. It may be easier to regard the trust in *Don King* as a trust of the benefit of the contracts rather than of the contracts themselves.

The reasoning in *Don King Productions* was applied in *Barber v Rasco International Ltd*,[31] to a contract which one of the partners had negotiated with BP but which the

---

[30] [1999] 2 All ER 218, CA.
[31] [2012] EWHC 269 (QB).

partnership agreement made clear was a partnership asset. Further it was held that the variations, extensions, and replacement BP contracts entered into with BP were all renewals, variations, or replacements of the original BP contract and so were all partnership assets. Again, following *Don King Productions*, this was said to be the case even if the variations etc occurred after dissolution but before it is dispersed during winding up.[32]

The width of what could be partnership assets has been shown by two recent cases. In *Campbell v Campbell*,[33] it was accepted by the judge that shares in a company operating a business controlled and/or conducted and/or profited from wholly or in part by the partners or some of them could be partnership assets. Further in *Goldup v Cobb*,[34] one partner in a firm of solicitors had acted as a coroner, bringing her net salary from that into the partnership accounts. She was also entitled to a pension from that post and, on her retirement, the other partners argued that those pension rights had also become partnership assets. The judge held that a partner's right to a personal pension could be a partnership asset. In fact, that was not really disputed, showing acceptance of the width of what can be such property. The real dispute in the case was whether it had actually become such an asset (see below).

Land held under a trust

6.11 Finally this interest is, of course, subject to the fiduciary duties imposed on partners and must not be used for private benefit or gain by the partners, and to the ordinary conveyancing rules imposed on the legal title of a trust of land—s 20(2) makes the latter quite clear. Under the Law of Property Act 1925 the first four partners named on a conveyance will be the trustees of the property (as joint tenants), holding for all the partners beneficially as tenants in common, and the fact that it is partnership property makes no difference to the rules relating to the legal estate held by the trustees. The Law Commissions made no attempt to define the nature of a partner's interest but made several recommendations consequent on the proposed introduction of legal personality. The property would then have belonged to the firm with the partners having rights against the firm. The principal opposition to the introduction of legal personality comes from the change in the registered ownership of land from trustees to the firm itself.[35]

---

[32] See para 5.17 above.
[33] [2017] EWHC 182 (Ch).
[34] [2017] EWHC 526 (Ch).
[35] Report, paras 9.19, 9.51, and 9.72.

Identifying Partnership Property

Express or implied agreement—surrounding circumstances

6.12 Returning to the words of s 20(1), partnership property can either be brought into the firm or acquired on account of the firm. Thus property brought in as capital is partnership property and subsequent acquisitions are also included.

6.13 In *Coward v Phaestos Ltd*,[36] the judge decided that s 20(1), at least insofar as it applies to subsequently acquired property, is not mandatory, however, and is always subject to contrary agreement either at the time or subsequently. Whether or not an item is partnership property is therefore a matter for agreement, express or implied and, at least at the outset of the partnership, any fiduciary duties between the partners will be moulded by the status of the asset. Of course fiduciary duties will be relevant to assessing the status of an asset after that date.

In *Goldup v Cobb*,[37] the judge stressed that the fiduciary relationship does not of itself create partnership assets, it applies to such assets once created. The question in the case was whether a personal pension payable to a partner from her office of coroner was a partnership asset. She had paid her net salary from that office into the partnership accounts. The judge held that there was no express agreement that the pension rights should become an asset and that on the facts it had not become one. Among other factors, the judge took into account the facts that the right to a pension pre-dated the partnership, the pension contributions were deducted from her salary at source, and the partnership received a 5.5 per cent supplement for each contribution.

The position is therefore simpler if the property is itemized in the accounts as partnership property or, as in *Don King Productions Inc v Warren*, there is an express agreement, the problems are usually only in construing the documentation, which can include the accounting treatment. This was the situation in *Strover v Strover*,[38] where each of three partners took out life assurance contracts to cover the effect of the death of the policyholder whilst still a partner. One partner retired and continued to pay the premiums. On his death it was held that the policy monies were partnership assets of the original, and not the successor, partnership.

In other cases the court will have to infer an implied agreement that the property was to be brought in or acquired as partnership property from the surrounding circumstances. These can include the subsequent treatment of the asset, or the partners' actions in complying with some formalities relating to the property, such as registering a trade mark. In the Singaporean case of *Ng Chu Chong v Ng Swee Choon*,[39] the trade

---

[36] [2013] EWHC 1232, Ch.
[37] [2017] EWHC 526 (Ch).
[38] [2005] EWHC 860 (Ch).
[39] [2002] 2 SLR 368.

mark was held to be partnership property because at one stage it could only be registered in joint names if they were partners, and it was the common intention of the partners to use the trade mark on their merchandise. It could not have been registered in the firm name.

Use in partnership not always sufficient to create partnership property—business efficacy and necessity

In *Miles v Clarke*[40] the two men were partners at will in a photography business. Miles was a well-known photographer who brought with him his reputation, whereas Clarke owned the lease of the studio and the equipment used in it. Miles also brought with him his existing negatives. Both partners, however, contributed to the stock in trade used in the business. The partners never agreed as to the formal listing of the assets, all that they agreed was to share the profits equally. On a dissolution the question arose as to who owned what. Harman J refused to imply any terms as to change of ownership so that Clarke retained the lease and equipment whilst Miles retained his previous goodwill and negatives. The only terms implied as to partnership property were those necessary to give business efficacy to the relationship, eg concerning the stock in trade, negatives taken during the partnership etc: 'Therefore, in my judgment, nothing changed hands except those things which were actually used and used up in the course of the carrying on of the business.'

6.14

In *Coward v Phaestos Ltd*,[41] a dispute arose as to whether very valuable investment software, mainly written by Dr Coward whilst a partner, was partnership property or remained the property of Dr Coward. Asplin J, after a detailed analysis of s 20(1), applied both the surrounding circumstances and business efficacy tests to decide that it had indeed become partnership property; any other decision would make no commercial sense. She rejected an argument based on the concept of a 'family partnership' so that each partner/spouse retained ownership. Unlike *Miles v Clarke*, 'the software which was created by Dr Coward, was created for the purposes of the partnership and was the bedrock of that business. The trading could not have been undertaken without it. It was the central tool by which the trading and investment operations of the business were to be carried out.'[42]

It is not uncommon for the freehold or leasehold of the firm's business premises to remain outside the partnership assets. In the Malaysian case of *Menon v Abdullah Kutty*,[43] the Full Court stated that merely because the partnership agreement required the business to be carried on in the premises leased by one partner it could not be inferred that

---

[40] [1953] 1 All ER 779.
[41] [2013] EWHC 1292 (Ch).
[42] [2013] EWHC 1292 (Ch) at [213]. On that analysis the skill of the photographer in *Miles v Clarke* seems equally necessary—but the surrounding circumstances were different.
[43] [1974] 2 MLJ 159. See also *Gian Singh v Devraj Nahar* [1965] 2 MLJ 12.

the premises had become partnership property. Nor had there been any contact with the owner of the freehold whose consent was necessary for any assignment of the lease. In a similar vein, in *Khan v Khan* where the partnership business consisted of letting properties,[44] the question arose as to whether all of those properties were partnership property. The judge held on the evidence that only those shown as fixed assets in the accounts were partnership assets. The mere fact that in relation to the others rent was produced for the partnership and the partnership defrayed the mortgage liabilities was not enough to say that they had been introduced as partnership property. This issue arises particularly in farming partnerships.

Farming cases

6.15 If there is no express agreement that the farm will become an asset of the partnership carrying on the farming business (usually a successor partnership to the original one or to sole ownership), the English courts are reluctant to imply one on the business efficacy test. Thus, in *Ham v Bell*,[45] it was accepted by the judge that it was

> not necessary to imply that the farm on which crops grow or animals are grazed is an asset of the partnership. Such a partnership can work perfectly well on the basis of the land-owning partners making the land available to the partnership for the use of a partnership business so long as it continues and that could happen perfectly well and naturally without any change in the ownership of a farm.[46]

That approach was followed in *Wild v Wild*,[47] on the basis that it was not normally necessary to imply a term that the farm land was a partnership asset. The partnership could operate entirely effectively on the footing that one partner retained ownership of the farm. That, said the judge, was a common arrangement in farming businesses.[48] A similar theme applies in Scotland as set out by the Inner House of the Court of Session in *Jack v Jack*,[49] where it was held that the partnership operated under an informal licence at will from the owner of the farm. There was no declaration of trust, no lease, and no formal licence to occupy, each of which would have created partnership assets.

The courts have also been involved in disputes relating to farming assets other than the farm itself. In *Davies v H and R Ecroyd Ltd*[50] two partners carried on a dairy-farming business, which began in 1983. The farm was expressly stated to remain the property of one of the partners. In 1984 the farm was allocated a milk quota, which was registered in the names of the partners. The partnership was dissolved in 1988 and it was claimed that the milk quota was a partnership asset. (Such quotas are valuable assets, which

---

[44] [2006] EWHC 1477 (Ch).
[45] [2016] EWHC 1791 (Ch).
[46] Ibid at [46]. This was so, even though the farm had, by mistake, been included in the farming accounts for the first few years.
[47] [2018] EWHC 2197 (Ch).
[48] Ibid at [41].
[49] [2016] CSIH 75.
[50] [1996] 2 EGLR 5.

can, subject to controls, be sold independently of the farm.) Much of the case was tied up with the technical question of whether the milk quota could be treated as a separate asset from the farm, the conclusion on that being that it could be severed but that in general it attaches to and runs with the land to which it relates. The question was therefore whether the partners were intending to treat the milk quota as being separate from the farm. Blackburn J, following the earlier case of *Faulks v Faulks* on the same point,[51] held that since the milk quota was acquired after the partnership had begun it was impossible to attribute any intention to the partners at that time. He also held that there was nothing in the evidence to indicate that the partners had ever treated the quota as being other than part of the farm. It was simply a licence to produce milk without penalty from the farm. There was no evidence that it was to be treated any differently from the farm.

In yet another farming case, *Moore v Moore* in Northern Ireland,[52] it was held that the presumption in s 20(1) was rebutted in respect of a number of cattle introduced by one partner, since the actions of the partners indicated the contrary. On the other hand it applied to pig slurry (brought by the partner from his own farm) used to fertilize the firm's land. It had become part of the common stock of the firm.

Strict construction of agreements

Even if there is an agreement, the courts will also construe it strictly before including a doubtful asset as being partnership property. In two cases, *Singh v Nahar*[53] and *Eardley v Broad*,[54] general words such as 'assets' have been held not to be specific enough to include a valuable lease. Evidence may, of course, point the other way, eg payment of insurance premiums relating to the asset, payment of rates or other taxes—but once again we are forced to the conclusion that there are no absolutes—each case has to be taken on its own facts. Mere use of the asset is clearly not enough as *Miles v Clarke*[55] and *Davies v H and R Ecroyd Ltd*[56] both show. The fact that the property, eg land, is registered in the name of one of the partners is not conclusive either way. It is possible, for example, as in *Singh v Nahar*,[57] for the court to imply that some assets owned by an existing business owner were brought into the partnership when he took a partner whereas others were not. The tests of surrounding circumstances and necessity will be applied.

6.16

---

[51] [1992] 1 EGLR 9.
[52] 27 February 1998.
[53] [1965] 1 WLR 412.
[54] (1970) 120 NLJ 432.
[55] [1953] 1 All ER 779.
[56] [1996] 2 EGLR 5.
[57] [1965] 1 WLR 412.

Property bought with partnership profits

6.17 If the dispute relates to property subsequently bought with partnership profits two other sections of the Act may apply. Section 21 provides:

> Unless the contrary intention appears, property bought with money belonging to the firm is deemed to have been bought on account of the firm.

Thus property so acquired is not automatically partnership property. It is also true that an asset acquired at the expense of an individual partner may still be a partnership asset. The fact that an asset was acquired out of the partnership account, however, puts the burden of proving that it is not a partnership asset onto the individual so claiming. It is important to note that s 21 only applies to property bought out of 'money belonging to the firm', ie money which is itself partnership property. As such, therefore, it does raise a presumption which needs to be rebutted.[58]

An example may show how this section works. In *Jones v Jones*,[59] two brothers, T and A, were general dealers and out of the profits of the partnership they bought a shop to use in the business. The land was conveyed to them as tenants in common. T died intestate. If the land was partnership property it was personalty under the doctrine of conversion and so passed to his next of kin; if it was not then it remained realty and descended to the heir (remember this distinction is now obsolete). Since the property had been acquired out of partnership profits and used for the partnership business the evidence was that it was partnership property and not owned by them as individuals.

The question as to whether the presumption in s 21 applies or has been rebutted can lead to extremely complex fact situations which the court has to unravel. For example, in *Badyal v Badyal*,[60] the parties traded allegations described as bordering on criminal and which involved various companies and some properties in India. The judgment ran to over 200 paragraphs, simply as to questions of fact, including the credibility of witnesses.

Purchase of land out of profits made by use of non-partnership land

6.18 The other section which applies to subsequent acquisitions is s 20(3). This deals only with one specific situation, however:

> Where co-owners of an estate or interest in any land, ... not being itself partnership property, are partners as to profits made by the use of that land or estate, and purchase other land or estate out of the profits to be used in like manner, the land or estate so

---

[58] For examples of a failure to rebut this presumption see *Longmuir v Moffat* [2009] CSIH 19, *Nadeem v Rafiq* [2007] EWHC 2959 (Ch), and *McKeown v Small* [2015] NZHC 1043.
[59] (1870) 4 SALR 12.
[60] [2018] EWHC 68 (Ch).

purchased belongs to them, in the absence of an agreement to the contrary, not as partners but as co-owners for the same respective estates and interests as are held by them in the land or estate first mentioned at the date of the purchase.

It is useful to remember that s 2(1) provides that co-ownership of land does not of itself make that land a partnership asset even though the profits from it are shared by the co-owners as partners. Just as that section applies to land already owned, s 20(3) applies to property bought out of those profits and used 'in like manner' to the original land.

Application to improvements
In such cases it is clear that something more than mere use of the property in the business is needed to make it a partnership asset. Although the section only applies to subsequent purchases, it has also been applied by analogy to improvements to the original property out of profits. Thus in *Davis v Davis*,[61] a father left his freehold business premises to his two sons as tenants in common. They carried on the business under an informal agreement and subsequently borrowed money by raising a mortgage on the premises. They used the money to expand the workshops. One brother died and it became important to decide (for intestacy purposes again) whether the improvements were partnership assets or not. North J applied s 20(3) even though it did not strictly cover the situation:

6.19

> In the present case, the money which was borrowed was not employed in paying for the additional piece of land which was brought into the business; if it had been the case it would have been exactly within that subsection; but the case seems to me so like that, that, although it is not literally covered by the subsection, the same law applies to it.

Contrary intention
Section 20(3) is different from s 21 in that it presupposes that the profits used to buy the land are the partners' own which they may spend at their will rather than profits which remain partnership money. Contrary intention can be shown, however, so that subsequent property may indeed become a partnership asset, even though the original land remains outside. There are many examples of this, cited by North J in a useful summary in *Davis v Davis*, including *Waterer v Waterer*.[62] There a nurseryman carried on a business with his son, although not in partnership. He died and left his estate, including the goodwill of the business and the land, to his sons as tenants in common. They carried on the business in partnership and bought more land for the purpose of the business, paying for it out of the father's estate. One son died and the others bought his share of the business, using money raised by a mortgage of the additional land. On the evidence and the fact that the new land had been included in the sale of the deceased brother's share, the judge was able to decide that the new land had been 'substantially involved' in the business and so had become a partnership asset.

6.20

---

[61] [1894] 1 Ch 393.
[62] (1873) LR 15 Eq.

Resulting trusts

6.21 Even if property is transferred or acquired in one partner's name so that there is no apparent co-ownership, the property may still be partnership property under the concept of a presumed resulting trust. In essence this applies where A and B jointly purchase an asset, which is then conveyed into A's name only. In certain circumstances, A may then be presumed to hold the property on trust for A and B. If A and B are partners it may well be that such an asset then becomes partnership property. The concept is only a presumption, however, and can be rebutted by evidence that B intended to make a gift of his share to A. But in the case of partnership with its fiduciary duties that may be very difficult to show.

A modern example of a resulting trust is the Australian case of *Carter Bros v Renouf*.[63] A partner took out a life assurance policy in his own name. When the firm was in difficulties the benefit of the policy was assigned to a creditor subject to a proviso for redemption. The policy was for a larger amount than the debt. When the partner died there was a dispute as to which set of creditors was entitled to the balance of the policy money after paying off the secured creditor. Since the premiums had been paid by the firm it was held that the benefit of the policy belonged to the partners; there was no evidence to rebut the presumption of a resulting trust. Thus the balance was available first to the partnership creditors.

A resulting or even a constructive trust can also arise if one person spends money on improving or extending the property of another. Thus if the firm uses its money to extend the business premises owned by one partner, it would be possible to argue that a limited interest arises in favour of the firm. The position is far from clear, however, and the better view is probably that such a trust, if it arises at all, is better classified as a constructive trust, ie one imposed by law on the grounds of equity rather than from a joint contribution to the purchase price. In any event it may well be that the investment can be classified as a loan and the judges in more recent cases have been careful to point out that a loan is a loan and does not give the lender rights in the asset as a constructive trustee. He has his rights as a creditor, and it is quite possible for the other partners to be creditors against the separate assets of one partner.

Business Premises: Leases and Licences

Problems of assignment

6.22 Many modern problems relating to partnership property revolve round the business premises of the firm. The simplest situation is where the freehold of the premises is itself

---

[63] (1962) 36 ALJR 67.

partnership property and so held by the partners as co-owners under the rules set out above. If the premises are held on a lease from a third party, however, so that the lease is a partnership asset, problems can arise on a change of partners. In such circumstances, can the old firm transfer the lease to the new firm, or surviving partners, even though there is a prohibition against an assignment in the lease? (Landlords take such covenants to protect themselves against finding themselves with unsuitable tenants by assignment.) In *Varley v Coppard*[64] it was held that the landlord's consent had to be obtained to any such assignment. One reason for this was that in that case the former partners would have ceased to be liable on the covenant in the lease if the assignment had gone through, since they were not parties to the original lease but were all tenants by assignment in the first place. Thus having themselves assigned the lease they could not be liable either under privity of contract (no contract with the landlord) or under privity of estate (being no longer tenants by assignment). In Australia in *Cook v Rowe*[65] the court held that the position would therefore be different if the retiring partners were in fact the original tenants and so would remain liable on the covenants even after the assignment on the basis of privity of contract. Whether a breach of a covenant against assignment should depend upon such technical considerations is a matter for doubt, however, and there are no English cases in support.[66]

Business tenancies

Since such a lease will usually be a lease of business premises the partners will be able to take advantage of Part II of the Landlord and Tenant Act 1954, as amended by SI 2003/3096, which enables a business tenant to claim renewal of a business tenancy at the end of the lease unless the landlord has a valid objection under the Act.[67] This valuable right is available where the membership of the firm is different at the time of claiming a renewal from that at the grant of the lease, under s 41A of the Act, introduced by s 9 of the Law of Property Act 1969. This reversed an unfortunate decision to the contrary.

6.23

The basic rule is that where partners are jointly tenants under a lease they must all join in any application for a new tenancy under the 1954 Act,[68] unless s 41A applies. That section allows an application if four conditions are satisfied. These are: first, the lease must be vested in at least two joint tenants; secondly, the demised premises must include premises occupied for the purposes of the business; thirdly, the business must at some time during the tenancy have been carried on by at least one of the joint tenants, either alone or in partnership with other persons; and fourthly, the business must now be carried on by at least one of the joint tenants, either alone or in partnership with

---

[64] (1872) LR 7 CP 505.
[65] [1954] VLR 309.
[66] If the issue is whether the lease itself is a partnership asset, failure to give consent to assign to the firm will count against it being such an asset: *Menon v Abdullah Kutty* [1974] 2 MLJ 159, FC.
[67] One being that he needs it for his own business. As to where that proposed business was alleged to be a partnership: see *Zafiris v Liu* (2005) 149 SJLR 147.
[68] *Jacobs v Chaudhuri* [1968] 2 QB 470.

other persons, with no part of the property being occupied under the tenancy for the purposes of a business carried on by the other joint tenants or tenants. In *Lie v Mohile*,[69] where both partners/tenants were still carrying on a business on the premises, an application by one of them for a new tenancy in his name only was rejected since it failed to comply with the fourth condition. The business was not being carried on 'by one or some only of the joint tenants'. It might have been different if he had been applying for a new tenancy for both partners.[70]

Similar rules applied to farming partnerships under the Agricultural Holdings Act 1986 but many of these controls were removed by the Agricultural Tenancies Act 1995. These Acts do not apply in Scotland. In practice considerable care is needed in drafting business leases, not only as to renewals but also as to rent review procedures, which have become part of life since inflation appeared on the scene. Failure to follow set procedures can be expensive for any business whether carried on in partnership or not.

Ownership by all partners outside the partnership

6.24 It is equally possible for the freehold or leasehold business premises to be owned by all the partners as co-owners and not as a partnership asset. No difference will arise in practice in the case of a leasehold interest from the position set out above, and the freehold, being held separately from the partnership property, will be governed by the ordinary rules of land law. One point to note, however, is that in such a case the partners, as co-owners, cannot grant a lease to themselves as partners. The House of Lords so held in *Rye v Rye*[71]—holding that, under s 72 of the Law of Property Act 1925, partners cannot do so. In such cases where a lease is attempted, the premises might well be construed as being partnership property in any event. Otherwise, one idea may be to form a company to hold the freehold which can then lease it to the firm, the firm paying rent and the partners receiving it back as dividends from the company. The point is that the rent comes equally off each partner's share of the profits, but is then distributed as dividends according to their respective shares in the property which need not necessarily be the same as the profit-sharing ratio.

Ownership by one or some partners outside the partnership

6.25 The most complex cases arise where the premises are owned by one or some of the partners and then used by the firm. The firm will almost certainly be using the premises either under a lease or a licence from the owner/partner. It is clear that the law allows him to grant a lease either to his co-partners or even, following s 72 of the Law of Property

---

[69] [2014] EWCA Civ 728.
[70] See *Featherstone v Staples* [1986] 1 WLR 861 and s 5 of the 1890 Act.
[71] [1962] AC 496, HL. But see Ch 1, above as to the possible effect of s 82 of the LPA 1925.

Act 1925, to all the partners including himself. It is also possible for one partner who holds a lease of property to grant an underlease to his co-partner and himself. If necessary the courts will enforce such an arrangement if there is a binding agreement to that effect as in *Toogood v Farrell*.[72] Strangely, however, it was held in *Harrison-Broadley v Smith*[73] that he cannot confer a licence on the whole firm, ie including himself. Whilst there are technical distinctions between leases and licences this does seem to be a peculiar one although it can be argued that in the absence of a statutory provision a partner cannot confer a licence upon himself.

The position of a partner/landlord is also unclear. As a partner he owes fiduciary duties to fellow partners but as a landlord he has certain rights both at common law and under various statutes. The exact relationship has never been clarified. One possible conflict could arise where the firm applies for a renewal of the tenancy under the Landlord and Tenant Act 1954, mentioned above, and the landlord/partner opposes it. Must he act for the benefit of the partnership as a whole or can he exercise his statutory rights as a landlord irrespective of such considerations? The answer will depend upon whether the court regards his activities in this respect as being within the scope of his fiduciary position or whether he is acting purely qua landlord and not in his capacity as a partner. In company law it has been held that a petition for relief by a shareholder/landlord failed because he was pursuing his interest as a freeholder and not as a member of the company,[74] but there are differences between that case and the partner/landlord. These include the fact that a shareholder is not a fiduciary and that he was seeking to enforce a right rather than being liable to account.

Where one partner owns the premises on which the partnership business is carried on, he or she is taken to have granted a licence to the other partner or partners to enter upon the premises for the purposes of the partnership business.[75] In *Lie v Mohile*,[76] this licence was held to continue for so long as the partnership business was being continued, even if it was being continued solely for the purposes of winding it up, for so long as the partner had a right to participate in running that business.[77] It did not end on a dissolution. On the other hand, although a lease granted for the duration of the partnership was upheld in *Pocock v Carter*,[78] later cases have stated that tenancies for an uncertain period are not allowed. Clearly a fixed-term lease is preferable and in the light of the lease-renewal protection in the statutes, not unduly hard on the other partners.

---

[72] [1988] 2 EGLR 233, CA.
[73] [1964] 1 WLR 456.
[74] *Re JE Cade and Son Ltd* [1992] BCLC 213.
[75] *Harrison-Broadley v Smith* [1964] 1 WLR 456.
[76] [2014] EWHC 3709.
[77] Eg until a receiver is appointed. Until then each partner has a right to participate in the business which is being wound up.
[78] [1912] 1 Ch 663.

Goodwill: A Note

6.26 All businesses generate goodwill, ie the difference between the value of the business as a going concern and the value of its assets. Partnerships are no exception to this and clearly the goodwill of the business will usually be a partnership asset (but remember *Miles v Clarke*[79] where the 'goodwill' attaching to the active partner when he entered the partnership remained his at the dissolution). In most cases questions as to whether goodwill has been transferred,[80] or as to valuing the goodwill or deciding on the effects of a transfer of goodwill, arise on a partial dissolution of a partnership. That is, where one or more of the partners wish to carry on the business and so must either buy the retiring or deceased partner's share of the goodwill or transfer a part of their share of the goodwill to an outgoing partner. Similar issues may arise on the introduction of a new partner who must buy himself into the firm, ie purchase a share of the goodwill. It can arise, however, in other cases, such as the valuation of property in a divorce settlement. Although it is still generally illegal to sell the goodwill of an NHS general practice under the Primary Medical Services (Sale of Goodwill and Restrictions on Subcontracting) Regulations 2004,[81] all other professional partnerships would appear to have a potential goodwill attached to them which needs to be valued in this way, despite the odd decision to the contrary. The absence of a restraint of trade clause may have an effect on the goodwill, particularly if a departing partner is free to set up on his or her own account.[82]

Identifying goodwill

6.27 There are two problems associated with goodwill: first as to identifying and valuing it and second the consequences for the vendor and purchaser of such a sale. In the absence of agreement in the partnership deed the position is governed entirely by case law and is unaffected by the Partnership Act. It is not, therefore, specifically a partnership problem and the following is simply a note of some of the points which can arise. First, what exactly is goodwill? Two classic statements are those of Lord Eldon in *Cruttwell v Lye*:[83] 'The goodwill which has been the subject of sale is nothing more than the probability that the old customers will resort to the old place'; and of Lord Macnaghten in *Trego v Hunt*:[84]

> It is the whole advantage, whatever it may be, of the reputation and connection of the firm, which may have been built up by years of honest work or gained by lavish expenditure of money.

---

[79] [1953] 1 All ER 779.
[80] This may have tax consequences: see, eg *Shorter v CEC*, 1 June 2001, VADT.
[81] SI 2004/906. See, eg *Rodway v Landy* [2001] EWCA Civ 471 and *Waltham Forest NHS Primary Care Trust, Secretary of State for Health v R (Malik)* [2007] EWCA Civ 265.
[82] *Short v Gray* HC Auckland Civ-2008-404-2232, 9 June 2010; *Wallace v Altan* [2018] NZHC 1337.
[83] (1810) 7 Ves Jr 335.
[84] [1896] AC 7, HL.

More graphically the Court of Appeal in *Whiteman Smith Motor Co v Chaplin*[85] divided up the goodwill into four animal groups. Some customers are 'cats' since they remain with the business whoever runs it; some are 'dogs', who will follow the proprietors wherever they go; others are 'rats' since they will drift away from both business and proprietors; and yet others are 'rabbits'—they come only because the premises are close by.

Recently, the Intellectual Property Enterprise Court has held, in the context of an action for passing off, that the burden of establishing goodwill is not high. It could be localized and even trading for a short period of time could give rise to an action for passing off.[86] For a more detailed modern analysis as to what goodwill actually consists of in the partnership context see *Castledine v RSM Bentley Jennison*.[87]

Professional partnerships

Recent cases have concerned the identification of goodwill in a professional partnership. In the Scottish case of *Finlayson v Turnbull* (No 1)[88] Lord Milligan adopted, without being fully able to apply it to his satisfaction, the criterion of the firm's 'capitalized profit-earning capacity' in relation to a solicitors' practice. But as was made clear in the New Zealand case of *Garty v Garty*,[89] that is only one possible method of valuing the goodwill in such cases. Apparent alternatives are the 'super profits multiple' or the 'fair market value'. The apparent simplicity of the latter is marred by the fact that such a method involves other, unspecified, methodologies. The former seems to involve a complex calculation of excess or 'super' profits and the application of an arbitrary multiplier. All this is somewhat heady stuff for lawyers and is best left to expert evidence, although the shortcomings of that approach can be seen in the case itself where the judge commented that within the accountancy profession there was a distinct dispute about which method was most appropriate for an accountancy firm. A simpler format was used in *Beaver v Cohen*.[90] Where two employed accountants had left the firm and taken some clients with them, the goodwill so taken was to be valued according to the recurring annual fees paid by the relevant clients. Those were limited to the clients who subsequently incurred a liability to pay fees to the defendants after the date of transfer, ie the active clients so transferred.

6.28

Consequences of a sale of goodwill

Lawyers are naturally more at home dealing with the consequences of a sale. Again I must stress that we are only dealing with the tip of the iceberg here but the following

6.29

---

[85] [1934] 2 KB 35, CA.
[86] *Martinez v Prick Me Baby One More Time Ltd* [2018] EWHC 776 (IREC).
[87] [2011] EWHC 2363 (Ch) at [7]–[12].
[88] 1997 SLT 613.
[89] [1997] 3 NZLR 66.
[90] [2006] EWHC 199 (Ch).

are three points which seem to have emerged from the cases, assuming that there is no contrary agreement.

(a) A person who acquires the goodwill alone may represent himself as continuing or succeeding to the business of the vendor.[91]

(b) The transferor may, however, carry on a similar business in competition with the purchaser though not under a name which would amount to a representation that he was carrying on the old business. He must not solicit or canvass the customers whose business has been transferred.[92] This second point applies equally to the partial transfer of goodwill by continuing partners to an outgoing partner as it does to the sale of goodwill to a third party, and to the transfer by an outgoing partner of his share of the goodwill to the continuing partners.[93]

(c) The transferor may therefore publicly advertise his new business, but may not personally or by circular solicit the customers of the old business.[94]

It is clear, therefore, that the purchaser of the goodwill should take additional steps to protect himself against competition from the vendors.

Goodwill as a partnership asset

6.30 The partnership agreement can, of course, provide what it will in relation to goodwill. It may give it a nominal or nil value.[95] In Chapter 3 we saw in the case of *Bridge v Deacons*[96] an example of the former so that a new partner paid very little for the goodwill but equally received little for it on his departure. Such solutions are, of course, the easiest course and place the emphasis instead on restricting the departing partner's activities. Alternatively the agreement may provide for some specific solution as to quantifying the goodwill, eg by reference to throughput of work or gross recurring fees. This again is now an easier option since precise records are kept in any event for VAT purposes (VAT being a tax on turnover). In *Finlayson v Turnbull (No 1)*,[97] Lord Milligan was unable to quantify the alternative profits-based approach with any accuracy due to lack of data. In the absence of any express agreement, goodwill is treated as any other asset of the firm, ie it belongs indirectly to all the partners in undivided shares which can only be ultimately realized on a partial or total dissolution of the firm. Until such realization, however, each partner retains his or her interest in it.

One question is whether the goodwill attaches to the firm or to a particular partner. One example is *Byford v Oliver*.[98] This concerned the goodwill attaching to the name

---

[91] *Churton v Douglas* (1859) John 174.
[92] *Trego v Hunt* [1896] AC 7, HL.
[93] *Darby v Meehan*, The Times, 25 November 1998.
[94] *Curl Bros Ltd v Webster* [1904] 1 Ch 685.
[95] See, eg *Summers v Smith* [2002] EWHC 694 (Ch).
[96] [1984] 2 All ER 19, PC.
[97] 1997 SLT 613.
[98] [2003] FSR 39.

SAXON which had originally been used by a heavy metal band carrying on business as a partnership. In 1985 Oliver left the band but it continued in many different manifestations, Byford being at all times a member of it. Oliver then joined another band which incorporated the word SAXON in its name and had now applied to register that name as a trade mark.[99] He was thus asserting that he had gained exclusive rights to use the name in the entertainment industry. Laddie J found that since there was no agreement, the basic principles of partnership property applied. In 1985, when Oliver left the partnership he had an interest in the realization of the firm's assets but he did not directly own, in whole or in part, the partnership name and goodwill. The position was that he had no right to use the name, but if the goodwill in the name earned prior to his leaving was still current, the partnership as it stood before Oliver's departure could sue the partnership as it now stood. The position would have been much better if the partners had expressly agreed that the name would remain with the remaining partners. Of course, in other circumstances the partners may agree not to realize the goodwill on a dissolution but to share it out—then each of them could use the name, as they owned a share in it directly and no longer through their interest in the partnership property.[100]

In *Bhayani v Taylor Bracewell LLP*,[101] there was a dispute between an employed solicitor and the employer firm as to who owned the goodwill generated by her. The case was decided, however, on the basis that she was no different from a partner in this respect. The court held that the goodwill would normally vest in the partnership. A solicitor, even an equity partner, was not a free agent. Her performance would be both assisted and constrained by the terms of the partnership and by the advice and pressure assisted by colleagues. Ultimately the quality of services of any individual solicitor was guaranteed by the firm. If the quality fell short, any compensation was available from the firm.

---

[99] This fell foul of two provisions of the Trade Marks Act 1994 since the application was held to be made in bad faith and was liable to a possible passing-off action.
[100] See *Burchell v Wilde* [1900] 1 Ch 551.
[101] [2016] EWHC 3360, IPEC.

7
DISSOLUTION AND WINDING UP

Dissolution

General and technical dissolutions

'In my beginning is my end,' wrote TS Eliot, and whilst it may seem unduly pessimistic it has to be said that many of the problems associated with partnerships are concerned less with their inception or active life than with their demise. We have seen how easily and informally a partnership can be created and run but, like most things in life, partnerships are easier to start than to finish. A dissolution can be the result of ill feeling and mistrust on all sides where every detail is a potential source of dispute. But of course not all dissolutions are like that—many arise on the death or retirement of one partner where the business is carried on by the surviving partner(s) often quite amicably. It is further quite clear that in England, where there is no separate legal personality, there is a dissolution (regarded now as a 'technical' dissolution) of the old partnership and the formation of a new one every time one partner retires or a new partner is admitted. Even in Scotland, where a partnership does have legal personality, it is dissolved on the death of a partner unless there is contrary agreement: see *Jardine-Paterson v Fraser*.[1] This has tax consequences and in the New Zealand case of *Hadlee v Commissioner of Inland Revenue*[2] it was held that the partnership agreement cannot avoid that basic proposition. Eichelbaum CJ made this very clear:

7.01

> no doubt it is competent for partners to agree in advance that in the event of a retirement the remaining partners will continue to practise in partnership but that does not overcome the consequence that the partnership practising the day after the retirement is a different one from that in business the previous day.

There are therefore two distinct situations, each of which is termed a dissolution. But in reality they have very different consequences. In the first, the whole business is finished as a going concern and has to be wound up, with each of the former partners receiving a share of the assets after the creditors have been paid. That is a general dissolution. In the other, sometimes referred to as a retirement, although there is a technical dissolution, the issue is solely as to valuing the outgoing partner's share.[3] The business will remain

---

[1] 1974 SLT 93.
[2] [1993] AC 524, PC, 229.
[3] See, eg *Summers v Smith* [2002] EWHC 694 (Ch) citing *Davidson v Waymen* [1984] 2 NZLR 115, CA, and *Kidsons v Lloyds Underwriters Subscribing Policy No 621/PK10000101* [2008] EWHC 2415 where it was held that s 38 had no application on a technical dissolution.

intact and be carried on by the remaining partners. The outgoing partner's rights are then only those of an unsecured creditor for that amount.[4] The essential question therefore is whether the business is being continued.

Where a partner retires leaving only one remaining partner, there may still be it seems a technical rather than a general dissolution. This is so, even though, of course, the partnership as a whole has ended. This distinction is important in ascertaining the outgoing partner's rights—is there to be a winding up or simply a buy out of the outgoing partner's share? In *Truong v Lam*,[5] the Court of Appeal in Western Australia found that there was a retirement rather than a general dissolution where the outgoing partner had agreed (impliedly in that case) that he should only receive the value of that share. It followed that his rights were only those of an unsecured creditor.

Insolvency may, of course, be involved in either case and this presents particular problems which are dealt with in Chapter 8. In this chapter it is assumed that there is no insolvency either of the firm or the individual partners. Let us start, however, with the first stage identified by the Law Commissions, the grounds upon which a partnership may be dissolved. These divide into three categories: contractual, automatic, and those made under court orders.

Contractual Grounds for Dissolution

Implied terms

7.02 Partnership has a contractual basis and so it is perfectly possible for the agreement itself to provide express terms as to when that agreement can be terminated. There is no general right to retire from a partnership, otherwise than by agreement. True to form, however, the Act also provides five implied terms to that effect, four of which are subject to the usual contrary agreement. We have in fact already encountered the first three, contained in s 32 of the Act, when we discussed the duration of a partnership in Chapter 2. Section 32 provides for a dissolution, unless there is an agreement to the contrary: (a) if a partnership is entered into for a fixed term by the expiration of that term; (b) if for a single adventure or undertaking by its termination;[6] and (c) if for an undefined time, by a notice[7] at any time given by one partner to his fellow partners.[8] In

---

[4] *Sobell v Boston* [1975] 1 WLR 1587.
[5] [2009] WASCA 217.
[6] This is a question of fact. See, eg *Say-Dee Pty Ltd v Farah Constructions Pty Ltd* [2005] NSWCA 469; *Sze Tu v Lowe* [2014] NSWCA 462; *Shanmugathaas v Paramanipurupen* [2018] NSWSC 1232.
[7] See, eg *Green v Hernum*, 2006 NLCA 46 and *ACC Bank plc v Johnston* [2011] 1 EHC 108 as to whether statements can amount to notice for this purpose. In Hong Kong a WhatsApp notice has been held to be sufficient: *Eva v Yin* [2018] HKDC 4.
[8] In that case the effective date of the dissolution (unless the contrary is specified) is the date when the notice is communicated to the other partners: *Unsworth v Jordon* [1896] WN 2; *Phillips v Melville* [1921] NZLR 571; *Harris v Burgess & Thorne* (1937) 4 DLR 219; *Arif v Yeo* [1989] SLR 849.

Chapter 2 we also encountered the relationship between this section and s 26 (partnerships at will)—remember that the key is that a partnership for a fixed term in s 32(a) includes any partnership with a time limit, however vague or uncertain, and that a partnership for an 'undefined time' in s 32(c) must be read in the light of that as including only totally open-ended agreements. It has also been suggested in Australia that if the partnership is formed to carry on a business (or businesses) then s 32(b) will apply so that s 32(c) cannot apply. Only when the business ceases will a dissolution take effect.[9]

The agreement itself may, of course, contain its own arrangements as to time and dissolution. If none of the above apply and there is no express or implied agreement,[10] a partner, eg in a fixed-term partnership which has not yet expired, will be effectively 'locked in' and the only remedy may be a dissolution by a court order.

Death, bankruptcy, and charging orders

Section 33 implies two further terms relating to dissolution. **7.03**

(1) Subject to any agreement between the partners, every partnership is dissolved as regards all the partners by the death or bankruptcy of any partner.
(2) A partnership may, at the option of the other partners, be dissolved if any partner suffers his share of the partnership property to be charged under this Act for his separate debt.

The winding up of a corporate partner does not amount to bankruptcy for the purposes of s 33(1). The bankruptcy of an individual divests him of his property, including his share in the firm, whereas a winding up does not have that effect on the company.[11]

Section 33(2) needs no contrary intention in the deed to oust it—it is only an option given to the partners where one partner's share in the partnership assets has been charged with payment of his individual debt under the procedure set out in s 23 of the Act—ie the involuntary assignment procedure which we have already discussed in Chapter 5. The Act does not provide for an automatic dissolution on such a charge being created since that was the very thing that s 23 was passed to prevent. What is unclear, however, is whether all the other partners have to agree to a dissolution under s 33(2). There is no authority on the point but the current view is that unanimity is required. This contrasts with the right of a single partner to dissolve the firm under s 32(c) or s 26.[12]

---

[9] *Cole v Lee* [2017] NSWSC 1011.
[10] See below.
[11] *Anderson Group v Davies* (2001) 53 NSWLR 401. Quaere the effect of the dissolution of a corporate partner vis-à-vis the death of an individual?
[12] The Law Commissions proposed radical changes to s 33(2) allowing for an expulsion rather than a general dissolution: Report, para 8.110.

Contrary intention—s 33(2)

7.04 It may be highly inconvenient for a large modern partnership to subject itself to the whole dissolution process under s 33(1) every time one partner dies or becomes insolvent.[13] In either case it will be much easier to value the relevant partner's share and provide some method of sorting things out whilst preserving the partnership business. It is usual to provide in most partnerships the necessary contrary intention to negative the full effect of s 33(1). An example can be seen in the Scottish case of *William S Gordon & Co Ltd v Mrs Mary Thompson Partnership*[14] (remember in Scotland a partnership does have a separate legal personality). The company was the landlord of two fields let to the defendant firm. The firm had three partners, one of whom, Mrs Mary Thompson, died in 1981. The landlords argued that by virtue of s 33(1) her death had dissolved the firm and so terminated the lease and they now sued the remaining partners for possession of the fields. The remaining partners relied on a clause in the partnership agreement that on such a death:

> the remaining Parties shall decide within two months of the death...either to wind up the partnership business or to take over the estate and assets of the partnership business and to carry on the business to the exclusion of the representatives of the deceased...with exclusive rights to the goodwill and use of the firm name.

They had in fact so continued the business and the Court of Session agreed that this clause amounted to a contrary agreement sufficient to act as an antidote to s 33(1). The chosen alternative allowed by the deed was not to wind up the firm but on the contrary to carry on the partnership business, and was thus another way of saying that the surviving partners could choose to carry on the partnership. Of course, each clause has to be construed on its own wording and a contrary decision was reached in *Inland Revenue Commissioners v Graham's Trustees*.[15]

In *McKeowen v Small*,[16] the New Zealand High Court found such an agreement from the fact that the partnership continued after the death of a partner and the evidence that this was agreed to by the deceased partner, partly as evinced from his will. In Canada, the court upheld a contrary agreement between the surviving partners and the legal representative of the deceased partner, the latter becoming a partner.[17]

Technically, of course, under English law, the old partnership would be dissolved and a new one commenced, so that a contrary agreement to s 33(1) in England can only be about whether a general winding up or a technical dissolution is to follow the death of a partner. In some cases the agreement provides contrary intention in the form of what is known as an automatic accruer clause whereby the outgoing partner's share automatically vests in the remaining partners on the date of his or her exit and providing for the

---

[13] Or even if he or she simply retires.
[14] 1985 SLT 112.
[15] 1971 SC (HL) 1.
[16] [2015] NZHC 1043.
[17] *Bohachewski v Bohachewski* 2018 SKQB 229.

financial entitlement of the outgoing partner. In such a case it has been held that there is no need for a general dissolution.[18] It is unlikely, following the reasoning in *Hadlee v CIR*,[19] mentioned above, that the contrary agreement provided for in that section could prevent a technical dissolution on the death of a partner, where, unlike the position in Scotland, a partnership has no legal personality separate from that of the partner.

Express clauses

There are also many examples of express dissolution clauses in partnership agreements which expand the available grounds for dissolution rather than ousting the implied terms in the Act. These are particularly important for professional partnerships where reputation and professional integrity are paramount. Thus in *Clifford v Timms*,[20] one dentist in a firm was held to be entitled to a dissolution, under a clause in the deed allowing him to do so if his partner was 'guilty of professional misconduct', where the other partner became involved in a company which produced scurrilous pamphlets etc as to the activities, both dental and sexual, of other dentists. Lord Loreburn LC was sufficiently outraged: 'for my part, if this be not disgraceful conduct, if it be not professional misconduct, I know not what the terms mean'. Sometimes in such cases 'conduct unbecoming' will suffice even though it is not directly related to the firm's business— remember the draper convicted of travelling on a train without a ticket in *Carmichael v Evans*.[21] Times, and standards, do of course change. Other express clauses relate to incapacity such as the one in *Peyton v Mindham*,[22] which we also discussed in Chapter 5 with reference to expulsion clauses. Remember also that when exercising the power of dissolution under all such clauses the partners remain subject to their fiduciary duty of good faith not to act solely for their own personal advantage. 7.05

Where the partnership agreement makes express provision for the dissolution of the firm the question arises whether a partner who is guilty of a material breach of the agreement can nevertheless exercise a contractual right to dissolve the firm. The answer, at least in Scotland, is no. In *Hunter v Wylie*,[23] the senior partners had withdrawn large sums of capital from the firm in breach of the partnership agreement. The court held that they had thereby forfeited their right to exercise a right to dissolve the firm based on that agreement, even though it was admitted that they may have been able to enforce other rights in the contract such as the right to remuneration. An interesting question which arises as a result of that decision is whether the answer would have been the same if the senior partners had been seeking to enforce a dissolution right based on an implied term under the Act.

---

[18] *Lawson v Wenley, Davies, Willis and Cross* [2012] NZHC 204.
[19] [1993] AC 524. See also *Summers v Smith* [2002] EWHC 694 (Ch).
[20] [1908] AC 112.
[21] [1904] 1 Ch 486.
[22] [1972] 1 WLR 8.
[23] 1993 SLT 1091.

Mutual agreement

7.06 Partnerships of course can always be ended by an express agreement of all the partners.[24] But in *Jassal's Executrix v Jassal's Trustees*,[25] the Court of Session held that a partnership can also be dissolved by mutual agreement of the partners as discovered from their acts, ie by implied rather than express agreement. This is a question of fact and in that case Lord Prosser had no doubts: 'It appears to me that the changes which they made evinced an intention to abandon all the essential features of a partnership venture.'[26]

That raises the question as to what circumstances will lead the court to hold that there has been such an implied mutual agreement to end that partnership relationship.[27] In *Chahal v Mahal*,[28] the Court of Appeal had to consider a case where some eighteen years earlier the assets and business of the firm had been transferred to a company. The court accepted that where such a transfer is accompanied by the issue of shares in the company to each of the partners beneficially then there would be an implied dissolution—the partners clearly intended the partnership to end. But that would not apply if there were other reasons for the transfer of the assets or business such as where there is an intention to start up a new business, improve the tax position, or revive a previous business. In such a case there would be no implied dissolution.[29] In the case itself, however, it transpired that one of the partners had never been issued with a share in the company and had not consented to the transfer of the assets to it. On those facts the Court of Appeal held that there could be no implied agreement to dissolve the firm.

In two similar cases where two doctors carried on practice in partnership but agreed to expand the partnership to include new doctors, the court found that there was clear evidence that the original partners had agreed to abandon the existing agreement although no concluded new agreement was ever finalized.[30] Accordingly the old partnership had ended.

The courts are, however, reluctant to infer an implied agreement, even if one partner ceases to be actively involved in the partnership business and continues only nominal activity.[31] Sometimes, as we have seen, this ground of dissolution is referred to as 'abandonment' which is discussed below at para 7.22. In the Australian case of *Fazio v Fazio*,[32] it was commented that abandonment may in fact connote two different types of

---

[24] See eg *Ilott v Williams* [2013] EWCA Civ 645.
[25] 1988 SLT 757.
[26] See also *Holdgate v The Official Assignee* [2002] NZCA 66. Cf *Rowlands v Hodson* [2009] EWCA Civ 1025.
[27] It is true that there is nothing express in the Act to allow for such agreements but both ss 19 and 32 are subject to contrary agreement which can be used to justify this approach: see *Hurst v Bryk* [2002] 1 AC 185 at 195 per Lord Millett and *Chahal v Mahal* [2005] EWCA Civ 898 at [21] per Neuberger LJ.
[28] [2005] 2 BCLC 655, CA.
[29] See *National Westminster Bank plc v Jones* [2001] 1 BCLC 98.
[30] *Firth v Amslake* (1965) 108 SJ 198; *Cheema v Jones* [2017] EWCA Civ 1706.
[31] See *Hodson v Hodson* [2010] EWCA 1042, applied in *Barber v Rasco International Ltd* [2012] EWHC 269 (QB).
[32] [2012] WASCA 72.

implied agreement. The usual one is an implied agreement for the mutual release of future, unperformed obligations which does not effect a release of the outgoing partner's interest or existing rights. The other is an agreed release of the outgoing partner's interest in the partnership to the others.

Illegality

There can, however, be no contracting out of s 34 of the Act. This is obligatory, although it only reflects the common law position:

7.07

> A partnership is in every case dissolved by the happening of any event which makes it unlawful for the business of the firm to be carried on or for the members of the firm to carry it on in partnership.

Again we are going over old ground—illegality was one of the subjects in Chapter 3. Most of the cases involve enemy aliens in time of war. Thus in *R v Kupfer*[33] the court was able to say: 'The declaration of war had the effect of dissolving the partnership by operation of law.'

Of course s 34 only applies if the event makes it unlawful either for the business to be carried on or for the members of the firm to carry it on in partnership. The latter concept was the subject of the decision of the Canadian Supreme Court in *Continental Bank Leasing Corporation v The Queen*.[34] By statute no bank could acquire an interest in a partnership. In that case a bank's subsidiary became a partner and the tax authorities sought to apply s 34 to dissolve the partnership. The court held that although the statute prohibited the bank from holding shares in its subsidiary whilst that company was a partner it did not prevent the subsidiary from being a partner. In determining who might be partners and what the lawful business of the partnership was, the law looked only to the partners and not those who invested or held shares in the partners.

But if s 34 does apply, even to only one of the partners, the effect is to dissolve the whole firm. Thus in *Hudgell Yeates & Co v Watson*[35] one of three solicitors in a firm forgot to renew his practising certificate without which he was forbidden to practise under the Solicitors Act 1974. The Court of Appeal was quite clear that this automatically ended the partnership under s 34 even though the partners were all unaware of the circumstances and in fact had continued as before. Waller LJ, reviewing the earlier cases, held that s 34 operates by force of law and not by any intention of the partners:

---

[33] [1915] 2 KB 321.
[34] (1998) 163 DLR (4th) 385.
[35] [1978] 2 All ER 363.

If the partnership was dissolved by force of law and since it is illegal for someone who is not qualified to be in partnership with a solicitor, it is inevitable in my view that if there is a partnership of solicitors it cannot include the unqualified man.

(For more details of this case turn back to Chapter 2 and the discussion of s 14 of the Act.)

Dissolution by the Court

Grounds for court order

7.08 Even if there is nothing in the agreement, express or implied, one partner may apply to the court for a dissolution order under one of six heads, and it is clear that the courts will not always allow an arbitration agreement to prevent access to the courts under these heads. We can take the six heads in order before returning to the arbitration question. They are set out in s 35 of the Act: 'On application by a partner the court *may* decree a dissolution of the partnership in any of the following cases':

(a) Mental incapacity

7.09 The actual wording of s 35(a) was repealed by the Mental Health Act 1959. Now, under the Mental Capacity Act 2005 the receiver or the other partners may apply to the Court of Protection for a dissolution which can be given if the person is unable to make a direction for him or herself.

(b) Permanent incapacity

7.10 Section 35(b) refers to a partner becoming 'in any other way permanently incapable of performing his part of the partnership contract'. Thus the analogy is with mental incapacity, formerly in para (a). It is of course, a question of fact in each case as to whether this situation has arisen. It will depend upon the partner's duties and it could hardly apply to a dormant or limited partner. The incapacity must be permanent, however, and in *Whitwell v Arthur*[36] evidence of an inprovement in the affected partner's condition (he had been subject to a stroke) prevented an order being made. As a result, express clauses, such as that in *Peyton v Mindham*,[37] usually specify a minimum period of incapacity.

(c) Prejudicial conduct

7.11 Section 35(c) requires proof of conduct by one partner which the court, having regard to the nature of the business, regards as 'calculated to prejudicially affect the carrying on of the business'. This heading includes conduct not directly connected with the

---

[36] (1863) 35 Beav 140.
[37] [1972] 1 WLR 8.

business and there is no need to prove actual loss or public knowledge—the test is objective: would a client knowing of this conduct have moved away from the business? In *Moore v Moore*,[38] the court rejected a claim under s 35(c) where there were only a few allegations, none of which had anything to do with the farming business of the partnership or how it was conducted. Two of them involved a person who had nothing to do with the partnership. They were all consistent with a response to the deterioration of the other partner's health and the need to protect the farm employees. There was no prejudice to the partnership business.

(d) Persistent breaches of the agreement
Section 35(d) requires evidence that the offending partner

7.12

> wilfully or persistently commits a breach of the partnership agreement, or otherwise so conducts himself in matters relating to the partnership business that it is not reasonably practicable for the other partner or partners to carry on the business in partnership with him.

The problem for the courts in such cases is to avoid the Draconian solution for petty internal squabbles and yet to end matters if the other partners really cannot continue with him. In *Cheeseman v Price*[39] the offending partner had failed to enter small sums of money received from customers into the accounts as he was required to do under the agreement. This had happened seventeen times and that was sufficient to tip the scales in favour of a dissolution. On the other hand, the incidents pleaded in *Moore v Moore* (above) did not justify a dissolution on this ground either. There was no evidence that it was not reasonably practical for the partnership to continue since they had nothing to do with the partnership. The court also rejected a claim under s 35(f)—see below.

As we shall see there is a clear overlap between dissolution on this ground and acceptance by the innocent partners of a repudiatory breach of the partnership agreement, which might be thought to end the contract and so the partnership.[40] In *Bishop v Goldstein*, the Court of Appeal made it clear that the two were not identical. Section 35(d) sets out a straightforward and unambiguous threshold test which does not depend upon repudiation. It follows that the precise contractual rules applicable to acceptance of repudiatory breach have no part to play in the court's exercise of its discretion under s 35(d). Discharge by breach, on the other hand, operates automatically so that the circumstances where it does or does not apply need to have a degree of legal certainty. Dissolution under this head is a matter for discretion and so has no such need. In *Lie v Mohile*,[41] it was held that acceptance of the alleged repudiation/persistent breach by continuing the partnership for a further three years negated this ground.

---

[38] [2016] EWHC 2202 (Ch).
[39] (1865) 35 Beav 142.
[40] But see para 7.20 below.
[41] [2015] EWHC 200 (Ch).

(e) Carrying on the business at a loss

7.13 Section 35(e) is straightforward: 'When the business of the partnership can only be carried on at a loss'. Current solvency will not prevent such an order being made if that situation cannot continue. On the other hand, there must be proof that making a profit is impossible in practice. In *Handyside v Campbell*[42] a partnership had been running at a loss but this was shown to be the result of the absence of the petitioning partner due to illness and that given proper attention the business could run at a profit. The judge, Farwell J, refused to make the order. The loss was attributable to special circumstances and not to any inherent defect in the business. Similarly in *PWA Corporation v Gemini Group Automated Distribution Systems Inc*,[43] the Canadian court refused a dissolution on the grounds of insolvency because under the partnership agreement further cash calls could be made against the partners to remedy the situation.

(f) Just and equitable ground

7.14 This wording, in s 35(f), has been the subject of many cases in company law because it has a direct counterpart in the Insolvency Act 1986 and has been applied by analogy to justify the winding up of a small 'partnership company'. Section 35(f) allows an order to be made '[w]henever in any case circumstances have arisen which, in the opinion of the court, render it just and equitable that the partnership be dissolved'. This would include a situation where the mutual trust, essential to a partnership, has broken down. In *Re Yenidje Tobacco Co Ltd*,[44] a company case based on earlier partnership cases, the following were suggested as examples of such circumstances: refusal to meet on matters of business or continued quarrelling and a state of animosity that precludes all reasonable hope of a reconciliation and friendly cooperation. In *Ebrahimi v Westbourne Galleries Ltd*[45] the House of Lords, in the company context, allowed a winding up where a company was formed on the basis of management participation by all and on the basis of mutual trust, and one member had been excluded from management. Since that decision there have been many cases involving such companies using the partnership analogy, such as in *Quinlan v Essex Hinge Co Ltd*,[46] where the petitioner was likened to a junior partner, although, in the company law context, such conduct will now rarely lead to a winding up.[47]

In the partnership case of *Moore v Moore*,[48] in addition to rejecting claims under s 35(c) and (d) (above), the judge also refused to apply s 35(f). The partnership was both long standing and very successful which both parties (until the recent deterioration of one partner's health) wished to see continued above all else. It would take more than a few

---

[42] (1901) 17 TLR 623.
[43] (1993) 103 DLR (4th) 609.
[44] [1916] 2 Ch 426.
[45] [1973] AC 360, HL.
[46] [1996] 2 BCLC 417.
[47] The likely remedy is for the petitioner to be bought out by the majority under s 994 of the Companies Act 2006.
[48] [2016] EWHC 2202 (Ch).

minor understandings to make it just and equitable to end the relationship. That, however, seems to miss the point as to how the partnership could continue in the circumstances. But the judge did not have to consider what should happen as he held that the partnership was in fact dissolved by the lack of one partner's capacity. By way of contrast, a winding up on the just and equitable ground was made in the Australian case of *Murray v Feros*.[49] The partners, running five pharmacies, were unable to work together, there was no applicable dispute resolution agreement, negotiations had failed to provide an agreement, and the major financier had stated that unless the disputes were settled within ninety days they would call in the loans, which would have a disastrous effect on the businesses.

If there is neither deadlock nor management exclusion, an alternative ground is where there has been a material change of circumstances so that the objects for which the partnership was formed can no longer be attained in the manner intended by the partners.[50]

In Australia it has been held that any order made under s 35(f) dissolves the firm as from the date of the commencement of the proceedings since that stands as a notice of an intention to dissolve the firm.[51]

Just and equitable ground—'no fault divorce'
In *O'Neill v Phillips*,[52] Lord Hoffmann emphasized that, in the corporate sphere, there **7.15**
is no right to winding up simply because the minority shareholder wants to leave. Thus in company law there is no concept of a 'no-fault' divorce and Lord Hoffmann doubted whether there would be in partnership law, at least if it was still possible for the business of the firm to be continued as agreed. There must be some actions leading to a breakdown in the relationship which dissolves the trust and confidence which is the foundation of partnership. In some cases, however, the conduct of the petitioner might mitigate against making an order:

> There may be circumstances in which the court might conclude that it is not right for a majority of partners simply to say relationships have broken down. We are unwilling to go on trading. We are not trading now. Please wind up the partnership.[53]

Lord Hoffmann's views on partnership law are subject to the possibility of the material change of circumstances ground.[54] But in general they are borne out by the decisions on s 35(f) in the partnership context. In *Sutherland v Barnes*[55] the Court of Appeal was concerned with the case of a professional partnership in circumstances such as those

---

[49] [2019] NSWSC 260.
[50] See, eg *Ellerforth Investments Ltd v The Typhon Group Ltd*, 429/07, 9 September 2009, Ont SC. See also *Re Neath Rugby Ltd* [2009] 2 BCLC 487, CA.
[51] *Yard v Yarhoo Pty Ltd* [2007] VSCA 35.
[52] [1999] 1 WLR 1092, HL.
[53] *Re Magi Capital Partners LLP* [2003] EWHC 2790 at [15]. See also *Root v Head* [1996] 20 ASCR 160.
[54] See the comments in *Re Neath Rugby Ltd* [2009] 2 BCLC 487, CA.
[55] 8 October 1997, CA.

suggested in *Re Yenidje Tobacco Co Ltd*.[56] Dr Barnes was a member of a partnership of general medical practitioners which had been set up by a deed in 1973 during the joint lives of the partners and their successors or any two of them. By the time of the court case there were six partners in the practice, three of whom had never signed the deed but were nevertheless found to be bound by it so that it was not a partnership at will. Dr Barnes fell out with his partners in 1982 when he violently opposed the provision of a free pregnancy testing service in the practice. From then on matters became worse. Dr Barnes refused to enter into any discussions concerning the future of the partnership, in particular the acquisition of new premises and an updating of the partnership deed. When the other partners decided to switch to a computerized records system he opposed it, writing to the supplier countermanding the order and attempting to block the wages paid to the staff concerned in operating the computer. A manual system had to be kept just for his patients. He also alleged irregularities in payments to the wife of the senior partner, asking the Revenue to investigate. He refused to agree to a dissolution.

On those facts the Court of Appeal had little difficulty in upholding the judge's order for a dissolution of the firm under s 35(f). The relationship of trust and confidence between Dr Barnes and his co-partners had irrevocably broken down as a result of the intransigent and unreasonable conduct of Dr Barnes. This was in no sense a question of a 'no-fault' divorce and the case also shows the difficulties which can arise where there is no provision in the partnership agreement for determination of the partnership in such circumstances.

In *Khurll v Poulter*,[57] the judge held that a property development partnership had become unworkable. As a result of the defendant's conduct, there was no longer any trust between the partners. Similarly in the Canadian case of *Tecle v Hassan*,[58] a partnership between two taxi drivers had deteriorated so much that one of them had been trying to extricate himself for more than three years. The other partner now had exclusive use of the main partnership asset (a taxi plate) and the plaintiff was deriving no benefit from it. On that basis the court held that it would be unjust and inequitable to force the plaintiff to continue the partnership and so dissolution was ordered. In *Lie v Mohile*,[59] another three-year dispute between two doctors involving amongst other things an invalid dissolution notice by M and an invalid expulsion notice by L (and two trips to the Court of Appeal) clearly amounted to a breakdown sufficient to justify a just and equitable winding up.

Application to commercial partnerships

7.16 Consideration of the section, in a commercial partnership situation, was undertaken by the Ontario Court in *PWA Corporation v Gemini Group Automated Distribution Systems Inc*.[60] A number of companies operating major airlines entered into a

---

[56] [1916] 2 Ch 426.
[57] 8 April 2003.
[58] 2012 ONSC 2233.
[59] [2015] EWHC 200 (Ch); cf *Moore v Moore* [2016] EWHC 2202 (Ch)
[60] (1993) 101 DLR (4th) 15, affirmed (1993) 103 DLR (4th) 609, CA.

partnership agreement for eighty years to use a joint computer reservation system. As part of the agreement they agreed to use the partnership system until the partnership was dissolved. PWA was short of cash and contracted with another airline. A condition in the contract required PWA to escape from its partnership obligations and PWA sought a dissolution on the just and equitable ground. Callaghan CJOC specified deadlock, substantial loss of substratum, and an unjustifiable loss of confidence as typical situations justifying a dissolution under this head. He rejected PWA's case on all three of these. The substratum (underlying purpose) of the partnership had not been lost—the business had been built up exactly as planned. In assessing whether there was a sufficient loss of confidence the court had to be satisfied that there was a valid basis to establish a lack of probity or good faith, or other improper conduct on the part of the other partners. There must be a serious departure from the proper conduct or management of the firm's affairs taking into consideration the history, structure, and operation of the partnership in question. This was not the case. Nor was there any evidence of deadlock on an operational day-to-day level. The mere fact that they could not agree on a restructuring plan was not evidence of deadlock. The judge concluded:

> This is a classic case of a 'purely commercial' partnership between sophisticated parties with a corporate relationship in a highly competitive field of endeavour. Deadlock is not established by the mere assertion that minority interest has been outvoted by a majority. Where a business with unequal control is constituted on the basis that decisions may be taken by the majority, as in this case, it would be neither just nor equitable to permit a disgruntled minority or one acting in its own self-interest to be able to dismantle the business and to frustrate the substantial investments of the other partners.

Ouster clauses

7.17 The final question which remains is can the partners effectively oust the jurisdiction of the courts by providing that all such disputes shall go to arbitration? The best answer was provided by Roxburgh J in *Olver v Hillier*,[61] where he considered that the court has a discretion in each case whether to allow the court action to proceed or to stay the case and allow the arbitration to go ahead. It is never an easy decision. After all, in a professional deed the partners have agreed to arbitration and so why not let them take the consequences? (Assuming that the arbitration clause is wide enough to cover dissolution—if it does not then the problem cannot arise.) On the other hand if the dispute relates to s 35(f), the just and equitable ground, it would seem to involve the exercise of judicial discretion which may persuade the courts to take matters into their own hands. That was certainly the basis of the actual decision

---

[61] [1959] 1 WLR 551.

in *Olver v Hillier* against staying the action. On the other hand if the dispute is more limited, eg as to the return of an alleged premium, perhaps an arbitration will be allowed: *Belfield v Bourne*.[62] Modern arbitration statutes preclude judicial review of an arbitrator's decision in most cases so that the distinction has since been sharpened and the matter is of more concern. One factor mitigating in favour of arbitration, however, is the lack of publicity attached to it, and the courts should be wary of allowing one embittered partner deliberately seeking publicity to harm his fellow partners in this way.[63]

Frustration of the Partnership Agreement

7.18 It is unclear whether an event which under the law of contract would frustrate the partnership agreement does in fact automatically dissolve the partnership relationship itself. Given that a number of potentially frustrating events are specifically covered by the Act (such as death or bankruptcy under s 33(1), illegality under s 34, and permanent incapacity under s 35(b)) it can be argued that the contractual doctrine is incompatible with the survival of the partnership. But, as we shall see, Lord Millett in *Hurst v Bryk*,[64] in the context of repudiation, doubted whether the application of contractual rules as to the termination of the contract automatically leads to the dissolution of the partnership itself. This view was then applied by Neuberger J in *Mullins v Laughton*,[65] so that it is quite possible that the doctrine of frustration is equally limited in its effect. The Law Commissions proposed that frustration should not break up the partnership without a court order to that effect.[66]

Rescission of the Partnership Agreement

7.19 A partnership agreement, like other contracts, may have been induced by a misrepresentation by one partner to another, be it a fraudulent, negligent, or innocent misrepresentation. In this respect the partner so induced can rescind the contract which, under s 41, has the effect of dissolving the partnership. In addition he may sue for damages if the misrepresentation is either fraudulent (in the tort of deceit) or negligent (under s 2(1) of the Misrepresentation Act 1967), although it is by no means clear whether under the general law there is such a remedy for an innocent misrepresentation (s 2(2) of the Misrepresentation Act is subject to dispute on this point). The law on misrepresentation has thus moved significantly since the Partnership Act was passed but s 41 of

---

[62] [1894] 1 Ch 521.
[63] See, eg *Re Magi Capital Partners LLP* [2003] EWHC 2790 at [10].
[64] [2002] 1 AC 185, HL.
[65] [2003] 4 All ER 94. That case decided that repudiation did not even end the contract; see para 7.20. Quaere as to frustration?
[66] Report, para 8.124.

the Act provides additional remedies for misrepresentation in the partnership context. Section 41 provides:

> Where a partnership contract is rescinded on the ground of the fraud or misrepresentation of one of the parties thereto, the party entitled to rescind is, without prejudice to any other right, entitled—
> (a) to a lien on, or right of retention of, the surplus of the partnership assets, after satisfying the partnership liabilities, for any sum of money paid by him for the purchase of a share in the partnership and for any capital contributed by him, and is
> (b) to stand in the place of the creditors of the firm for any payments made by him in respect of the partnership liabilities, and
> (c) to be indemnified by the person guilty of the fraud or making the representation against all the debts and liabilities of the firm.

The right to rescission applies even though there is no fraud or negligence.

In *Senanayake v Cheng*[67] a statement that the business was a 'gold mine' when in fact it had enormous bad debts enabled the court to rescind the contract.

The additional rights given by s 41 reflect the fact that entering into a partnership agreement brings about liabilities to third parties and thus the rights of subrogation in para (b) and indemnity in para (c) will apply even if the misrepresentation was innocent. The right to rescind is lost under the general law if there has been undue delay in claiming the remedy, if the affected partner has continued in the partnership after discovering the misrepresentation, or if a third party becomes involved. The effect of the Misrepresentation Act 1967 has been to reduce the scope of s 41 but it remains available as an alternative basis of claim.

It is not clear whether a partnership agreement can nullify the consequential rights under s 41.[68]

Repudiation of the Partnership Agreement

7.20 Another consequence of a partnership being essentially a contractual arrangement is that the contract could be discharged by a repudiatory breach by one party which is accepted by the other. Acceptance of repudiation usually amounts to a discharge of the contract. The question which arises, however, is what are the consequences of acceptance of such a repudiation in the partnership context.

---

[67] [1966] AC 63, PC.
[68] See *Neutral Capital CP LLC v 1156062BC Ltd* 2019 BCCA 258.

Contractual effect of repudiation

7.21 That question arose before the House of Lords in *Hurst v Bryk*.[69] Mr Hurst was one of twenty partners in a firm of solicitors. The firm was 'ill-starred'[70] and in 1990 eighteen of the partners, excluding Mr Hurst and Mr Simmons, served valid retirement notices under the agreement to take effect from 31 May 1991. But things got worse and on 4 October 1990 the nineteen partners other than Mr Hurst signed an agreement terminating the partnership with effect from 31 October 1990. Mr Hurst did not consent to this. The Court of Appeal found that the acceptance by Mr Hurst of his partners' repudiatory breach of contract dissolved the partnership and that finding was not challenged in the House of Lords. On the assumption that this was a correct statement of the effects of a repudiatory breach of a partnership agreement (although the majority of their Lordships doubted it—see below), the question was what was the effect of such a dissolution. Mr Hurst argued that, contrary to the situation in a normal dissolution, as between the partners he was automatically discharged from contributing to the firm's deficit, which had arisen mainly from rent due on one of the partnership leases. Such deficit, he argued, should be borne entirely by the other partners. (It was accepted that he would still remain liable to the landlord—the partnership contract has no effect on the rights of the creditor.)

That argument was rejected by the House of Lords. The effect of acceptance of a repudiatory breach is that both parties are discharged from further performance of their obligations under the agreement, but rights are not divested which have been unconditionally acquired. Thus rights and duties which arise by partial execution of the contract continue unaffected. Mr Hurst's liability to contribute to the accrued and accruing liabilities of the firm arose from the fact that the liabilities (for rent) were incurred by the firm whilst Mr Hurst was still a partner. The creditor could have sued any one of the partners, including Mr Hurst, for the whole debt under s 9 of the Act. Once the firm had undertaken liability for the rent, each partner was entitled (under normal partnership dissolution rules) to have that liability taken into account in ascertaining his share of the partnership profits or losses both before and after the dissolution and the doctrine of repudiation did not affect that right. Only by rescinding the partnership agreement as from its inception could he have avoided a liability to contribute to the deficit. The fact that he might have a right to damages for the breach of the agreement was independent of his liability to contribute to the deficit.

---

[69] [2002] 1 AC 185, HL.
[70] See the follow-up case of *Hurst v Bennett* [2001] 2 BCLC 290, CA.

Effect of repudiation on partnership relationship—abandonment/mutuality

7.22 But, as noted above, Lord Millett, with whom all the other Law Lords in the case agreed (except for Lord Nicholls of Birkenhead, who preferred to leave the question open), was clearly of the opinion that acceptance of a repudiatory breach of the partnership agreement should not amount to an automatic dissolution of the partnership itself. His main reason was that such a doctrine would be inconsistent with the discretion of the court as to whether to order such a dissolution under s 35(d), ie for wilful or persistent breaches of the partnership agreement. The court's discretion under s 35(d) stems from equitable principles and not common law doctrines such as repudiation. Lord Millett concluded:

> By entering into the relationship of partnership, the parties submit themselves to the jurisdiction of the court of equity and the general principles developed by that court in the exercise of its equitable jurisdiction in respect of partnerships. There is much to be said for the view that they thereby renounce their right by unilateral action to bring about the automatic dissolution of their relationship by acceptance of a re-pudiatory breach of the partnership contract, and instead submit the question to the discretion of the court.

Lord Millett also said that repudiation accepted by one innocent partner could not bind another innocent partner. This would not apply, however, to a two-person partnership.

In their initial Discussion Paper the Law Commissions questioned Lord Millett's analysis, mainly on the basis that the contract having been terminated, the relationship would then exist merely as a partnership at will, which the other partners could terminate immediately. This objection was discussed by Neuberger J in *Mullins v Laughton*,[71] where the issue actually arose for decision. The judge rejected the Commissions' argument on the basis that in the partnership context acceptance of a repudiatory breach did not even end the contract until the partnership itself had ended:

> Unlike a lease, where there is an interest in land which is effectively detached from the contract which created it, a partnership cannot be detached from the partnership agreement: the relationship is contractual, but it is subject to equitable principles and the provisions of the Partnership Act. Accordingly I am unconvinced that the continuing contract can be determined without the relationship being determined.

This argument that the contract and relationship are indivisible and therefore if the relationship is not ended then neither is the contract, can of course be put the other way with equal justification. If the contract was ended by acceptance of a repudiatory breach so would the relationship. Formation of a partnership depends entirely on the existence of an agreement. Equity then acts so as to define the obligations of the consequent

---

[71] [2003] 4 All ER 94.

relationship between the individuals concerned and, no doubt, with the consequences on the ending of that agreement. But why should it interfere with the normal contractual rules for ending that agreement, as opposed to sorting out the consequences of that ending as between the partners? Its application of fiduciary duties as between the individuals involved (there is no 'firm') will cover any problems without interfering in the operation of the ordinary rules of contract law and statutory interpretation as applied to s 1 of the Act. In their Final Report, however, the Commissions backed down and proposed that repudiation should not break up the partnership but could only give rise to an application to the court for a dissolution.

That in its turn gives rise to another objection to Lord Millett's analysis, which is that an innocent partner would be in a state of limbo until he applied to the court for a dissolution and the court made an order.[72] For Neuberger J, however, although that was not a negligible point, it was one without much force. Given the force of Lord Millett's reasoning and his dismissal of the objections, the judge in *Mullins v Laughton* consequently elevated that reasoning into a decision.

Neuberger J admitted that this was a difficult issue but subsequent first instance cases in England have followed his lead. In *Goldstein v Bishop*,[73] the judge not only followed *Mullins* but also refused to allow an exception for a two-person partnership. The Court of Appeal in that case decided the issue on different grounds but made it clear that they had no doubts as to the correctness of *Mullins*.[74] However, they considered the possibility of an exception for a two-person partnership to be 'an interesting question'.[75] Neither *Hurst* nor *Mullins* was a two-person partnership. That issue therefore remains open. But it is true as the courts suggest that in most cases the partners will all regard the partnership as having ended. *Lie v Mohile*,[76] was a two-partner case but the decision was that whatever the contractual effect of a repudiatory breach (serving an invalid notice of dissolution), the contract had since been affirmed by the other partner (continuing the partnership for a further three years).

Outside England, Lord Millett's views have had a mixed reception. Doubts were expressed by the New South Wales Court of Appeal in *Ryder v Frolich*.[77] In that case a clear repudiation of the partnership agreement, manifested by one of the partners walking away from the business and joining another one and the acceptance of that by the other, was considered to have ended the partnership. Since this could also be justified on the grounds of abandonment of the partnership (see below) the New South Wales Court of Appeal declined to decide the *Hurst v Bryk* point. But there is no doubt that they

---

[72] The only contrary authority is a decision of Harman J in *Hitchman v Crouch Butler Savage Associates* (1983) 80 LS Gaz 550. That case was reversed on appeal on other grounds.
[73] [2013] EWHC 881 (Ch). See also *Barber v Rasco International Ltd* [2012] EWHC 269 (Ch).
[74] *Golstein v Bishop* [2014] EWCA Civ 10 at [10].
[75] Ibid at [9].
[76] [2015] EWHC 200 (Ch).
[77] [2004] NSWCA 472 (21 December 2004). But the principle was approved by the British Columbia Court of Appeal in *Brew v Rozano Holdings Ltd* 2006 BCCA 346.

thought that ordinary principles of contract law ought to be applied to partnerships, notwithstanding the Act. The judges quoted, with approval, an article critical of Lord Millett's views, 'The Bonds of Partnership',[78] in which the authors argue that acceptance of a repudiatory breach is analogous to the retirement of the partner in breach rather than to a dissolution. Thus it has the effect of ending the contract so far as the partner who has exercised the right of discharge is concerned, leaving the other partners to decide whether to continue the business.

The doubts expressed in *Ryder v Frohlich* have since been adopted in subsequent Australian cases,[79] so there is a clear difference between the positions in England and Australia. A possible solution may be found in the position in Scotland which is considered below.

It is submitted that there seems some force in the criticisms of the Millett equitable entity view, but English law is currently to that effect. If so it creates problems in other areas where partnership law and the contractual doctrines interact. What, for example is the effect of frustration of the partnership agreement or indeed of abandonment of it, as used in *Ryder v Frolich*? That latter doctrine applies where it is plain from the conduct of the parties to a contract that neither intends that the contract should be further performed. The parties will be regarded as having so conducted themselves as to abandon or abrogate the contract.[80] Some support for the full application of the doctrine of abandonment may be gleaned from the acceptance by Neuberger LJ in *Chahal v Mahal*,[81] that full transfer of the partnership business and assets to a company in which each partner then takes an aliquot share would end the partnership.

A possible alternative solution to the problems raised by repudiation etc is presented by the decision of the Inner House of the Court of Session in *Forster v Ferguson, Forster, Macfie and Alexander*.[82] One partner was sentenced to five years' imprisonment for embezzlement of clients' funds. He was now seeking implementation of an obligation under the partnership agreement which allowed him to elect for payment to him of a pension for ten years instead of what was due to him in respect of his interest in the partnership. The Inner House by a majority held that as a result of his material breach of the contract he had lost his right to elect for the pension, although he had not lost his proprietary rights (which appeared to be non-existent). Partnership agreements are ones of mutuality. As Lord Clarke said in the case:

> The nature and extent of the respondent's conduct was an extraordinarily serious breach of that obligation. For the respondent to avoid the consequences of such conduct, which the law would otherwise apply, would require, in my opinion, very clear

---

[78] By E Peden and JW Carter (2000) 16 *Journal of Contract Law* 277.
[79] See *Fazio v Fazio* [2012] WASCA 72 at [412] and *Bonzalie v Cullu* [2013] NSWSC 1576 at [74].
[80] See, eg *DTR Nominees Pty Ltd v Mona Homes Pty Ltd* (1978) 138 CLR 423; *Cutts v Holland* [1965] Tas SR 69; *Lukin v Lovrinov* [1998] SASC 6614. See para 7.02.
[81] [2005] 2 BCLC 655, CA. See also *Cheema v Jones* [2017] EWCA Civ 1706.
[82] [2010] CSIH 38.

wording, indeed, in the partnership agreement.[83] To have that effect would require wording which made it clear that the other partners were abandoning their right to refuse to perform their obligations in the partnership agreement when faced with a material breach of contract striking at the very heart of the agreement between the parties.[84]

There are clearly problems with transposing this decision into English law given that we have no concept of material breach. But it may be a practical answer for some of the innocent partners caught in limbo by the English decisions.

General Dissolutions—Winding Up

7.23 The effect of a general dissolution is to finish the partnership as a going concern. The next step therefore is to wind up the business, ie to collect in and value the assets, pay off the partnership debts, and distribute the surplus, if any, to the former partners. Remember, this should be contrasted with a technical dissolution, ie any dissolution where the business per se is to continue in the hands of one or more of the former partners. That produces different problems which are dealt with later. For the moment we should concentrate on the mechanics of a general (and, as we have just seen, sometimes acrimonious) dissolution. The first question is who is to carry out the winding up? There are two basic choices: the existing partner or partners or a receiver appointed by the court. The third possibility, the appointment of a partnership liquidator with powers and duties defined by law, was proposed by the Law Commissions, who received considerable evidence of the defects of the current system. Their recommendations on solving the undoubted defects of the present unstructured system having now been lost, the situation remains unsatisfactory.

It is still not uncommon therefore for contentious dissolution proceedings to stretch out interminably and for costs to rise out of all proportion to the sums involved. Take two recent examples. In *Phillips v Symes*,[85] Peter Smith J described the dispute as having generated an unbelievable amount of litigation, including several interlocutory hearings, issue trials, two visits to the Court of Appeal, and a threatened petition to the House of Lords. By 2001, the only issue at stake was whether there was actually a partnership at all and if so what were the consequences of the subsequent falling out of the partners. Those proceedings had now reached 2006; the partnership was wholly insolvent. The judge made an order that all proceedings be stayed for two years and that, if no further applications were made on the current disputes during that time, all further applications would be barred. In *Sahota v Sohi*,[86] because of an inability of the parties

---

[83] The dissenting judge considered that the wording was so clear.
[84] [2010] CSIH 38 at [20].
[85] [2006] EWHC 1721 (Ch).
[86] [2006] EWHC 344 (Ch).

to settle their dispute the costs had escalated out of all proportion to the amounts and issues at stake. Disputes over a sum of approximately £17,000 had generated costs of £0.5 million. The judge found that one party was substantially at fault and awarded costs accordingly.

Winding Up by the Existing Partners

Partners, as we know by now, are all agents of each other whilst the partnership is a going concern and can bind each other to contracts etc if they are acting in the course of their actual, implied, or apparent authority. If it is decided that the partners are to conduct the winding-up operations personally then they continue to do so as agents for their fellow partners. Thus each will bind his fellow partners in the same manner as when the partnership was a going concern—and again questions of actual and apparent authority will be decided as questions of fact. Did the partner have actual permission to enter the contract on behalf of the firm or is the firm estopped from denying that he had authority because of their representations to that effect by words or conduct? Implied authority is, however, a question of law governed, whilst the partnership is a going concern, by s 5 of the Act (see Chapter 4 again). In this respect the position is altered in the case of a winding up, since s 5 is qualified by s 38:

7.24

> After the dissolution of a partnership the authority of each partner to bind the firm, and the other rights and obligations of the partners, continue notwithstanding the dissolution so far as may be necessary to wind up the affairs of the partnership, and to complete transactions begun but unfinished at the time of the dissolution, but not otherwise.

This section covers two things: (a) the implied authority of a partner following a general dissolution (but clearly not his actual or apparent authority), and (b) the fiduciary duties which are preserved for this purpose. The question of fiduciary duties on a dissolution has already been discussed in Chapter 5, the leading examples being *Chan v Zacharia*[87] and *Don King Productions Inc v Warren*.[88] It has been decided in *Kidsons v Lloyds Underwriters* Subscribing Policy No 621 PK10000101[89] that s 38 has no application in England to a technical rather than a general dissolution.

Extent of implied authority

Anything 'necessary to wind up the affairs of the partnership' is thus included in this implied authority and it is suggested that this authority should take precedence over the

7.25

---

[87] (1984) 154 CLR 178.
[88] [1999] 2 All ER 218, CA.
[89] [2008] EWHC 2415.

limitation as to completing transactions in existence at the date of dissolution. Clearly to dispose of stock is necessary for a winding up even though it will involve new transactions. An early example of s 38 is *Re Bourne*.[90] A surviving partner continued to run the business after the death of his partner until it was wound up. He continued the firm's bank account which was overdrawn at the date of the death and remained overdrawn until the final account. He paid money into and drew money out of the account, and to secure the overdraft he deposited the title deeds of certain partnership land with the bank. Did this bind the executors of the deceased partner? The Court of Appeal held that it did. A partner has a duty and the authority to do all such acts as are necessary for a winding up. Vaughan Williams LJ was quite clear: 'And if it is necessary for such winding up either to continue the partnership business, or to borrow money, or to sell assets... the right and duty are coextensive.'

The lack of cases in England on s 38 is due to the fact that the former partners, as the contracting parties, will normally remain personally both entitled and liable under the general law on pre-dissolution contracts.[91] It will only be in question when additional contracts or actions are sought. In the Australian case of *Belgravia Nominees Pty Ltd v Lowe Pty Ltd*,[92] one judge suggested that the word 'necessary' in the section should be regarded as meaning 'reasonably required'. That case arose in the context of whether to bring an action against a third party. On the other hand, Morritt VC, in *Boghani v Nathoo*,[93] held that s 38 does not entitle the continuing partners to engage in new contracts or bargains and only allows continuance of existing transactions if they are necessary for the winding up. New contracts could be made, however, if they are an inevitable part of satisfying the pre-dissolution contractual obligations. The case concerned the question as to whether to complete a hotel development and to borrow money to do so. The hotel project could be sold as a going concern (they were under no obligation to complete the development) and money could only be borrowed for a purpose within s 38.

The position in Scotland is different. There the partnership, having legal personality, was the party to pre-dissolution contracts. On dissolution that personality disappears and so s 38 is needed to allow the partners to act—they do not, however, become contracting parties as such.

In *Lujo Properties Ltd v Green*,[94] the Scottish court had to decide the effect of s 38 on a lease granted to the firm (remember in Scotland a partnership has legal personality) and the then partners as trustees for the firm. Following the dissolution of the firm it was held that, although the individual partners were no longer tenants under the lease

---

[90] [1906] 2 Ch 427. See also *Don King Productions Inc v Warren* [2000] Ch 341, [42].
[91] See *Inland Revenue v Graham's Trustees* 1971 SC (HL) 1 at 26–7 per Lord Upjohn. See also *Boghani v Nathoo* [2011] EWHC 2101 at [27] per Morrit C.
[92] [2015] WASCA 143.
[93] [2011] EWHC 2101 (Ch).
[94] 1997 SLT 225. See also *Sheveleu v Brown* [2018] CSIH 68, where the dispute concerned the meaning of an unfinished contract.

as the firm had ceased to exist, the lease was assignable and so formed an asset of the firm for the purposes of winding up. The effect of s 38 was to impose both rights and duties on the former partners for the purposes of winding up the firm so that the lease remained enforceable against the former partners including an obligation to pay a sum equivalent to the rent due under the lease.

The decision in *Lujo Properties* highlighted the problems of applying s 38 to a partnership with legal personality. The court did not seek to explain exactly how the rights and obligations under the lease passed from the former partnership, which no longer existed, to the former partners, who were never the tenants. In a similar case also on Scots law, *Inland Revenue Commissioners v Graham's Trustees*,[95] the House of Lords held that s 38 could not operate to confer any rights of possession or tenancy on the former partners, it simply required them to complete unfinished operations under conditions which would have applied if the lease had still existed.

This distinction between the English and Scottish authorities on the application of s 38 to a partnership with legal personality was highlighted in *975 Duncan v The MFV Marigold Pd 145*.[96] The latter seem to cast doubt on the partners' ability to enter into any new contractual commitments, especially new trading contracts. In that case the surviving partners had carried on trading for seven years and Lord Reed had no doubt that, even on the English authorities, s 38 could only confer authority for a limited time. Thus they had in fact formed a new partnership entity rather than continuing the old entity.

Effect on contracts of employment

In 2005 the Court of Appeal doubted the previously held general rule that a general dissolution of a partnership automatically ended any contracts of employment with that firm.[97] Any such general rule would seem to be inconsistent with the operation of s 38 and that was the subsequent decision of the New South Wales Court of Appeal in *Bromhead v Graham*.[98] It must depend upon whether such employees are required for the partners to carry out their functions under s 38.

7.26

Duty to wind up

In most cases a winding up will be carried out 'in-house' by the partners. It is cheaper, quicker, and more private than the alternative. It also preserves the confidentiality between the partners. Section 38 is construed as imposing a duty to wind up the firm and to complete existing transactions. It will therefore apply unless the court orders

7.27

---

[95] 1971 SC (HL) 1.
[96] 2006 SLT 975, CS (OH).
[97] *Rose v Dodd* [2005] ICR 1776.
[98] [2007] NSWCA 257.

otherwise and appoints a receiver because the lack of trust is terminal. One aspect of this duty means that failure to complete an existing transaction may give rise to an action for negligence by the third party so let down, eg by a firm of solicitors not pursuing an action so that it becomes statute-barred: see *Welsh v Knarston*.[99] Finally there is a proviso to s 38 whereby the firm is not bound by the acts of a bankrupt partner unless a partner has since held himself out as being a partner of the bankrupt.

Partnership Receivers

Appointing a receiver

7.28 Receivers may be appointed by the court even if the partnership is a going concern, in which case the person appointed will be a receiver and manager. In such cases some evidence of fraud or unfair conduct needs to be produced.[100] It is much more common, however, for the court to be asked to appoint a receiver on a dissolution to supervise the winding-up process or to manage the business pending the hearing of a petition and the making of consequent orders.[101] In cases where the relationship between the partners is hostile, lack of a receiver can give rise to problems, eg the right of access to partnership premises.[102] In the first case the receiver is a receiver and manager, in the second case the receiver is a receiver for sale and both are charged with acting in the best interests of all the partners. A receiver once appointed is the only person authorized to act and commence proceedings on behalf of the firm. In *Ong Kay Eng v Ng Chiaw Tong*,[103] it was held that the receiver could not carry on litigation brought by a partner. The Law Commissions noted that there are many problems associated with the appointment of a receiver. They cited one case where, eleven years after the appointment, one side was still challenging his actions. The other side had lost interest and it was likely that there would be no funds left for the partners and that the receiver would make a loss.

Professional partnerships

7.29 The court has an absolute discretion as to whether to appoint a receiver. Some recent decisions have, however, laid down a few guidelines for future reference. In *Floydd v Cheney*[104] an architect and his assistant/partner quarrelled and the latter disappeared with many documents relating to the business. When sued for their return he argued that there was a partnership and asked for the appointment of a receiver. The fact that a partnership was disputed did not preclude the appointment of a receiver, although it

---

[99] 1972 SLT 96.
[100] In Scotland, the equivalent is a judicial factor. See, eg *Rosserlane Consultants Ltd v Appointment of a judicial factor* [2008] CSOH 120.
[101] See, eg *Catch a Ride Ltd v Gardner* [2014] EWHC 1220; *Murray v Feros* [2019] NSWSC 260.
[102] See, eg *Latchman v Pickard,* 12 May 2005, Ch.
[103] [2001] 2 SLR 213, CA.
[104] [1970] Ch 602.

was a factor which the court could take into account. Another factor was that since the partnership involved a professional practice the court should be wary of appointing a receiver since such an appointment might harm the 'delicate blossom' of a professional man's reputation. On that basis, and the fact that he thought that it was unlikely that a partnership would in fact be established, the judge refused to appoint a receiver.

Continuation of business

In *Sobell v Boston*,[105] Goff J refused to appoint a receiver where one partner retired and the remaining partners were continuing the business. In other words, a receiver will not usually be appointed in a technical dissolution, ie where there is no winding up but simply the buying out of a retiring partner, even though such an appointment might speed up events. Such a partner's rights lie in s 42 of the Act (see below) and not in the appointment of a receiver. He also reiterated Megarry J's point vis-à-vis professional partnerships—in this case it was a firm of solicitors. The position is different if there is evidence of fraud, or the assets were somehow in jeopardy, or there are factors which 'warrant the attention of an impartial person appointed by the Court'.[106] In effect the only complaint in this case was the delay in payment and the unsatisfactory nature of s 42.

7.30

Single partner or receiver continuing the business

Two cases, one in England and one in Australia, show a marked difference in attitude to the appointment of a receiver for sale. Both cases involved a two-partner firm where one of the partners wished to continue running the business and the other one wished to realize his share of the business. In both cases there was no suggestion that the assets were in jeopardy (which would have led to the appointment of a receiver) but the parties were in dispute. In *Wedge v Wedge*[107] the Supreme Court of Western Australia, relying on English cases and authorities, decided that where a partnership is already in dissolution a receiver will be appointed almost as a matter of course, and certainly where there is a serious dispute between the partners. The appointment of a receiver for sale would give him the freedom to realize the assets in the most appropriate way.

7.31

But in *Toker v Akgul*[108] the Court of Appeal in England reversed an order by the judge which had appointed a receiver on the same basis and on similar facts as in *Wedge v Wedge*. Evans LJ doubted whether there was ever a practice of appointing a receiver as a matter of course. Waite LJ simply said that the judge was wrong to assume that this was the practice of the court. In this case there were alternatives, such as an action for a partnership account, which would be cheaper and more in keeping with the modest

---

[105] [1975] WLR 1587.
[106] *Anderson Group v Davies* (2001) 53 NSWLR 401 at 405 per Barrett J. In the case these included an intermingling of the financial affairs of the partnership and one of its corporate partners, and the fact that its profit and loss account did not reflect its trading operations. The receiver was appointed even though there was evidence that the business (a hotel) would suffer a consequent loss of staff morale.
[107] (1996) 12 WAR 489, SC.
[108] 2 November 1995, CA.

value of the partnership assets. That decision prompted the judge in a company case, *Wilton-Davies v Kirk*,[109] to comment that in the case of a receiver appointed with a view to realizing assets as distinct from one appointed to maintain assets, it was wrong to have a preconception that appointing a receiver was the normal thing to do. It was a matter of discretion, pure and simple.

An example of the exercise of this discretion is *Don King Productions Inc v Warren (No 3)*.[110] Following the dispute between the two boxing promoters as to the effect of contracts entered into by Warren and found by the courts to have been brought into the firm by him (see Chapters 5 and 6), King was awarded a freezing injunction against Warren and a protective regime as to dealings concerning the partnership assets was imposed by the court. King was concerned as to breaches of that order and regime by Warren and sought the appointment of a partnership receiver mainly to take over those contracts as being partnership assets. Although there was strong evidence of a breach of the order, the judge refused to appoint a receiver because there would be a real risk of substantial irreparable damage to Warren's business, since the publicity attached to such an appointment might well persuade boxers not to sign up with him in the future. Further there was evidence that to continue the order would be a better protection for King and the better course would be to accept assurances by Warren as to his future conduct which would allow the protective regime to continue and which had generally worked well from King's point of view.

On the other hand, in *Catch a Ride Ltd v Gardner*,[111] the court appointed a receiver and manager where the parties were at total loggerheads and where it was considered that no injunctive relief would be appropriate as it would only cause more dissention. It was estimated that any litigation to resolve the complex arrangements would take at least three years. The receiver was to take over the running of the business and neither partner was to be paid a salary in the meantime.

Remuneration of a receiver

7.32 A receiver appointed by the court is to be paid both his costs and his remuneration out of the assets of the firm. This is apparently so even though the receiver is a former partner who owes money to the firm which he cannot pay. This was the position in *Davy v Scarth*.[112] Davy and Scarth were partners. Davy died and Scarth was appointed as receiver by the court. The accounts showed that he had £1,392 in his hands as partnership assets and that in addition he owed the firm some £14,450. His remuneration as receiver was fixed at £280 and his costs at £48. The judge allowed him to deduct his fees

---

[109] [1997] BCC 770.
[110] [1999] 2 All ER 218, CA.
[111] [2014] EWHC 1220 (Ch).
[112] [1906] 1 Ch 55.

and expenses from the £1,392 before paying it over to Davy's executrix. Farwell J gave this graphic reason: 'I think he is entitled to have the remuneration, irrespective of his debt to the partnership, so as to keep himself alive while he is doing his work as receiver.'

On the other hand a receiver has no rights against the partners personally—he can only look to the assets of the firm. In *Boehm v Goodall*[113] a receiver made such a claim on the basis that he had been appointed with the consent of the partners. Warrington J in declining his request spelt out the true nature and position of a partnership receiver:

> Such a receiver and manager is not the agent of the parties, he is not a trustee for them, and they cannot control him. He may, as far as they are concerned, incur expenses or liabilities without their having a say in the matter. I think it is of the utmost importance that receivers and managers in this position should know that they must look for their indemnity to the assets which are under the control of the court. The court itself cannot indemnify receivers, but it can, and will, do so out of the assets, so far as they extend, for expenses properly incurred; but it cannot go further.

Despite various challenges the decision in *Boehm v Goodall* has been applied ever since, most recently by the Full Court of the Queensland Supreme Court in *Rosanove v O'Rourke*[114] and by the English Court of Appeal in *Choudhri v Palta*.[115] In that case the restriction to the assets of the firm was further limited since the only substantial asset in that case was subject to prior fixed charges in favour of two banks. The asset to the extent of those charges was not a partnership asset so that the receiver's claim for expenses etc (including the costs of this case) was deferred to those of the banks.

Liability of a receiver

It is clear that no action may be brought by a partner, or anyone else, against a receiver without the court's permission.[116] If permission is granted, then a partner may only claim for any loss sustained by him as a partner and not in any other capacity, eg as a prospective purchaser of the business.[117] These two propositions were upheld by the Court of Appeal in *McGowan v Chadwick*.[118] Mr McGowan successfully applied for the appointment of a receiver, Mr Grant. Mr Grant appointed Mr McGowan as his agent in running the business. In 1999 Mr Chadwick made an offer to Mr Grant to purchase the business for £10,000, plus writing off a debt owed to him of £12,000 and £5,000 receiver's expenses. This was rejected. So were several more that year, culminating in an offer of £250,000. That was also rejected but in June 2000, after several more manoeuvres, there was a sale to Mr Chadwick for £250,000. Mr Chadwick was now seeking

7.33

---

[113] [1911] 1 Ch 155.
[114] [1988] 1 QdR 171, SC.
[115] [1994] 1 BCLC 184, CA.
[116] *Re Maidstone Palace Varieties Ltd* [1909] 2 Ch 283 at 286 per Nevill J.
[117] *Skyepharma v Hyal Pharmaceutical Corporation* [2001] BPIR 163, Ont CA.
[118] [2002] EWCA Civ 1758.

permission to sue Mr Grant (a) for damages for failing to accept the original offer, and (b) for mismanagement of the business through his agent Mr McGowan. The Court of Appeal agreed with the judge that in effect these amounted to a single claim.

The first question was the test for allowing the action to proceed. Jonathan Parker LJ, giving a judgment with which both other members of the Court of Appeal agreed, said that there were no hard and fast rules in this area which was one of discretion. But the court must be satisfied that the claim is a genuine one. Whilst the receiver must be protected from vexatious or harrowing claims, justice must be done. But, assuming that the receiver had been in breach of his duties in failing to accept the original offer (which assumption has to be made in deciding leave to bring an action), virtually all the alleged loss accrued to Mr Chadwick as a purchaser and not as a partner. In particular any loss caused by the alleged mismanagement was not a loss suffered by Mr Chadwick *as a partner* except to the extent to which the purchase price received for the business was diminished.[119] On the facts therefore the only possible liabilities which might be recoverable were the receiver's fees and expenses from 1999 to 2000 (some £42,000) and possibly his litigation costs.

Return of Premiums

7.34 If one partner has paid a premium to the others on joining the firm he may be entitled to reclaim part of this on a dissolution. A premium has to be distinguished from a payment of capital or a purchase of part of the goodwill. The latter is an investment in the business and forms part of the partnership assets, whereas a premium is a 'joining fee' which goes to the other partner(s).[120] The premium is paid in return for being allowed to join the partnership and to remain a partner for a specified period. If the firm is dissolved prematurely, therefore, the payer has not received full consideration for his payment and can recover an appropriate amount from the other partner(s). Premiums, as I have said, are not capital and are thus considered separately (and indeed usually first) in a winding up. The Act deals with premiums in s 40 and they have been the subject of some complex case law. Although the Law Commissions surprisingly received evidence that s 40 was useful and proposed that it be retained,[121] it has a fairly antiquated ring to it. The following is a brief summary of the law in this area.

Section 40 codifies most of the pre-Act law exactly:

> Where one partner has paid a premium to another on entering into a partnership for a fixed term, and the partnership is dissolved before the expiration of that term

---

[119] Thus the increase in the price which Mr Chadwick had to pay was suffered by him as a purchaser and the receiver owed him no duty in that capacity.

[120] But where a contribution to capital has been made in anticipation of benefits (eg a share of profits) which never materialize, similar issuues arise. See *Old v Hodgkinson* [2009] NSWSC 1160.

[121] Report, para 13.22.

otherwise than by the death of a partner, the court may order the repayment of the premium, or of such part thereof as it thinks just, having regard to the terms of the partnership contract and to the length of time during which the partnership has continued; unless

(a) the dissolution is, in the judgment of the court, wholly or chiefly due to the misconduct of the partner who paid the premium, or

(b) the partnership has been dissolved by an agreement containing no provision for a return of any part of the premium.

Little further comment is needed. A partnership will presumably be for a 'fixed term' if it is not entirely open-ended (see the discussion on ss 26 and 32 in Chapter 2)—the pre-Act law was that there can be no recovery of a premium paid on the ending of a partnership at will since the payer was allowed to join a partnership which he knew could be ended at any time and he has thus received full consideration. There is equally no recovery on a dissolution caused by death (insolvency is not mentioned) or, under para (a), if the dissolution is caused by the misconduct of the payer. In *Brewer v Yorke*,[122] however, it was held that mere incompetence did not amount to misconduct for this purpose, at least in the absence of proof of damage caused by the incompetence. Paragraph (b) allows the parties, as usual, to contract out of the section. Where fraud is involved each case will depend upon its merits.

Since the payer will usually have received partial consideration for his payment he will receive only part of his premium back. This can be done on a simple mathematical basis—ie the proportion of the time remaining in the term to the whole term, but other factors may intervene. The payer may have already received valuable benefits, such as training or acquiring business contacts and acumen, which may well reduce the amount returnable. On the other hand the premium may itself have been induced by a misrepresentation in which case a substantial part of it will be recoverable.

Application of Assets on a Winding Up

Partners' rights in the assets of the firm

On a general dissolution the partners have certain rights as to how the firm's assets are to be dealt with. We have already spent some time in Chapter 6 defining both these assets and the nature of a partner's interest in them. The latter is usually described as a partner's lien which arises from s 39 of the Act but this is misleading in that it has little in common with the possessory liens like those of an unpaid vendor or garage (ie a right to retain goods until payment). It is, as we have seen, a form of equitable interest in the nature of a chose in action. Another possible analogy is with a floating charge, except that it does not crystallize

7.35

---

[122] (1882) 46 LT 289.

on a dissolution, for creditors will always be paid in priority to the partners and at the end of the day it is probably no more than an entitlement to a share of the surplus assets after the creditors have been paid. Whatever these rights are they arise from s 39:

> On the dissolution of a partnership every partner is entitled, as against the other partners in the firm, and all persons claiming through them in respect of their interests as partners, to have the property of the partnership applied in payment of the debts and liabilities of the firm, and to have the surplus assets after such payment applied in payment of what may be due to the partners respectively after deducting what may be due from them as partners to the firm; and for that purpose any partner or his representatives may on the termination of the partnership apply to the court to wind up the business and affairs of the firm.

The real importance of this section is that it separates partnership assets from an individual partner's assets and allows the former to be kept for partnership creditors rather than those of an individual partner. Thus, in the venerable case of *Skipp v Harwood*[123] the partners' lien was held to defeat a creditor of an individual partner seeking redress against partnership property. Remember that in *Don King Productions Inc v Warren*,[124] the argument that a non-assignable contract could not be 'realized' under s 39, and so could not be partnership property, failed. The court could find a way of 'realizing' the asset without prejudicing the other party to that contract (see Chapter 6). The precise rights of partners to be paid such surplus assets is explained at the end of this chapter.

Powers of the court in respect of the assets

7.36 In *Campbell v Campbell*,[125] the judge set out the powers of the court in relation to the division of assets on a winding up as between the partners (creditors will be paid first—see later). These powers are:

(i) to order a partition or in specie distribution of the assets and if necessary to order an equalization payment;[126]
(ii) to order partition of co-owned land, with or without beneficiary consent or an equalization payment;[127]
(iii) to order that one partner buys out the interest of the other (see below);
(iv) to order an account from a partner who has appropriated an asset for himself;
(v) to grant a mandatory injunction to one or more partners to take particular steps with regard to partnership assets if necessary to preserve or enhance their value;[128]

---

[123] (1747) 2 Swans 586.
[124] [1999] 2 All ER 218, CA.
[125] [2017] EWHC 182 (Ch) at [154].
[126] *Pick v Pick* [2007] All ER (D) 318; *Campbell v Campbell* [2017] EWHC 182.
[127] *Hopper v Hopper* [2008] EWHC 228 (Ch) using s 14 of the Trusts of Land and appointment of Trustees Act 1996. For another example of the use of that section see *Kingsley v Kingsley* [2019] EWHC 1073.
[128] See, eg *Badyal v Badyal* [2019] EWHC 467 (Ch).

(vi) to order a sale (see next paragraph);
(vii) to order the taking of accounts.[129]

Above all, the court has a discretionary supervisory power in the case of a winding up, of which these are a part. These can include enforcement of orders.

Realization by sale

The usual way of operating s 39 in a winding up is to realize the partnership assets by a sale, and any partner can apply to the court if necessary for such an order. But the courts have always held that s 39 does not give a partner an absolute right to demand a sale of all the assets, ie a full winding up. Thus where one or more partners wish to carry on the business, the outgoing partner may be regarded as having expressly or impliedly agreed to that. Thus in *Pearn v Berry*[130] the Court of Appeal refused to order the sale of a fishing boat on the dissolution of a two-man partnership. One of the former partners had continued to use the boat for some seven years after the dissolution and both partners had envisaged that this would be the position. Ordering a sale would solve none of the issues between the partners.

7.37

The Court's jurisdiction on realization by sale is very wide. In *Kotak v Kotak*,[131] the two partners, having fallen out, both agreed that the two properties held by the partnership should be sold. The properties were subject to a mortgage with the bank for a sum in excess of their likely sale price on the open market. There was an offer, however, in excess of that, from a company partly owned by one of the partners. The judge ordered a sale to that company subject to specific safeguards since it would produce more funds that a forced sale. He also noted that no sale could in fact take place unless the bank released its security, which it would only do if this was a reasonable price.

Another example of the ambit of s 39 is the decision of the Privy Council on an appeal from the Fijian Court of Appeal in *Latcham v Martin*.[132] In this case Latcham and Martin were partners in a firm called 'Brunswick Motors' in Fiji. The firm was dissolved in 1978 and the business had since been continued by Latcham. A dispute arose as to how Martin was to be bought out. The Fijian judge refused to order a sale of the assets under the Fijian equivalent of s 39 because such a course had ceased to be practical. The book value of the assets at dissolution was $379,901 and whilst their market value would have been established by a sale at that time, that could no longer be done. Latcham had continued to use the assets, four years had elapsed since the dissolution, and the nature and possibly the quality of the assets had changed. Instead the judge regarded Latcham as having purchased the assets in 1978 at their book value and awarded

---

[129] Ibid.
[130] 17 May 1998, CA.
[131] [2014] EWHC 3121 (Ch).
[132] (1984) 134 NLJ 745, PC.

Martin $257,387, representing the payment of the debt due to him from the firm and his share of the capital. The Fijian Court of Appeal dismissed Latcham's appeal. So too did the Privy Council. To permit Latcham to delay matters even further while the accounts of the partnership were reinvestigated at great expense would be a denial of justice. Section 39 does not require a sale. The court's power was not confined to ordering a sale but was a broader one, ie to wind up the affairs of the partnership in such a manner as to do justice between the parties.

Buy out or *Syers v Syers* orders

7.38 If the court takes the view that it would be preferable to require one or more of the partners to buy out the partner or partners petitioning for dissolution rather than to effect a full winding up then it is clear that it may do so. Such orders are known as *Syers v Syers* orders after the decision of the House of Lords in that case.[133] In practice these orders are not it seems often made. As Hoffmann LJ said in *Hammond v Brearley*,[134] the case is more frequently cited than applied, but he did apply it in that case where the outgoing partner's interest was small. In the corporate sphere, Lord Hoffmann, as he had by then become, established single-handedly in *O'Neill v Phillips*[135] a pattern that in nearly all quasi-partnership cases the remedy for an injured minority shareholder will be a buy out under s 996 of the Companies Act 2006 rather than a liquidation. Whether the same will happen in the partnership sphere is open to doubt, but such an order was made by Neuberger J in *Mullins v Laughton*.[136] That was on the basis that, despite his disapproval of the respondents' conduct, the petitioner's grounds for complaint were limited in their practical scope and he could not have objected to a retirement notice had it been served on him properly. It is also unclear as yet whether the principles set out in *O'Neill v Phillips* as to valuing a minority shareholder's interest in a quasi-partnership company will be applied to partnership law.[137]

The section, as it stands, does, however, provide the basic framework for a winding up. But, before we proceed to the final part of the process—the final account and distribution of the assets—we must first return to the problems associated with a partial dissolution, ie where the business is not being wound up but is being continued by one or more of the former partners.

---

[133] (1876) 1 App Cas 174, HL.
[134] 10 December 1992, CA.
[135] [1999] 1 WLR 1092, HL.
[136] [2002] EWHC 2761 (Ch). The report in [2003] 4 All ER 94 does not cover this point.
[137] This was left open in the Canadian case of *Valrut Investments Ltd v Norstar Commercial Developments* 2008 WL 949777 (Ont SC).

Technical Dissolutions

Although when one partner leaves a partnership the basic rule is that the whole firm is dissolved, it is not difficult to provide the contrary by an agreement so that the partnership business effectively continues as between the remaining partners.[138] This is what is known as a technical dissolution.

7.39

Problem areas

There are three general areas which present problems when one partner or partners so leave a partnership and the other partners carry on the business. First, the departing partner(s) should take steps to avoid liability for future debts etc of the firm. Second, their interest in the capital and undrawn profits of the firm must be valued and then purchased by the continuing partners, and third, whilst that process is going on, their rights as to the profits etc made by the firm between their retirement and the date when their shares are finally acquired by the other partners must be determined. The position is basically the same whether the former partners have retired, been expelled, or died, and whether the business is being carried on by one surviving or remaining partner as a sole trader or by two or more such partner(s) in partnership. Many variations are possible, particularly with professional firms, which will have buy-out agreements.[139] The common theme, which distinguishes a technical dissolution from a general dissolution, is that there is no winding up of the business.

7.40

Liability of Former Partner

We have already encountered the first of our three problems. We saw in Chapter 4 that a former partner can be liable to outsiders for debts etc incurred after his departure unless he complies with the notice provisions of s 36 and avoids being represented as a partner under s 14. In brief he must inform existing clients of the firm of his departure, put a notice to that effect in the *London* (or *Edinburgh*) *Gazette*, and, if he is wise, check that all the headed notepaper has been altered or destroyed. We need only mention in addition s 37 of the Act which provides:

7.41

> On the dissolution of a partnership or retirement of a partner any partner may publicly notify the same, and may require the other partner or partners to concur for that purpose in all necessary or proper acts, if any, which cannot be done without his or their concurrence.

---

[138] For an example of an agreement which failed to make this clear, see *Winter v Winter*, 10 November 2000.
[139] Sometimes the court will be required to interpret these, eg as to the date payment becomes due: *Liddle v Liddle* [2019] EWCA Civ 346.

In theory this section will not apply where a partner dies and the deed provides that there is no dissolution on such an event but it is unlikely that the court will accept such an argument. In effect this section is an example of the fiduciary duties of the partners and they are owed equally to the deceased's estate. The Law Commissions considered this to be an important section and recommended its retention.[140]

As between themselves the partners may have provided in the agreement for their liability for debts etc on a technical dissolution. Care must be taken in drafting such agreements, however. In *Hurst v Bryk*[141] the agreement provided that the 'successor partners' who continued to be partners after the date of a partner ceasing to be a partner in the firm would assume liability for all debts and liabilities of the firm. The Court of Appeal held that such a clause could not apply where only one of the former partners remained in the business, since one person could not be a partner on his own and so there could never be a sole 'successor partner'. (This issue was not contested before the House of Lords.)

Valuation of a Partner's Share in the Assets

Capital, assets, and profits

7.42 Valuation of assets is a skilled business normally outside the province of a lawyer. However, there are certain guidelines established by the cases as to the criteria to be used when ascertaining the sums due to an outgoing or deceased partner in a partial dissolution. In general such a partner will be entitled both to his share of the capital and assets of the firm and of the income profits made prior to his departure and not withdrawn by him during his time as a partner. Remember that *Popat v Schonchhatra*[142] established that in the partnership context the entitlement to a share in the capital of the firm relates only to the amount originally invested by the partners. The assets of the firm, over and above that figure, are much wider and are regarded as capital profits. These include all the assets brought into the partnership which must then be included in the accounting between the partners both at the start and end of the relationship, unless there is an agreement to the contrary. For an example see *Bennett v Wallace*.[143]

In practice the disputes seem to fall into two categories: first, is the outgoing partner's share of the capital and assets to be valued according to their book value, ie as shown in the previous accounts, or at their fair or market value? In the latter case the courts may also have to decide the appropriate method of valuing an asset, eg the work in progress of a professional firm,[144] or the value of an agricultural tenancy to be taken over by the

---

[140] Report, para 13.20.
[141] [1997] 2 All ER 283, CA.
[142] [1997] 3 All ER 800, CA.
[143] 1998 SC 457.
[144] *Browell v Goodyear*, The Times, 24 October 2000.

remaining partner where the outgoing partner was also the landlord.[145] Second, what exactly is meant by phrases such as 'profits', 'net profits', and 'undrawn profits' in such a context?

Valuation method

The starting point to decide whether an outgoing partner's share of the assets should be valued by reference to its (usually historic) book value or current market value is the House of Lords' decision in *Cruikshank v Sutherland*.[146] In that case the partnership accounts had always shown the assets of the firm at book value (ie at their value when they were brought into the partnership). The partnership agreement required a full and general account of the partnership dealing and of its property to be made each year. One of the partners died and the agreement required that his share be valued by reference to the accounts next prepared after his death rather than by reference to the accounts immediately before the death, which, remember, showed the assets at book value. The House of Lords held that since the agreement was entirely silent as to how such a *subsequent* account should be prepared for the purpose of valuing an outgoing partner's share and there was no previous practice as to how such an account should be prepared (no one had left the firm before), the account should be prepared on the basis that the assets should be valued as at market value and not historic book value. Thus the outgoing partner should be entitled to take his share of the firm's assets and capital profits. There was a distinction between the previous accounts prepared for the partnership as a going concern and the one to be prepared for valuing the outgoing partner's share.

7.43

Entitlement to market value—the position in Scotland

Cruikshank v Sutherland has been applied many times by the Scottish courts. In *Noble v Noble*[147] it was held that, in the absence of any agreement to the contrary, the historic value of a farm, the main partnership asset, as shown in the accounts was not intended to be a permanent valuation for the purpose of valuing an outgoing partner's share on a subsequent account. Such a partner was entitled to share in the capital profits of the firm. A similar view was taken by Lord Hunter in *Shaw v Shaw*[148] and by Lord Dunpark in *Clark v Watson*.[149] In the latter case, however, Lord Dunpark also said, obiter, that if the agreement did require the valuation of an outgoing partner's share to be taken from the accounts *prior* to the death of the outgoing partner (as distinct from accounts to be prepared for the period after his death) and those accounts showed the assets at book value, there would be a general rule that he was still entitled to have his share valued at market value. It might be different if he or she could be shown to have approved the

7.44

---

[145] *Greenbank v Pickles*, The Times, 7 November 2000, CA.
[146] (1922) 92 LJ Ch 136, HL.
[147] 1965 SLT 415.
[148] 1968 SLT (Notes) 94.
[149] 1982 SLT 450.

accounts; and even then it would have to be shown that he or she had approved the accounts as being appropriate not only for the partnership as a going concern but also as to how his or her share should be valued for ascertaining share of the assets on his or her death. A similar approach was taken by Lord Mayfield in *Wilson v Dunbar*.[150]

But it is clear that the parties may be taken to have agreed that the contrary should apply and that an outgoing partner is only entitled to a share in the book value of the assets. In another Scottish case, *Thom's Executrix v Russel & Aitken*,[151] Lord Jauncey found such a contrary agreement both from the agreement itself and the course of dealings between the partners (book values had been used on the retirement of two previous partners).

Construction of the agreement—the position in England and Wales

7.45 The very different position in English law was set out by the Court of Appeal in *Re White*.[152] In that case the partnership agreement required the outgoing partner's share to be ascertained from the accounts for the period prior to the death of the partner concerned, although they had not actually been prepared until after his death. The accounts had always shown the assets at historic value and that value had been used when two previous partners had left the firm. The partnership agreement also required that an outgoing partner should receive a just valuation of his share. The Court of Appeal decided that *Cruikshank v Sutherland*[153] was a decision only that each case depended upon the construction of the partnership agreement and any course of dealings between the partners. They also found that the subsequent Scottish cases were of the same effect. In this case the outgoing partner was entitled to a just valuation by reference to the agreed accounts for the period prior to his death (although not actually prepared until after his death) and not to an account yet to be prepared (for the period after his death) for the purpose, as in *Cruikshank*. Since all the partners had accepted previous accounts using book values and would not have been able to have done otherwise in the context of the previous partnership dealings, using that method of valuation provided a just valuation for the purposes of the agreement. It would have been unjust for a partner to have objected to that valuation.

In coming to this conclusion, the Court of Appeal rejected Lord Dunpark's statement in *Clark v Watson*, that in agreeing to a previous account a partner will only be bound if he accepted that valuation as being relevant to valuing his share on leaving the firm as well as for the continuing business of the firm. Although the deceased had not had the opportunity to approve the relevant account since it had been prepared after his death, albeit for a period prior to his death, he would not have been able to challenge it as not being a just valuation. How could a partner, after leaving the firm, be said to challenge a valuation which he would have regarded as a just valuation whilst the firm, including

---

[150] 1988 SLT 93.
[151] 1983 SLT 335.
[152] [2001] Ch 393, CA.
[153] (1922) 92 LJ Ch 136, HL.

himself, was continuing? Thus the deceased partner in this case could not have challenged the accounts even if he had been alive to do so.

The decision in *Re White* was followed by the Court of Appeal in *Drake v Harvey*,[154] reversing Mann J.[155] In that case the partnership deed provided that an outgoing (or deceased) partner should be paid the amount standing to the partner's credit as his or her share in the partnership belonging to the partner according to the annual accounts last before his or her exit. Those accounts valued the assets at historic cost but the relevant one had not been signed by the exiting partner. Mann J held that since the deed was silent as to how the assets were to be valued, the effect of *Cruickshank v Sutherland* was that fair value should then be used, there being no previous practice or agreement. For the Court of Appeal there was no such default rule or presumption of fair value. In *Cruickshank* the important point was that the share was to be valued by reference to a future account, not as here by reference to the last accounts. Further, in *Cruickshank*, the deed made no provision as to how such a valuation in that future account should be made, it was a different account drawn up for a different purpose. In this case the deed clearly referred to the previous account and so the usual valuation rules for such an account should be used.

It is clear therefore that in England, as distinct from Scotland, there is no presumption that fair value is to be applied. Each case is to be decided by construing the wording of the agreement and any prior course of dealings between the partners. Sometimes this can lead to a fair value being used. In *Gadd v Gadd*,[156] where the deed required an account to be prepared at a particular point of time with no indication as to whether historic cost or market vale should be used, the outgoing partner was entitled to have the assets included at market value. In *Ham v Ham*,[157] the Court of Appeal, whilst upholding the no presumption approach, was able to apply a fair value. In that case one major difference was that the clause applied on the termination of the partnership so that there were no continuing partners. The Court also took into account the nature of the business, which was farming and so income poor but asset rich, and the fact that the outgoing partner had the choice of taking his share of the assets or its monetary equivalent. If the first choice was at historic cost it was no choice at all.

Income profits

7.46 Turning from capital and capital profits to income profits, these will normally be calculated annually for tax and distribution purposes. Thus any outgoing partner's share of those profits due to him at his withdrawal can be ascertained by applying the

---

[154] [2011] EWCA Civ 838.
[155] [2010] EWHC 1446 (Ch).
[156] (2002) 08 EG 160.
[157] [2013] EWCA Civ 1301.

profit-sharing ratio to the profits so ascertained. Complications can, as ever, arise. In the absence of any agreement to the contrary it has been held in old cases that for partnership, if not for tax, purposes, the cash basis (ie sums actually received less money actually spent) will be used to calculate profits. In *Badham v Williams*[158] one partner was entitled to a fixed amount of profits until 1885 and from then on to a proportion of the profits. He left the firm in 1899 without having received any such share of the profits and the question arose as to whether he was entitled to a proportionate share of the money received after 1885 for work done prior to 1885. The judge applied the cash basis rule so that the outgoing partner was entitled to a share of all sums received since 1885, even though they were attributable to work done prior to that date. The cash basis is now only generally allowable for tax purposes for small businesses, however, and it is likely that the courts today would normally apply the earnings basis,[159] which reflects modern accountancy practice.

As we have seen, partners may decide on various ways of sharing the profits, paying themselves 'salaries' or 'interest' before sharing out the residue. Such complex arrangements can cause problems when assessing the amount of profits due to an outgoing partner. In *Watson v Haggitt*[160] the partners agreed to pay themselves a salary and to divide the 'net profits' after that equally. On the death of a partner, the survivor was to pay his estate one-third of the 'net annual profits'. Did this latter amount include provision for the salary payable to the continuing partner? No, said the Privy Council. Net profits in relation to a dissolution did not have the same meaning as given to it whilst the partners were alive. No allowance could be made for deduction of a salary.

Construction of terms of the agreements

7.47 Careful planning is needed in this area. One example is the case of *Smith v Gale*.[161] Three partners in a firm of solicitors kept their accounts on a cash basis. The junior partner agreed to be 'bought out' and an agreement was drawn up whereby he was to be paid a lump sum (for capital) and the amount of 'undrawn profits' due to him as certified by the auditors. The accounts showed this amount as £2,237—his share of the cash received less expenses. The other partners now claimed that this was a false amount since new premises had recently been bought on a mortgage and no deductions had been made from each partner's current (profit) account for the cost although the lump sum took the value of the premises into account. Undrawn profits, they argued, impliedly meant the current account less some provision for the cost of the premises. Goulding J rejected this argument (which would have reduced the figure to £13). The words 'undrawn profits' must bear their ordinary meaning—profits contained in the partner's current account. There had been no implied variation as alleged by the other partners and the original figure must stand. An expensive error for the other partners.

---

[158] (1902) 86 LT 191.
[159] In general terms this is similar to an invoice basis, which is also used in VAT.
[160] [1928] AC 127, PC.
[161] [1974] 1 WLR 9.

Another example is the case of *Hawthorn v Smallcorn*,[162] where an agreement provided for the retiring partner to be paid a sum 'in respect of his share of current assets less current liabilities as shown on the balance sheet'. A sum was duly paid but subsequently the firm received a repayment of VAT relating to a period prior to the partner's retirement. It was held that the agreement did not draw a line as to the assets as shown at that time, so that the right to the repayment was not a 'current asset' already accounted for by the sum paid under the agreement. The continuing partners had to account for the share of the repayment.

A different dispute arose in *Hammonds v Jones*,[163] where the issue was as to whether a departed partner could challenge the accounts by which his share was to be ascertained. The partnership agreement provided that any challenge to the accounts was to be decided by a majority of the partners and that their decision would be binding on all the partners. The question was whether all the partners included those, such as the respondent, who had left the firm during the year and so could not vote on the dispute. The Court of Appeal held that it did even though that meant that the term 'partners' meant different things in the same sentence of the agreement. To decide otherwise would be contrary to the purpose of the clause.

Law Commissions' proposals

In their final Report, the Law Commissions recommended the introduction of three default provisions for an outgoing partner, applicable therefore only in the absence of contrary agreement.[164] These were: **7.48**

(i) the right to his share of the partnership valued at the date of his withdrawal on the hypothesis that the assets were being sold as on a full dissolution; the price being the higher of
   (a) the liquidation or break-up value, and
   (b) the sale of the entire business as a going concern;
(ii) the right to a commercial rate of interest on that share from the date of withdrawal; and
(iii) an indemnity for any partnership debts or claims paid by him, without prejudice to any claims which the other partners may have against him.

The importance of these proposals, which may well never be implemented, is that they highlight the difficulties in this area which ought to be covered by the deed.

---

[162] [1998] STC 591.
[163] [2009] EWCA Civ 1400.
[164] Para 8.75.

Partner's Share in Profits etc after Dissolution

Choice of profits or interest

7.49 The process of valuing the outgoing partner's share can be a complex affair and thus take a long time, particularly if there is a reluctance by the remaining partners to settle matters. What right does the outgoing partner have vis-à-vis the profits made by the continuing partners from 'his' share of the assets during that period, ie from the partial dissolution to the final settlement? At first sight, s 42(1) provides the answer:

> Where any member of a firm has died or otherwise ceased to be a partner, and the surviving or continuing partners carry on the business of the firm with its capital or assets without any final settlement of accounts as between the firm and the outgoing partner or his estate, then, in the absence of any agreement to the contrary,[165] the outgoing partner or his estate is entitled at the option of himself or his representatives to such share of the profits made since the dissolution as the court may find to be attributable to the use of his share of the partnership assets, or to interest at the rate of five per cent per annum on the amount of his share of the partnership assets.

Outgoing partner—technical dissolution only

7.50 Section 42 only applies if the partner is an 'outgoing partner'. In *Hopper v Hopper*,[166] a father, mother, son, and daughter-in-law were partners at will in a fruit and vegetable wholesale business. The father died and the son and his wife continued the business. One of the questions which arose was the entitlement of the mother to a share of the post-death profits. The Court of Appeal, reversing the judge below, held that she was an outgoing partner for the purposes of s 42. There had been a technical dissolution on the death of the father and the business had been carried on in a new partnership by the son and his wife. In a technical dissolution, all non-participating former partners were 'outgoing partners' within s 42. There was no evidence that there had been any intention of a full winding up or that the mother had continued as a partner in the new firm under the pre-death profit-sharing arrangement.[167]

It follows from that decision and that of the subsequent decision by the Inner House of the Court of Session in *Sheveleu v Brown*,[168] that s 42 has no role where the business of the partnership is being carried on purely to effect a winding up. There are no 'continuing' or 'outgoing' partners. In those cases, the normal profit-sharing ratio will apply,

---

[165] Even if there is a contrary agreement, where there is still a duty to account for post-dissolution capital profits, interest can be awarded on those profits in equity. See *Hussar Estate v P & M Construction Ltd (No 2)*, 13 May 2005 (Ont SC), where the 5% figure in the section was adopted. See also *Lawson v Wenley, Davies, Willis and Cross* [2012] NZHC 204 at [61].

[166] [2008] EWCA Civ 1417.

[167] The parties, using common sense rather than the law, never actually considered that there had been any form of dissolution at all.

[168] [2018] CSIH 68. The court considered this issue in the context of the separate legal personality of Scottish partnerships.

although it may be that there might be some adjustment if some of the partners are more active in the business than others. This was suggested but not decided in *Sheveleu v Brown*.[169]

Section 42 has also been held in Australia to apply even where one partner retires and only one partner remains. This is where the retiring partner has agreed expressly or impliedly that he will only receive the price of his share.[170] In the absence of such an agreement then of course a winding up will ensue instead.

Such outgoing partners have a clear choice under the section—a share of the profits arising from the use of their share of the assets or 5 per cent interest on their share of the assets. We have already seen that a partner has to choose one or the other—he or she cannot have a receiver appointed because there is undue delay in coming to a final account[171]—the partner is merely an unsecured creditor for whichever sum he or she chooses to accept. (This has the unfortunate consequence that the former partner will cease to have an interest in the business and so lose any entitlement to attract relief from inheritance tax if the former partner dies before it is paid.[172])

The right to some return is in effect no more than an example of the fiduciary duties of partners. One example is the Privy Council decision in *Pathirana v Pathirana*,[173] where one of the partners continued the business (a petrol station) after the departure of his partner and exploited an agency agreement with an oil company for his own benefit even though it belonged to the firm. He had to account for his post-dissolution profits. We have already come across this case in connection with fiduciary duties in Chapter 5.

No application to capital profits

It has been held many times that s 42 has no application to post-dissolution capital profits as defined by the Court of Appeal in *Popat v Schonchhatra*,[174] ie to increases in the value of the partnership assets, as opposed to the original capital invested by each partner. This had previously been decided in both *Barclays Bank Trust Co Ltd v Bluff*[175] and *Chandroutie v Gajadhar*,[176] in the context of an outgoing partner taking the interest option under s 42. In *Popat v Schonchhatra*, the position was clarified in respect of ascertaining the share of profits option. The Court of Appeal in that case decided that, in the absence of any agreement to the contrary, the outgoing partner's share in

7.51

---

[169] [2018] CSIH 68 at [42].
[170] *Truong v Lam* [2009] WASCA 217.
[171] *Sobell v Boston* [1975] 1 WLR 1587.
[172] *Beckman v IRC* [2000] STC (SCD) 59.
[173] [1967] 1 AC 233, PC. See also *Hussar Estate v P & M Construction*, 7 March 2005 (Ont SC) where the liability extended to a situation where there was an apparent agreement to the contrary.
[174] [1997] 3 All ER 800, CA.
[175] [1982] Ch 172.
[176] [1987] AC 147, PC.

post-dissolution capital profits would be ascertained by reference to the implied term of s 24(1), ie on an equality basis. This was subsequently confirmed and applied by the Court of Appeal in *Emerson v Emerson*.[177] Two brothers were involved in a farming business, one of whom died in 1998. The dispute concerned the excess of the compensation monies received by the surviving partner, who had continued the business, for the slaughter of farm animals following the foot and mouth outbreak in 2001. The Court of Appeal held that the compensation payments were partnership assets and the excess over the value of the herd at the date of the brother's death represented a capital profit to which s 24(1) applied.

Post-dissolution income profits

7.52 Section 42 does apply to post-dissolution income profits. It provides for two alternative methods of ascertaining the former partner's share at his option. The first option is 'such share of the profits made since the dissolution as the court may find to be attributable to the use of his share of the partnership assets'. That is different from the pre-dissolution profit-sharing ratio—it is quantified instead by reference to the share of the assets rather than any previous agreement as to profits.

In ascertaining the former partner's share of the profits during this period the question arises whether s 24(3), which provides for the payment of interest on an advance by a partner to the firm, subject of course to any contrary intention, and which we met in Chapter 5, has any application once the firm has been dissolved. The point was left open by the New South Wales Court of Appeal in *Bartels v Behm*[178] but was clearly decided in the negative in the British Columbia Court of Appeal in *Klaue v Bennett*.[179] The wording of s 42 would seem to be in agreement with this conclusion, although it was not used to justify the decision.

On the other hand, where after the termination of the partnership but before winding up, one partner borrows money to enable partnership debts to be discharged, the other partner is liable to have his share of the interest paid on the loan debited against his share of the profits. This was the actual decision in *Bartels v Behm*.

Attributable to the use of his share of the partnership assets

7.53 As we have seen, s 42 requires the calculation of the share of post-dissolution income profits to be by reference to the use of the outgoing partner's share of the assets and not to any previous profit-sharing agreement, express or implied. The main question is whether the former is to be calculated in terms of his or her share of the total value of the assets of the business or his or her share of those assets after deducting any liabilities. In

---

[177] [2004] 1 BCLC 575, CA.
[178] (1990) 19 NSWLR 257.
[179] (1989) 62 DLR (4th) 367.

other words, is it by reference to his or her gross share or his or her net share of the assets? In *Taylor v Grier (No 3)*,[180] the judge held that it was clear that Parliament had intended only the net share to be used and since Mr Grier owed money to the partnership at the date of dissolution, his net share of the post-dissolution assets was nil. In *Sandhu v Gill*,[181] the Court of Appeal came to the same conclusion, overruling Lightman J who had held that it was the full proprietary interest of the outgoing partner in the partnership assets.[182]

The Court of Appeal came to this conclusion for a number of reasons. First, if the concept of the gross share was applied to the interest option under the section, it would produce the absurd result that the continuing partner would have to pay the outgoing partner interest on money owed *by him* to the firm. The creditor would be paying interest on a debt to the debtor. Given that, it was unlikely that the section would use the phrase 'share of the assets' to mean different things for the two options it provided. Second, the net profits interpretation accorded with the pre-Act cases;[183] and third, it was also the position with regard to the equivalent section in New Zealand.[184] The Court of Appeal also pointed out that their interpretation was not inconsistent with the judgment of Romer J in *Manley v Sartori*.[185] That case involved a different point, discussed in the next paragraph. The judge in that case was contrasting the rights of a partner under s 42 with those applicable to pre-dissolution profits and, *in that context*, said that the outgoing partner's rights were over all the assets of the firm.

But the Court of Appeal recognized that there were two serious counterarguments, which had weighed heavily with Lightman J. First, since s 41(a) of the Act uses express language to indicate the net share rather than the gross share of profits,[186] it seems strange that, if that was the intention in s 42, the same wording was not used. The Court of Appeal, however, considered that in other sections the phrase was used differently and that the language of the Act was not sufficiently homogenized to allow for such an inference to be drawn. In particular the net profits interpretation was in accordance with s 44, a section which was closer to s 42 in content. The second objection was that Nourse LJ, in *Popat v Schonchhatra*,[187] had obiter endorsed the gross profits interpretation of s 42. But on the basis that none of the pre-Act authorities were cited to Nourse LJ, that the case, and his judgment, were largely about s 24 which applies to the very different case of pre-dissolution profits, and the fact that the commercial unjustness of the

---

[180] 12 May 2003 Ch.
[181] [2006] Ch 466, overruling [2005] 1 All ER 990.
[182] That approach has since been applied in Scotland: *975 Duncan v The MFV Marigold Pd 145*, 2006 SLT 975.
[183] *Willett v Blanford* (1842) 1 Hare 253; *Simpson v Chapman* (1853) 4 De GM & G 154; and *Yates v Finn* (1880) 13 Ch D 839.
[184] See *De Renzy v De Renzy* [1924] NZLR 1065. Lightman J considered that he found this decision hard to follow.
[185] [1927] 1 Ch 157.
[186] 'The surplus of the partnership assets, after satisfying partnership liabilities.' Section 39 also uses similar language.
[187] [1997] 3 All ER 800 at 806, CA.

gross share interpretation was never considered, persuaded the Court of Appeal in *Gill* to come to the opposite, and, it is submitted, correct conclusion.

Deductions for management by remaining partner(s)

7.54 The position in relation to making an allowance for the management of the business by the remaining partner(s) was explained by Romer J in *Manley v Sartori*.[188] Whilst emphasizing that s 42(1) provides that the outgoing partner is prima facie entitled to a share of the profits proportionate to his share in the assets of the partnership, the judge considered it possible for the continuing partners to show that the profits have been earned wholly or partly by means other than by utilizing the partnership assets. They are entitled, for example, to an amount for their trouble in carrying on the business. He also outlined some of the factors which might be used by the continuing partners to rebut the presumption in the section:

> [I]t may well be that in a particular case profits have been earned by the surviving partner not by reason of the use of any asset of the partnership, but purely and solely by reason of the exercise of skill and diligence by the surviving partner; or it may appear that the profits have been wholly or partly earned not by reason of the use of the assets of the partnership, but by reason of the fact that the surviving partner himself provided further assets and further capital by means of which the profit has been earned.

That general approach was followed and explained by the Court of Appeal of Victoria in *Fry v Oddy*.[189] The issue there was as to how much of the profits of a solicitors' firm was due to the outgoing partner's share of the assets. The court considered that prima facie the profits of a partnership were attributable to its assets. Each case would then depend upon its own facts but in a modern legal practice profits were more attributable to the assets of the firm as opposed to the personal skills of each member of the firm. Ormiston JA suggested that whether the courts approached the matter as deducting from the profits what is attributable to the outgoing partner's share of the assets or by seeing how much is fairly attributable to his share did not matter. The ultimate solution is a question of fact to be judged from the evidence, of expert witnesses if necessary. In the case itself the dispute arose as to the value to be placed on the personal skills etc of the remaining partners. The court found no reason to upset the judge's findings which had differed from those of an expert witness.

Adjustments for management etc in relation to share of capital profits

7.55 In *Emerson v Emerson*,[190] the Court of Appeal having applied the rule that s 42 has no application to capital profits, which remain to be divided according to the

---

[188] [1927] 1 Ch 157.
[189] [1999] 1 VR 542, CA. This principle is now in statutory form in Western Australia.
[190] [2004] 1 BCLC 575, CA. See also *Beale v Trinkler* [2009] NSWCA 1093.

pre-dissolution ratio, nevertheless made a deduction for the cost to the surviving partner of keeping the livestock between the dissolution and the payment of the compensation. As the Court observed, farm animals are unlikely to stay alive and in good condition unless they are fed and cared for. This adjustment was made under the general indemnity principles applicable to trustees[191] on the basis that the surviving partner was indeed a trustee of the partnership business for the estate of his brother and on the basis that the surviving partner had acted reasonably in keeping the herd in condition.

Interest option in lieu of share of income profits

The alternative under s 42 to a share of profits is interest at 5 per cent on the partner's share of the partnership assets, ie as distinct from its capital. On the face of it this sounds a risky option since interest rates can vary and can be more than double or less than half that amount and in *Sobell v Boston*[192] Goff J suggested that an amendment increasing the rate should be considered 'by those charged with considering law reform'. The rate has not changed since 1890. An attempt to persuade the court to order a different rate under its statutory powers as a debt under s 43, failed in both *Williams v Williams*[193] and in *Dyce v Fairgreave*.[194] The scope of this interest option was clarified in the case of *Barclays Bank Trust Co Ltd v Bluff*.[195] A father and son carried on a farming partnership at will until the father died in 1972. The son carried on the business for several years, whilst negotiating with his father's executor, Barclays, for the purchase of his share of the business. Nothing was ever agreed, however, and in 1977 Barclays issued a summons asking for a declaration from the court that if it opted for the 5 per cent interest payment in lieu of profits, it would still be entitled to share in the increased value of the assets between dissolution and a final account. The farm had increased dramatically in value during that time as all land did in that period, the difference by the date of trial being about £60,000. The son's defence was based on two contentions. First, that an election for interest rather than a share of the profits excluded the right to all post-dissolution profits, including capital profits arising from an increase in the value of the assets. Second, that the bank had in any event already elected for interest and so could not opt for a share of profits, capital or otherwise.

7.56

No effect on right to capital profits
The judge rejected both arguments. On the main issue he decided that the word 'profits' in s 42(1) only included profits accruing in the ordinary course of carrying on the firm's business pending realization—in this case the earnings derived from the disposal, in

7.57

---

[191] See, eg *Carver v Duncan* [1985] 1 AC 1082 at 1120 per Lord Templeman.
[192] [1975] 1 WLR 1587.
[193] [1999] 9 CL 457.
[194] [2013] CSOH 155.
[195] [1982] Ch 172.

the ordinary course of trade, of livestock and produce. It did not include capital profits. Thus an election to take the 5 per cent interest instead of profits under the section had no effect on the executor's rights to a share in the increased value of the assets. In such cases the outgoing or deceased partner has a right to share in capital profits in addition to interest.

> Such increase in value cannot be regarded as having been brought about by the efforts of the [son] and it is difficult to see any rhyme or reason why he should have the whole benefit of it even if the [father's executor] has chosen to take interest of 5% per annum in lieu of a share of profits by way of income for the period between dissolution and sale of the partnership business. After all, the [son] is not the sole beneficial owner of the farm. He is a trustee of it for the deceased's estate and himself. In that situation a fortuitous accretion to the value of the farm ought surely to ensure to the benefit of all the beneficiaries interested in the property.

The decision is apparently contrary to the earlier Irish case of *Meagher v Meagher*,[196] but the position there was complicated by the fact that the income profits arose from buying and selling land. The judge in the *Barclays Bank* case regarded the alternative view as being inequitable and on principle he must be right. The key, as we have seen, is to distinguish between capital and income profits, only the latter being subject to s 42(1). In cases such as this therefore where a 5 per cent interest return is larger than a pro rata return on the profit basis, the interest option under s 42(1) is much more attractive than might originally be supposed.

The decision in the *Barclays Bank* case was approved by the Privy Council in *Chandroutie v Gajadhar*[197] on an appeal from Trinidad and Tobago. In that case a mother and son ran a grocery business in partnership. In 1973 the son and his wife ejected the mother and daughter from the premises and carried on the business themselves. The son died in 1975 and the daughter-in-law conducted the business for her own account. In 1978 the mother sued the daughter-in-law claiming a half-share in the business. Much of the case was concerned with whether the claim should have been brought against the son's executors (ie the other partner) and not the daughter-in-law as a third party and whether the delay in bringing the action was too great to allow it to proceed. The Privy Council held both points in favour of the mother and granted her a declaration of the amount she could claim against her daughter-in-law based on the reasoning in the *Barclays Bank* case. She had the right to a half-share of the partnership assets, valued at the date of their realization, and not merely a right to a half-share of the assets valued at the son's death (when the firm was dissolved), together with interest.

---

[196] [1961] IR 96.
[197] [1987] AC 147, PC.

Making an election

The *Barclays Bank* case also raised two points in relation to the son's second argument in that case that the bank had already made an election. This was based on two letters written by the bank's solicitors but the judge rejected this, first because the letters were ambiguous and subsequent actions by both sides showed that they still regarded the matter as open. An election under s 42(1) must therefore be clear and unambiguous to be effective. The second reason given by the judge was that in any event the bank was an executor and as such owed a fiduciary duty to the father's estate in making its choice. The bank could only have made an election, therefore, if it had considered the advantages and disadvantages of each course of action. For that it would have needed information as to the income profits made since dissolution, ie to see the farm accounts which had in fact been withheld from it. Thus the bank *as an executor* could not on the facts have made a valid election binding on the estate.

7.58

Contracting out

The partners may, of course, contract out of s 42(1), and s 42(2) provides an example of this:

7.59

> Provided that where by the partnership contract an option is given to surviving or continuing partners to purchase the interest of a deceased or outgoing partner, and that option is duly exercised, the estate of the deceased partner, or the outgoing partner or his estate, as the case may be, is not entitled to any further or other share of profits, but if any partner assuming to act in exercise of the option does not in all material respects comply with the terms thereof, he is liable to account under the foregoing provisions of this section.

It will be a question in each case whether the option has been exercised 'in all material respects' and, of course, the fiduciary duties will apply.

Transfer of Outgoing Partner's Share

Where a partnership business continues after the outgoing partner leaves the firm s 43 provides that his or her share will be a debt due to him or her from the other partners with effect from the date of his departure. The section therefore makes it clear that, subject to contrary intention, the obligation to pay the outgoing partner's share is a debt accruing at the date of the dissolution, even though the amount could not be actually ascertained until the accounts etc have been finalized.[198] The importance of it being

7.60

---

[198] See, eg *Purewall v Purewall* [2008] CSOH 147. It is a contractual debt not a trust obligation: *Chiam Heng Hsien v Chiam Heng Chow* [2014] SGHC 119.

regarded as a debt is that the statute of limitations will apply and after six years any claim will be statute-barred.[199]

It is not clear whether s 43 applies only to technical dissolutions or to all dissolutions. It fits slightly uneasily into a general dissolution since the 'debt' will fluctuate according to the affairs of the firm between dissolution and realization of the assets. But in *975 Duncan v The MVF Marigold Pd 145*,[200] Lord Reed, in the Court of Session, thought that, given that the intention of the section was to require the claim to be brought within the limitation period, it should apply to all dissolutions, and it is hard to see why that should not be. After all, even in a technical dissolution, the debt may fluctuate after it accrues, and Lord Reed also decided in that case that just because the debt accrued at the date of dissolution it need not be valued then. Section 42 precluded any such finding.

Another problem is that the section says nothing about how the share is to be transferred to the remaining partners, including transfer of title to any land etc held as partnership property. These matters have to be regulated by agreement between the partners, or failing that by implication from the Act (s 43 could be construed as implying that the debt due from the remaining partners is in return for the outgoing partner's share), or even the fact that it would be inconsistent with the concept of partnership that a former partner could have any share in the firm.

Distribution of Assets—Solvent Partnerships

Need for final accounts

7.61 Once the assets have been valued or realized the final stage in a winding up is to distribute the assets amongst all the partners in accordance with the final account. In the absence of some agreement,[201] the Court of Session said in *Bennett v Wallace*[202] that it is inherent in the nature of a partnership that all assets brought into the partnership should be included in the accounting between the partners, both at the start and at the end of the relationship. That was held, in the case, to include work in progress of a firm of solicitors. Again it must be emphasized that the position will be very different if any question of insolvency, either of the firm or the partners is involved (see Chapter 8).

One of the purposes of the taking of accounts, apart from ascertaining outside debts, is to establish what each partner is entitled to charge against the other partners. This may be amounts brought in or advanced or amounts not brought in or taken out by

---

[199] See, eg *Patel v Patel* [2007] EWCA Civ 1520.
[200] 2006 SLT 975.
[201] See *Lawson v Wenley, Davies, Willis and Cross* [2012] NZHC 204; c/f *Buchanan v Nolan* [2012] CSOH 132.
[202] 1998 SC 457.

others.[203] It may also involve questions as to whether occupation by a surviving partner of a non-partnership asset, following the dissolution of the partnership and before the winding up, requires payment to the former partners as co-owners of the asset.[204] It is also arguable that the licence granted to the partnership by the partners continues until the winding up.[205]

All actions between partners in respect of the discharge of liabilities or the distribution of assets on a winding up, eg where one partner pays all the creditors, are to be resolved by way of this final account. There is no separate action for a contribution or distribution unless accounts have already been taken, an asset unexpectedly arises, or a liability unexpectedly falls due, or where there would be no point in ordering an account. This was the decision of the Court of Appeal in *Marshall v Bullock*[206] where the action for an account was out of time and no alternative claim for contribution was allowed.

It seems that an action for recovery may be brought and no account is needed if a partner has partnership assets in his or her hands and nothing is due to him or her from the firm. If such a liability is clearly established then there would be no point in ordering an account.[207] In Australia, the Federal Court has held that the rule as to the taking of accounts has no application where one partner is seeking to recover money held by another partner as a fiduciary for him. To deny the action would be to promote unjust enrichment.[208]

Remember that it is the final account which also establishes the ultimate rights of the partners in partnership property.[209] The great importance of the final accounts was summed up by Peter Gibson LJ in *Marshall v Bullock*:

> Just as one cannot say what is the entitlement of a partner in respect of a partnership asset without the taking of an account, so one cannot say what is the liability of a partner in respect of a partnership liability discharged by another partner without that account being taken. The authorities show that unless the case is an exceptional one the court will not allow one partner to seek to recover from another partner a sum which is referable to a partnership asset save through an action for an account.[210]

But this does not apply where the action is brought against a partner by his former partners acting in another capacity. Thus in *Hurst v Bennett*,[211] the Court of Appeal allowed an action by four former partners against another former partner for payments made

---

[203] See, eg *Hungerford v Richardson* [2018] NSWSC 1543.
[204] See, eg *Kingsley v Kingsley* [2019] EWHC 1073.
[205] *Kingsley v Kingsley* [2019] EWHC 1073; *Lie v Mohile* [2014] EWHC 3709 at [9].
[206] [1998] EWCA Civ 561. Followed in *Ho Lai Ming v Chu Chik Leung* [2007] HKEC 1721.
[207] See *Holdgate v The Official Assignee* [2002] NZCA 66.
[208] *Momentum Productions Pty Ltd v Scotts* [2009] FCAFC 30.
[209] In the Australian case of *Rojoda Pty Ltd v Commissioners of State Revenue* [2018] WASCA 224, it was held that the partners' interest in the property is fixed once a surplus has been ascertained.
[210] Quoted with approval by Arden LJ in *Hurst v Bennett* [2001] 2 BCLC 290, CA.
[211] [2001] 2 BCLC 290, CA.

by them as trustees of a lease held for the benefit of the firm. There was a clear distinction between the right of a trustee to be indemnified and the right of a partner to be reimbursed for paying more than his share of partnership debts. Only the latter was subject to taking accounts.

Where the existing partnership accounts have been improperly kept, the partner responsible is not entitled to benefit from his failure to keep proper accounts and/ or tax returns. In such cases the courts are entitled to estimate the partnership profits and an adverse inference against the partner in default may well be drawn.[212]

Surplus assets and capital losses

7.62 The rules for distributing the assets where no insolvency is involved are contained in s 44 of the Act. Since all the partners are by definition solvent, the creditors of the firm will be paid in full and the only problems which arise are therefore among the partners themselves. There are in fact two possibilities: (a) where the firm has traded at a profit so that all its capital remains intact and there are surplus assets; (b) where it has traded at a loss so that after paying off the outside creditors part or the whole of the original capital has been lost. In (a) the question is who receives the surplus assets and in (b) who bears the capital loss. Section 44 provides some of the answers:

> In settling accounts between the partners after a dissolution of partnership, the following rules shall, subject to any agreement,[213] be observed:
> (a) Losses, including losses and deficiencies of capital, shall be paid first out of profits, next out of capital, and lastly, if necessary, by the partners individually in the proportion in which they were entitled to share profits;
> (b) The assets of the firm, including the sums, if any, contributed by the partners to make up losses or deficiencies of capital, shall be applied in the following manner and order:
>   1. In paying the debts and liabilities of the firm to persons who are not partners therein;
>   2. In paying to each partner rateably what is due from the firm to him for advances as distinguished from capital;
>   3. In paying to each partner rateably what is due from the firm to him in respect of capital;
>   4. The ultimate residue, if any, shall be divided among the partners in the proportion in which the profits are divisible.

---

[212] *Grays v Haig* (1855) 20 Beav 219; *Tan Liang Chong v Chou Lai Tiang* [2003] 4 SLR 775.
[213] In *Buchanan v Nolan* [2013] CSIH, the court held that where the agreement failed to provide any clear accounting rules in the circumstances which had arisen, s 44 would apply.

Surplus assets

Assuming that all the outside creditors have been paid, paragraph (b) therefore provides that partner/creditors are to be paid next, followed by repayments of capital, and then the surplus is to be divided in the profit-sharing ratio, irrespective of capital contributions. The reasons for divorcing the share of the ultimate residue from the original capital contributions were given in a unanimous judgment by the High Court of Australia in *Rowella Pty Ltd v Abfam Nominees Pty Ltd*[214] in ordering that the residue should be divided in accordance with the profit-sharing ratio in the agreement (40:60) even though the partner entitled to 40 per cent had contributed no capital to the firm:

7.63

> The ultimate residue to which para. (4) relates is the surplus remaining after external creditors have been paid (para. (1)) and the partners have received out of the assets of the partnership a return of the advances they have made and of the capital they contributed (paras (2) and (3)). The ultimate residue therefore does not include the capital of the partnership. Nor is it necessarily derived from the outlay of the capital contributed by the partners.

Since the partnership agreement did not provide any contrary agreement the section was allowed to take its course. The court refused to imply any contrary agreement from the original capital contributions alone.

Capital losses

The position is more complex where there has been a net loss of capital. There is by definition no surplus, and s 44(a) will apply so that, prima facie, the partners are bound to make good those losses in profit-sharing ratio (rather than in proportion to their capital entitlement). To take an example: A contributed £10,000, B £5,000, and C £2,000 into a partnership as capital but they shared profits equally. After paying off the creditors, only £11,000 capital remains so there has been a loss of £6,000 from the £17,000 originally invested. According to s 44(a) this loss must be borne equally, ie in profit-sharing ratio, so that each partner will have to contribute an additional £2,000 into the capital to restore it to its original amount. In effect this means that A will receive £8,000 net, B £3,000 net, and C nothing. In percentage terms, A will have lost 20 per cent of his investment, B 40 per cent, and C 100 per cent. Again, however, this rule can be varied by contrary agreement so that it is open to the partners to agree that losses shall be borne according to capital entitlement—in our example in the ratio 10:5:2 so that the percentage of loss of each partner will be the same.

7.64

Paragraph (a) was further explained by Joyce J in *Garner v Murray*.[215] In that case one of the partners was unable to contribute his share of the capital loss. The judge held that the other partners were not liable to make good his share so that his trustee in bankruptcy could not obtain any further assets in this way. Instead the loss will be borne by

---

[214] (1989) 168 CLR 301, HC.
[215] [1904] 1 Ch 57.

the solvent partners when the final distribution occurs under para (b) of s 44. Section 44(b) proceeds on the basis that capital contributions have been paid, but s 44(a) does not mean that contributions to losses should be equal, only that losses sustained by the firm should be borne equally.

An example should help to explain: A contributed £10,000, B £5,000, and C £2,000 capital into a partnership and they shared profits equally. After paying off the creditors only £8,000 capital remains, giving a loss of £9,000 so that under s 44(a) each partner is liable to contribute £3,000. If all the partners were solvent this would happen as in the example above and C would in fact have to contribute a further £1,000 (ie a 150 per cent loss). But suppose C is insolvent and cannot pay. *Garner v Murray* establishes that A and B need only contribute £3,000 and not £4,500 each, so that the capital available for distribution will be the £8,000 remaining plus the £6,000 contributed by A and B, ie £14,000. This will be distributed under s 44(b) according to capital entitlement.

Nothing in *Garner v Murray* affects outside creditors. A and B, in our example, will have to make good all outside debts in their loss-sharing ratios under the general principle of unlimited liability for partnership debts. The Law Commissions noted that there was a potential problem with the rule in *Garner v Murray* if a partner was already overdrawn on his capital account or became so after deducting his capital contribution. There is no concluded view as to whether that overdrawing should be included as a debt owed to the firm and taken into account as with any other debt or simply ignored. If it is taken into account, how does that fit with the idea that partners need not contribute capital they have not withdrawn?

The costs of the winding up etc rank as a deferred debt so that they will be paid after outside and partner creditors but before repayments of capital and distribution of surplus assets. If one partner owes money to the firm he cannot claim his costs until he has repaid his money. We have already mentioned the payment of a receiver's fees and expenses where the position is slightly different.

8

PARTNERSHIPS AND INSOLVENCY

Possibilities and Problems

In Chapter 7 we dealt with the issues arising when a partnership is dissolved and its assets have to be distributed amongst the partners after allowing for payment of the partnership debts. The position changes totally, however, if those debts exceed the partnership assets, ie if the firm is insolvent. The question then is not how much the partners will receive but rather how much the creditors will be paid in respect of their debts. The mechanisms used to answer that question are somewhat complex because of the various possibilities which may lead to the insolvency. As we have seen, partners are jointly liable for all debts of the firm, so that it is possible for the firm to be insolvent with respect to its own assets but for the partners, individually or collectively, to be able to make up the difference out of their own pockets. In that case the firm may be initially insolvent but the partners will remain solvent. **8.01**

The solvent partner(s) are then liable for the debts of the firm, but that claim may be lost if there is undue delay causing substantial and significant prejudice to the partner. That was the decision in *Mortgage Trust Ltd v Wilmett Solicitors*,[1] where the insolvency was caused by the substantial fraud of a partner and the partnership creditor had delayed bring an action.

Alternatively one partner may be insolvent in respect of his own private debts vis-à-vis his own assets. His private creditors will then wish to realize his share of the partnership assets in order to pay those debts. In such a case the other partners may be able to replace those assets out of their own resources and so there will be a bankrupt partner but the firm will remain solvent.

It is equally possible, however, for the bankruptcy of one partner to push the firm over the brink into insolvency, ie where the other partners cannot make up the loss of his interest in the partnership to the private creditors. This will certainly be the case where all the partners are insolvent. Alternatively the insolvency of the firm may cause a consequent bankruptcy of one or more of the partners who cannot meet their partnership liabilities.

In summary therefore, it is possible to have a bankrupt partner or partners with or without an insolvent partnership and to have an insolvent partnership with or without

---

[1] [2018] EWHC 488.

a bankrupt partner or partners. It is important to realize that in all these cases it is necessary to distinguish between partnership creditors (ie those whose debts are against the firm) and the separate private creditors of the individual partners, and between the assets of the firm and those of the partners (hence the need to identify partnership property as we saw in Chapter 6). In insolvency law parlance these are known respectively as the joint creditors, separate creditors, the joint estate, and the separate estates.

Applicable insolvency law

8.02 The different mechanisms under English law to deal with all these variations are to be found in the Insolvency Act 1986 which, by consolidating the Insolvency Act 1985 as well as other previous Acts, effectively changed the whole law on both personal and corporate insolvency. For partnerships, the law is contained in a series of statutory instruments. Selected provisions of that Act were applied to partnerships and partners initially by the Insolvent Partnerships Order 1986.[2] That Order was almost incomprehensible since it simply provided a list of amendments to the Act. In *Re Marr*,[3] Nicholls LJ spoke of the partners becoming 'enmeshed in the intricacies of the legislation relating to the winding up of insolvent partnerships'. As a result the government had a second go at the problem in the Insolvent Partnerships Order 1994,[4] which has replaced the 1986 version. This is somewhat more user-friendly in that it sets out (often in full) the amended sections of the Insolvency Act which now apply and deals with each of the possible reasons for the insolvency or insolvencies in turn. It also made some technical amendments to the 1986 rules, including one major change in the rights of the two types of creditor as against each other.

In addition it extended the concepts of a voluntary arrangement and an administration order, available to companies since 1986, to insolvent partnerships. These are intended as alternatives to a winding up of an insolvent firm in an attempt to allow the business to continue. It also applied several of the provisions of the Company Directors Disqualification Act 1986 to partners of an insolvent partnership (see below). Minor amendments to the 1994 Order were made by the Insolvent Partnerships (Amendment) Order 1996, and the Small Business, Enterprise and Employment Act 2015 (Consequential Amendments, Savings and Transitional Provisions) Regulations 2019.[5]

More substantial amendments, reflecting in the main changes made to the Company Directors Disqualification Act 1986 by the Insolvency Act 2000, were made by the Insolvent Partnerships (Amendment) Order 2001.[6] Changes made by the introduction of the EC Regulation on cross-border insolvency proceedings[7] were introduced by

---
[2] SI 1986/2142.
[3] [1990] Ch 773, CA.
[4] SI 1994/2421.
[5] SI 1996/1308; SI 2019/1058.
[6] SI 2001/767.
[7] Regulation 1346/2000 [2000] OJ L160/1.

the Insolvent Partnerships (Amendment) Order 2002.[8] That topic is beyond the scope of this book.[9] Major changes to the voluntary arrangement procedure brought about by the Insolvency Act 2000 were applied to partnerships by the Insolvent Partnerships (Amendment) (No 2) Order 2002.[10] But the major changes to the administration procedure for companies made by the Enterprise Act 2002 were not applied to partnerships until 2005 by the Insolvent Partnerships (Amendment) Order 2005.[11] There were a number of errors in the 2005 Order which were corrected by the Insolvent Partnerships (Amendment) Order 2006.[12]

Further amendments to the 1994 order were made following the changes to the Company Directors Disqualification Act and the Insolvency Act by Parts 9 and 10 of the Small Business Enterprise and Employment Act 2015 and Sch 6 to the Deregulation Act 2015. These amendments were made by the Deregulation and Small Business Enterprise and Employment Act (Consequential Amendments) (Savings) Regulations 2017[13] and the Insolvency (Miscellaneous Amendments) Regulations 2017.[14]

The resulting legislative framework governing the complex subject of partnership insolvency therefore simply adds to that complexity. In *Official Receiver v Hollens*,[15] Blackburne J commented that:

> the interrelationship of the IPO [Insolvent Partnerships Order 1994] and the 1986 Act is very far from straightforward even for those familiar with insolvency law and practice. Understanding how the scheme works is not assisted by its mode of presentation, namely a series of articles each applying and, by reference to separate schedules, modifying various provisions of the 1986 Act. The process of understanding is made more difficult by the fact that some of the articles provide for modifications to the 1986 Act by reference to modifications introduced by other articles so that it requires much cross-referencing and, at a practical level, much thumbing through the pages of the IPO to establish just what the schedule of modifications is which is to apply to the particular insolvency proceedings.

It was no wonder that the unrepresented bankrupt partners in that case were mystified by most of the proceedings. The law here is far from accessible. The bankrupt partners were a shade luckier in *Henry Butcher International Ltd v KG Engineering*,[16] where the Court of Appeal allowed an adjournment for them to obtain legal representation.

---

[8] SI 2002/1308.
[9] In essence it allows a liquidator appointed in proceedings covered by the Regulation to bring a petition against a partnership.
[10] SI 2002/2708.
[11] SI 2005/1516.
[12] SI 2006/622.
[13] SI 2017/540.
[14] SI 2017/1119.
[15] [2007] EWHC 753 (Ch).
[16] [2004] EWCA Civ 1597.

Partnership and partner insolvencies

8.03 The major change to partnership insolvency, introduced in 1986, remains, however, the same. The partnership itself, as distinct from the partners, is, in general, to be wound up as an unregistered company under Part V of the 1986 Act by the Companies Court rather than by reference to the personal insolvency provisions. (The converse applies in Scotland, see *Smith*.[17])

A partnership is, however, only to be treated as an unregistered company for the purposes of the winding up under Part V of the Insolvency Act. It is not an unregistered company for other purposes, so that where following the winding up of a partnership, the partners wished to form a company using a similar name, it was not subject to s 216 of the Insolvency Act which prohibits companies from re-using the same name following an insolvent winding up.[18]

Further, where the insolvency applies both to the firm and at least one partner, the petitions are to be dealt with in tandem in that court. In addition, the 1994 Order applies the concepts of voluntary arrangements and administration to partnerships. These alternatives (though sometimes a preamble) to full-blown insolvency proceedings are covered at the end of this chapter.

Since the 1994 Order runs to over 138 pages, several of which, as we have seen, have now been amended, and also refers to many other parts of the, much amended, Insolvency Act 1986, this chapter can do no more than attempt a summary of the procedures available on an insolvency, either of the firm or the partners, including the question of the priority of creditors. The detailed rules of procedure, discharge, and challenges to transactions etc, must be found in the specialist books on insolvency. Nothing more will be said of the case where although one partner is insolvent there is no effect on the firm's solvency since partnership is not then a specific issue in that partner's personal bankruptcy.

Bankrupt partner but no petition against the firm

8.04 The position is more complex, however, when one partner is made bankrupt as a result of inability to pay a partnership debt which may well make the partnership insolvent, but where for some reason there is no concurrent attempt to wind up the partnership.

This was the situation in *Schooler v Customs & Excise Commissioners*.[19] Mr and Mrs Schooler had been partners in a business which owed over £91,000 in unpaid VAT. The VAT authorities served statutory demands on both the partners for that amount. (Failure to pay such a demand normally leads to a bankruptcy petition.) Mr Schooler

---

[17] 1999 SLT (Sh Ct) 5.
[18] *Re Newtons Coaches Ltd* [2016] EWHC 3068.
[19] [1995] 2 BCLC 610, CA.

successfully negotiated an individual voluntary arrangement under the Insolvency Act 1986 in respect of his debts, including of course his liability for the VAT. The effect of that was to avoid his bankruptcy. Mrs Schooler failed to negotiate one in respect of her debts and so, having failed to pay, a bankruptcy order was made against her. She appealed to the Court of Appeal on the basis that no such order could be made against her without a concurrent petition to wind up the firm since both partners were jointly liable for the VAT debt.

The Court of Appeal dismissed this claim, principally because the 1986 Order, which applied to this case, expressly said that all partnership debts were also individual debts of each partner for the purposes of bringing a bankruptcy petition against a partner. The 1994 Order has no such provision but the Court of Appeal considered that the position would be the same because a partnership debt was clearly a 'debt owed by' a partner under s 267(1) of the 1986 Act and sufficient therefore to found a bankruptcy petition against each partner individually if unpaid, even though the others would be equally liable. The fact that Mr Schooler had entered into a voluntary arrangement was irrelevant—one partner so doing could not protect the other partners against liability for partnership debts. Otherwise the creditors would not be able to recover the money from even the solvent partners. Whilst this case may seem harsh it is no more than a natural extension of the principle of joint liability—a creditor may recover the debt from any of the partners.

We will now concentrate on those cases where a partnership is wound up as insolvent before looking at the alternatives of voluntary arrangements and administration orders as applied to partnerships.

The jurisdiction to wind up an insolvent partnership arises if it has in England and Wales either a principal place of business or a place of business at which business is or has been carried on in the course of which the debt arose which forms the basis of the petition. This does not apply if the business of the firm has not been carried on within the jurisdiction in the three years ending with the date of the petition.[20] In *Javelin Wholesale Ltd v Waypharm Limited Partnership*,[21] jurisdiction was taken in respect of a limited partnership (for which the rules are the same) on the basis that the address where the limited partnership chose to receive important documents[22] and where it was registered for VAT was in England, even though it did not trade in the jurisdiction. The fact that the debt had not been paid meant that the business transaction had not been completed so that it was carrying on business here.

---

[20] Section 221 of the Insolvency Act 1986 as modified by the 1994 Order.
[21] 22 May 2014, Case No 6563 of 2013 (Ch).
[22] An LP has to register a principal place of business. A partnership does not, but there must be an address for service and a VAT address.

Winding Up of an Insolvent Partnership Only

8.05 A partnership may be wound up as an unregistered company without bringing a concurrent petition against any partner under either art 7 or art 9 of the 1994 Order. Article 7, as amended by the 1996 Amendment Order, allows a petition to be brought by a creditor, an insolvency practitioner (a liquidator, administrator, temporary administrator, or bankruptcy trustee), the Secretary of State, or any other person other than a partner. This last category will include, eg the Financial Services Authority exercising its statutory functions. Article 9 only allows a petition to be brought by a partner or otherwise with leave of the court if there are eight or more partners. Such petitions can be brought on one of five grounds: (a) that the partnership has ceased to carry on business; (b) that it is unable to pay its debts; (c) that it is just and equitable to do so; (d) that a moratorium allowed prior to a partnership voluntary arrangement has ended and no such voluntary arrangement has been effected; or (e) if the firm has already been dissolved.[23] Only the second relates to insolvency as such; the others are useful to a partner if the unregistered companies procedure is preferred to a winding up as described in Chapter 7 or the Secretary of State wishes to act. The general definition of being unable to pay one's debts in the 1986 Act applies here. Detailed rules are provided by Schs 3 and 5 to the 1994 Order. Since there is no bankruptcy of a partner involved there is no need for special rules about the priority of the different sets of creditors.

In practice it seems that this procedure will be used only when, for a variety of reasons, a partner or creditor etc wishes to end (or threaten the end of) the partnership and there are really no problems about payment of the firm's debts at the end of the day. In particular it can be used by the Secretary of State to implement the disqualification provisions of the Company Directors Disqualification Act 1986 in relation to a partner (see below). It will not be used by a creditor where there is any doubt about the partners' ability to cover the firm's debts, following the decision in *Investment and Pensions Advisory Service Ltd v Gray*[24] that the private assets of a partner, as distinct from the partnership assets, will not be available unless the insolvency procedures have been applied to that partner.

Winding Up of an Insolvent Partnership and Concurrent Bankruptcy of the Partners

8.06 The most likely situation to arise in the insolvency of a partnership is that one or more of the partners will also be insolvent, whichever first triggers the other. Accordingly arts 8 and 10 of the 1994 Order allow either a member or a creditor to bring concurrent

---

[23] As introduced by the 2002 (No 2) Amendment Order. See below.
[24] [1990] BCLC 38.

WINDING UP OF AN INSOLVENT PARTNERSHIP & PARTNERS' BANKRUPTCY 287

petitions to wind up the partnership as an unregistered company and to bankrupt one or more of the partners. In both cases the partnership may be so wound up only if it is unable to pay its debts as defined in the 1986 Act or if after the moratorium allowed prior to a partnership voluntary arrangement has ended no such voluntary arrangement has been effected.[25] The relevant provisions of the 1986 Act are applied by Schs 4 and 6 to the Order. Many of the detailed rules apply so as to ensure that the two procedures are harmonized as much as possible. Thus the petitions are to be presented to the same court and on the same day. The partnership petition is to be heard first and the court is given wide powers to avoid difficulties arising from the two procedures.

Priority of creditors

As we have seen, the winding up of a partnership and the bankruptcy of the partners will involve two sets of creditors—the joint creditors of the firm and the separate or private creditors of each partner. Similarly there will be two available funds from which to pay them—the joint and separate estates.[26] It is clearly important therefore to decide the priority of the claims of these creditors in respect of each available fund. Even within each set of creditors there is priority for claims by employees for unpaid wages. These are the only preferred creditors after the various tax authorities were removed from the list in 2003. Other creditors may be secured creditors, eg a bank with a mortgage over property, who can realize their security in priority to all other creditors. Yet others will be deferred creditors, eg persons who have lent money to the firm under s 2(3)(d) or (e) of the Partnership Act 1890 and whose debts are postponed by s 3 of that Act (see Chapter 2). **8.07**

The rules for priority between joint and separate creditors were amended by the 1994 Order. The basic rule remains that the joint estate is primarily available for the joint creditors and the separate estates for the separate creditors and that if either is insufficient to meet the needs of their respective creditors, the unmet claims will then be transferred against the other. In a major change, however, if the joint creditors remain unpaid in full out of the joint estate, their claims for the unpaid balance will be apportioned amongst the several estates and they will then rank equally in respect of such claims with the ordinary separate creditors against those estates. There is no such provision with regard to unpaid separate creditors who must take after the joint creditors in respect of the joint estate.

In other words the joint creditors have first go at the joint estate and an equal go against the separate estates with the separate creditors, except for the preferred separate creditors who will continue to get first go at the separate estates. The ordinary separate

---

[25] See n 23 above.
[26] This distinction can be traced back at least to 1682: *Craven v Knight* (1682) 2 Rep in Ch 226. The rule was clear by 1715: *Ex p Crowder*, 2 Vern 706.

creditors will only therefore have an equal go at the separate estates with the joint creditors (for their unsatisfied joint debts) and last go at the joint estate if they cannot be met in full out of the separate estates. If this seems harsh the reality is that the joint creditors usually fare worse since partners have greater private assets than the joint assets so that equal treatment, as before 1994, would favour the separate creditors.

Sometimes the position is more complex, for example where a partnership creditor has securities over both the partnership assets and the assets of individual partners for repayment of the debt. In *Mc Clean v Chadwick*,[27] there were two secured creditors. One was the bank who had charges over both the partnership assets and individual assets owned by the insolvent partners. The other secured creditor only had a charge over the individual assets. The bank chose to enforce the charge against the individual assets to recover its debt, so exhausting the funds there available for the second creditor. The judge held that the doctrine of marshalling debts applied so that the bank should be taken in equity to have taken its money from the partnership assets, thus freeing up the individual assets for the second creditor. The judge also rejected an argument from the trustees in bankruptcy that this prejudiced the individual creditors since individual assets were then being used to pay partnership debts. Those assets were always available to pay partnership debts.

Disqualification from management of a company or LLP

8.08 Following the winding up of an insolvent partnership, with or without any concurrent bankruptcies of the partners, art 16 of the 1994 Order (as amended) applies certain provisions of the Company Directors Disqualification Act 1986, in some cases as modified by Sch 8 to that Order, as amended. In essence this allows the Secretary of State[28] to petition the court if the conduct of an officer of an insolvent partnership is such as to make him unfit to be concerned in the management of a company. A petition may also be brought against a person who has had significant influence over a disqualified officer. The Act itself applies to directors of insolvent companies and members of limited liability partnerships (LLPs) (applied by the LLP Regulations 2001). An officer of the partnership for this purpose is any partner or anyone who has been concerned with the management of the firm. If the court is satisfied that unfitness has been shown it must disqualify the officer from being involved in the management of a company or an LLP (but not a partnership) for at least two years. This provision will be useful to the Secretary of State where, eg a director of a solvent company (and so outside the Act) has been involved in an insolvent partnership of which his company was a partner. The intention is to prevent abuse of the limited liability provisions of the corporate form. Alternatively the Secretary of State is able to accept undertakings from a

---

[27] [2016] EWHC 2650 (Ch).
[28] Following a report by the liquidator or administrator.

partner or a person having significant influence over a partner equivalent to the effect of a disqualification order without taking legal proceedings. The effect of such an undertaking is the same as an actual order. In either case, a person acting in breach commits a criminal offence, and becomes personally liable for the debts of the company or LLP concerned. An application for an exception to an order or undertaking can be made to the court.

In addition, the court has power to make a compensation order against a disqualified partner if the conduct has caused loss to one of more of the creditors.

There has been a plethora of litigation over this Act with regard to directors of companies. What exactly does 'unfit' mean in any particular case, how long should the period of disqualification be etc, and reference should be made to books on company law for some guidance on these matters. The 1986 Act itself provides guidance as to the matters to be taken into account. As a general rule the courts have divided the cases into those involving non-fraudulent conduct and those involving fraud or breach of fiduciary duty, with the latter being given disqualification periods of between six and ten years and the former rather less than that. Their general attitude has, however, been mixed to say the least. Reference should be made to company law texts for the details.

Obviously the courts will consider the principles devised to deal with company directors in relation to partners. The analogy may not always be straightforward, however. For example, it has been held that a director can be disqualified simply for non-activity in relation to an insolvent company, on the basis that the director has lent his or her name to the company. In partnership law, inactive partners are not unknown, although they should be disclosed under the business names legislation. Such questions as these remain to be settled.

Joint Bankruptcy Petitions

Article 11 of the 1994 Order provides the partners with an alternative method of winding up an insolvent partnership under the bankruptcy rather than the company regime, where all the partners are also bankrupt. In such a case a joint bankruptcy petition may be presented by all the partners of an insolvent partnership. In such a case the personal bankruptcy provisions of the Insolvency Act 1986, as modified by Sch 7 to the Order, will apply and the partnership estate will be dealt with as part of the procedure for dealing with the separate estates. It is envisaged that a single trustee in bankruptcy will be appointed to administer all the estates involved. If he subsequently finds that there is a conflict of interest between his functions as trustee of the separate estates and as trustee of the joint estate he may apply to the court for directions. **8.09**

The rules as to the priority of debts between the joint and separate creditors are the same as those applicable to the situation where the partnership is being wound up

290   PARTNERSHIPS AND INSOLVENCY

as an unregistered company and there are concurrent petitions against the partners, described above.

Winding Up a Partnership after Separate Bankruptcy Petitions

8.10   If there is no petition to wind up the partnership as an unregistered company and the partners themselves do not bring a joint petition under art 11, what is the position vis-à-vis the partnership assets if the partners simply present individual bankruptcy petitions? That was the problem facing the Official Receiver in *Official Receiver v Hollens*.[29] Both partners were hopelessly insolvent, but the partnership had one asset, a van. No creditor appears to have been willing to bring a petition and the partners wished to keep the van (which would have been an excepted trade asset on an individual bankruptcy, but not on a partnership insolvency).

The Official Receiver successfully argued that the solution was for the court to exercise its discretion under the modified s 303 of the 1986 Act.[30] That section applies if in individual bankruptcy proceedings the court's 'attention is drawn' to the fact that the bankrupt is a partner. It may then make an order for the future conduct of the proceedings, give directions, and modify any provisions of the 1994 Order. The judge agreed that this section could and should apply in the case and ordered that the proceedings should continue as if the partners had brought a joint petition under art 11.[31] The pre-requisites for such an order were that the partnership in question must be insolvent (unable to pay its debts) and the order must be one which could have been made on an art 11 petition.

Partnership Voluntary Arrangements

8.11   Article 4 of the 1994 Order, as substituted by the 2002 (No 2) Amendment Order, applies Part I and Sch A1 of the 1986 Insolvency Act, as adapted by the substituted Sch 1 to the Order, to partnerships, allowing for partnership voluntary arrangements (PVAs) with creditors. The 2002 amendments reflect the changes to the Insolvency Act 1986 by the Insolvency Act 2000.[32] The procedure is in addition to voluntary arrangements which may be made in respect of an insolvent corporate partner or of a bankrupt partner in respect of their own assets and creditors under the 1986 Act provisions (art

---

[29] [2007] EWHC 753 (Ch).
[30] As applied by art 14(2) of the 1994 Order.
[31] Thus the van was lost. The perils of trading as a partnership and not as a sole trader.
[32] There may be slight amendments made in due course as a result of the Small Business, Enterprise and Employment Act 2015.

5 of the 1994 Order) as happened in *Schooler v Customs & Excise Commissioners*,[33] referred to earlier.

Effect of a partnership voluntary arrangement

The effect of a PVA is to enable an insolvent or potentially insolvent partnership to come to a legally binding arrangement with its creditors. If the procedure is followed it will bind even those creditors who have not agreed to it. Such an arrangement can be proposed by the members of the firm but only by the liquidator of the firm, if the firm is being wound up as an unregistered company, by the administrator if the firm is in administration (see below), or by the trustee if there is a joint bankruptcy petition by all the partners under art 11 of the 1994 Order. Thus the procedure can be used either before or after one of the insolvency orders has been made. **8.12**

The essence of the procedure is that a nominee must be appointed to implement the scheme who will either be the insolvency practitioner already involved in the insolvency or a qualified insolvency practitioner. Meetings of the partners and creditors must approve the scheme,[34] which cannot affect the rights of secured or preferred creditors without their consent. Where there is a dispute between the partners' meeting and that of the creditors, the latter is to prevail but any partner may apply to the court which may make any order it thinks fit. If the voluntary arrangement is approved, it binds all the creditors who were entitled to vote at the meeting or who would have been so entitled if they had had notice of it. An approved scheme can be challenged by a partner, any creditor bound by it, the nominee, or any liquidator, administrator, or trustee within twenty-eight days[35] on the grounds that the interests of a partner or creditor have been unfairly prejudiced or that there has been a material irregularity in the procedure.

An unopposed scheme will then be put into effect, with the nominee now being known as the supervisor. The hope is that the creditors will eventually be paid under the terms of the scheme and that the business will be able to continue. It is a criminal offence to make a false statement or to commit any fraudulent act or omission for the purpose of obtaining the approval of a voluntary arrangement.

Obtaining a temporary moratorium for 'smaller' partnerships

One of the perceived weaknesses of a voluntary arrangement was that, whilst all the creditors were bound after it was agreed, there was nothing to stop any creditor, prior **8.13**

---

[33] [1995] 2 BCLC 610, CA. See also *Golstein v Barnes* [2016] EWHC 2187 (Ch).
[34] The creditors must approve it by at least 75 per cent by value.
[35] If a creditor did not receive notice of the meeting, the twenty-eight-day period runs from when he or she became aware that the meeting had taken place.

to that, from pursuing a wrecking alternative remedy, such as petitioning for a winding up. The Insolvency Act 2000 sought to remedy this situation for 'smaller' companies and those changes were applied to PVAs by the 2002 Amendment (No 2) Order.[36] The idea is to allow a breathing space during which the PVA proposals can be put to the creditors. Under the alternative new provisions the partners can take steps to obtain a moratorium for a 'smaller' insolvent partnership: ie if its turnover is no more than £5.6 million, it has assets of not more than £2.8 million, and no more than fifty employees.[37]

To obtain a moratorium, the partners must submit their proposals for a PVA to the nominee and if his reply is favourable[38] and the PVA meetings called, then they can file the proposals and the nominee's reply with the court. The moratorium comes into effect on the date when those documents are filed with the court. It ends on the earlier of twenty-eight days or the holding of the PVA meetings.[39] The partners continue to manage the business although there are complex rules as to disposals of assets, especially those subject to a charge or other security, and the nominee is under a duty to monitor the partners, especially as to availability of funds. The effect of the moratorium is to prevent or stay any winding-up petition or order; any administration application; the enforcement of any security; the appointment of an agricultural receiver; any legal proceedings against the firm; any order under art 11 of the 1994 Order (joint bankruptcy petition); or any court order under s 35 of the 1890 Act for the dissolution of the firm.

After the meetings have been held, the PVA continues in much the same way as if no moratorium had been in existence. The publicity and complexity of these rules have made such PVAs uncommon. In addition the administration procedure is now more streamlined.

Partnership Administration Orders

8.14 Administration orders were introduced for companies in 1985 to provide an alternative to liquidation either as a form of company rescue by providing it with a breathing space from its creditors or for the better realization of its assets. The use of the procedure for companies proved to be, however, very low[40] and the process was recast by the Enterprise Act 2002 which substituted its Sch B1 for the 'old' Part II of the Insolvency

---

[36] By substituting, with some modifications, the amended Part 1 and Sch 1A of the Insolvency Act 1986 into the 1994 Order.
[37] This cannot happen if the partnership is already in administration, winding up, or a PVA, or subject to an agricultural receiver. Nor is it allowed if there has been an abortive PVA in the past year, or an order under art 11 of the 1994 Order (joint bankruptcy petitions) has been made.
[38] That the PVA has a reasonable chance of success and the firm enough funds to survive until then.
[39] The moratorium can be extended by a further two months if both meetings agree.
[40] This was mainly due to the ability of a floating-charge holder to block the procedure. That is not generally an issue for partnerships.

Act 1986. The 1985 version was applied to insolvent partnerships by art 6 of the 1994 Order. The 2002 version was, somewhat belatedly, introduced as a replacement by the Insolvent Partnerships (Amendment) Order 2005 with effect from 1 July 2005.[41] Thus Sch B1 of the 2002 Act (as amended) now applies to insolvent partnerships as modified by the 2005 Order.

Purpose of the administration

The administrator of a partnership must perform his functions with the objective of: (a) rescuing the partnership as a going concern; or (b) achieving a better result for the partnership's creditors as a whole than would be likely if the firm were wound up; or (c) realizing property in order to make a distribution to one or more secured or preferential creditors.[42] Those functions are in strict order of priority so that only if the first is not possible can the other two be contemplated, and then in that order. Thus the concept of partnership rescue is paramount, at least in theory. There are now three ways in which an administrator may be appointed.[43] One is by the holder of what is known as an agricultural floating charge. That is the only floating charge available against a firm. As such it is rather esoteric and the reader is referred to paras 14 to 21 of the Schedule as modified by the 2005 Order for the details. The other two procedures are by way of application to the court or an appointment by the partners themselves.

8.15

Appointment by application to the court

The court may only make an order if it is satisfied that the partnership is unable to pay its debts and that the order is reasonably likely to achieve the purpose of the administration.

8.16

An application for an administration order can be made by the partners or any or all of the partnership creditors. Bankrupt partners cannot make an application.[44] The applicant may apply for a specific person to be appointed administrator but the partners may nominate an alternative candidate. The court must then decide. That was the situation in *Northern Bank Ltd v Taylor*.[45] In the event the judge appointed the applicant's nominee as the bank was the principal (only) creditor of the partnership whereas the partners' nominee, having been unsuccessful in negotiating PVAs for the partners, might

---

[41] SI 2005/1516. The 'old' procedure applies to petitions brought before that date.
[42] Para 3 of Sch B1.
[43] Formerly only a court could appoint an administrator. An administrator may not be appointed if the firm is subject to a winding-up order unless the liquidator applies to the court. An administrator must be a qualified insolvency practitioner (see s 390 of the Insolvency Act 1986).
[44] But they may make representations that the application is not brought by the partnership: *Patley Wood Farm LLP v Brake* [2016] EWHC 1688 (Ch).
[45] [2014] NICh 9.

appear to be biased even though she clearly was not. There was a similar dispute in *National Westminster Bank plc v Msaada*,[46] where the court chose the bank's nominee over that of the partners on the basis that his proposals (orderly realization of the assets) had far more chance of success than those of the partners' nominee (slimming down the business and then carrying on) and had far more resources at his disposal. In *Patley Wood Farm LLP v Brake Group*,[47] the judge refused to appoint one of the trustees in bankruptcy of a partner as the administrator of the partnership on the grounds of the potential conflict of interest.

Whilst the court is considering the application there is an interim moratorium, similar to that which can be applied for in a PVA. Thus no winding-up order or joint bankruptcy order can be made, although a petition can be presented. The partnership is also free from any other actions by creditors to enforce their debts without the court's consent including any action for forfeiture by peaceable re-entry by a landlord for non-payment of rent or breach of any other condition. Because of these consequences the courts will strike out a petition which has not been properly presented. In *Re West Park Golf & Country Club*,[48] a petition was struck out where the partners presenting the petition had failed to disclose in their supporting affidavit the fact that there was a substantial secured creditor, the bank, which had not been consulted. The petition had been presented for the sole purpose of frustrating the bank in realizing its security.

Exercise of the court's discretion

8.17 As we have seen, the court, in making an administration order, must be satisfied that it will be likely to achieve the purpose of the administration. Frequently the administration is said to offer a better result than a liquidation for creditors. In *Patley Wood Farm LLP v Brake*,[49] this was said to mean that the prospect of a better result was real, not that it was a probability. In that case the administration was held to give a real chance of achieving a higher price for the assets that could be sold off, the likelihood of VAT recovery, and the saving of fees.

The court always has a discretion. To take two examples involving partnerships. The first is *Re Greek Taverna*.[50] The partnership in question had been formed in 1992 between Mr Harper and Mr Cotsicoros. Those two gentlemen had now fallen out to such an extent that they would not speak to each other and each ran the business on his own for part of the week. The two never met to discuss anything. The firm was overdrawn as to £17,000 with the bank and also owed Mrs Harper £8,000. Mrs Harper was in fact the petitioner for an administration order. The partnership was also in arrears in respect of its rent. The petition proposed that a Mr Rout, an insolvency practitioner, be appointed as administrator.

---

[46] [2011] EWHC 3423 (Ch); [2012] BCC 226.
[47] [2016] EWHC 1688 (Ch).
[48] [1997] 1 BCLC 20.
[49] [2016] EWHC 1688 (Ch).
[50] [1999] BCC 153.

As is required, Mr Rout had drawn up a report. That report indicated that the partnership was insolvent and that if it were wound up, with a forced sale of the business, it would produce a deficit of £68,000, ignoring the costs of the winding up. If an administration order were to be made, however, the business could be sold as a going concern which would produce an estimated surplus of £3,000. Further there would be an estimated profit of £9,000 if the business were continued for six weeks before sale. The petition was opposed by Mr Cotsicoros. That opposition was dismissed by the judge, however, on the basis that the only alternatives were either an insolvent winding up or an administration order, given the inability of the partners to come to any sensible arrangement, and that Mr Cotsicoros seemed incapable of accepting that things could not go on as they were. Nor did Mr Cotsicoros have any acceptable alternative (he was interested in buying the business but had not come up with any satisfactory offer).

In making the order sought, the judge came to the following conclusion:

> It does seem to me on the evidence that the alternative to an administration order is an imminent winding up of the partnership as an insolvent partnership. I am satisfied that there are grounds for the view expressed by Mr Rout to the effect that such a winding up would produce a far worse position for the creditors than is likely to be produced by the sale of the business as a going concern by an administrator. It seems to me that the evidence does establish that the making of an administration order will be likely to result in a more advantageous realisation of the partnership property than would be effected in the winding up and, indeed, may well result in the approval of a voluntary arrangement with the company's creditors.

In *Re DKLL Solicitors*,[51] a firm of solicitors was hopelessly insolvent. In particular it owed £1.7 million to HMRC and some £2 million to unsecured creditors. The partners applied for an administration order so that the administrator could immediately sell the business as a going concern for £400,000. That is known as a 'pre-pack' sale. HM Revenue & Customs opposed the application on the basis that such a deal would effectively disenfranchise the major creditor without any creditors' meeting taking place. But the judge allowed the application to proceed. A forced sale of the business would only realize some £105,000 and add some £44,000 worth of preferential claims from the employees. Not only would the administration achieve its purpose, but in its discretion the court would allow it to proceed. It would benefit the unsecured creditors, save the jobs of the employees, and cause minimum disruption to the firm's clients. The majority creditor did not have a veto in administration proceedings.

---

[51] [2008] 1 BCLC 112.

Appointment by the partners

8.18 The members[52] of an insolvent partnership may appoint an administrator unless one has already been appointed and that earlier appointment ceased within the last twelve months: paras 22 and 23 of the Schedule. Nor can such an appointment be made if there is a current winding-up petition against the firm. Five days' written notice of the proposal must be given to the holder of any agricultural floating charge, after which the partners have ten days in which to appoint an administrator. Notice of the appointment and its details must be filed with the court which triggers the interim moratorium. This includes a statutory declaration that the administrator consents to the appointment and that, in his opinion, the purpose of the administration is likely to be achieved. The appointment takes effect on that filing. The court may order the partners to indemnify any person who has suffered loss if the appointment turns out to be invalid: paras 29 to 34 of the Schedule.

Consequences of an order

8.19 If the court does make an administration order then there are profound consequences to enable the administrator to run the partnership in order to carry out the purposes of the administration. These are found in paras 42 and 43 of the modified Schedule:

(a) any existing winding-up or joint bankruptcy petition will be dismissed and none may be brought;[53]

(b) any agricultural receiver must vacate office and none can be appointed;

(c) no order for the dissolution of the partnership under s 35 of the Partnership Act 1890 can be made;

(d) no steps may be taken against the firm's assets or to repossess any goods without the consent of the administrator or the court;

(e) no landlord may exercise any right of forfeiture by peaceful re-entry for non-payment of rent or breach of any other condition, without the consent of the administrator or the court;

(f) no legal process may be instituted or continued (including enforcement) against the firm without such consent;[54]

(g) all business documents must state the name of the administrator and that he is managing the firm's affairs; and

(h) suppliers of utilities cannot make payment of pre-administration debts a precondition of further supplies.

---

[52] A majority will not suffice—para 105 of the Schedule which allows for appointment by a majority of the board of a company has not been applied to partnerships: *Patley Wood Farm LLP v Brake* [2016] EWHC 1688 (Ch).

[53] Except in the public interest or under s 367 of the Financial Services and Markets Act 2000.

[54] Such consent may be retrospective: *Fulton v AIB Group (UK) plc* [2014] NICh 8. Exceptionally, the court may allow a second creditor to enforce the security: *Promontoria (Chestnut) Ltd v Craig* [2017] EWHC 2405 (Ch).

The administrator has complete control of the firm's affairs and property, and is charged with carrying out the purpose(s) of the order. He has very wide powers and duties to this effect. He is the agent of the firm and his powers supersede those of the partners or partnership managers. He can even sell any partnership property free of any charge on it, although the chargee retains his priority as to the proceeds of the sale. He must initially draw up a statement of affairs of the firm, ie of its assets and liabilities, and must then formulate a plan to achieve the purpose(s) of the order. This must be approved by a meeting of the partnership creditors, with or without agreed modifications. A dissenting creditor has the right to apply to the court on the basis of unfair harm but he cannot sue the administrator for breach of duty except by way of a misfeasance summons under s 212 of the Insolvency Act 1986.[55]

Subject to that, the administrator then proceeds to carry out the plan, after which he will vacate office and the administration will end. If the plan does not work out then he can apply to the court to be removed and a winding up will almost inevitably follow. The details can be found in company law texts—there are no specific partnership issues.

Flexibility of administration

An example of the possibilities raised by the application of administration orders to partnerships is the case of *Oldham v Kyrris*.[56] The Kyrris family were partners in respect of several restaurants run on franchise agreements with Burger King and in premises sub-let from that well-known company. Two of the Kyrris family were named in the leases. In 1996 the firm stopped paying Burger King royalties due under the franchise agreements and rent due under the sub-leases. Burger King brought an action against the two named partners for arrears of £1.63 million rent and £630,000 royalties. Those two partners counterclaimed against Burger King on various matters. In April 1997 the Royal Bank of Scotland successfully presented a petition for an administration order against the firm in respect of debts of £2.85 million. This was on the basis that it would be a better way of realizing the assets than a winding up.

8.20

The administrators concluded that if the business was sold as a going concern it would raise £6 million and so pay off all the creditors. But to do that they needed the consent of Burger King who could end the sub-leases and the franchise agreements, thus destroying at one stroke the value of the partnership business. Burger King was willing to cooperate only if the overall settlement included the claims brought against the company by the two partners, who did not wish this to happen. Accordingly the administrators asked the court whether they could in effect take over that counterclaim as part of the administration.

---

[55] *Kyrris v Oldham* [2003] 2 BCLC 35.
[56] 21 July 1997.

The judge, Evans-Lombe J, held first that the counterclaim was a partnership asset. Any sums recovered would accrue to the firm and not just the two partners. He then said that the position of an administrator of a partnership was akin both to that of an administrator appointed over the assets of a company and to that of a partnership receiver appointed by the court, which we came across in Chapter 7. On that basis partnership assets, even those held in the name of individual partners, were under the control of the administrators to dispose of as they wished for the purposes of the administration. It followed that they could take over the counterclaim and deal with it as part of the overall settlement.

9
LIMITED PARTNERSHIPS

Origins and Development of the Limited Partnership

Limited partnerships, or LPs, were created by the Limited Partnerships Act 1907 (LPA) as a variation on the traditional partnership form. They can only be created by registration under s 4 of that Act. There is therefore no such thing as an informal limited partnership. *LPs are entirely different from limited liability partnerships, or LLPs, which are the subject of the following chapters.* LLPs are based on the corporate rather than the partnership form and their title is very misleading.

9.01

The intention behind the 1907 Act was to allow the partnership form to be used by those who simply wanted to invest in a business with the protection of limited liability (up to the amount invested) for the debts of the firm. The partners (known as general partners) who ran the business would have no such protection. The price paid by the limited partners for this protection was a ban on taking any management role in the firm. Breach of that would end the limited liability protection. But the growth of the private company (also introduced in 1907) effectively stultified any general use of LPs as general commercial vehicles. Limited liability, legal personality, and management could all be combined in the private company, and the disclosure and formal elements attached to such companies have been gradually reduced ever since.

For the major part of the twentieth century therefore the LP form was rarely used, the exception being in Scotland where they were ideally suited for holding agricultural tenancies.[1] Like Scottish partnerships, a Scottish LP (SLP) has legal personality, and that is one of the main reasons for the modern resurrection of the LP form in Scotland, although there are other factors which have also led to a more modest increase in the numbers of English LPs. LPs and SLPs have become a major vehicle of choice for the venture capital sector where the funds are managed in the United Kingdom. They are used in that context by private equity, real estate, and infrastructure managers.[2] They are also used for certain very large asset-backed pension schemes, oil and gas exploration and production purposes, and film production. There is, however, evidence of some abuse by SLPs in particular (see the end of this chapter).

---

[1] Since 2003, following the Agricultural Holdings (Scotland) Act 2003, however, that is no longer the case, but many such tenancies are still in existence.

[2] Research shows that venture capital contributes close to £30bn to GDP; see <http://www.bvca.co.uk/Portals/0/Documents/Research/TIN/Angel-and-VC-users-economic-impact-report.pdf>.

300   LIMITED PARTNERSHIPS

This substantial growth in the numbers and uses of LPs and SLPs has been spectacular. In 1998 there were 5.006 registered LPs and SLPs. By 2007 there were 20,000. In 2013 there were over 25,000 and by 2017 over 40,000, and in 2018 48,000. Given those numbers and the economic importance of LPs and SLPs, the Edwardian 1907 Act had to be re-evaluated. There have in fact been three such reforms enacted, the last two intended to 'modernize' the regime by a relaxation of some of the restrictions, but only for investment funds etc. These have created a separate category of LPs and SLPs but still within the framework of the 1907 Act. These are known as private fund limited partnerships (PFLP)

However, given the very recent rise in the number of registrations, particularly of SLPs, in suspicious circumstances, there are proposals for a more restrictive regime to be introduced.

The 1907 Act

9.02   The amended LPA 1907, apart from the formation sections, still basically contains a series of variations from general partnership law in relation to the rights and duties of limited partners. Thus much of the law applicable to general partnerships applies to LPs and PFLPs and their problems are to be resolved by reference to that law unless the Act provides otherwise. Section 7 of the LPA provides that the 1890 Act and the rules of equity and common law applicable to partnerships shall apply 'subject to the provisions of this Act'. Thus in England an LP has no legal personality and the general partners are in the same position as ordinary partners. This was made clear by Farwell J in *Re Barnard*.[3] He said that an LP was 'merely a combination of persons for the purpose of carrying on a particular trade or trades, and is in no sense strictly speaking a legal entity'. The general partners were fully liable for all the firm's debts.[4]

The LPA, however, creates three major differences between limited and ordinary partnerships, first as to the method and consequences of formation, second as to the financial position and flexibility of a limited partner, and third as to variations of the rules for the internal relationships and running of the firm.

The reform process

9.03   In August 2008, the then Department for Business, Enterprise and Regulatory Reform[5] issued a consultative document containing proposals to implement the Law Commissions' recommendations.[6] The original intention was to repeal the LPA and

---

[3] [1932] Ch 269.
[4] See also *Vanquish Properties (UK) LP v Brook St (UK) Ltd* [2016] EWHC 1508, to the effect that an LP cannot be a tenant.
[5] Currently (April 2015) the Department for Business, Energy and Industrial Strategy; but tomorrow?
[6] See <http://berr.gov.uk/files/file47577.pdf>.

replace it with sections to be inserted into the 1890 Act. This was to be effected by the use of a single legislative reform order (LRO) which allows for amendments to be made to primary legislation by a form of secondary legislation. Thirty-three responses were received which revealed strong opposition to some of the proposals from the Scottish landowning interests and 'extensive comments' from lawyers specializing in partnership law. As a result, the Department, in March 2009, concluded that it was not in a position to proceed with the LRO but would discuss with consultees how to proceed, given the broad support for many of the proposals.

In the event, the Department then decided to proceed by introducing a series of smaller LROs amending the LPA, starting with one dealing with the non-controversial but much needed clarification of the registration procedure. That LRO came into effect in October 2009 and is the first of these reforms.[7] It replaces s 8 of the LPA with four new sections.[8] The Department then stated that it intended consulting again on the introduction of further LROs. That was originally promised for late 2009 but it was delayed. In January 2010, the Department indicated that it intended to consult fairly quickly on a second LRO dealing with the relatively uncontroversial requirements of the details of registration of information with the Registrar of Companies. The Department also had some outline proposals for a third LRO which would cover more controversial areas such as the loss of limited partner status and their capital contributions. That, it was thought, would need more preliminary informal consultation before a full consultation was undertaken.

In fact, nothing then transpired until 2013 when the Treasury announced an intention to consult on bringing in some of the Law Commissions' proposals for venture capital (collective investment scheme) LPs and SLPs only. In that year some of these changes were actually made to those, relatively few, such LPs regulated by the Financial Conduct Authority (the second reform) by the Collective Investment in Transferable Securities (Contractual Schemes) Regulations 2013.[9]

In 2015, the Treasury published a consultation document and a draft LRO proposing a new revised regime for what were to be known as private fund limited partnerships (PFLPs).[10] These were to apply to both PFLPs and SPFLPs but not to other LPs.[11] The responses and firm proposals were set out in March 2016. As a result, the proposed changes, modified to some extent by the responses, were implemented by the

---

[7] SI 2009/1940.
[8] See the Sixth Report of the Regulatory Reform Committee, House of Commons, Session 2008–09, 25 June 2009.
[9] SI 2013/1884. The changes therein relate mainly to the liability of the general partner on a winding up and excluding certain financial activities from the concept of interfering with management. There are some exceptions from the definition of a collective investment scheme under the Financial Services and Markets Act 2000, s 235(5) which those regs will not apply to. But those exceptions have not been carried into the definition of a PFLP so that there is no need to delve into the complexities of the FSMA in registering an PFLP (see below).
[10] Proposal on using Legislative Reform Oder to change partnership legislation for private equity investments.
[11] Opposition had come from Scottish agricultural LPs.

Legislative Reform (Private Fund Limited Partnerships) Order 2017 with effect from April 2017, (the third reform).[12]

As a result, there are now LPs and SLPs which are partnerships subject to some differences from general partnership law, and PFLPs and SPFLPs[13] which have some of those differences but some others in addition. There are also proposals for further reforms to counter perceived abuse of LPs and SLPs. This may all be seen as a rather messy set up, so this chapter will therefore first describe the regime for those LPs which are not registered as PFLPs (private LPs). Then it will set out the modifications to that regime for PFLPs[14] and finally consider the proposals to counter abuse, some of which have been on the table since 2008.

Limited Partnerships which are not Private Fund Limited Partnerships (sometimes referred to as private limited partnerships)

Formation

Registration—reform proposals adopted

9.04 Private limited partnerships can only be formed (but not in England incorporated) by registration with the appropriate Registrar of Companies. Under the substituted ss 8A, 8B, and 8C of the LPA, the Registrar will register an LP on an application under s 8A. The application must state the name of the LP,[15] its general partnership business, the names of both the general and limited partners, the amount of capital contributed by each limited partner, the address of its principal place of business, and the term (if any) for its duration.[16] It must be signed or authenticated by each partner. On registration the Registrar will issue a certificate of registration under the new s 8C, which states that the named LP was registered on a certain date, gives its registered number, and that it is a registered LP. As an intended clarification to the old law, s 8C(4) provides that the certificate is conclusive evidence that the LP came into existence on the date of registration.

Effectiveness of the certificate of registration—fraudulent applications

9.05 The effect of this new provision on conclusiveness is that the LP exists as of that date of registration even if it does not actually comply with the definition of a partnership in s

---

[12] SI 2017/514.
[13] SLPs are also subject to additional restrictions outside the LPA under the Scottish Limited Partnership (Persons with Significant Control) Regulations 2017, SI 2017/694. These are considered at the end of this chapter.
[14] These relate to registration, interference in management, registration and transparency, capital contributions, winding up, and statutory duties. Some of these can be traced back to the Law Commissions' proposals. Other aspects of the general LP regime apply to PFLPs.
[15] As specified in s 8B.
[16] This is one of the areas where the law for PFLPs is different.

1 of the 1890 Act (see the following paragraph). Prior to registration an LP may or may not be a general partnership depending upon whether the elements in s 1 of the 1890 Act have been engaged. This is known as the *Khan v Miah* point on contemplated partnerships discussed in Chapter 1.

More importantly it has now been established that the certificate cannot be challenged even if it was obtained by fraud. In *Bank of Beirut SAL v HRH Prince Adel El-Hashemite*,[17] the defendant had fraudulently applied for and was granted a certificate of registration of an LP on the basis that the bank was the general partner and he was the limited partner. This was entirely false but the prince used the certificate for fraudulent purposes abroad. The bank was now seeking to have the certificate cancelled. The obligation in s 8A that the application be signed by or on behalf of each partner had not been complied with as the prince had no authority whatsoever to sign on behalf of the bank.[18] Nor indeed was there any partnership or any partners and the whole had been procured by fraud. Absent the conclusiveness provision, the judge stated that he would have cancelled the certificate. But after reviewing the cases on the certificate of incorporation relating to company law, which has a similar conclusiveness provision, and the explanatory document submitted by DBERR as to the purpose of introducing s 8C,[19] the judge held that the certificate could not be set aside by the court even though it was procured by fraud and forgery. Fraud does not unravel all in these circumstances.

One problem is that there is nothing in the LP Act[20] which currently allows the registrar to deregister an LP and it is doubtful whether there is any obligation to notify her of the dissolution or termination of the LP.[21] The judge sought to establish what a person searching the register would be able to find out in circumstances such as those in the case. It would be possible in a case such as this by a web search of the register in the bank's name to find out that the LP had been converted/closed and the fact that it had been obtained by fraud. If a copy of the certificate is asked for, then if there is a history of filing default the certificate would be annotated by hand. As counsel for the bank pointed out, this was not exactly a watertight procedure.

---

[17] [2015] EWHC 1451 (Ch). This applies to PFLPs as well.
[18] The registrar does not examine applications for validity or seek verification but simply checks that the application is in due form. The judge described the alternative as being impractical and wholly unreal.
[19] This was to protect innocent investors in venture capital schemes, which are mainly carried out by LPs, who agree to join an existing LP and become limited partners in good faith. They should not then be exposed to unlimited liability. The alternative would be to have to make extensive checks as to the regularity or otherwise of the application. Any possibility of interference by the court would frustrate that policy objective and upset the machinery of the whole venture capital industry. This of course has no bearing on the use of the certificate to defraud third parties as in the case.
[20] Unlike the provisions for companies and LLPs.
[21] It cannot really be regarded as a change in the character of the LP *during its continuance* as is required by s 9(1).

Other requirements

9.06 Section 8B contains new provisions relating to the name of all LPs. In addition to the general control on business names applicable to all partnerships, the name must end with the words 'limited partnership' or 'LP'.[22] Thus it must be designated as such.

Any changes to these particulars must be registered within seven days (s 9). The Registrar keeps an index of all LPs on the register and, having filed the application and any changes, he or she must acknowledge receipt by letter (ss 13 and 14).

Limited Partner's Liability

9.07 There must be at least one limited partner. That is defined in s 4(2A) as someone 'who shall at the time of entering such partnership contribute thereto a sum or sums as capital or property valued at a stated amount, and who shall not be liable for the debts or obligations of the firm beyond the amount so contributed'. Limited partners therefore are those who contribute a fixed amount of capital, which is the most they can lose if the firm is unsuccessful, though, of course, they may lose more in income terms from loss of profits if the losses are so apportioned within the firm. A company may be a limited or general partner. If a limited company is the sole general partner then everybody's liability is effectively limited. If a limited partner withdraws any part of his contributed capital he nevertheless remains liable for the full stated amount under s 4(3). It is clear, therefore, that there is a substantial legal distinction between general and limited partners in terms of financial commitment.

One of the purposes of public registration is that any creditor of the firm can discover the identity and liability of the limited partners, so if there is a change of status by a partner either way this must not only be notified to the Registrar within seven days, but if either a general partner is to be made a limited partner or a limited partner's share is to be assigned, this fact must also be notified under s 10 of the LPA in the *London* (or *Belfast* or *Edinburgh*) *Gazette*. (Since the *Gazette* is full of equally riveting topics it is only marginally more readable than a telephone directory.) Failure to do this renders such a change or assignment null and void for the purpose of avoiding liability.

Possible reforms on capital

9.08 The Department initially proposed that there should no longer be any legal requirement for a limited partner to contribute any capital. That would bring the law into line with the (legally untested) reality where the contribution is stated to be 1 per cent capital and 99 per cent a loan to the LP. If capital was contributed it was proposed that if it was in kind it should be valued as at the date of contribution for liability purposes. It was also proposed that a limited partner be allowed to withdraw capital, with a deferred

---

[22] Or, for those LPs with a principal place of business in Wales, the Welsh equivalent is allowed: 'partneriaeth cyfyngedig' or 'PC'.

liability for up to a year after the withdrawal was registered. Some of these proposals were introduced for PFLPs.

Trading losses

The Act limits the liability of limited partners to the amount of capital invested. It does not, however, limit their liability to bear losses out of their entitlement to a share of the profits. In *Reed v Young*,[23] the House of Lords upheld Nourse J's distinction between these two types of liability. It means that if the firm as a whole suffers a loss no creditor can sue limited partners for a contribution to the firm's assets above the limited amount agreed, but within the firm's accounts they may lose their right to undrawn or future profits by virtue of the agreement itself. In such cases, therefore, the limited partners have suffered a loss of the whole amount although they have not increased their capital liability. The tax advantages of thus claiming an allowable loss of the whole amount for tax purposes was negatived by s 48 of the Finance Act 1985.

9.09

Failure to contribute agreed sum

A limited partner's protection is therefore substantial, provided he or she complies with the 1907 Act. Failure to comply will simply make them general partners—s 6 is quite clear. There are two major ways in which such failure can arise. First, a limited partner, other than one in a PFLP, is required to contribute the capital as quantified in the registration statement. In *Rayner & Co v Rhodes*,[24] the plaintiffs were owed money by the limited partnership of Jones & Co. When Mr Rhodes was sued for his amount he claimed to be a limited partner and that he had already contributed the £5,000 he had agreed to contribute to the firm. In fact he had given a running guarantee for that amount to the firm's bankers for any overdraft and had deposited securities with the bank for the amount. Wright J decided that the 1907 Act required that money or its equivalent be transferred to the firm for its use. A guarantee was in no sense of the word a payment in cash or its equivalent—the firm had no access to the securities deposited with the bank nor could it enforce the guarantee. Mr Rhodes had merely assumed a future contingent liability. The registration statement had stated that Mr Rhodes had contributed £5,000 in cash and since that was wrong the Act had not been complied with and so there was no registration of Mr Rhodes as a limited partner. He had to be regarded as a general partner and treated as such.

9.10

Interference in management

The second way of failing to comply with the 1907 Act currently derives from s 6(1). It is worthwhile setting this part of the Act out in full:

9.11

> A limited partner shall not take part in the management of the partnership business, and shall not have power to bind the firm: Provided that a limited partner may by

---

[23] [1986] 1 WLR 649, HL.
[24] (1926) 24 Ll L Rep 25.

himself or his agent at any time inspect the books of the firm and examine into the state and prospects of the partnership business, and may advise with the partners thereon.

If a limited partner takes part in the management of the partnership business he shall be liable for all debts and obligations of the firm incurred while he so takes part in the management as though he were a general partner.

This section provides an insight into the policy of the LPA. A limited partner is to invest his capital and leave the running of the business to the general partners—a concept totally alien to the concept of an ordinary partnership (and even to some companies since *Ebrahimi v Westbourne Galleries Ltd*[25]). He is to be given only those rights necessary to protect his investment. If he goes beyond those rights he ceases to be a limited partner.

There are of course difficulties as to what amounts to interference in management. The Law Commissions proposed that there should be a definitive list of what a limited partner might do without losing limited liability protection.[26] That was not generally applied by the Department in 2008 but it has been enacted for PFLPs.

9.12 The proviso to s 6(1), which also applies to PFLPs, allows a limited partner to inspect the books of the firm'. The ambit of this right was the subject of a considerable dispute which had to be resolved by Norris J in two successive judgments in the case of *Inversiones Friera SL v Colyzeo Investors LP*. In his first judgment,[27] Norris J set out general guidelines which he hoped would resolve the dispute. He first noted that the right was important since the general partner was subject to the obligation of providing true accounts and full disclosure under s 28 of the 1890 Act. Obtaining information was not management. He then said that there was no point in going through a number of past cases since each case would be different. The purpose of the right of inspection is to allow the limited partners to inform themselves of the position of the partnership. On that basis the test is a functional one. The right extends to include everything needed either to establish the rights of the firm against a third party or to determine the rights of the partners between themselves. The motive or purpose behind the right was irrelevant.

Those guidelines failed to solve the dispute, however, and so the parties returned for a further resolution as to the details of the dispute.[28] Norris J made three further points as to deciding precisely which documents may be made available. First, that whilst only two of the limited partners had made the application, any documents made available to them must also be made available to all the limited partners. Second that the right of inspection does not require the general partner to create 'partnership books', nor to constitute partnership papers which are not already in existence. If there are none where there should be, then the right of inspection transfers to the primary documents

---

[25] [1973] AC 360, HL.
[26] This loss would, however, not be contingent on the third party being aware of the limited partner's activities as it is in Jersey for example.
[27] [2011] EWHC 1762 (Ch).
[28] [2012] EWHC 1450 (Ch).

in the possession of the general partner from which such books or records should have been created. Third where a list had been prepared by the general partner using the guidelines from the first hearing, the onus transfers to the limited partners to show in what way the list is not effective to fulfil those guidelines. The court expects the parties to behave in a reasonable manner.

Clearly, therefore, examining the books and looking into the state and prospects of the partnership business and, if necessary, even advising the partners on such matters will not usually be regarded as taking part in the management of the business. But there must be many fine distinctions to be drawn between the two in practice and these may be even more crucial since the most likely time for a limited partner to cross the dividing line is when the business is going downhill and it is at precisely that time that the potential liabilities as a general partner will be very real. If *Cox v Hickman*[29] had involved a limited partnership, however, it is hard to imagine that those taking over the business on a caretaker basis would have escaped being liable as general partners. It is perhaps ironic that such creditors, protected by s 2(3)(a) or (d) of the 1890 Act, are in a potentially better position than a limited partner in this respect.

Other Modifications of Partnership Law

Section 6(1) is thus a 'modification' of the general law of partnership. It should be noted that in addition to the veto on management activities it also provides that a limited partner has no power to bind the firm. That has no relevance, of course, to his liability by representation under s 14(1) of the 1890 Act nor to the liability of the firm so representing him as a general partner. All it means is that he has no implied authority to bind the firm but he may well have actual or apparent authority to do so. Nor does this have any effect on the firm's vicarious or direct liability for the acts of a limited partner under ss 10, 11, or 13.

9.13

The remainder of s 6 is also concerned with further modifications of the Partnership Act 1890 for the purpose of a limited partnership. These can be divided into four areas. First, following on the management restrictions in s 6(1), it is provided that any differences arising as to the ordinary matters connected with the partnership business can be decided by a majority of the general partners (in other partnerships the implied term of the agreement provides for a decision by a majority of all the partners). Second, as to the composition of the partnership, it is provided that another person may be introduced as a partner without the consent of the limited partner (in other partnerships there is an implied term that unanimity of all the partners is required for this but since a new partner cannot, in theory, bankrupt a limited partner by his deeds his consent is not thought necessary). Third, a limited partner may, with the consent of the general

---

[29] (1860) 8 HL Cas 268, HL.

partners (and a notice in the *Gazette*), assign his share to another who then becomes a full limited partner with all the assignor's rights. In ordinary partnerships an assignee of a partner's shares does not become a partner and has only a right to the income from it: he has no right even to inspect the books.

Derivative actions

9.14 Given the restriction on the authority of limited partners, it follows that no limited partner has authority to bring an action on behalf of the LP against a third party; that is the province of the general partner. But what if the general partner is not disposed to bring such an action? The answer has been provided by the judgment in *Certain Limited Partners in Henderson PFI Secondary Fund II LLP v Henderson PFI Secondary Fund II LP*.[30] In that case the limited partners wished to bring an action against both the general partner and the manager of the LP but did not wish to become liable either for costs or for the debts of the LP by interfering in management. The judge first held that any action against the general partner needed no permission from the court as that was a personal action belonging to each partner, not one belonging to the LP.

On the other hand, the action against the manager was a partnership action so that the limited partners would need to bring a derivative action—ie they would seek to bring an action deriving from the LP's right to do so. Derivative actions in the corporate sphere are now regulated by statute, but as the judge held, non-corporate derivative actions are allowed.[31] The case law established that there must be 'special circumstances' for the court to allow such actions. Although there was no formal requirement for a preliminary application for permission to bring the action, as there is for companies, such special circumstances had to be pleaded. In this case it was being considered as a preliminary issue.[32] Apart from the 'special circumstances' issue,[33] the court would look at whether there were any prospects of success or whether it was bound to fail, but would not otherwise entertain any assessment of the merits of the case. It would also consider whether there was a better alternative remedy.[34] On the other hand to bring the action would be a clear breach of s 6(1) of the LPA and thus open the applicants up to potential liability for costs if the action failed. Accordingly no order as to costs would be made at this stage.

Dissolution

9.15 The fourth area where the statutory rules are different concerns the grounds upon which a dissolution is presumed to have occurred. A limited partner has no right to

---

[30] [2012] EWHC 3259 (Ch).
[31] By a beneficiary on behalf of a trust for example.
[32] Which would seem prudent in most cases.
[33] In the case, the relationship between the general partner and the manager.
[34] The judge did not mention any consideration as to whether the applicants were fit and proper persons to conduct the case, which is used in corporate derivative actions.

dissolve the partnership by notice even if it is a partnership at will. He can only escape from the firm by assigning his share and then only with the consent of his fellow partners. Currently, therefore, his capital cannot be suddenly withdrawn at the first sign of trouble and in this respect at least a limited partner is like a shareholder in a private company. A creditor under s 2(3) of the 1890 Act is not necessarily subject to such restraints. Further, subject to contrary agreement, there is no implied dissolution on any of the following events, although there would be for an ordinary partnership: a charge on the limited partner's share in the firm in satisfaction of a private debt; the death of a limited partner; or the insolvency of a limited partner. Mental incapacity of a limited partner is only a ground for dissolution if his or her share cannot otherwise be realized. All these variations reflect the limited partner's status as an outside investor.

Private Fund Limited Partnerships

Since April 2017 LPs and SLPs, other than those regulated by the FCA, may register as PFLPs or SPFLPs if they satisfy the definition of PFLP. This followed a consultation in 2015 and was enacted by amendments to the LPA 1907 made by the Legislative Reform (Private Fund Limited Partnerships) Order 2017.[35] Such PFLPs are still LPs but they are treated differently to ordinary LPs in respect of registration, interference in management, capital contributions, winding up, and statutory duties. In other areas they are treated the same as LPs.   9.16

Definition, registration, and de-registration of a private fund limited partnership

The new regime will only apply to those LPs which are private fund LPs. These are as defined in s 8(3) by reference to s 235 of the Financial Services and Markets Act 2000. They are schemes which have arrangements with respect to any property, including money, the purpose or effect of which is to enable persons taking part to participate in or receive profits or income arising from the acquisition, holding, management, or disposal of the property or sums paid out of such profits or income. The participants are not to have day-to-day control over the management of the property, which is the province of the operator of the scheme and the investments are to be pooled.   9.17

PFLPs are specifically registered as such by the Registrar. For a new LP the application for registration under s 8A must be accompanied by an application for designation as a PFLP under s 8D. But such an application can also be made at any time after an LP

---

[35] SI 2017/514. Not all the proposals in the consultative document were implemented. Legal personality was considered but that could not be achieved by an LRO.

has been registered (s 8D(1)). The application for designation must state: the name and principal place of business of the PFLP; confirmation by the general partner that it fulfils the criteria for a PFLP; and, if it is already registered as an LP, its registered number and date of registration as such (s 8D(2)).

The Registrar will then issue a certificate of designation as a PFLP stating the firm's name, date of designation, and that it is so designated (s 8C(5)(7)). That certificate is conclusive evidence that it was so designated as of that date (s 8C(8)). A newly formed PFLP may get a combined certificate of incorporation and designation (s 8C(9)).

The original proposals to allow the Registrar to remove a PFLP from the register in certain circumstances[36] were not pursued on the grounds that it might leave limited partners liable for debts without their knowledge and that other LPs were not subject to it.[37]

Interfering in management—permitted activities

9.18 Section 6A sets out a 'white list' of activities which will not be considered as interference with management by a limited partner in a PFLP and so will not compromise their limited liability.[38]

This list is not exhaustive, however, so that other things may be regarded as not taking part in management (s 6A(4)(a)). On the other hand, it does not create any presumption either way for a private LP (s 6A(4)(b)). The list is set out in s 6A(2):

(a) taking part in a decision about: (i) the variation or waiver of the partnership agreement or associated documents; (ii) whether the general nature of the business should change; (iii) whether a person should become or cease to be a partner; and (iv) whether the partnership should end, or the term of the partnership should be extended;
(b) appointing a person to wind up the partnership;[39]
(c) enforcing an entitlement under the partnership agreement;[40]
(d) contracting with the other partners (excluding one allowing management);
(e) acting as a surety or guarantor for the partnership;
(f) approving the accounts;
(g) reviewing or approving a valuation of the assets;
(h) discussing the prospects of the business;

---

[36] On an application from the general partner or if there is no general partner by a limited partner, or if it is in fact moribund—subject in the last case to certain safeguards and the ability to apply for restoration to the register.
[37] Similar proposals for all LPs have been on the table since the Law Commissions' reports, but they may not yet be dead—see proposals for reform, below.
[38] Draft LRO, Art 2(5).
[39] See s 6(3B) below.
[40] Other than a right to take part in management.

(i) consulting or advising a general partner, manager, or adviser about the affairs of the partnership or its accounts;
(j) taking part in any decision regarding changes to the managers;
(k) acting or appointing an agent to act as a director, member, employee, officer, or agent of, or as a shareholder of the general partner or manager, provided it does not amount to management of the partnership;
(l) appointing an agent to represent the limited partner on a committee authorizing such a person to take any action which would not amount to management of the partnership, or revoking such an appointment;
(m) taking part in a decision as to how the partnership should exercise as an investor in another collective investment scheme (the master fund) unless exercising that right would increase the partnership's liability to the master fund over the amount contributed or agreed to be contributed to the master fund;[41]
(n) taking part in a decision approving or authorizing an action by the general partner or manager, in particular in relation to: (i) the disposal or acquisition of a business; (ii) the acquisition or disposal of a type of or a particular investment; (iii) the exercise of rights in respect of an investment; (iv) participation in a particular investment by the partnership; (v) the incurring, extension, variation, or discharge of a partnership debt; and (vi) the creation, extension, variation, or discharge of any other partnership obligation.

In addition, s 6A(3) provides that a conflict of interest is not on its own to say that the limited partner is interfering in management.[42] This list in itself indicates the modern usage of an LP as an investment vehicle. Most of it was contained in the original proposal and was heavily criticized at the time. It was amended following the responses to the 2015 consultation. It is interesting to note, however, that the Singapore LP introduced in 2008 actually has a similar, but not identical list, which does not seem to have raised any serious issues to date.

Capital contributions

The obligation on a limited partner to make a capital contribution does not apply to a limited partner in a PFLP (s 4(2B)). This accords with the previous practice whereby any such contribution was nominal, the investment being made in the form of interest-free loans or advances which could be withdrawn without infringing the rule on withdrawal of capital under s 4(3). That rule does not therefore apply to a PFLP first registered as an LP or PFLP after April 2017 (s 4(3A)). Any such capital already

9.19

---

[41] These are relevant to feeder funds.
[42] This avoids the strict equitable rule in cases such as *Boardman v Phipps* [1967] 2 AC 46, HL.

contributed to a PFLP first registered as an LP before that date, however, will be subject to the capital withdrawal rule (s 4(3B)).

Registered particulars, changes, and Gazette notices

9.20 A PFLP on registration with an application for designation as a PFLP need only give, in addition to the firm name, the name of the general and limited partners and the address of the proposed principal place of business (s 8A(3)). Any changes to those details must be registered within seven days (s 9). Notice of the cessation of a general partner in a PFLP must be put in the Gazette 'forthwith'. Such notice is a notice to a person dealing with the firm, but until it is included such a person may continue to rely on the former general partner still being such (s 10(1A),(1B),1(C)).

Other modifications on partnership law

9.21 In general the same modifications on the Partnership Act regime applicable to private LPs apply to PFLPs (s 6(5)). But there are further modifications for PFLPs in relation to fiduciary duties, apparent partners, and winding up.

Sections 28 (duty of honesty) and 30 (no competition) of the PA do not apply to limited partners in a PFLP (s 6(5)(f)). This is on the basis that they are inappropriate for passive investors with interests in several funds. They still apply to the general partner, as do other common law and equitable duties.

Section 36 (need to give notice on leaving a firm to avoid liability for future debts) will not apply to any limited partner ceasing to be a member of a PFLP (s 6(6)). Since there is no need to advertise the assignment of a share in a PFLP s 36(2), which provides that such a notice is effective for those who have not dealt with the firm before, will not work.

Winding up

9.22 Contrary to the general rule for private LPs (winding up by the partners or the court), if a PFLP has a general partner then, subject to contrary agreement, the winding up is to be done by the general partner (s 6(3A)). If there is no general partner, then the winding up must be by a person (not a limited partner) appointed by the solvent limited partners, again subject to any contrary agreement (s 6(3B)). However, those are all subject to any court order as to the winding up (s 6(3D)).

Proposed Reforms to Counter Abuse of the Limited Partnership Form

Evidence of abuse

Beginning in 2008 there was a rapid increase in the number of registrations of LPs, particularly of SLPs. The number of SLPs rose by 23,625 between 2007 and 2016, and in 2016 more SLPs were registered than in the previous century. It further emerged that most of these were registered by a handful of service agents (trust and company service providers (TCSPs))[43] and that they were 'opaque' in that they had corporate partners registered in jurisdictions with no disclosure provisions. They were controlled offshore, and they were used in some spectacular frauds.[44] They were particularly useful in money laundering schemes, providing anonymous ownership with an apparently respectable British business.[45]

9.23

Proposals for reform to counter abuse

It became clear to the Government that this could not be allowed to continue. In 2017 the Persons with Significant Control Regulations, applied to companies in an attempt to counter anonymity in response to money-laundering, were applied to SLPs.[46] The number of SLP registrations slowed down, although opaque SLP registrations continued, but there was a rise in the numbers of opaque English and Northern Irish LPs. In 2017 the Department for Business, Energy and Industrial Strategy issued a consultation paper suggesting four possible changes to counter abuse. In December 2018 the Department issued a response to that consultation, refining the four proposals. It noted that there were many important and legitimate uses of the LP forms but stated its intention to enact the following changes to the LP regime 'when parliamentary time allows'.

9.24

(i) All new LPs must be registered by an agent which can demonstrate that it is registered with an AML (anti-money laundering) supervisory body and which can provide evidence of this on the application form;[47]

(ii) All LPs must demonstrate an ongoing link to the United Kingdom either by having a principal place of business in the United Kingdom, demonstrating that

---

[43] In 2016/7 56 per cent of registrations were carried out by five such agents which were unregulated.
[44] Twenty SLPs formed part of a complex fraud used to raid US$1 billion from three Moldovan banks in 2014.
[45] One hundred SLPs were involved in moving vast sums out of Russia in just four years. See generally Transparency International UK, 'Offshore in the UK: Analysis of Scottish LPs in Corruption and Money Laundering', May 2017.
[46] Scottish Partnerships (Register of People with Significant Control) Regulations, SI 2017/694. These also required an SLP to provide an annual confirmation statement that it had delivered notice of any changes in the registered details to the Registrar.
[47] This will prevent any direct registration of an LP but that is very rare. Critics say that there will still be no effective fitness and properness test, no disclosure on registration particulars of corporate partners' registration location, and no enforcement budget.

they have legitimate business interests in the United Kingdom, or they have the services of an agent subject to an AML body which can provide a service address for the LP;[48]

(iii) On registration an LP must provide the date of birth and nationality of all partners and an indication of the nature of its business. In addition, it must file an annual confirmation statement, that all information on the register is correct. The PSC Regulations will not, however, be applied to English LPs;[49] and

(iv) (At last) the Registrar will be given powers to strike off moribund and dissolved LPs, giving due notice and with a right to be restored to the register.[50]

There is still nothing to allow the Registrar to strike off miscreant LPs in the public interest, to disqualify miscreant partners, and still little transparency or accountability.

---

[48] Critics say that having a meaningless UK maildrop address is no use as every single LP involved in a fraud was able to comply with this.

[49] Critics say that none of this confirms that the information is accurate and will simply increase the flow of unverified forms.

[50] Over 12,000 SLPs have already filed that the partnership is dissolved.

PART II
LLPs

10
LLPs: AN INTRODUCTION

A Note on Citation

Any text on LLP law must grapple with the indigestibility caused by the manner in which the provisions of company law are modified and adopted for LLPs. For the sake of readability a number of abbreviations are used in the chapters that follow when citing the Limited Liability Partnerships Act 2000 and the regulations made under it. The Act itself is referred to as the 'LLP Act 2000'. The three key sets of Regulations made under the Act are the Limited Liability Partnerships Regulations 2001,[1] the Limited Liability Partnerships (Accounts and Audit) (Application of Companies Act 2006) Regulations 2008,[2] and the Limited Liability Partnerships (Application of Companies Act 2006) Regulations 2009.[3] These are referred to as the 'LLP Regulations 2001', the 'LLP Accounts Regulations 2008', and the 'LLP Regulations 2009' respectively.

10.01

When citing provisions of company law applied to LLPs by the regulations, the convention adopted is to refer to the regulation and then, in parentheses, the section of the Companies Act 2006 (CA) or Insolvency Act 1986 (IA) that the regulation adopts or refers to in modified form. Thus 'LLP Regs 2009, reg 16 (CA, s 87)' refers to regulation 16 of the LLP Regulations 2009, which modifies and applies section 87 of the Companies Act 2006.

What is an LLP?

Like a company, but unlike an English partnership,[4] an LLP is a body corporate with limited liability. It has its own legal personality, distinct from its members, and full legal capacity. However, it is a far more flexible entity than a company: as in a general partnership, the members are largely left to organize their affairs as they see fit. As such, an LLP offers an attractive combination of characteristics drawn from both partnership and company law. It combines the flexibility of partnership with the significant benefit

10.02

---

[1] SI 2001/1090.
[2] SI 2008/1911.
[3] SI 2009/1804.
[4] Or, indeed, a Scottish partnership: although a Scottish partnership has legal personality, Scottish partners are personally responsible for the partnership's obligations.

of limited liability for its members that results from its separate personality and full capacity.

The Development of LLPs

10.03 LLPs came into being as a result of pressure from professional services firms in the mid 1990s, concerned as to their unlimited liability as traditional general partnerships in the face of an increasingly aggressive litigation culture. The business of such firms had reached such a size that the potential liabilities were huge, and the firms themselves had also grown to the extent that the risk of liability for the defaults of all other partners was becoming unacceptable, to say nothing of the cost of insuring that liability. The firms therefore sought a structure which would preserve the internal informality and tax arrangements of a general partnership, whilst also protecting the members of the firm from liability to those who dealt with the firm. By the late 1990s, various jurisdictions, most notably Jersey and various US states, had already taken steps to introduce limited liability for partnerships.

The genesis of the Limited Liability Partnerships Act

10.04 Partly in response to the concerns raised by professional partnerships, in 1995 the Law Commission undertook a feasibility investigation into reforms of the law of joint and several liability.[5] One possible solution to those concerns would have been to make reforms to the law of joint and several liability, so as to introduce fault-based limitations which would ensure that anyone (including a partner in a general partnership) would only be legally liable to the extent of their own culpability. However, this suggestion ran up against the fundamental concern that it would involve an unacceptable shift in the burden of risk onto the victim of the wrong. Other means of addressing the concerns therefore needed to be found.

Following a 1997 consultation paper that met with a generally favourable response,[6] in 1998 the UK Government therefore decided to introduce a Bill providing for a novel form of partnership that would allow for limitation of liability. As the Select Committee Report on the Bill stated:

> It is proposed to create a new legal vehicle for carrying on business, a Limited Liability Partnership (LLP), combining the internal arrangements of a general partnership with many of the external obligations of a company. An LLP will, unlike an English

---

[5] Common Law Team of the Law Commission and DTI, *Feasibility Investigation of Joint and Several Liability* (HMSO 1996).
[6] DTI, 'Limited Liability Partnerships: A New Form of Business Association for Professions' (URN 97/597).

partnership, be a body corporate, with whom clients and customers can contract and to whom banks can lend, with the possibility of a floating charge...

The fundamental problem which the proposed legislation addresses is the possibility that the assets of a partnership, and the personal assets of each and every partner, can be put at risk as a result of the negligence or incompetence of a single partner, over which the other partners have no control and of which they have no knowledge...[7]

The Report went on to note that the growth of large partnerships had strained the traditional partnership model: very large partnerships had developed in the fields of law and accountancy, comprising several hundred partners,[8] often personally unknown to each other, potentially located all over the world. The personal assets of partners in such firms could be put at risk by the actions of other partners over whom they had no control and of whom they might have no knowledge.

The Government's Explanatory Note to the Bill also outlined why unlimited liability amongst general partnerships had become a source of concern. Specifically cited were: (a) a general increase in the incidence of litigation for professional negligence and in the size of claims; (b) the growth in the size of partnerships; (c) the increase in specialization among partners and the coming together of different professions within a partnership; and (d) the risk to a partner's personal assets when a claim exceeds the sum of the assets and insurance cover of the partnership.[9]

The result of these efforts was the LLP Act 2000, which received Royal Assent in July 2000. Unlike previous efforts elsewhere to create partnerships with limited liability, which tended to create limited liability partnerships as non-corporate entities,[10] the LLP Act 2000 was intended to give rise to a new corporate body: incorporating the LLP as a separate legal entity from its members, and giving that entity unlimited legal capacity.[11] This corporate model of providing limited liability to a partnership has since proved to be popular, both nationally and internationally.

The LLP Act 2000 was also significant in imposing few restrictions on the sorts of businesses that could become LLPs. As set out at para 11.04, the only real restriction on the sorts of activities that can be conducted through an LLP under the Act is the requirement that the LLP be created for the purposes of conducting a business with a view to profit. By contrast, regimes elsewhere had been quite restrictive in this regard. For example, the Limited Liability Partnerships (Jersey) Law 1997 was originally passed with large accountancy firms in mind (indeed, it was drafted at the behest of two of them). It contained provisions that reflected this: under Article 6, a Jersey LLP had to provide

---

[7] Trade and Industry Committee, 'Draft Limited Liability Partnership Bill' (HC 59 1998–1999, 10 February 1999), paras 11–12 at <https://www.parliament.uk>.
[8] Partnerships of solicitors and accountants were exempt from the twenty-member limit that previously applied to partnerships under Companies Act 1985, s 716.
[9] Explanatory Note to the LLP Act 2000, para 9.
[10] See, eg the Limited Liability Partnerships (Jersey) Law 1997 (now replaced by the Limited Liability Partnerships (Jersey) Law 2013).
[11] LLP Act 2000, s 1(2)–(3).

a capital bond of £5 million to protect creditors in the event of its insolvency, a requirement that no small business could sensibly be expected to meet. It also required every partner to contribute effort and skill to the business (so one could not have a 'sleeping partner' of a Jersey LLP).[12] The LLP Act 2000 contains no such requirements.

The response to the Act

10.05 The LLP Act 2000 applies throughout the United Kingdom:[13] it has applied in Scotland since the original commencement date of 6 April 2001, and in Northern Ireland since 13 September 2004.[14] Across the whole of the United Kingdom, there are now 52,000 or so registered LLPs.[15] Since being introduced, the number of LLPs has gradually increased, peaking at over 60,000 in 2017 before falling back somewhat.

In November 1999, the Department of Trade and Industry (DTI) had suggested that around 90,000 of an estimated 600,000 partnerships in the United Kingdom might become LLPs.[16] Although, in the result, it might be thought that the LLP has proved less popular than anticipated, the crude numerical statistics disguise the importance of LLPs within the professional services sector in particular. Virtually all professional partnerships of lawyers, accountants, and other similar professional services firms of any substance are now LLPs. Furthermore, because they are taxed as partnerships (ie they are tax-transparent) they have also proved popular with venture capital and other businesses that might otherwise have chosen to incorporate as a company.

The demand for a flexible business structure with limited liability has also been felt outside the United Kingdom, and the perceived success of the UK legislation has inspired various other jurisdictions—particularly those in the common law world such as Singapore,[17] India,[18] Malaysia,[19] Guernsey,[20] and most recently Mauritius[21] and Pakistan[22]—to adopt a corporate model of LLP similar to that contained in the LLP Act 2000. Although some such jurisdictions (such as Ireland[23] and the Cayman Islands[24]) have preferred the US-style unincorporated model, they appear to be in the minority in terms of recent adopters.

---

[12] Limited Liability Partnerships (Jersey) Law 1997, Art 2.
[13] LLP Act 2000, s 19(4).
[14] Until 1 October 2009, LLPs in Northern Ireland were governed by delegated legislation in like terms to the LLP Act 2000.
[15] Though this comprises only 1.2 per cent of the entities registered at Companies House, the overwhelming majority (some 4 million) of which are private limited companies: Companies House: *Companies Register Activities: 2018 to 2019* (27 June 2019) at <https://www.gov.uk>.
[16] See HC Library Research Paper 00/54, *Limited Liability Partnerships Bill* (22 May 2000), p 9.
[17] Limited Liability Partnerships Act 2005.
[18] The Limited Liability Partnership Act 2008.
[19] Limited Liability Partnership Act 2012.
[20] Limited Liability Partnerships (Guernsey) Law 2013.
[21] The Limited Liability Partnerships Act 2016.
[22] Limited Liability Partnership Act 2017.
[23] Legal Services Regulation Act 2015: in Ireland, LLPs are permitted in the field of legal services only.
[24] Limited Liability Partnership Law 2017.

The success of the LLP Act 2000 has also inspired jurisdictions that had previously introduced LLPs to broaden the appeal of their own offerings. Thus the requirement of a £5 million capital bond in Jersey mentioned at para 10.04 was replaced from 2013 with the requirement that the LLP provide an annual statement of solvency. In turn, since 2017 that requirement has been abandoned all together; and whereas members of a Jersey LLP previously had to contribute 'effort and skill' to the LLP, they may now contribute capital instead.

The last twenty years have seen the international expansion of the LLP and its introduction as an important vehicle for commerce in economies across the globe. Although each legislative scheme inevitably differs—in particular with respect to the kinds of business that may incorporate as an LLP and as to the requirements of publicity and registration—in each case the impetus behind the introduction of the LLP has been largely the same: to provide additional protection to businesses that seek the benefits of limited liability with the structural flexibility and taxation benefits of a partnership. There has plainly been demand for such benefits, particularly in the professional and financial sectors.

Criticisms

10.06 The LLP is not without its critics, however. The advantage of limited liability to members is balanced by its disadvantage to creditors. The Trade and Industry Select Committee scrutinizing the Bill in 1999 expressed disquiet at the absence of any minimum capital requirement or guarantee from members, noting:

> We are . . . uneasy at the prospect of introduction of this new vehicle destitute of either minimum capital requirements or guarantees from members, and dependent on the perceived likelihood—or hope—that there will be some LLP assets available to creditors. As the Association of British Insurers put it, a regime under which liability is limited neither by shares nor by guarantee 'would appear to provide not for "limited liability entities" but "no liabilities" entities . . .' . . . The extent to which informed professionals and corporate clients, and potential creditors such as banks and landlords, will choose to enter into commercial relationships with an LLP is of course for them to determine. In the provision of some services, they may not in reality have much choice, if for example the majority of accountants were to take up that status.[25]

Critics have also complained that the concerns expressed as to professional liability in large firms that led to the Act in the first place were overblown and unsupported by evidence; and in any event there was no reason other than an overly precious attachment to 'partnership ethos' why firms seeking limited liability could not readily incorporate

---

[25] Trade and Industry Committee, 'Draft Limited Liability Partnership Bill' (HC 59 1998–1999, 10 February 1999), para 45 at <https://www.parliament.uk>.

as companies if so minded. Consistent with this view, the LLP Act 2000 has been described as 'part of a long line of concessions to the auditing industry'.[26] Certainly, the involvement of the large accountancy firms in promoting LLP legislation—in particular in Jersey, but also in the United Kingdom—has not gone unremarked. It has also been suggested that joint and several unlimited liability is in fact a welcome aspect of partnership law and acts as a salutary incentive to probity in professional life—though this is a view generally only held by those who are not subject to it.

The Legislative Scheme

10.07   The principal legislation concerning LLPs is divided between the LLP Act 2000 and the regulations made under it. No particularly compelling reason was offered as to why the legislation was split in this manner: in response to criticism, the Government observed merely that, if there was sufficient demand for it, no doubt legal publishers would find a way of presenting the legislation in a consolidated digestible form.[27]

The Act

10.08   The LLP Act 2000 is a framework Act, originally running to only nineteen sections. The general effect of its provisions can be quite shortly stated.

Section 1 declares what an LLP is, and identifies its key characteristics of a body corporate with unlimited capacity. It also gives effect to the Schedule to the LLP Act 2000, which contains provisions about the name of an LLP and the use of the identificatory suffix 'LLP'. Sections 2 and 3 set out the process of incorporation.

Membership of an LLP is addressed in ss 4–9. Section 4 identifies who the original members of the LLP are (viz those who subscribe to the incorporation document), and explains that 'any person' (therefore, either legal or natural) may become, or cease to be, a member of an LLP by agreement with the existing members. Section 5 provides for the LLP Agreement: the LLP equivalent of a partnership agreement, by which the members agree their respective rights and duties. Section 6 explains that members act as agents for the LLP, and s 7 addresses the rights of former members. Section 8 introduces the concept of 'designated members': that is to say certain members who have a particular role with regards to certain regulatory functions. Finally, s 9 provides for a public registry of members that must be kept up to date.

---

[26] Ibid, Memorandum submitted by Professor Prem Sikka, para 2.
[27] Trade and Industry Committee, 'Government Observations on the Fourth Report from the Trade and Industry Committee on the Draft Limited Liability Partnership Bill' (HC 529 1998–99, 14 June 1999), para 7 at <https://www.parliament.uk>.

Sections 10–13 make amendments to various tax statutes with respect to LLPs, and ss 14–17 are concerned with the power of the Secretary of State to make regulations to further regulate LLPs: in particular to deal with the application of company law, partnership law, and insolvency law to LLPs.

The regulations

Significantly more detail is to be found in the regulations. Essentially, the regulations take a magpie approach to various aspects of company and insolvency law, incorporating the relevant provisions of various statutes applicable to companies, with modifications to make them appropriate to LLPs.

10.09

Originally, the LLP Act 2000 was supplemented by one principal set of regulations: the LLP Regulations 2001. As originally promulgated, those regulations did two things. First, they incorporated provisions from the Companies Acts 1985, Insolvency Act 1986, Company Directors Disqualification Act 1986, and Financial Services and Markets Act 2000, with suitable adaptation to apply them to LLPs.[28] Secondly, they set out an assorted collection of 'default provisions' that apply to the internal management of an LLP to the extent the LLP Agreement does not provide otherwise.[29]

In October 2009, the Companies Act 2006 came into force. Wholesale amendment to the LLP Regulations 2001 would have been required to incorporate the relevant provisions from the new Act. However, it was decided instead that new regulations would be promulgated to address the 2006 Act, whilst leaving the existing regulations intact as to all other matters. The decision was also made (for no obvious reason except administrative convenience) to split the new regulations in two: provisions with respect to accounts and auditing went into the LLP Accounts Regulations 2008, and everything else into the LLP Regulations 2009. There are, therefore, now three sets of regulations that govern the application of company law to LLPs.

To further complicate matters, the various regulations do not apply a consistent method in adopting and adapting company law. The LLP Regulations 2001 did so (and, to the extent still in force, do so) by giving terse instructions as to how to convert company law into LLP law. This is generally done by identifying the provisions of the appropriate company law statute to be applied to LLPs, giving some general rules that apply when carrying out the application process (such as 'references to a company shall include references to a limited liability partnership' or 'references to a director . . . shall include references to a member of a limited liability partnership') and then, by means of long schedules to the regulations, identifying alongside each section number any further textual amendments necessary to make the provision applicable to LLPs.

---

[28] They also supplemented the LLP Act 2000 in other ways: in particular by setting out certain 'default provisions' that apply to LLPs to the extent the LLP Agreement does not provide otherwise.
[29] The default provisions are addressed further in Ch 14.

Bringing these various elements together is not easy. It is necessary to read the original company statute and the LLP Regulations 2001 together, piecing together the original wording and the scheduled amendments. At the same time, one must bear in mind any other instructions set out in the body of the regulation, whilst making such further modifications as the context might require.

Despite the convoluted drafting style, one potential advantage of adopting this approach to the incorporation of company law was that any minor changes in the underlying company statute would be automatically mirrored in the regulations as applied to LLPs without the necessity (except in the event of further modification being required) of amending the LLP Regulations 2001 themselves. In providing that the company law statutes 'shall apply' to LLPs, the legislation clearly intended that it is the statutes as they are in force from time to time that 'shall apply', and not the statutes frozen at the date of the LLP Regulations 2001.[30]

In drafting the LLP Accounts Regulations 2008 and the LLP Regulations 2009, however, the parliamentary draftsman adopted a different approach, and chose (for the most part) to reproduce the adapted sections of the Companies Act 2006 in their entirety in the regulations themselves. This is generally done by each regulation stating that a particular provision of the Companies Act 2006 'applies to LLPs, modified so that it reads as follows—', and then setting out that provision in modified form.

Whilst undoubtedly easier to read, a consequence of applying company statutory provisions to LLPs in this way means that any amendments to company law made to the Companies Act 2006 will only be mirrored by changes to LLP law if the LLP Accounts Regulations 2008 or LLP Regulations 2009 are also amended. Ordinarily, one would expect that to happen as a matter of course, but plainly the risk of error and confusion is heightened. For example, in the event that only the company law provision were amended, and no explanation were offered in the Explanatory Document as to why the LLP Regulations 2009 were not also being amended, one would be obliged to consider whether the failure to amend the LLP Regulations 2009 was intentional or an error; and if an error, whether one might be able to cure it by the process of statutory construction.[31]

The upshot of all this is that with effect from 1 October 2009 (when the Companies Act 2006 came into effect):

- The LLP Regulations 2001 remain generally in force except insofar as they address accounting, auditing, or general principles of company law. They incorporate (by way of cross-reference, as described above) various provisions of the Insolvency Act 1986, Company Directors Disqualification Act 1986, and the Financial Services and Markets Act 2000 as well as the provisions of the Companies Act 1985

---

[30] See *Feetum v Levy* [2005] EWCA Civ 1601, [2006] Ch 585 at [28] where Jonathan Parker LJ, without adverse comment, noted this proposition to be common ground.

[31] Applying the corrective principles identified in *Inco Europe v First Choice Distribution* [2000] 1 WLR 586, HL.

that still remain in force: in particular, those dealing with statutory investigations by BEIS.[32] They also set out the 'default provisions'.

- General company law provisions from the Companies Act 2006 are now contained in the LLP Regulations 2009. Those provisions are (for the most part[33]) set out in full in the body of the regulations, having been derived from the equivalent provisions in the Companies Act 2006.
- Provisions which apply company rules of accounting and auditing (which are mostly to be found in Parts 15 and 16 of the Companies Act 2006) are now contained in the LLP Accounts Regulations 2008. Again, those provisions are set out in full in the body of the regulations, having been derived from the equivalent provisions in the Companies Act 2006. The technical rules of accounting are to be found in the Small Limited Liability Partnerships (Accounts) Regulations 2008[34] and the Large and Medium-sized Limited Liability Partnerships (Accounts) Regulations 2008,[35] which apply modified forms of the equivalent Companies Accounts Regulations, in much the same style as the LLP Accounts Regulations 2008.

One day, perhaps, LLPs will merit a single coherent statute along the lines of the Companies Act 2006. Until then, the principal provisions will have to be unravelled from the ungainly combination of the LLP Act 2000 and the three sets of regulations. These have all been amended many times since enactment; and in the circumstances it is fair to say that no one should embark on a detailed consideration of technical LLP law without an annotated guide to the legislation or an inexhaustible well of patience. That said, in the result much of the law applicable to LLPs is a reasonably straight adaptation of company and corporate insolvency law and reference should be made to books on company law for a detailed commentary on both.

LLPs, Partnerships, and Companies

In terms of black letter law, the large-scale incorporation of technical company legislation demonstrates that an LLP has more in common with a limited company than with a partnership. That reflects the need to adopt company-style regulation and oversight as the quid pro quo for limited liability. Indeed, s 1(5) of the LLP Act 2000 expressly states that:

10.10

> Except as far as otherwise provided by this Act or any other enactment, the law relating to partnerships does not apply to a limited liability partnership.

---

[32] Ie the Department for Business, Energy and Industrial Strategy, as it is known at time of publication.
[33] There is still some old-fashioned cross-referencing to keep readers on their toes. For example, regs 31A–31N set out the rules with respect to the registration of 'people with significant control' of an LLP. They do so by seemingly switching at random between the two methods of incorporating the Companies Act rules.
[34] SI 2008/1912.
[35] SI 2008/1913.

The LLP is thus a form of body corporate subject to many of the controls imposed upon companies as the price for limited liability (eg preparation and disclosure of accounts, being subject to statutory investigations, and rules on names, addresses of members, auditors, registration, and disclosure). It is treated as a company for insolvency and winding up purposes. An LLP can essentially be regarded as akin to a company for most external purposes (eg as to its dealing with creditors, including the ability, denied to ordinary partnerships, to raise money through the security of a floating charge). It is, in the circumstances, unsurprising that the name 'limited liability partnership' has been variously branded unfortunate, intellectually dishonest, and a breach of the Trade Descriptions Act.

Both culturally and internally, however, an LLP has more in common with a partnership. Indeed, as Cranston J observed in *R (Sword Services Ltd) v HMRC*,[36] in ordinary language the term 'partnership' can refer to both a general partnership and an LLP, and the term 'partner' likewise can connote either a partner strictly so-called or indeed a member of an LLP.[37] Less forgivably, the term 'limited partnership' has sometimes been used to refer to an LLP: though that is simply a mistake rather than the use of ordinary language.[38]

Like partners in a general partnership, members of an LLP are largely left to their own devices in terms of deciding the rules that govern the relations between one another. Some company law rules do apply internally: perhaps most strikingly, the LLP Regulations 2009 apply the minority protection provisions of s 994 of the Companies Act 2006, though most well-drafted LLP Agreements have taken the opportunity (permitted by the LLP Regulations 2009) to exclude those provisions.

Of course, the similarities that exist between general partnerships and LLPs reflect the genesis of the LLP as an alternative to partnership, and the fact that many existing businesses have taken the opportunity to convert from partnerships to LLPs. One might think, though, that businesses would hesitate before applying the label 'partner' to someone who is not a true partner. To hold a member of an LLP out as a 'partner' might be said to suggest the existence of a partnership under the 1890 Act, and therefore amount to a representation that a person is acting (with unlimited liability) on behalf of himself and others.

In practice, however, the label 'partner' is frequently employed by LLPs themselves to describe their members, even if such usage is accompanied by an explanation (buried in an email footer or equivalent) that the term is being used in a non-technical sense. Customers of professional services firms—and, indeed, the professionals themselves—have long regarded the title 'partner' as the gold standard in the climb up the career

---

[36] [2016] EWHC 1473 (Admin), [2016] 4 WLR 113 at [60].
[37] In *Eaton v Caulfield* [2011] EWHC 173 (Ch) the judge referred to the governing document as a partnership agreement and an LLP agreement interchangeably, whilst in *Hilton v D IV LLP* [2015] EWHC 2 (Ch) the judge referred to a partnership deed throughout.
[38] One made repeatedly by the judge in *Tower Taxi Technology LLP v Marsden* [2005] EWHC 1084 (Ch).

ladder, and the cultural link between LLPs and partnerships seems too entrenched for more cautious practice to prevail. In some jurisdictions (such as Singapore) this use of everyday language even has statutory recognition inasmuch as the term 'partner' is used in equivalent LLP legislation there as the formal description for what the LLP Act 2000 more conservatively calls a 'member'. Although it may seem surprising that businesses would run the risk of holding out their members as partners—especially after going to the trouble of converting into LLPs in order to obtain the benefits of limited liability—the risk is probably overstated, provided the rules requiring an LLP to identify itself as such, addressed at para 11.24, are properly respected.

Another key area where the LLP is more characteristic of a partnership is taxation. Although tax laws change with bewildering frequency, one of the principal intentions of the reforms that created LLPs was to ensure that LLPs would be taxed in the same way as partnerships. Section 10 of the LLP Act 2000 itself made amendments to the tax legislation to provide that where an LLP is carrying on a trade, profession, or business with a view to profit it will be taxed for income tax and capital gains tax purposes as if it were a partnership and not a company. Section 11 applies similar principles to inheritance tax. (For VAT on the other hand an LLP will be the taxable person.)

In effect this means that for the most part an LLP is tax-transparent and will not itself be liable for tax (provided it is carrying on a business with a view to profit). The relevant taxation legislation achieves this result by imposing the legal fiction that the business is actually carried out by the members, and the LLP's assets are held by the members, rather than by the LLP.[39] Members will also bear liability for capital gains tax in like terms that would apply were they partners in a general partnership.[40]

Thus, although the LLP is in the main a modified form of company, it is a partnership for tax purposes. In addition there are provisions (originally introduced by s 76 of the Finance Act 2001) to prevent 'investment LLPs' and 'property investment LLPs' being used for tax avoidance purposes. These have been added to in subsequent Finance Acts. Inevitably the taxation treatment of LLPs has encouraged certain businesses to register as LLPs for purely fiscal reasons, often with the result that staff who would more appropriately be regarded as employees in receipt of a salary can find themselves being enticed with offers of 'partnership' and profit share in the LLP, without a complete appreciation of the effect this may have on their employment rights. Legislation has inevitably sought to keep up with such attempts: for example, the LLP may be required for tax purposes to treat as employees those members whose profit share is regarded as a form of 'disguised salary' regardless of their true status.[41]

It is still very early to divine a distinctly separate LLP law as opposed to simply applying the relevant corporate or partnership laws, but it is gradually emerging, particularly

---

[39] Income Tax (Trading and Other Income) Act 2005, s 863.
[40] Taxation of Chargeable Gains Act 1992, s 59A.
[41] Income Tax (Trading and Other Income) Act 2005, ss 863A–863G. See para 12.05.

in those areas where an LLP can be said to be truly *sui generis*. For example, one issue that case law has had to grapple with is whether a member of an LLP can also be an employee of the LLP. In this regard, company law and partnership law are diametrically opposed: a company director can be, and often is, an employee of the company. However, a partner cannot be an employee of the firm (a rule justified on the basis that one cannot employ oneself: see para 2.34). As we will see, a member of an LLP lies somewhere in between.

11

THE CORPORATE STRUCTURE

The Basic Requirements for an LLP

Section 2 of the LLP Act 2000 sets out the procedure under which an LLP is incorporated, and in so doing sets out the necessary conditions by which an LLP can be formed. Section 2(1)(a) states that for an LLP to be incorporated: **11.01**

> two or more persons associated for carrying on a lawful business with a view to profit must have subscribed their names to an incorporation document.

The language of this provision consciously echoes that of s 1 of the Partnership Act 1890.[1]

It is convenient to consider the criteria set out within s 2(1)(a) in turn.

'Two or more persons'

Unlike a company, an LLP cannot be incorporated by a single person. An LLP must comprise at least two persons at incorporation. Although the LLP Act 2000 does not explicitly impose any sanction on an LLP that fails to sustain that level of membership, the provisions of the Act are designed to ensure that an LLP will, in the ordinary course, have at least two members. In the event that membership falls below two, the court has the power to wind the LLP up.[2] A sole member of an LLP may also lose the benefit of limited liability under s 4A of the LLP Act 2000 if an LLP carries on business for more than six months without having at least two members.[3] **11.02**

'Person' for these purposes includes any legal person. A company can therefore be a member of an LLP. This is quite common,[4] often for legacy reasons (eg where a

---

[1] ie 'carrying on a business in common with a view of profit', though subscribers to an LLP will not be carrying on a business 'in common' with each other, as they are not partners. There is no meaningful difference (other than 110 years of linguistic evolution) between 'a view of profit' and 'a view to profit': *Ingenious Games LLP v HMRC* [2019] UKUT 226 at [301].

[2] LLP Regs 2001, Sch 3 (IA, s 122(1)(c)) (see para 10.01 for an explanation of statutory citations from the Regulations).

[3] See para 11.17. The draft LLP Regulations 2009 proposed that a modified form of Companies Act 2006, s 156 would also apply, entitling the Secretary of State to require the LLP to appoint another member, but this proposal was not implemented.

[4] According to the Government, as at 2014 over half of LLPs had at least one corporate member, of which half had no natural person as a member at all: Department for Business, Innovation and Skills (DBIS), 'Final Stage Impact Assessments to Part A of the Transparency and Trust Proposals (Companies Transparency): Opaque arrangements involving company directors' (June 2014, BIS/14/908A), Annex D, para 10, see <https://www.gov.uk>.

company converts its business into an LLP), or because of corporate investment in the LLP, or (perhaps more questionably) because those managing the LLP perceive benefit in doing so behind a company. There are no current plans for s 156A of the Companies Act 2006—which, when it comes into force, will require company directors to be natural persons—to apply to members of an LLP, though the Government has indicated it will keep this exemption 'under review'.[5]

Another LLP can therefore also be a member of an LLP, as can a Scottish partnership or Scottish limited partnership, each of which has legal personality (see paras 1.08 and 9.01). An LLP can even be formed without any natural person being a member at all, and there is no requirement that any member be resident or registered in the UK. There is no upper limit on the number of members an LLP may have.

Although for some purposes an English general partnership or unincorporated association can be considered to be a legal person,[6] it seems reasonably clear that partnerships and unincorporated associations cannot be members of an LLP as such. Instead, each partner/member must have separate membership of the LLP, or one or more of them must hold their rights in the LLP on behalf of the others. Although not expressly stated anywhere in the LLP Act 2000 or the LLP Regulations 2009, it is implicit in the provisions that require particulars of members to be recorded in the LLP's register of members that each member must be a single legal person.[7]

'Associated for carrying on'

11.03 The requirement that the subscribers should be associated for carrying on a business undoubtedly connotes that they must come together for the purpose of the LLP carrying on that business. Whether any or all of the subscribers must themselves intend to carry out that business as members of the LLP is a moot point. The Act does not require two or more subscribing members to associate for *forming* a business; rather they must associate for *carrying on* a business. The Act can therefore be read as suggesting that at least two of the subscribing members (if not all of them) must intend to be involved in the business of the LLP. So read, that would preclude off-the-shelf LLPs incorporated by company agents. There would seem no good reason to read the provision that narrowly, however, given the members themselves are not obliged, by virtue of their status, to contribute in any way to the LLP once business is underway.

---

[5] DBIS consultation paper, 'Scope of Exceptions to the Prohibition of Corporate Directors' (November 2014, BIS/14/1017), paras 68–73, see <https://www.gov.uk>.
[6] By reason of the broad definition given to the word 'person' under the Interpretation Act 1978, Sch 1. See also the example at para 4.33.
[7] LLP Regs 2009, reg 18 (CA, s 164(d)).

'A lawful business with a view to profit'

Undoubtedly, the word 'business' must be given a broad meaning: as under the Partnership Act 1890, it includes 'every trade, profession and occupation'.[8] The express limiting factors are that the business must be 'lawful' and 'with a view to profit', and in those circumstances there would seem to be no real reason to restrict the scope of permitted 'business'.

11.04

Whilst the issue of lawfulness relates to the business rather than the proposed means of carrying it on, a business will not be lawful if its conduct would necessarily be unlawful. The ambit of lawfulness for these purposes is likely to be identical to that applicable under what is now s 7(2) of the Companies Act 2006. Thus business whose conduct is criminally unlawful is caught,[9] as is business that involves the performance of illegal contracts.[10] It is suggested that any business would likely be unlawful for these purposes if a contract to conduct that business would necessarily be considered contrary to public policy: not least because of the inevitable effect that this would have on the LLP Agreement relating to such an LLP.

The business must be conducted 'with a view to profit'. There must therefore be a causative link between the business and the intended profit, but it would seem not to matter how any profit is to be distributed or shared. This is likely to require a common-sensical approach similar to that applicable to general partnerships (see para 1.24) and the question of whether the subscribers subjectively[11] intend the business to be conducted with a view to profit should simply require them to model themselves on Mr Micawber.[12] Charities, clubs, and societies are all precluded on this basis.

In principle, there is no reason why an LLP, once formed, cannot change into a non-profit-making or non-business organization, but this is unlikely to be desirable. Doing so will result in the LLP ceasing to be taxed as a partnership.[13] It might also (depending on the circumstances) justify a winding up petition on public interest grounds,[14] or on the just and equitable ground.[15] Indeed, it could even put the membership personally at risk in the event of wrongful trading etc.

---

[8] LLP Act 2000, s 18.
[9] *R v Register of Joint Stock Companies ex p More* [1931] 2 KB 197 (the illegal sale of lottery tickets).
[10] *R v Register of Companies ex p A-G* [1991] BCLC 476 (the business of prostitution).
[11] *Ingenious Games LLP v HMRC* [2019] UKUT 226 at [303]–[340] contains a review of English and Commonwealth case law in support of the conclusion that 'a view to profit' is a purely subjective test, but that profit need not be the predominant aim. Although the question arose in the context of taxation statutes, the analysis is of general application and would apply also to the meaning of the phrase in s 2.
[12] 'Annual income twenty pounds, annual expenditure nineteen nineteen and six, result happiness. Annual income twenty pounds, annual expenditure twenty pounds ought and six, result misery', Charles Dickens, *David Copperfield* (1850).
[13] Income Tax (Trading and Other Income) Act 2005, s 863; Corporation Tax Act 2009, s 1273
[14] LLP Regs 2001, Sch 3 (IA s 124).
[15] LLP Regs 2001, Sch 3 (IA s 122(1)(e)).

The Process of Incorporation

11.05 In order to incorporate an LLP, s 2 of the LLP Act 2000 requires three steps to be taken. First, the founding members—who, as just discussed, must be 'associated for carrying on a lawful business with a view to profit'—must subscribe their names to an incorporation document.[16] Second, a statement must be made by one of the subscribers or a solicitor to the effect that the subscribing members have indeed associated for carrying on such a business;[17] and third the incorporation document and the confirmatory statement must be delivered to the Registrar of Companies (in England, Scotland, or Northern Ireland as appropriate).[18]

The incorporation document is the fundamental constitutional document for the LLP, and must be in the form required by the Registrar of Companies.[19] The form for the incorporation document and statement in support are currently combined on Form LL IN01 issued by Companies House.

The incorporation document is required to set out the following particulars:

- the name of the LLP;
- the 'situation' of the registered office;
- the address of the registered office;
- certain required particulars of the subscribing members;
- the identity of the 'designated members';
- a statement of 'initial significant control'.

Name

11.06 As with companies, there are some restrictions on the names that can be employed for an LLP. First, it must end with the acronym 'LLP', 'llp' or the words 'limited liability partnership'.[20] Second, as with companies, only permitted characters can be employed, and certain prohibited or offensive expressions must be avoided.[21] Third, the name must not be the same name as an existing company, LLP, or other registered entity, and rules set out the precise tolerance permitted in this regard.[22] A procedure to challenge an LLP's registered name, equivalent to that provided for companies, also exists.[23] The

---

[16] LLP Act 2000, s 2(1)(a).
[17] LLP Act 2000, s 2(1)(c).
[18] LLP Act 2000, s 2(1)(b)–(c).
[19] LLP Regs 2009, reg 60 (CA s 1068).
[20] LLP Act 2000, Sch, para 2. Under para 7, it is an offence for a person who is not an LLP to carry on business using these suffixes.
[21] LLP Regs 2009, regs 8–10 (CA, ss 53–57, 65).
[22] LLP Regs 2009, reg 11 (CA, ss 66–68).
[23] LLP Regs 2009, reg 12 (CA, ss 69–74).

rules applicable to the recycling of an insolvent company's name apply to members of LLPs, including both criminal and civil sanctions.[24]

Once registered, an LLP may change its name at any time (by filing form LL NM01).[25] A change in name takes effect from the date on which the Registrar issues a certificate to that effect.[26] A change of name does not affect the rights or duties of an LLP or render defective any legal proceedings by or against it under its old name.[27]

Situation and address

Like a company, an LLP must at all times have a registered office located within the United Kingdom.[28] As the LLP Act 2000 is UK-wide, this therefore requires the subscribing members to choose a 'situation' (ie the relevant legal jurisdiction of the United Kingdom in which the LLP is to be registered: England and Wales, Scotland, or Northern Ireland) and to choose an address within that jurisdiction. Each such jurisdiction has its own Registrar of Companies and Companies House. Once registered, an LLP can change its address within its chosen jurisdiction[29] (by filing form LL AD01) but (subject to the exception noted in the next paragraph) cannot change the jurisdiction or 'situation' of its registered office, which is fixed for all time.

11.07

An LLP with a registered address physically located within Wales may choose to identify 'Wales' rather than 'England and Wales' as its situation: this permits it to use the Welsh language equivalents of the various permissible LLP suffixes in its name,[30] and to communicate with the Registrar of Companies in Welsh.[31] Such an LLP may subsequently amend its incorporation document to vary its registered situation between 'Wales' and 'England and Wales' as appropriate (by filing form LL AD05).[32]

An LLP's registered office serves as its principal communication hub: it is where the LLP must take formal service of documents, and it provides the seat of the LLP for jurisdiction purposes. The location of the registered office is a matter that is recorded at Companies House, and any change in that location must be notified. The registered office also serves as the default point of inspection for various documents that the LLP must make available in various circumstances, such as its accounting records, its registers of members and those with significant control, and its registrable charges.

---

[24] LLP Regs 2001, Sch 3 (IA, ss 216–217).
[25] LLP Act 2000, Sch, para 4.
[26] LLP Act 2000, Sch, para 5(4).
[27] A fairly obvious point, but one the legislature felt the need to express in LLP Act 2000, Sch, para 6.
[28] LLP Regs 2009, reg 16 (CA, s 86).
[29] LLP Regs 2009, reg 16 (CA, s 87).
[30] LLP Act 2000, Sch, para 2(2). The Welsh for LLP is PAC.
[31] LLP Regs 2009, reg 68 (CA, ss 1103–1107).
[32] LLP Regs 2009, reg 17 (CA, s 88).

Members' particulars

11.08 The incorporation document is required to give the particulars of the subscribing members that will be entered into the LLP's register of members and register of members' residential addresses.[33] These are two registers that an LLP is obliged to keep up to date for the purpose of recording the details of its members (see para 11.25).[34]

In the case of an individual member, the required particulars are the member's name (and any former name), a service address, country of residence, date of birth, and whether the member is a designated member.[35] In the case of a member that is a body corporate (such as a company, or another LLP) or other legal person (such as a Scottish partnership), the required particulars are the member's name, the address of its registered or principal office, certain particulars of its registration in its state of incorporation,[36] and whether it is a designated member or not.

Designated members

11.09 The incorporation document is required to identify the proposed 'designated members' of the LLP. These are members who are given certain administrative functions under the modified Companies Act legislation as applied to LLPs. By and large, these comprise the compliance obligations that would, under company law, be placed on company directors: signing and filing accounts, appointing auditors, filing documents at Companies House, and so forth.

The Act permits LLPs to register on the basis that all their members from time to time will be treated as designated members, or on the basis that only certain named members will be treated as designated members.[37] An LLP may switch between these two forms of designation by filing form LL DE01.

The choice made at registration is given statutory effect by s 8 of the LLP Act 2000. Where the LLP has elected that only certain named members will be treated as designated members, it must give notice of any change in the designated members by filing a notice (on form LL CH01) that a member's status has changed.[38] The members may, by agreement, appoint new or replacement designated members or remove an existing designated member at any time, but in the event that the number of designated

---

[33] LLP Act 2000, s 2(2ZA).
[34] LLP Regs 2009, reg 18 (CA, s 162).
[35] LLP Regs 2009, reg 18 (CA, s 163).
[36] For a UK company or LLP this would simply be its registered number at Companies House; otherwise the particulars will vary as to whether the member is an EEA company under the First Company Law Directive or not: see LLP Regs 2009, reg 18 (CA, s 164).
[37] LLP Act 2000, s 2(2)(f).
[38] LLP Act 2000, s 9.

members falls below two, then every member of the LLP automatically becomes a designated member.

Statement of initial significant control

Finally, the incorporation document is required to identify any person who, on incorporation, will be 'a person with significant control' (PSC) or registrable relevant legal entity (RLE) with respect to the LLP and to give their particulars.[39] Since 30 June 2016, pursuant to the Small Business, Enterprise and Employment Act 2015, company law has required unlisted companies to declare who owns or controls them, in an effort to instil greater transparency into corporate ownership. The same rules apply to LLPs and companies, and are addressed in further detail at para 11.27.

11.10

The Legal Consequences of Incorporation

If satisfied that the requirements of s 2 have been met, the Registrar will register the incorporation document and statement in support and issue a certificate of incorporation, stating the name and registered number[40] of the LLP, the date of its incorporation, and the situation of its registered office. The practice remains for the happy occasion also to be announced by the Registrar in the London Gazette (or its Edinburgh or Belfast equivalent).[41] A certificate of incorporation is conclusive evidence that the requirements of s 2 have been complied with, and that the LLP has been incorporated by the name specified in the certificate.[42] The conclusive nature of the certificate does not prevent the Crown from challenging the Registrar's determination to register by way of judicial review,[43] but, in most practical senses, once an LLP has been registered it exists as a legal person until such time as it is formally wound up and dissolved.

11.11

An LLP must commence trading within a year of incorporation, or risks being wound up by the court.[44]

---

[39] LLP Regs 2009, reg 3A (CA, s 12A).
[40] Registered numbers for LLPs begin with the prefix 'OC' in England and Wales, 'SO' in Scotland, and 'NC' in Northern Ireland.
[41] LLP Regs 2009, reg 61 (CA, s 1064) in the absence of regulations (under LLP Regs 2009, reg 60 (CA, s 1116)) permitting an alternative means of public promulgation.
[42] LLP Act 2000, s 3(4). Unlike the equivalent Companies Act 2006 provision, s 15, this provision curiously uses the present tense, which might be read as indicating that the certificate is conclusive evidence that the requirements of s 2 continue to be met from time to time. That is obviously not intended; besides which s 2 is not drafted in such a way as might permit it to give rise to a continuing representation.
[43] *R v Register of Companies ex p A-G* [1991] BCLC 476 (Div Ct).
[44] LLP Regs 2001, Sch 3 (IA, s 122(1)(b)).

Upon incorporation, the LLP comes into existence as a body corporate with its own legal personality, and with unlimited legal capacity. Its initial members are the subscribers to the incorporation document.[45]

Attribution and vicarious liability

Attribution

11.12 As an artificial person, an LLP—like a company—cannot act other than through human agency. Rules are therefore required in order to decide whose acts, and where appropriate whose states of mind, are to be attributed to the LLP so that they may be treated as the acts and states of mind of the LLP itself. These rules are known as the rules of attribution. In an LLP context, the rules will principally be established by consideration of the various statutory provisions governing LLPs, the provisions of its LLP Agreement, and the general law of agency. Of key significance is s 6(1) of the LLP Act 2000, which provides that every member of an LLP is the agent of the LLP.

The authority of members to act on behalf of the LLP is considered at para 11.14. In most cases, where a member acts with full authority on behalf of the LLP, the attribution of that member's acts to the LLP poses few problems. For example, a member of an LLP who enters into a contract on behalf of the LLP with authority to do so causes the LLP to contract. By the process of attribution under the law of agency, the member's acts are those of the LLP. Similarly, where a third party makes a claim against an LLP based on the allegedly wrongful actions of a member performed on behalf of the LLP—misrepresentation, say—the ordinary rules of agency may suffice to attribute both the acts and state of mind (if relevant) of the member to the LLP. This is not a form of vicarious liability: it is primary liability based on attribution.[46]

However, the position can often be more complex. The context may show that it would be more appropriate to attribute one person's state of mind to an LLP than another. It may often be appropriate to attribute to the LLP the mental state of what, in company law, is often called 'the directing mind and will' of the LLP. The identity of the directing mind and will may depend on the context in which the question arises: the directing mind and will for one purpose may not be the directing mind and will for other purposes. Thus, in the leading case of *Meridian Global Funds Management Asia Ltd v Securities Commission*,[47] when considering a breach of securities regulations a company was attributed with the conduct and knowledge of the (culpable) senior portfolio manager, rather than the (innocent) board or managing director. It was more appropriate to have regard to the state of mind of the former rather than the latter having

---

[45] LLP Act 2000, s 4(1).
[46] Though where the rules of agency do not permit attribution, the LLP may of course still be vicariously liable: that is to say not liable for its own wrong, but liable for the wrong of its member, acting in the course of the LLP's business.
[47] [1995] 2 AC 500, PC.

regard to the purpose of the securities regulation: thus, in context, the portfolio manager was treated as the 'directing mind and will' of the company.

Further complexity arises where a member has acted wrongfully vis-à-vis the LLP: in those circumstances it would utterly negate the member's duty to the LLP if the member's knowledge of his or her own wrongdoing were attributed to the victim of that wrong. In such a case, therefore, the member's knowledge will not ordinarily be attributed to the LLP.[48]

Vicarious liability

On analysis, it may be that acts that are wrongful cannot be attributed to the LLP. However, they remain the acts—and also the wrongs—of the LLP's servant or agent. In such a case, the question may arise as to whether the LLP can be made vicariously liable for the wrong in question. Section 6(4) of the LLP Act 2000 attempts to codify the concept of vicarious liability where the wrongful act is committed by a member of the LLP. It states:

11.13

> Where a member of a limited liability partnership is liable to any person (other than another member of the limited liability partnership) as a result of a wrongful act or omission of his in the course of the business of the limited liability partnership or with its authority, the limited liability partnership is liable to the same extent as the member.

This provision is modelled on s 10 of the Partnership Act 1890 (addressed at paras 4.24–4.35) and many of the same considerations will apply. There are small differences: the word 'ordinary' that qualifies 'course of business' in s 10 is missing from s 6(4); and s 6(4) does not refer to 'any penalty', but is limited to third party liability. The scope of s 6(4) would therefore seem to be in one sense wider and in another narrower than s 10, though given that s 10 has been interpreted as broadly corresponding with the common law doctrine of vicarious liability,[49] it is probably the case that the omission of the word 'ordinary' will give rise to no meaningful point of distinction. As with s 10, the section will impose vicarious liability not just for torts but also equitable wrongs such as dishonest assistance.

In cases that fall outside s 6(4) the common law doctrine of vicarious liability will apply where the wrongdoer is an employee.[50] However, it is unlikely to apply where a member is liable to another member—a scenario excluded from s 6(4). The exclusion of the LLP's statutory vicarious liability in such a case would be meaningless if liability could always be achieved at common law instead, and it must therefore have been intended that vicarious liability would not arise where the exclusion applies. Although the reasoning that seemingly excludes or limits such liability in the case of partners under s 10 of the 1890 Act (that the partnership cannot be vicariously liable to a partner, because

---

[48] *Bilta (UK) Limited v Nazir (No 2)* [2005] UKSC 23, [2006] AC 1.
[49] See para 4.25.
[50] See Jones (ed), *Clerk & Lindsell on Torts* 22nd edn, Sweet & Maxwell, 2018, Ch 6.

otherwise the victim would be suing himself) does not apply to an LLP, it seems likely that the draftsman of s 6(4) was seeking to achieve the same outcome. But is it really the case that an LLP is vicariously liable when (say) a member is injured at work by reason of the negligence of an employee of the LLP acting in the course of the LLP's business, but has no liability where the wrongdoer happens to be a member? Similar difficulties arising in the context of general partnerships remain unresolved.[51]

Members' authority

11.14 Section 6(1) of the LLP Act 2000 provides that every member is the agent of the LLP. The effectiveness of any agency depends on the ambit of authority granted by the agent's principal. As between an LLP and its members, that is a matter that ought to be addressed in the LLP Agreement: though if it is not, it may well be that the correct starting point is that prima facie a member has complete authority on behalf of the LLP. On ordinary principles of agency, the LLP will be bound by anything done by a member (or any other person who is authorized to act as agent) acting within their authority.

Apparent authority

11.15 Where a person's agent acts beyond his or her express authority, the common law rules of apparent (or ostensible) authority will apply in order to determine whether the principal is bound or not.[52] However, s 6(2) seeks to codify the doctrine of apparent authority where the agent is a member. It provides that:

> . . . a limited liability partnership is not bound by anything done by a member in dealing with a person if—
> (a) the member in fact has no authority to act for the limited liability partnership by doing that thing, and
> (b) the person knows that he has no authority or does not know or believe him to be member of the limited liability partnership.

It is implicit that an LLP is bound by the acts of a member when the converse is true. So where a third party (T) deals with a member (M) who lacks actual authority, the LLP will be bound to T where T (a) knows or believes that M is a member of the LLP, but (b) is not aware of M's lack of authority.

There are three consequences to this provision that should be noted.

First, one curious (and surely unintended) effect of s 6(2) is that where T deals with M but wrongly believes M to be a senior employee rather than a member, the LLP will not be bound by anything done by M outside M's actual authority. On the other hand, where T deals with a person who actually *is* a senior employee, the LLP will be bound

---

[51] See para 4.31.
[52] See Watts (ed), *Bowstead & Reynolds on Agency* 21st edn, Sweet & Maxwell, 2018, 3-001ff.

on ordinary principles of agency if that employee had apparent authority to act as they did. There is a distinct lack of coherence here; and unless the common law rules of apparent authority can somehow sit alongside s 6 so that s 6(2) does not preclude liability in such circumstances, there is a risk of the LLP avoiding liability that it ought, properly, not to be able to avoid. It is, however, difficult to read s 6(2) as allowing this.

Second, all agents are subject to a duty of strict liability as to their authority: an agent will be in breach of contract with their principal if they exceed the authority expressly or impliedly granted to them. Therefore, where M acts outside the authority granted by the LLP, but nevertheless so that the LLP is bound to T by M's actions, the LLP may well have a claim against M to indemnify the LLP for any loss caused.[53]

Third, in accordance with the law of agency, where M acts outside the authority granted by the LLP, but the LLP is not bound (eg because, as in the example above, T is misled into thinking that M has authority to act for the LLP, but does not believe M to be a member), M may be liable to T on the basis of breach of warranty of authority.[54] Whether that is satisfactory recompense for the LLP seemingly being able to avoid liability to T is, perhaps, another matter.

The corporate veil and limited liability

The 'corporate veil' that applies to companies will apply also to LLPs. The corporate veil is the metaphorical divide that separates the LLP as a legal person from its members, a distinction which has stood, at least since the middle of the nineteenth century, as a fundamental doctrine of company law, and upon which the concept of limited liability is grounded. As Lord Macnaghten put it in a passage from the seminal case of *Salomon v Salomon & Co Ltd* that might equally describe the metamorphosis of a partnership to an LLP:

11.16

> The company is at law a different person altogether from the subscribers to the memorandum; and, although it may be that after incorporation the business is precisely the same as it was before, and the same persons are managers, and the same hands receive the profits, the company is not in law the agent of the subscribers, or trustees for them. Nor are the subscribers as members liable, in any shape or form, except to the extent and in the manner provided by the Act.[55]

The status of limited liability granted to members of a company or an LLP is directed to two matters. The first such matter is the members' liability to contribute to the assets of the company or LLP in the event of its insolvency. In this regard, s 1(4) of the LLP Act 2000 explains that members of an LLP have 'such liability to contribute to its assets in

---

[53] Ibid 6-002ff.
[54] Ibid 9-060ff.
[55] [1897] AC 22, HL at 51.

the event of its being wound up as is provided for by virtue of this Act'. That is a matter ultimately governed by the provisions of the Insolvency Act 1986:[56] as applied to LLPs, s 74 of the Insolvency Act 1986 provides that members are liable to contribute only to the extent that they have agreed to do so. It is therefore entirely a matter for the LLP Agreement as to what (if any) liability should arise. Their liability is as limited as they choose to make it.

Secondly, and more broadly, the status of limited liability also connotes that members are not liable for the individual debts of the LLP as they arise. This is not a matter addressed in express terms by the LLP Act 2000. Rather, it is simply a consequence of the LLP's separate legal personality,[57] and the fact that the members act only as agents for the LLP, rather than on their own account or for each other.[58] On general principles, the LLP alone is liable for the debts and liabilities it contracts.

Exceptions

11.17 There are nevertheless exceptions to limited liability. For example, as with company directors, insolvency legislation contains a variety of provisions to require contribution from LLP members in the event of default, or so as to preserve the *pari passu* principle of insolvency. They are addressed below in Chapter 17. A member who is disqualified from being a member of an LLP under the Company Directors Disqualification Act 1986 is also jointly and severally liable with the LLP for debts incurred during their membership.[59]

Furthermore, the limited liability granted to members of an LLP is circumscribed by the LLP Act 2000 itself. Section 4A provides that if an LLP carries on business with only one member for more than six months, then the sole member is jointly and severally liable with the LLP for the payment of any of the LLP's debts that are contracted whilst he or she knows that the LLP is carrying on business with only one member. Unlike a company, therefore, an LLP must have at least two members in order to retain the benefits of limited liability.[60] Indeed, the fact there is only one member of an LLP is a ground on which the LLP may be wound up[61] or removed from the register.[62]

Lifting the veil

11.18 There are also occasions when the court will lift or 'pierce' the veil, treating the company as indistinguishable from the person or persons who control it. The law in this respect has been authoritatively restated in *Petrodel Resources v Prest*.[63] There, the Supreme Court held that the court could pierce the veil for the purpose of depriving

---

[56] LLP Regs 2001, Sch 3 (IA, s 74).
[57] As a matter of English law at least: see *Rayner (Mincing Lane) Ltd v Department of Trade* [1989] Ch 72, CA at 176 per Kerr LJ.
[58] LLP Act 2000, s 6(1)
[59] By s 15: see para 12.15.
[60] Though there is no reason in principle why the second member could not be a company wholly owned and controlled by the first member, or indeed why two companies together cannot form an LLP.
[61] LLP Regs 2001, Sch 3 (IA, s 122(1)(c)).
[62] LLP Regs 2009, reg 51 (CA, s 1003).
[63] [2013] UKSC 34, [2013] 2 AC 415.

the company's controller(s) of the advantage that might otherwise be gained from the company's separate legal personality. It would do so when the controller sought to use the company to deliberately evade or frustrate an existing legal obligation, liability, or restriction. The same analysis will apply to LLPs.

In practice, the principle under which the court will lift the corporate veil is one of limited application. That is because, in most cases where the court might be minded to do so, the fraudulent behaviour of the company's controller is likely to provide other means of preventing the controller from evading liability. It is only necessary to pierce the veil where the controller has otherwise truly managed to evade his or her responsibilities. When applied to LLPs, the need to pierce the veil is perhaps more limited still, given the requirement—in practice at least—that an LLP should contain two members. In short, there is no obvious reason why a fraudster would make use of an LLP for such a scheme when a company would do just as well, without the added problem of finding a second member. On the other hand, as members of an LLP can be purely legal persons, it is not difficult to envisage circumstances in which an LLP with one or more corporate members might be used as part of a sham structure for the purpose of assisting an individual in evading liability.

Capacity

In the words of s 1(3) of the LLP Act 2000, an LLP 'has unlimited capacity'. The various complications and difficulties that arise when a partnership assumes liabilities, executes documentation, acquires property, or litigates will therefore not arise. The LLP can do all these things itself, and in its own name. It can subscribe for shares in a company, form another LLP, or even enter into partnership.   **11.19**

Pre-incorporation contracts and deeds
An LLP that has yet to come into existence obviously has no capacity at all, and—with one exception—the rules that govern contracts and deeds that purport to be entered into with companies prior to incorporation set out in s 51 of the Companies Act 2006 apply equally to LLPs. That is to say: **11.20**

> a contract that purports to be made by or on behalf of an LLP at a time when the LLP has not been formed has effect, subject to any agreement to the contrary, as one made with the person purporting to act for the LLP or as agent for it, and he is liable on the contract accordingly.[64]

It would also seem to follow that the person purporting to act for the LLP may take the benefit of a contract that they enter into in these circumstances.[65]

---

[64] LLP Regs 2009, reg 7 (CA, s 51). The same rule applies to deeds by s 51(2).
[65] *Braymist Ltd v Wise Finance Co Ltd* [2002] EWCA Civ 127, [2002] Ch 273.

Note that a company cannot by adoption or ratification obtain the benefit of a contract purporting to have been made by or on its behalf before it came into existence.[66] The same will be true of an LLP. Instead, a new contract will be required and ordinary contractual principles of novation will apply.

The exception relates to the LLP Agreement itself, as to which s 5(2) of the LLP Act 2000 provides that:

> an agreement made before the incorporation of a limited liability partnership between the persons who subscribe their names to the incorporation document may impose obligations on the limited liability partnership (to take effect at any time after its incorporation).

The intention behind this provision is presumably that an LLP Agreement may be executed by all the members prior to incorporation, so that it will bind the LLP without any further formality once it is incorporated. It is, however, questionable whether s 5(2) achieves this goal: not only does it say nothing about rights that the LLP Agreement might seek to grant to the LLP, but it also fails to make clear the interrelation with the general rule under the Companies Act 2006, s 51. After all, a pre-incorporation agreement that seeks to 'impose obligations on the limited liability partnership' would, in the ordinary course, fall within s 51. So does it take effect as envisaged by s 51 pending incorporation? In all events, it would be advisable for an LLP, once incorporated, to formally become a party to any LLP Agreement that is intended to bind it.

Post-incorporation contracts and deeds

11.21 After incorporation, an LLP may contract in the same way as a company: ie either in writing 'under its common seal' or simply by way of an agent acting with express or implied authority further to the principles of attribution discussed at para 11.12.[67]

An LLP is not required to have a common seal, but if it has one it can also execute a document by affixing that seal to it. Alternatively, two members may sign, or one member may sign in the presence of an attesting witness.[68] Where one of the signing members is itself a corporation, it may be that an individual will have to sign in more than one capacity: eg once as the first signatory on behalf of the LLP and once as a director/member of the second signatory on behalf of the LLP. In such a case, that person must sign separately in each capacity.

A deed must not only be executed to take effect, but must also be unconditionally 'delivered', usually by exchange with a counterparty. Delivery will be presumed upon execution, unless the contrary is proved.[69]

---

[66] *Natal Land & Colonization Co Ltd v Pauline Colliery & Development Syndicate Ltd* [1904] AC 120, PC.
[67] LLP Regs 2009, reg 4 (CA, s 43).
[68] LLP Regs 2009, reg 4 (CA, s 44).
[69] LLP Regs 2009, reg 4 (CA, s 46).

Finally, in favour of a purchaser in good faith for valuable consideration, it is provided that a document will be deemed to have been duly executed by an LLP if it 'purports' to be signed on behalf of the LLP by two members or by a member in the presence of an attesting witness.[70] Perhaps surprisingly, the precise impact of this provision is unclear: on the one hand, an LLP is probably bound where a member executes a document without express authority, or where a member without authority forges the signature of a member with authority;[71] but it is not so obvious that two people who are not members—indeed, who may be wholly unconnected to the LLP—can by means of forgery cause the LLP to execute a document that binds the LLP vis-à-vis a purchaser in good faith.[72]

Litigation

LLPs sue and are sued in their own name. Provision has been made under Part 6 of the Civil Procedure Rules (CPR) for the service of claim forms and other documents on LLPs at their 'principal office', or at any place of business within the jurisdiction with a real connection to the claim.[73] The alternative service regime under the Companies Act 2006 is also applied.[74] Unfortunately, the provisions of CPR 6 do not completely address the position of LLPs. In particular, certain documents in litigation must be served 'personally' on parties, and although CPR 6.5 explains how personal service can be effected on a company or partnership, it fails to state how personal service can be effected on an LLP. It may be that, by analogy with the provisions for partnership, service can be personally effected by leaving it with a member of the LLP; or it may be that, by analogy with the provisions for companies, service can be personally effected by leaving it with 'a person holding a senior position' within the LLP (who may not necessarily be a member). A party seeking to effect personal service on an LLP would be advised to seek to meet both tests.

11.22

CPR 39.6, the rule that permits a company to be represented at trial by an 'employee' with the permission of the court, applies to LLPs as it does to all other corporations. It is inherent in this rule that a company director (who may or may not be an employee) may represent the company with the court's permission; and it must be equally inherent that a member of an LLP (who is never an employee: see para 12.08) may represent the LLP with the court's permission.

---

[70] LLP Regs 2009, reg 4 (CA, s 44(4)): though, unhelpfully, the equivalent provision for companies is in fact contained in Companies Act 2006, s 44(5).
[71] *Lovett v Carson Country Homes Ltd* [2009] EWHC 1143 (Ch), [2009] 2 BCLC 196. Though might LLP Act 2000, s 6(2) preclude liability in certain cases? See para 11.15.
[72] Ibid [98]–[102]. Despite the judge's equivocation, it is difficult to believe this was the intended effect of s 44(5). Such a conclusion would result in the Companies Act 2006 having radically changed the law in this respect: see *Ruben v Great Fingall Consolidated* [1906] AC 439, HL.
[73] CPR 6.3(3), CPR 6.9 at entry 4, and CPR 6.20(3).
[74] LLP Regs 2009, reg 75 (CA, ss 1139–1140). These rules permit service of documents on LLPs and their members at their registered addresses. Note that in the case of members, these rules apply regardless of the purpose of the document, and regardless of whether the document relates to the LLP. They therefore provide a potentially useful method of service on a member of an LLP in respect of litigation or other matters wholly extraneous to the business of the LLP: *Re Energy Corrector Ltd* [2019] EWHC 144 (Ch) at [30]–[33].

In most other respects, LLPs will litigate as companies do. They are undoubtedly amenable to the common law 'derivative action' jurisdiction of the courts,[75] whereby in the event that those managing the LLP decline (or are unable) to allow it to pursue a legal remedy, in certain circumstances a member may bring a claim in the name of an LLP, subject to the permission of the court.[76] Furthermore, it is likely that the 'rule against reflective loss' would apply to LLPs, so as to prevent a member from suing for damage done to his or her share or interest in the LLP consequent to damage done to the LLP itself: instead, the member must procure the LLP to sue for the damage it has suffered (provided it has a cause of action). The rule against reflective loss is designed to ensure that where both the company and a shareholder could sue in respect of the same loss (the shareholder's loss being the loss of value of shares in the company and therefore parasitic), only the company may sue.[77] There would seem no reason not to apply the same logic to members of LLPs.

Disclosure obligations

11.23 As with companies, the law imposes certain obligations on LLPs as the quid pro quo for limited liability. These obligations are intended to allow those who deal with LLPs to be made aware that they are dealing with an entity with limited liability, to learn the identity of those who comprise its membership and those who control it, and to discover information as to the LLP's assets and liabilities.

Once the LLP has been incorporated, the incorporation document and statement in support become public documents available for inspection at Companies House (though some personal information, such as residential addresses, is first expunged). The certificate of incorporation is similarly a public document. The provisions of the Companies Act 2006 with respect to public inspection apply:[78] in practical terms, this currently means that these documents, and all other formal documents submitted to the Registrar, can be found in PDF format on the Companies House website.[79] Note that there is no requirement to register or publish the LLP Agreement, either at incorporation or subsequently.

During the LLP's lifetime, a number of continuing disclosure obligations apply. These are set out in the paragraphs that follow.

---

[75] *Harris v Microfusion 2003-2 LLP* [2016] EWCA Civ 1212. However, the statutory jurisdiction for derivative actions under the Companies Act 2006 has not been applied to LLPs. Such claims will therefore fall within CPR 19.9C.
[76] For full treatment, see Joffe et al, *Minority Shareholders: Law, Practice, and Procedure* 6th edn, OUP, 2019, Ch 2.
[77] *Prudential Assurance v Newman (No 2)* [1982] Ch 204, CA.
[78] LLP Regs 2009, reg 66 (CA, ss 1085–1086).
[79] <https://beta.companieshouse.gov.uk>.

Display of name

An LLP must announce itself as such, by displaying its registered name at its registered office, any alternative inspection location (or 'SAIL': see para 11.25), and any other location where it carries on business. Detailed rules in this regard are contained in regulations which apply equally to companies and LLPs.[80]

11.24

An LLP must also display its registered name on all business correspondence and documentation, including letters, notices, and invoices, as well as on its websites.[81] Business correspondence, order forms, and the LLP's websites must also carry the LLP's registered number, the address of its registered office, its situation (ie the part of the UK in which it is registered), and (in most cases) the fact that it is an LLP.[82]

Failure to comply with these rules exposes the LLP and its designated members to the risk of criminal prosecution. The LLP may also find itself unable to enforce a contract executed in breach of the rules if its counterparty can show that it is unable to pursue some claim against the LLP by reason of a breach of the rules, or if the breach has caused it to suffer some financial loss in connection with the contract.[83]

Register of members

The register of members is one of three registers that an LLP is required keep;[84] the other two being the register of members' addresses,[85] the register of persons with significant control.[86] These registers should not be confused with the register maintained by the Registrar of Companies under s 1080 of the Companies Act 2006 (sometimes referred to in the legislation as the 'central register'),[87] though (as explained below) it is possible now for an LLP to use the central register in place of maintaining its own registers.

11.25

The register of members records the names of every member of the LLP, along with various other prescribed particulars. In the case of individual members,[88] those are an address for service (which may simply be the registered office of the LLP, or indeed any other address), the country of residence, and date of birth. In the case of members who are corporations or other artificial persons,[89] those are the registered or principal office and relevant registration particulars (such as company number). In both cases, the register must record whether the member is a designated member or not.

---

[80] Company, Limited Liability Partnership and Business (Names and Trading Disclosures) Regulations 2015, SI 2015/17, Pt 6, given effect by LLP Regs 2009, reg 14 (CA, s 82).
[81] SI 2015/17, reg 24.
[82] SI 2015/17, reg 25.
[83] LLP Regs 2009, reg 14 (CA, s 83).
[84] LLP Regs 2009, reg 18 (CA, s 162(1)).
[85] LLP Regs 2009, reg 18 (CA, s 165(1)).
[86] LLP Regs 2009, reg 31E (CA, s 790M(1)).
[87] A confusion that appears to have been made in *Polegoshko v Ibragimov* [2015] EWHC 1669 (Ch), where the court ordered rectification of the central register under LLP Regs 2009, reg 67 (CA, s 1096), apparently in the belief that it was thereby rectifying an LLP's register of members.
[88] LLP Regs 2009, reg 18 (CA, s 163).
[89] LLP Regs 2009, reg 18 (CA, s 164).

It is important to note that the register of members is not definitive: rather, it records the LLP's understanding of who is a member, and represents a person's status as such to third parties. Accordingly, there is no equivalent provision to Companies Act 2006, s 112(2) which defines members of a company by reference to their entry in the register of members. Nor is there an express provision under which the court may rectify the register of members, though the court can of course compel the LLP to reflect a person's true status at the suit of that person, and an inherent power to this effect therefore exists.[90] Whether a person actually is a member or not is addressed at para 12.01.

Traditionally, a company kept its statutory records, including its register of directors and register of members, at its registered office. An LLP may still choose to keep its statutory registers in that way—whether in paper form or electronically. However, two alternative options are also available to it.

First, an LLP may specify (by filing form LL AD02) a 'SAIL address'—that is an address that serves as a 'single alternative inspection location'. This allows the LLP to keep its register of members (and other inspectable registers and documents) at a place other than the LLP's registered office, so that the right of members or the public to inspect the LLP's records can be carried out somewhere more (or maybe less) convenient. As its name suggests, an LLP may have only one SAIL, and must record (by filing form LL AD03 or LL AD04) the transfer of inspectable documents and registers from its registered office to its SAIL and vice versa.

Second, as a result of reforms introduced with effect from 30 June 2016 by the Small Business, Enterprise and Employment Act 2015, an LLP may elect to keep its registers centrally, on the central register maintained by the Registrar of Companies.[91] If this method is chosen, then rather than updating its books manually, the LLP must file updates at Companies House in addition to its other reporting requirements. This delegates the administration of keeping the LLP's statutory registers to the Registrar of Companies. It essentially elides the central register maintained by the Registrar with the LLP's own registers. The price for that convenience is that the LLP's own registers become public documents available for instant inspection via the Companies House website: though that is, perhaps, no great price to pay given that the information will in the ordinary course mostly appear also on the central register anyway, as explained below.

If the LLP chooses to keep its own register of members, it may be inspected by any person, members and non-members alike, though non-members must pay a fee. The location of the register—whether the LLP's registered office or its SAIL—must also be notified to the Registrar. There are no particular requirements as to the form in which registers must be kept, and they may therefore be electronic rather than physical.

---

[90] Compare *Speed Investments Ltd v Formula One Holdings (No 2)* [2004] EWCA Civ 1512, [2005] 1 WLR 1936. See also n 87.

[91] LLP Regs 2009, reg 18A (CA, ss 167A–167E) (register of members and register of members' residential addresses); LLP Regs 2009, reg 31K (CA, ss 790W–790ZD) (PSC register).

Failure to notify the Registrar of the location, and failure to permit inspection, are both offences. Any designated member who is 'in default' with respect to such a failure likewise commits an offence.[92]

An LLP must also maintain a register of residential addresses of individual members, stating their 'usual residential address' though there is no statutory requirement to make this available for inspection except by court order.[93] The contents of this register are treated as 'protected information' that, whether held by the LLP or by the Registrar, may only be used or disclosed in certain limited circumstances.[94]

Notification of membership changes to the Registrar

Whether or not the LLP elects to keep its register centrally, it is required to give notice to the Registrar of all changes in the membership, so that these can be recorded on the central register. Thus when the membership of the LLP changes, or when the particulars in the register of members changes, or when the identity of the designated members changes, the LLP must additionally ensure that notice of the change is delivered to the Registrar within fourteen days of the change.[95] Appointment and termination of membership are addressed by forms LL AP01 and LL TM01 respectively; changes of a member's particulars by form LL CH01 or form LL CH02 depending on whether the member is an individual or a corporation. This information will appear on the central register (and the Companies House website) regardless of whether the LLP elects to keep its own register of members. In practice, therefore, even if an LLP chooses to keep its own register of members and does not elect to use the central register, much of the same information will still be available to the public via Companies House.[96]

11.26

The PSC register

LLPs are obliged to maintain a register of 'people with significant control' (PSC).[97] This is another innovation introduced by the Small Business, Enterprise and Employment Act 2015 in the name of corporate transparency. The regulations are to be found in a new Part 21A of the Companies Act 2006, as supplemented by provisions contained in the Register of People with Significant Control Regulations 2016.[98] Those are applied to LLP via the provisions of a new Part 8A of the LLP Regulations 2009.[99] The legislation is highly complex, though the Department for Business, Energy and Industrial Strategy

11.27

---

[92] LLP Regs 2009, reg 18 (CA, s 162).
[93] LLP Regs 2009, reg 18 (CA, s 165), reg 19 (CA, s 244).
[94] LLP Regs 2009, reg 19 (CA, ss 241–246). These include a byzantine procedure by which the Registrar may determine to publish a member's residential address if there is evidence to suggest that the member's service address is not an effective medium of communication or service.
[95] LLP Act 2000, s 9.
[96] There are some modest distinctions in content of what is recorded and in terms of the timing of the obligation to record it. For example, if the register is kept centrally, a member's full date of birth is published. If not, the day is omitted under LLP Regs 2009, reg 66 (CA, s 1087A).
[97] LLP Regs 2009, reg 31E (CA, s 790M).
[98] SI 2016/339.
[99] Introduced by the Limited Liability Partnerships (Register of People with Significant Control) Regulations 2016, SI 2016/340.

(BEIS) has published guidance on the regulations (running to over 100 pages in its most recent edition[100]) that can be found via its website. Some of that guidance is 'statutory guidance' and is therefore material in the interpretation of the various regulations.

The intention is to allow the identity of those who ultimately control companies and LLPs (and certain other entities) to be apparent from the register. As one might imagine, the notion of defining 'significant control' in the context of LLPs proves a particular challenge, given the varied and informal ways that an LLP may choose to manage itself, but the government has managed to make the regulations equally complex for both LLPs and companies. Essentially, a person is a PSC if they fulfil one or more of five conditions:[101]

- the right to more than 25 per cent of the assets on a winding up;
- more than 25 per cent of the voting rights;
- the right to appoint the majority of management;
- the exercise of 'significant influence or control' over the LLP (a concept that is glossed in the legislation and in statutory guidance);
- the exercise of 'significant influence or control' over a trust or partnership that falls within the above categories.

Whilst the first three conditions would not ordinarily be expected to present much difficulty, it is easy to see how, in the context of an LLP, identifying what voting rights should qualify as giving significant control, or who qualifies as 'management', may prove troublesome.

An LLP is under a statutory obligation to gather the requisite information and record it in a PSC register and to keep it up to date.[102] The PSC register records the name, date of birth, nationality, and country of residence of each PSC, their service address and residential address (the latter being protected information and may therefore only be used or disclosed in certain circumstances[103]), and the date on which they became, or ceased to be, a PSC. There are also rules with respect to identifying the condition or conditions that are fulfilled with respect to each PSC.[104]

By definition, a PSC is an individual; however, the regulations also address the position where significant influence or control is exercised by companies, LLPs, or other entities that themselves have a PSC register. Such entities are called 'Relevant Legal Entities' (RLEs). Essentially, the scheme of the legislation is designed to ensure that where an individual exercises significant influence or control over an LLP through an RLE, the

---

[100] BEIS, 'Register of People with Significant Control: Guidance for Registered and Unregistered Companies, Societates Europaeae, Limited Liability Partnerships, and Eligible Scottish Partnerships (Scottish Limited Partnerships and Scottish Qualifying Partnerships)' (Version 4, June 2017), see <https://www.gov.uk>.
[101] LLP Regs 2009, reg 31B (CA, s 790C) to be read with reg 31M (CA, Sch 1A).
[102] LLP Regs 2009, reg 31C (CA, ss 790D–790J).
[103] LLP Regs 2009, reg 31H (CA, s 790T).
[104] LLP Regs 2009, regs 31D–31E (CA, ss 790K, 790M).

individual will appear on the PSC register of the RLE, whilst the RLE will appear on the PSC register of the LLP.[105]

Like the register of members, the PSC register is either kept at the registered office, at the LLP's SAIL, or it can be held centrally by the Registrar (though in this case the consent of PSCs is also required).[106] It must be made available to inspection by any person, without charge. The criminal penalties that seek to ensure compliance with the requirements pertaining to the register of members also apply to the PSC register.[107]

Registration of charges

Just as an LLP can hold its own property, it can charge its property (eg its land, intellectual property, debts and so forth) as security, by way of fixed or floating charge. The ability to grant a floating charge was one of the potential advantages over general partnerships noted by the Select Committee Report on the Bill that became the LLP Act 2000 (see para 10.04). **11.28**

The Companies Act 2006 rules that apply to the registration of company charges apply, with suitable modifications, to LLPs. Those rules were extensively rewritten in 2013 in order to modernize the system of registration and to bring the English and Scottish rules into uniformity. It is the rules as rewritten that are now incorporated into the LLP Regulations 2009 with suitable modifications.[108]

Registrable charges—and that now means most of them—are void as against a liquidator, administrator, or creditor of the LLP unless registered. Registration requires the LLP to deliver to the Registrar a 'statement of particulars' together with a certified copy of any instrument, within twenty-one days of creation of the charge.[109] The required particulars will vary depending on the precise nature of the charge, but they will include the name of the chargee, and a description of the property charged, or (in the case of a floating charge) an indication of whether all the property and undertaking of the LLP is charged. Failure to do so is not an offence, but if the charge is not registered in time then not only is it void against the categories of person described above, but the money secured under it becomes immediately payable.[110] Late registration is possible, provided a court order is first obtained.[111] Once registered, the charge will be given a unique code, and the statement of particulars and any instrument are placed on the central register.[112]

---

[105] Ibid.
[106] LLP Regs 2009, reg 31K (CA, ss 790W–790ZD).
[107] LLP Regs 2009, reg 31F (CA, ss 790N–790O).
[108] LLP Regs 2009, reg 32 (CA, ss 859A–859Q). Transitional provisions contained in the Limited Liability Partnerships (Application of Companies Act 2006) (Amendment) Regulations 2013, SI 2013/618, reg 8 address charges created prior to 6 April 2013.
[109] LLP Regs 2009, reg 32 (CA, ss 859A–859E).
[110] LLP Regs 2009, reg 32 (CA, s 859H).
[111] LLP Regs 2009, reg 32 (CA, s 859F).
[112] LLP Regs 2009, reg 32 (CA, s 859I).

Rules also exist to ensure that the Registrar is made aware of the appointment of a receiver or manager (whether in court or out of court), so that it can be noted against any relevant registered charge. Failure to do so is an offence (committed by the person making the appointment, rather than the LLP or its members), though there are no civil consequences to such a failure.[113] Provision also exists by which the satisfaction of a charge, or the release of property from it, can be recorded.[114]

A copy of the charge itself must be kept by the LLP at its registered office or its SAIL, available for public inspection (by creditors and non-creditors alike, though non-creditors must pay a prescribed fee).[115] As with the register of members, the location of the register must be notified to the Registrar. Failure to notify the Registrar of the location, and failure to permit inspection, are both offences.

In addition to the individual registration of charges, an LLP may choose to keep a register of debenture holders. If it does, provisions exist setting out the particulars that must be recorded and the right of debenture holders, members, and the public to inspect the register (in the case of the public, for a fee).[116]

Annual confirmation statements

11.29 An LLP must deliver a 'confirmation statement' to the Registrar at least annually (on form LL CS01).[117] This is a simplified version of the old annual return. The statement confirms that all the key information required to have been delivered in the period under confirmation has been duly delivered. That is to say: any notification of change in the LLP's registered office, of change in membership, and of change in the location where records are kept. If the LLP has elected to have its records kept centrally by the Registrar, the statement must confirm that all information necessary to update the relevant registers has been submitted. As with other registration requirements, non-compliance is addressed by criminal penalties against the LLP and the designated members.[118]

Records and accounts

11.30 Quite apart from any obligation that may arise from the regulated nature of any business conducted by an LLP, an LLP must keep 'adequate accounting records': that is to say, records that are sufficient to show and explain the LLP's transactions, to disclose with reasonable accuracy, at any time, the financial position of the LLP at that time, and to enable the members of the LLP to ensure that any accounts required to be prepared comply with the relevant requirements of the Companies Act 2006.[119] The records must

---

[113] LLP Regs 2009, reg 32 (CA, s 859K).
[114] LLP Regs 2009, reg 32 (CA, s 859L).
[115] LLP Regs 2009, reg 32 (CA, ss 859P–859Q).
[116] LLP Regs 2009, reg 21 (CA, ss 743–748).
[117] LLP Regs 2009, reg 30 (CA, ss 853A–853B).
[118] LLP Regs 2009, reg 31ZA (CA, s 853L).
[119] LLP Accounting Regs 2008, reg 6 (CA, ss 386, 388).

be available for inspection by the members and must be preserved for at least three years, though in practice tax legislation will require records to be maintained for longer. The records need not be kept at the registered office or SAIL. A failure to comply with these obligations is an offence committed by the LLP and any member (designated or not) who is in default.[120]

As is the case with companies, the precise content of the LLP's obligations to publish annual accounts depends on the size of the LLP in terms of turnover, balance sheet, and employees. In broad terms, and subject to exemptions for dormant entities and the like, the members of an LLP are under a statutory obligation to produce a profit and loss account and balance sheet at the end of each financial year that give a true and fair view of the state of affairs of the LLP for the relevant financial period.[121]

Information on the required contents of the accounts, which will ordinarily be prepared in accordance with Generally Accepted Accounting Practice under FRS 102, can be found in specialist texts. Once those accounts are approved by the members, the designated members are obliged to file them with the Registrar, along with any required auditors' report and 'energy and carbon report' (the latter being an innovation introduced from April 2019 under which larger LLPs must report annually on emissions, energy consumption, and energy efficiency).[122] In the ordinary course, that must happen within nine months of the end of the relevant financial year.[123] Non-compliance is addressed by criminal penalties against the designated members and a civil penalty imposed on the LLP.[124]

---

[120] LLP Accounting Regs 2008, reg 6 (CA, ss 387, 389).
[121] LLP Accounting Regs 2008, reg 9 (CA, s 394). Detailed regulations are set out in the Small Limited Liability Partnerships (Accounts) Regulations 2008, SI 2008/1912 and the Large and Medium-sized Limited Liability Partnerships (Accounts) Regulations 2008, SI 2008/1913.
[122] LLP Accounting Regs 2008, reg 17 (CA, s 441).
[123] LLP Accounting Regs 2008, reg 17 (CA, s 442).
[124] LLP Accounting Regs 2008, reg 22 (CA, ss 451–453).

12
MEMBERSHIP

Who is a Member?

Commencement of membership

Section 4(1) of the LLP Act 2000 provides that a limited liability partnership's (LLP) first members are the subscribers to the incorporation document. Thereafter, the members of the LLP may admit any other member by agreement. Section 4(2) states: **12.01**

> Any other person may become a member of a limited liability partnership by and in accordance with an agreement with the existing members.

The use of the preposition 'by' is unfortunate. It suggests that an agreement must be reached between the proposed new member and the existing members themselves, so that an agreement between the proposed new member and the LLP would not suffice. However, the provision has been interpreted as allowing the existing members to authorize the LLP to enter into the necessary agreement with the proposed new member.[1] In practice, it is common for new members to join an LLP in this manner. Although a decision that a person should be admitted as a member prima facie requires unanimity,[2] it is open to the existing members (typically within the LLP Agreement) to decide that they will be bound by a lower threshold. There is no requirement under s 4(2) that the agreement be in writing. Even entry of a person's name into the register of members is not determinative, though it is, of course, prima facie evidence of an agreement under s 4(2).[3]

The consequences of membership

The effect of a person becoming a member of an LLP depends on the precise terms of the agreement by which they join. There is no requirement that members have equal rights and obligations under the LLP Agreement, and no requirement that a member should receive a share of profits from the LLP. But in the ordinary course the result of **12.02**

---

[1] *Reinhard v Ondra* [2015] EWHC 26 (Ch) at [29]. Strictly, of course, even if the existing members authorize the LLP to enter into such an agreement on its own behalf, the agreement is still made 'by' the LLP rather than 'by' the existing members, but the common sense of this interpretation is obvious.

[2] Not least because of the default rule in LLP Regs 2001, reg 7(5).

[3] Registration appears to affect the substantive rights of a member in only one circumstance: ie only registered members count for the purposes of an application to investigate an LLP's affairs under LLP Regs 2001, Sch 2 (CA 1985, s 431(2)) (see para 10.01 for an explanation of statutory citations from the Regulations).

admission is that a new member will become a full party to the LLP Agreement, and subject to the rights and obligations set out in it.

It follows that a person admitted to an LLP by agreement will assume both the rights and obligations provided for by that agreement, as well as the statutory rights and obligations that are consequent to membership (see para 13.05). These rights are inherent to all members. As Proudman J observed in *Eaton v Caulfield*:

> [T]here is no concept of a member in name only. Members are creatures of statute with statutory rights and obligations.[4]

Degrees of membership?

12.03 By the same token, the difficulties in distinguishing between 'true partners' in a general partnership and those who may appear to be partners, but are not, do not arise in the case of an LLP. In a general partnership, 'salaried' or 'fixed-share' partners may, on analysis, turn out to be true partners if their rights and obligations include the appropriate indicia of partnership; but they might instead not be partners at all, and may have some other status such as that of employee. This is an objective question of substance rather than form: see paras 2.37–2.42. In partnership, therefore, the label applied by the partners is not determinative. By contrast, in an LLP, the label chosen by the parties *is* essentially determinative: it is for the parties to decide whether a person should join the LLP, and if that is what they agree in accordance with s 4(2), then that of itself is sufficient. Section 4(2) does not admit of the sort of analysis one might apply to determine whether a person is a partner or not.[5] So-called 'salaried' and 'fixed-share' members are full members of an LLP.[6]

It is therefore possible for someone to be a member of an LLP in circumstances in which, were the LLP a partnership, they would not be a partner in a partnership. In light of this, whilst all members are vested with the statutory rights and obligations of membership, the full consequences of membership cannot be identified with uniformity: as will be seen, some members may, by virtue of their relative status, owe lesser fiduciary duties than others; tax or pension legislation may treat some members differently on the basis of how they are remunerated; some members may have statutory rights denied to others.

What, then, is the position where the rights or duties contractually vested in an intended member are inconsistent with membership of an LLP? Given the inherent flexibility of the contents of those rights and duties, this will not be a common occurrence. The scenario most likely to occur is where a contract provides (whether expressly or by

---

[4] [2011] EWHC 173 (Ch) at [47].
[5] Though a person's purported admission to membership might, in an appropriate case, be regarded as a sham and therefore ineffective, in accordance with the ordinary principles that apply to sham transactions: *Snook v London and West Riding Investments Ltd* [1967] 2 QB 786, CA at 802.
[6] See para 12.05.

implication) that a person shall be both a member and employee of the LLP. As set out at paras 12.08 to 12.10 it seems these are mutually exclusive statuses, so the court would need to resolve the resulting contradiction either by denying the member's employment or denying their membership.[7] The latter course could lead to an outcome where a person is treated as a contractual party to the LLP Agreement without actually being a member of the LLP—a potentially difficult situation to unravel.

Termination of membership

The methods of termination and their consequences are addressed in Chapter 16. **12.04**

'Salaried members'

The fact that anyone can be a member of an LLP simply by agreement runs the risk that the favourable tax arrangements will be abused, and businesses will convert to LLP status to take improper advantage of the tax rules. A 2013 Treasury consultation document stated: **12.05**

> Current tax rules mean that individuals who are members of an LLP are taxed as if they are partners in a partnership established under Partnership Act 1890 (traditional partnership) even if they are engaged on terms closer to those of employees. This produces unfairness in the tax system as an individual member of an LLP who is treated as a partner receives more favourable treatment of income tax and National Insurance Contributions ('employment taxes') than an individual who is an employee engaged on similar terms. As a result, LLPs can be used to disguise employment and to avoid employment taxes. There is evidence that LLPs are increasingly being used and marketed on that basis.[8]

As a result, significant changes to LLP/member taxation were introduced by the Finance Act 2014.[9] These are intended to achieve the result that certain members— referred to in the legislation as 'salaried members'—are taxed as employees (and subject to employee PAYE, national insurance and pension treatment, including compulsory enrolment) if, by reference to various statutory tests, they do not share sufficiently in the profits and losses of the LLP, they do not have sufficient influence over its affairs, and they have not made sufficient capital contribution. It is important to note that although taxed as employees, salaried members are not actually employees but are full members of the LLP.

---

[7] *Reinhard v Ondra LLP* [2015] EWHC 26 (Ch) at [46], [375]. See also subsequent proceedings at [2015] EWHC 1869 (Ch) in which the court had to decide between the two possibilities.
[8] HMRC, 'Partnerships: A review of two aspects of the tax rules' (20 May 2013).
[9] Amending the Income Tax (Trading and Other Income) Act 2005, by the addition of ss 863A–863G.

In very broad terms, a member (M) is treated as a salaried member if three conditions (labelled A, B, and C in the legislation) are fulfilled:

> Condition A: If it is reasonable to expect that at least 80% of M's performance related income is 'disguised salary': ie a sum which is not variable in accordance with the LLP's profits and losses;
>
> Condition B: If M does not have significant influence over the affairs of the LLP;
>
> Condition C: If M's capital contribution to the LLP is less than 25% of their disguised salary.

A member who meets all three conditions is taxed as an employee, and the LLP is therefore required to pay the various employment taxes that their employment would attract. Unsurprisingly, the legislation resulted in a flurry of amendments to affected LLP Agreements, generally by introducing an element of profit-related remuneration so as to overcome the first condition.

Shadow members

12.06 A 'shadow member' is a person who is not a member of the LLP, but is nevertheless someone 'in accordance with whose directions or instructions the members of the LLP are accustomed to act'.[10] A shadow member will therefore have no rights or duties under the LLP Agreement, and is not a member except for the purposes of the particular statutory provisions in which the status is engaged: that is to say certain provisions of the Insolvency Act 1986—in particular wrongful trading and the adjustment of withdrawals[11] and various criminal sanctions—and the disqualification provisions of the Company Directors Disqualification Act 1986 (CDDA 1986).[12] Shadow membership is not, therefore, membership in any true sense: the concept is, rather, a statutory construct to make third parties liable for certain consequences in the event of insolvency or wrongdoing.

Directors of a holding company are not, by virtue of that status alone, shadow directors of the subsidiary company. By the same logic, it would follow that the directors of a corporate member of an LLP will not be shadow members of the LLP itself merely because, acting in their capacity as directors, they instruct the corporate member to exercise its rights and duties with respect to the LLP in a particular way.[13]

---

[10] LLP Regs 2001, reg 2, Sch 3 (IA, s 251).
[11] LLP Regs 2001, Sch 3 (IA, ss 214-214A).
[12] LLP Regs 2001, reg 4(2).
[13] *Re Hydrodan (Corby) Ltd (in liquidation)* [1994] BCC 161 (Ch) at 164 per Millett J. See also *Revenue & Customs Commissioners v Holland* [2010] UKSC 51, [2010] 1 WLR 2793, in the context of de facto directors.

De facto members

Unlike the status of shadow director, the status of 'de facto director' of a company has no statutory recognition, but is wholly judge-made. In company law, a de facto director is a person who assumes the responsibilities of a director despite not being validly appointed as such—most often simply because of oversight in the performance of some formality, or perhaps because his or her term of office has unknowingly expired.[14] Generally speaking, de facto directors are treated as de jure directors for the purposes of company and insolvency legislation. As a result, the various provisions of company and insolvency legislation that impose liability on a director for wrongdoing or which can lead to disqualification apply equally to a de facto director. In addition, acts performed by de facto directors are treated as valid acts of a company, with Companies Act 2006, s 161 further providing that the acts of a person acting as director are valid despite any defect in his or her appointment.

12.07

The ability to treat a 'de facto director' as a true director is significantly assisted by the fact that company and insolvency legislation does not provide an exhaustive definition for the term 'director'—merely stating that it includes a de jure director, but without limiting it to such a person.[15]

Does LLP law recognize the concept of a 'de facto member'—that is to say a person who has not been validly made a member under s 4(1) or s 4(2) of the LLP Act 2000 but nevertheless acts as a member and is willingly held out by the LLP as being a member?

There are good reasons why it should, though getting to such an outcome may not be straightforward. The term 'member' is not as loosely defined in the LLP Act 2000 as the term 'director' is in companies legislation, and Companies Act 2006, s 161 does not apply to LLPs. Instead, s 18 of the LLP Act 2000 requires the term 'member' to be construed 'in accordance with section 4'. It is therefore difficult, if not impossible, to see how a person who has *not* been validly appointed under s 4 can be a 'member' for the purposes of the LLP Act 2000 without the assistance of some sort of estoppel, the existence of which will depend on the facts. The LLP Regulations 2001 and 2009 do not define 'member' either, but by reason of Interpretation Act 1978, s 11, the definition in the LLP Act 2000 will apply 'unless contrary intention appears'.[16] So assuming the definition in s 18 is exhaustive, it seems to follow that where the legislation refers to a 'member', that can (subject to estoppel) only mean a de jure member.

---

[14] A person may also be a de facto director simply by virtue of assuming direction of the company, and becoming part of its governing structure. In *Holland* (n 13) the majority of the Supreme Court held that this required them to actually perform acts as a director of the company: so a person who acted as director of a corporate director of a company would not thereby be a de facto director of that company. See also *Smithton Ltd v Naggar* [2014] EWCA Civ 939, [2015] 1 WLR 189 at [20]–[45].

[15] *Re Lo-Line Electric Motors Ltd* [1988] Ch 477 at 488 per Sir Nicholas Browne-Wilkinson V-C. See also n 21.

[16] 'Where an Act confers power to make subordinate legislation, expressions used in that legislation have, unless the contrary intention appears, the meaning which they bear in the Act.'

Even if this is right, the effect on the LLP will be limited. There is, generally speaking, no requirement for an LLP to act through its members: it may act through any human agent, member or not, provided that person is vested with authority. In addition, any person who acts on behalf of the LLP will owe appropriate duties to the LLP when doing so arising from the role they have assumed, validly appointed member or not.

In any event, given the lack of formality required under s 4(2), a de facto member may rapidly become a de jure member by an agreement founded on mutual conduct, though that may depend on the capacity of the person to actually be a member,[17] and the ability of the LLP and existing members to enter into such an agreement, having regard to the terms of the LLP Agreement between them.

But questions remain. For example, is a 'de facto member' a member for the purposes of applying s 44 of the Companies Act 2006[18] (execution of documents), or under the specific rules of authority that apply in s 6(2) of the LLP Act 2000?[19] And can a de facto member's conduct be sanctioned by the courts in the same way as a de facto director's conduct can?[20] It is difficult to justify excluding such a person from the definition of 'member' in these scenarios; and one can imagine that the courts will look to find a way to avoid doing so.[21]

Members and Employees

12.08 Section 4(4) of the LLP Act 2000 represents one of the great mysteries of LLP law. It states:

> A member of a limited liability partnership shall not be regarded for any purpose as employed by the limited liability partnership unless, if he and the other members were partners in a partnership, he would be regarded for that purpose as employed by the partnership.

At first blush, the intent behind this provision would appear to be to ensure that a member's employment status is unaffected by whether the organization of which they

---

[17] A corporate body may not have that capacity under its constitution. An individual may not have that capacity if they have some alternative incompatible status: eg employee (see para 12.08).
[18] LLP Regs 2009, reg 4 (CA, s 44). See para 11.21.
[19] See para 11.15.
[20] Most significantly by disqualification under CDDA 1986, and in respect of claims under Insolvency Act 1986, ss 212, 214, 214A.
[21] It might be thought that Insolvency Act 1986, s 251 and CDDA 1986, s 22(4), both of which are adopted by the LLP Regs 2001, might be relevant here. Under those provisions, a director 'includes any person occupying the position of director, by whatever name called' subject to the instruction in reg 4 to substitute 'director' with 'member'. However, on close analysis these provisions do not assist. That is because, as explained in *Re Lo-Line Electric Motors Ltd* (n 15), a de facto director falls outside this wording (which simply addresses nomenclature for a de jure director). Rather, it is the absence of any exhaustive definition of the term 'director' that allows the courts to construe the term as including a de facto director where appropriate. On the other hand, since an exhaustive definition *is* supplied for the term 'member' by LLP Act 2000, s 18 a similar line of reasoning cannot be adopted.

are a part is an LLP or partnership. Section 4(4) would thus seem to require the application of a statutory hypothesis—that the LLP is a partnership and the members, including the person concerned (M), are partners. On that hypothesis, M will only be an employee of the LLP if M would have been an employee of the hypothetical firm.

That is all very well, until one recalls that (on an orthodox understanding of the law, at any rate) a partner in a partnership can never be an employee, as a result of the rule that a person cannot employ himself.[22] But if that is right, then the condition of the section could never be fulfilled, and M could never be regarded for any purpose as employed by the LLP. The answer to s 4(4) would always be the same: a member of an LLP shall never be regarded for any purpose as employed by the LLP. So what would be the point of the condition?

One way of making sense of s 4(4) could be to treat the hypothetical partnership as a *purported* hypothetical partnership: thus M is not an employee unless, if M and the other members were *held out* as partners in a partnership, M would be regarded as an employee. Another possibility—to much the same effect—would be to gloss over the words 'he and', and simply ask what M's status would be if the other members were partners. One would essentially be incorporating into s 4(4) the conundrum that arises as to the status of a 'salaried partner' or 'fixed share partner': if the LLP was a partnership, on which side of the line would M fall: partner or not? If the former, then s 4(4) precludes M from being regarded as an employee. If the latter, s 4(4) would not preclude it.

Tiffin v Lester Aldridge LLP

This second approach was the one adopted by the Court of Appeal in *Tiffin v Lester Aldridge LLP*.[23] In that case, speaking for a unanimous Court of Appeal, Rimer LJ proposed construing s 4(4) as follows:

12.09

> Section 4(4) requires an assumption that the business of the LLP has been carried on in partnership by two or more of its members as partners; and upon that assumption, an inquiry as to whether or not the person in question would have been one of such partners. If the answer to that inquiry is that he *would* have been a partner, then he could not have been an employee so will not be, nor have been, an employee of the LLP. If the answer is that he would *not* have been a partner, there must then be a further inquiry as to whether his relationship with the notional partnership would have been that of an employee. If it would have been, then he will be, or would have been, an employee of the limited liability partnership.[24]

---

[22] See para 2.34 and *Cowell v Quilter Goodison Co Ltd* [1989] IRLR 392, CA.
[23] *Tiffin v Lester Aldridge LLP* [2012] EWCA Civ 35, [2012] 1 WLR 1887. Steps towards similar reasoning can be found in the earlier judgment of the Employment Appeal Tribunal in *Kovats v TFO Management LLP* [2009] ICR 1140, addressed in *Tiffin* at [33]–[34].
[24] *Tiffin v Lester Aldridge LLP* (n 23) at [32]. Jackson LJ and Sir Nicholas Wall P agreed with Rimer LJ's judgment.

There is much sense to this suggestion, even if it does strain the statutory language (though s 4(4) is hardly the only provision in the LLP Act 2000 whose drafting leaves something to be desired). Rimer LJ's interpretation gives s 4(4) a statutory purpose which is coherent, inasmuch as it ensures that a partnership's decision to incorporate does not affect the employment status of those working at the firm, and ensures that, in addressing the newly fashioned LLP, courts did not treat membership as equivalent to employment. It also has the distinct advantage of allowing the test under s 4(4) to admit of more than one possible answer. If correct, whilst it would mean that many (if not most) members of LLPs would not be regarded as employees, it would allow protection for those more junior members who had very limited rights in the LLP, and who would not, in a partnership, be regarded as true partners. Thus an LLP that offered membership to its employees with a view to evading employment rights legislation—with respect to matters such as unfair dismissal, redundancy, or parental leave—would likely be unsuccessful in doing so if the membership offered lacked the indicia of true partnership.

Clyde & Co LLP v Bates van Winkelhof

12.10 Rimer LJ's proposed construction was adopted without adverse comment by the Court of Appeal in *Clyde & Co LLP v Bates van Winkelhof*.[25] That case did not concern the question of whether a member of an LLP was an employee, but rather whether the member was a worker. Under the Employment Rights Act 1996, 'worker' is a broader category than 'employee' and includes not only those who work under a contract of employment, but also those who undertake work or services for another person (other than a client or customer).[26] In addressing that question, the Court of Appeal took the view that s 4(4) applied to both employees and workers: so a member could not be a worker unless the necessary condition were fulfilled. It then applied the test derived from *Tiffin* in order to determine whether, if the business of the LLP had been carried out in partnership, the claimant would have been one of the partners. It held she would have been. It went on to find that partners in a general partnership could not be workers any more than they could be employees, and so the claimant could not be regarded as a worker.

However, when the case reached the Supreme Court,[27] matters took a very different turn. In overruling the Court of Appeal's judgment, the Supreme Court took the view that s 4(4) did not apply to workers. The question of whether the claimant was a worker was therefore entirely a matter of construction of the Employment Rights Act 1996, without reference to the LLP Act 2000. Construing the former, it held that the claimant was, indeed, a worker.

---

[25] [2012] EWCA Civ 1207, [2013] 1 All ER 844 at [42], revd (n 27).
[26] Employment Rights Act 1996, s 230.
[27] *Clyde & Co LLP v Bates van Winkelhof* [2014] UKSC 32, [2014] 1 WLR 2047.

But on the way to that conclusion the Supreme Court made wider observations, of significance to both the law of partnership and the law of LLPs. As to the former, Lady Hale DP questioned the proposition that a partner could not be an employee: her observations in this regard have already been considered at para 2.34. As to the latter, she also took the opportunity to reject Rimer LJ's interpretation of s 4(4). In Lady Hale's view, the statute should be applied literally because (whatever the position might be in England), there was a good argument that partners in a Scottish partnership could be employees of the partnership, so s 4(4), read literally, did serve some function after all. She held:

> ... once it is recognised that the 2000 Act is a UK-wide statute, and that there is doubt about whether partners in a Scottish partnership can also be employed by the partnership, then there is no need to give such a strained construction to section 4(4). All that it is saying is that, whatever the position would be were the LLP members to be partners in a traditional partnership, then that position is the same in an LLP. I would hold, therefore, that that is how section 4(4) is to be construed.[28]

It is arguable that Lady Hale's observations here are not part of the *ratio decidendi* of the case and are therefore not binding as a matter of precedent: after all, she concluded that s 4(4) was not engaged, because the words 'employed by' did not refer to workers,[29] so her observations on how s 4(4) worked were hardly a necessary part of her reasoning. However, in *Reinhard v Ondra LLP*, Warren J expressed the view that these were not obiter observations.[30] His conclusion in this regard was not reasoned. It might, itself, arguably also be seen as obiter.

Until the matter is clarified, it seems that Lady Hale's views must therefore be regarded as definitive as to the interpretation of s 4(4). That is unfortunate. Her interpretation is, with respect, somewhat improbable. And if she is right, then so long as the rule against dual status in partnerships exists, a member of an LLP—no matter how limited their rights—cannot be an employee. Thus, in contrast to the position that would apply under Rimer LJ's interpretation, an LLP that offered membership to its employees with a view to evading employment rights legislation might very well succeed in doing so, insofar as those rights applied only to employees.

Members and Workers

As explained at para 12.10, the Supreme Court in *Clyde & Co LLP v Bates van Winkelhof*[31] considered that the question of whether a person was a 'worker' for the

12.11

---

[28] Ibid at [21].
[29] Ibid at [23].
[30] *Reinhard v Ondra LLP* [2015] EWHC 1869 (Ch) at [38].
[31] *Clyde & Co LLP v Bates van Winkelhof* (n 27).

purposes of employment legislation was one that fell to be determined on the construction of s 230(3)(b) of the Employment Rights Act 1996, without reference to s 4(4) of the LLP Act 2000.[32] The construction of that provision was addressed at para 2.35 in considering whether a partner can be a worker. The statutory test is likely to be easier to meet in the case of a member of an LLP than in that of a partner, because the difficulties that arise in the application of the statutory test to a partner will not arise in the case of an LLP: it will generally be straightforward to determine whether a member of an LLP is performing work or services 'for another party to the contract whose status is not by virtue of the contract that of a client or customer'. In *Roberts v Wilsons Solicitors LLP*,[33] it was common ground that the former managing partner of an LLP firm of solicitors was a worker under this legislation. Indeed, all members who provide services to the LLP will typically be 'workers' for the purposes of employment legislation under which 'worker' status affords certain rights, particularly with respect to 'whistle-blowing' and disciplinary procedures.

Disqualification from Membership

12.12 Regulation 4(2) of the LLP Regulations 2001 applies the whole of CDDA 1986 to members and shadow members of an LLP, subject to any amendments listed in Sch 2 (though at present Sch 2 is empty).[34] A person against whom an order is made under the Act may be disqualified from being a member of an LLP or director of a company.

Disqualification of LLP members

12.13 In circumstances in which a director of a company can be disqualified from acting as such (for up to fifteen years in some cases) a member of an LLP can similarly be disqualified.

Regulation 4(2) does this by providing that the provisions of CDDA 1986 'shall apply to limited liability partnerships' and that the Act is to be read so that references to a company include an LLP and references to a director include a member. This means that a member of an LLP whose behaviour merits disqualification can be (and in certain cases must be) disqualified from being a director of a company as well as a member of an LLP.

---

[32] Lord Clarke SCJ would have dissented on this point.
[33] [2016] ICR 659 (EAT), affd [2018] EWCA Civ 52, [2018] ICR 1092.
[34] As to the possibility of the Act applying to 'de facto members' see para 12.07.

Disqualification of company directors

12.14 It is probably the effect of reg 4(2) of the LLP Regulations 2001 that a company director who has proved themselves unfit for office can be (and in certain cases must be) disqualified from being a member of an LLP. Such an interpretation gives effect to the inclusionary language referred to above, and is supported by the fact that reg 4(2) provides that CDDA 1986 applies to LLPs rather than, specifically, to members of LLPs: thus it can be read as applying to protect LLPs as well as applying to sanction their members. There is no doubt that s 15(c) of the LLP Act 2000 is sufficiently wide to permit the regulations to have this effect, and there seems to be no good reason why reg 4(2) should not be read accordingly.[35] It would surely be a curious thing if the Act protected companies from unfit members, but did not protect LLPs from unfit directors.

Grounds for disqualification

12.15 Under s 6 of CDDA 1986, the court has a duty to make a disqualification order under s 1 if it is satisfied that a person has acted as a director of a company or member of an LLP which has become insolvent, and where that person's conduct as a director or member makes him or her unfit to be concerned in the management of a company or LLP. This might be regarded as something of a blunderbuss in the case of LLPs, in that it would require disqualification even from membership of an LLP that did not, by the terms of the LLP Agreement, grant the member in question any management rights or responsibilities, but this is a consequence of the statutory equation between directors and members. The court also has a duty to make an order in the event of certain infringements of competition law.[36] In certain cases, a disqualification undertaking can be accepted in lieu of a disqualification order.[37]

There is extensive case law on what is considered unfitness for office,[38] the procedural aspects (including human rights issues), and the tariff of length of time to be imposed. It is an offence to act in contravention of a disqualification order or disqualification undertaking.[39]

Under s 15 of CDDA 1986, a person who is involved in the management of an LLP whilst disqualified (or a who takes instructions given by someone he knows to be disqualified) is personally liable for the debts incurred by the LLP during that period of management (or during the period of the instructions).[40] Note that CDDA 1986, s

---

[35] This view is supported by Mithani, *Directors' Disqualification* LexisNexis, Looseleaf. 2337–41, but not shared by Whittaker and Machell, *The Law of Limited Liability Partnerships* 4th edn, Bloomsbury, 2016, 37.2. Respectfully, the former view is more persuasive. Admittedly, though, it would have been clearer had Parliament simply amended the principal text of CDDA 1986 instead of incorporating the Act via the Regulations.
[36] CDDA 1986, ss 9A–9E.
[37] CDDA 1986, ss 1A, 7.
[38] See also CDDA 1986, Sch 1.
[39] CDDA 1986, s 13.
[40] CDDA 1986, s 15.

15(4) provides that for the purposes of s 15 a person involved in the management of a company includes a director of that company: when translated to LLPs, this means that mere membership of an LLP will engage liability under s 15, whether or not accompanied by any actual management role.

Although most disqualifications are made under s 6 following insolvency, disqualification orders may also be made on various discretionary grounds. These are: (a) the commission of particular offences in connection with the promotion, formation, management, or liquidation etc of a company or LLP,[41] (b) certain breaches of companies legislation,[42] (c) fraudulent trading under Companies Act 2006, s 993 or certain other fraudulent conduct,[43] (d) conviction of certain offences under foreign companies legislation,[44] (e) general unfitness for office,[45] (f) the exercise of influence over a person who has been disqualified (on certain grounds),[46] (g) certain competition law infringements,[47] (h) a finding of liability for fraudulent or wrongful trading under Insolvency Act 1986, ss 213–214.[48] In some instances, the Secretary of State may accept a disqualification undertaking instead of seeking an order from the court.

Undischarged bankrupts

12.16 It is an offence for an undischarged bankrupt[49] to act as a director of a company or member of an LLP, or directly or indirectly to take part in or be concerned in the promotion, formation or management of a company or LLP without the permission of the court.

---

[41] CDDA 1986, s 2.
[42] CDDA 1986, ss 3, 5.
[43] CDDA 1986, s 4.
[44] CDDA 1986, s 5A.
[45] CDDA 1986, s 8.
[46] CDDA 1986, ss 8ZA, 8ZD.
[47] CDDA 1986, s 9A.
[48] CDDA 1986, s 10.
[49] Or a person subject to certain related personal bankruptcy processes. Note also CDDA 1986, s 12 which applies to judgment debtors under a County Courts Act 1984 administration order.

13

RIGHTS AND DUTIES OF MEMBERSHIP

The Member's Share

Membership of an LLP brings with it various rights and duties. The disparate bundle of rights and duties of membership can be regarded as together forming the member's 'share' in the LLP.   **13.01**

The terms 'interest' and 'share' are used interchangeably in the legislation to describe the various rights (and concomitant obligations) in the LLP; though it has been suggested that the term 'share' should be reserved for the totality of the contractual or statutory rights and obligations of a member which attach to membership, while an 'interest' is one or more components of that share.[1] This makes good linguistic sense, even if the distinction is not wholly respected in the legislation.

It is also clear that a member's share comprises both alienable and inalienable rights. Thus s 7(1) of the LLP Act 2000 (considered in more detail in para 13.02) recognizes the assignability of a member's share, though makes it clear that the assignee may not interfere in the management or administration of the LLP.[2] A member's share is therefore a combination of (a) purely personal rights that have no financial value in themselves (to participate in management, to exercise statutory rights granted to members and so forth) and (b) potentially valuable financial rights that are capable of being treated as property, and thus assigned and mortgaged etc.

The effect of assignment and bankruptcy on a member's share

As a person can only be admitted to membership by way of agreement under s 4(2) of the LLP Act 2000, a member's share cannot be assigned to another person in its totality so as to make the assignee a member. Nevertheless, the financial interests comprised within a share are capable of assignment. In addition, in the event of a member's bankruptcy or insolvency, the member's share will automatically vest in the member's trustee in bankruptcy/liquidator by way of a statutory assignment.[3]   **13.02**

---

[1] *Reinhard v Ondra* [2015] EWHC 26 (Ch) at [57] per Warren J approving Whittaker and Machell, *The Law of Limited Liability Partnerships* 3rd edn, Bloomsbury, 2009, 8–18 (see now 4th edn, 2016).

[2] The right to assign may be excluded or restricted in the LLP Agreement. Under the default provisions, assignment requires the unanimous consent of all members: LLP Regs 2001, reg 7(5)—see para 14.09.

[3] LLP Regs 2001, Sch 3 (IA, ss 145, 306) (see para 10.01 for an explanation of statutory citations from the Regulations). Note that although the bankrupt member may remain a member in the absence of a term in the LLP Agreement to the contrary, it would be an offence for them to 'act as' a member without the permission of the court

Just as assignment of a member's interest or share in the LLP to a third party does not make the assignee a member of the LLP, it should go without saying that such an assignment does not cause the assignor to cease to be a member. Even if the financial rights are assigned, other rights inherent in membership will remain vested in the member.

It is unfortunate, therefore, that s 7 of the LLP Act 2000—which regulates assignments of such interests—is entitled 'Ex-members'. Although some of the circumstances in which s 7 applies will arise on termination of membership, some do not. Section 7(1) states:

> This section applies where a member of a limited liability partnership has either ceased to be a member or—
> (a) has died,
> (b) has become bankrupt or had his estate sequestrated or has been wound up,
> (c) has granted a trust deed for the benefit of his creditors,[4] or
> (d) has assigned the whole or any part of his share in the limited liability partnership (absolutely or by way of charge or security).

Section 7(2) goes on to provide:

> In such an event the former member or—
> (a) his personal representative,
> (b) his trustee in bankruptcy, the trustee or interim trustee in the sequestration, under the Bankruptcy (Scotland) Act 2016, of the former member's estate or the former member's liquidator,
> (c) his trustee under the trust deed for the benefit of his creditors, or
> (d) his assignee,
> may not interfere in the management or administration of any business or affairs of the limited liability partnership.[5]

The use of the pronoun 'his' in s 7(2)(b)–(d) adds further confusion, since linguistically this would seem to refer to 'the former member' despite none of the triggering events for s 7(2)(b)–(d) resulting in termination of membership. Section 7(2) is clearly trying to do too much in too few words, and the 'his' in paragraphs (b)–(d) must be read as referring back to the member of the LLP referred to in s 7(1), who may or may not be a former member. The explanatory note to s 7 is, in this regard, more coherently drafted than the section itself.

---

whilst they remain an undischarged bankrupt: LLP Regs 2001, reg 4 (Company Directors Disqualification Act 1986, s 11(1)). A bankrupt member is in a potentially awkward situation: they cannot act as a member, but if they seek to terminate their membership they may extinguish the financial benefits that have been assigned, in law, to their trustee. That would be a breach of their duties under the Insolvency Act 1986.

[4] This subsection refers to a Scottish insolvency procedure akin to a voluntary arrangement.

[5] Section 7(3) then provides that subsection (2) does not affect any right to receive an amount from the LLP in the event of termination/death/assignment. Though quite how s 7(2) could have been interpreted as providing otherwise is a mystery.

In consequence, and despite any suggestion to the contrary apparent from s 7, neither assignment of a member's share nor insolvency will automatically terminate membership. Nor (it is suggested) should s 7(2) be read as preventing a member who has assigned an interest in the LLP to a third party from interfering in the management or administration of the LLP. Indeed, in the event of an assignment, such rights remain vested in the assignor.

The Sources of Members' Rights and Duties

13.03 The rights and duties of members are derived from (a) the LLP Agreement, (b) statute: in particular, the LLP Act 2000 and the regulations made under it, and (c) various common law and equitable rules.

The LLP Agreement

13.04 Section 5(1) of the LLP Act 2000 provides that, subject to any other statutory provision, the rights and duties of the members between themselves, and the rights and duties between members and the LLP, are governed by agreement. Almost invariably, both sets of rights and duties are set out in the same agreement: namely the LLP Agreement. This is addressed in Chapter 14.

Statutory rights and duties

13.05 In addition to the rights and duties set out in the LLP Agreement, there are miscellaneous other rights granted to and duties imposed upon members that can be found in statute, principally the Companies Act 2006 (as modified). Most of those have already been addressed in Chapter 11. Although the majority of administrative duties under the Companies Act 2006 are imposed only on designated members, some of the Act's duties are enforceable against members as a whole (in particular the duty to maintain financial records and with respect to accounts: see para 11.30). A further important right (unless excluded) is the right to petition for unfair prejudice. This is addressed, along with the right to seek a just and equitable winding up, at para 13.19.

Common law and equity

13.06 To the extent not expressly addressed by the LLP Agreement, equitable or tortious duties may also arise. These are addressed immediately below.

Members' Fiduciary Duties

13.07 'Fiduciary duties' is the umbrella term applied to certain duties of equitable origin that arise where a person assumes responsibility for the management of the property or affairs of another. They comprise the duty of loyalty, a duty of good faith, a duty not to profit from one's position (the 'no profit' rule), and a duty not to place oneself in a position of conflict of interest (the 'no conflict' rule). They are duties that are peculiar to those in a fiduciary relationship.[6] Section 5 of the LLP Act 2000 is silent as to whether the two relevant relationships that it governs, ie that between the members and an LLP and that between the members and each other, are fiduciary ones. It is convenient to consider these two relationships separately.

Fiduciary duties between members and the LLP

13.08 In *F&C Alternative Investments (Holdings) Ltd v Barthelemy*,[7] Sales J rejected the suggestion that fiduciary duties arose between members and the LLP automatically. He held that in determining the existence and extent of such duties, it was necessary 'to look at the specific roles and responsibilities arising in the particular context in question' and the control exercised by the member in question over the affairs or property of the LLP in order to determine whether, and if so what, fiduciary obligations might arise.[8]

The existence of fiduciary duties owed by members to the LLP must therefore 'be assessed having regard to the specific context created by the factual background and the contractual framework constituted by [the LLP Agreement]'.[9]

However, since the members are agents of the LLP (under s 6 of the LLP Act 2000) it seems fairly obvious that the courts will generally find that the members, when they are acting as agents, owe the fiduciary duties of an agent to the LLP.[10]

Specific attention should also be paid to default rules (9) and (10), under which a member cannot compete with the LLP without the consent of the LLP (see para 14.13) and a member must account for any benefit derived from the LLP's business without the consent of the LLP (see para 14.14). These are both aspects of the no-conflict rule. Unless the LLP Agreement expressly or implicitly provides otherwise, all members will be subject to these fiduciary duties regardless of their role or responsibility.

---

[6] *White v Jones* [1995] 2 AC 207, HL at 271; *Bristol and West Building Society v Mothew* [1998] Ch 1, CA at 16.
[7] [2011] EWHC 1731 (Ch), [2012] Ch 613.
[8] Ibid at [218].
[9] Ibid at [245].
[10] Ibid at [219] as applied in *Recovery Partners GP Ltd v Rukhazde* [2018] EWHC 2918 (Comm), [2019] Bus LR 1166 at [95]–[98], [329]–[331].

Subject to these caveats, members who conduct the business of the LLP will almost certainly owe appropriate fiduciary duties to the LLP that reflect the fact they are entrusted with a role that requires them to act for the benefit of another. The contents of the particular fiduciary duties likely to arise by virtue of a member's management of the LLP's business will be similar to those which apply to both partners and company directors, and are addressed at paras 5.05–5.19. Although the fiduciary (and other) duties owed by company directors to their company are now codified in the Companies Act 2006, those codified provisions do not directly apply to an LLP's members. Nevertheless, s 170(4) requires the statutory provisions to be interpreted in the same way as the underlying common law rules or equitable principles from which they are derived. Accordingly, case law with respect to directors' statutory duties under the Companies Act 2006 is likely to be material when considering the fiduciary (and other) duties of members to the LLP.[11]

Informed consent by the LLP

The analogy with companies must, however, be applied with care. Not only do the statutory duties of directors extend beyond their equitable or common law origins in some respects, but the rules and procedures as to informed consent will inevitably differ. Informed consent can permit what would otherwise be a breach of the duties to avoid a conflict of interest or not to make a profit from one's position. In the case of a company, this traditionally required the consent of the shareholders in general meeting. However, companies' articles often permitted disclosure of the circumstances of a potential breach to be made to the board, who could consent on behalf of the company; and that procedure now has statutory recognition.[12] There are no such rules in the case of an LLP. A member will therefore have to make disclosure to the LLP itself in some effective manner. If there is a management committee, they would presumably have authority to receive such disclosure on behalf of the LLP; if not, then seemingly disclosure would have to be made to all other members. As to consent, must all members consent, or would a majority suffice? That will likely depend on the terms of the LLP Agreement and the context in which consent is sought. It may also turn on whether the granting of consent is an 'ordinary matter' for the purposes of default rule (6).[13] In most cases, it probably would be.

13.09

---

[11] See, by way of example, the application of the codified duties to members of an LLP in *McTear v Eade* [2019] EWHC 1673 (Ch) at [139]–[140], though as the court emphasized, the existence of these duties depends on the specific role played by the relevant member. See also *Riley v Reddish LLP* [2019] 6 WLUK 96 (Ch) at [40] for a case in which a claim that a member owed the codified duties of a director was held by Nugee J to be demurrable in the absence of 'some specific transaction or management or factual basis to generate evidence that the member played any particular role likely to generate fiduciary duties'.

[12] Companies Act 2006, ss 175 and 177 specifically permit disclosure of a potential conflict to be made to the board, which may consent to the transaction on behalf of the company.

[13] LLP Regs 2001, reg 7(6). See paras 14.10 and 15.02.

Remedies

13.10 The traditional remedies for breach of fiduciary duty include equitable compensation and an account of profits wrongfully made. Exceptionally, a fiduciary can also be required to forfeit a right to fees paid or payable by the principal if the breach is particularly serious or dishonest. It has been held that this extends to the profit share of a member of an LLP, provided that profit share can be regarded as a form of remuneration for services to the LLP.[14]

Fiduciary duties between members themselves

13.11 Whilst partners owe fiduciary duties to each other because of the lack of a body corporate, directors and shareholders in a company do not generally owe them to the (other) shareholders. There are some very limited situations where the courts have held that fiduciary duties are capable of arising between directors (or controlling shareholders) and individual shareholders, but those depend on the existence of a 'special relationship' arising out of the particular facts in issue.[15]

Generally speaking, it is to be expected that the company approach will be applied to LLPs rather than the partnership approach. This is for a number of reasons. First, whereas partners are agents for each other, that is not the case in an LLP, where members are agents for the LLP.[16] Second, the LLP Act 2000 specifically provides that the law relating to partnerships does not apply to an LLP except to the extent provided for by statute.[17] Third, the imposition of duties to the LLP itself tends against the existence of duties owed to individual members, which—to the extent imposing such duties would serve any additional purpose at all—might simply cut across or even conflict with the duties owed to the LLP.[18] Fourth, the LLP Act gives wide discretion to the parties as to how an LLP is to be managed, and it seems doubtful that one could universally regard the relationship between members as necessarily fiduciary.

On the other hand—and perhaps surprisingly—default rule (8) provides that:

> Each member shall render true accounts and full information of all things affecting the limited liability partnership to any member or his legal representatives.[19]

Why this duty should be owed by one member to another, rather than to the LLP, is not clear. In all likelihood, it is simply the result of an unthinking transposition from

---

[14] *Hosking v Marathon Asset Management LLP* [2016] EWHC 2418 (Ch), [2017] Ch 157. See para 16.13.
[15] *Sharp v Blank* [2015] EWHC 3220 (Ch), [2017] BCC 187; *Peskin v Anderson* [2001] BCC 874, CA. In *Sharp*, the 'special relationship' was described by Nugee J at [12] as 'something over and above the usual relationship that any director of a company has with its shareholders'.
[16] LLP Act 2000, s 6(1).
[17] LLP Act 2000, s 1(5).
[18] Eg, what is the position where the members are under a fiduciary duty of full disclosure to each other but there are serious doubts about the conduct of one member? To disclose information to him or her may compromise their coexisting fiduciary duty to act in the best interests of the LLP.
[19] LLP Regs 2001, reg 7(8).

s 28 of the Partnership Act 1890 (from which the wording is derived). Although the wording of the rule might be said to suggest the existence of broader duties of a fiduciary nature between the members, the better view is that it does not.

In *Barthelemy*, Sales J also considered the extent to which duties might arise between members of an LLP themselves.[20] After rejecting the suggestion that a duty of good faith necessarily arose between the members, he concluded that:

> In view of the wide range of governance structures which parties are free to contract for, it is difficult to make generalisations about the circumstances in which a duty of good faith or other fiduciary duties as between the members in a limited liability partnership may arise. It is necessary to refer back to basic equitable principles in order to decide whether and what fiduciary obligations arise in the context of a limited liability partnership.[21]

Accordingly, it seems that there is no basis for the establishment of fiduciary duty between the members themselves except where the facts specifically warrant it.[22] That said, there is no reason why the parties to an LLP Agreement cannot provide that the members owe each other duties of good faith and other fiduciary duties, whether generally or as regards particular matters. Where an LLP has converted from a partnership, and where the LLP has opted for a flat management structure, such provisions are not uncommon, and reflect the 'partnership ethos' under which the LLP operates.

Members' Duty of Care to the LLP

Whether the duty has tortious, contractual, or equitable origins, a duty of care will undoubtedly be owed by a member to the LLP in the performance of the member's functions and the conduct of the LLP's business. The equivalent duty that partners owe to each other is analysed at para 5.04.

13.12

As to the standard of care required, s 174 of the Companies Act 2006 codifies the position with respect to directors, requiring a director to exercise the care, skill, and diligence that would be exercised by a reasonably diligent person with (a) the general knowledge, skill, and experience that may reasonably be expected of a person carrying out the function carried out by the director in relation to the company, and (b) the

---

[20] *F&C Alternative Investments (Holdings) Ltd v Barthelemy* (n 7) at [207]–[213].
[21] Ibid at [211].
[22] It has nevertheless been suggested that a limited obligation of good faith between members themselves might arise where certain fundamental matters are in issue—eg on the incorporation of the LLP itself, the admission of a new member, the amendment of the LLP Agreement, or liquidation of the LLP—so as to require disclosure of facts or matters material to the decision: see Whittaker and Machell, *The Law of Limited Liability Partnerships* 4th edn, Bloomsbury, 2016, 13.26. There is much to be said for that view, though these are perhaps instances of circumstances where a 'special relationship' can be found to justify the imposition of such duties.

general knowledge, skill, and experience that the director has. Although this provision does not apply to members of an LLP, it is itself derived from the statutory test in s 214 of the Insolvency Act 1986 (which defines 'wrongful trading', and which does apply to an LLP[23]). Unless the LLP whilst solvent is entitled to expect a different standard of care from its members than the LLP in insolvency, it seems very probable that the statutory expression of the duty represents the expected standard of care to be applied, subject of course to anything in the LLP Agreement.

Whatever the correct standard (whether under s 174 or the potentially higher standard of 'culpable negligence' or 'gross negligence' suggested by some of the partnership cases[24]) the possibility of liability has practical implications for a member's limited liability status. That is because, subject to anything to the contrary in the LLP Agreement, a member who causes the LLP to act negligently towards a client or customer would be liable, by reason of that member's own negligence to the LLP, to indemnify the LLP for its liability to that client or customer. Thus even though the member may not be directly liable to the client, he or she would still be liable to the LLP. This is no different from the position of a director of a company who acts in breach of duty under s 174 of the Companies Act 2006.

Exclusion of liability

13.13 Unlike the liability of a director, that of a member of an LLP can be limited or excluded by agreement, and an LLP can indemnify its members against all manner of liabilities (other than fraud[25]). Section 232 of the Companies Act 2006, which curtails the right of a company to provide such an indemnity, does not apply to LLPs.

Relief from liability

13.14 As with a director, s 1157 of the Companies Act 2006 permits the court to relieve a member, wholly or in part, from liability for negligence, default, breach of duty, or breach of trust provided the member 'acted honestly and reasonably' and ought, in all the circumstances, 'fairly to be excused' from liability.[26] The discretion is likely to be exercised in much the same way as it is exercised for directors: ie sparingly.[27]

---

[23] LLP Regs 2001, Sch 3 (IA, s 214).
[24] Esp *Lane v Bushby* [2000] NSWSC 1029, discussed at para 5.04.
[25] *Armitage v Nurse* [1998] Ch 241, CA at 251–6.
[26] LLP Regs 2009, reg 77 (CA, s 1157).
[27] Morse (ed), *Palmer's Company Law* Sweet & Maxwell, Looseleaf, 8.3425.

Members' Duties to Third Parties

Liability for one's own wrongs

It would be a mistake to assume that limited liability means that a member can never be liable to a third party with whom they deal on behalf of the LLP. Of course, where a contract exists between the third party and the LLP, then unless the member is party to that contract as a matter of law, the member will be a stranger to it and therefore cannot be personally liable on it. But where the member commits a tort against a third party the member will be personally liable for his or her own wrong, in the same way that a director will be personally liable for his or her own wrong.[28] This should hardly be controversial, but it still required a judgment from the House of Lords to make the position clear. As Lord Hoffmann explained in a case involving the tort of deceit:

13.15

> My Lords, I come next to the question of whether [the director] was liable for his deceit. To put the question in this way may seem tendentious but I do not think that it is unfair. [The director] says, and the Court of Appeal accepted, that he committed no deceit because he made the representation on behalf of [the company] and it was relied upon as a representation by [the company]. That is true but seems to me irrelevant. [The director] made a fraudulent misrepresentation intending [the customer] to rely upon it and [the customer] did rely upon it. The fact that by virtue of the law of agency his representation and the knowledge with which he made it would also be attributed to [the company] would be of interest in an action against [the company]. But that cannot detract from the fact that they were his representation and his knowledge.[29]

Therefore, whether or not the LLP is also liable under the rules of attribution[30] or vicarious liability,[31] a member remains liable for his or her own wrong. A member cannot excuse his or her wrong by saying 'I was committing this tort on behalf of the LLP'. This is a relatively straightforward principle to apply in torts of intention, or in negligence where physical harm results. However, in cases of economic loss resulting from negligence, a member's potential liability will depend on establishing whether the member personally owed a duty of care to the third party. Here, whilst they still cannot say 'I was committing this tort on behalf of the LLP' they may well be able to say 'I did not actually commit a tort because I did not owe you a duty care'.

---

[28] This is implicitly acknowledged, in the case of an LLP, by the terms of LLP Act 2000, s 6(4).
[29] *Standard Chartered Bank v Pakistan National Shipping Corp (Nos 2 & 4)* [2002] UKHL 43, [2003] 1 AC 959 at [20].
[30] Para 11.12.
[31] Para 11.13.

Assumption of responsibility

13.16 Generally speaking, a duty of care for economic loss requires a 'special relationship' to exist between the parties, based on an 'assumption of responsibility'.[32] Where, on an objective view of the facts, such a relationship exists, and where it is reasonably relied upon, a duty of care may arise. The court will not impose a duty unless it is fair, just, and reasonable to do so, and there is therefore an element of policy consideration in the finding of a duty of care in any particular circumstance.

Thus in any case where the question arises as to whether any agent is liable to his or her principal's client, the answer turns on whether the agent assumed personal responsibility to that client. The leading case in a corporate context is *Williams v Natural Life Health Foods Ltd*.[33] There, potential investors entered into a franchise agreement with the company, relying on financial projections provided by the director. The projections were negligent, and the issue was whether the director was personally liable to the franchisees for their losses. The House of Lords held that liability turned simply on 'whether the director, or anybody on his behalf, conveyed directly or indirectly to the prospective franchisees that the director assumed personal responsibility towards the prospective franchisees'.[34] On the facts, no such assumption of responsibility was conveyed; nor did the franchisees reasonably rely on any such assumption.

It has been suggested that the courts may be more willing to find a 'special relationship' in the case of a firm providing professional services because of the personal and fiduciary nature of those services. Thus in the Hong Kong case of *Yazhou Travel Investment Co Ltd v Bateson Starr*[35] the judge suggested that the fact a client might see an individual as 'his solicitor' and that solicitor might see the client as 'his client' suggested an assumption of responsibility by the individual solicitor, personally, to the client. This might be regarded as a surprising outcome: and where the risk of personal liability might arise, an LLP will doubtless consider excluding liability by its members, subject of course to the provisions of the Unfair Contract Terms Act 1977/Consumer Rights Act 2015.

Said v Butt

13.17 One potential restriction on the liability of company directors to third parties arises from the so-called rule in *Said v Butt*.[36] This is the rule that directors cannot be liable for the tort of procuring a breach of contract by their company provided they act bona fide within the scope of their authority.

---

[32] *Hedley Byrne & Co v Heller & Partners Ltd* [1964] AC 465, HL.
[33] [1998] 1 WLR 830, HL.
[34] Ibid at 835H.
[35] [2005] PNLR 31 (HK CFI).
[36] [1920] 3 KB 497 (KB).

Although much criticized as an anomaly,[37] the rule survives, and benefits both directors and officeholders such as receivers and administrators.[38] There is no reason to doubt that it would apply to members of an LLP who, acting bona fide, cause the LLP to commit a breach of contract. Directors (and therefore members of an LLP) can, however, be liable where they procure a tort by the LLP: on general principle, to procure or authorize a third party to commit a tort gives rise to joint liability for that tort with that third party.[39]

Members' Duties to Creditors

If the directors of company know, or should know, that it is insolvent or that it is probable that it will become insolvent, their duty to act in the best interests of the company for the benefit of its shareholders is displaced by a duty to have regard to the interests of creditors. It is now the creditors' money which is at risk from their decisions. The same is true of an LLP, and members will therefore owe duties to act in the interests of the LLP's creditors in this eventuality.[40] **13.18**

Minority Protections

The remedies of a petition for relief on the grounds of unfair prejudice, and a petition to wind up a company on the just and equitable basis apply also to LLPs, and may afford significant protection to a member who considers that the affairs of the LLP are being conducted in a harmful or prejudicial manner. The detail of these remedies, and how they interrelate, is complex, and reference should be made to specialist texts.[41] **13.19**

Unfair prejudice

The remedy to petition the court for relief on the basis that the LLP's affairs are being conducted in a manner that is unfairly prejudicial to the interests of one or more members is contained in ss 994–996 of the Companies Act 2006.[42] As with companies, the remedies available in the case of unfair prejudice in the conduct of the affairs of an LLP are broad. The most common remedy is likely to be one that provision is made for the purchase of a member's share in the LLP, and therefore an exit from the LLP: any order **13.20**

---

[37] Eg *Welsh Development Export Agency v Export Finance Co* [1992] BCLC 148, CA at 173 per Dillon LJ.
[38] *Lictor Anstalt v Mir Steel UK Ltd* [2011] EWHC 3310 (Ch), [2012] 1 All ER (Comm) 592 at [54].
[39] Watts (ed), *Bowstead & Reynolds on Agency* 21st edn, Sweet & Maxwell, 2018, 9-120.
[40] *McTear v Eade* [2019] EWHC 1673 (Ch) at [141]–[148] (ICC Judge Jones).
[41] Joffe et al, *Minority Shareholders: Law, Practice, and Procedure* 6th edn, OUP, 2019.
[42] LLP Regs 2009, reg 48 (CA, ss 994–996).

to that effect will need to take care to identify what the share comprises and the basis upon which it is to be valued.[43] Only a member of the LLP has locus standi to petition. The assignee of a member's share or any interest in the LLP has no such right.

Excluding the right

13.21 The right to petition for unfair prejudice can be excluded in the LLP Agreement, but only by unanimous agreement, recorded in writing.[44] Where, for example, the parties have provided some alternative mechanism to resolve the sorts of disputes that might otherwise be addressed by a petition for unfair prejudice, it may often be convenient to exclude the remedy. However, where the remedy is excluded without some alternative mechanism being in place, the LLP runs the risk that the court will accede to a disgruntled member's application to wind it up on the just and equitable basis, there being no alternative viable mechanism for redress.

Quasi-partnerships

13.22 There is, as yet, no authority that addresses the concept of the 'quasi-partnership' in the context of an unfair prejudice petition against an LLP. 'Quasi-partnership' is the term given to a company where the association between the shareholders is based on a personal relationship, such that unfair prejudice can be found not just in the breach of the company's articles or the improper exercise of a power, but also by reference to broader equitable considerations where the strict terms do not fully reflect the understandings upon which the shareholders have associated together.[45] Furthermore, when valuing a quasi-partnership the ordinary practice is not to value the petitioner's interest on a pro rata basis, without any discount to reflect that the holding is a minority holding.[46]

Although many LLPs will, self-evidently, bear the hallmarks of quasi-partnerships as being founded on the personal relationship between the members,[47] the rights and expectations of members will also usually be the subject of detailed agreement. Such agreement is likely to leave little room for any equitable overlay, and the existence of detailed terms has often been said to exclude the introduction of equitable considerations in a company context.[48] Furthermore, given the relative lack of formality required to create an LLP Agreement, it may well be that factors that, in a company setting, would be held to give rise to equitable considerations might, in an LLP setting, be capable of creating contractually binding terms.

---

[43] For the sorts of difficulties that might arise where the basis of valuation is unclear, see *Hailes v Hood* [2007] EWHC 1616 (Ch).
[44] LLP Regs 2009, reg 48 (CA, s 994(3)).
[45] See generally *Re Saul D Harrison & Sons plc* [1995] 1 BCLC 14, CA at 19 and *O'Neill v Phillips* [1999] 1 WLR 1092, HL at 1098–9.
[46] *Re Bird Precision Bellows Ltd* [1984] Ch 419 (Ch).
[47] In *Ebrahimi v Westbourne Galleries Ltd* [1973] AC 360, HL at 379, Lord Wilberforce noted that the necessary personal relationship may well be found where a pre-existing partnership has been converted into a company. That is, of course, just as true of an LLP, if not more so.
[48] *Re a Company (No 005685 of 1988)* [1989] BCLC 427 (Ch) at 440.

Just and equitable winding up

13.23 The LLP Regulations 2001 permit a winding up order to be made against an LLP on the basis that it is just and equitable to do so.[49]

Standing of members

13.24 Any member (or former member) of an LLP will have standing to present a petition if they are a creditor of the LLP or if they fall within the term 'contributory' as it appears in s 124(1) of the Insolvency Act 1986.[50] By s 79(1), a member (or former member) is a 'contributory' if they are liable to contribute (however notionally) to the assets of the LLP in the event of it being wound up.[51] Shareholders in a company limited by shares are liable to contribute to the amount unpaid on their shares, and (even when shares have since been fully paid up) the requirement that a petitioner be a contributory is rarely a significant hurdle in the case of a shareholder. However, the same cannot be said of the member of an LLP, whose liability to contribute can be excluded all together. Thus it would seem that a member whose liability to contribute is entirely excluded by the LLP Agreement cannot be a contributory and cannot therefore petition for just and equitable winding up (unless they can do so as a creditor).

It is difficult to believe that this was intended, particularly as a just and equitable winding up can be sought against a perfectly solvent LLP, in respect of which the existence of any sort of obligation to contribute on a winding up is in a practical sense completely irrelevant. The outcome is particularly perverse, given that, unlike a shareholder, a member may well have a significant interest in bringing about the winding up of an LLP, as membership itself may come with onerous obligations. It is yet to be seen how the courts will reach the obviously desirable result that *any* member should be entitled to petition for just and equitable winding up. The most promising route to this result is probably to translate the language of s 124(1) which also permits 'the directors' (collectively) to petition for winding up to mean not just 'the members' (collectively), but also 'each member' (individually).[52]

Grounds for relief

13.25 The principles on which the court will grant a petition are the same as for companies: deadlock, lack of probity in management, exclusion from management and so forth.[53] The existence of equitable considerations that supplement the LLP Agreement, as in the case of unfair prejudice, will also be relevant.

---

[49] LLP Regs 2001, Sch 3 (IA, s 122(1)(e)). This provision is based on s 122(1)(g) as it applies to companies.
[50] LLP Regs 2001, Sch 3 (IA, s 124(1)).
[51] LLP Regs 2001, Sch 3 (IA, s 79). Though not if their only liability arises as a result of fraudulent or wrongful trading, or under the s 214A clawback provision.
[52] A construction proposed by Whittaker and Machell, *The Law of Limited Liability Partnerships* 4th edn, Bloomsbury, 2016, 31.23, whilst acknowledging that the argument seems 'difficult'.
[53] LLP cases include *Eaton v Caulfield* [2011] EWHC 173 (Ch), [2011] BCC 386 at [69] (breakdown); *Tower Taxi Technology LLP v Marsden* [2005] EWHC 1084 (Ch) (loss of substratum; though petition struck out).

Arbitration and other remedies

13.26 It is likely that, as is the case with a company, the right to petition the court for a just and equitable winding up of an LLP cannot be excluded by agreement as a matter of law.[54] Even then, the courts will likely uphold an arbitration clause that requires any underlying dispute that might give rise to a right to present a petition to be determined by arbitration.[55] Such clauses are quite common in LLP Agreements. Furthermore, the existence of some alternative remedy (such as a petition for unfair prejudice) is an important consideration as to whether the court will grant the relief sought. It is part of the statutory formulation under s 125 of the Insolvency Act 1986, applicable to both companies and LLPs, that the court should not grant such relief if there is some other remedy that the petitioner is unreasonably failing to pursue.

---

[54] *Re Peveril Gold Mines Ltd* [1898] 1 Ch 122, CA at 131. See also the concession to this effect in *Re Magi Capital Partners LLP* [2003] EWHC 2790 (Ch) at [10].

[55] *Re Magi Capital Partners LLP* (n 54) at [16]; *Fulham Football Club (1987) Ltd v Richards* [2011] EWCA Civ 855, [2012] Ch 333 at [83] (obiter); *Salford Estates (No 2) Ltd v Altomart* [2015] Ch 589, CA.

14

THE LLP AGREEMENT

The Scope of the LLP Agreement

Section 5(1) of the LLP Act 2000 states: **14.01**

> Except as far as otherwise provided by this Act or any other enactment, the mutual rights and duties of the members of a limited liability partnership, and the mutual rights and duties of a limited liability partnership and its members, shall be governed—
> (a) by agreement between the members, or between the limited liability partnership and its members, or
> (b) in the absence of agreement as to any matter, by any provision made in relation to that matter by regulations under section 15(c).

This section therefore anticipates that members' rights and duties, both between the members themselves and between a member and the LLP, will be addressed by agreement: ie by the LLP Agreement.

The wording of s 5(1)(a) is also adopted in the LLP Regulations 2001 and 2009 and the LLP Accounting Regulations 2008 to define the (inter-changeable) terms 'LLP Agreement' and 'limited liability partnership agreement'. Those terms are used (albeit sparingly) in the modified provisions of the Companies Act 2006 and Insolvency Act 1986 in lieu of references to a company's articles.[1]

Supplementing the terms of the LLP Agreement, there are eleven default provisions set out in regs 7 and 8 of the LLP Regulations 2001, any one of which will apply in the absence of any provision in the LLP Agreement addressing the issue covered by the specific default provision.

'Between the members' or 'between the LLP and its members'

Section 5(1)(a) comprises two limbs: the first provides for agreement to be made between the members, without the LLP being a party. The second provides for agreement between the LLP, on the one hand, and the members on the other. An LLP Agreement **14.02**

---

[1] LLP Regs 2001, reg 2, Sch 3 (IA, s 436) for the purposes of various provisions of the Insolvency Act 1986; LLP Accounting Regs 2008, reg 47 (CA, s 539) for the purposes of establishing a parent/subsidiary relationship and with respect to the appointment of auditors; LLP Regs 2009, reg 79 (CA, s 1173) for the purposes of unfair prejudice remedies under reg 48 (CA, s 996) (see para 10.01 for an explanation of statutory citations from the Regulations).

may in fact comprise several different agreements, particularly where arrangements are not wholly committed to writing.

Almost invariably, however, the LLP itself must be a party to the LLP Agreement. That is because an agreement between the members alone cannot grant rights to or impose liabilities on the LLP, particularly as the Contracts (Right of Third Parties) Act 1999 does not apply to LLP Agreements.[2] Accordingly, such an agreement could only govern the relationship between the members themselves; and the LLP must be a party if the members are to have any rights against it (and vice versa) other than those provided for by statute or set out in the default provisions.

There is no reason why the rights and duties that arise between the LLP and a particular member could not be governed (in whole or in part) by an agreement between the LLP and that particular member, to which the other members are not a party and under which they have no rights. For example, LLPs will often conclude 'entitlements letters' with individual members that contain bespoke arrangements as to that member's financial entitlements. Whether such bespoke arrangements actually fall within s 5(1) or the statutory definition of LLP Agreement in the regulations is unlikely to matter provided all members' rights and obligations interrelate coherently.

Formalities

14.03 Section 5(1) does not require the LLP Agreement to be in writing, and there is therefore no reason why an LLP Agreement cannot be made or varied orally, or by conduct, or by a combination of these means and a written agreement, subject of course to the terms of any written agreement preventing it.[3] Although s 5 itself is silent on the point, the statutory definition of LLP Agreement in the regulations[4] expressly acknowledges that an LLP Agreement might arise by implication.

There are two specific qualifications to this. The first is that a power to expel cannot arise by implication—it must be expressly provided for.[5] The second is that if the parties wish to exclude the remedy for unfair prejudice, they must do so unanimously and their agreement must be recorded in writing.[6] More broadly, any relevant formalities under the Law of Property Act 1925 or the Law of Property (Miscellaneous Provisions) Act 1989 must also be observed.[7]

---

[2] Contracts (Rights of Third Parties) Act 1999, s 6(2A).
[3] Such as a 'no-oral variation' clause, as to which see *Rock Advertising Ltd v MWB Business Exchange Centres Ltd* [2018] UKSC 24, [2019] AC 119. Such a clause is highly advisable in a written LLP Agreement for this reason.
[4] See n 1.
[5] LLP Regs 2001, reg 8 addressed at para 16.05.
[6] LLP Regs 2009, reg 48 (CA, s 994(3)).
[7] Particularly where the LLP Agreement deals with real property. That may be the case if (for asset protection reasons) land is not vested in the LLP, but is instead held by some of the members on trust for the LLP.

If the parties do enter into a formal written agreement, then there are no obligations to register that agreement or make it available to third parties. There is not even any specific statutory requirement that the agreement must be made available to members, though such an obligation would likely arise as an express or implied term of the LLP Agreement itself.[8] This may be a particular concern where the LLP Agreement has been amended over time, or where it contains provisions that permit its variation without the express consent of each individual member.[9]

Default Provisions

Regulations 7 and 8 of the LLP Regulations 2001 set out eleven default provisions which will apply in the absence of any agreement on the point in the LLP agreement. Despite the protestation in s 1(5) of the LLP Act 2000 that the law relating to partnership does not apply to LLPs, these are based on various provisions applicable to partners as set out in ss 24–30 of the Partnership Act 1890. There are no default provisions as to meetings, resolutions etc and none of the Companies Act provisions or Model Articles on those points have been applied to LLPs. It is difficult to regard the 'default provisions' as anything other than a work in progress: they fall woefully short of providing a comprehensive regime akin to that under Table A or the Model Articles, and by no stretch of the imagination could they stand as substitute for a properly drafted LLP Agreement. In short, any LLP that finds itself falling back wholesale on the default provisions is likely to be in serious trouble.

14.04

Regulation 7 (which introduces ten of the eleven provisions) describes the default provisions as 'rules' that determine 'the mutual rights and duties of the members', and 'the mutual rights and duties of the limited liability partnership and the members'—language that consciously echoes s 5(1) of the LLP Act 2000, which defines the scope of the LLP Agreement. Whether the default provisions apply or not depends on establishing whether the matters they address are already addressed in the LLP Agreement itself, such that the default provisions are excluded expressly or by necessary implication. It is also possible that a particular default provision may help elucidate the meaning of a particular express term in the LLP Agreement, provided it is otherwise apparent that the express term is intended to operate in a manner similar to the default provision.[10]

Note that reg 7 states that the default rules apply subject to the 'terms' of any LLP Agreement. This includes implied terms. It is therefore possible for a term to be implied into an LLP Agreement that is inconsistent with the default rules if the circumstances

---

[8] See esp default rule (7) (LLP Regs 2001, reg 7(7)) discussed at para 14.11 which requires 'books and records' to be made available to members. A written LLP Agreement would likely fall within that provision.
[9] Compare also the position with contracts of employment, where there may be an implied obligation to bring collectively negotiated terms to an employee's attention: *Scally v Southern Health and Social Services Board* [1992] 1 AC 294, HL.
[10] As they did in *Hilton v D IV LLP* [2015] EWHC 2 (Ch).

justified it. This accords with the language of s 24 of the Partnership Act 1890, from which many of the default rules are drawn.

It is necessary to take each default term in turn.

(1) Right to an equal share in capital and profits

14.05 Default rule (1) states:

> All the members of a limited liability partnership are entitled to share equally in the capital and profits of the limited liability partnership.

This provision is derived from s 24(1) of the Partnership Act 1890 (see paras 5.26–5.29). There is no reference to losses, however, since any losses are borne by the LLP and thus automatically reflected in the member's diminished share in the LLP. Technically, capital is the fixed sum contributed to an entity's assets, and is to be distinguished from the totality of the assets themselves, the difference between the two being capital profits. In a partnership, it is clearly established that capital profits are not included in 'capital', so fall to be distributed equally, or in accordance with the partners' profit share, rather than in accordance with any agreement as to capital.[11] In a company, by contrast, shareholders have a claim to the whole of the assets of the company in accordance with their interest in the share capital. An LLP would seem to follow a partnership in this regard, rather than a company.

Default rule (1) says nothing about how profits are actually to be divided. Ordinarily revenue profits must first be established or declared by the LLP, before they can be allocated and distributed to members. The progression from declaration to distribution may be instantaneous and automatic; or it may be that profits, once declared, are held in the LLP's reserves until being allocated by being paid into a member's current account. As to distribution of capital and capital profits on termination, see para 16.11.

(2) Right to an indemnity

14.06 Default rule (2) states:

> The limited liability partnership must indemnify each member in respect of payments made and personal liabilities incurred by him—
> (a) in the ordinary and proper conduct of the business of the limited liability partnership; or
> (b) in or about anything necessarily done for the preservation of the business or property of the limited liability partnership.

---

[11] *Popat v Shonchhatra* [1997] 3 All ER 800, CA discussed at para 5.26.

This is a direct application of s 24(2) of the Partnership Act 1890 and what is said at para 5.32 therefore applies equally to LLPs.

(3) Right to manage

Default rule (3) states: **14.07**

> Every member may take part in the management of the limited liability partnership.

Again, this is a direct application of s 24(5) of the Partnership Act 1890 (as to which, see para 5.21), substituting 'the limited liability partnership' for 'the partnership business', which reflects the separate legal personality of an LLP. How a right to 'take part' is to be exercised is not stated, but prima facie one would expect each member to have an equal vote in the direction of the LLP. A failure to permit a member to take part in the management of the LLP where such a right arises may be very relevant to a winding up petition on the just and equitable ground or a petition for unfairly prejudicial conduct under s 994 of the Companies Act 2006 (again as applied to LLPs). Those matters are discussed at para 13.19.

(4) No right to remuneration

Default rule (4) states: **14.08**

> No member shall be entitled to remuneration for acting in the business or management of the limited liability partnership.

This is derived from s 24(6) of the Partnership Act 1890 (as to which, see para 5.22), replacing the words 'the partnership business' with 'the business or management of the limited liability partnership'. The intention is that members are to be remunerated purely by whatever agreement is reached as to their profit share (which may, of course, make allowance for a member's contribution to the business or management of the LLP), such that no member should be entitled to any further reward unless specifically agreed.

(5) No right to assign

Default rule (5) states: **14.09**

> No person may be introduced as a member or voluntarily assign an interest in a limited liability partnership without the consent of all existing members.

The equivalent provision in the Partnership Act 1890 is s 24(7) (as to which, see para 5.33). However, that provision does not include the restriction on voluntary assignment that appears in default rule (5).[12] The assignment of a member's interest or share in the LLP is further regulated by s 7(1)(d) of the LLP Act 2000, which provides that the assignee may not interfere in the management or administration of any business or affairs of the LLP.[13] It may be that the default rule is intended also to prevent a sub-assignment of a member's share, as it purports to apply to any person—though the opening words of reg 7 itself limits the default rules to the relationship between members and the LLP.

(6) Majority rule

14.10 Default rule (6) states:

> Any difference arising as to ordinary matters connected with the business of the LLP may be decided by a majority of the members, but no change may be made in the nature of the business of the LLP without the consent of all the members.

This is a straight application of s 24(8) of the Partnership Act 1890 (as to which, see paras 5.23–5.24). As with s 24(8), the wording seems to contemplate a neat dichotomy between everyday 'ordinary matters' (in which the majority rule applies) and matters relating to the nature of the business itself (in which it does not). That dichotomy barely works in the case of a general partnership, and it certainly does not work for a complex corporate entity such as an LLP. For example, significant constitutional changes to an LLP such as an increase in capital cannot sensibly be considered to be 'ordinary matters connected with the business of the LLP' but nor do they relate to the nature of the business. These matters are explored further at paras 15.02 to 15.05.

(7) Books and records

14.11 Default rule (7) states:

> The books and records of the limited liability partnership are to be made available for inspection at the registered office of the limited liability partnership or at such other place as the members think fit and every member of the limited liability partnership may when he thinks fit have access to and inspect and copy any of them.

This provision is based on s 24(9) of the Partnership Act 1890 (as to which, see para 5.25). 'Books and records' are not defined, but the term has been construed as being equivalent to the phrase 'books of the firm' that appears in s 6(1) of the Limited

---

[12] In partnership law there is no such implied restriction on assignment (though the right is frequently restricted by agreement); however, the assignee receives very limited rights (see paras 5.44–5.46).
[13] Para 13.02.

Partnership Act 1907 (as to which, see para 9.12). Thus the test is a 'functional' one, and the right appears to extend to any document necessary to establish the rights as between members themselves, as between members and the LLP, and as between the LLP and any third party.[14] The right is plainly wider than the statutory right to have access to the 'accounting records' under s 388 of the Companies Act 2006 (as applied to LLPs).[15]

(8) Duty to account

Default rule (8) states: **14.12**

> Each member shall render true accounts and full information of all things affecting the limited liability partnership to any member or his legal representatives.

This provision is derived from s 28 of the Partnership Act 1890 (as to which, see para 5.10). As noted at para 13.11, it imposes a fiduciary duty as between the members themselves, rather than between a member and the LLP. There is no equivalent provision in company law where, save in exceptional cases, all duties are owed to the company.

(9) Duty not to compete

Default rule (9) states: **14.13**

> If a member, without the consent of the limited liability partnership, carries on any business of the same nature as and competing with the limited liability partnership, he must account for and pay over to the limited liability partnership all profits made by him in the business.

This section is derived from s 30 of the Partnership Act 1890 (as to which, see para 5.19), and imposes a fiduciary duty on members not to compete with the LLP. Save to the extent that this provision is displaced by the LLP Agreement, all members (regardless of how lightly involved they may be in the business of the LLP) will owe such a duty to the LLP. It is not apparent whether a grant of consent under this provision would be an 'ordinary matter' under default rule (6) or not. Whilst this is inevitably fact specific, it is suggested that it usually would, and the consent of the LLP may therefore be given by a majority unless the LLP Agreement provides otherwise.

---

[14] *Hilton v D IV LLP* (n 10) at [34]–[35]. There, HHJ Pelling QC adopted the broad approach taken by Norris J to s 6 of the 1907 Act in *Inversiones Fiera SL v Colyzeo Investors LP* [2011] EWHC 1762 (Ch).

[15] LLP Accounting Regs 2008, reg 6 (CA, s 388).

(10) Improper benefit

14.14 Default rule (10) states:

> Every member must account to the LLP for any benefit derived by him without the consent of the LLP from any transaction concerning the LLP, or from any use by him of the property of the LLP, name or business connection.

This application of s 29(1) of the Partnership Act 1890 (as to which, see paras 5.11–5.18) calls for the same comments as under (9) above. However, the question also arises as to whether the apparent qualification on the fiduciary duty derived from *Aas v Benham*[16] also applies to LLPs. In that case, a partner was held to be entitled to use information he had acquired as a partner for his personal purposes, provided he did so outside the scope of the firm's business so that he was not competing with the firm. Ordinarily, fiduciary duties are strict, and a fiduciary is obliged to account for a benefit regardless of whether it could have been exploited by the principal. In *O'Donnell v Shanahan*,[17] the Court of Appeal sought to confine this exception to partnerships, holding that a company director could not profit from any information belonging to the company, regardless of whether that information fell within the scope of the company's business.

The basis for the distinction made in *O'Donnell* is that most companies are constitutionally capable of engaging in any business that the board of directors may think appropriate: so a director should not second-guess whether the company might wish to exploit particular information. However, the same may not be true of a partner, where the business of the partnership is usually circumscribed by the partnership agreement which cannot be altered except by the consent of all.[18] Accordingly, the scope of a partner's fiduciary duty is itself circumscribed by the scope of the partnership business.

Applying this analysis to LLPs, it is suggested that the limitation derived from *Aas v Benham* (to the extent it represents good law) ought to apply where the business of the LLP is circumscribed by the LLP Agreement, though only perhaps if the scope of the LLP's business cannot be amended, save by unanimous consent of all the members.

(11) Expulsion

14.15 Regulation 8 of the LLP Regulations 2001 contains a single rule, dealing with expulsion. It is based on s 25 of the Partnership Act 1890. It differs from the default provisions set out in reg 7 inasmuch as it is plain from its terms that it cannot be excluded by implication. It is not so much a default provision as a requirement for particular formality in respect of a power of expulsion. It is addressed at para 16.05.

---

[16] [1891] 2 Ch 844, CA. See para 5.15.
[17] [2009] EWCA Civ 751, [2009] 2 BCLC 666.
[18] Ibid at [68]–[69] per Rimer LJ.

A Duty of Good Faith

14.16 A duty of good faith can arise as an aspect of the fiduciary duty of loyalty (see para 13.07) or in the context of a discretion exercised under a decision making power (see para 15.07). It is also capable of subsisting in its own right as an express or implied contractual common law duty. Such a duty is often to be found expressly set out in an LLP Agreement, requiring the members to act in good faith towards the LLP; and/or perhaps towards each other. Where expressly provided for, the contents of the duty will be a matter of construction; however, generally speaking it has been said that:

> ... a contractual obligation of good faith does not require a party to act in the interests of the other party or to subordinate its own legitimate interest to the interests of the other party; although it does require it to have due regard to the legitimate interests of both parties.[19]

Whether such a duty might be implied where the LLP Agreement is silent is a moot point. The (not dissimilar) duty of mutual trust and confidence that applies in the employment relationship is an instance of where a term is implied as an incident of a legal relationship (rather than on the usual 'business efficacy'/'officious bystander' test[20]) and cannot therefore be exported to the very different context of an LLP.

In *Flanagan v Liontrust Investment Partners LLP*,[21] Henderson J rejected a claim that implied duties of mutual trust and confidence or good faith were owed by the members between themselves (or by the LLP to the members), on the basis that, on the facts of that case, the ordinary test for the implication of terms was not met. He also relied on Sales J's reasoning in *Barthelemy*[22] to the effect that a fiduciary duty of good faith was not a necessary incident of an LLP Agreement.

It would therefore seem that where an LLP Agreement does not expressly include any obligation of good faith, or indeed of mutual trust and confidence, none will be implied unless on the facts of the case the ordinary test for the implication of terms is met. The mere fact that the relationship between the parties arises in the context of an LLP is not, of itself, sufficient.

---

[19] *Macquarie International Health Clinic Pty Ltd v Sydney South West Area Health Service* [2010] NSWCA 268 at [147] cited in *F&C Alternative Investments (Holdings) Ltd v Barthelemy* [2011] EWHC 1731 (Ch), [2012] Ch 613 at [255].
[20] *Marks & Spencer plc v BNP Paribas Securities Services Trust Co (Jersey) Ltd* [2015] UKSC 72, [2016] AC 742.
[21] [2015] EWHC 2171 (Ch) at [248]–[249].
[22] *F&C Alternative Investments (Holdings) Ltd v Barthelemy* (n 19).

Amending the Agreement

14.17 Subject to any term to the contrary, any amendment to the LLP Agreement will require unanimity of all members. As a matter of contract, members will only be bound if either they specifically agree to the amendments proposed, or if they have already signed up to a process whereby amendments can be made other than unanimously. For reasons of convenience, an LLP Agreement will typically contain a provision that permits amendments to be made by a majority, or even by a minority where management is concentrated in a small subset of members. Indeed, one sometimes sees such a power vested in a single member as a 'reserved matter'.

A power to amend is, of course, prima facie capable of effecting remarkable and potential unforeseeable change on the LLP and the rights and obligations of its members. Despite the apparent belief of those in whom such powers are frequently vested, such powers are not unfettered. The general rule is that a power to amend can only be exercised for the purpose for which it is granted: ie a purpose within the reasonable contemplation of the parties to the contract granting it. Thus in *Hole v Garnsey*,[23] an apparently unfettered power of amendment was exercised to alter the rules of an industrial and provident society so as to require members of the society to subscribe for additional shares, as a way of raising funds. The amendment to the rules was struck down as being outside the power, according to its proper interpretation. Lord Atkin stated that the operation of the clause was limited to 'matters which are within the scope of the administration of the venture as originally framed' and did not extend to 'fundamental' matters such as the purposes of the association or the sums required to be contributed to it by way of capital.[24] Unsurprisingly, the additional financial burden appears to have weighed significantly with the court. Lord Tomlin added:

> In construing such a power as this, it must, I think, be confined to such amendments as can reasonably be considered to have been within the contemplation of the parties when the contract was made, having regard to the nature and circumstances of the contract. I do not base this conclusion upon any narrow construction of the word 'amend' in Rule 64, but upon a broad general principle applicable to all such powers.
>
> If no such principle existed I see no reason why a dairy society in Wiltshire should not by means of the exercise of such a power as the one under consideration find itself converted into a boot manufacturing society in Leicester with an obligation on the members to contribute funds to the new enterprise.[25]

The principle stated in *Hole v Garnsey* is, in essence, the common law equivalent of the 'proper purpose rule' in equity under which a fiduciary or otherwise limited power must be exercised for the purpose for which it is given.[26] There seems to be no real

---

[23] [1930] AC 472, HL.
[24] Ibid at 495–6.
[25] Ibid at 500.
[26] See, further, para 15.08.

difference between the common law and equitable rules in practice: ultimately, whether the issue is addressed in terms of contractual construction or the equitable rule, one must ask the same question: does the proposed amendment fall within the power to amend, properly understood?[27]

Remedies for Breach

In the ordinary course, breach of an LLP Agreement will give rise to a claim for damages against the parties in breach.[28] That may include the LLP if the wrongdoing can be attributed to it. Injunctive relief may be available on ordinary principles to prevent a threatened breach or to restore the position to the status quo ante. The LLP Agreement may itself provide alternative or additional rights. Breach of the LLP Agreement may also ground a petition for unfair prejudice or for the just and equitable winding up of the LLP (see para 13.19). 14.18

Rescission

There is no reason to doubt that the remedy of rescission is available in principle in respect of an LLP Agreement. Although there is no express statutory acknowledgment of this,[29] all things being equal it is difficult to see why the remedy should not exist: rescission is an equitable doctrine sufficiently flexible to ensure that it does not operate to the prejudice of third parties, such as other members of the LLP not caught up in the relevant wrongdoing, or an LLP's creditors. It will only be available where restitutio in integrum is possible and where the agreement to be impugned has not been affirmed. 14.19

Although the remedy ought to be available in all cases where the courts are prepared to rescind a contract—misrepresentation, mutual or unilateral mistake, duress, and undue influence—the most likely vitiating factor in the context of an LLP will be a misrepresentation. In such a case, the Misrepresentation Act 1967 will apply, so that the court may (additionally or alternatively) award damages for negligent misrepresentation under s 2(1); or it may award damages in lieu of rescission under s 2(2).

---

[27] The issue has often arisen in respect of the restructuring of pension schemes, though of course the relevant factors will depend on context. See *British Airways plc v Airways Pension Scheme Trustee Ltd* [2018] EWCA Civ 1533, [2018] Pens LR 19 at [43]–[54] per Patten LJ, dissenting in the result, [85]–[100] per Lewison LJ, and the cases cited therein.
[28] See eg *Flanagan v Liontrust Investment Partners LLP* (n 21) at [239], [244(5)].
[29] As there is under Partnership Act 1890, s 41.

Availability of the remedy

14.20 Rescission is a remedy by which a party can undo their agreement to enter into a contract, or to vary or discharge a contract. In the context of an LLP, the remedy could therefore apply to (a) a person's agreement to become a member under s 4(2), (b) a member's agreement to vary the LLP Agreement, and (c) a member's agreement to cease to be a member under s 4(3).

The remedy would seemingly not apply to an agreement to form an LLP once the LLP has been incorporated, however: a subscriber becomes a member automatically under s 4(1), and once the LLP has come into existence as a legal person, restitutio in integrum is not possible without the LLP being dissolved. In such a case, a subscriber who claims to have been misled would have to seek to wind up the LLP or petition for unfair prejudice.

Application of the remedy

14.21 However, it is one thing to say that the remedy applies; it is quite another to say how it applies. As we have seen, an LLP Agreement is a multiparty arrangement between the members and the LLP. Where a misrepresentation is made to a single member or prospective member on behalf of all other relevant parties—ie all the other members and the LLP—or where the misrepresentation can be attributed to them under the rules of agency, then there is usually no difficulty: the LLP Agreement (or its variation, or the member's agreement to retire) will be rescinded as between the misled member and the others, and will remain in force as between the remaining members.

However, where the misrepresentation is made by only some of the other members, and where some of the other members are wholly innocent of misrepresentation, the parties fall into three camps: the victims seeking rescission because they have been misled (V), the guilty who misled them (G), and the innocent third parties to the representation who did not (T). Given the lack of mutual agency between members, this is a scenario more likely to occur in the context of an LLP than a general partnership, though it could arise in any multiparty contractual situation.

The multiparty scenario presents numerous difficulties. So far as an LLP Agreement is concerned, V cannot exercise the remedy of rescission against G unless it is also exercised against T. Otherwise, the effect of rescission would not be restitutio in integrum, but the creation of (probably unworkable) novel contractual arrangements between V and T and between G and T, but not between V and G. Conversely, to allow V to exercise the remedy against both G and T despite T's lack of culpability might prejudice T.

The position of the LLP itself may also be difficult to analyse. Where all the members are guilty of misrepresentation, it may be relatively straightforward to attribute their wrongdoing to the LLP: but in the three-camp scenario, the question may arise whether the LLP is in camp G or T, and as to the effect that has on the available remedy.

There is no one answer to these issues, and a surprising dearth of authority. Similar issues arise in the context of whether V can accept a repudiatory breach of contract committed by G but not T. Those issues have contributed to the conclusion that the doctrine of repudiation does not apply to LLPs (see para 14.22). In the context of rescission, all one can probably say with any certainty is that a court is likely to be wary to ensure that rescission does not prejudice innocent members of the LLP who did not engage in the conduct said to vitiate the victim's agreement.

Repudiation

14.22 It is now established—at least as a matter of first instance authority—that a general partnership cannot be dissolved by acceptance of a repudiatory breach of the partnership agreement. Nor can the partnership agreement be severed from the partnership relationship, so that the agreement is terminated whilst the partnership relationship remains intact. These matters were discussed at paras 7.20–7.22.

The rationale for this rule in the case of a general partnership is that partnership is a relationship subject to the court's equitable jurisdiction. Whether a person should cease to be a partner by reason of the other partners' breaches is therefore a matter for the court's discretion under s 35(d) of the Partnership Act 1890;[30] and as the partnership agreement and relationship of partnership are indivisible, neither can be determined by acceptance of a repudiatory breach.[31]

That rationale would not apply to an LLP, which is a creature of statute, quite apart from the effect of s 1(5) of the LLP Act 2000. Nevertheless, there are powerful reasons why an LLP Agreement should not be capable of repudiation, and the High Court has held that it cannot.

Flanagan v Liontrust Investment Partners LLP

14.23 The matter arose for consideration in *Flanagan v Liontrust Investment Partners LLP*.[32] In that case, F claimed that the LLP had committed a repudiatory breach of the LLP Agreement, which F had accepted. F's motive in advancing this argument was not to argue that he thereby ceased to be a member of the LLP, but rather that he ceased to be

---

[30] *Hurst v Bryk* [2002] 1 AC 185, HL at 195–6.
[31] *Mullins v Laughton* [2002] EWHC 2761 (Ch), [2003] Ch 250 at [91].
[32] *Flanagan v Liontrust Investment Partners LLP* (n 21). The issue did not arise on appeal at [2017] EWCA Civ 985. In *Wilsons Solicitors LLP v Roberts* [2018] EWCA Civ 52, [2018] 1 BCLC 306 at [50]–[51], the Court of Appeal was prepared to assume that *Flanagan* was correctly decided on this point.

a party to the LLP Agreement, and remained a member subject to the default terms. These were significantly more favourable to him than the terms applicable under the Agreement, not least because they would entitle him to a share of profits under default rule (1), rather than his fixed profit share under the LLP Agreement.

This was an unattractive argument. It would have meant that F's relationship with the LLP would be subject to one regime, whilst all other members would remain subject to the LLP Agreement. It would also follow that F would have management rights under default rule (3), and could not be expelled from the LLP under reg 8. It is not difficult to see how such consequences could quickly give rise to conflict between the two regimes and spiral into incoherence.

Henderson J held that the question of whether an LLP Agreement could be determined by acceptance of a repudiatory breach depended on the proper construction of s 5(1) of the LLP Act 2000. Specifically, in providing that the rights and duties of members were to be determined by agreement, and, in the absence of agreement by the default rules, did Parliament intend for a regime under which a repudiatory breach could lead to the default regime applying to a some members, whilst the contractual regime continued to apply to other members? Henderson J held that it cannot have so intended, given that the risk of incoherence was 'all but self-evident'.[33] Any other conclusion would be 'offensive to common sense'.[34]

One might fairly observe that this is a problem in any multiparty contract. As noted at para 14.21 in the context of discussing rescission, there may be contractual parties who are not involved in the breach, and the question of how repudiation should operate in such cases (eg how does it affect the relations between the parties accepting the breach and the innocent parties? How does it affect the relations between the parties accepting the breach inter se?) is a vexing one. Arguably, the fact that such problems arise in a complex contractual matrix should not, of itself, prevent an innocent party from terminating the contract for breach even if the consequences of doing so will require some working out and may force the parties to negotiate further. However, as Henderson J pointed out, the fact that such difficulties can arise in any multiparty contractual situation does not mean that Parliament intended them to arise under s 5(1). He concluded:

> In my view it is reasonably possible to construe the statutory scheme in such a way, without doing any violence to the wording of either section 5 or the default rules. I would accept Liontrust's submission that it is implicit in the statutory regime for the internal governance of LLPs that, in relation to any particular matter, an LLP and all of its members for the time being must be subject to the same set of rules, whether those rules are contained in an exhaustive section 5 agreement, or (in the absence of any section 5 agreement) in the default rules alone, or in a combination of a section 5

---

[33] *Flanagan v Liontrust Investment Partners LLP* (n 21) at [231].
[34] Ibid at [239].

agreement and the default rules. This does not mean, of course, that the rules have to treat all the members alike, or that the rules may not themselves be subject to amendment or modification in accordance with procedures to which all have previously agreed. But it does mean, in my judgment, that there is no place for operation of the doctrine in relation to section 5 agreements, save perhaps where the LLP has only two members.

Another way of expressing the same principle is to say that, once a section 5 agreement has been made, it will continue to bind the LLP and the members until either it is terminated by common agreement, or it is varied in accordance with a procedure to which all the relevant parties have previously subscribed. It is only in such circumstances, in my judgment, that there could be 'the absence of agreement as to any matter', within the meaning of section 5(1)(b) of LLPA 2000, in relation to a matter which was previously covered by the section 5 agreement, so as to allow the matter to be governed for the future by the default rules.[35]

Assuming this is the correct approach, a number of questions remain.

First, might it not be the case that acceptance of a repudiatory breach has some consequence other than the engagement of the default rules? Could it, for example, terminate membership of the LLP? The possibility that the acceptance of a repudiatory breach might terminate membership of the LLP was not, of course, F's case; it was instead canvassed by the LLP as an alternative to its primary case that the doctrine did not apply. Henderson J rejected this possibility summarily, principally relying on the fact that the acceptance of a repudiatory breach of the LLP Agreement did not fall within any of the recognized methods of termination under s 4(3).[36] His judgment in this regard is obiter, and may not therefore be the final word on the matter. Whilst it is probably right that discharge of the LLP Agreement cannot automatically lead to termination of membership (the two concepts not being indivisible as they are in a general partnership), it might be argued that on the true construction of reg 7 of the LLP Regulations 2001 acceptance of a repudiatory breach terminates a member's rights and obligations under the LLP Agreement but without engaging the default rules. That would leave the member with the limited statutory rights of membership under the Companies Act 2006 and a right under s 4(3) of the LLP Act 2000 to resign on reasonable notice (discharge of the LLP Agreement having ipso facto discharged any agreement 'as to cessation of membership'). Thus acceptance of a repudiatory breach could, perhaps, ultimately provide an exit route from the LLP under which the member could then resign and sue for damages for breach of contract.

Second, if the doctrine did apply, how would repudiation work in practice? Even if the LLP Agreement comes to an end between the accepting members and the guilty members/LLP, it would prima facie only be terminated as between those parties. It would

---

[35] Ibid at [234]–[235].
[36] Ibid at [237].

therefore remain in force between the accepting members and any members not in breach, between the accepting members inter se (if more than one), between the guilty members inter se, and between the guilty members and the LLP. As Henderson J observed in *Flanagan*, this is a problem that can arise in any multiparty contract, though its resolution appears especially intractable in the case of an LLP.

Third, what about the 'two member' situation mentioned by Henderson J? Generally, of course, a two-member LLP will require a three-party LLP Agreement. Given the judge's reasoning, it is odd that he thought that this might be an exception: because if the effect of accepting a repudiatory breach is that the default rules applied, a two-member LLP still faces the risk of inconsistency and incoherence unless the default rules apply not just between the accepting member and the guilty member/LLP but also as between the LLP and the guilty member as well. In truth, a two-member exception only makes sense if the consequence of accepting a repudiatory breach is termination of the innocent party's membership.

Resignation and a claim for damages

14.24 It is worth noting that in many cases the reason why a member may wish to accept a repudiatory breach is because they wish to achieve an outcome whereby (a) they are no longer a member of the LLP and (b) they can sue for damages for breach of the LLP Agreement, and perhaps other wrongs as well. From a contractual perspective, that is an outcome that is ordinarily achieved by treating the breaches of the contract as repudiatory, and accepting the breaches. However, in the context of an LLP (or indeed a general partnership), the same result can often be achieved by other means. Thus if a member has the right to resign or is able to negotiate their departure from the LLP, it is a question of causation as to whether losses, including post-termination losses suffered by reason of ceasing to be a member, are the result of the LLP's breaches of contract; and the courts have tended to look benevolently on claimants who resign and sue for breach of contract where those breaches were sufficiently serious to justify the claimant's decision to quit the firm.

In *Wilsons Solicitors LLP v Roberts*,[37] the Court of Appeal held that it was open to a member who had been lawfully expelled from an LLP to sue for post-termination losses, provided those loses were attributable to the prior wrongs committed by the LLP. In other words, lawful termination of the LLP Agreement—whether by the act of the LLP or by the member in question—does not necessarily break the chain of causation in respect of wrongs committed during a person's membership, and a member who finds themselves in a situation where their continued membership of the LLP is

---

[37] *Wilsons Solicitors LLP v Roberts* (n 32).

intolerable may be able to resign and sue for damages, including damages that are consequent to the termination of the LLP Agreement.[38]

Frustration

Frustration of a contract takes place when a supervening event significantly changes the nature of the outstanding contractual rights and/or obligations from what the parties could reasonably have contemplated at the time of its execution that it would be unjust to hold them to the contract. In such an event, the contract is discharged. **14.25**

As discussed at para 7.18, it seems doubtful that the doctrine of frustration applies to a general partnership. That conclusion is based on a similar analysis to that applied to the question of repudiation in *Hurst v Bryk*[39] and *Mullins v Laughton*.[40] As noted at para 14.22, the logic of those cases does not directly apply to an LLP. Indeed, having regard to the basis on which the court has held that the doctrine of repudiation does not apply to an LLP Agreement, there would seem to be considerably less objection to the doctrine of frustration applying, given that the frustration of the agreement would be universal, affecting all parties to it equally. The risk of incoherence identified by Henderson J in *Flanagan*[41] would not therefore arise.

That said, it is unlikely that the doctrine applies. The doctrine does not apply where the contract anticipates the event in question, and the fact that the LLP can be wound up on the just and equitable basis arguably provides a remedy for any event that might otherwise be regarded as frustrating the LLP Agreement. There are also formidable objections to the doctrine if the effect would be that the parties fall back on the default terms, as this could impose a radically different regime to that agreed and one ill-suited to the LLP in question. That might itself be just as uncontemplated and unjust as the original frustrating event. For these reasons, the better view is that whilst a supervening frustrating event may provide ample ground to wind up the LLP, it should not automatically lead to the discharge of the LLP Agreement as a matter of law.

---

[38] See also *Golstein v Bishop* [2014] EWCA Civ 10, [2014] Ch 455, in which a partnership was terminated by mutual consent. The claimant could nevertheless claim losses consequential to the dissolution, his agreement to dissolve the partnership having been caused by the defendant's breaches of it.
[39] *Hurst v Bryk* (n 30).
[40] *Mullins v Laughton* (n 31).
[41] *Flanagan v Liontrust Investment Partners LLP* (n 21).

15
DECISION-MAKING

The Decision-Making Process

Even the most rudimentary of LLP Agreements is likely to contain provisions explaining how decisions are to be made on behalf of the LLP, including whether some sort of board or management committee should be constituted and what powers should be vested in it. In the absence of such provision, however, default rules (3) and (4) will apply so that every member is entitled to take party in the management of the LLP, and no member is entitled to remuneration for doing so.[1]

15.01

The default rules provide significantly less assistance in terms of *how* decisions are to be made. It is implicit that (subject to the terms of the LLP Agreement) decisions should be made by each member expressing their vote, and that every member should have an equal vote. Beyond that, though, the position is unclear.

The flexible nature of an LLP means that LLP Agreements can address the issue of decision-making in a wide variety of ways. It is not uncommon for certain decisions to be reserved to a subset of members or even a single member; and where that single member is a company, it can then make use of its own board procedures to regulate the decision-making process. Of course, such decisions must still be made in the best interests of the LLP. Furthermore, such a process may raise difficult questions—such as the extent to which the directors of the corporate member owe any duty of care to the members of the LLP, or may themselves be shadow members of the LLP.[2]

What follows is subject to any terms of the LLP Agreement to the contrary.

Ordinary matters connected with the business

Default rule (6) provides that 'ordinary matters connected with the business of the LLP' are to be decided by a majority of members. This means a majority of all members, rather than just a majority of members voting. The words 'ordinary matters' are drawn from s 24(8) of the Partnership Act 1890. They clearly include the day-to-day conduct of the LLP's business, whatever it might be, and clearly exclude fundamental matters relating

15.02

---

[1] See paras 14.07 and 14.08.
[2] See para 12.06.

to the nature of the business. But the extent to which they extend to matters such as the timing of the payment of profits or other matters internal to the management of the business is surprisingly unclear. At para 5.23, it was suggested that ordinary matters related to the running of the firm as opposed to the structure of the firm, and that would seem a useful rule of thumb as to what an 'ordinary matter' is under default rule (6).

Extra-ordinary matters

15.03 Default rule (6) specifically provides that changes to the nature of the business require unanimity. Again, this means unanimity of all members of the LLP, not just those voting.

What about other extra-ordinary matters? Default rule (6) is silent as to these. In partnership law, it seems well established that all issues going to the fundamental nature of the business conducted require unanimity (see para 5.23). Given its genesis, it is arguable that default rule (6) should be approached on the same basis, and so all fundamental matters affecting the business of the LLP should be subject to a requirement of unanimity. However, the position is complicated by (a) the existence of company law powers vested in an LLP by statute and (b) the corporate nature of an LLP.

Statutory powers

15.04 Where a right is vested in the LLP by legislation, questions of how the right is to be exercised can be regarded as questions of statutory interpretation. A consideration of the nature of the right, the consequences of its exercise, and how it would be exercised by a company, may assist to determine whether unanimity or a majority vote is required, or even (perhaps) whether a majority of those voting would suffice. Most powers vested in an LLP by the Companies Act 2006 and Insolvency Act 1986 are, in the case of a company, vested in directors who (under the Model Articles) act by a majority of those voting. Subject to any indication given by default rule (6) to the contrary, it is arguable that a decision that could be made by such a majority of a company's board cannot sensibly have been intended to require the unanimous assent of the members of an LLP. That may suggest that a majority will suffice, as it would for an 'ordinary matter'. It is, perhaps, in this aspect more than any other that the absence of Model Articles for an LLP is most keenly felt.

Corporate decision-making at common law

15.05 The position is further complicated by the corporate nature of an LLP. At common law a decision made by a corporate body is made by a majority of members voting at a meeting attended by a majority of all members.[3] Does this common law rule have any

---

[3] *Merchants of the Staple of England v The Governor and Company of the Bank of England* (1887) 21 QBD 160, QB, at 165.

application to decisions made by LLPs? If so which ones, and how does it relate to default rule (6)? Until an especially deficient LLP Agreement falls for interpretation by the courts, these questions will likely remain unanswered.[4]

However, if the common law rule does apply to decisions made by the LLP, then it will potentially give rise to a (probably unintended) distinction between (a) any contractual term or statutory provision which depends upon a decision to be made by the LLP itself, and (b) any term or provision that depends upon a decision to be made by the members of the LLP. The former is a decision by an incorporated body; the latter is not.

The *Duomatic* principle

15.06 The *Duomatic* principle[5] is the name given to the common law rule under which a valid decision can be reached regardless of necessary formalities (including those as to meetings, notice, and so forth), provided all persons who have a right to vote give their fully informed assent. It can be used in a wide variety of circumstances, including to ratify breaches of duty. Although principally applicable to companies, the rule applies to other entities as well. It undoubtedly applies to LLPs.

The Exercise of Discretion

15.07 Powers granted by the LLP Agreement or by statute to members, or to a managing committee of members, may have far reaching consequences, and the question arises as to the constraints that exist of the exercise of those powers and the discretion to invoke them. The first question will be what the scope of the power is and whether it is subject to any implicit restrictions. The second question will be how the power is to be exercised, and whether there is any restraint on the discretion granted. Inevitably the answer to these questions must depend on the terms and effect of the power that is being exercised, but there are certain principles that are likely to be of general application when the exercise of a discretion might affect the rights of others.

Good faith and proper purpose

15.08 Although it is possible that a power granted in an LLP Agreement is intended to be exercised purely in the interests of the person exercising it (such as the right to retire),

---

[4] Whittaker and Machell, *The Law of Limited Liability Partnerships*, 4th edn, Bloomsbury, 2016, 17.12 suggest an extensive role for the common law rule. Frankly, though, it represents an unwelcome complication, and the courts may be reluctant to agree.
[5] From *Re Duomatic Ltd* [1969] 2 Ch 365 (Ch).

most powers typically found are of a management nature, and will have to be exercised in the interests of the LLP itself. They are therefore likely to give rise to a fiduciary duty to exercise them in good faith.[6] Indeed, even in cases where the decision-maker is entitled to have regard to his or her own interests and the decision does not appear to engage the corporate interest of the LLP, the exercise of any contractual discretion is still likely to require good faith. In *Socimer International Bank v Standard Bank London*, Rix LJ observed that:

> . . . a decision-maker's discretion will be limited, as a matter of necessary implication, by concepts of honesty, good faith, and genuineness, and the need for the absence of arbitrariness, capriciousness, perversity and irrationality. The concern is that the discretion should not be abused.[7]

It is 'trite law'[8] that a power must also be exercised for the purpose for which it was granted, rather than some collateral purpose. For example, a power to impose amendments upon an LLP Agreement binding all the members cannot be used to fundamentally change the business of the LLP or impose an obligation on members to invest further capital, as that is unlikely to have been the purpose of the power.[9] This may be apparent simply as a matter of the proper construction of the LLP Agreement's terms, but—certainly where a power that is to be exercised in the interests of the LLP appears on its face to be unfettered—it may be a rule that is best understood as an aspect of the doctrine of 'fraud on a power'[10] under which a power must be exercised for a proper purpose. This finds expression in s 171(b) of the Companies Act 2006: 'A director of a company must . . . only exercise powers for the purposes for which they are conferred.'[11] In *Eclairs Group Ltd v JKX Oil & Gas plc*, Lord Sumption SCJ further explained that '[a]scertaining the purpose of a power where the instrument is silent depends on an inference from the mischief of the provision conferring it, which is itself deduced from its express terms, from an analysis of their effect, and from the court's understanding of the business context.'[12]

Rationality

15.09 The constraints imposed by the court on the decision-making process may focus not just on the state of mind and intentions of the decision-maker, but also on an objective

---

[6] See para 13.07.
[7] [2008] EWCA Civ 116, [2008] 1 Lloyd's Rep 558 at [66].
[8] *Re Courage Group's Pension Schemes* [1987] 1 WLR 495 (Ch) at 505 per Millett J.
[9] See, further, *Hole v Garnsey* [1930] AC 472, HL discussed at para 14.17.
[10] *Duke of Portland v Lady Topham* (1864) 11 HLC 32, HL at 54. 'Fraud', here, merely means that the power has been exercised for a purpose, or with an intention that is beyond the scope of, or not justified by, the instrument creating it: see *Vatcher v Paull* [1915] AC 372, HL at 378.
[11] Whilst not directly applicable to members of an LLP, the codified duties of directors are strongly indicative of the scope of a member's duties to the LLP when exercising powers on its behalf. See para 13.08. For detailed commentary on this duty see Morse (ed), *Palmer's Company Law*, Sweet & Maxwell, Looseleaf, 8.2506.
[12] [2015] UKSC 71, [2016] BCC 79 at [30].

consideration of the process of decision-making, if not its outcome. In *Braganza v BP Shipping Ltd*,[13] the Supreme Court proposed that concepts borrowed from administrative law should be imported into the judicial assessment of contractual discretions. As Lady Hale DP explained:

> There is an obvious parallel between cases where a contract assigns a decision-making function to one of the parties and cases where a statute (or the royal prerogative) assigns a decision-making function to a public authority. In neither case is the court the primary decision-maker. The primary decision-maker is the contracting party or the public authority. It is right, therefore, that the standard of review generally adopted by the courts to the decisions of a contracting party should be no more demanding than the standard of review adopted in the judicial review of administrative action.[14]

Under the so-called *Wednesbury* test applicable to judicial review,[15] the court does not substitute its own decision for that of the decision-maker, but applies a two-limb test. The first limb focuses on the decision-making process: have the right matters been taken into account? The second limb focuses on the outcome of the process: is the result so outrageous that no reasonable decision-maker could have reached it?[16]

Since *Braganza*, this approach has been widely implemented in all manner of contractual situations, and there is every reason to assume that the *Braganza* criteria should apply to decisions made by members of an LLP, to at least some degree. Again, everything turns on an assessment of what procedural protections a decision seemingly requires, having regard to the purpose of the discretion and its context.[17] Who does it affect? Does the decision involve an assessment of fact or the exercise of a judgment?

In practice, the real difficulty is likely to come from the first limb of the *Wednesbury* test and the extent to which a court will scrutinize the matters that are relevant and irrelevant to a decision. In particular, must the decision-maker seek out further facts before passing judgment? Courts will have to be astute not to hold business people to the standard of public officials unless it is appropriate to do so. In *Braganza* itself, Baroness Hale acknowledged that allowance must be made for the vagaries of commercial judgment, and accepted that it would be unrealistic to expect an exhaustive examination of every issue.[18]

Where *Braganza* applies, it has been held that it is for the person challenging the decision to demonstrate that there are grounds for thinking that the decision-maker has exercised the discretion unreasonably. Once that is done, the burden transfers to the decision-maker to show that the decision was reasonable.[19]

---

[13] [2015] UKSC 17, [2015] 1 WLR 1661.
[14] Ibid at [19].
[15] *Associated Provincial Picture Houses Ltd v Wednesbury Corp* [1948] 1 KB 223, CA.
[16] *Braganza* (n 13) at [24].
[17] Ibid at [31].
[18] Ibid.
[19] *Hills v Niksun Inc* [2016] EWCA Civ 115, [2016] IRLR 715 at [23]–[26] per Vos LJ.

Natural Justice and Giving Reasons

15.10 A power that has express procedural requirements attached to it must be exercised in accordance with those procedural requirements. We saw this in the context of expulsion clauses from a general partnership (see para 5.39).

The more difficult question is whether there is an implicit obligation to follow the requirements of natural justice or to give reasons.

Natural justice

15.11 The courts are not consistent as to what 'natural justice' entails; it is apparently a 'flexible term which imposes different requirements in different cases'[20] and is 'an expression sadly lacking in precision'.[21] The standards of expected behaviour will therefore vary from case to case. It may simply be synonymous with a duty to act fairly in the circumstances, though it will generally include giving a person adversely affected the right to be heard. In *Gaiman v National Association for Mental Health*, Megarry J noted:

> ... there is a tendency for the court to apply the principles [of natural justice] to all powers of decision unless the circumstances suffice to exclude them. These circumstances may be found in the person or body making the decision, the nature of the decision to be made, the gravity of the matter in issue, the terms of any contract or other provision governing the power to decide, and so on ... This, of course, does little by way of providing a clear test: but as the authorities stand, it may not be possible to do much more than say that the principles of natural justice will apply unless the circumstances are such as indicate to the contrary. Certainly I would say that the cases show a tendency to expand the scope of natural justice rather than constrict it.[22]

That was said in 1970, and a new era of judicial activism in administrative law was well underway.[23] Yet despite the general direction of travel, there is still no particular requirement of natural justice in a purely contractual non-judicial determination.[24] Accordingly, the question is whether, within the context of an LLP, the nature of the rights in issue and the relationship between the parties should impose such a requirement. There is, of course, a strong case for arguing that decisions that deal with a person's livelihood or property should be subject to appropriate safeguards.[25] However,

---

[20] *McInnes v Onslow-Fane* [1978] 1 WLR 1520 (Ch) 1530 per Megarry J.
[21] *R v Local Government Board ex p Arlidge* [1914] 1 KB 160, CA at 199 per Hamilton LJ.
[22] [1971] Ch 317, CA at 333.
[23] Woolf et al, *De Smith's Judicial Review*, 8th edn, Sweet & Maxwell, 2018, 6-044.
[24] *Bernhard Schulte GmbH & Co KG v Nile Holdings Ltd* [2004] EWHC 977 (Comm), [2004] 2 Lloyd's Rep 352 at [95] (Cooke J, addressing expert determinations).
[25] Hence the requirement of natural justice in the case of trade associations and political parties: *Lee v The Showmen's Guild of Great Britain* [1952] 2 QB 329, CA at 342 per Denning LJ; *John v Rees* [1970] Ch 345 (Ch) at 397 per Megarry J. Those are, of course, not commercial enterprises like an LLP.

the position in partnership law is unclear (see para 5.40) and one could hardly expect the position to be any clearer when it comes to considering LLPs.

As with a partnership, the existence of some sort of right to challenge the determination (by arbitration) may well cure any alleged defect in procedure: but otherwise, the right to challenge may ultimately have to be exercised before a court.

Natural justice in a corporate setting

Gaiman concerned the exercise of a power of expulsion from a company limited by guarantee. The existence of the company, like that of the LLP, will potentially complicate the picture. In holding that principles of natural justice did not apply to a decision to expel members from a company limited by guarantee,[26] Megarry J stated:

15.12

> Where there is corporate personality, the directors or others exercising the powers in question are bound not merely by their duties towards the other members, but also by their duties towards the corporation. These duties may be inconsistent with the observance of natural justice, and accordingly the implication of any term that natural justice should be observed may be excluded. Furthermore, Parliament has provided a generous set of statutory rules governing companies and the rights of members, as contrasted with the exiguous statutory provisions governing trade unions and the even more exiguous provisions governing clubs. Yet again, the authorities . . . indicate the extent to which the courts will go in enforcing the provisions of the articles, even where those provisions appear to operate harshly or unjustly. These considerations seem to me to militate against the application of the principles of natural justice in this field.[27]

The first half of this passage is plainly applicable to LLPs, though the second half is arguably less so. The provisions of the Companies Act applicable to LLPs include few rules governing the relationship between the LLP and its members. But even though the existence of a corporate body must be taken into account, *Gaiman* does not stand for the proposition that the principles of natural justice should never be implied in such a setting. That is because any conflict can be resolved by ensuring that the flexible components of natural justice are moulded in such a way as to be consistent with duties owed to the corporate entity.[28]

Much will turn on the nature of the decision. A determination that requires particular grounds to be made out (eg misconduct) is more adept to include requirements

---

[26] The facts were unusual. The company was not a commercial enterprise but a charitable body in the field of mental health, whose membership had been infiltrated by a group of Scientologists. The board expelled a large number of members summarily on the basis that they were believed to have views antithetical to the company's aims. The members were not therefore deprived of any meaningful proprietary rights, and their livelihood was unaffected.

[27] *Gaiman* (n 22) at 335.

[28] *Dymoke v Association for Dance Movement Psychotherapy UK Ltd* [2019] EWHC 94 (QB) at [62]–[64] per Popplewell J.

of natural justice than a discretion that is simply at large.[29] The gravity of the consequences is also an important factor.[30]

Reasons

15.13 Giving reasons may disclose flaws in the decision-making process that would not otherwise be apparent. For that reason (amongst others) decision-makers will usually prefer to give as terse an explanation for the exercise of their discretion as possible, if they say anything at all. On the other hand, without some understanding of the basis on which a power was exercised, a person affected will have no way of knowing if the power has been lawfully exercised. Accordingly, the greater the imbalance in the parties' rights, and the greater the impact of the decision, the more disposed the court will be to require reasons to be given. In the Scottish partnership case of *Greck v Henderson Asia Pacific Equity Partners (FP) LP*, the judge baldly stated:

> ... where the discretion is exercised, reasons ought usually to be given, not necessarily in any formal way but in some manner sufficient to indicate to interested parties what decision has been taken and why.[31]

This overstates the case. Yet, certainly in the employment sphere, giving a reason for matters such as a suspension, garden leave, or refusal of a bonus is regarded as an aspect of the duty of mutual trust and confidence.[32] Although such a duty is not automatically imported into an LLP Agreement as it is into an employment contract, it is difficult to resist the inference that any consideration of these sorts of issues will likely lead to the same conclusion. In any event, pre-action disclosure and data protection rights may make it impossible to avoid reasons being provided one way or another. In the specific context of an LLP, particularly where a right to information as to the LLP's business exists (under default rule (8) or otherwise), it may be impossible to prevent light being shed on the decision-making process.

The forensic value of procedural propriety

15.14 In a private law context, the principal purpose of any requirement to insist on a fair hearing or to give reasons ought to be to ensure that the decision reached has been reached lawfully. In many respects, natural justice can be seen as a forensic counterpart

---

[29] *Gaiman* (n 22) at 336. See also *Eclairs Group Ltd v JKX Oil & Gas plc* [2013] EWHC 2631 (Ch), [2014] 1 BCLC 202. There, Mann J considered *Gaiman* in detail before concluding that questions of natural justice did not arise in the context of a decision made by a board based on whether it had 'reasonable cause to believe' a particular fact. The board was under no duty to carry out a wide-ranging enquiry before considering its state of mind. The issue did not arise on appeal.
[30] *Gaiman* (n 22) at 337.
[31] [2008] CSOH 2 at [76] (Lord Glennie).
[32] See eg *Keen v Commerzbank AG* [2006] EWCA Civ 1536, [2007] IRLR 132 at [44].

to the lawful exercise of a discretion. Procedural fairness is a tool that a decision-maker may use, and is often well advised to use, to ensure the decision is lawful. A failure to give reasons may not be a ground of complaint in itself, but may point to a lack of good faith, or suggest that there was in fact no rational reason for the decision. And the absence of a fair hearing may lead a decision-maker failing to take account of all relevant matters, because they do not know what might be said against the decision.

It may be too much to hope that *Braganza* leads to a reassessment and rationalization of the case law in this field; but, unless and until it does, decision-makers who are tasked with determining whether particular grounds for a decision are made out or not may be best advised to err in favour of ensuring that there is a measure of procedural fairness to any determination that has a significant effect on the rights of members, particularly where that determination involves the assessment of a member's conduct. Reticence in justifying a controversial decision rarely presents well to a judge.

Statutory rights

15.15 Employment law favours procedural safeguards. Although members do not have the statutory rights of employees, it should be noted that if a member is, in law, a worker (which is likely)[33] then they will have a statutory right to be accompanied by a representative to a disciplinary or grievance hearing at their request, provided that request is reasonable.[34]

The Consequences of an Unlawful Decision

15.16 So far as third parties are concerned, the doctrine of apparent authority and s 6(2) of the LLP Act 2000 may cause the acts of a member to have some legal effect even if they are the product of an unlawful decision.[35] Thus a decision of the management board that the LLP should contract with X Co may have been flawed, but it will not usually prevent the creation of a contract with X Co unless s 6(2) provides otherwise.

But in the context of internal matters—eg powers to expel, to raise capital, to amend the LLP Agreement—the question arises as to the legal effect of flawed decision-making. There are essentially three possible outcomes when a flawed decision is made on behalf of an LLP: (a) the decision is void, and therefore a complete nullity,[36] or (b) it is

---

[33] See para 12.11.
[34] Employment Relations Act 1999, s 10.
[35] See para 11.15.
[36] In practice, a decision that is void may be validated subsequently—either formally by ratification, or by an informal process such as acquiescence over time: see *Abbatt v Treasury Solicitor* [1969] 1 WLR 1575, CA at 1583 (Lord Denning MR).

voidable, and therefore, whilst valid, liable to be set aside on a challenge (whether in arbitration or before the courts), or (c) the decision is a valid determination.

In determining which of these outcomes applies, a distinction is often drawn between (a) the situation where the decision-maker acts outside the scope of the power and (b) the situation where the decision-maker acts within the scope of the power but exercises the power improperly. Although well established, this is potentially a difficult distinction: after all, depending on how a power is analysed, one could argue that the scope of the power includes the manner of its exercise. For example, a power must be exercised in good faith: so if a decision-maker acts in bad faith, are they acting entirely outside the power because a decision in bad faith is not a decision at all, or are they exercising the power, albeit improperly? It all turns on how one defines the power.

Acting outside the scope of the power

15.17 Traditionally, the common law has regarded conduct that is ultra vires as simply void, because those purporting to exercise the power were not competent to do so.[37] This will undoubtedly be the case where the LLP or its members purports to exercise a power that simply does not exist (eg a power of expulsion where none is provided for). Such a decision will be a nullity and of no effect. The same will be true if the power is vested in member X but wrongly exercised by member Y, or if it is exercised outside a required timeframe. These are all instances where the decision-maker simply lacked capacity to make the decision purportedly made: it fell outside the scope of the power granted. A decision made in bad faith is often treated as void.[38] The same may (perhaps) be true of a power exercised for an improper purpose.[39]

Improper exercise of the power

15.18 What if the decision-maker has capacity, but exercises the power improperly: eg the result is irrational or the wrong factors are taken into account? In equity, where a trustee must exercise a fiduciary power in the interests of a beneficiary, the wrongful exercise of the power is deemed void if the decision-maker had no power to make the decision; but is merely voidable if the decision-maker had the power but exercised it improperly.[40]

---

[37] *Ashbury Railway Carriage & Iron Co Ltd v Riche* (1874–75) LR 7 HL 653, HL at 672.
[38] *Blisset v Daniel* (1853) 10 Hare 493 (Ch) (see para 5.41).
[39] *Cloutte v Storey* [1911] 1 Ch 18, CA. This is much more questionable: see *Pitt v Holt* [2013] UKSC 26, [2013] AC 108 at [62], [93].
[40] *Pitt v Holt* (n 39) at [93]. As to the exercise of directors' powers, see *Howard Smith Ltd v Ampol Petroleum Ltd* [1974] AC 821, PC.

A decision made on behalf of an LLP may be subject to similar considerations, at least where fiduciary duties are engaged. The law in this respect—lying as it does at the crossroads between the common law and equity—has yet to be rationalized. But, tentatively, it is likely that fiduciary decisions that are made in bad faith, for an improper purpose, or irrationally, will be voidable (if not void).

Not all flaws in the decision-making process will vitiate a decision, however. Where iduciary duties are not engaged, it may be that the flaw in the process is merely a breach of contract. For example, a decision-maker may be obliged to act with reasonable care and skill, though it has never been suggested that a lack of reasonable care in making a decision should give rise to a right to have the decision set aside—at most it may give rise to liability for damages.[41]

---

[41] See Nolan, 'Controlling Fiduciary Power' [2009] CLJ 293, 309.

16
TERMINATION OF MEMBERSHIP

Methods of Termination

As we will see, the cessation of a person's membership of an LLP can be achieved by: **16.01**

- the member's death or dissolution;
- agreement, whether ad hoc or by the terms of the LLP Agreement permitting or requiring a member's retirement or expulsion. Mutual abandonment falling short of an actual agreement may also perhaps suffice;
- reasonable notice under s 4(3) of the LLP Act 2000;
- rescission of the LLP Agreement;
- a petition for unfair prejudice (where permitted) seeking the buy-out of the member's share;
- in extremis, the winding up of the LLP itself, on the just and equitable ground or otherwise.

Section 4(3) of the LLP Act 2000 states:

A person may cease to be a member of a limited liability partnership (as well as by death or dissolution) in accordance with an agreement with the other members or, in the absence of agreement with the other members as to cessation of membership, by giving reasonable notice to the other members.

The Act thus recognizes the first three methods of termination of a person's membership of an LLP listed above: by the death of the member (or dissolution of a corporate member), by agreement, or by reasonable notice.

The Act does not make clear whether the methods of termination set out in s 4(3) are comprehensive, and leaves open the question of whether membership of the LLP can be terminated on other grounds. As we have seen, however, there seems no reason why a person's agreement to become a member, and their subsequent accession to the LLP Agreement, might not be rescinded on the usual grounds that apply to rescission of a contract—ie misrepresentation, mistake, duress, and undue influence—provided restitutio in integrum is still possible.[1] And termination is an outcome that can be achieved by the remedy of unfair prejudice where it applies, and by a winding up of the LLP.[2] These three further methods of termination are addressed elsewhere in this work.

---

[1] See para 14.19.
[2] See para 13.19.

On the other hand, it seems that the doctrines of frustration and termination for repudiatory breach probably do not apply to an LLP Agreement and, consequently, cannot terminate a person's membership of the LLP.[3]

'By death or dissolution'

16.02 Although the first method of termination recognized by s 4(3) is implicit rather than explicit, it is clearly the intention that death or dissolution should, eo instante, result in termination of membership.[4] This is consistent with the fact that membership cannot be assigned: just as membership itself cannot be transferred to an assignee or a trustee in bankruptcy,[5] so it cannot be transferred to a personal representative (or the Crown as bona vacantia).

'Agreement with the other members'

16.03 The second method of termination of membership recognized by s 4(3) is by agreement. The agreement may be an ad hoc agreement to retire, or it may be contained within the LLP Agreement itself. In the latter case, s 4(3) therefore admits of methods that may not be consensual in their application. Such an agreement includes a clause permitting the LLP to remove a member on grounds of personal insolvency or age[6] (usually under the euphemism of 'compulsory retirement') as well as under an express power of expulsion. Power of expulsion are addressed further at para 16.05.

Note that the wording of s 4(3) permitting retirement by agreement 'with the other members' appears to be deficient in the same way as s 4(1), in that it does not expressly include an agreement between the departing member and the LLP alone.[7] As with s 4(1), it is probably nevertheless possible to treat the LLP as being implicitly authorized to make such an agreement with a member who wishes to retire.

There is no requirement that the agreement be in writing.

Abandonment?

16.04 If a member treats his or her membership as terminated, and the LLP and other members do likewise, their conduct may be sufficient to give rise to an agreement within s 4(3). Even if not, however, there is no reason why an estoppel by convention could not

---

[3] See para 14.22.
[4] Confusingly, however, s 7(1)(a) of the LLP Act 2000 suggests that death is distinct from cessation of membership. This is the consequence of poor statutory drafting.
[5] See para 13.02.
[6] Subject to the Equality Act 2010: see eg *Seldon v Clarkson Wright & Jakes* [2012] UKSC 16; *Murray v Maclay Murray & Spens LLP* [2018] IRLR 710 (EAT). Equality Act 2010, s 45 specifically prohibits unlawful discrimination by LLPs (and also by persons intending to incorporate an LLP).
[7] See para 12.01.

arise to prevent the effectiveness of a member's departure from being denied, particularly if the member's name is removed from the register of members without any objection. The possibility of 'abandonment' being a ground of termination for a general partnership was explored at para 7.22. The objections to that possibility in the case of a general partnership stem from Lord Millett's analysis in *Hurst v Bryk*[8] based on the supervisory role exercised by the courts of equity. That objection does not apply to LLPs. Although the point is free from authority, there is no obvious reason why an estoppel could not, in an appropriate case, bind all parties to treat a person's membership as having effectively ceased even in the absence of an agreement under s 4(3).

Expulsion

Regulation 8 of the LLP Regulations 2001 states: **16.05**

> No majority of the members can expel any member unless a power to do so has been conferred by express agreement between the members.

This applies s 25 of the Partnership Act 1890 (as to which, see para 5.37) so that, as with a general partnership, there is to be no implied power of expulsion from an LLP.

The LLP Agreement should set out how a power of expulsion is to be exercised. For example, the members may agree to vest that power in a particular majority (or even in a particular minority, eg where management is concentrated in limited body of members), or agree that its exercise is subject to procedural requirements.

A power of expulsion is expropriatory in nature, in that it forcibly deprives a member of his or her membership share. It will therefore be construed strictly.[9] It is almost inevitable that such a power will be construed as requiring its exercise to be conducted in good faith. The principles outlined at paras 5.37–5.41 and the considerations addressed there will apply as much to an LLP as to a general partnership: viz (a) is the expulsion within the terms of the power; (b) to the extent the rules of natural justice apply, have they been complied with; and (c) has the power been exercised in good faith?

To the extent a power of expulsion involves the exercise of a discretion, see paras15.07ff. The question as to whether the rules of natural justice require a fair hearing or reasons to be given for a power of expulsion is considered at para 15.10.

'Reasonable notice'

Finally, in the absence of agreement, a member can retire on reasonable notice. The **16.06** words qualifying reasonable notice—ie 'in the absence of agreement with the other members as to cessation of membership'—are not especially clear, but they must be

---

[8] [2002] 1 AC 185, HL.
[9] *Eaton v Caulfield* [2011] EWHC 173 (Ch), [2011] BCC 386 at [25].

referring to the situation where the agreement fails to make express provision for unilateral retirement, rather than the situation where the parties are unable to reach agreement as to the terms of retirement. They therefore operate as a form of default provision, and apply to the extent not implicitly or explicitly excluded by the LLP Agreement. On that basis, it follows that it is open to the parties to expressly preclude the possibility of retirement from an LLP if so minded.

The words 'notice to the other members' appears to be deficient in not permitting notice to the LLP itself. This is a deficiency similar to that noted in s 4(2).[10] Again, this can probably be cured by treating the LLP as being authorized by the members to receive such notice, though the scope for dispute in a contentious resignation is obvious, as is (as it always is) what qualifies as 'reasonable'. In the latter regard, a reasonable notice period is intended to strike a balance between the competing rights of the individual seeking to leave the business and those that remain; consequently case law on reasonable notice in the employment context is likely to be relevant, and the courts can be expected to take a similar approach. Key considerations would therefore likely include the seniority of the member, their role in the organization and length of involvement in the business, and the nature of that business.[11]

Again, there is no requirement that notice be in writing.

Consequences of Termination

16.07 It is convenient to consider separately (a) the consequences of termination with respect to third parties, and (b) the consequences of termination with respect to the relationship between the former member and the LLP.

External consequences

16.08 Section 6(3) of the LLP Act 2000 states as follows:

> Where a person has ceased to be a member of a limited liability partnership, the former member is to be regarded (in relation to any person dealing with the limited liability partnership) as still being a member of the limited liability partnership unless—
> (a) the person has notice that the former member has ceased to be a member of the limited liability partnership, or
> (b) notice that the former member has ceased to be a member of the limited liability partnership has been delivered to the registrar.

---

[10] See para 12.01.
[11] *Hill v CA Parsons & Co Ltd* [1972] Ch 305, CA; *Clark v Fahrenheit 451 (Communications) Ltd* [2000] 6 WLUK 65 (EAT).

The wording of s 6(3) is ambiguous. Section 6 as a whole concerns the authority of members when acting as agents for the LLP. Having regard to the other provisions of s 6,[12] one might surmise that the intended effect of s 6(3) is that a third party dealing with a former member should be entitled to assume that the former member remains an agent for the LLP unless the former member's cessation of membership has been notified in accordance with either paragraph (a) or (b). The explanatory notes to the section indicate that this is, indeed, the intended effect of s 6(3): ie that the LLP should be bound by the acts of the former member unless the test in either paragraph (a) or (b) is met.

However, that is not what s 6(3) actually says: by its terms it only applies when a third party is 'dealing with the limited liability partnership', and to treat a third party who deals with a former member as dealing with the LLP itself is simply to beg the question. If the intended effect of s 6(3) is to ensure that LLPs remain bound by the acts of former members where cessation of their membership has not been properly notified, then it is necessary to read the words 'dealing with the limited liability partnership' as though they said 'dealing with the former member purportedly on behalf of the limited liability partnership'.

Section 6(3) could be interpreted very differently, however, and in a manner that operates to the potential detriment of the former member. Suppose, for example, that the members of an LLP agree to guarantee the LLP's obligations under its lease, on terms that the guarantee should last only so long as they remain members. In such a case, might s 6(3) bite so as to extend the liability of a former member whose resignation has not yet been notified to either the Registrar or the landlord? This would depend on whether the landlord could be regarded as a person 'dealing with' the LLP for the purposes of s 6(3). If so, then the effect of s 6(3) would be that, as between the landlord and the former member, the former member would still be regarded as being a member of the LLP, and would therefore remain liable on the guarantee. This interpretation treats s 6(3) as a counterpart to ss 14(1) and 36(1) of the Partnership Act 1890, though this does not seem to have been intended.

However s 6(3) is to be approached, it is important that, on termination, notice is given to the Registrar as soon as possible that the person in question has ceased to be a member. Consideration should be given to notifying particular third parties who might be able to take advantage of s 6(3). Under s 9(1) of the LLP Act 2000, the LLP is in any event required to ensure that notice to the Registrar is delivered within fourteen days.[13]

---

[12] See paras 11.13–11.15.
[13] See para 11.26.

Internal consequences

16.09 The only provision of the LLP Act 2000 that addresses the consequences of termination as between the departing member and the LLP is s 7(2).[14] This provides that a former member cannot interfere in the management or administration of the LLP. That is surely self-evident (though there is no reason why the LLP Agreement could not provide for some residual rights to continue to exist, and to the extent necessary s 7(2) must therefore be capable of being disapplied by agreement).

Beyond that, the LLP Act 2000 is silent as to the effect of a member's cessation of membership as between the former member and the LLP. Once a person is no longer a member then the rights and obligations that are incidental to membership will no longer apply to them. But that leaves significant questions unanswered as to the rights of departing members. In particular, are they entitled to the return of any capital paid to the LLP? Or to capital profits? Are they, in other words, entitled to receive something in return for giving up their former share in the LLP, now extinguished and—in effect—released to the LLP itself, and if so how is that share to be valued?

These are similar issues to those that arise in the case of a technical dissolution of a general partnership.[15] They are matters that, of course, one would expect to see addressed in the LLP Agreement, and ultimately the question will likely turn on the interpretation of that agreement. A number of general observations can, however, be made: though these are of course subject to any terms to the contrary.

Entitlement to profits

16.10 Ordinarily, one would expect a former member who was entitled to share in the LLP's profits to be entitled to any unpaid profit share with respect to any previous fully completed accounting year. Almost invariably, the calculation of annual profits can only take place once the LLP's financial year has ended, and there is therefore often a lag between the year end and the declaration and payment of profits. In the meantime, any member who leaves the LLP will do so with an accrued right to profit with respect to that year.

Unless a member's retirement coincides with the LLP's year end, the question of profits for the existing accounting year will also arise. Assuming the member has been receiving drawings on account of those profits, there are three principal ways that the parties might choose to address the situation. First, the member could have no entitlement to profit at all: requiring them to repay any drawings. That seems improbable, though of course there is nothing to stop it being agreed. Second, the member could be entitled to retain drawings taken, but with no further right or

---

[14] Set out at para 13.02.
[15] See para 7.41.

liability to repay. That has the benefit of simplicity, and could be expressly agreed for reasons of convenience. Third, the member might be entitled to a partial pro rata share of profits, up to the date of departure. Although this method would obviously require such profits to be specifically calculated, in most cases this is likely to accord with the parties' intentions, as it affords a member a share in profits for so long as they remain a member. That is the assumption behind default rule (1) and is likely to be the assumption behind any LLP Agreement, even if default rule (1) is disapplied.

It seems unlikely that a member would be entitled to profits after their departure: ie between the date of termination and the final settlement of any payment owing to the former member. Although this is an issue that often arises in the case of a general partnership, there is no equivalent to s 42 of the Partnership Act 1890[16] and the possibility that a former member could be entitled to such profit share runs contrary to default rule (1).

Repayment of capital

Members' capital constitutes funds provided to the LLP as an equity investment, as a price of membership, in the same way that a shareholder may pay a company to acquire shares. Whether funds provided to an LLP by members are provided by way of loan or capital investment is a question of fact. A loan will be repayable on its terms. But is there any requirement for the LLP to repay a departing member's capital as a matter of course? **16.11**

Given that any requirement for a member to pay to acquire capital in the LLP will be found in the LLP Agreement, one would expect the LLP Agreement also to make provision as to the repayment of that capital. If it does not, it will be a question of whether a right to repayment can be implied. Again, default rule (1) assumes that all members are entitled to share in both the profits and capital of the LLP. Although the default rule says nothing as to the realization of that capital, the right would be fairly meaningless unless it assumed that members could obtain repayment of capital from a solvent LLP on their departure. Such a conclusion accords—as Nourse LJ put it in when considering the right of a partner's repayment of capital in *Popat v Shonchhatra*[17]—with 'the common sense of the matter', and the court is unlikely to have much difficulty in implying a right to repayment of capital if necessary.

Capital profits and goodwill

Perhaps the most difficult question is whether a departing member can claim a share of capital profits—ie the value of the LLP's assets accrued over time, in excess of their initial book value—including a share in the goodwill of the LLP. This is often a vexed question **16.12**

---

[16] See para 7.50.
[17] [1997] 3 All ER 800, CA at 805.

in a general partnership, where such assets are of course owned by the partners themselves. In the case of an LLP, the assets belong to the LLP[18] and there is no indication in default rule (1) that a member should have any personal entitlement to share in them.

If a member is not entitled to a share in the LLP's assets on departure, this means that the value of the assets will ultimately pass to the members as at the date of dissolution, who may well receive a windfall. This would contrast with the position of company shareholders who can generally expect the value of their shares to reflect, indirectly, the value of the company's underlying assets from time to time.

In the absence of any indication that a departing member has a right to share in the LLP's assets beyond revenue profits and capital (properly so-called), it seems simply to be inherent to the nature of an LLP that such assets remain vested in the LLP until dissolution.[19]

Although there is as yet no authority on point, a degree of support for this conclusion can be gained from the case of *Hailes v Hood*.[20] There, Morgan J had to interpret a settlement agreement, under which the claimant, a former member of an LLP, was entitled to receive 'a proper valuation of his share' in the LLP. The question for the court was whether such a valuation equated to a proportionate share of the full net asset value of the LLP, including any goodwill, or whether the claimant was entitled only to a share of profits (having contributed no actual capital). Although the judge preferred the former argument as a matter of construction of the particular settlement agreement, he observed on the way to this conclusion that upon termination of his membership the claimant would, in the ordinary course, have been entitled only to a share of profits and he would not have been entitled to share in the assets of the LLP.[21]

Forfeiture of profits

16.13 The circumstances of a member's departure from the LLP may raise the question as to whether, by reason of the member's conduct, the member can be forced to forego financial rights to which the member may otherwise be entitled, quite apart from any liability the member may have to the LLP for any misconduct.

The case of *Hosking v Marathon Asset Management LLP*[22] was noted at paras 5.03 and 5.22, and raises the possibility that a member might be required to forfeit a share of profits received whilst engaged in the commission of breaches of fiduciary duty. Whilst it is a longstanding principle of equity that an agent might be made to forfeit remuneration in such circumstances, *Hosking* appears to extend the right of forfeiture to a partner/member's profit share, at least where the profit share is in the nature of remuneration.

---

[18] As to goodwill generated whilst a person is a member of an LLP, see *Bhayani v Taylor Bracewell LLP* [2016] EWHC 3360 (IPEC).
[19] In this respect, an LLP is in a similar position to a company limited by guarantee.
[20] [2007] EWHC 1616 (Ch).
[21] Ibid at [67]. The contrary was not argued however.
[22] [2016] EWHC 2418 (Ch), [2017] Ch 157.

Post-Termination Controls

Once a person's membership of an LLP has ended, few obligations contained in the LLP Agreement are likely to remain. In addition to those terms necessary to achieve any financial reconciliation between the former member and the LLP, and to impose a continued obligation of confidentiality, those that do will likely be in the nature of restrictive covenants: whether against dealing with the LLP's clients, or soliciting clients, employees, or members away from the LLP, or against trading in competition with the LLP. These are also a common feature of partnership agreements, and such clauses are considered at paras 3.06–3.11.

16.14

Covenants in restraint of trade

The principles as to the doctrine of restraint of trade and the consequent validity of restrictive covenants are the same in whatever context they arise: they must protect a legitimate interest and go no further than is reasonable having regard to both the parties' and the public interest.[23] However, we have seen that in practice the courts are more suspicious of such clauses in an employment context than in a partnership context. This is a reflection of the fact that, generally speaking, there is an absence of mutuality in an employment situation when compared with a partnership situation. That is not to say that all partners are treated with the same broad brush: as discussed at para 3.06, restrictions that may be agreed with a full equity partner may not be fair if imposed on a junior fixed-share partner.

16.15

Restrictive covenants agreed by members of an LLP can be expected to be treated by the courts in the same way, and the approach set out in the opinion of the Privy Council in *Bridge v Deacons*[24] will apply. Although, strictly speaking, there may not be mutuality between a departing member and the LLP, there will usually be mutuality between the members themselves, and the fact that restrictive covenants are imposed for the benefit of all will likely carry significant weight with the court, as it does in the partnership context.

Implied restrictions on solicitation?

One potential point of divergence between LLPs and partnerships concerns implied restrictions that arise in the absence of express terms. Cases such as *Trego v Hunt*[25] (see para 6.28) have established that whilst a departing partner can set up in competition to the firm (subject to express terms agreed), he or she cannot solicit or canvass the

16.16

---

[23] *Esso Petroleum Co Ltd v Harper's Garage (Stourport) Ltd* [1968] AC 269, HL.
[24] [1984] 1 AC 705, HL.
[25] [1896] AC 7, HL.

customers of the firm away from the firm, even in the absence of an express covenant to this effect. This conclusion is apparently justified on the basis that on departure the partner transfers his or her share of goodwill to the remaining members of the firm, and it would be a derogation from grant to then make use of that same goodwill. This may not realistically reflect the circumstances in which most partners leave their firm, but the principle remains good law. How it translates to an LLP, where the goodwill is vested in the LLP itself and is not sold on a member's departure, remains to be seen: is it enough to engage the implied restriction on solicitation that a departing member can be seen as a vendor of his or her membership share in the LLP?

17

INSOLVENCY AND DISSOLUTION

The Insolvency Act Regime

17.01 Regulation 5 of the LLP Regulations 2001 applies virtually all the provisions of the Insolvency Act 1986 (as modified by Sch 3 to the Regulations) with regard to the winding up and insolvency of companies to LLPs. Thus LLPs may make voluntary arrangements, be subject to administration orders, and be wound up (voluntarily or compulsorily) in the same way as companies, leading to the appointment of a liquidator and, ultimately, to the LLP's dissolution.[1]

Voluntary winding up

17.02 Under s 84(1) of the Insolvency Act 1986 as modified, an LLP may be wound up voluntarily when it determines that it is to be wound up.[2] The required majority of members voting to reach such a determination is a matter for the LLP Agreement. In the absence of specific provision, default rule (6) provides that unanimity is required for there to be any change in the nature of the LLP's business, and such language would seem apt to include the LLP's winding up.[3] Once so determined, the voluntary winding up of an LLP—whether as a members' voluntary winding up (if the LLP is solvent) or a creditors' voluntary winding up (if it is not)—will proceed in the same manner as a company's voluntary winding up.

Compulsory winding up

17.03 The grounds on which an LLP may be compulsorily wound up are set out in s 122(1) of the Insolvency Act 1986 as modified.[4] As single member companies are now possible, the ground in sub-paragraph (c)—if the number of members is reduced below two—is

---

[1] Notoriously, the terminology used is the inverse of that for a partnership: a partnership dissolution leads to a winding up of its affairs, whereas a corporate winding up order leads to a dissolution. Who says insolvency lawyers do not have a sense of humour?

[2] LLP Regs 2001, Sch 3 (IA, s 86(1)) (see para 10.01 for an explanation of statutory citations from the Regulations).

[3] See paras 14.10 and 15.03. This view is shared by Totty, Moss, and Segal, *Insolvency* Sweet & Maxwell, Looseleaf, I2-23. Contrast Whittaker and Machell, *The Law of Limited Liability Partnerships* 4th edn, Bloomsbury, 2016, 31.1 who suggest a simple majority should suffice.

[4] LLP Regs 2001, Sch 3 (IA, s 122(1)).

unique to LLPs. The other grounds all have their equivalents in s 122 as it is applied to companies. Most notable amongst these are s 122(1)(d)—that the LLP is unable to pay its debts—and s 122(1)(e)—that the court is of the opinion that it is just and equitable that the LLP should be wound up, addressed in para 13.23.[5] Insofar as a petition for the winding up of the LLP might be presented by a member, the observations as to standing in para 13.24 apply generally.

As to the inability to pay debts, the same rules that apply to companies apply with respect to proof of insolvency. Thus in addition to the other methods recognized under s 123, an LLP will be deemed unable to pay its debts if a statutory demand is made and the debt is not paid within three weeks.

Voluntary arrangements

17.04 Company voluntary arrangements—generally known as CVAs—enable a company to make a formal proposal to its creditors which, on acceptance, will bind all creditors provided three-quarters in value vote in favour. The procedure applies to LLPs in the same way as it does to companies.[6]

Administration

17.05 LLP administrations proceed like company administrations, and an administrator can be appointed over an LLP under Sch B1 to the Insolvency Act 1986 as modified if the LLP is or is likely to become unable to pay its debts, and if one of the statutory purposes of administration is likely to be achieved by an administration order.[7] Pre-pack administrations (under which the terms of an immediate sale of the business are negotiated prior to the administration order being made) are likely to be just as popular—and just as controversial—with LLPs as they are with companies.[8]

Receivership

17.06 Although administrative receivership has largely given way to administration, the provisions of the Insolvency Act 1986 with respect to receivership apply to LLPs in the same way as they do to companies. As a consequence of the availability of other insolvency processes, including in particular administration, receivers are much less likely to be appointed over an LLP than they are over a partnership.[9]

---

[5] The equivalent provisions for companies are s 122(1)(f) and s 122(1)(g) respectively.
[6] LLP Regs 2001, Sch 3 (IA, ss 1–7B).
[7] LLP Regs 2001, Sch 3 (IA, Sch B1, para 3).
[8] See eg *Re Halliwells LLP* [2010] EWHC 2036 (Ch), [2011] 1 BCLC 345.
[9] As to which see para 7.28.

The LLP in Liquidation

17.07 Whether by way of a voluntary or compulsory winding up, the liquidation of an LLP has the same consequences as a company winding up. The authority of members to act on behalf of the LLP will cease, a liquidator will be appointed, and the liquidator will get in and realize the assets of the LLP and distribute them to creditors and those entitled in accordance with the rules of insolvency. The liquidator acts as agent for the LLP, with the specific powers set out in Insolvency Act 1986, ss 165–168 and Sch 4. It follows that the liquidator can exercise any contractual powers in the LLP Agreement that are vested in the LLP, and that may extend to any powers vested in specific members or committees of members, where those powers are held by members as agent for the LLP. Subject to the following points, an LLP liquidation will proceed in similar manner to a company liquidation.

Contributions by members

17.08 Although the limited liability of members of an LLP can effectively mean no liability at all, s 1(4) of the LLP Act 2000 provides for the possibility of members contributing to the assets of an LLP on its winding up 'as provided for by virtue of this Act'. Such liability has been imposed via the LLP Regulations 2001 by the introduction of a modified s 74 and a new s 214A into the Insolvency Act 1986. These are in addition to any liability under the well-established provisions of the Insolvency Act applicable to companies and directors. Thus liability for fraudulent trading under s 213 (carrying on business with intent to defraud creditors) or wrongful trading under s 214 (carrying on business at a time when it ought to have been appreciated that insolvent liquidation could not be avoided) may be imposed on members of an LLP. The law with respect to the unravelling of transactions at an undervalue (s 238) and preferences (s 239) also applies to insolvent LLPs and may therefore require members to return assets to an insolvent LLP.

Section 15A of the Company Directors Disqualification Act 1986 also permits the court to make a compensation order against a member or former member of an insolvent LLP who has been disqualified under the Act in circumstances in which their conduct caused loss to one or more creditors of the LLP. Such an order can be made on the application of the Secretary of State within two years of the disqualification order (or acceptance of the disqualification undertaking as appropriate). This is a relatively new provision, and it remains to be seen how it will interrelate with the remedies and powers granted to a liquidator under the Insolvency Act 1986.[10]

---

[10] See Mithani, *Directors' Disqualification* LexisNexis, Looseleaf, 2651–64.

Voluntary contributions: s 74

17.09 As modified, s 74 of the Insolvency Act 1986 allows for the enforcement of any agreement between the members,[11] or between a member and the LLP, that a member will, in circumstances which have arisen, be liable to contribute to the assets of the LLP in the event that the LLP goes into liquidation. Such a member is liable, to the extent agreed, to contribute to the LLP's assets, up to an amount sufficient for paying off its debts and expenses, and for the consequent adjustment of the contributions of the other members as between themselves.[12] Any such agreement can be made between any of the parties and at any time. This provision applies to former members, provided the obligation is capable of being construed as surviving cessation of membership.

The position of members of an LLP is thus similar to that of members in a company limited by guarantee, except that there is no obligation to make such an agreement, and it is entirely a matter for the LLP and its members to decide.

Enforced contributions: s 214A

17.10 Section 214A of the Insolvency Act 1986 is entitled 'adjustment of withdrawals'. It allows the court to declare, on the application of the liquidator, that a member is liable to contribute such amount to the assets of an LLP as it thinks proper if certain conditions are met. These conditions are:

(a) that within two years prior to the commencement of the winding up the member withdrew any property of the LLP (in any form, including a share of the profits) (s 214A(2)(a));

(b) that at the time of the withdrawal the member knew or had reasonable grounds for believing either that the LLP was unable to pay its debts, or that it would become so as the result of that withdrawal and any other withdrawals made by the members contemporaneously or contemplated at that time (s 214A(2)(b)); and

(c) that the member knew or ought to have concluded that after each withdrawal relevant for (b), there was no reasonable prospect that the LLP would avoid going into insolvent liquidation (s 214A(5)).

If those conditions are fulfilled the court cannot order the member to contribute more than the total amount of withdrawals made in the two-year period.

Condition (c) is based on the criteria for wrongful trading in s 214, and the wording closely follows s 214(2)(b). As with s 214, it is expressly provided—in s 214A(6)—that the consideration of what a member ought to have concluded is to be assessed by reference to the position of a reasonably diligent person with the general knowledge, skill, and experience that may reasonably be expected of a person carrying out the

---

[11] How a liquidator, who acts as agent for the LLP, is able to enforce an agreement between the members alone is not explained. Ordinarily, any such agreement would in any event be made with the LLP, as part of the LLP Agreement.

[12] LLP Regs 2001, Sch 3 (IA, s 74).

same functions as were carried out by the member in question, and the actual general knowledge, skill, and experience possessed by that member.[13] Case law with respect to wrongful trading under s 214 is likely to be relevant in making this assessment.[14] It has, generally, been found to be a difficult condition for a liquidator to meet.

It is not clear whether condition (b) is to be approached in the same way. This is an additional hurdle that finds no equivalent expression in s 214. In particular, in assessing whether a member has reasonable grounds for believing the LLP is unable to pay its debts, should inquiry be limited to the matters known to the member, or should it extend to the grounds that ought to have been known to him or her?

Identifying the withdrawals that are to be 'contemplated' under (b) is also likely to be problematic. the intention of the legislation is that it is not just the effect of the withdrawal made by the member in question that is to be taken into account, but the cumulative effect of all contemporaneous withdrawals, both made and in contemplation. But over what timescale? Profit is commonly taken from an LLP by regular drawings: so is a member obliged to contemplate the consequences of the next month's drawings as well?

Under s 214A(3), where the conditions are met the court may declare that a person must make such contribution to the LLP's assets as the court thinks proper (if any). Claims are capped by s 214A(4) at the aggregate of 'the amounts or values of all the withdrawals referred to in subsection (2)'. The wording is unclear, but this seems to mean all withdrawals of the type identified in s 214(2)(a) made within the two-year period, whether or not the mental element in s 214(2)(b) is fulfilled by the member making them. Thus a member making a single tainted withdrawal might be liable to repay all withdrawals made within the two-year period, even if made during a time of undoubted solvency.

Because the remedy under s 214A is compensatory rather than restitutionary, it must follow that a member against whom an order is made cannot subsequently prove in the liquidation with respect to any impugned withdrawal.[15] An order under s 214A requires contribution to the LLPs assets. It does not rescind the payment, so as to restore the debt that the withdrawal discharged (as it might be under s 239 in the case of a preference). If this is right, the title to the section—'adjustment of withdrawals'—is something of a misnomer.

It remains to be seen how, in practice, s 214A will interrelate with s 214 (and indeed with s 239 which allows the court to set aside preferences).[16] So far, the only successful reported case is *McTear v Eade*.[17] There, Insolvency and Companies Court (ICC)

---

[13] LLP Regs 2001, Sch 3 (IA, s 214A(6)).
[14] See in particular *Re Hawkes Hill Publishing Co Ltd* [2007] BCC 937 (Lewison J sitting as a judge of the Birmingham County Court) and *Re Ralls Builders Ltd* [2016] EWHC 243 (Ch), [2016] BCC 293 at [166]–[179].
[15] For the opposing view, see Blackett-Ord and Haren, *Partnership Law* 5th edn, Bloomsbury, 2015, 25.95.
[16] See Finch and Freedman, 'The Limited Liability Partnership: Pick and Mix or Mix Up?' [2002] JBL 475, 502–9 for consideration of some of the difficulties presented by s 214A.
[17] *McTear v Eade* [2019] EWHC 1673 (Ch). The earlier Scottish case of *Milne v Rashid* [2018] CSOH 23, [2018] 2 BCLC 673 failed on the third condition.

Judge Jones drew a close comparison with s 214. In particular, as to the calculation of compensation, he held that the starting point was to require the member to repay the amount of profit withdrawn, but that it was also relevant to consider (as one would under s 214) the extent to which the LLP's continued trading during the time which withdrawals were made resulted in an increase in the net deficiency of its assets. In other words, it would be relevant to consider whether the net effect of continuing to trade through the period in which the profits were taken may have improved the financial position of the LLP: it may be that the creditors would have been no better off if the LLP had entered liquidation at a time before the profits were taken. If so, it might not be fair to disgorge all the profits made by the members during that period.

By its terms, liability under s 214A extends to shadow members.[18]

Claims by members

17.11 Undoubtedly, claims by members that are not brought in their capacity as members rank equally with claims made by outsiders. However, the issue is not so clear with respect to claims brought by members in their capacity as members.

In its application to companies, the Insolvency Act 1986 provides that certain claims by shareholders are subordinated to claims by the general body of unsecured creditors. Specifically, s 74(2)(f) provides that sums owing to shareholders with respect to dividends and profits rank behind debts owing to other creditors. The corollary of this is that claims that arise from a person's status as shareholder will rank behind the claims of other creditors, though shareholders will rank equally with other creditors for any other liability.

However, s 74 as modified for LLPs contains no such provision. Does it follow that the claims of members qua members (eg to unpaid profit share under the LLP Agreement) rank equally with the claims of outsiders? Not necessarily. There are typically two such claims that a member might have qua member: a claim to capital and a claim to accrued but unpaid profits.

Claims to capital

17.12 In *McTear v Eade*, ICC Judge Jones held that members' claims for repayment of their capital were not debts that ranked equally with the claims of unsecured creditors.[19] The judge was dismissive of the s 74 argument—perhaps excessively so—but the judgment was undoubtedly correct in the result. It is inherent in the nature of capital that it is exposed to the risk of loss, and it is therefore only be repaid to the extent the LLP has assets to be able to do so. Put another way, a member's claim to capital is not a creditor's

---

[18] As to the possibility of the section applying to 'de facto members' see para 12.07.
[19] *McTear v Eade* (n 17) at [118].

claim to a debt. Rather, it is a claim to the property of the LLP, and such claims are only met once an LLP's liabilities have been met.

Claims to profit
Subject to the terms of the LLP Agreement, until profits have been declared and allocated, and until a profit share has actually accrued to a member, profits remain the property of the LLP and cannot be proved for by members. Once profits are allocated, however, the position seems to be different. The view of most commentators is that allocated but unpaid profits are provable debts.[20] There is as yet no authority on these matters; though in *McTear v Eade* the court held that the LLP's claim for repayment of drawings taken on account of profit share was not a claim in respect of which the members could set off some other debt owing to them.[21] The court's reasoning is somewhat truncated, but this finding appears to be based on the assumption that the member's claim to profits (on account of which the drawings had been paid) was not a debt in insolvency, but was a claim to the property of the LLP. If so, the result may be explicable on the basis that there had been no formal allocation of profits.

17.13

Either way, a member of an LLP pursuing an unpaid profit share is in a more precarious position than an employee of a company (whose claims to salary are not just debts in the insolvency, but preferential debts at that). So far as a salaried member or fixed-share member is concerned, their position may depend in part on whether their remuneration is paid out of profits as a matter of construction of the LLP Agreement. If not, then it ought to be a provable debt in any event.

Arrangements and Reconstructions

Schemes of arrangement

The LLP Regulations 2009 apply Companies Act 2006, ss 895–900 to LLPs.[22] In company law these sections provide a procedure whereby a compromise between a company and its shareholders or between a company and its creditors may be given legal effect (especially against dissentients) by a court order, provided a set approval procedure (basically 75 per cent approval of those affected, measured in terms both of number and value) has been followed. This procedure is known as a scheme of arrangement. Such schemes can range from the simple compounding of a company's debts to a significant restructuring of a company or its amalgamation with another entity.

17.14

---

[20] Blackett-Ord and Haren, *Partnership Law* 5th edn, Bloomsbury, 2015, 25.89 (the authors take the same view as to capital, however); Totty and Moss, *Insolvency* Sweet & Maxwell, Looseleaf, I2-27; Whittaker and Machell, *The Law of Limited Liability Partnerships* 4th edn, Bloomsbury, 2016, 33.5.
[21] *McTear v Eade* (n 17) at [136].
[22] LLP Regs 2009, reg 45 (CA, ss 895–900).

By applying these sections to LLPs, LLPs are able to come to an arrangement binding on all creditors, with the approval of only a majority of them, as a potential alternative to liquidation. Furthermore, the sections also apply to arrangements between an LLP and its members. As between companies and their shareholders, schemes of arrangement are sometimes used by companies to effect fundamental constitutional changes where there is less than unanimous consent, or even to effect a merger between two companies. In the LLP context this would seem to be contrary to the idea that internal matters are best left to the members to agree upon. It is certainly a long way from the partnership ideal that no one can be made a partner in a different partnership without consent.

Nevertheless, the effect of the application of these sections as between an LLP and its members is, therefore, that, provided the requisite procedure is followed, a majority of the members may effect a merger of the LLP with another LLP or company, or perhaps fundamentally change the constitutional rights of members, so as to bind any dissenting minority of the members. Of course, the court's consent is required to bring this about and it may prove to be the case that the courts will be less willing to approve such schemes than they are with companies, where they are mainly concerned to see that all the formalities have been complied with. Time will tell.

Again, this is an area where reference should be made to books on company law for the details of the sections. One possible area of difficulty is that the scheme must be approved by the requisite majority of each 'class' of creditors or member (as appropriate) where there are different classes.[23] As applied to LLPs, it may be difficult to establish whether all members are equal or some are different, ie with interests different enough to constitute a separate class and so requiring the requisite approval of that class.

Cross-border mergers

17.15 The LLP Regulations 2009 also apply the Companies (Cross-Border Mergers) Regulation 2007 to LLPs.[24] These are unlikely to be much used. They allow a form of cross-border amalgamation, but not in a way practised in the United Kingdom.

Voluntary reconstructions

17.16 The LLP Regulations 2001 apply s 110 of the Insolvency Act 1986 to LLPs.[25] That section allows a company that is being, or that proposes to be, voluntarily wound up to transfer all or part of its undertaking to another company, in what is known as

---

[23] LLP Regs 2009, reg 45 (CA, s 899(1)).
[24] LLP Regs 2009, reg 46 (SI 2007/2974).
[25] LLP Regs 2001, Sch 3 (IA, s 110).

a reconstruction.[26] As applied to LLPs this means that the members, having proposed or instituted the members' winding up, may also authorize the liquidator to transfer the whole or part of its business or property to another LLP or to a company.[27] The liquidator will then receive an interest in the transferee company or the transferee LLP (presumably, in the latter case, by way of the LLP becoming party to the transferee's LLP Agreement or receiving an assignment of rights under it), which become assets of the liquidation for distribution amongst the members, or can alternatively agree arrangements whereby members receive some valuable benefit from the transferee.

The process supposes unanimous agreement amongst the members. Any member who opposes the reconstruction may give written notice of dissent to the liquidator within seven days. Under s 111 of the Insolvency Act 1986, the liquidator must then either withdraw the sale or buy out the member at an agreed price (determined by arbitration if necessary).[28]

A reconstruction will be void (unless sanctioned by the court) in the event that the LLP is wound up compulsorily within a year.[29]

Investigations

Investigations by the Department for Business, Energy and Industrial Strategy (BEIS), the responsible government department, are conducted under provisions that remain enacted by Part XIV of the Companies Act 1985. Those are applied to LLPs by Sch 2 to the LLP Regulations 2001. In outline, these allow inspectors appointed by the Secretary of State to conduct an investigation into the affairs of an LLP either on the application of the LLP or at least one-fifth of the registered members,[30] or under a court order.[31] In addition the Secretary of State may order an investigation if it appears that the affairs of the LLP are being conducted with intent to defraud creditors, or for any fraudulent or unlawful purpose, or in a manner unfairly prejudicial to some of the members, or where those setting up the LLP have been guilty of fraud, misfeasance, or other misconduct, or where the members have not been given all the information about its affairs which they might reasonably expect.[32] There is, however, no specific power to investigate the ownership of an LLP as there is with companies.[33]

17.17

---

[26] The LLP Regs 2001 also amended s 110 in its native form (ie as it applies to companies) so as to permit the assets to be transferred to an LLP.
[27] The modified section actually states 'to another company ... or to a limited liability partnership', a clear slip in the drafting.
[28] LLP Regs 2001, Sch 3 (IA, s 111).
[29] LLP Regs 2001, Sch 3 (IA, s 110(6)).
[30] LLP Regs 2001, Sch 2 (CA 1985, s 431).
[31] LLP Regs 2001, Sch 2 (CA 1985, s 432(1)).
[32] LLP Regs 2001, Sch 2 (CA 1985, s 432(2)).
[33] Cf CA 1985, ss 442–446.

The inspectors have wide powers of investigation. They can compel the production of documents or other evidence from any person who may be in possession of information relating to a matter they believe to be relevant to the investigation.[34] They can also investigate subsidiary or holding companies or LLPs to the extent necessary for the purpose of their original investigation.[35] It is the duty of members and 'agents' of the LLP and former members and agents to co-operate with the inspectors,[36] and failure to do so may be a contempt of court.[37] 'Agents' includes bankers, solicitors, auditors.

Upon conclusion of their investigation, the inspectors will produce a report to the Secretary of State. That report, together with any interim reports directed, will be provided to the court (if the investigation was conducted consequent to a court order), and may also be published or provided to particular persons.[38] The report is admissible in legal proceedings, including in disqualification proceedings under the Company Directors Disqualification Act 1986.[39]

The Secretary of State also has a freestanding power to require an LLP to produce documents or information, whether or not a fully-fledged investigation is underway.[40]

The powers under the Act are backed with a right to enter and search premises under warrant,[41] and those who disclose information under the Act (including those who volunteer information in good faith) are exempted from liability that might otherwise arise for breach of confidence.[42] The Act also contains miscellaneous criminal provisions relating to the destruction or falsification of documents, and for furnishing false information.[43]

The potential consequences of investigations are various, but include an application to wind up the LLP on public interest grounds,[44] applications to disqualify persons from acting as members of LLPs or company directors in the future, as well as criminal proceedings for any wrongdoing discovered.

---

[34] LLP Regs 2001, Sch 2 (CA 1985, s 434(2)).
[35] LLP Regs 2001, Sch 2 (CA 1985, s 433).
[36] LLP Regs 2001, Sch 2 (CA 1985, s 434(1)).
[37] LLP Regs 2001, Sch 2 (CA 1985, s 436).
[38] LLP Regs 2001, Sch 2 (CA 1985, s 437).
[39] LLP Regs 2001, Sch 2 (CA 1985, s 441).
[40] LLP Regs 2001, Sch 2 (CA 1985, ss 447–447A).
[41] LLP Regs 2001, Sch 2 (CA 1985, s 448).
[42] LLP Regs 2001, Sch 2 (CA 1985, s 44A).
[43] LLP Regs 2001, Sch 2 (CA 1985, ss 449–450).
[44] LLP Regs 2001, Sch 3 (IA, s 124A).

Striking Off the Register

Striking off consequent to winding up

An LLP will be dissolved once its winding up has come to an end. That is, generally, three months after completion of the liquidation.[45] The LLP is thereupon removed from the register.

17.18

Striking off by the Registrar

In addition, there is a power to strike off an LLP:

17.19

- where the Registrar has reasonable cause to believe that it is not carrying on business or is not 'in operation' and the LLP does not respond to inquiries as to its status;[46]
- where an LLP is being wound up, required returns have not been filed, and the Registrar has reasonable cause to believe that no liquidator is acting or the affairs of the LLP are fully wound up;[47]
- on the application of a majority of members (if more than two), or all members (if two or fewer), supported by a declaration to the effect that the LLP is dormant and has not engaged in certain specified activities.[48]

Once the striking off has been advertised in the Gazette, the LLP is officially dissolved, though without prejudice to the possible liabilities of members of the LLP, which continue and may be enforced as if the LLP had not been dissolved.[49]

Bona vacantia

As with a company, if an LLP owns property when it is dissolved, that property vests in the Crown as bona vacantia. The provisions of the Companies Act 2006 apply as to the potential disclaimer of that property by the Crown.[50] There are no LLP-specific issues that arise.

17.20

---

[45] LLP Regs 2001, Sch 3 (IA, ss 201–205).
[46] LLP Regs 2009, reg 50 (CA, s 1000).
[47] LLP Regs 2009, reg 50 (CA, s 1001). There is a duty to strike off in this eventuality.
[48] LLP Regs 2009, reg 51 (CA, 2006 ss 1003–1011).
[49] LLP Regs 2009, reg 50 (CA, s 1000(6)–(7), s 1001(4)–(5)), reg 51 (CA, s 1003(5)–(6)).
[50] LLP Regs 2009, regs 52–55 (CA, ss 1012–1023).

Restoration

17.21 The same procedures also exist as to the possible restoration of the LLP to the register.[51] Where the LLP was struck off by the Registrar on grounds that the LLP appeared to be defunct, administrative restoration (on application to the Registrar) may be possible. Otherwise, an application to court can be made, subject to a limitation period of six years from the date of dissolution.[52] If restored, it is as if the LLP had never been removed from the register. Again, no LLP-specific issues arise.

---

[51] LLP Regs 2009, regs 56–58 (CA, ss 1024–1034).
[52] LLP Regs 2009, reg 57 (CA, s 1030); though there is no time limit to restore an LLP for the purposes of pursuing a claim for personal injury against it.

INDEX

abandonment 7.06, 7.22, 16.01, 16.04
accident and injury in course of firm's business 1.09
accountancy partnerships 1.02, 1.27, 1.29, 1.31, 10.04–10.06
account, duty to 5.03, 5.11, 5.17, 14.12
account of profits 5.45, 13.10
  secret 5.03
accounts/accounting requirements
  access to books 5.25, 14.11
  corporate partners 1.37
  entitlement 5.47
  final accounts, necessity for 7.61
  Generally Accepted Accounting Practice 11.30
  intentional partnerships 2.05
  limited liability partnerships (LLPs) 10.09, 11.30
  membership of LLPs - rights and duties 13.05
  preparation and disclosure 10.10
  records 11.30, 14.11
acknowledgment of service 3.19
acts or instruments in firm name 4.10
actual authority
  contracts: partners' liability 4.03–4.04, 4.11
  misapplication of property: liability 4.36
  private limited partnerships 9.13
  vicarious liability 4.28, 4.36
  winding up 7.24
administration 8.03, 17.05
administration orders 8.02, 8.04, 17.01
  appointment by application to court 8.15–8.17
  appointment by partners 8.18
  consequences of an order 8.19
  court's discretion 8.17
  flexibility of administration 8.20
  purpose of administration 8.15
administrators: appointment 8.15
advances 5.31
age
  of majority 3.04
  minors and freedom to contract 3.04
  and termination of LLP membership 16.03
agency 1.28
  common law and equity 1.10
  contracts: partners' liability 4.02–4.05, 4.17–4.18, 4.20

freedom to contract 3.04
group partnerships 1.31–1.32
impact of LLPs 1.30
intentional partnerships 2.12
legal controls on partnerships 3.01
limited liability partnerships (LLPs) 11.12, 11.14–11.15
LLP Agreement 14.21
management and control 5.25
agreed sum, failure to contribute 9.10
agreement
  construction 7.45, 7.47
  contrary 2.08, 9.22
  duration of 2.05
  effect of 5.02
  formal partnerships 2.05
  from an association 1.12
  grave or persistent breaches of 5.38, 7.12
  limitations in 4.04
  mutual 2.10, 7.06
  oral 1.10, 4.03, 5.02
  with other members and termination 16.03–16.05
  strict construction 6.16
  written *see* written agreement
  see also express or implied agreement; LLP Agreement; repudiation
agricultural tenancies 9.01
alternative trust solution 4.22
annual confirmation statements 11.29
annuities 2.27
anti-money laundering (AML) supervisory body 9.24
apparent authority
  contracts: partners' liability 4.03–4.04, 4.09, 4.11
  decision-making 15.16
  limited liability partnerships (LLPs) 11.15
  misapplication of property: liability 4.36, 4.38, 4.40, 4.42
  private limited partnerships 9.13
  vicarious liability 4.24
  winding up 7.24
apparent partners 9.21
arbitration 7.17, 13.26
  agreement 5.24, 7.08
  clauses 3.03

assets 7.42
  capable of being partnership property, limits on 6.10
  circulating 6.01
  distribution - solvent partnerships
    capital losses 7.62–7.64
    final accounts, necessity for 7.61
    surplus assets 7.62–7.64
  fixed 6.01
  goodwill as 6.30
  identification of
    agreements, strict construction of 6.16
    business efficacy and necessity 6.14–6.15
    express or implied agreements - surrounding circumstances 6.12–6.13
    farming cases 6.14–6.15
    land purchased from profits made by use of on non-partnership land 6.18–6.20
    profits, property bought with 6.17
    resulting trusts 6.21
  misuse of 5.19
  partition or in specie distribution 7.36
  personal, risk to 10.04
  surplus 7.62–7.64
  use of for personal benefit 5.13–5.14
  see also partnership property; valuation of partner's share in assets; winding up
assignment
  business premises: leases and licences 6.62
  commercial 5.44
  involuntary 5.44–5.45, 5.50, 7.03
  membership of LLPs - rights and duties 13.02
  no right of 14.09
  personal 5.44
  voluntary 5.44–5.45
association
  freedom of 3.03, 3.12
  no requirement for written agreement for 2.04
  partnerships by 2.13
attribution 11.12, 11.21, 13.15
auditing/auditors 1.37, 10.09, 11.30
authority
  express 11.21
  limited liability partnerships (LLPs) 11.14–11.15
  misapplication of property: liability 4.37
  types of 4.03
  see also actual authority; apparent authority; implied authority
automatic accruer clause 7.04

bankruptcy
  concurrent 8.06–8.08
  corporate partners 1.35
  dissolution 7.03–7.04
  duration of liability 4.55, 4.59
  intentional partnerships 2.07
  joint petitions 8.09, 8.12
  membership of LLPs - rights and duties 13.02
  partner bankrupt but no petition against firm 8.04
  petitions 8.10
  undischarged bankrupts and disqualification 12.16
  see also insolvency
Belfast Gazette 9.07
beneficial interest 6.08–6.10
body corporate 10.02, 10.10, 11.08, 11.11
bona vacantia 17.20
bonus, refusal of 15.13
book value 7.42–7.45, 16.12
borrowing powers 1.30
Braganza criteria 15.09
branch offices 1.31, 1.34
bribery 4.26
burden of proof 2.03, 2.41, 4.57
business activities *see* ordinary course of business
business in common 2.43
business efficacy 2.04, 6.14–6.15
business names
  acts or instruments in 4.10
  change of name 11.06
  disclosure 3.16
  display of 11.24
  limitations on choice of 3.15
  limited liability partnerships (LLPs) 11.06
  passing-off actions 3.17
  permitted additions 3.14
  private limited partnerships 9.06
  public domain and partnerships 3.19
  use and disclosure of 1.11
business premises *see under* partnership property
business purposes 1.14–1.19
  company formation 1.19
  contemplated partnerships 1.15
  excluded relationships: co-ownership 1.18
  self-employment and employees 1.16
  single commercial venture 1.17
business reality 1.10
buy-out agreements 7.38, 7.40

capacity
  corporate partners 1.36
  freedom to contract 3.04
  intentional partnerships 2.05
  legal 10.02

INDEX 433

legal controls on partnerships 3.03
limited 15.17
limited liability partnerships
    (LLPs) 11.19–11.22
  post-incorporation contracts and
    deeds 11.21
  pre-incorporation contracts and deeds 11.20
  see also authority; mental incapacity
capital 5.27, 7.42
  and assets (or property) distinction 5.26
  claims 17.12
  contributions 5.30, 9.19
  gains 5.26
  losses 7.62–7.64
  payment of 7.34
  profits
    -earning capacity 6.28
    and goodwill 16.12
    no application to 7.51
    no effect on right to 7.57
    share of 7.55, 14.05
  reforms 9.08
  repayment 16.11
  see also venture capital
cash basis rule 7.46
certificate of designation 9.17
certificate of incorporation 9.17, 11.11, 11.23
certificate of registration 9.05
change of partners
  conditional clauses 5.36
  contrary intention 5.33–5.35
  implied requirement for unanimous
    consent 5.33
  and liability duration 4.49–4.51
charging orders 5.49–5.50, 7.03–7.04
choses in action 6.09, 7.35
claims by members 17.11–17.13
  capital claims 17.12
  profit claims 17.13
close connection test 4.25
collective investment scheme 9.03
commencement of formal
    partnerships 2.05–2.06
common law
  corporate decision-making 15.05
  and equity 1.10, 13.06
  membership of LLPs - rights and duties 13.06
  partnership law 1.10
community of benefit,
    establishing 2.16–2.18, 2.22
Companies House 11.07, 11.09, 11.23,
    11.25–11.26
company law 10.08–10.10, 11.12, 11.15,
    12.07, 17.14

company voluntary arrangements
    (CVAs) 17.04
compensation 5.03, 5.10
  equitable 1.10, 13.10
  order 8.08, 17.08
competition law 12.15
composition of partnership 9.13
compulsory registration of information on
    formation 3.01
compulsory retirement 5.43, 16.03
compulsory winding up 17.01, 17.03, 17.07
conditional clauses 5.36
conduct
  course of 5.02
  duty of care 5.04
  legal controls on partnerships 3.01
  membership of LLPs 12.15
  prejudicial 7.11
  unfair 7.28
  unlawful 11.04
  see also misconduct
confidence
  loss of 7.15
  see also mutual trust and confidence
confidentiality
  conflict of interest and duty - unauthorized
    personal profit 5.15
  good faith 5.06
  management and control 5.25
  partnership property 6.04
  termination 16.14
  winding up 7.27
conflict of interest
  charging orders against partners 5.50
  expulsion clauses 5.42
  joint bankruptcy petitions 8.09
  partnership administration orders 8.16
  private fund limited partnerships 9.18
  see also conflict of interest and duty -
    unauthorized personal profit;
    no-conflict rule
conflict of interest and duty - unauthorized
    personal profit 5.09–5.10
  direct profit from partnership
    transaction 5.12
  errant partner's share of the benefit 5.18
  liability, duration of 5.17
  no-conflict rule 5.11, 5.15
  no-profit rule 5.11, 5.15–5.16
  partnership opportunity, misuse of 5.15–5.16
  secret profit 5.12
  use of partnership asset for personal
    benefit 5.13–5.14
consensus ad idem 2.05, 3.03

consent
  assignment of partnership share 5.44
  contract and equity 5.02
  duration of liability 4.52
  express 1.09, 2.05
  honesty and disclosure 5.10
  implied/inferred 1.09, 2.05
  informed 13.09
  mutual 2.08
  unanimous 5.23, 5.33
consequent orders 7.28
constitution 1.35, 1.39, 4.55
construction, principles of 2.05
constructive trusts 1.10, 1.13
  conflict of interest and duty - unauthorized personal profit 5.17
  legal controls on partnerships 3.01
  misapplication of property: liability 4.40–4.42, 4.44
  partnership property 6.21
contemplated partnerships 1.15, 9.05
continuation of business 7.30
continuity *see* legal personality and continuity *under* partnerships
contracting out 7.59
contracts
  breach of 4.26
  contractual agreement, express 1.12
  contractual effect of repudiation 7.21
  contractual rules in intentional partnerships 2.05
  and equity 5.01–5.03
  formation 1.10
  freedom to contract 2.05, 2.08, 3.03–3.05
  liability *see* contracts: partners' liability
  pre-dissolution 7.25
  ratification 4.05
  scope of 2.05
  single continuing 4.50
  statutory provisions 1.28
  variation 1.10
  vitiation 1.10
  see also contractual grounds *under* dissolution; privity of contract; repudiation; rescission
contracts - partners' liability
  agency concepts 4.02–4.05
  authority, types of 4.03
  limitations in the agreement 4.04
  ratification 4.05
  see also implied authority, exclusion of
contrary agreement 2.08, 9.22
contrary clause 5.33
contrary intention 5.33–5.35

assets distribution - solvency 7.64
contract: implied terms 5.20
dissolution 7.01–7.02, 7.04
duration of liability 4.54
evidential difficulties 5.35
financial affairs 5.26–5.29
intentional partnerships 2.08 2.08–2.10
land purchased from profits made by use of on non-partnership land 6.20
management and control 5.23
membership of LLPs 12.07
partnership law 1.09
partnership property 6.13, 6.17
private limited partnerships 9.15
transfer of outgoing partner's share 7.60
valuation of partner's share in assets 7.44
valuation of partner's share in profits post-dissolution 7.52
contributions by members 17.08–17.10
  enforced contributions 17.10
  voluntary contributions 17.09
control
  two or more persons (carried on in common) 1.22
  see also management and control
conversion doctrine 6.06, 6.17
co-ownership 1.18, 2.01, 6.05
corporate decision-making at common law 15.05
corporate manslaughter 4.33–4.34
  see also gross negligence manslaughter
corporate model 10.04
corporate partners 1.35–1.37
corporate structure of limited liability partnerships (LLPs)
  basic requirements
    associated for carrying on 11.03
    lawful business with a view to profit 11.04
    two or more persons 11.02
  incorporation: legal consequences
    apparent authority 11.15
    attribution 11.12
    capacity 11.19–11.22
    corporate veil and limited liability 11.16–11.18
    litigation 11.22
    members' authority 11.14–11.15
    post-incorporation contracts and deeds and capacity 11.21
    pre-incorporation contracts and deeds and capacity 11.20
    vicarious liability 11.13
  see also disclosure obligations and limited liability partnerships (LLPs)

incorporation process
    designated members 11.09
    members' particulars 11.08
    name 11.06
    situation and address 11.07
    statement of initial significant
        control 11.10
corporate veil and limited liability 11.16–11.18
corporations: statutory powers 1.12
course of dealings and intentional
    partnerships 2.05, 2.12
court orders 2.07
    see also under dissolution
courts
    partnership administration orders 8.15–8.17
    powers of in respect of assets 7.36
creditors
    deferred 8.07
    did not know they were partners at time of
        retirement 4.60
    financial involvement, association by 2.22
    formation and establishment of
        partnerships 2.03
    insolvency and dissolution 17.02
    joint 8.01, 8.07, 8.09
    limited liability partnerships (LLPs) 11.28
    membership of LLPs 13.18
    partnership 8.01
    partnership property 6.02
    preferred 8.12
    priority 8.03, 8.07
    private 8.01, 8.07
    secured 8.07, 8.12
    separate 8.01, 8.07, 8.09
    unsecured 8.17, 17.11
    see also insolvency
credit, pledging 4.11
criminal offences 4.32–4.35
    business names, choice of 3.15
    can firm be convicted of an offence? 4.33
    corporate manslaughter 4.33–4.34
    freedom to contract 3.05
    liability 4.23
    Scotland 4.35
    winding up 8.08
    see also in particular fraud
cross-border mergers 17.15

damages
    business names, choice of 3.17
    claim for 14.24
    conflict of interest and duty - unauthorized
        personal profit 5.11
    contract and equity 5.03
    duty of care 5.04
    honesty and disclosure 5.10
    limited liability partnerships (LLPs) 1.02
    LLP Agreement 14.18
    management and control 5.22
    rescission of partnership agreement 7.19
    restraint of trade 3.11
    see also compensation; fines; injunctions;
        restitution
data protection rights 15.13
death/deceased partners
    corporate partners 1.37
    dissolution 7.01, 7.03–7.04
    duration of liability 4.50, 4.55, 4.59
    financial involvement, association by 2.21
    frustration of partnership agreement 7.18
    intentional partnerships 2.07
    joint and several liability 4.45
    legal personality in Scotland 1.08
    membership termination of
        LLPs 16.01–16.02
    partnership property 6.13, 6.19–6.20, 6.26
    premiums, return of 7.34
    private limited partnerships 9.15
    technical dissolution 7.40
    valuation of partner's share in assets 7.42–7.46
    valuation of partner's share in profits
        post-dissolution 7.50, 7.57
    winding up 7.25
    see also intestacy
debts
    common law and equity 1.10
    corporate partners 1.35
    deferred 2.27
    duration of liability 4.49
    group partnerships 1.31
    incurred after retirement: liability 4.55–4.60
    partnerships 1.12
    private 8.01
    subpartnerships 1.34
deceit 3.17, 7.19, 13.15
decision-making and limited liability
        partnerships (LLPs)
    discretion 15.07–15.09
        good faith and proper purpose 15.08
        rationality 15.09
    Duomatic principle 15.06
    extra-ordinary matters 15.03–15.05
        corporate decision-making at common
            law 15.05
        statutory powers 15.04
    natural justice 15.11–15.12
    ordinary matters connected with
        business 15.02

decision-making and limited liability
        partnerships (LLPs) (cont.)
    procedural propriety, forensic value of 15.14
    process 15.01–15.06
    reasons 15.13
    statutory rights 15.15
    unlawful decision, consequences
        of 15.16–15.18
        acting outside scope of power 15.17
        improper exercise of power 15.18
deductions for management by remaining
        partner(s) 7.54–7.55
deed of settlement companies 1.28
de facto members 12.07
default provisions see under LLP Agreement
Department for Business, Energy and Industrial
        Strategy (BEIS) 9.24, 10.09, 11.27, 17.17
Department for Business, Enterprise and
        Regulatory Reform (DBERR) 9.03, 9.05
Department of Trade and Industry
        (DTI) 3.12, 10.05
    Limited Liability Partnership - A New Form of
        Business Association for Professions 1.02
    'think small first' policy 1.04, 1.29
dependants, provision for 2.21
derivative actions/claims 3.20, 9.14, 11.22
designated members 10.08, 11.09
designation, certificate of 9.17
directing mind and will 11.12
directors 1.10
    disqualification 12.14
    membership of LLPs 12.06,
        13.12–13.14, 13.17
disciplinary procedures 12.11
disclosure
    auditors' remuneration 1.37
    charging orders against partners 5.50
    common law and equity 1.10
    conflict of interest and duty - unauthorized
        personal profit 5.16
    contract and equity 5.01
    good faith 5.08
    group partnerships 1.32
    impact of LLPs 1.30
    legal controls on partnerships 3.01
    membership of limited liability partnerships
        (LLPs) - rights and duties 13.09
    of names of partners 3.16
    partners 3.03, 5.09–5.10
    pre-action 15.13
    private companies 1.29
    voluntary disclosure letters 5.07
    see also disclosure obligations and limited
        liability partnerships (LLPs)

disclosure obligations and limited liability
        partnerships (LLPs)
    annual confirmation statements 11.29
    name, display of 11.24
    notification of membership changes to
        Registrar 11.26
    people with significant control (PSC)
        register 11.27
    records and accounts 11.30
    register of members 11.25
    registration of charges 11.28
discretion 15.07–15.09, 16.05
discrimination
    contractual and statutory problems 1.07
    direct 3.04
    expulsion clauses 5.37
    freedom to contract 3.04
    indirect 3.04
'disguised salary' 10.10, 12.05
dishonest assistance 4.23, 4.40–4.43, 11.13
dishonesty 5.10
dismissal, unfair or wrongful 2.34, 2.36,
        2.41, 12.09
disputes
    intentional partnerships 2.07
    legal controls on partnerships 3.01
    partnerships 1.01, 1.04
    public domain and partnerships 3.19
    resolution procedure 1.13
    resolution procedure, see also arbitration
    see also arbitration
disqualification 8.08
    insolvency and dissolution 8.05, 17.17
    liability by representation 2.31
    limited liability partnerships (LLPs) 11.17
    order 17.08
    undertaking 17.08
    see also under membership of limited liability
        partnerships (LLPs)
dissolution
    assets distribution - solvent
        partnerships 7.61–7.64
        capital losses 7.62–7.64
        final accounts, necessity for 7.61
        surplus assets 7.62–7.64
    charging orders against partners 5.50
    conflict of interest and duty - unauthorized
        personal profit 5.17
    contractual grounds 7.02–7.06
        bankruptcy 7.03–7.04
        charging orders 7.03–7.04
        contrary intention 7.04
        death 7.03–7.04
        express clauses 7.05

INDEX

implied terms 7.02
mutual agreement 7.06
corporate partners 1.37
court orders
  application to commercial partnership 7.16
  carrying on business at a loss 7.13
  grounds 7.08–7.16
  just and equitable ground 7.14–7.17
  mental incapacity 7.09
  no fault divorce 7.15
  ouster clauses 7.17
  permanent incapacity 7.10
  persistent breaches of the agreement 7.12
  prejudicial conduct 7.11
duration of liability 4.55
employees, workers and partners 2.36
expulsion clauses 5.37, 5.41
and fiduciary duties 5.09
financial affairs 5.31
financial involvement, association by 2.17
freedom to contract 3.05
frustration of partnership agreement 7.18
general dissolution 7.01, 7.23–7.24, 7.26, 7.35, 7.60
illegality 7.07
implied 7.06
intentional partnerships 2.07–2.08, 2.10–2.12
international partnerships 1.39
legal personality in Scotland 1.08
liability by representation 2.31
liability of former partner 7.41
limited liability partnerships (LLPs) 11.11
management and control 5.21–5.22, 5.24
membership termination of LLPs 16.01–16.02
ouster clauses 7.17
partial 6.08, 7.42, 7.4
partnership property 6.03, 6.14, 6.26, 6.30
partnerships 1.04
premiums, return of 7.34
private limited partnerships 9.05, 9.15
repudiation of partnership agreement 7.20–7.22
rescission of partnership agreement 7.19
rights of assignee on 5.46–5.47
salaried and fixed share partners 2.39, 2.41
technical dissolution 7.01, 7.04, 7.23, 7.30, 7.39–7.40, 7.50, 7.60, 16.09
termination of LLP membership 16.12
total 6.08
transfer of outgoing partner's share 7.60
vicarious liability 4.35

see also insolvency and dissolution of limited liability partnerships (LLPs); receivers; valuation of partner's share after dissolution; winding up
documents, falsification or destruction of 17.17
Duomatic principle 15.06
duration of liability
  actual notice 4.57
  change of partner, effect of 4.49–4.51
  conflict of interest and duty - unauthorized personal profit 5.17
  debts incurred after retirement 4.55–4.60
  guarantees 4.54
  notice in the *Gazette* 4.58
  novation 4.52–4.53
  presumption of liability 4.56
  Scotland 4.51
  single continuing contract 4.50
  third party did not know he was a partner 4.59
duration of partnerships 2.07–2.12, 7.02
  fixed-term 2.08–2.12, 7.02
  undefined 2.08, 7.02
duress 14.19, 16.01
duties of partners 1.09, 9.02, 14.01
  breaches of 4.23, 5.40
  conflict *see* conflict of interest and duty - unauthorized personal profit
  duty not to compete 5.19
  flagrant breach of 5.37
  non-compete rule 9.21, 14.13
  see also duty of care; fiduciary duties/breach of fiduciary duties; membership of limited liability partnerships (LLPs) - rights and duties; no-conflict rule; no-profit rule
duty of care 5.04, 13.12–13.14, 15.01

economic loss resulting from negligence 13.15
economic or social regulation 3.05
Edinburgh Gazette 9.07
election, making 7.58
embezzlement 7.22
employees and workers
  business purposes 1.16
  contractual and statutory problems 1.07
  formation and establishment of partnerships 2.03
  limb (a) workers 2.35
  limb (b) workers 2.35, 2.37
  and members of LLPs 12.03, 12.08–12.11
  partners as 2.34–2.35
  remuneration 2.20
Employment Appeal Tribunal 2.36
employment contracts and winding up 7.26

employment law 1.11–1.12
enemy aliens 3.04
energy and carbon report 11.30
entitlements letters 14.02
equality 5.26–5.28
equalization payment 7.36
equitable duties *see* good faith
equitable relationship 1.11
equitable wrongs *see* knowing assistance; knowing receipt
equity 1.28
  and contract 5.01–5.03
  membership of LLPs - rights and duties 13.06
  partnership law 1.10
  private 9.01
  see also fiduciary duties/breach of fiduciary duties
errant partner's share of the benefit 5.18
establishment *see* formation and establishment of partnerships
estoppel
  contracts: partners' liability 4.03
  duration of liability 4.56
  liability by representation 2.33
  partnerships by 2.28
  partnerships by association 2.13
European Union 1.18, 1.29, 1.37–1.39
evidential burden 5.28
excluded relationships: co-ownership 1.18
exit right 5.21
ex-members of LLPs 13.02
express authority 11.21
express clauses 7.05, 7.10
express or implied agreement 1.10, 2.04, 2.07, 2.13, 7.06
  assets, identification of 6.12–6.13
  contract: implied terms 5.20
  contract and equity 5.02
  decision-making 15.08
  financial affairs 5.26
  honesty and disclosure 5.10
  intentional partnerships 2.05
  partnership property 6.05
express terms 2.09
express trusts 4.43–4.44
expulsion 2.12, 14.15, 7.40, 16.01, 16.05
expulsion clauses 5.20, 7.05
  abuse of power 5.41–5.43
  express clauses: necessity 5.37
  natural justice 5.40
  terms of clause, complying with 5.38–5.39
extra-ordinary matters 15.03–15.05

fair hearing 16.05
fair market value 6.28, 7.42–7.45
falsification or destruction of documents 17.17
family and business relationships 1.14
farming cases 1.01, 6.14–6.15, 8.15, 8.18, 9.01
fiduciary duties/breach of fiduciary duties
  application to prospective partners 5.08
  charging orders against partners 5.50
  common law and equity 1.10
  dissolution, application to 5.09
  formation and establishment of partnerships 2.02
  impact of LLPs 1.30
  intentional partnerships 2.12
  liability of former partner 7.41
  LLP Agreement 14.12–14.14, 14.16
  membership of LLPs 12.03
  misapplication of property: liability 4.41
  partnership property 6.04, 6.11, 6.13, 6.25
  private fund limited partnerships 9.21
  repudiation 5.09, 7.22
  salaried and fixed share partners 2.41
  subpartnerships 1.34
  termination of LLP membership 16.13
  two or more persons (carried on in common) 1.20
  valuation of partner's share in profits post-dissolution 7.50, 7.58–7.59
  vicarious liability 4.26
  winding up 7.24, 8.08
  see also confidentiality; duties of partners; good faith; membership of limited liability partnerships (LLPs) - rights and duties
fiduciary liabilities: extension 1.32
financial involvement, association by 2.13, 2.28
  community of benefit, establishing 2.16–2.18
  debts, deferred 2.27
  dependants, provision for 2.21
  goodwill, sale of 2.25
  losses, sharing of 2.17
  opposition of interest, establishing 2.16–2.18
  partners or creditors 2.22
  profit-sharing as evidence of partnership 2.15
  remuneration of employees 2.20
  written agreement, necessity for 2.24
financial matters
  advances 5.31
  equality 5.26–5.28
  group partnerships 1.31
  indemnities 5.32
  interest on capital contributions 5.30
  limited partnerships 9.02
  losses 5.29
  records 13.05
  rights 13.01
  see also financial involvement, association by

financial sector partnerships 10.05
fines 1.08
　　see also sanctions, criminal and civil
firm names see business names
fixed charge 1.37, 11.28
fixed share partners 2.35, 2.42, 12.03,
　　12.08, 17.13
　　growth of 2.37
　　semi-retirement issues 2.38
　　substance not form 2.40
fixed-term partnerships 2.08–2.09,
　　2.11–2.12, 7.02
flexibility of limited partners 9.02
floating charge 1.29, 1.37, 7.35, 8.15,
　　8.18, 11.28
forfeiture 5.03, 5.22
forgery 9.05, 11.21
formal partnerships
　　commencement 2.05–2.06
　　duration - partnerships at will 2.07–2.12
　　partnership agreement or deed 2.05
formation and establishment of
　　　　partnerships 1.19
　　association 2.13
　　compulsory registration of information
　　　　on 3.01
　　financial involvement see financial
　　　　involvement, association by
　　importance 2.02
　　intentional partnerships see formal
　　　　partnerships
　　liability see representation, liability by
　　limited partnerships 9.02
　　partners, employees and workers 2.34–2.36
　　persons having status as partner 2.43
　　questions to be asked 2.01–2.04
　　written agreement, no requirement for 2.04
　　see also fixed share partners; formation under
　　　　private limited partnerships; salaried
　　　　partners
forms
　　LL AD 01 11.07
　　LL AD 02 11.25
　　LL AD 03 11.25
　　LL AD 04 11.25
　　LL AP 01 11.26
　　LL CH 01 11.09, 11.26
　　LL CH 02 11.26
　　LL CS 01 11.29
　　LL DE 01 11.09
　　LL IN 01 11.05
　　LL NM 01 11.06
　　LL TM 01 11.26
Foss v Harbottle rule 3.20

fraud
　　assignment of partnership share 5.47
　　certificate of registration 9.05
　　expulsion clauses 5.41
　　financial affairs 5.32
　　honesty and disclosure 5.10
　　insolvency and dissolution 8.01, 17.08, 17.17
　　liability by representation 2.28
　　limited liability partnerships (LLPs) 11.18
　　limited partnerships 9.23
　　membership of LLPs 12.15, 13.13
　　misapplication of property: liability 4.37,
　　　　4.39, 4.41
　　on a power 15.08
　　premiums, return of 7.34
　　receivers 7.28, 7.30
　　vicarious liability 4.25–4.26, 4.29
　　winding up 8.08
freedom of association 3.03, 3.12
freedom to contract 2.05, 2.08, 3.03–3.05
freedom to trade under a chosen business name 3.03
freezing injunction 7.31
frustration of partnership agreement 7.18, 7.22,
　　14.25, 16.01

garden leave 15.13
general partners/general partnerships 9.01–9.02,
　　9.07, 9.13–9.14
　　limited liability partnerships (LLPs) 10.03–10.04,
　　　　11.04, 11.10, 11.13
　　membership of LLPs 12.03
　　private fund limited partnerships 9.21
　　termination of LLP membership 16.10
good faith
　　application to prospective partners 5.08
　　common law and equity 1.10
　　contract and equity 5.01, 5.03
　　decision-making and LLPs 15.08, 15.16
　　dissolution 7.05
　　employees, workers and partners 2.35
　　expulsion clauses 5.37, 5.40–5.42
　　fiduciary principle 5.05
　　financial affairs 5.32
　　formation and establishment of partnerships 2.02
　　freedom to contract 3.04
　　limitations on 5.07
　　limited liability partnerships (LLPs) 11.21
　　LLP Agreement 14.16
　　management and control 5.24
　　membership of LLPs - rights and
　　　　duties 13.07, 13.11
　　profit-making 1.26
　　termination of LLP membership 16.05
　　width of 5.06

goodwill
   animal group labels - cats, dogs, rats and rabbits 6.27
   business names, choice of 3.17
   and capital profits 16.12
   conflict of interest and duty - unauthorized personal profit 5.17
   medical partnerships 3.07
   partnership property 6.14, 6.20
   purchase of part of 7.34
   restraint of trade 3.09
   sale of 2.25, 2.27
   termination of LLP membership 16.16
   see also under partnership property
gross negligence manslaughter 4.34
gross returns 2.01
group association agreement 2.33
group partnerships 1.31–1.33
   business names, choice of 3.14
   fiduciary liabilities: extension 1.32
   multi national firms 1.33
guarantees 4.54

head offices 1.31, 1.39
head partnerships 1.34
holding-out principle 1.31, 2.28, 2.31–2.33
homicide 4.34
honesty, duty of 5.09–5.10, 5.37, 9.21

illegality
   dissolution 7.07
   financial affairs 5.32
   freedom to contract 3.05
   frustration of partnership agreement 7.18
   intentional partnerships 2.05
   legal controls on partnerships 3.03
   limited liability partnerships (LLPs) 11.04
impact of LLPs 1.30
implied agreement *see* express or implied agreement
implied authority
   acts or instruments in firm name 4.10
   another business 4.14–4.15
   contracts: partners' liability 4.03–4.04, 4.07, 4.13
   exclusion of
      alternative trust solution 4.22
      application to partnership 4.19
      undisclosed principal 4.18, 4.20
      wording 4.21
   imputed notice 4.16
   kind of business 4.09
   limited liability partnerships (LLPs) 11.21
   misapplication of property: liability 4.36, 4.38–4.39, 4.41
   modern developments 4.13
   pledging credit 4.11
   in the usual way 4.12
   vicarious liability 4.08, 4.28
   winding up by existing partners 7.24–7.26
implied terms 2.05, 2.09, 5.20, 5.23, 7.02
improper benefit 14.14
improper employment of trust property in partnership 4.40
improper manner, means or purpose 4.08, 15.17
incapacity, permanent 7.10, 7.18
income profits 7.46–7.47
   post-dissolution 7.52–7.53
incorporation
   certificate 9.17, 11.11, 11.23
   limited liability partnerships (LLPs) 11.05, 11.23
   partnerships up to 1890 1.28
   see also under corporate structure of limited liability partnerships (LLPs)
indemnity 2.05, 5.32, 7.19, 14.06
individual members 1.15, 11.02, 11.08
informal partnership relationship 2.04
inheritance tax 10.10
initial significant control statement 11.10
injunctions 3.11
   business names, choice of 3.17
   conflict of interest and duty - unauthorized personal profit 5.11
   freezing 7.31
   LLP Agreement 14.18
   management and control 5.21, 5.23
   mandatory 7.36
injury, consequential 4.24
insolvency
   bankrupt partner but no petition against firm 8.04
   business purposes 1.17
   corporate 1.37, 8.02
   cross-border 8.02
   dissolution 7.01, 7.13
   financial affairs 5.32
   financial involvement, association by 2.27
   joint bankruptcy petitions 8.09
   legal controls for partnerships 3.02
   limited liability partnerships (LLPs) 10.04, 10.08–10.10, 11.16–11.17
   membership of LLPs 12.06–12.07, 12.15, 13.12
   partnership and partners 1.11–1.12, 8.03–8.04
   and partnership property, link with 6.02
   partnership voluntary arrangements (PVAs) 8.11–8.13

personal 8.02
possibilities 8.01–8.04
practitioner 8.12
private limited partnerships 9.15
problems 8.01–8.04
public domain and partnerships 3.18
statutory provisions 8.02
termination of LLP membership 16.03
see also insolvency and dissolution of limited liability partnerships (LLPs); partnership administration orders; receivers; winding up
insolvency and dissolution of limited liability partnerships (LLPs)
  administration 17.05
  company voluntary arrangements (CVAs) 17.04
  compulsory winding up 17.01, 17.03
  cross-border mergers 17.15
  investigations 17.17
  receivership 17.06
  schemes of arrangement 17.14
  striking off the Register 17.18–17.21
    bona vacantia 17.20
    by the Registrar 17.19
    restoration 17.21
  voluntary reconstructions 17.16
  voluntary winding up 17.1–17.02
  see also liquidation of limited liability partnerships (LLPs)
intention
  subjective 1.25
  see also contrary intention
intentional partnerships *see* formal partnerships
interest 13.01
  on capital contributions 5.30
  payments 2.22
  or profits, choice of 7.49–7.50, 7.56–7.58
  rate, fixed 2.27, 5.31
  valuation of partner's share in assets 7.46
interim moratorium 8.16, 8.18
international partnerships 1.38–1.40
  see also European Union
intestacy 6.06, 6.19
investment industry regulation 3.02

Jersey 1.02–1.03, 10.03–10.06
joint bankruptcy petitions 8.09, 8.12
joint estate 8.01, 8.07
joint and several liability 4.45–4.47, 8.01
  costs 4.47
  legislation 4.46
  limited liability partnerships (LLPs) 10.04, 10.06, 11.17

joint ventures 1.13, 1.15, 4.15, 5.21–5.22
judgements 1.39–1.40
junior partners 5.22
jurisdiction 1.33, 8.04, 11.22
  see also international partnerships
just and equitable winding up 7.14–7.17, 11.04, 13.05, 13.21, 13.23–13.26, 14.18, 14.25
  arbitration 13.26
  grounds for relief 13.25
  standing of members 13.24

Khan v Miah point on contemplated partnerships 9.05
knowingly being represented as a partner 2.30
knowing receipt 4.23, 4.40–4.44

land held under trust 6.11
land purchased from profits made by use of on non-partnership land 6.18–6.20
  application to improvements 6.19
  contrary intention 6.20
law and equity rules 1.09
leases 1.01, 6.22–6.23
  see also business premises: leases and licences *under* partnership property
legal certainty 7.12
legal controls on partnerships
  business names *see* business names
  freedom of association 3.12
  freedom to contract 3.04–3.05
  private controls 3.01–3.03
  public controls 3.01–3.03
  public domain *see* public domain and partnerships
  public interest 3.02–3.03
  restraint of trade *see* restraint of trade
legal personality
  corporate partners 1.37
  de facto 1.07
  employees, workers and partners 2.35
  financial affairs 5.31
  impact of LLPs 1.30
  legal controls for partnerships 3.02
  limited liability partnerships (LLPs) 1.02, 10.02, 11.11, 11.16, 11.18
  limited partnerships 9.01
  LLP Agreement 14.07
  partnership property 6.11
  partnerships up to 1890 1.28
  public domain and partnerships 3.19–3.20
  see also under partnerships; Scotland
legal privilege 5.06
legislative reform order (LRO) 9.03
legitimate interests 3.06, 3.10

INDEX

legitimate protection 3.09
liability
  avoidance for future debts 9.21
  contracts *see* contracts: partners' liability
  debts incurred after retirement 4.55–4.60
  deferred 9.08
  direct 4.37, 9.13
  duration *see* duration of liability
  duty of care 5.04
  exclusion of 13.13
  of former partner 7.41
  joint and several *see* joint and several liability
  limited *see* limited liability
  of limited partners *see under* private limited partnerships
  misapplication of property *see* misapplication of property: liability
  nature of 4.45–4.47
  for one's own wrongs 13.15
  for other wrongs 4.23
  primary 4.30, 4.37, 4.42, 11.12
  property *see* misapplication of property: liability
  receivers 7.33
  relief from 13.14
  strict 4.33, 11.15
  unlimited 5.21, 10.04
  see also representation, liability by; vicarious liability
licences *see* business premises: leases and licences *under* partnership property
limitation periods 5.01, 5.03, 7.60, 17.21
limited liability partnerships (LLPs) 1.02, 9.01
  body corporate 10.02
  citations 10.01
  corporate structure *see* corporate structure of limited liability partnerships (LLPs)
  criticisms 10.06
  decision-making *see* decision-making in limited liability partnerships (LLPs)
  definition 10.02
  development 10.03–10.06
    statutory provisions 10.04–10.05
  disqualification from 8.08
  dissolution *see* insolvency and dissolution in limited liability partnerships (LLPs)
  fault-based limitations 10.04
  insolvency *see* insolvency and dissolution in limited liability partnerships (LLPs)
  Jersey 1.03
  Law Commission review of partnership law 1.04
  legal capacity 10.02
  legal personality 10.02
  legislative scheme 10.07–10.09
  legislative scheme, statutory provisions 10.08–10.09
  limited liability 10.02, 11.16–11.18
  liquidation *see* liquidation of limited liability partnerships (LLPs)
  membership *see* membership of limited liability partnerships (LLPs); membership termination of limited liability partnerships (LLPs)
  partnerships and companies 10.10
  personal assets 10.04
  see also LLP Agreement
limited partnerships 9.07
  abuse, countering 9.24
  abuse, evidence of 9.23
  formation *see* formation and establishment of limited partnerships
  origins and development 9.01–9.03
  reform process 9.93
  statutory provisions 9.02
  two or more persons (carried on in common) 1.23
  see also private fund limited partnerships (PFLPs); private limited partnerships
liquidation of limited liability partnerships (LLPs)
  claims by members 17.11–17.13
    capital claims 17.12
    profit claims 17.13
  contributions by members 17.08–17.10
    enforced contributions 17.10
    voluntary contributions 17.09
litigation 3.02, 3.19–3.21, 11.22
  costs 1.04
LLP Agreement 10.08, 11.20
  amendment 14.17
  decision-making 15.01, 15.05, 15.07–15.08, 15.13, 15.16
  default provisions 14.04–14.15
    account, duty to 14.12
    assign, no right to 14.09
    books and records 14.11
    capital and profits, right to equal share in 14.05
    expulsion 14.15
    improper benefit 14.14
    indemnity, right to 14.06
    majority rule 14.10
    manage, right to 14.07
    non-compete duty 14.13
    remuneration, no right to 14.08
  frustration 14.25

good faith 14.16
insolvency and dissolution 17.02, 17.07,
    17.11, 17.13, 17.16
membership of LLPs 12.01, 12.03,
    12.05–12.07, 12.15
membership of LLPs - rights and
    duties 13.03–13.06, 13.08–13.09, 13.11–
    13.12, 13.21–13.22, 13.24–13.26
remedies for breach 14.18
repudiation 14.21–14.24
    *Flanagan v Liontrust Investment Partners
    LLP* 14.23
    resignation and claim for damages 14.24
rescission 14.19–14.21
    application of remedy 14.21
    availability of remedy 14.20
scope 14.01–14.03
    between members or between LLP and its
        members 14.02
    formalities 14.03
termination of LLP membership 16.01,
    16.03, 16.05–16.06, 16.09–16.11, 16.14
locked-in partner 7.02
loss(es) 5.29, 5.48
    carrying on business at 7.13
    consequential 4.24
    reflective 11.22
    sharing of 2.17
    trading 9.09
loyalty 13.07, 14.16

majority voting 5.23–5.24, 14.10, 15.04
management
    committee 13.09
    intentional partnerships 2.05
    interference in 9.11–9.12, 9.18
    internal 10.09
    limited partnerships 9.01
    participation 5.21
    right to 14.07
    see also management and control
management and control
    majority voting 5.23–5.24
    management rights 5.21
    partnership books, access to 5.25
    remuneration - share of the profit 5.22
    see also legal controls on partnerships
managing partner/management group 5.21
manslaughter *see* corporate manslaughter
market value 6.28, 7.42–7.45
material change of circumstances 7.14–7.15
medical partnerships 3.03, 3.07
membership of limited liability
    partnerships (LLPs)

commencement 12.01
consequences 12.02–12.03
de facto members 12.07
degrees of membership 12.03
disqualification 12.06–12.07, 12.12–12.16
    company directors 12.14
    grounds 12.15
    LLP members 12.13
    undischarged bankrupts 12.16
employees and members 12.03, 12.08–12.10
    *Clyde & Co LLP v Bates van
    Winkelhof* 12.10
    Tiffin v Lester Aldridge LLP 12.09
salaried members 12.03, 12.05, 12.08
shadow members 12.06, 12.12
termination *see* termination of membership
    of limited liability partnerships (LLPs)
workers and members 12.11
see also membership of limited liability
    partnerships (LLPs) - rights and duties
membership of limited liability partnerships
    (LLPs) - rights and duties
    creditors 13.18
    duty of care 13.12–13.14
        liability, exclusion of 13.13
        liability, relief from 13.14
    fiduciary duties 13.07–13.11
        between members and LLP 13.08–13.10
        between members themselves 13.11
        informed consent 13.09
        remedies 13.10
    just and equitable winding up 13.21
    member's share 13.01–13.02
        assignment and bankruptcy, effects
            of 13.02
    sources of rights and duties 13.03–13.06
        common law and equity 13.06
        LLP Agreement 13.04
        statutory rights and duties 13.05
    third parties 13.15–13.17
        assumption of responsibility 13.16
        liability for one's own wrongs 13.15
        Said v Butt 13.17
    unfair prejudice 13.05, 13.25–13.26
    see also minority protections and membership
        of LLPs
membership statement 3.19
membership termination of limited liability
    partnerships (LLPs)
    abandonment 16.04
    agreement with other members 16.01,
        16.03–16.05
    death 16.01–16.02
    dissolution 16.01–16.02

membership termination of limited liability partnerships (LLPs) (cont.)
  expulsion 16.05
  external consequences 16.08
  internal consequences 16.09–16.13
    capital profits and goodwill 16.12
    capital repayment 16.11
    profits, entitlement to 16.09–16.10
    profits, forfeiture of 16.13
  methods 16.01–16.06
  post-termination controls
    restraint of trade c 14–16.15
    solicitation, implied restrictions on 16.16
  reasonable notice 16.01, 16.06
mens rea 4.33
mental element 17.10
mental incapacity 3.04, 7.09, 9.15, 15.17
mental state *see* directing mind and will
middle partners 5.22
minority protection 10.10
  just and equitable winding up 13.05, 13.23–13.26
    arbitration 13.26
    grounds for relief 13.25
    standing of members 13.24
  unfair prejudice 13.19–13.22
    excluding the right 13.21
    quasi-partnerships 13.22
minors and freedom to contract 3.04
misapplication of property: liability 4.23
  direct liability 4.37
  improper employment of trust property in partnership 4.40
  primary liability 4.37
  receipt in ordinary course of business 4.39
  receipt within apparent authority of partner 4.38
  vicarious liability 4.37
    for breaches of express trusts 4.43
    for dishonest assistance and knowing receipt 4.41–4.43
misappropriation 4.36–4.37, 5.12
misconduct
  conflict of interest and duty - unauthorized personal profit 5.16
  decision-making 15.12
  dissolution 7.05
  expulsion clauses 5.38, 5.41
  management and control 5.21
  premiums, return of 7.34
  termination of LLP membership 16.13
misfeasance 17.17
  summons 8.19

misrepresentation
  business names, choice of 3.17
  contract and equity 5.02
  innocent 7.19
  intentional partnerships 2.05
  liability by representation 2.28, 2.30
  limited liability partnerships (LLPs) 11.12
  LLP Agreement 14.21
  negligent 14.19
  rescission of partnership agreement 7.19
  termination of LLP membership 16.01
  vicarious liability 4.31
mistake 2.05, 5.02, 14.19, 16.01
money-laundering 9.23–9.24
morality and moral culpability 3.04–3.05
moratorium
  interim 8.16, 8.18
  temporary 8.13
multinational firms 1.33
multiparty contractual situation 14.21, 14.23
multiparty contractual situation, *see also* two or more persons partnership
mutuality 3.06, 7.22
mutual trust and confidence 5.01, 5.21, 5.33, 7.14–7.15, 14.16, 15.13

names *see* business names
national insurance 1.12, 1.30, 3.02, 12.05, 17.09
natural justice 5.37, 5.40–5.41, 15.11–15.12, 16.05
necessity 5.32, 6.14–6.16
negligence
  culpable 5.04, 5.32, 13.12
  duty of care 5.04
  and economic loss 13.15
  gross 5.04, 5.32, 13.12
  liability by representation 2.30
  limited liability partnerships (LLPs) 1.02, 10.04, 11.13
  membership of LLPs - rights and duties 13.15
  ordinary 5.32
  rescission of partnership agreement 7.19
  vicarious liability 4.28, 4.31
  winding up 7.27
no-conflict rule 5.11, 5.15, 13.07–13.08
'no fault divorce' 7.15
nomination clause 5.36
non-compete rule 5.19, 9.21, 14.13
non-profit-making or non-business organization 11.04
no-profit rule 5.01, 5.11, 5.15–5.16, 13.07
notice
  actual 2.05, 4.57, 4.60
  dissolution 7.02

INDEX

duration of liability 4.56
imputed 4.16
intentional partnerships 2.07–2.08, 2.10, 2.12
and liability avoidance for future debts 9.21
misapplication of property: liability 4.44
partnerships at will 2.11
public domain and partnerships 3.19
reasonable 16.01, 16.06
salaried and fixed share partners 2.39, 2.41
written 2.11, 2.32
see also notice in *Gazette*
notice in *Gazette* 4.58, 4.60, 7.41, 17.19
Belfast 9.07
Edinburgh 9.07
London 9.07, 11.11
private fund limited partnerships (PFLPs) 9.20
private limited partnerships 9.13
novation 4.52–4.53, 11.20
nullity 1.39
number of partners *see* size of partnerships

offer and acceptance *consensus ad idem* 3.03
opposition of interest, establishing 2.16–2.18, 2.22
oral agreement 1.10, 4.03, 5.02
ordinary course of business 4.15, 4.23–4.27, 14.10, 15.02
close connection test 4.25
contracts: partners' liability 4.08–4.09 4.11, 4.14, 4.23
misapplication of property: liability 4.36–4.43
personal dealings 4.27
vicarious liability 4.28–4.29
ordinary partnerships 9.02
ostensible authority *see* apparent authority
outsiders *see* third parties
ownership
beneficial 6.03
legal controls on partnerships 3.01
see also co-ownership

parental leave 12.09
participation in business required 1.21
particulars of members 11.08
partners
agreement, effect of 5.02
apparent 9.21
books *see* accounts/accounting requirements
change of *see* change of partners
charging orders 5.49–5.50
contract: implied terms 5.20
contract and equity 5.01–5.03

disclosure 5.09–5.10
duties *see* duties of partnerships
as employee distinction 2.34, 2.36
fiduciary relationships 5.01
financial involvement, association by 2.22
fixed share *see* fixed share partners
general *see* general partners/general partnerships
honesty 5.09–5.10
insolvency 8.03–8.04
interest *see under* partnership property
prospective 5.08
rights in assets of firm 7.35
salaried *see* salaried partners
share in assets *see* valuation of partner's share in assets
share valuation *see* valuation of partner's share after dissolution
standard of care and skill, assessment of 5.04
as worker 2.35
partnership law 1.12, 10.08
common law and equity 1.10
Partnership Act 1890 1.09
relevant statutes 1.11
partnership property
business premises: leases and licences
assignment problems 6.22
business tenancies 6.23
ownership by all partners outside the partnership 6.24
ownership by one or some partners outside the partnership 6.25
definition 6.07
formation and establishment of partnerships 2.02
goodwill 6.26–6.30
consequences of sale of 6.29
identification 6.27–6.28
as partnership asset 6.30
professional partnerships 6.28
joint purchase only 1.18
law 1.12
partner's interest, nature and consequences of
assets capable of being partnership property, limits on 6.10
beneficial interest 6.09
enforcement only on partial or total dissolution 6.08
land held under trust 6.11
premises, right to enter under warrant 17.17
problem areas
beneficial ownership 6.03
conversion doctrine 6.06
co-ownership issues 6.05

446 INDEX

partnership property (*cont.*)
    fiduciary duties 6.04
    identification of property, necessity for 6.01
    insolvency, link with 6.02
    see also assets; misapplication of property: liability; valuation of partnership assets
partnerships
    administration *see* administration orders
    agreement *see* agreement
    at will *see* partnerships at will
    business purposes 1.14–1.19
    changing role 1.27–1.30
        impact of LLPs 1.30
        private companies: growth and development 1.29
        up to 1890 1.28
    and company or LLP: distinction 1.01
    contemplated 1.15, 9.05
    control *see* management and control
    corporate partners 1.35–1.37
    defined 1.01–1.02
    duration *see* duration of partnerships
    establishment *see* formation and establishment of partnerships
    fixed-term 2.08–2.09, 2.11–2.12, 7.02
    flexibility to vary arrangements
        group partnerships 1.31–1.33
        subpartnerships 1.34
    formal *see* formal partnerships
    formation *see* formation and establishment of partnerships
    general *see* general partners/general partnerships
    as a going concern: rights of assignee 5.45
    head 1.34
    insolvency *see* insolvency
    international partnerships - jurisdiction 1.38–1.40
    joint ventures, relationship with 1.13
    law *see* partnership law
    legal control *see* legal controls on partnerships
    legal personality and continuity 1.01, 1.04–1.08
        continuity 1.06
        contractual problems 1.07
        Scotland 1.08
        statutory problems 1.07
    management *see* management and control
    of necessity 1.20
    ongoing issues 1.37
    opportunity, misuse of 5.15–5.16
    ordinary 9.02
    professional *see* professional partnerships
    profit-making 1.24–1.26
    property *see* partnership property
    public domain *see* public domain and partnerships
    as relationships 1.01
    shares *see* assignment
    two or more persons (carried on in common) 1.20–1.23
    see also limited liability partnerships; limited partnerships; private fund limited partnerships (PFLPs); private limited partnerships; quasi-partnerships; two or more persons partnership
partnerships at will
    continuing terms into 2.12
    current situation 2.10
    dissolution 7.02
    duration 2.07–2.12
    following fixed-term partnership 2.09
    notice, form of 2.11
    salaried and fixed share partners 2.39, 2.41
partnership share, assignment of
    losses 5.48
    rights of assignee on dissolution 5.46–5.47
    rights of assignee whilst partnership is a going concern 5.45
partnership voluntary arrangements (PVAs) 8.11–8.13
passing-off actions 1.10, 3.03, 3.17, 6.27
penalty, consequential 4.24
pensions 9.01, 12.03, 12.05
perpetual succession 1.08
personality *see* legal personality
personal profit *see* conflict of interest and duty - unauthorized personal profit
personal rights 13.01
personal welfare, protection of 3.05
person with significant control (PSC) register 11.10, 11.27
persons of unsound mind *see* mental incapacity
physical harm 13.15
power, abuse of 5.24
    acting outside scope of power 15.17
    compulsory retirement 5.43
    expulsion clauses 5.41
    improper exercise of power 15.18
    unreasonableness 5.42
premises, right to enter under warrant 17.17
premiums, return of 7.34
pre-pack sale 8.17
presumed authority *see* implied authority
primary liability 4.30, 4.37, 4.42, 11.12
principal place of business 9.24

INDEX 447

private companies 1.29, 9.01
private controls 3.01–3.03
private fund limited partnerships (PFLPs)
    9.01–9.03, 9.11–9.12
  capital contributions 9.19
  changes 9.20
  definition 9.17
  de-registration 9.17
  Gazette notices 9.20
  honesty, duty of 9.21
  management, interference in - permitted
    activities (white list) 9.18
  no competition 9.21
  notice and liability avoidance for future
    debts 9.21
  registered particulars 9.20
  registration 9.17
  Scottish 9.03, 9.16
  winding up 9.22
private limited partnerships
  formation 9.04–9.06
    business name 9.06
    effectiveness of certificate of registration -
      fraudulent applications 9.05
    registration - reform proposals
      adopted 9.04
  liability of limited partners
    agreed sum, failure to contribute 9.10
    capital reforms 9.08
    management, interference in 9.11–9.12
    trading losses 9.09
  statutory reform 9.13–9.15
    derivative actions 9.14
    dissolution 9.15
  see also private fund limited partnerships
    (PFLPs)
privity of contract
  contracts: partners' liability 4.02
  duration of liability 4.52
  intentional partnerships 2.05
  partnership law 1.09
  partnership property 6.22
privity of estate 6.22
procedural propriety, forensic value of 15.14
professional integrity 7.05
professional partnerships 10.05, 10.10
  accountancy partnerships 1.02, 1.27, 1.29,
    1.31, 10.04–10.06
  dissolution 7.05, 7.15, 7.40
  goodwill 6.28
  medical partnerships 3.03, 3.07
  receivers 7.29–7.30
  solicitors' partnerships 1.27, 1.31, 3.03, 3.08–
    3.10, 10.04–10.05

profit-based approach 6.30
profit-earning capacity 6.28
profit-making 1.24–1.26
  gross and net profits distinguished 1.26
  profit motive 1.24–1.25
  profit-sharing 1.24–1.25
profit-related remuneration 12.05
profit(s) 5.27, 7.42
  account of 5.45, 13.10
  capitalized profit-earning capacity 6.28
  capital *see under* capital
  carrying on a lawful business with a view
    to 11.05
  claims 17.13
  entitlement to 16.09–16.10
  forfeiture of 16.13
  and goodwill 16.12
  gross profits 7.53
  income 7.46–7.47
  or interest, choice of 7.49–7.50
  land purchased from profits made by use of
    on non-partnership land 6.18–6.20
  net profits 7.53
  no application to 7.51
  property bought with 6.17
  remuneration - share of the profit 5.22
  right to equal share in 14.05
  secret 5.03
  super profits multiple 6.28
  see also conflict of interest and duty -
    unauthorized personal profit;
    no-profit rule
profit-sharing agreement 1.13
profit-sharing as evidence of partnership 2.15
profit-sharing ratio 5.28, 5.30, 5.45, 7.46, 7.50,
  7.52, 7.63–7.64
promoters 1.19
proper purpose rule 14.17, 15.08
property *see* partnership property
prosecution 1.05, 1.08
prospective partners 5.08
public controls 3.01–3.03
public domain and partnerships 3.18–3.21
  litigation 3.19–3.21
  right of individual partner to sue for wrong
    done to partnership 3.20
  right of partner not to be joined as claimant in
    partnership action 3.21
publicity requirements 10.05
public interest 3.02–3.03, 3.06–3.07,
  11.04, 17.17
public investment 3.01
publicity requirements, *see also* notice in *Gazette*
public policy 3.02, 3.05, 3.07–3.09, 3.15, 11.04

quasi-partnerships 1.29, 2.28, 13.22

rationality 15.09
real estate 9.01
realization by sale 7.37
realty and personalty distinction 6.06
reasonableness test 3.07, 3.09
reasonableness test, *see also Wednesbury* test of reasonableness/irrationality
receipt
  in ordinary course of business 4.39
  within apparent authority of partner 4.38
  see also knowing receipt
receivers 17.06
  appointment of 7.28–7.31
    continuation of business 7.30
    liability 7.33
    professional partnerships 7.29
    remuneration of receiver 7.32
    single partner or receiver continuing business 7.31
recklessness 2.30
records 11.30, 14.11
recycling of insolvent company's name 11.06
redundancy 2.36, 12.09
registered office 11.07, 11.24, 11.28, 11.30
Registrar of Companies
  limited liability partnerships (LLPs) 11.07, 11.11, 11.25, 11.27–11.28, 11.30
  limited partnerships 9.03
  notification of membership changes 11.26
  private limited partnerships 9.04
  striking off by 17.19
  termination of LLP membership 16.08
registration 1.28, 9.20, 10.08, 11.25
  certificate 9.05
  of charges 11.28
  private limited partnerships 9.04
  procedure 9.03
  requirements 10.05
  restoration of LLP to the register 17.21
  see also Companies House; incorporation; Registrar of Companies; striking off the Register
relevant legal entities (RLEs) 11.10, 11.27
reliance, necessity for 2.31–2.32
remedies 5.03, 7.19, 13.10, 14.18
  see also damages; fines; injunctions; restitution
remuneration
  of employees 2.20
  no right to 14.08
  of receiver 7.32
  right to 7.05

share of the profit 5.22
  see also salaried partners
representation
  association by 2.13
  by words or conduct 4.38
  see also representation, liability by
representation, liability by
  knowingly being represented as a partner 2.30
  necessity for representation 2.29–2.30
  reliance, necessity for 2.31–2.32
  true nature of liability 2.33
  written notice of being a partner 2.32
repudiation 7.20–7.22
  abandonment/mutuality 7.22
  common law and equity 1.10
  contractual effect 7.21
  dissolution 7.12
  and fiduciary duties 5.09
  freedom to contract 3.04
  frustration of partnership agreement 7.18
  LLP Agreement 14.21–14.25
  termination of LLP membership 16.01
reputation 3.17, 3.19, 7.05, 7.29
rescission 5.10–5.11, 7.19, 14.19–14.21, 16.01
reserved matter and agreement amendment 14.17
resignation and claim for damages 14.24
responsibility, assumption of 13.16
restitutio in integrum 14.19, 16.01
restitution 1.10, 5.18
restoration of LLP to the register 17.21
restraint of trade 16.14–16.15
  enforcement of clauses 3.11
  intentional partnerships 2.05
  legal controls on partnerships 3.03
  medical partnerships 3.07
  solicitors' partnerships 3.08–3.10
  validity assessment 3.06
restriction order 3.19
restrictive covenant *see* restraint of trade
resulting trusts 6.21
retirement
  compulsory 5.43, 16.03
  contract and equity 5.03
  decision-making 15.08
  dissolution 7.01
  intentional partnerships 2.07
  liability of former partner 7.41
  LLP Agreement 14.21
  partnership property 6.13, 6.26
  receivers 7.30
  repudiation of partnership agreement 7.21
  semi-retirement issues 2.38

technical dissolution 7.40
termination of LLP membership 16.01
valuation of partner's share in assets 7.44, 7.46
valuation of partner's share in profits post-dissolution 7.50
see also duration of liability; pensions
rights 1.09, 9.02, 14.01
  alienable 13.01
  of assignee on dissolution 5.46–5.47
  of assignee whilst partnership is a going concern 5.45
  inalienable 13.01
  of partner not to be joined as claimant in partnership action 3.21
  see also membership of limited liability partnerships (LLPs) - rights and duties

SAIL (single alternative inspection location) address 11.25, 11.27–11.28, 11.30
salaried partners 12.03, 12.05, 17.13
  growth of 2.37
  membership of LLPs 12.08
  semi-retirement issues 2.38
  Stekel v Ellice decision 2.39–2.40
  subsequent cases on 2.41
  substance not form 2.40
  valuation of partner's share in assets 7.46
salary, 'disguised' 10.10, 12.05
sale, realization by 7.37
sanctions, criminal and civil 11.06, 12.06
schemes of arrangement 17.14
Scotland
  agricultural leases 1.01
  business purposes 1.18
  common law and equity 1.10
  creating a status 1.10
  crimes 4.35
  dissolution 7.01, 7.04
  duration of liability 4.51, 4.58
  employees, workers and partners 2.34
  joint and several liability 4.45
  legal controls on partnerships 3.01
  limited liability partnerships (LLPs) 10.05, 11.02, 11.08, 11.28
  limited partnerships 9.01, 9.03
  membership of LLPs 12.10
  partnership property 6.08
  partnerships 1.01
  repudiation of partnership agreement 7.22
  subpartnerships 1.34
  valuation of partner's share in assets 7.44–7.45
  vicarious liability 4.33

  winding up 7.25
  see also Scottish limited partnerships (SLPs); Scottish private fund limited partnerships (SPFLPs)
Scottish limited partnerships (SLPs) 9.03, 9.23–9.24
Scottish private fund limited partnerships (SPFLPs) 9.03, 9.16
self-employment 1.16, 2.35, 2.37
semi-retirement issues 2.38
senior partners 5.22
separate estates 8.01, 8.07
severance words 6.05
sexual harassment 4.26
shadow members 12.06, 12.12, 15.01
single commercial venture 1.16–1.17
single member companies 7.31, 15.01, 17.03
situation and address 11.07
situation and address, *see also* SAIL (single alternative inspection location) address
situational conflict *see* no-conflict rule
size of partnerships 3.12, 10.04, 11.02
sleeping partners 5.21
smaller partnerships and temporary moratorium 8.13
solicitation, implied restrictions on 16.16
solicitors' partnerships 1.27, 1.31, 3.03, 3.08–3.10, 10.04–10.05
special circumstances 9.14
specialization among partners 10.04
special relationship 13.11, 13.16
special resolution 5.39
standard of care and skill, assessment of 5.04
statement in support 11.23
status as a partner, persons having 1.10, 2.43
statutory powers (extra-ordinary matters) 15.04
statutory rights 15.15
Stock Exchange listing 3.01
striking off the Register 17.18–17.21
  bona vacantia 17.20
  by the Registrar 17.19
  restoration 17.21
subordination argument (employees and workers) 2.35
subpartnerships 1.34
subrogation 7.19
super profits multiple 6.28
surrounding circumstances 6.13–6.14, 6.16
suspension 15.13
Syers v Syers orders 7.38

taxation issues
  business purposes 1.17
  changing role of partnerships 1.27

taxation issues (*cont.*)
  dissolution 7.01
  financial affairs 5.30
  formation and establishment of
      partnerships 2.02–2.03
  group partnerships 1.31
  impact of LLPs 1.30
  inheritance tax 10.10
  legal controls on partnerships 3.02
  legal personality in Scotland 1.08
  limited liability partnerships 10.03, 10.05,
      10.08, 10.10
  membership of LLPs 12.03, 12.05
  partnerships 1.11–1.12
  person having status as a partner 2.43
  private limited partnerships 9.09
  profit-making 1.25
  public domain and partnerships 3.18
  salaried and fixed share partners 2.42
  valuation of partner's share in assets 7.46
  see also value added tax (VAT)
temporary moratorium for smaller
      partnerships 8.13
termination 9.05, 12.04
third parties
  assignment of partnership share 5.48
  continuity 1.06
  contract and equity 5.01
  contracts: partners' liability 4.02–4.04,
      4.07–4.11, 4.17–4.20
  decision-making 15.16
  did not know they were a partner 4.59
  duration of liability 4.54
  duty of care 5.04
  intentional partnerships 2.05
  liability by representation 2.28
  liability of former partner 7.41
  limited liability partnerships (LLPs) 11.12,
      11.15, 11.25
  LLP Agreement 14.11, 14.19, 14.21
  membership of LLPs 12.06, 13.15–13.17
    assumption of responsibility 13.16
    liability for one's own wrongs 13.15
    rights and duties 13.02
  misapplication of property: liability 4.38
  partnership law 1.09
  partnership property 6.09
  private limited partnerships 9.12,
      9.14–9.15
  public domain and partnerships 3.19–3.21
  rescission of partnership agreement 7.19
  subpartnerships 1.34
  termination of LLP membership 16.07–16.08
  vicarious liability 4.25, 4.27, 4.29

  winding up 7.25, 7.27
tort 4.08, 4.23, 5.32, 13.17
  common law and equity 1.10
  duration of liability 4.48
  joint and several liability 4.45
  liability 4.23
  vicarious liability 4.24–4.35, 11.13
transactional conflicts *see* no-conflict rule
transfer of outgoing partner's share 7.60
trust
  breaches of 4.23
  contract and equity 5.03
  land held under 6.11
  utmost (*uberrimae fidei*) 5.10
  see also mutual trust and confidence
trust and company service providers
      (TCSPs) 9.23
trusts
  express 4.43–4.44
  resulting 6.21
  see also constructive trusts
two or more persons partnership 1.20–1.23,
      1.25, 14.23
  control 1.22
  limited partnerships 1.23
  participation in business required 1.21
  repudiation of partnership agreement 7.22

ultimate residue 7.63
unanimity
  consent: implied requirement 5.33
  decision-making 15.03–15.04
  insolvency and dissolution 7.03, 17.02, 17.16
  LLP Agreement amendment 14.17
unauthorized personal profit *see* conflict
      of interest and duty - unauthorized
      personal profit
unconscionable bargain 3.04
undisclosed principal 4.18–4.20, 4.22
undue delay causing substantial prejudice 8.01
undue influence 3.03–3.04, 14.19, 16.01
unfair dismissal 2.34, 2.41, 12.09
unfair harm 8.19
unfair prejudice 13.19–13.22, 13.25–13.26
  excluding the right 13.21
  LLP Agreement 14.03, 14.07, 14.18, 14.20
  membership of LLPs - rights and duties 13.05
  quasi-partnerships 13.22
  termination of LLP membership 16.01
unfair treatment 5.25
unfitness for office 8.08, 12.15
  see also compulsory retirement; mental
      incapacity
unincorporated associations 11.02

unjust enrichment 5.03, 7.61
unlawful decision, consequences of 15.16–15.18
unlawful purpose 17.17
unlisted companies 11.10
unravelling of transactions at undervalue 17.08
unregistered company 8.03, 8.06, 8.09–8.10, 8.12
unsound mind *see* mental incapacity
usual authority *see* implied authority
utmost trust (*uberrimae fidei*) 5.10

valuation of partner's share after dissolution
  capital profits, no application to 7.51
  contracting out 7.59
  deductions for management by remaining partner(s) 7.54–7.55
    share of capital profits 7.55
  interest option in lieu of share of income profits 7.56–7.58
    election, making 7.58
    no effect on right to capital profits 7.57
  post-dissolution income profits 7.52–7.53
    attributable to use of his share of partnership assets 7.53
  profits or interest, choice of 7.49–7.50
    choice of, outgoing partner: technical dissolution only 7.50
valuation of partner's share in assets
  assets 7.42
  capital 7.42
  income profits 7.46–7.47
  income profits, construction of terms of agreements 7.47
  Law Commissions' proposals 7.48
  profits 7.42
  valuation method 7.43–7.45
    construction of agreement 7.45
    market value 7.44
    Scotland 7.44
value added tax (VAT) 1.07, 3.18, 10.10
variation of contract 1.10
venture capital 1.01, 9.01, 9.03, 10.05
vicarious liability 4.08, 4.23, 4.37
  for breaches of express trusts 4.43
  common law and equity 1.10
  contracts: partners' liability 4.09
  crimes 4.32–4.35
  limitations on liability 4.29
  limited liability partnerships (LLPs) 11.13
  membership of LLPs rights and duties 13.15
  ordinary course of business 4.24–4.27
  primary liability of wrongdoer 4.30
  private limited partnerships 9.13

wrongs between partners 4.31
wrongs within partner's authority 4.28
vitiation of contract 1.10
voluntary arrangements 2.27, 8.02–8.03
  company (CVAs) 17.04
  individual 8.04
voluntary contributions *see* national insurance
voluntary disclosure letters 5.07
voluntary reconstructions 17.16
voting
  by majority 5.23–5.24, 14.10, 15.04
  group partnerships 1.31
  limited liability partnerships (LLPs) 11.27
  salaried and fixed share partners 2.37
  see also unanimity
vulnerable persons 3.04

warranty of authority, breach of 2.28
Wednesbury test of reasonableness/irrationality 5.42, 15.09
whistle-blowers' protection 2.35, 12.11
wilful default and financial affairs 5.32
winding up 8.02–8.03
  after separate bankruptcy petitions 8.10
  buy out or *Syers v Syers* orders 7.38
  by existing partners 7.24–7.27
    contracts of employment, effect on 7.26
    duty to wind up 7.27
    implied authority, extent of 7.25–7.26
  compulsory 17.01, 17.03, 17.07
  conflict of interest and duty - unauthorized personal profit 5.17
  fiduciary duties 5.09
  general dissolution 7.04, 7.23
  of insolvent partnership and concurrent bankruptcy of partner 8.06–8.08
    creditors, priority of 8.07
    disqualification from management of company or LLP 8.08
  of insolvent partnership only 8.05
  international partnerships 1.39
  joint bankruptcy petitions 8.09
  limited liability partnerships (LLPs) 10.10, 11.02, 11.04, 11.11, 11.16
  LLP Agreement 14.07, 14.20
  management and control 5.21–5.22
  membership of LLPs - rights and duties 13.19, 13.21
  partnership administration orders 8.17–8.19
  partnership property 6.04, 6.10, 6.25
  partnership voluntary arrangements (PVAs) 8.13
  partners' rights in assets of firm 7.35
  powers of courts in respect of assets 7.36

winding up (*cont.*)
  private companies 1.29
  private fund limited partnerships (PFLPs) 9.21–9.22
  realization by sale 7.37
  salaried and fixed share partners 2.39, 2.41
  termination of LLP membership 16.01
  voluntary 17.1–17.02, 17.07
  see also dissolution; just and equitable winding up
withdrawals
  adjustment 12.06, 17.10
  tainted 17.10
workers *see* employees and workers

written agreement 1.21
  contracts: partners' liability 4.03
  employees, workers and partners 2.36
  necessity for 2.24
  no requirement for 2.04
written notice 2.11, 2.32
wrongful acts or omissions 4.24, 4.36, 11.13, 12.06
wrongful trading 11.04
  insolvency and dissolution 17.08, 17.10
  membership of LLPs 12.06, 12.15, 13.12
wrongs
  between partners 4.31
  within partner's authority 4.28